D1174334

SCHRODERS

SCHRODERS

Merchants & Bankers

Richard Roberts

MACMILLAN

First published 1992 by
THE MACMILLAN PRESS LTD
Houndmills, Basingstoke, Hampshire RG21 2XS
and London
Companies and representatives
throughout the world

ISBN 0–333–44511–2

A catalogue record for this book is available
from the British Library.

Copy-edited and typeset by Povey–Edmondson
Okehampton and Rochdale, England

Printed in Great Britain by
Butler & Tanner Ltd,
Frome, Somerset

Contents

List of Maps

List of Figures

List of Tables

List of Plates

Preface

Schroders: Merchants & Bankers is a history of one of the City of London's oldest and most important merchant banks. In the nineteenth century, it played a central role in financing world trade and in raising long-term capital for governments and railway companies. Today it is a public company conducting business worldwide and is a leading provider of international merchant and investment banking services. Yet very little is known about the historical development of the firm since there has been virtually nothing published on the subject. Thus it was exciting and challenging to be invited by the firm to write a history, being given full access to all its records and every other co-operation.

There are several long-term themes in the history of Schroders. First, the important role of the founding family, which continues to this day. Indeed, an important reason why the firm has a lower public profile than some of its peers has been the family's concentration on business and its limited involvement in British high society and politics. Second, probably more than any other London merchant bank its business orientation has been outward looking, leading to a heavy involvement in Germany and to the establishment of a fully fledged firm in New York in 1923, a unique initiative. Third, is its disciplined and unflamboyant, though in no way conservative, style of conduct of business. In combination these long-term traits largely explain why the firm still exists and is at the forefront of its industry.

There are several points to be made about my approach to writing the book. First, it is a history of the firm, not the Schroder family. Second, the bulk of Schroders' records until the mid-twentieth century comprise financial accounts and it is these data which provide the framework of the story, although the formal presentation of financial analysis forms a minor proportion of the text. Third, I have devoted considerable attention to the key decision-takers since historically the performance of merchant banks has been highly dependent upon the initiative, imagination and judgement of their partners or leading directors. Fourth, I have endeavoured to produce a chronologically evenly balanced account of the evolution of the firm in London, New York and internationally from the early nineteenth century to 1973. This is followed by a full, but qualitatively different, description of subsequent developments, particularly the reorientation of the business in the 1980s.

Recent years have seen the publication of several impressive histories of merchant banks and merchant banking. These studies greatly assisted my understanding of the development of the merchant banking industry

and helped to identify how Schroders differs from its peers. I have
intentionally provided quite extensive accounts of the evolution of
London and New York as international financial centres considering
that this contextual information is important for comprehension of the
development of the Schroder firms.

An innovation which I believe will help many readers, though some
may regard it as distracting, is to provide conversions in the text of some
financial figures in 1990 values. The purpose is to permit the reader to
have an indication of the magnitude of statistics of capital, profits and
certain key numbers whose scale is obscured by inflation. The conversions are based upon the conversion multiples listed in Appendices
V(i) and V(ii), which are derived from well-known retail price series.
Retail prices are the most commonly used yardstick of inflation, but it
should be borne in mind that the rate of retail price inflation is not
necessarily identical with the rate of financial asset inflation, particularly
in the short-term. Moreover, inflation-adjusted figures from the past
understate the relative significance of activities because of the expansion
of aggregate economic activity. Thus the conversions provided in the text
should be regarded as indicative not definitive figures. Since any
conversion will be virtually immediately out of date, the beginning of the
decade of the 1990s was chosen as the conversion point and the
converted numbers are flagged by the phrase 'in 1990 money'.

RICHARD ROBERTS

Acknowledgements

My first acknowledgement is to Professor Donald Coleman, who suggested me as author to Schroders when the firm decided to commission a history. He has continued to be associated with the project and his comments have been very helpful. I should like to thank very much George Mallinckrodt, Bruno Schroder and Geoffrey Williams, the directors of Schroders most involved who have been highly supportive. I am also grateful to Philip Mallinckrodt, who assisted me in the initial stages of research. He contributed to aspects of the financial analysis and undertook much of the work on the German sources. He has been closely involved throughout and I owe much to his insights and observations. Further research assistance was very ably provided by Martin Todd.

I should like to express my thanks to the Schroder family, especially Charmaine Mallinckrodt, and to Henry Tiarks, for their help and hospitality; also to Erik Gasser for encouraging the firm to commission a history. With respect to the early history of the firm, I would like to acknowledge the work undertaken by Eduard Eggers, who over many years collected documents about the early history of the Schroder family which are deposited in the Staats Archiv in Hamburg. I am also grateful for the work done by Paul Bareau, assisted by Dr Roger Alford, in 1954 when a history of the firm was first contemplated in connection with the celebration of its 150th anniversary. With respect to the history of the firm in the twentieth century, I should like to express my gratitude to the people with whom I conducted interviews. In London: The Earl of Airlie; Jonathan Backhouse; Win Bischoff; Maurice Buckmaster; Toby Caulfeild; Alec Cairns; Francis Cater; David Forsyth; Dennis Garrett; Erik Gasser; John Hull; Bernard Knight; Robert Lunt; Laurance Mackie; John May; Sir Leslie Murphy; Ken Pearch; The Earl of Perth; Robin Pilkington; Sir Ashley Ponsonby; Lord Richardson; Philip Robinson; Jan Stuijt; Edward Tucker; Michael Verey; Sir Charles Villiers; William Wiltshire. In New York: John Bayley; Edmund Bartlett; Francis Bessenyey; Norbert Bogdan; George Braga; Donald Brown; Peter Carpenter; Canon Clements; Burgis Coates; Alden Cushman; Sherman Gray; John Howell; Frederick Klingenstein; Charles Meares; Chris Meili; Polly Lada-Mocarski; Gerhard Laube; Ernest Leimroth; Otto Leuteritz; Gottfried Lucas; Arno Mayer; Prestley McCaskie; Barbara Noble Robinson; Fred Seeley; Karl Streeck; James Wolfensohn.

Much of the research and writing was undertaken at Schroders and I would like to thank all members of the firm who have assisted me, in particular Alistair Forsyth, Andrew Gaulter, Michael Gwinnell, Terry

Mellish and Ulf Sudeck. My thanks for efficient and cheerful secretarial assistance to Hiltrude Dembina, Sarah Falshaw, Angela Lee, Louise Sanderson and Angela Yeoman.

I have received generous help from many people outside the firm. The following kindly agreed to be interviewed; Dr Hermann Abs; Eduard Eggers; Rodolphe d'Erlanger; Robert Gibson Jarvie; Walter Gleich; Graham Greenwell; John Kinross; Sir John Mallabar. I would like to thank the following for their assistance in providing access to the records in their charge: John Evans of the British Merchant Bankers Association; Edwin Green of the Midland Bank; Henry Gillett, John Keyworth and John Pullinger of the Bank of England; Simone Mace of N. M. Rothschild & Sons; John Orbell of Baring Brothers. I must also record my thanks to Professor Vincent Carosso, Dr Stephanie Diaper, Dr David Kynaston, Michael Moss and Alison Turton. Of course, responsibility for errors of fact or judgement rest with the author.

Most of the pictures which appear in the plate sections were provided by Schroders or members of the Schroder family. In addition I am grateful to all those who have provided pictures of themselves or of relatives. The drawing of the opening of the Tokyo–Yokohama railway appears by courtesy of the *Illustrated London News*. The Japanese print of the opening of the Tokyo–Yokohama railway and the picture of the Liverpool docks appear by kind permission of the Mansell Collection. The picture of Leadenhall Street in the early 1840s and the exterior view of 145 Leadenhall Street appear by kind permission of the Guildhall Library. The picture of The Earl of Perth appears by courtesy of the Associated Press. The photograph of Lord Richardson is by Godfrey Argent; the photograph of John Hull is by Rex Coleman of Baron; the photograph of The Earl of Airlie is by Murdoch, MacLeod Assocs Ltd, London; the photograph of George Mallinckrodt is by Richard Greenly; and the photographs of Bruno Schroder, Win Bischoff and the Schroders plc board are by Ben Rice.

RICHARD ROBERTS

A Note on Names and Terminology

The family name was Schröder until 1868, when Johann Heinrich Schröder, the founder, was made a baron and he and his descendants became Baron von Schröder. Although the 'von' was used by the family in Germany, they never used it in England or the United States. Helmut Schroder, who was born in England, dropped the umlaut upon his marriage in 1930. Since the death of Baron Bruno Schröder in 1940, all the family have used the spelling Schroder. In the text, the name appears as Schröder until 1939 and Schroder thereafter. When there is ambiguity about identity because of similarity of names, individuals are distinguished by a suffix, for instance Christian Matthias II.

The following abbreviations are sometimes used in the text for the names of the senior partners.

Schroder Family

Full name	*Abbreviation*
Johann Heinrich Schröder (Baron from 1868)	Johann Heinrich
Johann Heinrich Wilhelm Schröder (known in England as John Henry William Schröder) (Baron from 1868) (Baronet from 1892)	John Henry
Wilhelm Heinrich Schröder (known in England as William Henry Schröder) (Baron from 1868)	William
Bruno Schröder (Baron from 1904)	Baron Bruno (from 1904)
Helmut Schroder (title of Baron not used)	Helmut

The London firm was called J. Henry Schröder & Co. from its foundation until 1957, although after 1939 the umlaut was used less frequently. The name of the private company formed in 1957, J. Henry Schroder & Co. Ltd, was registered without an umlaut. In the text the name appears with an umlaut prior to 1939 and without thereafter. The name of the New York firm never had an umlaut. The following abbreviations are sometimes used for firms in the text:

Firm

Full Name	*Abbreviation*
J. F. Schröder & Co. (1801–33)	–
J. Henry Schröder & Co. (1818–1939)	Schröders
J. Henry Schroder & Co. (1940–57)	Schroders
J. Henry Schroder & Co. Ltd (1957–62)	Schroders
Helbert, Wagg & Co. (1848–1962)	Helbert, Wagg
J. Henry Schroder Wagg & Co. Ltd (since 1962)	Schroder Wagg
J. Henry Schroder Banking Corporation (1923–77)	Schrobanco
Schroder Trust Company (1936–77)	Schrotrust
J. Henry Schroder Bank & Trust Company (1977–86)	Schrobanco
Schroders Limited (1959–82)	Schroders
Schroders plc (since 1982)	Schroders
Wertheim & Co. (1927–86)	Wertheim
Wertheim Schroder & Co. (since 1986)	Wertheim Schroder

Generic Terminology

The appropriate generic term for Schroders and the firms conducting similar businesses over the nineteenth and twentieth centuries is potentially confusing. In the nineteenth century such firms were known as 'merchants' and then as 'merchants and bankers'. 'Merchant bank', the modern term, did not come into general use until the turn of the century, though to avoid muddle it has been used anachronistically in the text as a designation for Schroders and its peers in earlier years. 'Accepting house' was another term which came into use in London at the beginning of the twentieth century, referring to firms engaged in accepting, particularly those that were members of the 'Accepting Houses Committee', the association formed by a score of such firms shortly after the outbreak of the First World War. 'Issuing house' was another term current from the late nineteenth century, denoting a firm whose principal business was the issuing of securities. This included most of the members of the Accepting Houses Committee, though most of the sixty-or-so firms which in 1946 became members of the Issuing Houses Association did not conduct accepting business and were not embraced by the term 'accepting house'. 'Investment bank' and 'commercial bank' are US terms denoting, respectively, firms conducting securities' underwriting and deposit-taking/lending activities, which have been legally separated since the 1930s. 'Investment bank' has been used in the City since the Second World War, but 'merchant bank' is still the usual generic term for firms such as Schroders.

Financial Terminology

'Billion' is used in the text following American usage and means one thousand million.

'Net profits' means profits *less* the 4 per cent interest charge for the use of partners' capital. The 'return on capital' for J. Henry Schröder & Co. for the years 1852–1939 is *inclusive* of the 4 per cent interest charge for the use of partners' capital. Thus in some years, such as 1935 and 1939, although J. Henry Schröder & Co. made negative net profits it made a positive return on capital.

Percentages are calculated to the nearest whole number and may not sum to 100 because of rounding.

Part I

Hamburg and London

1654–1918

1

Origins in Quakenbrück and Hamburg

1654–1821

The founder of J. Henry Schröder & Co., the firm from which Schroders has developed, was Johann Heinrich Schröder, who arrived in London from his native city of Hamburg aged seventeen early in 1802, in the midst of the Napoleonic Wars. He was a member of a prominent and prosperous north German merchant family and it is with his ancestors and relatives, and their business activities, that the story of Schroders begins.[1]

The first member of the Schröder family about whom biographical information survives is Bernhard Schröder, who was born in the village of Bützfleth in 1654.[2] Bützfleth lay alongside a customs post at which tolls were collected by the Duchy of Bremen from the busy shipping on the estuary of the River Elbe, the nearest town being Stade, a small but well fortified settlement.[3] At the time of Bernhard's birth the Duchy of Bremen was in the possession of Sweden, perhaps giving rise to a mistaken suggestion that the Schröders originated from Sweden. It was bounded by the estuaries of the Weser and the Elbe upon which lay respectively the independent cities of Bremen and Hamburg. It was to these great Hanseatic ports that the most enterprising of Bernhard's descendants moved. But Bernhard himself also made an important migration – he moved from the countryside to the town and henceforth the Schröders were urban dwellers.

As a young man Bernhard Schröder settled in Verden, a market town some eighty miles from Bützfleth at the southernmost tip of the Duchy of Bremen (see Map 1.1). Verden's prosperity was based upon its location near the junction of the Weser and Aller rivers, along which travelled goods bound from Bremen to Minden and Hanover. As the north German economy recovered from the devastation wrought by the campaigns of the Thirty Years War (1618–48) opportunities appeared for commercial enterprise and application to reap rewards. Bernhard made a successful career as a tobacco manufacturer, eventually becoming the proprietor of his own works. In 1684 he married Anna Wiebe, the 21-year-old daughter of a brewer who was a burgher of Verden, and the match must have assisted Bernhard's entry into the ranks of the townsmen.[4] There were seven children born of the marriage, four boys and three girls. It was the youngest child, Anthon, baptised in

3

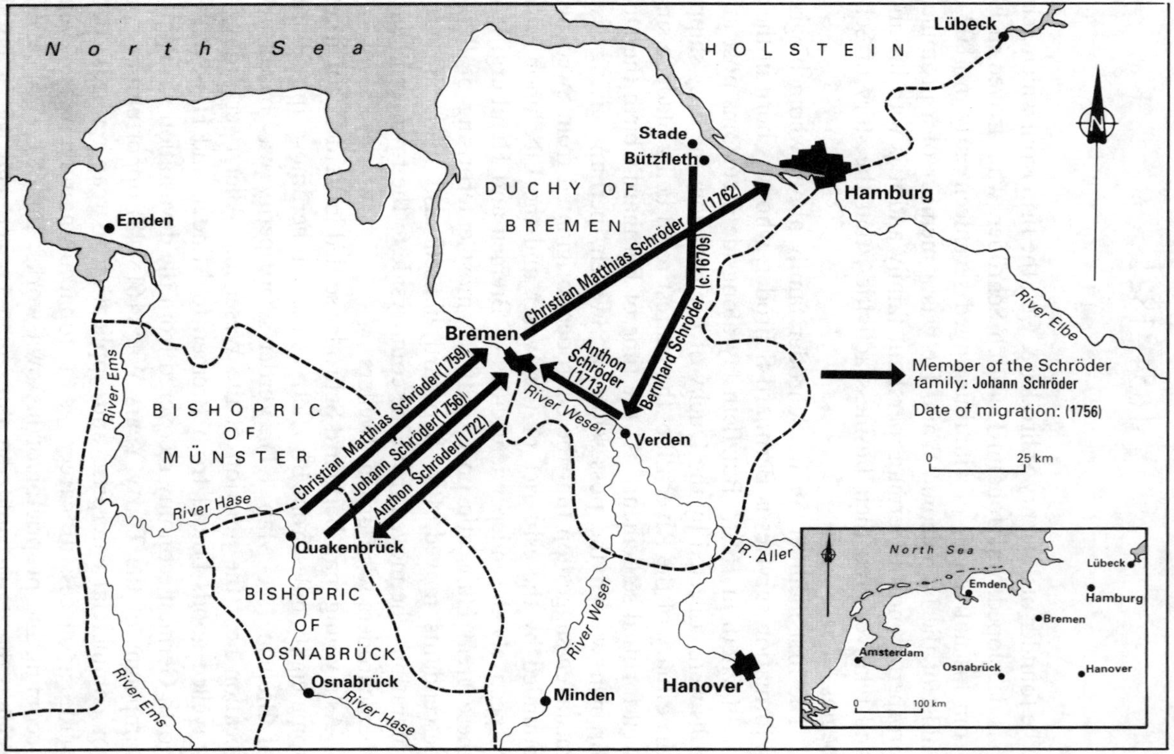

Map 1.1 Migrations of members of the Schröder family in the seventeenth and eighteenth centuries

the church of St Johann in Verden on 17 October 1697, who established the Schröders as a mercantile dynasty.

In 1713, at the age of sixteen, Anthon Schröder was apprenticed to a textile merchant named Thomas Blothe in Bremen, an important centre of the textile trade. There he may perhaps have met Johann Baring, a textile apprentice of exactly the same age, though in 1717 Baring left Bremen to serve an apprenticeship with an English wool-merchant in Exeter.[5] His sons subsequently founded the London merchant bank Baring Brothers & Co. In 1720, now a qualified journeyman, Anthon joined the firm of another Bremen textile merchant, Diedrich Schütte, and two years later he moved to Quakenbrück where he took up employment with Johan Schütte, the brother of his erstwhile master.

Quakenbrück, 50 miles to the south-west of Bremen in the Bishopric of Osnabrück, was a thriving town of some 2000 inhabitants. Local tradesmen prospered on the victualling requirements of the garrison of soldiers who guarded the nearby border crossing between the Bishoprics of Osnabrück and Münster. Quakenbrück was also an important market town on account of the convergence there of goods moving north to south along the River Hase, *en route* to and from the North Sea ports of Emden and Bremen, and east and west along the *Hellweg*, the traditional trade route from Amsterdam to Bremen and beyond to Poland. A volume of impressions of northern Germany written by a traveller in 1798 commented upon 'the noticeable elegance of the houses of Quakenbrück, which seem to have been copied from the Dutch. Trade here is flourishing and one can count many, in some cases very rich, businessmen. All the industry reflects well on the inhabitants. The trade is mainly forwarding business, and it is from this that this small town derives its importance'.[6]

Anthon Schröder settled in Quakenbrück and in 1725 he married Anna Kramer, the daughter of a wealthy merchant and alderman whose substantial residence and counting house was prominently positioned on the town's large market square.[7] In 1730 he established his own firm, Anthon Schröder & Co., trading in a wide range of goods, the first of the many Schröder merchant firms. The business flourished and Anthon became very prosperous, moving in 1760 into the large house on the market square. As one of Quakenbrück's leading citizens he also took an active part in civic affairs, becoming a town councillor in 1750 and serving as an alderman from 1767 to 1778. The family, comprising three daughters, each of whom married a local man, and five sons, was closely-knit, so much so that the parents deferred their Golden Wedding celebrations for a year awaiting the return of their second son from Portugal where he had gone to buy wine. Anthon died in May 1784, aged 87 – longevity would seem to be a Schröder family trait – just six months before the birth of his grandson, Johann Heinrich Schröder.

6

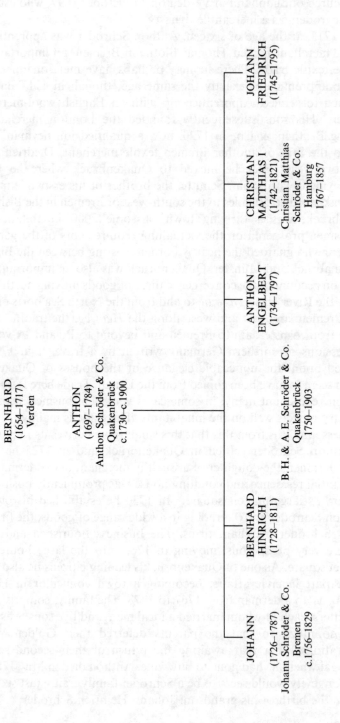

Figure 1.1 Merchant descendants of Bernhard Schröder (1654–1717)

BERNHARD
(1654–1717)
Verden

ANTHON
(1697–1784)
Anthon Schröder & Co.
Quakenbrück
c.1730–c.1900

JOHANN
(1726–1787)
Johann Schröder & Co.
Bremen
c.1756–1829

BERNHARD
HINRICH I
(1728–1811)

ANTHON
ENGELBERT
(1734–1797)
B. H. & A. E. Schröder & Co.
Quakenbrück
1750–1903

CHRISTIAN
MATTHIAS I
(1742–1821)
Christian Matthias
Schröder & Co.
Hamburg
1767–1857

JOHANN
FRIEDRICH
(1745–1795)

Each of Anthon's five sons became a merchant (see Figure 1.1). In 1750 his second and third sons, Bernhard Hinrich and Anthon Engelbert, aged respectively 22 and 16 years, established a firm of wine merchants, B. H. & A. E. Schröder & Co., in Quakenbrück and built a successful business distributing Bordeaux wine in north Germany. The wine arrived at Emden, on the North Sea coast, from where it was transported in large barrels called *oxhofts* by barge along the rivers Ems and Hase and then by wagon to the Schröder wine store in Quakenbrück. By 1782 the firm was conducting business on a large scale, for in that year it took delivery of 1200 oxhofts, amounting to a remarkable 270,000 litres of wine. The firm of B. H. & A. E. Schröder & Co. remained in Schröder family ownership until 1903. Today the successor firm, C. Kruse & Co., still distributes a schnaps called 'Schröder's Alte Liebe'.[8]

Johann, the eldest of Anthon's sons, initially joined his father's firm but in 1756 he moved from Quakenbrück to Bremen where he established his own merchant firm, Johann Schröder & Co. Johann's business marked the beginning of the creation of a network of Schröder family firms which did business together and assisted each other with commercial information. A series of letters written in 1767 by Johann to his father and brothers reveals close co-operation between the Schröder firms in Bremen and Quakenbrück and dealings with the firm of Johann's brother-in-law in Westphalia.[9] From the port of Bremen, two days' journey from Quakenbrück, Johann despatched wines, spirits, coffee, sugar, salmon, herring, lemons, rye and cloth, receiving in return consignments of textiles and foodstuffs such as smoked ham. Johann also undertook currency transactions for his father and brothers, since in Bremen he was able to get a better rate of exchange for the Dutch guilder, in which they often received payment, than was possible in Quakenbrück. More adventurously, Johann began to participate with other merchants in the joint financing of ship voyages. A letter of 31 January 1767, for instance, records the safe arrival in Lisbon of a cargo of sugar from Bahia, Brazil, on which he hoped to make a profit of 3000 shillings – about £85, the annual income of an English small farmer of the day.[10] Most likely it was the example of Johann's enterprises that inspired his younger brother, Christian Matthias, to become an international merchant.

Christian Matthias Schröder and his Enterprises, 1767–89

It was Christian Matthias, the fourth son of Anthon Schröder of Quakenbrück, who established the Schröders as a leading merchant family in Hamburg. Born on 30 January 1742 in Quakenbrück, he was destined for the Church and received an education fitting for that vocation. However, at the age of seventeen he abandoned his ecclesiastical training following a visit to his brother in Bremen and embarked upon a career as a merchant. Christian Matthias began his apprenticeship with Johann Schröder & Co. in Bremen in 1759, but in 1762 he moved to the much larger port of Hamburg.

The 'Free Imperial City of Hamburg' was an independent city state within the Holy Roman Empire. In the Middle Ages it had been a member of the celebrated Hanseatic League, which provided protection for its members' merchants who dominated North Sea and Baltic trade. The League was succeeded by a loose alliance between Hamburg, Bremen and Lübeck, and Hamburg continued to thrive, emerging as the foremost German port and a flourishing cultural centre, the population growing from 20,000 to 90,000 between 1550 and 1750. Its prosperity arose from trading ties with the Western European seaboard, the New World and the Baltic, and its location at the mouth of the Elbe, which made much of Central Europe its hinterland. By the mid-eighteenth century, it was a major participant in the system of international trade in colonial produce, only Amsterdam and London surpassing it in importance (see Map 1.2). From the entrepôts of the Portuguese, Spanish, French and British empires its merchants procured much-sought-after colonial produce, such as sugar, coffee, tobacco and spices. A significant factor in Hamburg's success was the tolerance of the city's authorities towards foreign residents and non-Lutherans; by the 1580s there were sizeable merchant communities of Dutch Calvinists, Italian Catholics and Portuguese Sephardic Jews, and a century later an influx of Huguenots escaping the suppression of Protestant worship in France. Nevertheless, it remained a staunchly Lutheran city with a constitution which enshrined the authority of the Lutheran church, and the most numerous of the immigrants were fellow Lutherans from the surrounding region of Lower Saxony, amongst them Christian Matthias Schröder.[11]

At the time of Christian Matthias's arrival in 1762 Hamburg's trade was booming because of the city's neutrality in the Seven Years War, but the end of the war the following year was marked by a commercial crisis.[12] Christian Matthias's employer, the firm H. Moller Wwe. und Tamm, was a casualty, a harrowing but instructive experience for the young man, whose responsible conduct made a most favourable impression and he emerged from the episode with 'honourable trust'.[13] Somehow Moller resumed business and Christian Matthias continued his apprenticeship. Early in 1767, with his training coming to an end in July, Christian Matthias came to an important decision about his career. In a letter to his father dated 17 February 1767 he explained that he

Map 1.2 Hamburg and international trade in the eighteenth century

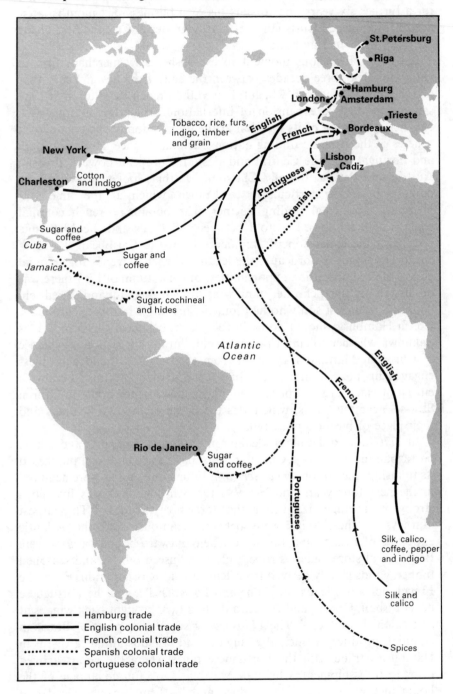

St.Petersburg

Riga

Hamburg
Amsterdam

London

Trieste

Bordeaux

Tobacco, rice, furs,
indigo, timber
and grain

English

French

Lisbon
Cadiz

New York

Portuguese

Cotton
and indigo

Spanish

Charleston

Sugar and
coffee

Cuba

Sugar and
coffee

Jamaica

Sugar, cochineal
and hides

*Atlantic
Ocean*

English

French

Rio de Janeiro

Sugar
and coffee

Portuguese

Silk, calico,
coffee, pepper
and indigo

Silk and
calico

---------- Hamburg trade
―――――― English colonial trade
― ― ― ― French colonial trade
·············· Spanish colonial trade
–·–·–·–·– Portuguese colonial trade

Spices

intended to decline the contract he had been offered tying him to Moller
for a further six years and to start his own business. Six months later,
aged 25, he formed Christian Matthias Schröder & Co., the first of the
Schröder firms in Hamburg.

It was an auspicious moment to establish a new merchant firm in
Hamburg. The three decades between the end of the Seven Years War
and the onset of the wars which followed the French Revolution of 1789
saw a considerable expansion of international trade. Hamburg was a
beneficiary because of its location at the intersection of the commercial
spheres of the Atlantic trading nations, Britain, France, Holland, Spain
and Portugal, and the Central and Eastern European powers, Prussia,
Austria and Russia. Initially Christian Matthias looked westwards to
develop business, particularly to France, which at the time was
Hamburg's principal trading partner. The booming French colonial
trade, which multiplied tenfold between the 1720s and the 1780s due
largely to the expansion of shipments from the Caribbean island of
Santo Domingo to Bordeaux, the leading French entrepôt for colonial
goods, offered promising opportunities. In the autumn of 1767 there was
discussion in the Schröder family as to whether Johann Friedrich,
Anthon's youngest son who had joined Christian Matthias Schröder &
Co. in Hamburg, should go to Bordeaux on behalf of the firm.[14] It is
unknown whether Johann Friedrich went, but the suggestion is evidence
of Christian Matthias's ambition from the outset to build a business
engaged in international trade. In 1768 Christian Matthias became a
citizen of Hamburg and purchased a large three-storey house in Grimm
Strasse, near the docks, which was the home of the two brothers and
their place of business until 1805.

In 1776, after a decade of dealing in imports and exports and taking
participations in cargoes, Christian Matthias Schröder & Co. purchased
its first ship, the 70 ton *Anna Gertruth*. Four more vessels were acquired
in the next four years and by 1780 the Schröder fleet was five ships
strong, its average size during the next three decades.[15] The earliest
journeys of these ships were between Hamburg and the Atlantic
entrepôts of France and Portugal. Their outward-bound cargoes were
Baltic naval stores such as rope, sailcloth, linseed oil, tar and seasoned
timber, goods mostly derived from Russia, and Russian grain. From the
French ports Bordeaux, Bayonne and La Rochelle, and the Portuguese
ports Lisbon, Oporto and Figueira da Foz they brought back wine, salt
and colonial produce.[16] The 1770s saw a surge of imports of Brazilian
colonial produce, principally sugar, and a substantial growth in
Hamburg's trade with the Portuguese ports where the goods arrived
prior to transshipment. Christian Matthias took full advantage of the
boom in trade in Brazilian produce and his firm became a leader in

Hamburg's trade with Portugal. In the 1770s Christian Matthias was also modestly engaged in trade with England, employing a small 45-ton barque on the North Sea crossing, and in 1780 he became a member of the *England Fahrer Gesellschaft* (the Company of Merchants Trading with England).[17]

In the 1780s and 1790s Portugal and France continued to be the usual westward destinations of Schröder ships, though now they called first at the Baltic ports of Riga, Pernau or Libau to take on cargoes such as timber or grain, which was presumably more profitable than loading in Hamburg, and occasionally at Archangel in the White Sea and Vyborg, a timber port in the Gulf of Finland. This pattern was inaugurated in 1781 when two vessels sailed east upon leaving Hamburg to the Russian Baltic port of Pernau before journeying to Figueira da Foz. In 1782 the Schröder brothers took delivery of three new ships, the *Neptunus* and the *Rebecca*, each 100 tons, and the *Vriendschap*, 140 tons, which replaced some of the smaller vessels and raised the total tonnage of the fleet from 307 tons to 490 tons. Christian Matthias was also very actively engaged in the shipment of luxury consumer goods, such as wine, sugar, coffee and textiles, from Hamburg to St Petersburg, Russia's capital and the principal port for imports with a population of 220,000 in the 1780s. The first transatlantic crossing by a Schröder ship was in 1782 when Christian Matthias's largest ship visited the West Indies, presumably to collect sugar. The end of the American War of Independence of 1776–83 brought a restoration of peace between Britain and France, which had supported the insurgent colonists, and the lifting of the British blockade permitted a revival of trade between Hamburg and the French ports. For the following decade and a half the Schröder brothers' westward trade focused upon long-haul business with French and Portuguese ports, entirely forsaking North Sea trade with England from 1783 to 1797.[18]

Besides building up their business with great success, Christian Matthias and Johann Friedrich took active parts in the civic life of Hamburg. The administration of Hamburg was based on the constitution of 1712, according to which sovereignty resided in the joint authority of the Senate, an executive body comprising four *Bürgermeister* and 24 senators (13 merchants and 11 lawyers), and three civic colleges in which the burghers were represented by their parish administrators. The constitution also enshrined Lutheranism as the official religion of the city state.[19] As Lutherans, the Schröder brothers were able to achieve full citizenship, Christian Matthias becoming a burgher in 1768 only six years after his arrival, and they both assumed considerable burdens of civic responsibilities. Christian Matthias served as a poor relief official in the parish of St Catherine and an administrator of the city's orphanage; a collector of customs duties and the burgher tax; a captain of the militia in the 1780s; and an officer of the artillery in the 1790s and as a member of the Chamber of Commerce. Johann Friedrich took on a similar set of civic duties: poor house administrator; tax administrator; and member of the Chamber of Commerce and one of the civic colleges. These responsibilities promoted the social advancement of the Schröder brothers in their adopted city, but it is unlikely this was their only motive. Civic service was already an established family tradition amongst the Schröders, inspired by a sense of duty deriving from their devout Lutheranism.

Commercial success and civic service paved the way for Christian Matthias and Johann Friedrich to enter the ranks of Hamburg's leading citizens. Their advancement was also fostered by their marriages into families of established eminence. On 25 May 1773 Christian Matthias married Louise Mutzenbecher, the fifteenth and youngest child of a prosperous Hamburg merchant. Elizabeth Tamm, Johann Friedrich's bride in 1780, was the daughter of a senator and bore the name of a family illustrious in the affairs of the city since the Middle Ages. In 1787 Christian Matthias purchased a 40-acre country property at Eimsbüttel, five miles north-west of Hamburg. The *Schröderhof*, as it became known, was a long, single-storey house surrounded by gardens laid out as a park with meadows, which became the family's summer residence. Faith, fortitude, duty and family were Christian Matthias's tenets of life, according to the letter he wrote to his children in 1779 counselling them on conduct:

> Be devout, love piety and virtue, and rest your happiness in righteousness, and the true obedience to the foremost duty of every Christian to love his neighbour . . . Endeavour to be gentle and noble in character. Remember that wrath is not right before God. Should things on this world not go so well or as you would wish, reconcile yourselves to it with Christian resignation. Heed not adversity and stand fast to God. Keep up true friendship and concord with your kith and kin, help one another faithfully for then you will be safest from the persecution of your enemies . . . I pray God that he may keep you and your children to the thousandth generation in his peace and blessing.[20]

Each of Christian Matthias's six sons became a merchant (see Figure 1.2). The eldest pair, Christian Matthias II and Anthon Diedrich, joined their father in his firm. The third, Johann Friedrich, was dispatched to London, where he was joined a couple of years later by Johann Heinrich, the fifth son. The other two, Hermann Engelbert and Georg Wilhelm, were sent east and formed firms in the Russian Baltic ports of

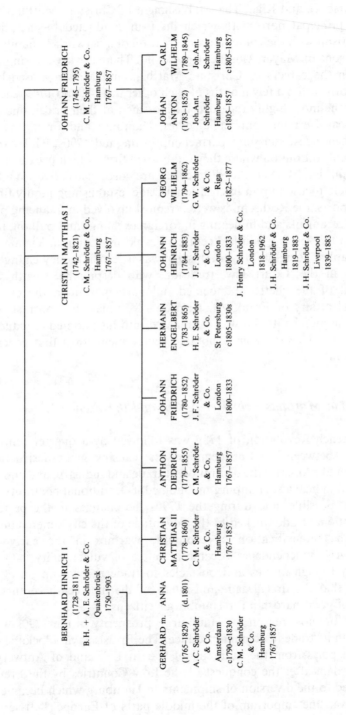

Figure 1.2 Merchant descendants of Christian Matthias Schröder (1742–1821)

Christian Matthias Schröder & Co. abbreviated to C. M. Schröder & Co.

St Petersburg and Riga. The establishment of Christian Matthias's sons in the principal ports with which his firm conducted business invites comparison with the contemporary creation of a network of family firms by the sons of Mayer Amschel Rothschild. There are several similarities between the careers of Christian Matthias and Mayer Amschel: they were born within a few months of each other in 1742 and 1743; each was one of the most highly regarded businessmen of their era in one of the two great German commercial cities, Hamburg and Frankfurt; both took their eldest sons into partnership in the mid-1790s, while younger sons went to London where they established firms which became leading merchant banks. Yet the differences are also instructive. While the Schröders focused upon international trade, establishing family firms in major ports, the Rothschilds were foremost involved in financing princes and governments and in dealing in foreign exchange and bullion, having firms in five leading political centres: Frankfurt, London, Vienna, Paris and Naples. Socially, Mayer Amschel was a Jewish money changer and banker in the 'Court Jew' tradition, who despite his wealth was a resident of the ghetto and denied full participation in the civic and political affairs of Frankfurt. Christian Matthias, by contrast, was a Lutheran merchant who was assimilated into his adopted city and even became its *Bürgermeister*, a notable achievement for a first generation immigrant.

Christian Matthias Schröder & Co. and the French Wars

The French Revolution of 1789 was followed by a quarter century of warfare between the European powers, causing great destruction of people and property, the disruption of trade and industry, and enormous political upheavals. Hamburg maintained its traditional neutrality for as long as possible, and during the 1790s the changes in the pattern of international trade worked to the advantage of the city's merchants, but with the intensification of economic warfare in the early 1800s Hamburg's independence became a source of vulnerability.[21] Occupation by foreign armies and obstacles to trade thrown up on all sides meant that the first decade-and-a-half of the nineteenth century were years of great hardship for Hamburg's citizens.

The foremost reason for Hamburg's prosperity in the 1790s was the boom in its trade in colonial produce. The British naval blockade of the French ports from the outbreak of war in 1793 and of Antwerp and Amsterdam after the conquest of the Low Countries by the French in 1795 led to the diversion of shipments to Hamburg which became more than ever 'the emporium of the middle parts of Europe'.[22] It served as the principal distribution centre for the whole Continent, including France, for both sugar and coffee.[23] Business with London, the leading international entrepôt, increased dramatically, the volume of British shipments to Hamburg growing from 6000 tons in 1789 to 60,000 tons in 1800.[24]

Christian Matthias's business thrived in the 1790s and his standing amongst Hamburg's merchants was further enhanced, becoming head of the Chamber of Commerce. From 1793, in view of the British blockade of the French ports, he focused on the trans-shipment of Russian produce directly from the Baltic ports to Portugal, and of colonial produce from Portugal to Hamburg. To undertake these voyages he acquired two new ships, the 120-ton *Aurora* and the 150-ton *gute Henriette*, which were launched at Eckenförde near Lübeck in 1793. Each spring, once the ice in the Baltic had melted, the ships set sail for the Russian ports, whose export trade grew rapidly in the 1790s and 1800s, collecting cargoes of naval stores and also grain, hides and tallow, which became increasingly important exports following the Russian annexation of the rich agricultural regions of Poland and the Black Sea steppes in 1792. Simultaneously, there was a boom in imports of luxury goods, notably sugar and coffee, to St Petersburg.[25] Christian Matthias and his sons were active participants in these developments, establishing an enduring pattern of activity – the trades in grain, tallow and sugar with Russia being specialities of the Schröder firms for many years.

The Portugal trade, the other important dimension to Christian Matthias's business, also underwent great changes. Portuguese neutrality ensured that Brazilian sugar and coffee, appearing in Europe for the first time, could be transshipped to northern Europe without interference from the British or French navies, and Brazilian exports boomed, as did the port of Lisbon, which was described by a German visitor as a scene of 'activity and opulence . . . after London . . . the first commercial place in the world'.[26] The United States acted as a neutral entrepôt for Caribbean produce in the war years of the 1790s, explaining why Christian Matthias's ships began to call at American ports. In 1795 the *gute Henriette*, which had sailed from Hamburg to Riga and thence to Oporto, journeyed to Charleston, South Carolina, before returning to Hamburg. The next year, it again visited Charleston, this time via Tenerife, and in following years other Schröder ships visited Baltimore and New York. In 1797, Schröder ships called at London for the first time since 1781, reviving Christian Matthias Schröder & Co.'s trade with England.

In the midst of the boom of 1795, Johann Friedrich died of tuberculosis, which must have been a heavy blow for Christian Matthias both personally and in the business. At the time of his death the brothers and their families still shared the Grimm Strasse townhouse, and Christian Matthias naturally assumed responsibility for Johann Friedrich's widow and children. He took as his new partner Gerhard Schröder, the 30-year-old son of his elder brother, Bernhard Hinrich I, one of the founders of the Quakenbrück wine merchants B. H. & A. E. Schröder. Gerhard had formerly run his own firm A. C. Schröder & Co. in Amsterdam but the French occupation in 1795 forced him, like many other Amsterdam merchants and bankers, to flee to Hamburg. In 1796 the partnership was cemented by Gerhard's marriage to one of Christian Matthias's daughters, one of many marriages between Schröder cousins in the eighteenth and nineteenth centuries that reinforced the close ties between the Schröder family firms. In the busy latter years of the 1790s the partners were assisted by Christian Matthias's elder sons, Christian Matthias II and Anthon Diedrich, who at the turn of the century were aged 22 and 21 respectively. They, like their younger brothers, Johann Friedrich, aged 20, Hermann Engelbert, aged 17, Johann Heinrich, aged 16, Georg Wilhelm, aged 6 and their cousins Johann Anton, aged 18, and Carl Wilhelm, aged 11, had grown up in the *milieu* of a bustling place of business a stone's throw from the berths of the Schröder ships. International trade was in the air they breathed, and all became international merchants.

Hamburg's flourishing trade with London led to political problems with Britain's enemies. In 1799, France declared an embargo on Hamburg vessels, accusing the city of siding with the British. The French embargo coincided with the arrival in northern Europe of large shipments of colonial merchandise via Lisbon and London, leaving Hamburg merchants holding large stocks. The ensuing Hamburg Crisis, which began in August 1799, saw the bankruptcy of more than 150 firms.[27] British interception of neutral shipping to prevent supplies of war materials reaching France provoked mounting resentment on the part of the northern European powers. In 1800, Russia, Sweden, Denmark and Prussia formed the League of Armed Neutrality, a common front to force Britain to stop its searches and seizures of their shipping by closing the Baltic to British trade. To this end, Hamburg, the principal point of distribution of British goods, was occupied by the Prussians and then the Danes. The bombardment of Copenhagen in April 1801 by Admiral Nelson led to the detachment of Denmark from the League and secured the restoration of Hamburg's independence, while the lifting of the French embargo was secured soon after by the payment of a large fine. No record remains of how Christian Matthias Schröder & Co. coped with the Hamburg Crisis or the subsequent troubles, but his appointment as a senator on 19 August 1799, in the midst of the crisis, suggests that his public standing had never been higher. Each senator was the protector of a guild, Christian Matthias's responsibility being for the prestigious Goldsmiths' Guild. It was during these difficult and volatile years, but with their father's success and reputation as backing, that Johann Friedrich and Johann Heinrich established themselves in London, and Hermann Engelbert in St Petersburg.

Hamburg's trade revived in the period of peace which followed the signing of the Treaty of Amiens between Britain and France in March 1802, but fourteen months later hostilities resumed, ushering in a disastrous decade for Hamburg's merchants. In the summer of 1803 French troops occupied the Electorate of Hanover, a possession of the British Crown which since 1721 had included the Duchy of Bremen. The French closed the estuaries of the Elbe and the Weser to British shipping, and in retaliation the British Navy imposed a blockade, bringing hardship to Hamburg and Bremen. To make matters worse the French forced the Hanseatic cities to make loans which were used to pay for the army of occupation, and French customs police were introduced to enforce the suppression of trade with Britain. Despite these impediments Christian Matthias continued to conduct business, his ships calling each spring at Riga or Pernau before sailing to Portugal, or occasionally to the Caribbean or the United States.

Besides depriving Britain of a continental foothold, the occupation of Hanover strengthened Napoleon's hand in the political reorganisation of Germany. This had been begun in February 1803, when the constitution of the Holy Roman Empire was drastically reformed, sweeping away a myriad of princelings and reducing the number of free imperial cities from fifty-two to six. The great Hanseatic cities, Hamburg, Bremen and Lübeck, were three of the survivors, thanks, it was rumoured, to the payment of large bribes.[28] Central Germany was reconstructed as a set of medium-sized states which were rallied into a French-dominated alliance, the Confederation of the Rhine, and French ascendancy in central Europe was made complete by Napoleon's victories over the Austrians at Austerlitz in December 1805 and the Prussians at Jena in October 1806. But the war with Britain continued, the defeat of the French fleet at Trafalgar in 1805 putting paid to his plans for invasion. Napoleon thus determined to stop British trade with the Continent, believing that this would cause the collapse of its finances and render it incapable of paying subsidies to continental allies. To this end, on 14 November 1806, a month after the battle of Jena, Hamburg was occupied by French troops and two days later Napoleon promulgated a set of measures proscribing all forms of trade with Britain, known as the 'Continental System'.

The occupation of Hamburg and the Continental System led to a new wave of failures of Hamburg merchants and hardship amongst the inhabitants. The French military administration seized all goods of British origin and declared forfeit profits earned in trade with Britain. The Hamburg Savings Bank was seized, on the pretext that it had British deposits, and the Hamburg Poor-House, one of the most notable civic charitable foundations of Europe, was requisitioned as a military barracks.[29] The Continental System was applied by France, the Low Countries, the Confederation of the Rhine, Denmark, Prussia, Austria and Spain, and Russia was brought into the fold by the Treaty of Tilsit in June 1807. Despite Napoleon's threats, Portugal continued to trade with Britain, prompting a French invasion in the summer of 1807. With most of Portugal under French occupation, London became the principal entrepôt for Brazilian exports and henceforth Brazilian trade was conducted directly with foreign ports, an important development for Hamburg merchants when peace was restored.

The business of Christian Matthias Schröder & Co. must have suffered as a result of these developments but the standing of the firm appears to have been undiminished – a saying amongst Hamburg merchants at the time being 'As sound as Christian Matthias'.[30] When it was suggested that his firm might be in difficulties because of Hamburg's problems, he responded, 'Ich empfinde das gar nicht, mein Feld ist die Welt' ('I don't see it like that at all, my field is the world').[31] Perhaps Christian Matthias's confidence was based on the presence of his sons in London and St Petersburg, who probably had with them much of the family fortune for safe-keeping and maybe some of the Schröder ships. Christian Matthias began to withdraw from active participation in the business in 1807, handing over control of the firm to his sons, Christian Matthias II and Anthon Diedrich. He divided his time between a magnificent townhouse at 63 Rodingsmarkt, which he purchased in 1805, the *Schröderhof* in Eimsbüttel, and a new estate *Ruhleben* ('quiet life') on the Plöner See in Schleswig-Holstein. His fortune was estimated in 1808 (during the depression caused by the French occupation) at one million Bancomarks – £200,000 in sterling of the day – a sum which might have purchased a stately home and 20,000 acres in England.[32] In his retirement he concentrated upon his senatorial duties and served on the committee established to organise the quartering of French soldiers upon the hostile townsfolk.

Despite the Continental System and the occupation, Hamburg merchants continued to trade with Britain using Heligoland, an island 30 miles off the North German coast, as a staging post under British naval protection for the smuggling of British goods. Most probably the contraband shipments included goods despatched to their native city by Johann Friedrich and Johann Heinrich in London. Bourienne, the first French governor, estimated that there were 6,000 smugglers in Hamburg alone and during his lax administration false certificates of origin for ship cargoes were readily available from the Hamburg Senate, and were accepted by French customs officials if accompanied by a bribe.[33] In 1810 Napoleon replaced Bourienne with Marshal Davout, a 'stern but upright man of discipline [an] honest fanatic of Napoleonic statesmanship', who zealously suppressed the trade in British contraband.[34] In December 1810 the Hanseatic cities, as well as Holland and various German territories as far as the Baltic, were annexed to France, Hamburg becoming 'une bonne ville de l' Empire Française' within the new *Département des Bouches de l'Elbe* (Map 1.3). The 1712 constitution was abolished, the Senate being replaced by a 'conseil municipal' supervised by a French prefect, and the Code Napoleon legal system was introduced. Hamburg's trade came to a halt upon the annexation, with 300 ships laid up in the harbour, deserted quays, and only one of the 400 sugar refineries in operation.[35] With business at a standstill, his civic duties terminated and his wife in poor health, Christian Matthias retreated to his estate in Schleswig-Holstein.

The tightening of the tourniquet on British trade provoked a financial crisis in Britain but did not cause the collapse of its war effort. In fact, it led to the defection of Russia and Sweden from the Continental System, the Russian nobility resenting being deprived of revenues from the export of timber, grain and other produce of their estates, and of imports of colonial produce. It was probably upon Russia's resumption of trade with Britain in 1811 that Georg Wilhelm, Christian Matthias's youngest son, established the merchant firm G. W. Schröder & Co. in Riga. Napoleon responded to the defections with military reprisals occupying Swedish Pomerania and invading Russia in the summer of 1812, a move which proved most ill-judged.

News of French reverses in Russia inspired an insurrection in Hamburg in March 1813 and the French were expelled from the city. But in May 1813 French troops, commanded by the fearsome Marshal Davout, reappeared and laid siege to Hamburg, which prudently surrendered. Enormous reparations were demanded by the French as punishment for the city's disloyalty, and when payment was not forthcoming Davout seized the reserves of the Bank of Hamburg, an institution which was a vital source of credit and finance for Hamburg's merchants.[36] The inhabitants were put to work on strengthening the fortifications and many were expelled from the city and starved. Hamburg's tribulations came to an end at last following Napoleon's defeat at the Battle of Nations at Leipzig in October 1813, which led to the retreat of French troops back across the Rhine in the face of the advancing Russian and allied troops who entered Paris in March 1814. Hamburg's independence was recognised by the post-war peace treaties and once again it became a free city state.

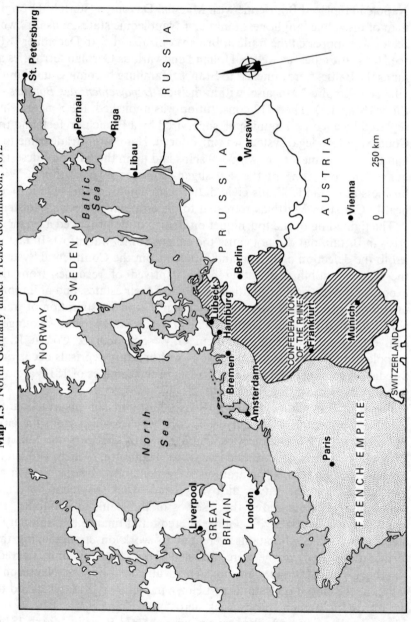

Map 1.3 North Germany under French domination, 1812

When the French arrived at the Elbe in 1803 Hamburg was a prosperous and well-run city with a population of 130,000. A decade later the population was impoverished, many merchants were ruined, the administration was in chaos, and the inhabitants numbered fewer than 100,000.[37] Christian Matthias played a leading part in the administration of the city in the period of reconstruction which followed the departure of the French.[38] He resumed his seat in the Senate, which again became the forum for government with the restoration of the constitution of 1712, and on 12 June 1816 he was made *Bürgermeister*, one of the four heads of the city state. He died in office on 6 July 1821, aged 79.

The Business Legacy of Christian Matthias Schröder

At the time of the death of Christian Matthias there were Schröder family firms in half-a-dozen northern European ports. His six sons ran enterprises in Hamburg, London, St Petersburg and Riga, a geographical distribution which reflected the Atlantic and Baltic pattern of Christian Matthias Schröder & Co.'s business. There were further Schröder firms conducted by Christian Matthias's nephews in Bremen, Amsterdam and Hamburg. Moreover, there were also the family firms in Quakenbrück. In the next couple of generations, during the second and third quarters of the nineteenth century, offshoots of these houses multiplied the network of Schröder firms (see Map 1.4). In Europe, firms were founded in Liverpool in 1839 and in Trieste in 1843; in the United States: in New Orleans in 1848 and New York in 1856; and in South America: in Rio de Janeiro, Lima and Aguadilla on the island of Puerto Rico. Furthermore, in the second half of the nineteenth century, J. Henry Schröder & Co. did business with Busing Schröder & Co. of Batavia (Jakarta) and Singapore, with which there was a family connection.

Such international networks of family firms were not new. The Bardi and Peruzzi in fourteenth-century Tuscany and the Medici of Florence in the following century had partnerships which conducted merchanting and banking activities all over Western Europe.[39] Subsequently, networks of family firms became familiar features of international trade, being particularly associated with merchants of Huguenot, German, Greek and Jewish origin. The strength of an international network of family firms, an 'international house' as it has been called, was the trust which could be placed in the honesty and diligence of fellow family members at a time when overseas commercial transactions often took many months and were conducted without the protection of legal redress across national boundaries.[40] Of equal importance was the

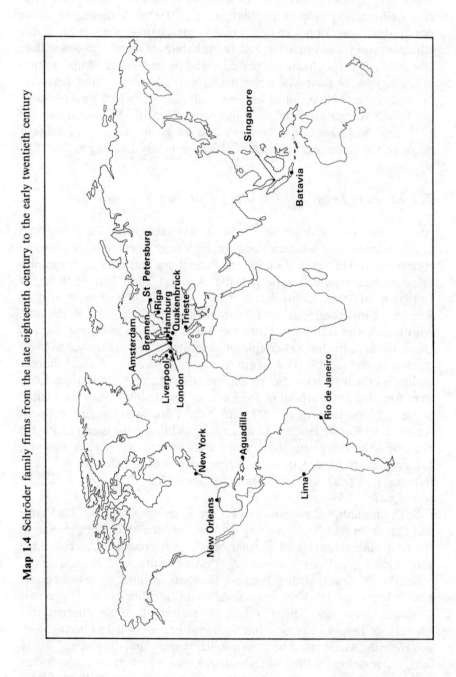

Map 1.4 Schröder family firms from the late eighteenth century to the early twentieth century

Aguadilla
Name unknown

Amsterdam
A. C. Schröder
(c.1790–1830)
B. H. Schröder & Co.
(c.1830–1890)
J. Herman Schröder
(c.1890–1920)

Batavia (Jakarta) & Singapore
Büsing, Schröder & Co.
(c.1870s)

Bremen
Johann Schröder & Co.
(1756–1829)
G. H. & P. D. Schröder
(c.1830–1870)
B. H. Schröder Söhne
(c.1850–1880)

Hamburg
Christian Matthias Schröder & Co.
(1767–1857)
Johan Anton Schröder & Co.
(c.1805–1857)
J.H. Schröder & Co./Schröder, Mahs & Co.
(c.1819–1883)
Schröder Gebrüder & Co.
(1846–1968)
Christian Schröder & Co.
(1858–1900)

J. G. Schröder & Co.
(1858–c.1920)
Anthon Schröder & Co.
(1859–c.1920)
Schröder & Südeck
(c.1890–1920)
Poelchau & Schröder
(c.1870–1950)

Lima
C. M. Schröder & Co.
(c.1870–1930)

Liverpool
J. H. Schröder & Co.
(1839–1883)

London
J. F. Schröder & Co.
(1800–1833)
J. Henry Schröder & Co.
(1818–1962)
Schröder, Böninger & Co.
(1860–1872)

New Orleans
Schröder, Mummy & Co.
(1848–1857)

New York
Troost, Schröder & Co.
(1856–1857)

Quakenbrück
Anthon Schröder & Co.
(1730–1880s)
B. H. & A. E. Schröder
(1750–1903)

Riga
G. W. Schröder & Co.
(c.1812–1877)

Rio de Janeiro
Herman Schröder
(c.1840–1860)

St Petersburg
H. E. Schröder & Co.
(c.1802–1865)

Trieste
A. & Ch. M. Schröder
(1843–1898)

commercial intelligence provided by family correspondents which permitted accurate credit evaluation and assessment of risks, reducing the hazards of international banking business.

J. Henry Schröder & Co.'s membership of the Schröder international house was vitally important to its success and to the pattern of the development of its business. The hub of the Schröder international house was Hamburg, which in the nineteenth century became more than ever the leading port of northern continental Europe conducting a worldwide commerce though retaining its strong ties with London and the Russian Baltic ports. J. Henry Schröder & Co. and the other Schröder firms benefited from the dynamic expansion of Hamburg's trade. Furthermore, the Schröder family sustained its close involvement in the city's commercial and civic affairs, several branches being eminent amongst the mercantile and social elite. The Schröder international house was first and foremost a mercantile network, the business of the Hamburg Schröder firms and most of the overseas houses being international trade and shipping. J. Henry Schröder & Co.'s specialisation in financing trade was exceptional and in its early stages owed much to servicing the requirements of other family firms for financial accommodation. The mercantile focus of the Schröder network of family firms is an important factor in explaining why J. Henry Schröder & Co. did not enter the purely financial activity of issuing foreign loans until the second half of the nineteenth century, many decades after Barings and Rothschilds.

Christian Matthias's achievements and values were enduring influences upon the Schröder family. His reputation for integrity and judgement gave an immediate advantage to his offspring and relations in their business undertakings. His civic services bestowed prestige upon his descendants and inspired emulation. Moreover, his strong orientation to his home and his family set an example to succeeding generations. The Schröder family was notably endogamous, there being a score of marriages between direct descendants of Christian Matthias in the nineteenth century. This pattern reflected and reinforced the tightly-knit nature of the Schröder family and Schröder firms. It also contributed to their continuing prosperity by preserving the family fortune, fostering the conduct of business together and the exchange of commercial information.

Christian Matthias Schröder & Co. was the leading Schröder firm in Hamburg from the 1760s to the 1850s. From 1807 it was directed by Christian Matthias's eldest sons, Christian Matthias II and Anthon Diedrich. Like their father, they also took active parts in the civic life of Hamburg, and in 1821 Christian Matthias II succeeded his father as a senator. Subsequently his eldest son, Christian Matthias III, succeeded as the head of the family firm. During the 1820s, 1830s and 1840s,

Schröder ships, named after female members of the family, plied their way to South America and to the Baltic, and the firm conducted a large business as an importer of coffee, spices, grain, wine and textiles. In the 1850s it played an important part in the establishment of the German settlement in Joinville, Brazil. In the United States, a younger son of Christian Matthias II and a second cousin formed Schröder, Mummy & Co. in New Orleans in 1848, with an eye to participating in the cotton trade, and in 1856 a brother-in-law formed Troost, Schröder & Co. in New York, a mercantile house which conducted a general commission business.

A significant development in the business of Christian Matthias Schröder & Co. was the commencement of the financing of the trade conducted by other merchants.[41] In the early 1850s it led the way in the financing of exports from Scandinavia and developed a large business providing trade credits on account of shipments of Swedish iron ore to Portugal.[42] Defaults by merchants engaged in this business in the commercial crisis of 1857 endangered the survival of the firm. Johann Heinrich offered support to his elder brothers but the position was so hopeless that Christian Matthias Schröder & Co. was obliged to close, the most spectacular casualty of the crisis which led to the failure of 200 Hamburg merchant firms. To relieve the hardship of his ruined relatives, Johann Heinrich provided them with pensions. Following the crisis of 1857 there was no doubt that Johann Heinrich was the senior figure in the Schröder family or that J. Henry Schröder & Co. in London was the premier Schröder firm. It was Johann Heinrich, the fifth son of Christian Matthias, who had inherited his father's business acumen and discipline and who developed his legacy to the greatest extent.

2

Johann Heinrich Schröder in London, Hamburg and Liverpool

1800–49

Johann Heinrich Schröder was born on 12 December 1784 and died 98 years later on 28 June 1883. At his birth the Industrial Revolution was in its infancy but by the time of his death factory production, railways, steamships and the electric telegraph were commonplace in the industrial nations. The creation of the modern industrial economy was accompanied by an enormous increase in international trade, in the development of which Johann Heinrich's firms were involved. During the course of his lifetime he was a partner in four merchant firms conducting international trade. Initially, he joined J. F. Schröder & Co., the firm of an elder brother with whom he was in business for a decade and a half in London. Upon the dissolution of their partnership at the end of 1817 he formed his own firms in London and Hamburg and subsequently another in Liverpool – the three leading European seaports of the era. The business built by Johann Heinrich was an international trading organisation with a growing emphasis on trade finance in London, the world's foremost financial centre.

The shipment of commodities, particularly sugar, coffee, cotton, indigo, tallow and grain, from producer countries to consumer markets was the activity with which Johann Heinrich's firms were principally involved. As merchants, they conducted business both as principals and as agents. Operating as principals, merchant firms purchased, shipped and sold goods on their 'own account', assuming all risks and receiving all profits, or on 'joint account' with other firms, sharing the risks and rewards. These were the ways in which Christian Matthias Schröder & Co. conducted business. Merchants also acted as agents for merchants in other cities. Acting as agents, they organised the shipment, insurance and sale of cargoes for a commission. This was less risky and required less capital, but the rewards were commensurately more modest than successful own account or joint account transactions. The firms of Johann Heinrich acted both as principals and as agents for one another and for the other Schröder family firms.

In the first half of the nineteenth century much of the trade in the import of commodities to Europe was conducted on a 'consignment' basis.[1] Merchants in market centres, notably London, Liverpool and Hamburg, received cargoes of produce despatched by planters or merchants in the places of origin. The goods were sold and the proceeds remitted to the shipper or held as a balance on his behalf, depending on the arrangements between the parties, the consignment merchant taking a percentage commission for his services. Although in principle the role of the consignment merchant was that of an agent, in fact he often assumed part of the risks of the transactions because it became common practice for an advance to be made to the shipper of up to two-thirds or three-quarters of the likely value of the consignment.[2] Advances to shippers were furnished in the form of bills of exchange; that is, an order signed by the consignment merchant promising payment on presentation of the bill at a future date, by which time he would have sold the goods received on consignment and be in a position to pay. If the shipper required cash prior to the maturity of the bill he could sell it to a local bank or some other party who in due course would present it for payment by the consignment merchant.

Exporters, whether operating on a consignment basis or by outright sale of goods, preferred payment in bills endorsed by a well-known firm of impeccable reputation. This gave rise to the specialist activity which in time came to be called 'merchant banking', the practice of certain high-standing merchant firms guaranteeing payment of bills of exchange issued by firms of lesser standing and receiving a commission for providing this service.[3] Upon presentation of the bill, the merchant firm would acknowledge responsibility for payment by writing 'accepted' across the face. Such bills became known as 'acceptances' and the firms which provided this service as 'accepting houses', or alternatively 'merchant banks'. Typically, payment was due 90 days after acceptance and in the meantime the bills were traded in the money market. The increasing specialisation of certain London merchants upon acceptance business in the early nineteenth century led to the provision of credit facilities for clients on a regular rather than *ad hoc* basis by means of the granting of a 'letter of credit', which was an authorisation to a client to issue bills of exchange up to an agreed limit, an arrangement known as a line of credit. Firms granting letters of credit, such as Schröders, engaged a network of merchants and bankers in other cities to act as correspondents or agents, who agreed to make payment upon the presentation of bills issued under the firm's letters of credit.

In theory, any merchant of repute could provide endorsements and bills could be denominated in any currency, but during the nineteenth century it was the London merchant banks and the sterling bill of exchange which predominated. There were several reasons for this. First, in the words of a contemporary witness, the 'almost complete annihilation of the commerce of Amsterdam, formerly the first commercial city of Europe', following the French invasion of 1795.[4] Second, the enormous increase in trade passing through British ports, the port of London in particular, during the French wars. Third, the existence of a rapidly growing market in bills of exchange arising from domestic transactions, which provided an institutional framework for trading bills originating from international trade (known as a 'bill on London'). Fourth, Britain's adoption of the gold standard in 1819, which made the sterling bill of exchange a universally acceptable medium for the finance of international trade; in 1832 Nathan Rothschild told a parliamentary inquiry that Britain 'is the Bank for the whole world . . . all transactions in India, in China, in Germany, in the whole world, are guided here and settled through this country'.[5] Johann Heinrich's London firm, J. Henry Schröder & Co., was an active participant in the development of the sterling bill of exchange as the foremost instrument for the finance of international trade. 'Merchants & Bankers' was the term by which J. Henry Schröder & Co. styled itself until well into the twentieth century.

J. F. Schröder & Co., 1800–33

The outbreak of war with France in 1793 was followed by a boom in British trade, the value of exports, many of which were re-exports of colonial produce, doubling in the years 1793–1801.[6] The rapid increase was a consequence of the suppression of enemy commerce by the British Navy, which led to the routeing of shipments of colonial produce via Britain and to the expansion of the output of the British West Indies. The fastest growing market for British exports was Germany, shipments quadrupling in value in the years 1793–98. Three-quarters of these cargoes were colonial produce, particularly sugar, and, as already related, Hamburg was much the most important recipient, serving as the principal point of distribution on the Continent for West Indian produce and for British manufactures. The Hamburg Crisis of 1799 caused a downturn in trade, but in 1800 British exports to Germany reached a record £12 million, which constituted 55 per cent of total British exports, and the trade boom continued until 1803.

Christian Matthias responded to the increase in British trade by establishing members of his family in London. The first to arrive was Bernhard Hinrich II, a younger brother of Christian Matthias's partner and son-in-law, Gerhard. On 31 May 1797 the 21-year-old Bernhard Hinrich II became member 208 of Pilgrim Lodge, a freemasons' lodge founded in London in 1779 whose members were mainly foreign merchants trading in London.[7] Nothing is known of his business activities but most likely he acted as a commission agent for his uncle and brother, purchasing cargoes of colonial produce for them and despatching them to Hamburg.

Bernhard Hinrich II was joined in London by his 20-year-old cousin, Johann Friedrich, third son of Christian Matthias, who on 26 February 1800 became Pilgrim Lodge member 232. He appears to have arrived with family capital since he immediately set up his own firm, J. F. Schröder & Co., which is recorded in a London street directory of 1801 at 35 Throgmorton Street in the City.[8] The development of J. F. Schröder & Co. must have been assisted by his election as a member of Lloyds in 1801, enabling him to conduct the insurance underwriting of ships and cargoes.[9] Another advantageous move was his marriage in 1802 to Isabella Bustard, the eldest daughter of a partner of the merchant firm Richard Bustard & Marwood of 12 Laurence Pountney Lane in the City, a match which warranted a mention in the *Gentleman's Magazine*.[10] Johann Friedrich had been in business for less than two years when he was joined in London by his younger brother, Johann Heinrich, who was admitted as a member of Pilgrim Lodge on 27 January 1802, a month after his seventeenth birthday. It is probable that Johann Heinrich became a partner in his brother's firm in 1804, the year traditionally ascribed to the foundation of J. Henry Schröder & Co. in London. For a decade and a half the Schröder brothers developed their business together in London, prospering despite the war and the unsettled political and economic conditions.

J. F. Schröder & Co. specialised in sugar, a trade which had long been of importance to Christian Matthias Schröder & Co.[11] Sugar was the most important commodity in Hamburg's trade with Britain in the opening years of the nineteenth century, and early ledgers of the West India Dock Company establish that in 1805 the firm rented storage space in eight of their warehouses, accommodation which was used almost exclusively for sugar.[12] In addition to its activities as a sugar merchant, the firm acted from the outset as an acceptor of bills of exchange. In April 1802, Nathan Rothschild, the founder of N. M. Rothschild & Sons, who was still conducting business as a textile merchant based in Manchester, presented three bills to J. F. Schröder & Co. for acceptance.[13] The bills represented payment by Jacob Marcus of Amsterdam, an acceptance client of the firm, to three Manchester cotton merchants who had sold them to Rothschild.

The admission of Johann Friedrich to the Russia Company in London in November 1807 suggests that the Schröder brothers were endeavouring to develop trade in the Baltic to compensate for the downturn in trade with Hamburg following the French occupation of the city.[14] By the early nineteenth century the Russia Company, which had been granted a monopoly of trade between England and Russia by Queen Elizabeth I in the sixteenth century, had lost most of its privileges, but membership still afforded some benefits.[15] Johann Heinrich's application for membership was considered by the Court of the Russia Company in February 1808, three months after his brother joined, but he was turned down for failing to attend the meeting, a most uncharacteristic lapse that suggests he was absent abroad.[16] The timing of the Schröder brothers' applications is intriguing and may have been prompted by the moves to instigate a convoy system for British trade with the Baltic at this moment.[17]

Napoleon's tightening of the blockade on British trade with the Continent in 1810 led to a commercial crisis in Britain. A North American visitor to London wrote that:

> There is a general stagnation of commerce . . . all entrance to Europe being completely shut up . . . Merchants have either become bankrupt, or retired, while they could, from business. Their clerks are all discharged, and gone into the army, or country. Those merchants who formerly kept ten or fifteen clerks, now have two or three. There are now many thousands half-starved, discharged clerks, skulking about London; in every street you see, 'A counting-house to let' . . . The Royal Exchange is miserably attended; no foreigners, but about a dozen Hamburgers, very few Americans . . . Such a time as this was never known in England.[18]

Trade with Germany came almost to a halt in 1811 and for the first time during the French wars communication between London and Hamburg became impossible.[19] These years saw a wave of bankruptcies amongst merchant firms in London but J. F. Schröder & Co. weathered the storm.

The repudiation of the Continental System by Russia and Sweden in 1811, that marked the beginning of its break-up, led to a vigorous recovery of British exports, which doubled in the years 1811–15. Hermann Engelbert (the brother of Johann Friedrich and Johann Heinrich), who had gone to St Petersburg where he had established the firm H. E. Schröder & Co., seized the opportunity presented by the resumption of trade between Russia and Britain to meet the pent-up demand for sugar from the prosperous population of the Russian capital. In 1812, he purchased a sugar mill at the Baltic port of Katherinenhof, receiving supplies of West Indian raw sugar forwarded by his brothers in London. One such shipment was in July 1814, for which J. F. Schröder & Co. received payment in the form of a bill of exchange bearing the names of H. E. Schröder & Co. and E. H. Brandt & Co., the London firm of another well-known Hamburg mercantile family, which acted as acceptor.[20] Georg Wilhelm, Christian Matthias's youngest son, also established a merchant firm in Russia, G. W. Schröder & Co. in Riga, which probably specialised in the timber trade. A reference by Johann Friedrich to 'my Riga house' in correspondence with Rothschilds establishes that the firms were doing business together in 1831, and the accounts of J. Henry Schröder & Co. show that it was a client until 1877.[21]

There are several indications that a revival of the business of J. F. Schröder & Co. was well under way by 1813. First, Johann Heinrich became a member of Lloyds, an unnecessary action unless there were cargoes to be insured.[22] Second, Johann Friedrich and his family, now comprising a son and two daughters, moved to Dulwich, which was then on the very outskirts of London. Since their arrival in the City the Schröder brothers appear to have lived on the premises of the firm, as was customary at the time, but Johann Friedrich's new residence, Dulwich Lodge, was a substantial mansion set in 26 acres of land and brought with it tenure of pew Number One in Dulwich College Chapel.[23] The following year the firm moved from 37 Old Broad Street, its home since 1802, to premises at 3 St Helens Place, with a counting-house at 33 Great St Helens.

Trade between London and Hamburg grew rapidly in 1814 upon the end of the French occupation, and the business of J. F. Schröder & Co. must have benefited greatly. The revival of commercial shipping by the continental countries following the restoration of peace in Europe presented the firm with an opportunity to develop the trade finance side of its business. A batch of letters survives from February and March 1817 between J. F. Schröder & Co. and F. W. Karthaus Reinicke & Co. of New York concerning shipments by the latter firm of cotton, rice and tobacco from the port of Savannah, Georgia, on consignment to Karthaus Hasenclever & Co. in Amsterdam.[24] Karthaus Reinicke received payment by bills of exchange issued by Karthaus Hasenclever and endorsed by the London firm, which also arranged the insurance of the shipments at Lloyds, 'at the lowest premium and with safe underwriters'. There is also a reference in the correspondence to a shipment of goods from Baltimore, Maryland, to 'your brothers in Hamburg' – Christian Matthias Schröder & Co. – for which the London firm acted as acceptor. In fact, all the parties to these transactions were related, since the Schröders had marriage ties to the Hasenclevers and there was a family connection between Karthaus Reinicke and Karthaus Hasenclever. These letters shed some light on J. F. Schröder & Co.'s operations as a provider of acceptance credit, indicating in particular the importance of family connections in the early years of this activity.

By the time of the Karthaus Reinicke correspondence the Schröder brothers had been in business together in London for fifteen years. They had built a thriving enterprise conducting both consignment and acceptance activities with the firms of their brothers in Hamburg, St Petersburg and Riga, and with other clients. Johann Friedrich was content with these achievements but Johann Heinrich had further ambitions. In contrast to his brother he was unmarried and the absence of his name from the street directories of the day suggests that he was still living on the premises of J. F. Schröder & Co. Moreover, probably it was he who undertook the extensive travelling which was necessary to maintain contact with the family and clients in order to be able to undertake sound business. In 1817, Johann Heinrich decided to return to Hamburg to make that city his home and on 31 December the partnership between the brothers was dissolved.[26]

Following the change in the partnership, J. F. Schröder & Co. continued, but with declining vigour. Johann Friedrich appears to have ceased to take an active part in its affairs some time in the 1820s, being reported in 1835 to be 'very opulent and retired from the business for many years'.[25] The decision to liquidate the firm in 1833 probably owed much to the death of his only son in 1830, which left him without a male heir. Freed of the necessity to have access to the City, Johann Friedrich and his family moved to the countryside. In 1834, he purchased Northbrook House, a Georgian manor near Bentley, Hampshire, where he lived until his death in 1852. Although Johann Friedrich made his home in England it is clear that he kept in contact with his German family who were beneficiaries of bequests in his will. In 1845, a party of Hamburg cousins was entertained at Northbrook House. The following year he visited his German relations on a continental tour, which included France and Italy, being provided with letters of introduction by the Rothschilds.[27] Neither of the daughters of Johann Friedrich married and both predeceased their mother. Upon her death in 1868 the direct family line of Johann Friedrich came to an end.

The Three Firms of Johann Heinrich Schröder

The dissolution of the partnership between the Schröder brothers in London at the end of 1817 enabled Johann Heinrich to reorganise his business activities. It was the prelude to the creation of a unique network of firms in London, Hamburg and Liverpool which made Schröders different from the other merchant banking firms established in the City. At the beginning of 1818 Johann Heinrich founded his own firm in London, under the English name J. Henry Schröder & Co., and in 1819 he established a second firm, J. H. Schröder & Co., in Hamburg. The concurrent conduct of two firms in London and Hamburg was a bold business strategy in the era of the horse-drawn carriage and the sailing ship. Success required the support of trustworthy partners. For partners Johann Heinrich initially turned to his family, choosing merchants related by marriage in both London and Hamburg (see Figure 2.1). It also necessitated a formidable stamina for lengthy and uncomfortable travel. In 1830, the trip from Hamburg to London, as Johann Heinrich's eldest son vividly recalled many years later, took fourteen days by overland coach to Calais, and from Dover to London a further two.[28] Johann Heinrich made the return journey at least once a year during the 1820s, 1830s and 1840s.

There are few surviving records which offer insight into the personality of Johann Heinrich Schröder, but it is known that he was very hard-working, ambitious and highly self-disciplined, traits which go a long way in explaining his outstanding success as a businessman. Family folklore was full of tales of his impeccable punctuality and of his intolerance of lapses in time-keeping by others; he even, it is said, called off an engagement to a girl who was unpunctual because he foresaw that it would be a source of friction between them. He had rigorous standards and could turn stern if disappointed. 'You lack all knowledge of men and the world,' he reprimanded his youthful and recently appointed agent in St Petersburg, Heinrich Schliemann, in 1846, 'prattle too much, have too high expectations, and are infatuated with brainless chimeras . . . Take pains to become a sensible human being, acquire good, unassuming manners, don't dream of Spanish castles in the sky.'[29] But he also was a shrewd judge of character and recognised ability, and his letter to Schliemann finished 'however, since I am confident that you will mature, I will give you another chance'. He had strongly-held religious convictions and a highly developed sense of duty towards his family and the community, though unlike his father and other relations he did not become involved in the civic life of Hamburg.

From 1818, Hamburg was Johann Heinrich's home. On 26 January 1819, aged 34, he married Henriette von Schwartz, the 20-year-old daughter of Heinrich von Schwartz, a Hamburg merchant and the Prussian consul-general in Hamburg. In 1824, aged 40, he became a citizen of the city-state. That year he purchased a house set in a park overlooking the estuary of the River Elbe on the outskirts of the city at Othmarschen, and three years later an imposing town house in one of the best streets, 21 Grosse Bleichen, which became home and office. Doubtless personal and family sentiments counted for much in his decision to return to the city of which his father was a *Bürgermeister* but commercial considerations must also have played a part. Hamburg's

Figure 2.1 Connections between the Schröder, Bustard, Gill and Mahs families

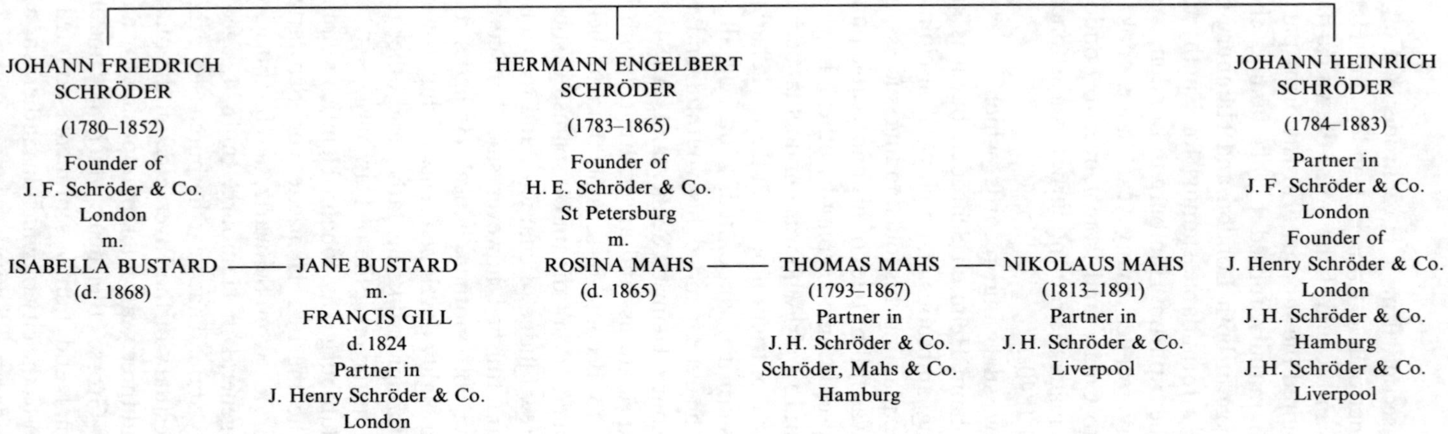

JOHANN FRIEDRICH SCHRÖDER

(1780–1852)

Founder of
J. F. Schröder & Co.
London
m.

HERMANN ENGELBERT SCHRÖDER

(1783–1865)

Founder of
H. E. Schröder & Co.
St Petersburg
m.

JOHANN HEINRICH SCHRÖDER

(1784–1883)

Partner in
J. F. Schröder & Co.
London
Founder of
J. H. Henry Schröder & Co.
London
J. H. Schröder & Co.
Hamburg
J. H. Schröder & Co.
Liverpool

ISABELLA BUSTARD ——— JANE BUSTARD

(d. 1868)

ROSINA MAHS ——— THOMAS MAHS

(d. 1865)   (1793–1867)

Partner in
J. H. Schröder & Co.
Schröder, Mahs & Co.
Hamburg

NIKOLAUS MAHS

(1813–1891)

Partner in
J. H. Schröder & Co.
Liverpool

m.
FRANCIS GILL

d. 1824

Partner in
J. Henry Schröder & Co.
London

trade recovered rapidly following the departure of the French, the number of ships entering the harbour almost doubling in the years 1814–18.[30] In the three decades between Johann Heinrich's return to his native city and his retirement, Hamburg's trade rose threefold, the tonnage of shipping using the port rising from 174,000 tons in 1818, to 252,000 tons in 1830, 337,000 tons in 1840, and 548,000 tons in 1850. By mid-century, Hamburg was the largest port not only of Germany but also of continental Europe, and the fourth largest port in the world after London, Liverpool and New York.

The expansion of Hamburg's trade and the city's prosperity in the nineteenth century was based on the great increase in worldwide commerce which came about as a result of industrialisation and the widespread adoption of free trade. Hamburg's outward-looking cosmopolitan merchants thrived in this environment and opposed any loss of independence of the city state, an attitude which enraged German nationalists, one of whom complained that they 'knew "every town on the Mississipi" from personal experience, and had been "twenty times in London", but had never visited Berlin at all'.[31] The connection with Britain was especially strong and important, it being the source of half of Hamburg's imports in the first half of the century.[32] Textile produce, that is yarns, raw cotton, manufactured silk, woollen and cotton goods, and indigo for the manufacture of textile dyes, constituted about two-thirds of the total, the rest being mainly metal goods, engineering products and West Indian produce, notably coffee, raw sugar and rum. Much the most important of the goods exported via Hamburg to Britain was raw wool, though grain was also shipped in significant quantitites following the repeal of the British restrictions on entry in 1846. In the 1820s, Hamburg merchants developed direct trade with the countries of Latin America which became possible with the end of Spanish and Portuguese rule on the continent and the slackening of colonial authority in the West Indian islands, importing large volumes of coffee, raw sugar and tobacco. Hamburg's other major trading partners were France and the United States, from which large shipments were received of wine and raw cotton, respectively. Russia, on the other hand, declined in importance as a source of imports to Hamburg, though it remained a significant market for exports and re-exports of goods from Hamburg.

At the outset Johann Heinrich was the sole partner of J. H. Schröder & Co., his Hamburg firm, but in 1826 he took Thomas Mahs as his partner and the firm became Schröder, Mahs & Co.[33] (see Figure 2.1). Mahs was the brother-in-law of Johann Heinrich's brother, Hermann Engelbert, the head of H. E. Schröder & Co. of St Petersburg. The Mahs family was a well-known Hamburg merchant family prominent in trade with Russia. Thomas Mahs' grandfather had settled in St Petersburg in the mid-eighteenth century and in 1779 was appointed consul-general of Prussia. Mahs himself was born in St Petersburg in 1793 and it was not until 1825 that he went to live in Hamburg, lodging in Johann Heinrich's household. In 1826, he became a citizen of Hamburg but his ties with Russia remained strong and in 1829 he became Russian vice-consul in Hamburg, an office he held for twenty years. Johann Heinrich's choice of Mahs as his partner in his Hamburg firm indicates that trade with Russia was an important aspect of its business in the 1820s. Most probably this concerned the shipment of goods such as sugar and coffee imported from Cuba and Brazil to H. E. Schröder & Co. in St Petersburg, G. W. Schröder & Co. in Riga and the several Mahs family firms.

An insight into J. H. Schröder & Co.'s endeavours to develop business with Latin America is provided by the survival of a fragment of correspondence with Rothschilds. In August 1832, J. Henry Schröder & Co. asked Nathan Rothschild (who acted as the financial agent of the Brazilian government in London) for a letter of introduction to his correspondents in Brazil for Theodore Otte, who was making a trip there on behalf of J. H. Schröder & Co. 'for the purpose of forming new connections amongst houses which are in the habit of sending the produce of that country for sale in Europe'.[34] The request was explained on the grounds that 'there is great difficulty of obtaining letters of introduction from houses which are in the Brazil trade on grounds of jealousy'. Besides confirming Johann Heinrich's interest in developing Latin American trade, the letter indicates the close co-operation of his Hamburg and London firms in the conduct of their business.

London at the end of the French Wars was the largest port in the world. Between 1816 and 1850 the tonnage of vessels engaged in foreign trade which entered and cleared the port of London rose from 1.2 million tons to 3.3 million tons, reflecting the major expansion of international trade in these years.[35] An important factor in the growth of international trade was the development of the provision of financial and commercial services in the City of London. The City provided four fundamental services for international trade: ship chartering; marine insurance; commodity markets; and trade finance. The ship charter market, where shipowners and merchants met to transact business, was located at the Baltic Coffee House in Threadneedle Street (see Map 2.1). In 1823, the patrons formed the Baltic Exchange, imposing a form of regulation upon the market by the requirement of membership to conduct business. As the name suggests, many of those who did business in the Baltic Exchange were involved in trade in Baltic goods, and the commodity markets in timber, grain and tallow were located there. The markets in colonial produce were housed in Mincing Lane at the London Commercial Sale Rooms which opened in 1811 in response to the

Map 2.1 The City of London, *c.* 1850. Principal financial institutions and addresses of J. Henry Schröder & Co.

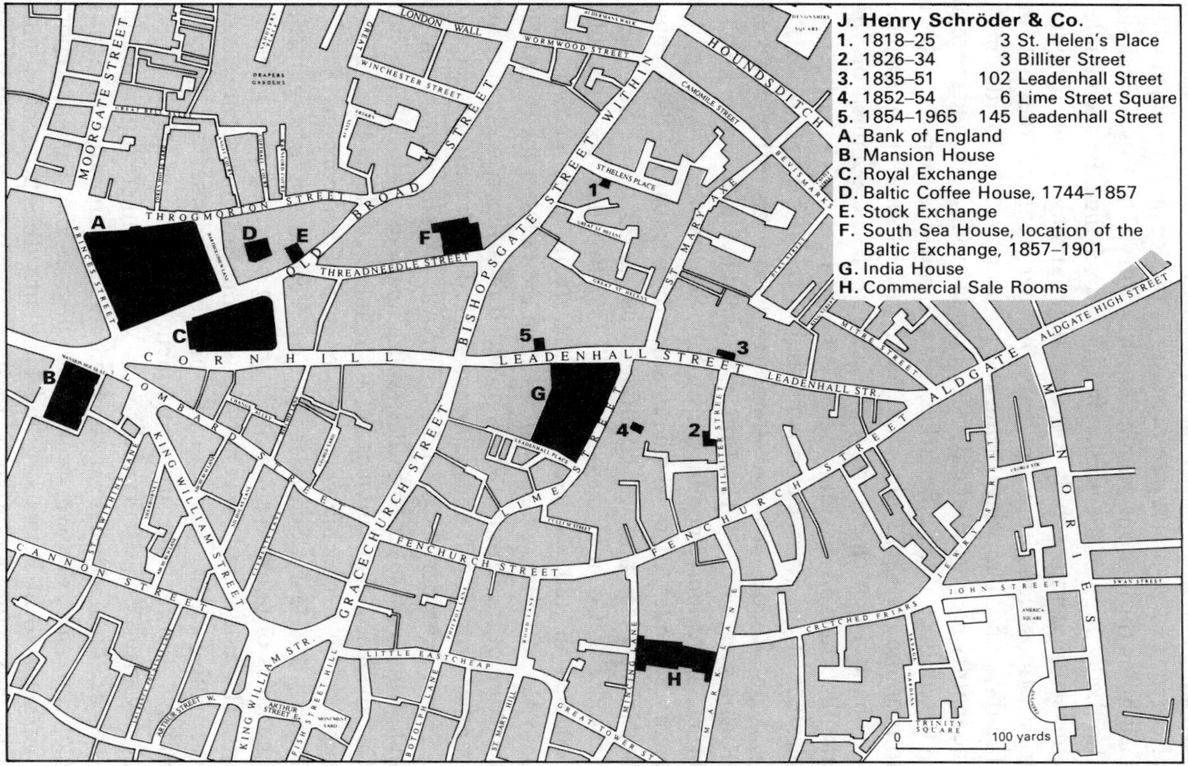
J. Henry Schröder & Co.
1. 1818–25 3 St. Helen's Place
2. 1826–34 3 Billiter Street
3. 1835–51 102 Leadenhall Street
4. 1852–54 6 Lime Street Square
5. 1854–1965 145 Leadenhall Street
A. Bank of England
B. Mansion House
C. Royal Exchange
D. Baltic Coffee House, 1744–1857
E. Stock Exchange
F. South Sea House, location of the Baltic Exchange, 1857–1901
G. India House
H. Commercial Sale Rooms
100 yards
MOORGATE STREET
LONDON WALL
WORMWOOD STREET
HOUNDSDITCH
WINCHESTER STREET
THROGMORTON STREET
OLD BROAD STREET
THREADNEEDLE STREET
BISHOPSGATE STREET WITHIN
ST MARY AXE
PRINCES STREET
CORNHILL
LEADENHALL STREET
LEADENHALL STR.
ALDGATE
ALDGATE HIGH STREET
MINORIES
LOMBARD STREET
KING WILLIAM STREET
GRACECHURCH STREET
FENCHURCH STREET
LIME STREET
BILLITER STREET
CANNON STREET
LITTLE EASTCHEAP
MINCING LANE
MARK LANE
JEWRY STREET
JOHN STREET
CRUTCHED FRIARS
GREAT TOWER ST
FISH STREET HILL
BOTOLPH LANE
ST MARY HILL
TRINITY SQUARE

requirement for improved accommodation for the auction of cargoes. Marine insurance was provided by the members of Lloyds, which had been a membership market since 1769. In 1774, the members moved out of Lloyds Coffee-house into premises in the Royal Exchange, which was their home throughout the nineteenth century. The Royal Exchange was also the location of the market in bills of exchange. By the middle of the nineteenth century bills of exchange arising from foreign trade transactions constituted perhaps 40 per cent of the bill market, Tuesdays and Thursdays being the customary days for dealings.[36] As the century progressed the Bank of England took more and more interest in the conduct of the bill market, and its growing supervisory role helped to promote the City's pre-eminence in international trade finance.

Johann Heinrich returned to London in the summer of 1819, six months after his wedding in Hamburg. In July 1819, he became a member of the Russia Company and in the 1820s and 1830s J. Henry Schröder & Co. was one of the thirty or so firms in London known as 'Russia merchants'.[37] His firm may well have taken over much of the business previously conducted by J. F. Schröder & Co., since it was J. Henry Schröder & Co. which remained the occupant of the premises at 3 St Helens Place and the counting-house at 33 Great St Helens, J. F. Schröder & Co. moving back to 37 Old Broad Street, the building it occupied in 1802–14 (see Map 2.1). Nothing is known about the activities of J. Henry Schröder & Co. in the 1820s or the early 1830s, but a picture of the firm in 1835 is provided by a report on the credit rating of other firms drawn up by Barings.[38] Trade with Russia was the forte of J. Henry Schröder & Co. and the firm was prominent in the shipment of indigo and raw sugar to St Petersburg, particularly to H. E. Schröder & Co. Evidence also survives of a shipment of 40 bottles of mercury, supplied by Rothschilds, to a client in St Petersburg in 1844.[39] From Russia, J. Henry Schröder & Co. received on consignment large quantities of tallow from a St Petersburg merchant called Solodovniec-off. The tallow trade was notorious in the early nineteenth century for speculative activity and simply to survive episodes such as the 'cornering' of the market and its subsequent collapse in 1830–31 was an achievement.[40] J. Henry Schröder & Co.'s other important business was the shipment of sugar to Hamburg, probably to J. H. Schröder & Co., on an 'extensive' scale according to the Barings report. The shipments to St Petersburg and Hamburg were probably financed by bills of exchange endorsed by the London house on behalf of the other Schröder firms, and most likely it was also already providing this service for other merchants. The Barings report concluded that 'there can be no doubt that there is considerable prosperity in the House and that they are first rate in point of credit'.

Johann Heinrich's London partner in 1818–24 was Francis Gill, an English merchant who was married to Jane Bustard, a sister of the wife of Johann Friedrich (see Figure 2.1 on page 34). Following Gill's death in August 1824 a new partnership was formed with Hermann Otto von Post, a 34-year-old merchant, the son of a Bremen lawyer, who had set up in business on his own account in the City a few years earlier.[41] The terms of the partnership are unknown, but it appears unlikely that von Post contributed substantially to J. Henry Schröder & Co.'s capital, since he was referred to by Barings in 1835 as 'a confidential German clerk who signs by procuration for the house'. Johann Heinrich spent several months each year in London, during which time he took rooms in Clapham near to his brother in Dulwich. In 1826, the firm moved from St Helens Place to 9 Billiter Street, an address it shared with half a dozen other firms (see Map 2.1 on page 37). In 1835, it moved to 102 Leadenhall Street, a big building set back from the road which housed about fifteen firms of merchants, shipping agents and insurance brokers.[42] The reasons for the moves are unknown but they may have been prompted by the need for additional accommodation since between 1829, when records begin, and 1849, the staff increased from five to ten, suggesting that the firm was prospering. This was an average staff size for a merchant firm at mid century, though Barings and Rothschilds had as many as forty clerks at this time.[43]

In July 1839, Johann Heinrich established a third firm, J. H. Schröder & Co. in Liverpool, of which initially he was the sole proprietor.[44] The capital of the new firm was £50,000, a fairly typical sum for modest-sized merchant banks of the day, such as George Peabody & Co. or Frühling & Goschen.[45] However, Johann Heinrich informed the Bank of England's Liverpool branch that he was prepared to commit a further £150,000 to the undertaking should it be required, indicating substantial wealth.[46] To manage the firm he engaged Nikolaus Mahs, a younger brother of Thomas Mahs, his partner in Hamburg and a relation by marriage; and Charles Pickering, a local man from the family of Pickering Brothers, Liverpool corn merchants. Pickering and Mahs were taken into partnership by Johann Heinrich in October 1842, apparently to satisfy the Liverpool branch of the Bank of England, which was unwilling to allow the firm to open a drawing account in the absence of a resident partner.[47]

The basic business of J. H. Schröder & Co. of Liverpool was the receipt of consignments of cotton from the southern United States. At the time of its formation the cotton trade was reviving following a drastic downturn during the commercial crisis of 1836–37, which had bankrupted several of the leading transatlantic consignment merchants and weakened others, for instance W. & J. Brown & Co., the forerunner of Brown, Shipley & Co., which survived only with massive assistance from the Bank of England.[48] The disarray amongst the established firms enabled J. H. Schröder & Co. to establish itself in Liverpool, an opportunity which was also seized by Frederick Huth & Co., another Anglo-German merchant firm.[49] Other London firms of merchants and bankers which established a presence on Merseyside were Antony Gibbs & Co. in 1805, Barings in 1832, and Kleinworts in 1858.[50] These Liverpool offshoots conducted business on the basis of bills endorsed by their metropolitan parents, thereby boosting the development of the trade finance business of the London houses. J. H. Schröder & Co. also acted on behalf of Schröder, Mahs & Co. as an agent for textile shipments to Hamburg, a role assisted by the presence of Nikolaus Mahs in Liverpool. Such shipments might have been financed by bills guaranteed by J. Henry Schröder & Co. in London, thus uniting all three of Johann Heinrich's firms in a common purpose.

　　J. Henry Schröder & Co. celebrated its thirtieth anniversary in 1848. By this time it was a soundly established and well-reputed firm of moderate size, making profits of perhaps £15,000 per annum – about £500,000 in 1990 money.[51] The distinctive features of its business were its specialisation in certain colonial and Baltic produce and its strong ties with Hamburg; all but one of the sixteen clerks who were employed at J. Henry Schröder & Co. in 1829–49 had German surnames. Its peer group was a set of mostly Protestant Anglo-German merchant firms in the City, of which some leading members were D. H. & J. A. Rücker & Co., established in 1800; E. H. Brandt & Co., in 1805; Frederick Huth & Co., in 1809; Frühling & Goschen, in 1814; C. J. Hambro & Sons, in 1839; and subsequently Kleinwort, Sons & Co., in 1855. Hamburg was the place of origin of most of these firms, and all retained strong ties with Germany for many years after their establishment in London. Hambros and Brandts were heavily involved in trade in Baltic goods, Emanuel Henry Brandt acting as agent in London for the firm formed by his brother William in Archangel in 1802, a relationship similar to that of J. Henry Schröder & Co. and the family firms in St Petersburg and Riga. Colonial produce played a large part in the business of all these firms, Frühling & Goschen, for instance, being described in 1835 as 'almost entirely in the exporting of colonial produce on commission to Germany', while Rückers were 'a very old West India and Hambro [Hamburg] house . . . they have a very fair share in the export of colonial produce to the Continent'.[52] Cuban sugar was of great importance both to Huths and Kleinworts. Frederick Huth, the founder of Huths, was born in Stade on the River Elbe in 1777, served his apprenticeship in Hamburg and was a partner of a firm in Corunna which specialised in the import of sugar before establishing his own firm in London. His

1. Anthon Schröder of Quakenbrück, founder of the first of the Schröder family firms

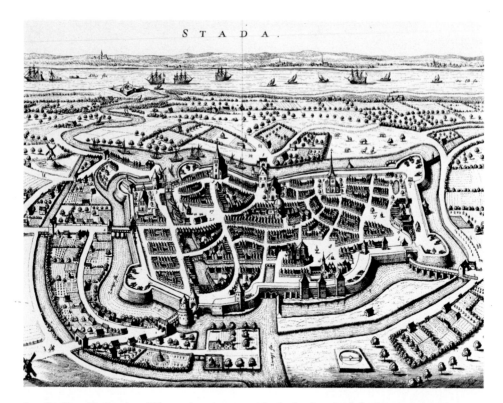

2. Stade, with the river Elbe and customs post in the background, in the seventeenth century

3. The market place in Quakenbrück. The large house in the centre was the home of the Schröder family

4.   Christian Matthias Schröder, founder of the business in Hamburg and *Bürgermeister*

5. The *Schröderhof* in Eimsbüttel, summer home of Christian Matthias Schröder

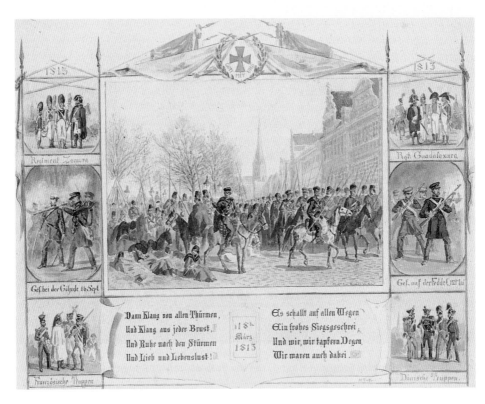

6. Scenes of Hamburg under the French occupation in 1813

7. (*left*) Johann Heinrich
   Schröder, founder of
   J. Henry Schröder & Co.

8. (*right*) Henriette, wife of
   Johann Heinrich Schröder

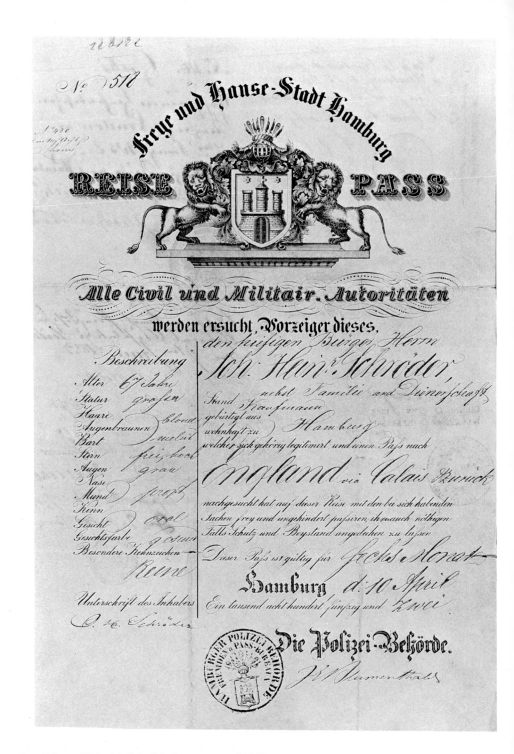

9. Johann Heinrich Schröder's passport of 1845

10. Arrival of Johann Heinrich Schröder and his family at Dover on the Hamburg–London journey in the 1820s

11. The port of Hamburg in 1834

12. The City of London soon after the formation of J. F. Schröder & Co. The Bank of England (*right*) and The Mansion House (*facing*) in 1809

13. The port of Liverpool in the 1850s, the heyday of J. H. Schröder & Co., Liverpool

The brothers of Johann Heinrich Schröder

14. (*left*) Johann Friedrich Schröder, senior partner of J. F. Schröder & Co., London

15. (*bottom left*) Hermann Engelbert Schröder, St Petersburg

16. (*bottom right*) Georg Wilhelm Schröder, Riga

Partners of Johann Heinrich Schröder in London, Hamburg and Liverpool

17. (*left*) Hermann Otto von Post, London

18. (*bottom left*) Thomas Mahs, Hamburg

19. (*bottom right*) Charles Pickering, Liverpool

20.   Grosse Bleichen, Hamburg townhouse

21.   House at Othmarschen overlooking the river Elbe

22. Schwansee, the country estate in Mecklenburg purchased in 1846

23. Rear view of Schwansee

24. *Schröderstiftung*, the Hamburg home for the elderly, erected and endowed by Johann Heinrich Schröder

close connections with Spain led to the specialisation of his firm in trade with South America during the nineteenth century, crossing paths with Schröders sometimes as a competitor, sometimes as a partner.[53] Alexander Kleinwort, the founder of Kleinwort, Sons & Co., was a generation younger than Johann Heinrich or Frederick Huth, being born in 1815, the son of a Hamburg lawyer.[54] Having served his apprenticeship in Hamburg he spent fifteen years in Havana with a sugar export house prior to his arrival in London. In the late nineteenth century and early twentieth century it was Kleinworts whose acceptance business most closely resembled that of Schröders and was its most formidable rival in the City.

In 1849, Johann Heinrich reorganised the partnerships of both his London and Hamburg firms, moves which suggest his withdrawal from active participation in business. In London, Hermann Otto von Post took retirement after twenty-three years' service and Johann Heinrich's eldest son, John Henry, aged 24, and Alexander Schlüsser, an older and more experienced merchant, became partners. In Hamburg, Schröder, Mahs & Co. was dissolved and the partners established the separate firms J. H. Schröder & Co. and Thomas Mahs & Co. Mahs retired in 1865 and returned to St Petersburg. In 1855 Johann Heinrich took Ernst Friedrich Vogler, his senior clerk, into partnership, an arrangement which continued until the liquidation of the firm following Johann Heinrich's his death in 1883. Nothing is known of J. H. Schröder & Co.'s business activities in these decades, but it probably became more and more an outpost of J. Henry Schröder & Co. of London, which emerged in the second half of the nineteenth century as much the most important of the firms founded by Johann Heinrich. London's pre-eminence is reflected in the relative size of Johann Heinrich's interest in the capital in his three firms at the time of his death: £153,000 Hamburg; £244,000 Liverpool; and £1,058,000 London.

Johann Heinrich was approaching his 65th birthday in 1849, so age was probably an important factor in his decision to retire. Perhaps also prompting him to seek a quieter life were the commercial crisis of 1847–48, the revolutions in many European countries in 1848, and the brief occupation of Hamburg by the Prussians in 1849, all of which must have been disruptive to the business of his firms. Maybe the persuasive inducement was the lure of his country estate at Schwansee in Mecklenburg, about 60 miles north-east of Hamburg, which he purchased in 1846. Charitable works absorbed him in retirement of which the most notable was the erection of a home for the elderly, the Schröder Stiftung, to which in 1850 he made an endowment of 1.5 million Bancomarks, £110,000 in sterling of the day – around £4.5 million in 1990 money. In 1868, in recognition of his benefactions the

King of Prussia made him a Prussian Freiherr, Baron Johann Heinrich von Schröder, a very unusual honour for a Hamburg merchant.

Besides business, Johann Heinrich's greatest interest was his family. There were nine surviving children, three sons and six daughters. The eldest and youngest sons, Johann Heinrich and Wilhelm, were given charge of their father's London and Liverpool firms, while the middle son, Carl, inherited the family estate at Schwansee and pursued the life of a country landowner. All three were generally known by the English forms of their names, respectively John Henry, William and Charles – used henceforth in the text – which was a common practice amongst Hamburg's Anglophile merchant families; indeed, Johann Heinrich's inheritance valuation, though written in German, refers to him as 'John Henry Schröder', reflecting his identification with London despite his residence in Hamburg.[55] Five of his daughters married Hamburg merchants or merchant bankers: Helene, a partner in the highly regarded firm Conrad Hinrich Donner, and Harriet, a member of the eminent Godeffroy family, while Francisca, Eveline Sophie, and Clara Louise married Schröder cousins. The husbands of Eveline Sophie and Clara Louise were the brothers Bernhard Hinrich II and Johann Rudolph I, the grandsons of Christian Matthias's elder brother Bernhard Hinrich I, one of the founders of the Quakenbrück wine merchants B. H. & A. E. Schröder & Co. This pair of sons-in-law had inherited the family's enterprise and application in full measure, and in 1846 they established their own firm, Schröder Gebrüder, which in the second half of the nineteenth century became the leading Schröder firm in Hamburg.

3

Emergence as Leading Merchant Bankers

1849–71

The reconstruction of the partnership in 1849 was an important turning point in the history of J. Henry Schröder & Co. For the first time the firm had two full resident partners who devoted themselves to the development of its business. One measure of their achievements is the increase in the number of clerks from ten in 1849 to twenty-five in 1870. Another yardstick is the growth of the capital from £244,000 in 1852, the first year for which figures are available, to £890,000 in 1870 – from about £9 million to £31 million in 1990 money. By the latter date Schröders and Kleinworts were the largest of the City's Anglo-German houses, though still considerably smaller than Rothschilds or the leading Anglo-American firms, Barings and Brown, Shipley. Table 3.1 shows the capital of some leading merchant banks around 1870, though these figures may not have been recorded on the same basis.

The success of J. Henry Schröder & Co. in the 1850s and 1860s was above all a tribute to the partners' abilities and application, though they enjoyed the advantages of a well-established name, an existing network of clients and family correspondents, and the capital of the experienced and wealthy senior partner in Hamburg. Also conducive to success was the rapid growth of international trade, stimulated by reductions in tariff barriers and increases in international capital flows, estimates suggesting a two-and-a-half-fold increase between 1850 and 1870, creating buoyant demand for the shipping, insurance, commodity and trade finance services in which the City specialised.[1] London was also the leading international capital market in which was raised the vast volume of funds required to finance the railway building and the other infrastructure developments which led to the integration of new regions into the world economy. The intermediaries between the borrowers of funds and investors were the same firms that specialised in the provision of international trade finance, merchant banks such as J. Henry Schröder & Co.

The two new resident partners were John Henry William Schröder and Alexander Schlüsser. The former, who was born in Hamburg in 1825 (as Johann Heinrich Wilhelm, but was always known by the English names John Henry), was the eldest of Johann Heinrich's sons. From an early age he was destined for the partnership of J. Henry Schröder & Co.,

Table 3.1   Capital of some leading merchant banks c.1870

Merchant Banks	Year	Capital £ million
N. M. Rothschild & Sons	1875	6.51
Baring Brothers & Co.	1870	2.1
Brown, Shipley & Co.	1875	1.2
Kleinwort, Sons & Co.	1870	0.91
J. Henry Schröder & Co.	1870	0.89
C. J. Hambro & Son	1870	0.67
J. S. Morgan & Co.	1870	0.66
Frederick Huth & Co.	1870	0.5
Wm Brandt Sons & Co.	1877	0.18

Note: Information on other firms unavailable.

Sources: Stanley Chapman, *The Rise of Merchant Banking* (London: George Allen & Unwin, 1984) p. 44; J. Henry Schröder & Co., balance sheets; Kathleen Burk, *Morgan Grenfell 1838–1988* (Oxford: Oxford University Press, 1989) p. 264; Stephanie Diaper, 'Kleinwort, Sons & Co. in the History of Merchant Banking, 1855–1966' (unpublished PhD thesis, University of Nottingham, 1983) p. 52.

paying his first visit to London in 1830, aged five, on one of his father's trips. In 1841, aged sixteen, he joined the office, learning the basics of the business under von Post's supervision. His marriage in 1850 to Dorothea Eveline Schlüsser, the niece of Alexander Schlüsser, created a family bond between the three London partners. At the time of the wedding, John Henry was living in the household of Adolphus Klockmann, a German sugar merchant with strong Cuban connections, in Acacia Road, Marylebone, an affluent villa suburb then on the edge of London.[2] John Henry and his wife took up residence in fashionable Bayswater where they lived in the 1850s and early 1860s amongst neighbours who were Members of Parliament and peers of the realm. In 1864, the same year that he became English by naturalisation, John Henry purchased 'The Dell' at Englefield Green, Surrey, a large house with 160 acres of land which abutted Windsor Great Park, which was henceforth his home. The following year he joined the Society of Merchants Trading to the Continent, the merchant bankers' dining club established in 1801, the first partner of the firm to become a member. In 1868, upon his father becoming a Prussian *Freiherr* he became known as Baron John Henry Schröder.

Alexander Schlüsser was born in St Petersburg in 1803, where his father was the founder of Schlüsser & Co., a merchant firm with which

Schröders did business until the First World War. The family firm was inherited by an elder brother, Wilhelm, the father of John Henry's bride, and Alexander came to London to seek his fortune. He engaged the services of the Revd William Gurney, Rector of St Clement Danes, a City church, as tutor, and subsequently married his daughter. In 1829 he became a partner in Perkins, Schlüsser and Mullens, a firm of wine merchants, and apparently made the acquaintanceship of John Henry in 1845. His appointment to the partnership of J. Henry Schröder & Co. was a reflection both of the need for an older partner to work with the 24 year old John Henry and of the continuing significance of Russian trade to the firm. Subsequently, Schlüsser's adopted daughter Agnes married Henry Tiarks, a Schröder clerk who was promoted to the partnership in 1871. The complex web of personal and professional ties between members of the Schröder, Mahs, Schlüsser, Horny and Tiarks families is depicted in Figure 3.1.

In the 1850s and 1860s Johann Heinrich provided some 80 per cent of the firm's capital and received, under the terms of the new partnership articles, 50 per cent of profits after interest on partners' capital. Despite his retirement he continued to be the senior partner and kept a close watch on its affairs, requiring an annual report from John Henry each summer in Hamburg. John Henry and Alexander Schlüsser, the executive partners, contributed the remainder of the capital roughly equally and each received 25 per cent of the profits as remuneration for their work. (In the 1860s, the founder relinquished a further 5 per cent of his share of profits which was divided between an 'associate' partner, who received a salary and a small share of profits but was not exposed to losses, and the office manager.) These arrangements were mutually advantageous. Johann Heinrich's commitment of capital enabled J. Henry Schröder & Co. to conduct a much higher volume of business than would otherwise have been possible, while his funds earned an attractive rate of return. The allocation of profits to the executive partners enabled them gradually to build up their interest in the firm so that when the founder's capital was eventually withdrawn the disruption to business could be minimised. In fact, Johann Heinrich's longevity meant that the partnership of 1849 came and went before this problem had to be faced.

Consignment and Accepting Business

Both consignment and accepting business continued to be important to Schröders in the 1850s and 1860s. Gradually, trade finance superseded consignments as the firm's principal activity, although in 1870, the

46

Figure 3.1 Connections between the Schröder, Schlüsser, Tiarks and Horny families

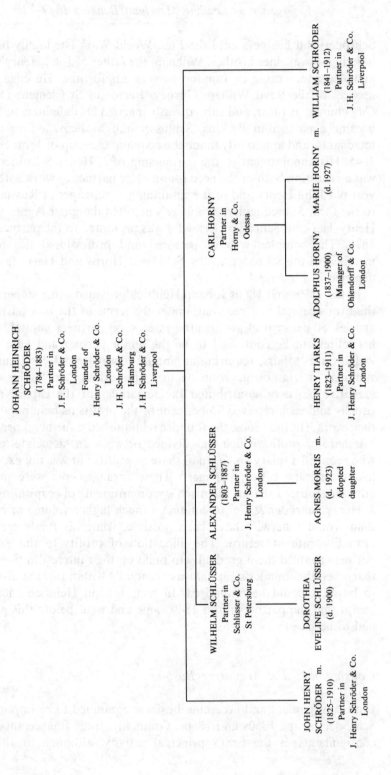

earliest year for which it is possible to differentiate revenues from the two sources, consignments were still of major importance, generating £41,000 while acceptance commissions earned £55,000. In the years 1852–70, the firm's combined revenues from accepting and consignments grew fourfold from £24,000 to £96,000 (see Figure 3.2). From 1853 the firm also had occasional earnings from the issue of securities, of which details are available only from 1861. In 1863, and again in 1870, issuing revenues were substantial, but in other years they were very small and it was accepting and consignments which were much the most important of the firm's activities in 1849–70.

Schröders' acceptance and consignment commission earnings grew continuously during the 1850s until the commercial crisis of 1857–58. Surprisingly, the Crimean War of 1854–56, in which Britain and France confronted Russia, seems to have had little adverse impact on the firm's business despite its large involvement in Russian trade. But the crisis of 1857–58 led to the failure of thirty-one clients – nineteen of them Hamburg firms including four Schröder family firms – inflicting losses on the London firm. Growth resumed in 1859 but the outbreak of the American Civil War in 1861 caused a setback to the expansion of world trade and had a detrimental impact on the business of J. Henry Schröder & Co. until the end of the hostilities in 1865. The following year saw the collapse of the leading discount house Overend Gurney & Co., which struck the City with 'the shock of an earthquake' and brought down many firms.[3] Schröders was left almost unscathed by the episode and a couple of months after the crisis was described by the Bank of England as 'excellent in every respect'.[4] It was thus able to take advantage of the

Figure 3.2   J. Henry Schröder & Co., combined consignment and acceptance commissions and issuing revenues, 1852–70

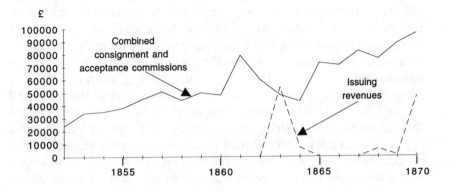

shake-out which followed the crisis and its business grew rapidly in the latter years of the 1860s.

The provision of acceptance credits was a form of banking business and like any banking operation was conducted on the basis of ratios which kept risks within bounds. But prudent practices also restricted revenues and there was always a temptation to relax standards to boost returns. There were two prudential principles which governed the conduct of accepting: the first, regarding the size of individual credits; the second, the volume of total credits. The risk of losses from defaults on the part of clients, such as suffered by Schröders as a result of the crisis of 1857–58, was minimised by undertaking business on a small scale with a large number of clients. However, this was administratively expensive and there was a natural tendency for the scale of business with particularly trusted clients to increase. The volume of total credits was governed by the size of the firm's capital, a ratio of capital to acceptances of 1:4 being regarded as the upper limit to the prudent conduct of accepting. Of course, the higher the volume of acceptances relative to capital, the more profitable the business, though the greater the risk of ruin through a conjunction of bad debts. In the 1850s and in the second half of the 1860s the capital-to-acceptances ratio of J. Henry Schröder & Co. was 1:3.4, though during the years of the American Civil War it dropped to an average of 1:2.5. Comparable information is available only for Kleinworts and Hambros, which had ratios averaging 1:2.5 and 1:1.1 in the second half of the 1860s, suggesting a rather adventurous conduct of accepting in these years by the Schröder partners.[5]

Over the years 1848–68, J. Henry Schröder & Co. provided acceptance credit facilities to a total of 652 merchant firms around the world, whose names were listed in a 'conditions book', in which the terms on which the firm would endorse their bills were set out.[6] These suggest that a fairly typical Schröder acceptance credit of the 1850s and 1860s was around £10,000. The records of Baring Brothers and George Peabody & Co. indicate a 'commission war' between merchant banks in the late 1840s and early 1850s.[7] Schröders' conditions book confirms a decline in commission rates in these years, stabilising in the 1850s at ½ per cent for three months' drafts and 1 per cent for six months' drafts. Confirmation was charged at ½ per cent and the arrangement of insurance at ¼–½ per cent. Banking operations, such as remittances against funds in hand or purchases of drafts or bonds, were done for ⅛–¼ per cent. Interest charged on accounts in debt was commonly bank rate, with a minimum of 5 per cent, while interest allowed on accounts in credit was generally 1 per cent below bank rate, though often no interest whatsoever was paid, such interest-free balances being regarded as part of a merchant bank's remuneration for the provision of services.

Table 3.2   Geographical location of the acceptance credit clients of J. Henry Schröder & Co., 1848–68

	Number of clients	Per cent
EUROPE AND RUSSIA		
Germany		
Hamburg	101	
Bremen	30	
Altona	8	
Stettin	7	
Berlin	3	
Other	25	
Total	174	27
Baltic and Northern Russia		
St Petersburg	41	
Moscow	22	
Riga	14	
Other	34	
Total	111	17
Mediterranean, Black Sea and Central Europe		
Trieste	37	
Odessa	25	
Vienna	10	
Marseilles	1	
Other	22	
Total	94	14
Western Europe		
Antwerp	14	
Paris	14	
Amsterdam	6	
Rotterdam	2	
Other	11	
Total	47	7
United Kingdom		
Manchester	10	
Liverpool	7	
London	1	
Other	2	
Total	20	3

Table continued over

Table 3.2 continued		Number of clients	Per cent
AMERICAS AND ASIA			
West Indies			
Cuba		53	
Puerto Rico		10	
Other		3	
Total		76	12
North America			
New York		29	
New Orleans		8	
Other		7	
Total		44	7
South America			
Brazil	– Rio de Janeiro	17	
	– Bahia	8	
	– Others	5	
Chile	– Valparaiso	5	
Argentina	– Buenos Aires	6	
Peru	– Lima	6	
Venezuela		6	
Mexico		7	
Other		–	
Total		60	9
Asia			
Singapore		4	
Calcutta		3	
Hong Kong		2	
Other		17	
Total		26	4
TOTAL		652	100

Source: J. Henry Schröder & Co., conditions book 1848–68.

The conditions book for 1848–68 permits the identification of the geographical distribution of Schröders' clients, which is shown in Table 3.2, and gives some idea of the trades in which they were involved. Two-thirds of the clients, 446 firms, were located in Europe and Russia. The business of these merchants was the importation of commodities, principally foodstuffs, which were often of tropical origin. Merchants in the Russian ports of St Petersburg and Riga were also involved in the export of grain, tallow and Baltic produce, and Odessa's business revolved around the grain trade. The 206 clients located in the Americas and Asia were mostly engaged in the export of primary produce to Europe, and to a lesser extent to the United States. The most important export trade financed by the firm in the 1850s and 1860s was the shipment of sugar from Cuba to Europe and the United States. Other trades of major importance were the shipment of grain and flour from New York to London; cotton from New Orleans to Liverpool and Hamburg; coffee from Brazil to Europe and the United States; guano from Peru to Germany; indigo from India to Russia; and there was a long list of less significant commodities – tallow, cotton, nitrates, rum, cochineal, tobacco, rice, silk, leather hides, petroleum, wool, silk, gold and silver. It should be noted that there is hardly any mention of shipments of manufactured goods.

Hamburg, where there were 101 clients (plus another eight in adjacent Altona), remained much the most important commercial centre with which the firm conducted business. Hamburg's trade benefited greatly from the increase in international trade, the tonnage of shipping entering the port rising from 547,000 tons in 1850 to 1.4 million tons in 1870.[8] More than ever, Hamburg was the leading port of continental Europe and the expansion of its commerce led to the growth of the city's population from 200,000 to 350,000 in these years. There were sixty-five clients in other German cities, thirty of them in the rapidly growing port of Bremen. Overall, German firms comprised a quarter of Schröders' clients in 1848–68.

Russia continued to be of great importance to J. Henry Schröder & Co. in the 1850s and 1860s. In these years there were forty-one clients in St Petersburg, fourteen in Riga – where contacts with merchant firms were especially close because of the presence of members of the Schröder, Mahs and Schlüsser families – and twenty-two in Moscow. Schröders' agent in St Petersburg in the 1850s and early 1860s was Heinrich Schliemann, who is best known for his discovery of the site of the ancient city of Troy. Schliemann, the son of a Mecklenburg pastor, began his career in Hamburg and in 1844 joined B. H. Schröder & Co. of Amsterdam as a clerk, as did a younger brother. In 1846, having taught himself Russian and established important contacts in the Russian indigo trade, he was despatched to St Petersburg to represent the firm. The following year, aged 25, he set up his own firm specialising in the import of indigo, though also representing B. H. Schröder & Co. and Johann Heinrich's Hamburg and London firms. Schliemann was a bold and highly successful merchant and in a few years amassed a fortune.

The Crimean War presented great opportunities for dealing in war materials and commodity speculation in other goods and he was able to double his capital in a single year. His autobiographical notes and his letters suggest no interruption of contact with Schröders or other British and French merchants during the hostilities, which may explain why there was no downturn in Schröders' business in 1854–56.[9]

For forty years Schliemann was in regular correspondence with the Schröder firms, informing them of market conditions and commercial opportunities in Russia or wherever his travels took him. In Italy in 1864 he suffered the first attack of the ear ailment which was ultimately to kill him, probably brought on by sea-bathing, in whose therapeutic benefits he had a fanatical belief. At the suggestion of Johann Heinrich he consulted a doctor in Bavaria who was able to restore him to health. By way of convalescence Schliemann undertook a journey to India, in order, as he explained, 'to find out how indigo grows and how it is processed, in which business I have been for the last 23 years'.[10] Already a rich man, he decided upon his return from the East to retire from business in order to pursue his archaeological interests. Accordingly, he converted the capital of his business into a portfolio of bonds, including large holdings of the Cuban and US railway bonds issued by Schröders, which he deposited for safekeeping, along with his will, with the firm in London. In 1868 he commenced the archaeological inquiries which were to culminate in the discovery of Troy. Schliemann's memoirs recorded that his 'honoured friends' in London assisted his excavations by sending him essential tools, including 'the very best English wheelbarrow' and 'a large supply of tins of Chicago corned beef, peaches, the best English cheese, and ox-tongues, as well as 240 bottles of the best English pale ale. I was the sole consumer of these 240 bottles of pale ale, which lasted me for five months and which I used as a medicine to cure constipation, from which I had been suffering for more than 30 years, and which had been aggravated by all other medicines, and particularly by the mineral waters of Carlsbad. This pale-ale-cure proved perfectly effectual'.[11]

The years from the mid-1830s to the mid-1850s saw a vigorous expansion of grain exports from southern Russia, the bulk being shipped through the port of Odessa.[12] The increase was especially rapid in 1846–53 following the abolition of the import tariff by Britain, the Ukrainian share of British grain imports rising from 3 per cent to 50 per cent before the outbreak of the Crimean War put paid to the trade. Much of Odessa's export trade was despatched to London on a consignment basis, and J. Henry Schröder & Co. was a major recipient. Its Odessa clients included the Russo-German firms Ernest Mahs & Co. and Horny & Co., with which the Schröder partners had family connections, and the leading Jewish merchants Ephrussi & Co. and Raffalovich & Co. The foremost foreign merchant in the Odessa grain trade in these years was John Ralli, whose business career has some striking parallels with that of Johann Heinrich: born in 1785 on the Greek island of Chios, he came to London where in 1818 he established a merchant bank, Ralli Brothers, which in the mid-nineteenth century specialised in trade in tallow and indigo, and from 1826 had an office in Manchester to participate in the cotton trade.[13] The export of grain from Odessa resumed at the end of the Crimean War and grew apace for a while, but the advent of North American supplies from the 1860s sent the trade into rapid decline, and Schröders' activity waned accordingly.

The prominent position of J. Henry Schröder & Co. amongst London merchant firms engaged in trade with Russia led to the involvement of John Henry in the affairs of the Baltic Exchange. In February 1854, he was elected to its governing body, the Baltic Committee, and in 1857–89 served as a director of the Baltic Company Ltd, which was established in 1857 as proprietor of the Exchange's new premises at South Sea House.[14] He was one of the leading instigators of these long overdue improvements to the Exchange's accommodation, and played an active part in the affairs of the Baltic Exchange as a member of the Baltic Committee until the 1870s.[15]

The presence of Schröder family firms in Trieste (the principal port of the Austro-Hungarian Empire), Amsterdam and Antwerp helps to explain the concentrations of Schröder clients in these European cities. Paris and Vienna were capital cities in which local merchants supplied the requirements of the large number of consumers. London too was a capital city, yet there was only a single Schröder client there, probably because the partners saw no advantage in tying up resources servicing a well-provided market while higher profit margins were to be had overseas. In Lancashire, by contrast, there were seventeen clients whose business derived from the activities of J. H. Schröder & Co. in Liverpool.

The 1850s were highly successful years for Johann Heinrich's Liverpool house. By the end of the decade it was the fourth largest recipient of consignments of cotton in Liverpool, ahead of all the other offshoots of London accepting houses, though ten years earlier its name had not featured on a list of the city's top thirty cotton merchants.[16] In these years the firm was run by Charles Pickering and the chief clerk, Julius Servaes, who was made an associate partner in 1856. Nikolaus Mahs, who had been taken into partnership along with Pickering in 1842, resigned to form his own firm in 1851, and for many years subsequently acted as Russian consul in Liverpool. The outbreak of the American Civil War in 1861 halted the shipment of cotton from the southern states to Lancashire. Hardship ensued for all connected with the cotton industry, and the downturn in J. H. Schröder & Co.'s activities as cotton consignment merchants led to the placement of funds which could not be used in the business on deposit with J. Henry Schröder & Co. in London. By the end of 1861 this balance was £61,810, which must have represented a large part of the northern firm's capital. In following years, as other opportunities for business became available, the sum on deposit declined, and in 1865, the final year of the war, it disappeared. The revival of business coincided with the appointment of Johann Heinrich's youngest son, William Henry Schröder, aged 25, to the partnership in 1866. The same year William married Marie Horny, the daughter of a partner in Horny & Co., the Russo-German Odessa grain merchant which was an important Schröder client (see Figure 3.1 on page 46). From 1868 he was known as Baron William Schröder.

Cuba was the location of fifty-three Schröder clients, a concentration second only to Hamburg. In these years the island produced around a quarter of world sugar output and was the single most important source of this commodity, which explains the firm's strong connections. Amongst its clients was the leading Havana sugar merchant Scharfenberg, Tolme & Co. Records remain of a typical acceptance transaction in 1861 between Scharfenberg, Tolme and another Schröder client, the St Petersburg import merchant Carr & Co., which is depicted in Figure 3.3.[17] On 16 February 1861, Schröders received a copy of a letter which had been sent three weeks earlier by Carr & Co. to Scharfenberg, Tolme & Co. instructing the latter 'to purchase for our account 1500 to 2000 boxes of Havana sugar (white and dry sugar) at or under 10 to 10.5 Reals', which were to be sent to St Petersburg [1]. Carrs applied to Schröders for a letter of credit [2] and then informed Scharfenberg, Tolme that 'should their purchase be effected, our friend Messrs J. Henry Schröder & Co. in London will accept your draft for the amount of your invoice . . . as they will confirm to you by letter'. Schröders instructed their agent in Cuba [3] to provide Scharfenberg, Tolme & Co. with a letter of credit issued on behalf of Schröders incorporating an undertaking to accept a bill of exchange when presented in London provided that it was accompanied by specified shipping documents [4]. Scharfenberg, Tolme then executed the purchase of sugar in Havana and arranged for its shipment to the Baltic port of Kronstadt. Doubtless the firm took heed of Carr & Co.'s complaint that 'most of the early cargoes last season arrived here much damaged and this was in some instances caused by leaky ships and we therefore call your attention to this circumstance and trust you will select a good seaworthy vessel for our sugar'. Having despatched the sugar, Scharfenberg, Tolme presented documents evidencing proof of shipment to their local bank in Cuba and issued a bill of exchange to the value of the purchase price, plus the cost of freight, insurance and premiums totalling 15 per cent, as payment for

Figure 3.3 Acceptance transaction between Carr & Co., St Petersburg, Scharfenberg Tolme & Co., Havana, and J. Henry Schröder & Co., London, in 1861

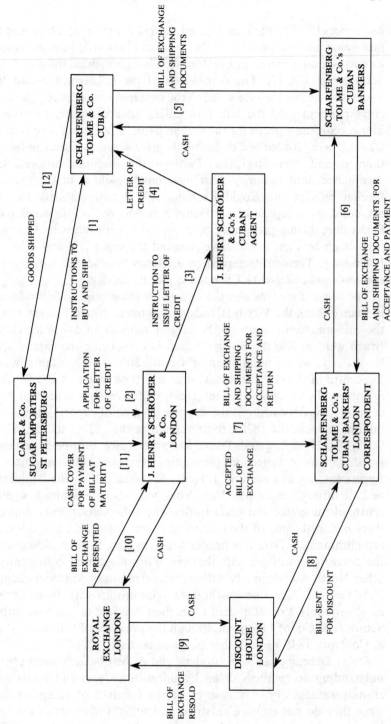

its services [5]. The bank purchased the bill for cash, at a discount to the face value but at a profit over its costs, and forwarded the documents to its correspondent bank in London [6], which presented them to J. Henry Schröder & Co. [7]. The firm accepted the bill, which meant that it undertook to pay the face value to the bearer 90 days hence. The London correspondent sold the bill, now called an acceptance, to a discount house, realising a profit for the Cuban bank [8]. Although the acceptance was still being traded at a discount, its price was now nearer to face value than it had been in Cuba. Perhaps the discount house held the acceptance until maturity or it may have resold it in the market for foreign bills at the Royal Exchange [9]. Upon maturity the holder presented the acceptance to J. Henry Schröder & Co. [10] which paid the face value, having previously been provided with funds by Carr & Co., [11] which by then would have received the sugar [12] and sold it in St Petersburg. The profits earned by J. Henry Schröder & Co. came from commissions charged to Carr & Co. for its services.

The sugar trade was also the reason for the groups of Schröder clients in Puerto Rico, the Virgin Islands and Bahia in North Eastern Brazil. In the mid-nineteenth century the largest number of Schröder clients in Brazil were in Rio de Janeiro, which besides being the capital and the largest city, with a population of around 200,000 inhabitants, was then the centre of the coffee trade. Coffee overtook sugar as Brazil's leading export in the 1830s and by the 1850s coffee exports generated half the country's export earnings, the average volume of exports rising from 10 million sacks in the 1830s, to 26 million in the 1850s, and 29 million in the 1860s. Hamburg and Trieste were the major European destinations for shipments of coffee and the leading Hamburg coffee importer H. H. Eggers & Co. was a client of J. Henry Schröder & Co., the families being related through marriage. New York was also becoming a significant centre of the coffee and sugar trades, and Schröders' twenty-nine clients there included some of the leading importers of these commodities. The establishment of Troost, Schröder & Co. in New York in 1856 assisted in the development of ties with the New York mercantile community. The other North American city with a concentration of Schröder clients was New Orleans. The London house's relationship with these firms was most probably a development from their conduct of business with J. H. Schröder & Co. of Liverpool, though the presence of Schröder, Mummy & Co. from 1848 was another point of contact.

On 31 December 1870, Schröders' end of year balance sheet contained outstanding acceptances of £3.2 million. Such year-end totals are not entirely satisfactory as measures of the conduct of accepting activity since they do not capture seasonal and other variations in the level of business, but they are the usual and only available yardstick.

Table 3.3 Acceptances of some leading merchant banks, 1870

31 December	£ million
Baring Brothers & Co.	6.70
J. Henry Schröder & Co.	3.22
Kleinwort, Sons & Co.	2.35
C. J. Hambro & Son	0.98
N. M. Rothschild & Son	0.91
Wm Brandt Sons & Co.	(1871) 0.10

Note: Information on other firms unavailable

Sources: Stephanie Diaper, 'The History of Kleinwort, Sons & Co. in Merchant Banking, 1855–1966' (unpublished PhD thesis, University of Nottingham, 1983) p. 144 ; Philip Ziegler, *The Sixth Power: Barings 1762–1929* (London: Collins, 1988) p. 202; J. Henry Schröder & Co., balance sheets.

Information about the acceptance activity of the other merchant banks at this time is incomplete, what is available being shown in Table 3.3, which establishes that in 1870 Schröders was conducting a larger acceptance business than Kleinworts, and a much larger business than Hambros, Rothschilds or Wm Brandt Sons & Co. (as the firm E. H. Brandt & Co. was styled from 1859).[18] Brown, Shipley & Co. and J. S. Morgan & Co. (the forerunner of Morgan Grenfell), the other leading Anglo-American houses, also had large acceptance businesses, though it seems unlikely that they surpassed Schröders'.[19] In fact, by 1870, Schröders' acceptance business was probably second only to Barings', a major advance in the standing of the firm since 1849.

Commencement of Bond Issuing

Underlying the expansion of international trade in the second half of the nineteenth century was the economic development of many regions of the world through the construction of railways and port facilities, and the establishment of new plantations and mines. The funds required were raised by the issue of long-term bonds, usually with maturities of 20–30 years, in the financial centres of Europe by foreign governments, municipalities and other authorities, and by private companies, notably railway companies. Rightly or wrongly, the market believed that lending to overseas borrowers carried higher risks than domestic investment, and demanded higher returns.[20] Whereas British government bonds provided nominal yields of around 3 per cent, investors expected 4–6 per cent from sound overseas sovereign borrowers. Similarly, domestic railway debentures paid around 4–6 per cent, while the rate for overseas railways and municipalities was about 5–7 per cent. Borrowers who were perceived to be of higher than normal risk needed to offer additional premiums to persuade investors to part with their money.

London handled the lion's share of international bond issues because of the abundance of British savings, the contacts with borrowers arising from its pre-eminence in international trade finance, and the role of sterling as *the* medium for the conduct of international financial transactions.[21] Prior to 1914, the City was the leading international capital market, intermediating the supply and demand for long-term funds and acting, as Cornelis Rozenraad, President of the Federation of Foreign Chambers of Commerce in London, observed in a discussion on overseas investment in 1909, as 'honest broker working in all parts of the world, taking over – to a great extent with the money of her customers – the loans of other nations. In a word, although the investment power of Great Britain is very great, London is the principal intermediary between Europe and other parts of the world for the placing of foreign securities issued here'.[22] The natural corollary of London's leading role as a primary market was that it had the largest and most liquid secondary market in international securities.

The firms which were best placed to act as intermediaries in the rapidly growing international bond market were the merchant banks. Their contacts in foreign lands made them uniquely qualified to appraise the creditworthiness of borrowers, and the appearance of a name such as J. Henry Schröder & Co. on a bond reassured investors and greatly enhanced the marketability of the security. Furthermore, their networks of clients and correspondents in other commercial centres gave them ready-made distribution systems for the securities. Generalisations about the part played by the merchant banks in the conduct of issues are difficult, since they acted in a variety of roles and market practice was continually evolving. What is certain, however, is that the conduct of large issues of bonds on behalf of overseas borrowers could be a highly profitable business.

Between 1853 and 1914, J. Henry Schröder & Co. played a part in bond issues totalling £162 million, perhaps 4 per cent of the £4 billion or so sterling securities issued in Britain for overseas borrowers in these years.[23] The destinations of these funds echoed the pattern of the firm's consignment and accepting clients, since by and large they led to its introduction to borrowers. The countries of South America and the Caribbean were the recipients of £88 million, just over 50 per cent of the total. Europe and Russia received £42 million, the United States £20 million, and other regions £12 million. Virtually all the funds, those raised by sovereign borrowers as well as those destined for companies, were earmarked for particular purposes, as was the usual practice in the international capital market before the First World War. Railway building was the use to which the bulk – £110 million in total – was put. Banking, mining, plantations and a variety of other purposes absorbed £52 million. Most of these investments led directly to increases in the export of primary produce, notably sugar, cotton, coffee, nitrate and wheat, the commodities in which J. Henry Schröder & Co. specialised as a provider of acceptance credit trade finance.

The transportation of sugar, the commodity in which the Schröder firms in London had specialised for 50 years, was the purpose of J. Henry Schröder & Co.'s first bond issue, which was made on behalf of a Cuban railway company in 1853. Cuba's first railway was opened as early as 1837, only a decade after the first commercial exploitation of the technology in Britain and considerably before anywhere else in Latin America, because of the enormous savings which could be made in transport costs. Using railways the cost of carrying a box of sugar from the inland plantations to the port of Havana declined from $12.50 to $1.25.[24] Rising demand from European and North American consumers led to increased Cuban sugar output, which expanded from 220,000 tons in 1849 to 449,000 tons in 1861, prompting further railway building, and by the beginning of the 1860s 640 kilometres of track had been opened. From the 1850s J. Henry Schröder & Co. played a very important role in the development of the Cuban railway system (see Map 3.1 on page 60). In 1853 it issued £200,000 bonds on behalf of the Matanzas and Sabanilla Railroad Co. for the improvement of a line connecting the port of Matanzas to an inland sugar growing area. The loan was bought outright by the firm and sold to the public at a 10 per cent premium to the purchase price. The bonds provided a 7 per cent yield, a fairly high return for an overseas railway company reflecting the unfamiliarity of the capital market with both the borrower and the sponsor. In 1855, Schröders made a second issue for a Cuban railway company, the Jucaro Railroad Co., raising £100,000. The outbreak of the American Civil War in 1861 led to the closure of the substantial Louisiana sugar industry. This gave a boost to Cuban producers, who promoted further extensions of the island's railway system to expand their output yet further. In 1861, Schröders issued £250,000 bonds for the Havana and Matanzas Railroad Co., the first of several loans raised for this client. The bonds, which had a coupon of 7 per cent, were bought by the firm at 90 and sold to the public at 95, giving investors a yield of 7.4 per cent. There were further loans for the Havana and Matanzas of £100,000 in 1863 and £400,000 in

Map 3.1 United Railways of the Havana system, c. 1914

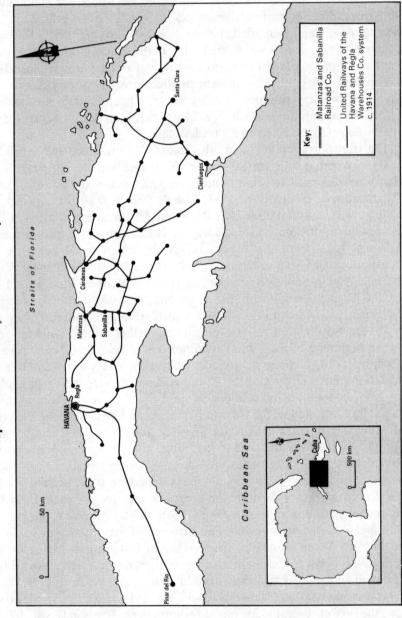

1865, and another £300,000 was raised for the Matanzas and Sabanilla line in 1863. Overall, in the dozen years 1853–65 J. Henry Schröder & Co. raised £1.5 million – around £50 million in 1990 money – for the development of the Cuban railway system, assuming a dominant role in Cuban railway finance which reinforced the firm's prominent position in the finance of the sugar trade. Naturally, it provided the usual paying agency and registration services for the duration of the bonds, which sustained the relationships between the parties, and when in subsequent years additional capital was needed, the Cuban railway companies again turned to the London firm.

The shipment of cotton and tobacco from the Mississippi hinterland to New Orleans was the purpose of the New Orleans, Jackson and Great Northern Railroad Co., whose promotors proposed to build a 550-mile line to connect the port of New Orleans with Nashville, Tennessee, by way of Jackson, Mississippi.[25] The scheme got under way in 1851 with strong political and financial support from the city of New Orleans and the state of Louisiana. Nevertheless, the Great Northern soon found itself short of money and became dependent upon advances provided by a New Orleans bank controlled by the most active of the company's directors, James Robb, a prominent and wealthy city councillor and Louisiana state senator. In the summer of 1853 Robb visited London, hoping to raise further funds for the Great Northern through a bond issue. Interest amongst British investors in American railroad bonds had been nurtured in previous years by Barings, Rothschilds and George Peabody & Co., and most probably it was to those houses that Robb first applied for assistance, but the unsettled condition of the New York securities market, which began in the autumn of 1853 and persisted until 1857, made the leading London issuing houses unwilling to adopt new US commitments.[26] Somehow Robb obtained an introduction to J. Henry Schröder & Co., perhaps through cotton trade contacts with J. H. Schröder & Co. of Liverpool or maybe from the recently established New Orleans firm Schröder, Mummy & Co. In November 1854, the London house provided a cash advance of £50,000 to the Great Northern secured against City of New Orleans bonds, pending a moment when market conditions were favourable to an issue.[27] On 11 August 1856, an agreement was signed by Schlüsser, acting for J. Henry Schröder & Co., and Robb, for the issue in London of £450,000 bonds, at par with an 8 per cent coupon, providing an exceptionally attractive yield.[28] Schröders acted as agent for the sale of the bonds, receiving a sales commission of 2.5 per cent of nominal value. The firm was also appointed agent in London for interest and redemption payments, for which services it received respectively 1.5 per cent and 1 per cent commissions.

James Robb's travelling companion on his visit to London in 1853
was a fellow Great Northern director, John Slidell, a New Yorker by
birth, who moved to New Orleans in 1819 to escape the scandal that
followed his participation in a duel.[29] He emerged as an important figure
in Louisiana politics in the 1840s, and in 1845 was appointed US
Commissioner to Mexico. In 1853 he entered the US Senate and for most
of James Buchanan's term in the White House, from 1856 to 1860, he
was the power behind the President. Upon the outbreak of the Civil War
in 1861, Slidell was appointed, because of his diplomatic experience, as
the Confederacy's representative in France. In this capacity he again
encountered J. Henry Schröder & Co. and it may have been he who
introduced John Henry to Emile Erlanger, a key figure in the history of
the firm from the 1860s to the 1880s.

Emile Erlanger was born in 1832 in Frankfurt, where his father was a
prominent Jewish banker.[30] He entered the family firm at the age of
seventeen, and in 1859, aged 27, he established his own private banking
firm, Emile Erlanger & Cie, in Paris. John Henry and Emile Erlanger
had much in common: both were born into established financial families
in Germany; they were of similar age; they were cosmopolitan in
outlook, energetic and ambitious. They became lifelong friends and in
the 1880s and 1890s Erlanger was frequently a member of the shooting
parties in Scotland organised by John Henry. They died within a year of
each other. Temperamentally there were differences. Erlanger was a
gambler who took great risks and generally reaped spectacular rewards.
'This man Erlanger is a dangerous one,' wrote a rival banker in 1863, 'he
has the quickest intelligence I have ever been thrown in contact with and
he is well calculated to exercise great influence over other minds not so
active, but I judge him to be ambitious, selfish, daring and
unscrupulous'.[31] John Henry, though possessing a keen eye for
opportunity, preferred to act as an agent rather than a principal, and
to make gradual but sure progress. Evidently the two men found that
their ambitions and ways of working were complementary, and for
several projects initiated by Erlanger in Paris in the 1860s it was J. Henry
Schröder & Co. which acted as agent and manager in London. Such co-
operation between bankers in the two leading international financial
centres, London and Paris, flourished in the 1860s, encouraged by
contacts developed during the Crimean War, when firms had linked up
to finance military supplies for the Anglo-French forces, and by the
trade treaty between Britain and France of 1860.[32]

Bond issues on behalf of foreign governments of questionable
creditworthiness had been virtually unmarketable in London since the
1820s, when there had been a rash of defaults by Latin American
countries. But the year 1862 saw 'a distinct turn' in favour of foreign

sovereign loans on the part of investors and a record eight such issues were made, including several highly speculative ones.[33] One of them was a 60 million franc loan for the government of Egypt which was brought out in the spring by a syndicate of Frankfurt banks acting in collaboration with Emile Erlanger & Cie in Paris, though it was in London that the bulk of the bonds were sold, with Frühling and Goschen acting as agent. The Egyptian government was a borrower of poor standing and the 7 per cent bonds were priced at a discount to par of 16–18 per cent yielding 8.5 per cent, terms tempting enough to attract a fourfold over-subscription. It has been estimated that after the deduction of commissions, charges and the discount, the Egyptian authorities received no more than 65 per cent of the nominal value of the bonds.[34] In its audacity, this loan was a rehearsal for the even more controversial issue on behalf of the Confederate States of America, which was offered to the public by Emile Erlanger & Cie and J. Henry Schröder & Co. a year later, and also took advantage of the new bull market in sovereign issues.

Confederate Cotton Loan, 1863

The American Civil War between the secessionist Confederacy of southern slave-owning states and the Union of northern states began in early 1861. It was by no means a contest of equals. By every material measure of martial capacity the South was inferior. Northerners outnumbered southerners by 22 million to 9 million, of whom some 3.5 million were slaves. The North had 80 per cent of American industrial plant, and the manufacturing capacity of the South soon proved inadequate to meet the needs of the Confederate Army. The Union Navy dominated the seas and from early on imposed a maritime blockade that severely curtailed southern trade with Europe. Yet the Confederate cause was not entirely hopeless. The Confederacy was fighting a defensive war for a cause that enjoyed enthusiastic popular support among southern whites. For the North to suppress the secession it would be necessary for its armies to occupy the South. For the South to achieve its independence it was enough to persuade the North that the sacrifices required were too great to warrant the preservation of a united nation. Any assistance which the South could muster from abroad could only make the North's ambition more difficult to realise, and hasten its abandonment.

In the early days of the Civil War southerners held high hopes of diplomatic intervention by Britain and France to bring the war to an end. There was considerable sympathy for the Southern plantation owners amongst the landowners who dominated their governments, and the Emperor Napoleon III of France was rumoured to be well disposed towards the South. Above all, Southern expectations were based on the dependence of the European cotton textile industries upon supplies of raw material from the Southern states, Britain receiving 80 per cent of supplies from this source.[35] At the outset of the war the South deliberately withheld cotton shipments to starve the British and French textile industries of supplies, calculating that the ensuing distress would lead their governments to apply pressure on the North to halt the hostilities. However, by the spring of 1862 it was clear that the most that the South could expect from the major European powers by way of support was the protection of the shipping rights of neutrals to carry Southern goods and supplies, and the embargo strategy was dropped. By then the South was desperately in need of foreign currency with which to purchase war materials and essential goods from Europe, which could only come from sales of cotton.

Although hampered by the Northern naval blockade, the export of cotton continued during the war since fast ships were able to run cargoes to West Indian islands where they were transferred to neutral vessels for shipment across the Atlantic. The Confederate government itself was a major seller of cotton, having a large stock as a result of the subscriptions to a loan of September 1861 paid by planters in kind. The summer of 1862 saw the sale in Europe of Confederate Cotton Certificates, which gave entitlement to government cotton for collection at a Southern port, it being up to the owner to organise running the blockade. The foreign currency thus raised was useful but by no means sufficient to meet the requirements of the Confederacy, and it became evident that any scheme to increase the financial resources of the South would be favourably received in Richmond, Virginia, the Confederate capital. So far as Lancashire was concerned the quantities shipped did little to relieve the 'cotton famine' which was intensifying rather than abating as stocks were exhausted. The result was a sharp rise in the price of cotton. On the eve of war the price of 1lb of New Orleans 'middling' cotton in the Liverpool market had been 7d. By the end of 1861, it had risen to 12d. and a year later it had reached 20d. The increase in cotton prices coupled with the desperation of the South for additional finance set enterprising minds to work.

The proposal for a bond issue secured by a 'cotton guarantee' appears to have been made first by Felix Carteret, a retired French civil servant whose help as a financial adviser had been enlisted by a Southern patriot living in Paris.[36] Carteret interested Erlanger and in September 1862 they discussed the idea with Slidell. Carteret reappeared in the story a year or so later when he and some others pursued Erlanger through the courts in an attempt to extract from him commissions which they claimed were due to them. On 28 October 1862, an agreement to issue a loan was signed between Erlanger and Slidell which was despatched to Richmond, Virginia, for ratification. In the winter of 1862 Erlanger was engaged in negotiations regarding the amount of the loan, the coupon and the commission charges. He was also conducting discussions of a different kind with Mathilda Slidell, James Slidell's 19-year-old daughter, which led to their marriage in October 1864. In February 1863 it was agreed to issue bonds with a nominal value of £3 million at 90.[37] Erlanger undertook to buy the issue at 77 and the difference, plus a 5 per cent underwriting commission, was his profit on the transaction. The bonds had a 7 per cent coupon, which meant a yield to investors of 8 per cent.

When James Spence, the Liverpool merchant who was acting as the agent for the sale of the Cotton Certificates, heard of these terms he protested that the yield was too low to ensure the success of an issue on behalf of an unrecognised rebel regime at war with its more powerful neighbour. Southern politicians, on the other hand, who saw the loan as an assertion of Confederate sovereignty as well as a financial measure, opposed a higher yield on the grounds that it would constitute an advertisement of the poor creditworthiness of the South. In any case, investors in the Confederate Cotton Loan were much less interested in the yield than in the 'cotton clause'. This feature, described by *The Economist* as 'peculiar', 'attractive', and 'the gambling element', entitled bondholders to convert into cotton held in warehouses in the South, and the cotton option was the most valuable part of this highly innovative convertible bond.[38] The conversion price was 5.4d. per lb, which was very attractive at a time when New Orleans 'middling' cotton was quoted in Liverpool at 22d. per lb. Even with the deduction of freight and insurance costs there was scope for enormous profits whenever it proved possible to obtain possession of the cotton. *The Economist*'s judgement was that 'we can scarcely imagine any combination of circumstances under which middling New Orleans shall go as low as 6d. or even 7d. per lb for several years to come'. The danger that title to the collateral cotton would not be recognised in the event of the South losing the war was dismissed as 'so slight that, of itself, it need not deter any man from sharing in an 8 per cent loan'.

As with the Egyptian loan of 1862, Erlanger decided to issue the bonds simultaneously in several European markets, this being an already established practice of the international capital market. Finding an agent in London must have presented a problem since the leading Anglo-American firms, notably Barings, Rothschilds, Brown, Shipley and George Peabody & Co. were all aligned with the North. John K. Gilliat & Co., a well-known firm of London merchants established in the eighteenth century with strong ties to the Southern states, was invited to act as agent for the loan but declined to get involved. Perhaps James Slidell then suggested to his future son-in-law that he should approach Schröders, the firm which had proved so accommodating over the raising of funds for the Great Northern railroad. John Henry agreed to handle the business and J. Henry Schröder & Co. made its first appearance as an issuer of a sovereign loan – albeit for a borrower of rather less than triple-A standing.

The prospectus for the Confederate Cotton Loan appeared on Tuesday 19 March inviting subscriptions in Paris and Frankfurt, where it was handled by the Erlanger family firms; in Amsterdam, where B. H. Schröder & Co. acted as agent; and in London and Liverpool. Three days later the lists were closed after £15 million had been subscribed in London and £1 million elsewhere 'in order not to increase further the difficulty of allotting to the satisfaction of all subscribers'.[39] A representative of the South in London wrote jubilantly to the Treasury Secretary of the Confederacy of the 'brilliant success' of the issue[40] which he reported was attributed by Erlanger to the 'high standing and influence' of J. Henry Schröder & Co.[41] Rothschilds took a rather different view of the matter: 'The Confederate Loan,' wrote a partner to August Belmont, their New York agent, 'was of so speculative a nature that it was very likely to attract all wild speculators . . . It was brought out by foreigners, and we do not hear of any respectable people having anything to do with it . . . We ourselves have been quite neutral and have had nothing to do with it'.[42]

Schröders' role in the issue did not come to an end with the closing of the subscription lists. The firm was charged with the management of the issue until full payment had been received from subscribers. Payment for the Confederate Cotton Loan bonds was divided, as was usual practice, into several parts; subscribers paid 5 per cent on application and successful applicants then had to pay a further 10 per cent on allotment, which meant before the end of March. There were three further calls of 10 per cent, due on 1 May, 1 June and 1 July, and three calls of 15 per cent, due on 1 August, 1 September and 1 October, making a total of 90 per cent, the full amount since the issue was made at a 10 per cent discount. April was the danger period, since if confidence in the loan lapsed then holders might decided to write off the 15 per cent which they had already paid rather than throw good money after bad. However, once the first call on 1 May, and even more so the second on 1 June, had been paid there was every expectation that bondholders would make the other payments rather than forfeit their investments. In the meantime it was essential to sustain the price of the bonds, which meant the conduct of a support operation in the market by Schröders.

Immediately after issue the Confederate bonds rose to a 100 per cent premium on their partly-paid price, as might be expected given the scale of oversubscription. However, agents of the Union were hard at work waging war in the market against the Confederate Cotton Loan. On 28 April, three days before the crucial first call was due, Erlanger wrote to the Confederate Secretary of the Treasury to explain developments:

> The progress of the Loan has not been quite so satisfactory as the great favour shown it in the beginning led us to anticipate . . . [it] encountered a most determined opposition by parties in the Northern Interest who were, not without reason, frightened at the extraordinary popularity of the Loan and the demonstration it involved in favour of the South. Rumours of a second and larger issue at an early date, the existence of Cotton Warrants, Certificates and similar securities, together with false reports of the great want of food in the Southern Army and other unprincipled assertions were spread in all directions, and backed as they were by immense speculative sales found sufficient credence to bring about a reaction in the mind of a number of allottees . . . In ordinary cases it is perfectly immaterial whether a Loan after it has been fully subscribed for advances or recedes in price. Fluctuations are the rule on every Bourse . . . If we had had to deal with an ordinary Loan we should therefore have left the price to regulate itself by the Common Law of supply and demand . . . But in the present instance we felt that the Loan having assumed a political bearing and great importance being attached to its depression by the Northern party we should not be doing our duty were we to treat it merely as a question of finance.[43]

To counter the 'bear' activities of the Northern agents Schröders made purchases in the market to support the price of the bonds. Initially the purchases were made for Erlanger's account but soon it became necessary to call upon the £450,000 which the Confederacy had received from the subscriptions upon application and allocation. On 6 April 1863, James Mason, the Confederate ambassador to Britain, agreed that Schröders could purchase up to £1 million (nominal value) of the Cotton Loan bonds if necessary. This proved insufficient and on 24 April consent was given for the purchase of a further £500,000 (nominal value) of the bonds. Overall bonds with a face value of £1,517,000 were purchased during April. The support operation was a success, since it achieved its objective of sustaining the market price of the bonds, and holders duly paid the 1 May call and subsequent ones. However, the Confederacy was left holding half the bonds it had just issued.

Predictably, there was a dispute between Erlanger and the government as to whether his commission was to be calculated on the initial sale of the whole issue or on the amount that ended up in the hands of investors, which was eventually resolved by his payment in bonds with a nominal value of £302,000.[44]

Erlanger's large bondholding led to his involvement in blockade running. J. Henry Schröder & Co. was an ideal partner for this undertaking, not only because of its role in the Confederate Cotton Loan issue but also on account of its contacts in Cuba and the southern states. Soon after the issue Erlanger and Schröders formed the European Trading Company to conduct blockade running between Havana and Mobile, Alabama, where its agent was H. O. Brewer & Co., a local commission merchant firm.[45] The European Trading Company's steamship *Denbigh* arrived in Havana in December 1863 and in the following year and a half made thirteen round trips before running aground in May 1865. Contemporary estimates suggest that the earnings from a single successful return run were sufficient to pay the entire capital cost of a vessel and generate a modest profit. Plainly the operations of the *Denbigh*, which could carry 500 bales of cotton, were highly profitable. In June 1864 Erlanger and Schröders came up with yet another project concerning Southern finance, the establishment of a Confederate bank in London with a capital of £10 million, but this came to nothing.[46]

Schröders' activities on behalf of the Confederacy provoked sanctions on the part of the Union government. In the spring of 1863 the US consul in Hamburg refused to certify the validity of a notarial signature because the document to which the signature was attached contained the firm's name. A few months later, in July 1863, there was another episode in New York. 'Some bills for about £2000 drawn on Messrs Schröder by Messrs Scharfenberg & Co. of Havana, for a cargo of sugar shipped to Amsterdam, were sent as a remittance by another firm to their agent in Quebec,' reported *The Times*. 'That gentlemen – Mr W. H. Smith, an English subject – being about to return to Havana, brought the bills in question to New York, whence he intended to sail to Havana. His trunks were searched by a Customs-house officer, and the drafts on Messrs Schröder being found in them, he was detained as a prisoner and the drafts impounded. Subsequently, he was released and allowed to sail, but the drafts were not returned to him'.[47]

The Confederate Cotton Loan was one of the most remarkable episodes in the history of the international capital market. Ultimately the Confederacy received cash proceeds of £1.6 million and many of the repurchased bonds were used to settle outstanding debts.[48] Though the sums raised fell short of the nominal amount of the issue, it was an unrivalled achievement to secure so much funding for an unrecognised regime in the throes of a civil war. It was not the Confederacy that lost as a result of the Cotton Loan but the speculators who bought the certificates which upon the defeat of the South became, in the words of Erlanger's grandson, 'good only for papering walls'.[49] Erlanger's gross receipts were £154,000 in cash plus whatever he made from the sale of cotton exchanged for the £302,000 in bonds (at nominal value) which were the basis of his blockade-running activities.[50] However, Erlanger incurred considerable costs, including brokerage charges and Schröders' commissions, which he told the Confederate authorities amounted to an 'unprecedented expenditure'.[51] The exact extent of his profits are unknown, but they must have been very substantial. Schröders' profits from its involvement in the Confederate Cotton Loan were recorded as £37,637 – a handsome £1.3 million in 1990 money – and John Henry used his share to buy 'The Dell'. It was an auspicious start to the relationship between J. Henry Schröder & Co. and Emile Erlanger & Cie.

Even before the final call had been made for the Confederate Cotton Loan, Schröders and Erlangers were conducting another issue together. Hitherto the Kingdom of Sweden had raised funds in Frankfurt, but Swedish diplomatic support for Denmark in the dispute with Prussia over Schleswig-Holstein made it inexpedient to issue a loan in Germany.[52] Erlanger seized the opportunity and offered to bring out a loan for Sweden in London, using Schröders as his agent for the issue. In October 1863, the Swedish government passed a law authorising 'Schröders and other associated capitalists' to raise £2,223,000 which was to be used for the construction of railways in Sweden.[53] A prospectus offering bonds with a 4.5 per cent coupon at a price of 92.5, giving a modest yield of 4.86, which reflected the good standing of the borrower, appeared in April 1864. The issue was well received, particularly on the Continent where it was distributed by a consortium of four firms including the Erlanger family's Frankfurt and Paris firms, Emile Erlanger receiving the title of Baron from the grateful Swedish crown. Later that year Baron Erlanger brought out a loan for the government of Tunis, a much less creditworthy client which had to provide investors with a yield of 7.29 per cent to secure their favour. Schröders assisted with the placement of the bonds in London and its agent Heinrich Schliemann visited Tunis to negotiate on behalf of Erlanger and the firm.[54]

In the aftermath of the Crimean War the Russian government instigated an ambitious programme of railway construction to facilitate the movement of troops around the country and to promote economic development. The late 1860s saw a new phase of the programme and in 1867–68 bond issues totalling £18 million were made in London for the construction of railways in Russia.[55] One of the objectives was the completion of a railway connection between St Petersburg and Odessa.

The contract to raise the £1.7 million required for the construction of the final Charkow–Krementschug section was awarded to Ephrussi & Co. and Raffalovich & Co., the Odessa grain merchants for whom Schröders acted as consignment merchants in London. Following negotiations in Paris, where a branch of the Raffalovich family had established residence, Schröders undertook to act as agent for the issue in November 1868 of £1.3 million bonds in London, another tranche being issued through the Disconto-Gesellschaft in Berlin. The bonds, which were guaranteed by the Russian government, had an 81-year maturity, a coupon of 5 per cent and were priced at 80, giving investors a yield of 6.25 per cent. Despite adverse press comment on the 'reckless course' of Russian railway issues, which it was alleged had flooded the market, the issue was several times over-subscribed.[56]

The late 1860s saw large scale borrowing to finance reconstruction in the southern states following the American Civil War. Erlanger was contractor for two of these loans and Schröders acted as his agent for the tranches brought out in London. In 1869, funds were raised for the Alabama & Chattanooga Railway Co., under the guarantee of the State of Alabama, and in 1870 for the State of Alabama itself. It was necessary to offer high returns to attract funds and the yields were 9.9 per cent and 8.5 per cent respectively. Investors were right to be wary since the administration of most southern states had fallen into the hands of 'carpet baggers' and much of the proceeds of the loans disappeared in fees and commissions paid to politicians, and in 1872 both the State of Alabama and the Alabama & Chattanooga Railroad Company defaulted. During the 1870s Erlanger acquired large shareholdings in defaulted southern railway companies such as the Alabama & Chattanooga and was able to put together a regional network spanning Alabama, Louisiana, Tennessee and Kentucky, which became known as the Erlanger System.[57] This was floated on the London Stock Exchange in 1881 as the Alabama, New Orleans, Texas & Pacific Junction Railways Co. In 1883 J. Henry Schröder & Co. sponsored an issue of £800,000 6 per cent debentures on the company's behalf. This bold venture came to grief in the mid-1880s because of insufficient traffic, and went into voluntary liquidation in 1887.[58]

Japan Customs Loan, 1870

Japan's drive for modernisation and industrialisation began in earnest following the political changes of 1868 known as the Meiji Restoration. The new ministers supported improvements in communications for military, political and economic motives, and in November 1869 the government decided to build the country's first railway, connecting Tokyo, the capital, a city of several million inhabitants, with the port of Yokohama.[59] Lacking the necessary funds, the Japanese government took advantage of an offer of finance from Horatio Nelson Lay, a flamboyantly named Englishman who had arrived in Japan in July 1869 announcing that he represented a powerful consortium of financiers who had £3 million available for lending.[60] Lay's career in the Orient had begun twenty years earlier when he had been sent to China by the British consular service.[61] Subsequently he had become a senior customs administrator for the Chinese government, but had left its employment in the mid-1860s on account of dissatisfaction with his conduct of the purchase of a flotilla of gunboats in Europe. In December 1869, an agreement was signed between Lay and the government whereby he undertook to furnish £1 million at 12 per cent interest secured on the customs revenue.

It was understood by the Japanese government that the funds would be privately subscribed by Lay's consortium, but a second agreement, which was signed the same day making no reference to the earlier one, appointed Lay as commissioner for the Japanese government to raise the £1 million on any terms and from any persons he thought fit. On the basis of the second agreement Lay approached Rothschilds and other firms with a view to making a public issue, but was unable to find a London house which would handle the business.[62] He then turned to Emile Erlanger in Paris who agreed to make the issue in conjunction with Schröders in London. In April 1870, Schröders successfully brought out the 10-year £1 million Imperial Government of Japan Customs Loan, receiving a 1 per cent commission for its services. Although the Japanese government had agreed to pay Lay 12 per cent interest for the funds, Schröders was able to make the issue bearing a 9 per cent coupon at a price of 98, giving a yield to investors of 9.18 per cent, a high yield relative to established sovereign borrowers but not for a country which was completely unknown in the international capital market and had been closed to foreigners for centuries.

When the Japanese government learned that the funds had been raised by a public issue and of the discrepancy between the 12 per cent interest which Japan paid to Lay and the 9 per cent which he and Erlanger paid to bondholders there was outrage.[63] Perhaps the Japanese had also learned that Erlanger was related through his wife, Martha Slidell, to Commodore Perry, the United States naval commander who in 1856 had humilated Japan by the bombardment of Yokohama and the forced signature of a much resented trade treaty. In June 1870, a decree was issued which cancelled all the powers granted to Lay by the agreements of December 1869 frustrating his intention of pocketing the 3 per cent difference in interest rates. Lay decided that he had had enough of high finance and the following year he became a barrister, the last year in which it was unnecessary to sit a qualifying examination, and had a successful career at the Middle Temple. However, his legal expertise proved of no avail in the conduct of his defence against the suit brought against him in the Court of Chancery in 1873 by the members of the consortium who had sent him to Japan, who successfully sued him, claiming a share in the profits which he and Erlanger had made on the issue of the Japan Customs Loan.[64]

The Japanese had nothing but praise for the role of J. Henry Schröder & Co. in introducing the bonds to the market and were pleased by their subsequent performance. By the summer, the bonds were trading at a premium to all other foreign securities, this being attributed to the growing appreciation amongst investors of Japan's commercial and political strengths, of which the issue itself aroused awareness. Schröders was retained as paying agent until the maturity of the issue in August 1882, receiving ½ per cent commission for its services. Following the completion of the redemption of the bonds Joseph Foreman, Schröders' office manager, was presented with a Japanese vase by the Minister of Finance, Prince Matsukata Masayoshi, 'as a mark of our esteem for the trouble you have taken'.[65]

Three months after the issue of the Japan Customs Loan war broke out between France and Prussia. The seige of Paris by the Prussians and the subsequent episode of the Commune disrupted the functioning of the French capital as an international financial centre in the early 1870s, and Emile Erlanger moved to London. Initially Schröders continued to act as agent for bond issues originated by Erlanger and it was in this capacity that in December 1871 the firm issued £210,000 6 per cent bonds on behalf of the Amoor River Navigation Company. This undertaking had been formed a few months earlier to exploit a 20 year concession by the Russian government to provide a regular postal, passenger and freight service on the Amoor River and its tributaries that provided access to East Siberia and Manchuria from the Pacific Ocean, one of the earliest attempts to unlock the economic potential of Siberia. However, the demand for riverboat services fell short of expectations and the company went into default in December 1874 and thereafter paid only a third of the rate of interest promised in the prospectus. Erlanger established his own firm in London and soon began to conduct issuing business under his own name, including a loan for the Republic of Costa Rica in which Schröders prudently took no part. Costa Rica had neither the ability nor the intention of honouring its liabilities to bondholders and the loan was soon in default. As a result, in 1875 Erlanger had the disconcerting experience of being summoned before a Select Committee of the House of Commons which was investigating the practices of loan contractors such as himself.[66] But his firm survived the scandal and subsequently became a highly regarded and reputable merchant bank.

Financial Performance and Organisation of the Firm

The bulk of the revenues of J. Henry Schröder & Co. in the 1850s and 1860s were derived from the activities already discussed – accepting, consignments and issuing. Detailed information is unavailable for the 1850s but in 1861–70 these generated 84 per cent of total revenues, much the largest amount deriving from acceptance and consignment commissions (which cannot be disaggregated in these years) (see Table 3.4). The other important source of revenue was 'net interest' which produced 9 per cent of total revenues in 1861–70. Net interest was the revenue from interest paying assets, government bonds, for instance, less a charge of 4 per cent levied for the use of the partners' capital. Such fixed interest charges were, and are, a normal practice in partnerships and are usually closely related to the yield on government bonds. One of the factors which determined the level of net interest revenues was the type of assets in which the firm's funds were invested, the shorter the maturity of the asset the lower the rate of return. Information about Schröders' assets in the 1850s and 1860s is incomplete, but it is clear that they were very liquid, a very high proportion comprising cash and bills

Table 3.4   J. Henry Schröder & Co., sources of revenues, 1861–70

	1861–70 Annual average £000s	*Per cent*
Accepting Consignments }	72	72
Issuing	12	12
Net interest	9	9
Other[1]	7	7
Total	100	100

1. Freight, postage, insurance, sundry merchandise, etc.

Source: J. Henry Schröder & Co., profit & loss accounts.

of exchange, the most liquid form of earning asset. Another constraint upon net interest revenues was that the firm did not take deposits, though it did hold balances for clients, and the partners' capital constituted a much higher proportion of liabilities than would have been the case for a bank, though it is not possible to be precise about the ratio of partners' capital to other liabilities prior to 1870.

There were two types of costs incurred in the conduct of J. Henry Schröder & Co.'s activities: operating costs, of which the largest component was staff wages and salaries, and bad debts. No information is available about costs in the 1850s but in the years 1861–70 operating costs averaged £9,500 per annum while bad debts, which fluctuated considerably from year to year, averaged £20,000 per annum. Thus in the 1860s, and there is no reason to believe that the 1850s were different, bad debts were twice as costly for Schröders as operational expenses. Plainly the key to success, and indeed survival, in the merchant banking business in these years was the management of risk to minimise bad debts. This was achieved by adherence to the prudential principles already discussed, by a constant vigilance in respect of the business of clients, and by curtailing credit when trading conditions became hazardous. Thus it was that Schröders survived the surges of bad debts in the commercial crises of 1847–48, 1857–58 and 1866, which brought down other merchant banking firms.

Figure 3.4   J. Henry Schröder & Co., net profits after interest on partners' capital, 1852–70

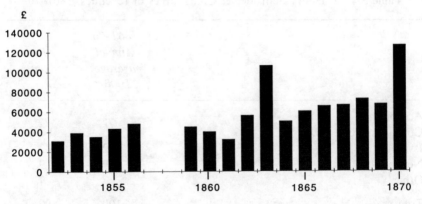

Note: Information unavailable for 1857 and 1858.

Any liability for income tax was borne by the partners.

Figure 3.5   J. Henry Schröder & Co., return on capital and annual rate of inflation, 1852–70

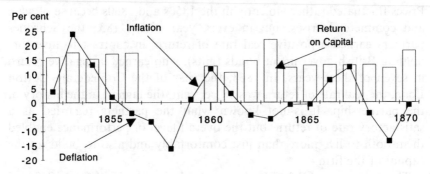

Note: Returns for 1857–59 cannot be calculated because of missing information.

The 'real' return on capital is the difference between the nominal return on capital depicted above and the annual rate of inflation.

Profits in 1852–70 – after deduction of the 4 per cent interest on partners' capital – are shown in Figure 3.4. There was no tax on the partnership's profits although the partners as individuals paid income tax, then at very modest levels, on their earnings. In the 1850s, profits averaged £35,000 – about £1.1 million in 1990 money – in the first half of the decade and £42,000 in the second half (though no information is available for the years 1857 and 1858) but slumped to £32,000 in 1861 because of a rash of bad debts brought about by the outbreak of the American Civil War. In 1863, thanks largely to the Confederate Cotton Loan, they surged to £106,000 – about £3.8 million in 1990 money – the first time that issuing activity produced a massive bonus on top of the firm's 'bread and butter' business.[67] The following year profits fell back to a more 'normal' level of £50,000 and in 1864–69 they averaged £63,000. In 1870, once again inflated by large issuing proceeds, profits soared to £126,000.

To assess the performance of a firm it is necessary to relate profits to the scale of the resources which produce them. Figure 3.5 shows Schröders' rate of return on capital, including the annual 4 per cent paid on partners' capital, for the years 1852–70. Schröders' return on capital averaged 16.7 per cent in 1852–56 and 14.5 per cent in 1860–70. These were much higher rates than were available to 'portfolio investors', whose highest possible returns were 5–7 per cent on foreign bonds or 6–9 per cent on domestic equities.[68] An important investment consideration is inflation, which complicates the use of rates of return as a yardstick of performance, the 'real rate' of return on capital in Figure 3.5 being the difference between the depicted nominal return and the inflation rate. Prices fluctuated rather violently in the 1850s and 1860s because of wars and commercial crises, but in every year except 1853 the Schröder partners earned a positive real rate of return, in contrast to investors holding British government bonds (gilts), who earned a negative return in seven of these years. In 1863, the year of the Confederate Cotton Loan, the real rate of return was 28 per cent, the highest in the history of the partnership. It is not known what the partners regarded as a satisfactory rate of return, but the overall level of performance enabled them both to live more than just comfortably and also to build up the capital of the firm.

The expansion of Schröders' business during the 1850s and 1860s led to some important changes in the organisation of the firm. In the first place, the growing number of clerks, who numbered 10 in 1849, 17 in 1860 and 25 in 1870, necessitated more space. In 1852 the partners rented 6 Lime Street Square, of which the firm was the sole occupant, and in 1854 paid £6,500 for a freehold building at 145 Leadenhall Street, which became the address of the firm for the following century[69] (see Map 2.1 on page 37). This was the first time that J. Henry Schröder & Co. had owned its premises, a change of policy which may have owed something to the booming City property market. A rise in demand for office and warehouse accommodation in the 1850s, resulting from the rapid increase in international trade, led to an extensive redevelopment of old residential dwellings as offices.[70] Schröders joined in the building boom, which in July 1859 was reported by the *Building News* to be 'in active progress in all directions included within a radius of a mile of the Royal Exchange . . . on the northern side of Leadenhall Street, opposite to the Hide and Leather Market, the large block of houses, Nos 145 and 146, are condemned and the old materials of which they are composed are to be sold to Messrs Pullen & Son, on Monday'.[71] Ten months later, the same publication reported the completion of a 'large structure' to the designs of D. A. Cobbett, an architect practising at 57 Fenchurch Street.[72] The plainness of the exterior of the building was remarked upon disapprovingly by the paper, but most probably the Schröder partners were delighted with a facade which did not distract the eye from the imposing portal that they specified was to be 'twelve feet in height from the pavement to the ceiling thereof and shall be as near as circumstances permit similar to the entrance corridor and passage leading to the Counting House in the occupation of Messrs Antony Gibbs & Sons . . . except that the same is to be faced with Portland Cement and not Stone'.[73]

The expansion of personnel led to the establishment of a layer of management between the partners and the clerks. In 1854, the year of the move to Leadenhall Street, the partners appointed Theodore Karck, who had joined the firm in 1840, as its first office manager, his duties being the supervision of the clerks and the premises. Karck came from a well known Hamburg merchant family and a relative, Ferdinand Karck, was a close business associate of Alexander Kleinwort, the founder of Kleinwort, Sons & Co. In time he might have been promoted to the Schröder partnership, but he resigned in 1862, probably to take up an offer of a partnership in another firm since in 1868 he was elected a member of the exclusive Society of Merchants Trading to the Continent. Karck's resignation was followed by the promotion of two of the clerks, Otto von der Meden and Henry Tiarks, into managerial positions. Von der Meden was made associate partner, sitting in the partners' room and assisting with the running of the business and the partnership correspondence, and participating in profits but without liability for losses. Tiarks, who became Schlüsser's son-in-law in 1862, was appointed office manager in succession to Karck.

Within merchant banks there were several categories of clerks. Barings' salary sheets of the 1830s and 1840s divided the clerks systematically into three classes. 'Class three' clerks, usually known as 'juniors', were young men learning the business of banking and awaiting promotion to a position of greater responsibility. They had routine responsibilities such as opening the mail and making the pressed copies of letters, and acted as assistants to the more senior clerks. They shared these tasks with the 'volunteers', the sons of merchants whose preparation for entering the family business was to spend several years, usually abroad, working with 'friends'. At Schröders, volunteers with the names Tamm, Horny, Merck, Gildemeister, Schlüsser and, inevitably, Schröder, all of which were borne by firms with which J. Henry Schröder & Co. had close relations, passed through the office during the lifetime of Johann Heinrich.

'Class two' clerks, known as ledger clerks, were mostly employed in keeping the firm's books, though they might also undertake some correspondence work. There was a clear salary differential between the juniors and the ledger clerks, the latter receiving two or three times as much as the former. The 'class one' clerks were the correspondence clerks and those charged with particular duties such as oversight of the ledgers, supervision of the paperwork associated with bills of exchange, or the purchase of insurance at Lloyds. Often they commanded several languages and had experience in a number of firms in various countries. Their remuneration was two or three times the average salary of the ledger clerks.

The annual average earnings of Schröders' clerks at the beginning of the 1850s were: juniors, £73; ledger clerks, £124; and correspondence clerks, £193.[74] This meant that they all had sufficient means to sustain a middle-class style of life which it has been calculated required an income of at least £60 per annum.[75] However, only the correspondence clerks met the yardstick of £150 per annum which Mrs Beaton's *Book of Household Management* specified as the minimum for the employment of a servant, which was her definition of a comfortable middle-class life.[76] Even their incomes fell well short of the £300 per year which contributors to the correspondence column of *The Times* in 1858 felt was necessary for a 'gentleman' to earn before he could marry.[77] By the early 1870s, however, the average salary of Schröders' correspondence clerks had risen to £319 per annum, conferring upon them the status of 'gentleman'. The ledger clerks had also enjoyed an increase to £160 per annum, but the remuneration of the juniors had fallen to £54 per annum.

In these years Schröders' clerks were predominantly German, reflecting the overwhelmingly German character of the firm. Between 1829 and 1892 the firm engaged 179 clerks, 70 per cent of whom had recognisably German surnames and it was not until 1843, twenty-five years after the foundation of the firm, that a clerk with an obviously English surname, Norbury, was engaged. E L Cheese, who joined as a junior in 1887, recalled that all the clerks spoke German and there were often sons of German clients working as volunteers in the office.[78] This was also true of Kleinworts, where half the staff were of foreign origin in the late nineteenth century.[79] The reasons for this are clear. Schröders did much of its business with Hamburg merchants or German-speaking merchants in Russia, and many of its clients in other parts of the world, notably South America, were of German origin. Furthermore, German clerks had a reputation for efficiency and hard work. Investigations by the London Chamber of Commerce following complaints that English clerks were 'being pushed from their stools by competitors from Germany' in the 1880s, established that, in firms conducting extensive overseas business, two-fifths or more of the staff were commonly foreign.[80] Their employers told the enquiry that foreign clerks, especially German ones, were better educated than Englishmen and had superior command of foreign languages, but the spokesmen for their English counterparts maintained that the reasons for their employment was that they were willing to accept lower wages and to work longer hours.

Another dimension to the German character of the firm is the lifestyle and interests of the partners and senior clerks. In the mid-nineteenth century, with the exception of John Henry, all the partners and senior clerks of J. Henry Schröder & Co. lived in the leafy villa suburbs of south London that were developed from the 1820s as residential quarters for prosperous City merchants.[81] Street directories of the middle decades of the century record von Post in Clapham New Park; Schlüsser at 'The Priory', Balham; Karck in Camberwell; von der Meden at 'Coventry Hall'; Streatham; and Tiarks at 'The Lawns', Clapham Common.[82] Amongst their neighbours were members of other Anglo-German merchant families such as the Brandts, the Huths and the Kleinworts. Another was Julius Caesar Czarnikow, who in 1861 founded C. Czarnikow Ltd, a leading sugar importer which became an important Schröder client.[83] The diary kept by Agnes Tiarks, the wife of Henry Tiarks, suggests that the partners and senior clerks of Schröders who lived in south London saw a lot of each other socially in the 1860s and early 1870s, though not with the regularity of the partners and senior clerks of Kleinworts who dined together every Sunday evening.[84]

A focal institution of the German mercantile community in south London was the German Evangelical Church, Denmark Hill. It was founded in January 1854 by a Lutheran congregation comprising eighty German families of 'substantial means'.[85] A pastor was appointed, with guidance from the Revd Johann Gerhard Tiarks, the father of Henry Tiarks, and an appeal was launched for funds to build a church. Letters were sent to a couple of hundred firms and individuals in London and to prospective benefactors in Germany. Prince Albert headed the list of forty-six contributors, who included the names of partners of Schröders, Kleinworts and Huths. The German Evangelical Church, seating 300 for Sunday morning services in German, was consecrated in December 1855. Its congregation included Schlüsser, Karck and Tiarks, and several partners of Kleinworts, who were very active in its affairs.

John Henry, though preferring fashionable Bayswater to Balham as a place of residence, was a leading benefactor of London's German institutions and charities. He was a subscriber to the appeal launched in 1843 to build a hospital in Hackney to serve the German community of London's East End, many of whom were very impoverished and worked in dangerous and unpleasant occupations such as sugar refining and salt processing. Donations to the cause were also made by Alexander Schlüsser, and the Revd Johann Tiarks and his merchant brother Heinrich Tiarks, and Bernhard Hinrich Schröder and Christian Matthias Schröder II of Hamburg.[86] John Henry served as treasurer of the German Hospital, which opened on 15 October 1845, the birthday of the King of Prussia[87] and in March 1862 he became a trustee of London's oldest German institution, the Hamburg Lutheran Church (later called the German Lutheran Church) which had been founded in 1699 as a place of worship for Hanseatic merchants residing in the City.[88] It was there that he had married Eveline Schlüsser in 1850. In the early 1870s, John Henry and Richard Brandt, a fellow trustee who was a partner of

Wm Brandt Sons & Co., organised the relocation of the church from the City to the vicinity of the German Hospital in Hackney. Subsequently, other members of the Schröder family in London and the Tiarks family also became trustees and since the turn of the twentieth century the affairs of the trustees of the German Lutheran Church have been administered from Schroders.

In the 1850s and 1860s, John Henry and Alexander Schlüsser turned J. Henry Schröder & Co. from a modest Anglo-German merchant firm into a prominent merchant bank. By 1870, Schlüsser was 67 years old and 'riche comme un prince', as Heinrich Schliemann noted in his diary after a visit in 1866. His retirement the following year led to a rearrangement of the partnership and a new phase opened in the history of the firm.

4

Boom, Recession and Recovery

1871–92

The years 1871–73 saw 'a convulsion of prosperity' in the industrial economies, to use Benjamin Disraeli's contemporary description.[1] There was a boom on the London stock market, which saw a rash of bond issues on behalf of borrowers of very doubtful standing, and a 'fever of speculation' on the Continental bourses.[2] In Germany, the upsurge was especially vigorous, being fuelled by the massive war indemnity paid by France following its defeat in the Franco-Prussian War of 1870–71. The end of the boom was heralded by the crash of the Vienna bourse in May 1873 and soon the industrial nations were in recession, which meant bankruptcies, bond defaults and a slowing in the rate of growth of international trade. The slackening of demand in the major European economies and the United States exacerbated the growing imbalance between the supply and consumption of primary produce and triggered the start of an era of declining prices which lasted until the mid-1890s. The underlying cause was the rapid increase in output of foodstuffs, minerals and other raw materials due to the integration of the American prairies and other frontier lands into the international economy, brought about by the construction of railways and the growth of ocean-going steam shipping. Stagnant or falling export revenues made it difficult for public and private borrowers in regions such as Latin America to service their external debts, and there were many defaults. Investors became wary of the bonds of overseas borrowers and the volume of issues made on their behalf in London slumped in the mid- and late 1870s. Moreover, their incomes were hit by the low nominal interest rates and small dividends which were the consequences of the profits squeeze that accompanied the falling price level, inducing a perception of hardship amongst *rentiers* and businessmen that led to the era becoming known to contemporaries as the 'Great Depression'.

Estimates of the growth of foreign trade suggest a slowdown from 1873, the annual rate of growth measured by value declining from 4.3 per cent in 1853–72 to 2.7 per cent in 1873–92.[3] This was an unfavourable development for the merchant banks, since international trade was the basis of their acceptance business. Corroborative evidence of slack demand for the trade finance services of the merchant banks is provided

81

by estimates of the volume of bills of exchange deriving from the finance of international trade in the London money market, which suggest at least a lull in the expansion of acceptance business and perhaps even a decline in the late 1870s and early 1880s.[4] Finally, the consignment business of the merchant banks went into decline because of changes in commercial techniques arising from the growth of international telegraph communication by undersea cables, a business manual of the day observing that they 'have almost annihilated space and time . . . swamping many an ordinary merchant of moderate means'.[5] These adverse developments in the business of the London merchant banks are reflected in the fortunes of Barings, Morgans and Kleinworts, which experienced downturns in activity or prosperity in the mid-1870s.[6]

The US and German economies resumed rapid growth in the early 1880s and both boomed for the rest of the decade.[7] New issues for US borrowers in the London capital market picked up from 1880, which benefited City houses with strong American connections.[8] In the second half of the decade the countries of Latin America (particularly Argentina) and Australia also became large borrowers in the London capital market, and the years 1888–90 saw an overseas issuing boom of unprecedented magnitude, though by now there were new competitors challenging for the business and the merchant banks were gradually losing market share.[9] The City firm which benefited more than any other from the new issues boom of the late 1880s was Barings, which handled the lion's share of Argentinian issues, and the financial crisis of 1890 which ensued from the follies of the bull market has become known as the Baring Crisis. The aftermath was another acute slump in issues for overseas borrowers in the early 1890s. On the commercial side of the merchant banks' business, the 1880s appear to have seen a pick-up in the growth of sterling trade finance, though consignment business continued to decline. The more favourable environment is reflected in the performance of Barings, Morgans and Kleinworts, which expanded and prospered in the 1880s.

For J. Henry Schröder & Co., in contrast to the other merchant banks, the early and mid-1870s were boom years. The reason was the firm's appointment from 1872 to 1876 as the principal agent for the worldwide distribution of Peruvian guano. Thus while the other firms were in recession, Schröders' profits grew from £129,000 in 1871 to £201,000 in 1876, the capital from £890,000 to £1,914,000, and the clerks employed by the firm from twenty-five to thirty-six. From 1876, however, Schröders' business underwent a drastic decline. Not only did the guano agency come to an end, but each of the trades in which the firm had specialised for half a century or so was adversely affected by developments of one sort or another, troubles which led to gross bad debt losses of £185,000 – equivalent to 10 per cent of capital – in the second half of the 1870s. Even the industrialisation of the US economy, which assisted the recovery of the other firms, was of little benefit to Schröders because of its continuing orientation towards the commodity-producing southern states. While the profits of other merchant banks revived, Schröders' plummeted and in 1884 were a mere £2000.

Managerial shortcomings were identified as a problem by a partner in Brown, Shipley & Co., who in August 1875 wrote of Schröders, 'the management is very bad in London and especially in Liverpool'.[10] But there was a special factor which inhibited a dynamic response on the part of the London partners to their problems: the imminent withdrawal of the bulk of the firm's capital by the nonagenerian senior partner, Johann Heinrich. This was eventually effected in two stages, the first in 1878 and the second on his death in 1883. As a result, the capital of the firm fell from £1,914,000 in 1876 to £679,000 in 1883. The years surrounding the withdrawal of capital marked the low point of Schröders' fortunes and in the latter half of the 1880s the firm staged a strong revival. The recovery was achieved by the development of business with new clients and new initiatives, facilitated by the more favourable operating environment, particularly the new issues boom in the closing years of the decade. In the years 1885–90, profits revived from £22,000 to £152,000, the clerks increased from twenty-six to thirty-one and by 1892 the partners' capital had recovered to £1,095,000, approximately the same level as in 1871.

Schröders' partnership was reconstituted following Schlüsser's retirement in 1871. As before, Johann Heinrich provided the bulk of the firm's capital, and after interest on partners' capital received half the net profits. The other partners were John Henry, who furnished about a fifth of capital; Otto von der Meden, the office manager in the 1860s; and Schlüsser's son-in-law, Henry Tiarks, each of whom received profit shares larger than their contributions to capital as remuneration for their executive responsibilities. In 1878, there was a slight rearrangement of the profits participations, which boosted those of von der Meden and Tiarks, suggesting that they were assuming a greater role in developing the business.

John Henry was 46 years old in 1871 and had been in the firm for thirty years. During the 1870s he continued to play the principal role in the development of the business, though he appears to have been able to combine this with such other pursuits as fox-hunting; from 1872 to 1881 he rented Bicester Hall for the hunting season and rode with the Bicester hounds forty to fifty times each winter.[11] Other leading merchant bankers of the day (Lord Rothschild, for instance) behaved similarly, believing the spectacle of a merchant banker at leisure suggested a peace of mind which inspired confidence in the soundness of his firm.[12]

Nevertheless, such absences from the office were only possible so long as others could be relied upon, and it is apparent that Tiarks, von der Meden and John Henry's private secretary, Carl Albrecht Bingel, assumed more and more of the burdens as the years went by.

Henry Frederic Tiarks was born in London in 1832. His father, the Reverend Johann Gerhard Tiarks, came to England from Jever in Oldenburg in 1821, aged 27, and from 1827 until his death in 1858 was pastor of the Reformed Lutheran Church in London's East End. He was also chaplain to the Duchess of Kent and a prominent figure in the Anglo-German community. The Reverend Tiarks' younger brother, Heinrich Friedrich Tiarks, also moved to London, where he was a City merchant and consul general for the Duchy of Oldenburg. In 1835, he was described as 'almost entirely in the export of colonial produce to Hambro [Hamburg] . . . his means cannot be large but he is quite safe for anything he may undertake'.[13] In the 1840s, he was one of the first merchants in London to trade in nitrate, a commodity in which Schröders developed a speciality forty years later. Henry Tiarks attended the Mercers' School, a school founded by one of the City livery companies, which he left in 1847, aged fifteen, to join J. Henry Schröder & Co. as a junior clerk, an engagement arranged by von Post, who was a member of his father's congregation. In 1853, at the age of 21, he was sent abroad as a 'volunteer' to work in other firms, most probably to improve his command of German and French. During the 1860s he travelled on behalf of J. Henry Schröder & Co. to France, Hamburg and northern and southern Russia, being away for thirteen months in 1861– 62. Upon his return from this trip he was made office manager and married an adopted daughter of Alexander Schlüsser (as also did a brother of his).[14] Thereby Henry Tiarks established a claim to be Schlüsser's successor in the Schröder partnership and a family link was forged with John Henry through their wives. It was Tiarks who conducted the negotiations with Raffalovich in Paris in 1868 which led to Schröders' appointment as agent for the Charkow–Krementschug loan, a success which marked a significant step towards the partnership.

In the 1860s and early 1870s the Tiarks lived in Clapham, near the Schlüssers, who they saw every Saturday, and the von der Medens, who were also regular social companions. Every summer Agnes Tiarks and her growing family, which eventually comprised eight daughters and three sons, sojourned at a seaside resort, usually Worthing, where they were joined at weekends by Henry, business permitting. Each autumn the couple took a month-long holiday in the West Country touring the coastal towns and villages and staying with Henry's brother at Loxton, Somerset. In October 1875 they made their first continental tour, to Switzerland, and thereafter took a European holiday every few years. At

Christmas they usually stayed with the Schröders at The Dell for a few days. In June 1877, the Tiarks family moved to 'Foxbury', a 40-room mansion set in 57 acres at Chislehurst, Kent, built for them in a restrained Gothic style to the design of David Brandon, a fashionable country house architect.[15] In the 1880s, they saw rather less of other members of the firm and developed a wider circle of friends, many of whose families were prominent in the City, such as de Zoete, Ralli, Hoare, Foster, Braithwaite and especially Lubbock, two of the Tiarks' daughters marrying sons of Sir Nevile Lubbock, the brother of Lord Avebury, a very prominent City figure in the late nineteenth century and Liberal MP for Maidstone, Kent.[16] Henry Tiarks' growing prominence in the Schröder partnership was recognised by his peers in the City in 1875 when he was invited to join the Society of Merchants Trading to the Continent.

Otto von der Meden was born in Hamburg in 1827 and joined J. Henry Schröder & Co. as a clerk in 1847 and had been associate partner since 1862. Upon his promotion to full partner, Werner Kelbe was appointed associate partner, and a new office manager, Adolphus Schmidt, was recruited from Kleinworts. Both were of German birth, as was George Stielow, who replaced Schmidt in 1877 when the latter absconded with £1,381 – £50,000 in 1990 money. The new management team introduced important changes to the firm's organisation and bookkeeping system in July 1871. The thirty-two clerks were divided into functional departments: a Bill Department, headed by the cashier, which handled the acceptance credit business and insurance; a Goods Department, which had responsibility for consignment trade and shipping arrangements; and a Bookkeeping Department, overseen by the bookkeeper, which looked after client balances and advances, and the journal and cash book. Hitherto the accounts had been organised alphabetically by client, but henceforth they were divided on a geographical basis so that clerks became expert on the firm's clients and activities in particular parts of the world. The announcement of the new arrangements included a reminder of the clerks' terms of employment: 'We expect all gentlemen to be in their places at 10 o'clock at the latest and that they take one hour and no longer for their luncheon. The time of departure can only be regulated by the amount of work to be done and we repeat that to work this system properly all the books must be kept up to the day in every particular'.[17] This structure, with additions on the securities side of the business, lasted until the 1920s.

Johann Heinrich, although 87 years old in 1871, continued to be the senior partner and to take a close interest in the firm's affairs. His iron will was a trait of character to the end of his long life; his last words, aged 98, on his death bed, were, according to the family legend, 'I die voluntarily' and, turning his face away from his family to the wall, he expired. Thereupon John Henry became the firm's principal proprietary partner, providing four-fifths of the capital in the 1880s and 1890s. As the new senior partner, he continued to play an active role in the development of the business and under the terms of the new partnership agreement of 1883 received half the profits. His partners, Tiarks and von der Meden, received a third and one sixth respectively as compensation for their executive responsibilities. From 1883 Tiarks' role in the partnership became increasingly significant and he deserves much of the credit for the firm's successful recovery from the nadir of the early 1880s. In these years he also emerged as a well-known City figure, playing an active role in the affairs of the London Produce Clearing House, of which he was a founder in 1888; the Baltic Exchange Company, becoming a director in 1889; and as Governor of the Royal Exchange.

Peruvian Guano Business of the 1870s

Prior to 1870, Schröders had no special connection with the guano trade or with Peru. Between 1871 and 1878, however, the profits of the Peruvian Department, the department which was established to conduct the guano agency activities, generated a third of total revenues. Moreover, considerable amounts of the firm's acceptance and issuing business in these years derived from guano shipments or Peruvian loans, so that possibly half the firm's revenues in the first half of the 1870s were attributable to its involvement with Peruvian guano. The profits of the Peruvian Department surged upwards from 1871 to 1877, more than compensating for declining acceptance and consignment revenues (see Figure 4.1). Not only was the Peruvian connection vital to the firm's prosperity in these years, but it firmly established Schröders' connection with mainland South America, prompted the establishment of important new ties in Hamburg, and led the firm into its first venture capital investment in Britain; all in all it was one of the most remarkable episodes in the history of the firm.

The precise origins of Schröders' involvement are unknown but it was certainly through Parisian connections, presumably Erlanger or Raffalovich, that it came about. Schröders' partner was Auguste Dreyfus, the head of Dreyfus Frères & Cie, a Parisian merchant firm, who on 17 August 1869 was appointed contractor for guano sales by the Peruvian government. The deposits of guano (solidified bird-droppings which were used as fertiliser by farmers) occurred on uninhabited offshore islands which were owned by the state, and export revenues

Figure 4.1 J. Henry Schröder & Co., revenues from accepting, consignments and Peruvian Department profits, 1871–92

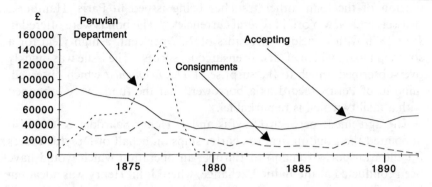

from sales were the bedrock of Peruvian public finance from the 1840s to the 1870s. For many years, sales of guano were made on behalf of the Peruvian government by consignment merchants, most notably Antony Gibbs & Sons of London, who remitted the proceeds minus a commission for their services. These arrangements were criticised for over-generosity towards the consignees and it has been estimated that in the 1850s and 1860s the government received only 60–70 per cent of sales revenues.[18] In 1869, new arrangements were devised which raised the participation of the Peruvian state in the sales revenues, and Dreyfus, who was backed by the French bank Société Genérale, was the first of the new monopoly contractors. By the terms of the 'Dreyfus Contract' he undertook to organise the sale of 2 million tons of guano at a price of £12.50 per ton, generating revenues of £25 million, and to advance a substantial sum to the Peruvian government.[19]

Overseas borrowing by Peru began in the early 1820s, soon after independence, but in 1826 it defaulted on its debts. The advent of guano revenues in the 1840s made possible a settlement with bondholders in 1849, and in the 1850s and 1860s several Peruvian loans were issued upon the security of receipts from guano sales. In August 1869 a loan for £290,000 was issued in London by the merchant bank Thomson, Bonar & Co., on behalf of the Peruvian government, to finance the building of the country's first railway. The signature of the Dreyfus Contract enhanced the standing of Peruvian bonds in the international capital market, doubling in price according to one account, making possible much larger fund-raising for the government's ambitious programme of railway construction.[20] Dreyfus was appointed contractor for the issue of a loan totalling £11,920,000, a very large sum by contemporary standards, to finance lines to connect coastal ports with inland centres of production of

commodities such as silver and copper. In April 1870, Dreyfus appointed
J. Henry Schröder & Co. as agent for the issue in London of the sterling
portion of the loan, other tranches being issued in Paris, Hamburg,
Brussels and New York in several currencies.[21] The bonds were offered in
June 1870 with a yield to investors of 7.27 per cent, a high yield for a
sovereign loan, which evidently ensured its success. The issue was quickly
oversubscribed, much to the surprise of *The Economist* which observed,
mindful of Peru's record as a borrower, that the funds were 'obtained
with a facility which is remarkable'.[22]

The agreement between Dreyfus and J. Henry Schröder & Co. also
appointed the London firm to charter ships on behalf of Dreyfus Frères
for the transport of guano to Europe, an operation which would have
been conducted at the Baltic Exchange, where John Henry was a leading
figure. The conduct of business from Paris became impossible following
the outbreak of the Franco-Prussian War in July 1870, which seems to
have led to Schröders playing a larger part in Dreyfus's guano business
than originally envisaged. On 2 February 1871, less than a week after the
capitulation of Paris to the besieging Prussian Army, Schröders signed a
second agreement with Dreyfus Frères by which the London firm was
appointed 'Central Agents' for the distribution of Peruvian guano in the
British Empire and continental Europe, with the exception of France.[23]
By the terms of the new contract, Schröders agreed to advance Dreyfus
Frères £800,000 in cash plus £600,000 in the form of an acceptance credit
facility, in return for which the firm would receive a 1.5 per cent
commission on sales in the United Kingdom and a 1 per cent
commission on sales elsewhere, perhaps £350,000 on the sale of the 2
million tons. In addition, moreover, there was the prospect of a
substantial volume of acceptance credit business with low risk because of
the firm's detailed knowledge of the trade, and the profits from its
participations in the issue of loans. Nevertheless, the £1.4 million
advance and credit facility was considerably in excess of the partners'
total capital of £947,000 and constituted a very bold approach to the
conduct of business. Perhaps the Bank of England's Liverpool branch
learned of the scale of Schröders' commitment, for an enquiry was made
of the Bank of England in London, which gave the reassuring reply that
'the state of affairs in France in connection with the guano engagements
of J. H. Schröder & Co., London, has not affected them, and they
continue to be A1 in all respects'.[24]

Preparations for the commencement of the Peruvian guano agency
were made during 1871. In the summer, Schröders established the
Peruvian Department with its own personnel and separate premises at 15
Leadenhall Street, later moving to East India Avenue. A network of
eighteen wholesale agents was created to handle the distribution of the

guano in ports of the United Kingdom, continental Europe, Australia and various Atlantic and Pacific islands. Other merchant firms were appointed by the wholesale agents as retail agents to conduct sales to retailers or farmers. In Hamburg, Ohlendorff & Co. was made wholesale agent and Schröder Gebrüder and Vorwerk Gebrüder became its retail agents, the activities of all being financed by acceptance credits provided by J. Henry Schröder & Co. from 1871. This marked the beginning of Schröders' important relationships with these Hamburg firms.

In July 1871, while these arrangements were being made, Dreyfus signed a contract with the Peruvian government for the issue of a second foreign loan for the massive amount of £36.8 million – as much as £1.3 billion in 1990 money – of which £21.8 million was earmarked for the consolidation of existing debts, and £15 million for further railway construction. The scale of the new loan, known as the Peruvian Government 5 per cent Consolidated Loan of 1872, necessitated not only its simultaneous issue in several European financial centres, but also the formation of an issuing syndicate to conduct the business. Issuing syndicates for the issue of foreign loans were an innovation of the late 1860s, according to a contemporary authority.[25] The purpose was to enable the private partnerships to spread the risk and mobilise greater capital resources to compete with the new joint stock banks. The initial offering of the 5 per cent Consolidated Loan was to be £15 million, and the Dreyfus Syndicate contracted to purchase £4 million of the bonds, which was known as taking the securities 'firm', and to act on an agency basis on behalf of the Peruvian government for the sale of the remainder, such partial underwritings being common at the time. The Dreyfus Syndicate comprised Dreyfus Frères, which underwrote 33 per cent of the funds; Société Genérale, 25 per cent; J. Henry Schröder & Co., 20 per cent; and the remainder was underwritten by B. Premsel of Amsterdam and Stern Bros.[26] The last was a firm established in London in the 1830s by Frankfurt-based relations of the Rothschilds, who like them specialised in the issue of foreign sovereign loans. Schröders had recently played a part in marketing the bonds of the Italian Tobacco Monopoly Loan, issued by Sterns in 1868, and its position in the Peru loan may have been reciprocity.

The Peruvian Government 5 per cent Consolidated Loan was brought out in March 1872 simultaneously in London, Paris and Amsterdam, with J. Henry Schröder & Co. and Stern Bros acting as joint lead-managers. The bonds, which had a 5 per cent coupon, a 26-year maturity and were secured on public guano revenues, were purchased by the syndicate at 75 and offered to the public at 77.5, giving investors a 6.45 per cent yield. By the spring of 1872 investors were beginning to be wary of lending to Latin American governments, which appeared to have an insatiable appetite for borrowing. *The Economist*'s view of the Peruvian offer was 'whatever way we look at the transaction, it is a very doubtful one'; the public agreed, and only £4.2 million was subscribed.[27] This was enough to relieve the syndicate of their contractual obligations at a profit, which was doubtless a great relief in Leadenhall Street, since Schröders' exposure in the deal was £800,000 on a capital base of £1.1 million. Hitherto the firm had acted as principal only for the small Cuban railway loans and its lead-management of a syndicate for a large sovereign loan was an important milestone in its development as an issuing house. For Peru, the failure of the loan was a 'complete disaster' and exacerbated the country's mounting financial chaos.[28] Over the next four years Schröders assisted the Peruvian government with placements of a further £15 million of the bonds, at large discounts to the issue price, receiving commission payments for its services.

Ohlendorff & Co., the Peruvian Department's wholesale agent in Hamburg, was established in the 1840s by Baron Albertus Ohlendorff to import guano into central Europe.[29] Ohlendorff's partner was Adolphus Horny, the brother of Marie Horny, the bride of William Schröder of Liverpool. In the early 1860s, Ohlendorff & Co. developed a process of treating guano with sulphuric acid, producing a product with enhanced fertilising properties, which was known as 'dissolved guano'. In January 1872, Dreyfus Frères, Schröders and Ohlendorff formed a company, also called Ohlendorff & Co., in London to produce dissolved guano in Britain, Belgium and other European countries. It was a substantial manufacturing undertaking with a capital of £500,000, subscribed 50 per cent by Dreyfus Frères and 25 per cent each by Ohlendorff and Schröders. Adolphus Horny became managing director of the new firm, which established its head office at 15 Leadenhall Street, where Dreyfus Frères also had its London office. An 8-acre site was purchased on the north bank of the Thames in West Ham, the focal point of London's chemical industry in the nineteenth century.[30] Construction of the Ohlendorff process plant began in 1872 and production in 1873, whereupon Dr Augustus Voelcker, Britain's leading agricultural chemist, was appointed consultant analyst, and under his guidance 'Ohlendorff's Dissolved Peruvian Government Guano' was awarded the Gold Medal at the Paris Exhibition of 1878.[31]

The process of producing dissolved guano was observed soon after the commencement of operations by Dr Edward Ballard, medical officer of the Local Government Board, the government body with responsibility for public health. Guano, supplemented by fish heads, was churned up with sulphuric acid, inducing a temperature of 140° Fahrenheit and dissolving the guano. The mixture was then spread on the floor of a large shed to cool. The following day it was 'picked' by hand, to remove the stones and lumps which led to complaints from farmers, and then packaged for sale. 'There are abundant vapours given off in the process,' observed Ballard, 'watery vapour, hydrochloric acid, arising from the decomposition of the chlorides in the guano, arsenic, and some organic substance which imparts to the vapours a cheesy smell in addition to the acid odour.'[32] The obnoxious fumes which emanated from the Ohlendorff works led to complaints from residents on the south side of the river, and in March 1874 the West Ham Board of Health passed a resolution censuring Ohlendorff & Co. for 'not abating the nuisances'.[33] Early in 1875 the Board resolved to prosecute Ohlendorffs on account of the air pollution caused by the factory but this proved unnecessary because of the installation of new machinery that enclosed the mixture until cooling had taken place, thus eliminating the worst of the fumes.[34] Ohlendorff & Co. prospered but Schröders' shareholding was sold in 1883 upon the liquidation of Johann Heinrich's estate. A new firm, the Anglo-Continental Guano Works Company, owned entirely by the German Ohlendorff company, was established to continue the business of the London firm.[35] The annual visits paid to the works by Baron Ohlendorff and his sons were long remembered in the locality; after completing their tour of inspection the frock-coated visitors would remove their white gloves and toss them to the workforce, who scrambled for them.[36] A close relationship was sustained between Schröders and the Anglo-Continental Guano Works Company, which remained in occupation of the offices at 15 Leadenhall Street, and Adolphus Horny continued as manager until his death in 1900. The firm was one of Schröders' largest acceptance credit clients in the 1890s and 1900s. During the First World War it was sequestrated as enemy property by the British government and was eventually acquired by Fisons in 1937.

Shipments of guano consigned to Schröders began to arrive in 1871. They were landed at the Victoria Dock, close to the Ohlendorff plant, where the firm rented warehouses with a storage capacity of 5,000 tons.[37] The volume of guano handled by the firm during the period of its agency is unknown; a contemporary estimate by a disgruntled Peruvian bondholder was 650,000 tons in 1873–75[38], which seems rather small, but in 1876 there was a surge in shipments which necessitated additional storage facilities for 50,000 tons at the Victoria Dock.[39] Schröders' appointment as Central Agent for Peruvian guano expired in November 1876, though sales from stocks continued until 1882 when the Peruvian Department was wound up.

Early in 1876 the Peruvian government, whose advances from Dreyfus had run out, declared a 'momentary interruption of punctuality' on the service of its loans.[40] Thereupon the Schröder partners became much involved with the efforts of the Corporation of Foreign Bondholders to secure the resumption of payments by the Peruvian government. These continued until the establishment in 1890 of the Peruvian Corporation, which took over the government's obligations and also many of its assets.[41] Settlement was delayed by the War of the Pacific in 1879–83 between Peru and Bolivia in alliance against Chile. The causes of the conflict were many, but they revolved around longstanding Chilean claims over the Peruvian province of Tarapaca and the Bolivian province of Antofagasta which were rich in nitrate deposits. The outcome was a resounding victory for Chile, which extended its national territory by a third. Following the conclusion of peace in October 1883 there was a rapid expansion of Chilean nitrate production, a development which provided Schröders with a sequel to its Peruvian guano business and led to the establishment of close ties with Chile.

Decline of Consignments and Development of Accepting

In the heyday of Schröders' Peruvian guano business, 1871–78, the firm's annual revenues averaged £197,000 (see Table 4.1). Acceptance commissions, £69,000, were the largest source, though the contribution of the Peruvian Department, £64,000, was only a little less. Consignments generated half as much as acceptances, £30,000, while issuing, net interest and other activities together produced £34,000. In the years 1879–84, total revenues averaged only £63,000. It was not only the virtual demise of Peruvian Department profits that caused the fall, but every other source of revenues slumped: acceptances averaged £36,000; consignments, £16,000; and issuing, £3,000. The years 1885–92 saw a revival of revenues to an annual average of £105,000 which was mainly due to the recovery of acceptance commissions to £46,000 and a sharp increase in issuing revenues to £40,000. But why did Schröders' business fare so badly in 1879–84, and how was the recovery in the second half of the 1880s achieved?

Schröders' consignment business stagnated in the early 1870s and went into long-term decline from 1876. The communications and marketing developments which underlay the decline of the merchant banks' consignment business have already been discussed, but the contraction of the firm's activity was accelerated by changes particular to the tallow, grain and sugar trades – the most important goods it received on consignment. The tallow trade waned in the 1860s with the advent of kerosene oil lamps, which also meant a shift in the pattern of trade away from Russia, since it was the Pennsylvania oilfield that supplied the world's petroleum requirements in the early days of the

Table 4.1   J. Henry Schröder & Co., sources of revenues, 1871–92

| | *1871–78* | | *1879–84* | | *1885–92* | |
	Annual average £000s	*Per cent*	*Annual average £000s*	*Per cent*	*Annual average £000s*	*Per cent*
Accepting	69	35	36	57	46	44
Consignments	30	15	16	25	10	9
Issuing and underwriting	12	6	3	5	40	38
Net interest	9	4	2	3	2	2
Other[1]	13	7	4	6	7	7
Total	133		61		105	
Peruvian Department	64	32	2	3	–	–
Total	197	100	63	100	105	100

1. Freight, postage, insurance, sundry merchandise, etc.

Source: J. Henry Schröder & Co., profit & loss accounts.

industry. Likewise, the grain trade was shifting from the Baltic and the Black Sea to the Atlantic, because American grain was superior in quality and cheaper. Lastly, developments in the Cuban sugar industry (discussed below) put paid to that source of consignment cargoes.

While the business of the Produce Department declined, that of J. H. Schröder & Co. of Liverpool and the other cotton consignment merchants virtually disappeared following the opening of the Atlantic Telegraph in 1866, which permitted direct contact between buyers and sellers, thus eliminating their role. The firm's difficulties were heightened by the managerial deficiencies to which the Brown, Shipley partner referred in 1875. Charles Pickering, who had been there from the outset, was a spent force and retired in 1881, while Baron William Schröder preferred the life of an English country gentleman to that of a Liverpool merchant. From 1865 he lived in the Cheshire countryside at 'The Rookery', a large house set in 170 acres. He was a well-known figure in Cheshire society and in 1888 served as Sheriff of the county. He was a stalwart of the Cheshire Hunt and an enthusiastic yachtsman and member of the Royal Yacht Squadron. From the 1890s he rented a 45,000-acre Scottish sporting estate, the Attadale Estate on the west coast near the Isle of Skye, which he subsequently purchased in 1910. His obituary in a local newspaper in 1912 dwelt long upon his sporting interests and his support for rural pastimes, but made no mention of J. H. Schröder & Co. of Liverpool, which was long forgotten.[42] From 1869 onwards the accounts of J. Henry Schröder & Co. show large balances on account of the Liverpool house, suggesting that its capital was not being actively employed in business, and in 1883, upon the death of Johann Heinrich, the firm was wound up. Julius Servaes, who joined J. H. Schröder & Co. in 1845 and had been a partner since 1856, and his son, Julius Max Servaes, set up their own firm conducting a general agency and commission business, which acted as the London firm's Liverpool agent from 1883 until the Second World War.

The geographical dispersion of the 586 acceptance clients listed in the conditions book covering the years 1869–94 is shown in Table 4.2. The fall in the number of Schröders' acceptance clients in northern Russia, from 111 in 1848–68 to 69 in 1869–94, was the result of the problems that beset the Russian tallow and grain trades, described above. Another factor was the retirement of Heinrich Schliemann and the consequent demise of the finance of indigo shipments to Russia. Moreover, demand for indigo was declining because of competition from synthetic dyestuffs, and the depression of this trade contributed to the fall in clients in Asia from twenty-six to ten. The conditions book for 1848–68 contains the names of fifty-three Cuban clients; that for 1869–94 a mere ten. This was a consequence of the 10-year war which began in 1868 to overthrow the Spanish colonial administration, which caused great destruction to sugar mills and plantations and brought an end to the 'golden age' of the Cuban sugar industry.[43] Many of the island's sugar merchants were ruined by the decade of hostilities, among them Scharfenberg Tolme & Co. Another casualty was the Bay of Havana and Matanzas Railroad Co., which defaulted on bond payments in 1871. In 1874, J. Henry Schröder & Co. made a £750,000 preference share issue on behalf of this client which was part of a capital reconstruction organised in London by the bondholders led by Adolphus Klockmann, John Henry's landlord at the time of his wedding in 1851.

The shifts in the pattern of the geographical location of Schröders' clients revealed by the conditions books also point to the sources of the recovery of the firm's acceptance business in the latter half of the 1880s. Of particular significance are the increases in the number of clients in Hamburg, New York and London. Hamburg was the location of the largest number of Schröder clients listed in both conditions books; 101 in 1848–68 and 158 in 1869–94. The rapid progress of German industrialisation led to the rise in tonnage entering the port from 1.9 million tons in 1871 to 5.6 million tons in 1892.[44] Hamburg itself began to become a major industrial centre during the anomalous political

Table 4.2   Geographical location of the acceptance credit clients of
J. Henry Schröder & Co., 1869–94

	Number of clients	*Per cent*
EUROPE AND RUSSIA		
Germany		
Hamburg	158	
Bremen	30	
Altona	6	
Stettin	2	
Berlin	4	
Total	200	33
Baltic and Northern Russia		
St Petersburg	28	
Moscow	23	
Riga	11	
Other	7	
Total	69	12
Mediterranean, Black Sea and Central Europe		
Odessa	33	
Trieste	22	
Vienna	16	
Marseilles	4	
Other	3	
Total	78	13
Western Europe		
Antwerp	30	
Paris	27	
Amsterdam	2	
Rotterdam	7	
Other	9	
Total	75	12
United Kingdom		
Manchester	10	
Liverpool	7	
London	11	
Total	28	5

Table continued over

Table 4.2 continued	*Number of clients*	*Per cent*
AMERICAS AND ASIA		
West Indies		
Cuba	10	
Puerto Rico	4	
Other	2	
Total	16	3
North America		
New York	62	
New Orleans	2	
Other	11	
Total	85	14
South America		
Brazil – Rio de Janeiro	4	
– Bahia	3	
– Others	2	
Chile – Valparaiso	9	
Argentina – Buenos Aires	2	
Peru – Lima	5	
– Others	2	
Venezuela	4	
Mexico	–	
Other	4	
Total	35	6
Asia		
Hong Kong	4	
Singapore	1	
Calcutta	1	
Other	4	
Total	10	2
TOTAL	596	100

Source: J. Henry Schröder & Co., conditions book 1869–94.

1880s, a development that was stimulated by the tariff protection for manufacturing which came with the city's entry into the German Customs Union under pressure from Bismarck, which was agreed in 1881 and came into force in 1888.[45] This marked the end of Hamburg's autonomy, though its entrepôt trade was safeguarded by the establishment of an extensive duty-free port area.

Much of Germany's import trade in the late nineteenth century was financed in London by sterling bills of exchange, of which J. Henry Schröder & Co. was a leading provider. Schröders' extensive Hamburg client list included leading firms that combined merchanting and banking, such as M. M. Warburg, Münchmeyer & Co., J. C. Godeffroy & Co., L. Behrens & Sons, Conrad Hinrich Donner, H. J. Merck & Co., H. H. Eggers, the leading coffee firm, and the steamship line C. Woermann Linie, besides several Schröder family firms. Godeffroy & Co. was saved by Schröders' support in the crisis of 1873, the marriage of one of Johann Heinrich's daughters to a member of the family doubtless being an important consideration.[46] So extensive were Godeffroy's business interests in the Pacific, particularly Samoa, and in South America, that the head of the house was called the 'King of the South Seas', and when the firm again got into trouble in 1879 Bismarck considered its survival to be of such importance to the development of the German empire that it was bailed out by the government. In the 1870s and the first half of the 1880s credits outstanding to such Hamburg firms were usually in the range £2,000–£20,000, though very occasionally they were as much as £50,000. But by the latter half of the 1880s and early 1890s half a dozen or so Hamburg firms regularly had credits outstanding in excess of £20,000, and availments of £100,000 by these firms, which were all involved in the shipment or distribution of Chilean nitrate, were not uncommon. Schröders' connection with nitrate began with the appointment of Schröder Gebrüder as a distribution agent by Antony Gibbs & Co., which had extensive nitrate interests in Chile, following a trip to London by one of the partners at the beginning of the 1880s.[47] Schröders was soon providing financial facilities on a large scale for Hamburg's leading nitrate importers: by 1890 credits outstanding to these firms were Vorwerk Gebrüder, £222,000, Schröder Gebrüder, £136,000, F. H. Jacobson, £91,000 and F. Laeisz, £54,000 – very large sums for a firm with a capital of £1.1 million. Schröders also began to finance merchants conducting nitrate export trade in Valparaiso, Chile, of which the most important was Weber & Co., which had credits outstanding of £54,000 in 1890.

The rapid growth of the US economy in the 1880s led to increases in imports of many foodstuffs and raw materials which were largely financed by sterling acceptance credits. Demand for such facilities led to the increase in Schröders' New York client list from twenty-nine firms in 1848–68 to sixty-two firms in 1869–94. In the 1870s, most had German names, many of which were readily recognisable as associates of prominent Hamburg firms, such as Amsinck, Godeffroy, Gossler and

Moller. But from the second half of the 1880s the proportion of Anglo-Saxon names, particularly corporations, increased. Many were involved in the sugar industry. Cuban sugar production recovered following the return of peace in 1878, and by the early 1880s output was back to the level of the 1860s.[48] In the post-civil war years a new pattern of business emerged in the Cuban sugar industry whereby American refineries secured their supplies not from merchants but by sending agents who bought directly from growers. In 1877, Schröders began to finance the purchases of the New York refiners Mathiesen & Weichers and in the early 1880s it acquired several more such clients: Havermeyer & Elders in 1881; Arbuckle Brothers in 1882; and the Brooklyn Sugar Refining Company in 1883. In the first half of the 1880s the credits used by these firms were in the range £5,000–£20,000, but in the second half of the decade there was a dramatic increase and credits were often in excess of £100,000. In 1888, Henry Osborne Havemeyer, the scion of a sugar dynasty of German origin, organised a consortium of American sugar refineries, which included Schröders' clients, into the American Sugar Refining Co. (the so-called Sugar Trust) which came to produce 70–90 per cent of sugar consumed in the United States until broken up by anti-trust legal action.[49] The American Sugar Refining Co. became a Schröder client, with outstanding acceptances of £391,000 in 1891. In the same year, the Spreckels Sugar Refinery, a new client, had credits of £172,000 and the brokers Lewisohn Brothers, clients since 1887, credits of £85,000, which meant that acceptances totalling £648,000, half Schröders' capital, were outstanding to three US sugar firms, a very bold way indeed to conduct the business of a merchant bank.

London firms were conspicuous by their absence as clients of J. Henry Schröder & Co. in the 1850s and 1860s, but in the 1870s and 1880s there were eleven acceptance credit clients on its doorstep. Most were merchant firms with German names whose business was probably the shipment of commodities purchased in the London markets to Hamburg or other German ports. Of particular significance was the commencement in 1884 of the provision of acceptance credits for C. Czarnikow Ltd, one of London's leading sugar brokers, but in the 1880s and early 1890s these were not on the scale of the credits provided for the New York refiners and brokers, and rarely exceeded £20,000. In 1888, Henry Tiarks and Julius Caesar Czarnikow, the colourful founder of C. Czarnikow Ltd, played leading parts in the establishment of the London Produce Clearing House, which became London's futures market for sugar and other 'soft' commodities.[50]

Between 1871 and 1875, the period of the guano agency, Schröders' total acceptances rose from £2.8 million to £4.6 million. In these years the acceptance activities of most other merchant banks declined and the scale of its business almost caught up with Barings, the sector leader whose acceptances had probably fallen to about £5 million by 1875. But Schröders' acceptances declined sharply after 1875 and by 1878 were a mere £1.8 million; Kleinworts', on the other hand, rose because of the firm's expanding US activity, and in 1879 it overtook Schröders.[51] In the 1880s, Barings and Kleinworts were larger acceptors than Schröders, and by the early 1890s so was Morgans, probably as a result of new business from US clients, who abandoned Barings following the Baring Crisis of 1890. The recovery of Schröders' acceptance activity in the second half of the 1880s was the result of the development of new business with new clients, notably the US sugar refiners and the Hamburg nitrate importers. In both cases, the scale of the credits granted to individual clients escalated rapidly in the late 1880s because of mergers amongst the commodity importers and processors, which led to the emergence of firms conducting business on a much larger scale than hitherto. To service these clients it was necessary to provide commensurately larger credits, and by the early 1890s the aggregate acceptances of the largest half dozen or so of Schröders' clients equalled the capital of the firm. Formerly, the business had been run on the

Table 4.3 Acceptances of some leading merchant banks, 1875, 1884, 1892

31 December	1875 £ million	1884 £ million	1892 £ million
Baring Brothers & Co.	(1870) 6.7	(1890) 15.0	3.9
J. Henry Schröder & Co.	4.6	2.3	3.9
Kleinwort, Sons & Co.	1.8	2.8	5.5
C. J. Hambro & Son	1.1	1.9	1.5
N. M. Rothschild & Sons	1.9	0.9	3.4
J. S. Morgan & Co.	n/a	n/a	4.2
Antony Gibbs & Sons	(1883) 0.8	0.5	0.6
Wm Brandt Sons	(1874) 0.1	0.2	0.7

n/a = not available

Note: Information on other firms unavailable.

Sources: Stephanie Diaper, 'The History of Kleinwort, Sons & Co. in Merchant Banking, 1855–1966' (unpublished PhD thesis, University of Nottingham, 1983) p. 144 ; Philip Ziegler, *The Sixth Power: Barings 1762–1929* (London: Collins, 1988) p. 202; Kathleen Burk, *Morgan Grenfell 1838 – 1988* (Oxford University Press, 1989) p. 278; J. Henry Schröder & Co., balance sheets.

principle of minimising bad debt risk by creating a large number of small credits. The new pattern greatly increased the hazards of the business, but if nothing went wrong it could prove highly profitable.

Revival of Issuing in the Late 1880s

The second half of the 1880s saw initiatives to diversify and develop Schröders' business. In 1885, the firm established a relationship with the Wall Street brokerage house Ladenburg, Thalmann & Co. to conduct joint operations in US securities, apparently an innovation on the part of a London merchant bank.[52] The nature of these activities was twofold; first, to market US securities to European investors, the stock being purchased by Ladenburg, Thalmann in New York and sold by Schröders in Europe; second, arbitrage operations to exploit differences in stock prices between the New York market and European markets. The scale of their joint account operations grew rapidly: in 1886 Schröders' commitment of funds was already £139,000; by 1892 it was £550,000, half the firm's capital. Though the securities arbitraged were generally high-class, usually the bonds of well-known US railroad companies, the development of this activity inevitably reduced the liquidity of the balance sheet and thus increased the firm's exposure to the risk of illiquidity in a commercial crisis.

These years also saw moves by both Baron John Henry Schröder and Henry Tiarks to strengthen Schröders' ties with the marine insurance industry, which had long been closely connected with the merchant banks. In 1885, John Henry became deputy chairman of the North British and Marine Insurance Company, of which he had been a director since 1863, and served as chairman from 1889 to 1900.[53] This appointment doubtless explains why he became a member of Lloyds in 1890.[54] A related outside appointment was his election as a director of the West India Dock Company in 1888.[55] Tiarks joined the board of the Royal Exchange Assurance and was chairman of the Sea Committee, the marine branch of the business, in the 1890s.[56] He served as Governor of the Royal Exchange Assurance in the opening years of the twentieth century and was succeeded in 1904 by his son-in-law's father, Sir Nevile Lubbock.

Schröders' recovery was boosted by the upturn in international securities issues in the London market in the late 1880s. Figure 4.2 shows the firm's annual revenues from issuing between 1865 and 1892, and total UK sterling securities issues for overseas borrowers, indicating the general level of market activity. The chart illustrates the volatility of revenues from issuing and the close correspondence between the level of

Figure 4.2   J. Henry Schröder & Co., issuing and underwriting revenues, and sterling issues for overseas borrowers, 1865–92

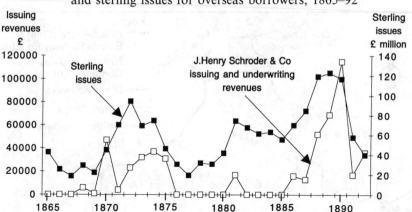

Source: Sterling issues – Mathew Simon, 'The Pattern of New British Portfolio Foreign Investment, 1865–1914', in A. R. Hall (ed.) *The Export of Capital from Britain 1870–1914* (London: Methuen, 1968) p. 38.

the firm's issuing revenues and market activity. A notable feature is the great upsurge in Schröders' earnings from issuing in 1888–90.

The revival of the Cuban sugar industry in the early 1880s was assisted by new investments in the island's railways. In 1881 and 1886, Schröders made issues on behalf of the Havana Railways Co., the island's oldest railway company and one of the largest, to raise funds for extensions to its system. Then, in the late 1880s, the decline in the world sugar price prompted steps to rationalise the Cuban railway system to cut costs, a process in which Schröders was closely involved. In 1889, several companies operating railways and port facilities in the Havana area amalgamated to form the United Railways of the Havana and Regla Warehouses Co., a firm with 457 kilometres of track and capital of £1.4 million (see Map 3.1 on page 60). The following year Schröders made an issue on its behalf which raised £1.6 million to extinguish outstanding debts of the constituent companies, and for extensions. The bonds, which were secured on the company's property assets and had a 37-year maturity, had a 5 per cent coupon and were priced at 95, giving a yield to investors of 5.26 per cent.

The Chilean nitrate industry was also the recipient of a substantial volume of capital raised by J. Henry Schröder & Co. in the late 1880s and early 1890s, ten of the twenty-one issues conducted by the firm in 1887–92 being made on behalf of companies active therein. In the aftermath of the War of the Pacific the Chilean government was eager to promote the exploitation of its newly acquired nitrate deposits for fiscal

Map 4.1 Antofagasta (Chili) and Bolivia Railway and the Nitrate Railway, 1910

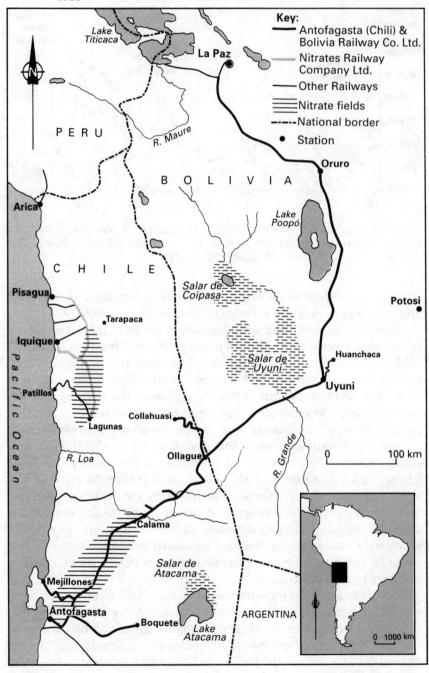

reasons, and supported the construction of railways which would make this possible. In 1884, the Antofagasta Nitrate and Railway Co., which had pioneered the development of the nitrate fields in the 1860s, and the Huanchaca Co., whose traditional business was silver production in Bolivia, began jointly to develop a railway system for the region.[57] This was acquired in its entirety in 1887 by the Huanchaca Co., whose president, Melchor Concha y Toro, had ambitious plans for its development to link the Chilean Pacific port of Antofagasta with the Bolivian silver mines in the Andes mountains (see Map 4.1). For finance he turned to the London capital market, Schröders issuing two loans for the Huanchaca Co. and its railway in 1887 which together raised £1.26 million. According to the memoirs of Emile Erlanger's son, it was an introduction from Baron Erlanger, who was a friend of Concha y Toro's brother-in-law, the president of the Chilean Banco Mobiliario, that secured the appointment of Schröders as issuing house to raise the funds to finance the extensions.[58] The following year it brought out a loan of £1.15 million on behalf of the Antofagasta (Chili) and Bolivia Railway Company Ltd, a British-registered company formed to acquire the railway interests of the Bolivian Huanchaca Co. This development was another step in the domination of the nitrate industry by British capital following the War of the Pacific and it has been estimated that by 1890 70 per cent of the output of the industry was in British hands.[59] Further funds for development were raised by Schröders, acting jointly with Frederick Huth & Co. (which had a long-established presence in Chile), in 1889, 1890, 1891 and 1892, which financed further railway construction and the acquisition of the Huanchaca Company's mining concessions in Chile and Bolivia. In total Schröders participated in raising £5.75 million for the Antofagasta railway in 1887–92.

The issues on behalf of the Antofagasta (Chili) and Bolivia Railway and the Huanchaca Co. served as an introduction to further issues on behalf of Chilean railway companies. In 1888, Schröders sponsored a large £2 million bond issue on behalf of the Nitrates Railway Company, the line which dominated the transportation of nitrate in the province of Tarapaca, and an issue of £400,000 bonds for the Arauco Co., which operated coal mines and associated railways in the south of the country. Both these companies were promoted by John North, the so-called 'Nitrate King'. North, a highly controversial figure, was a Yorkshire-born mechanical engineer who went to South America to supervise railway construction and made a fortune by purchasing enormous nitrate interests at very low prices during the War of the Pacific.[60]

The usual issuing procedure adopted for the Chilean railway issues, and for most of the issues conducted by Schröders in the late 1880s and early 1890s, was for the firm to act not as an agent but as a principal, purchasing all the securities from the company and issuing them to the public, taking the difference between the negotiated purchase and sale prices, less costs, as its profits. Besides bringing the bonds to the market it was often necessary to make advances to issuing clients pending a moment when the bonds would be favourably received by investors, which could tie up considerable funds. These developments in issuing practice increased the firm's exposure to risk, but also enhanced the profitability of successful transactions.

The Antofagasta (Chili) and Bolivia Railway loan of April 1889 marked the beginning of Schröders' relationship with the City solicitors Slaughter and May. Hitherto, Ashurst, Morris, Crisp had usually acted as solicitors to the issues conducted by Schröders and thus when William Slaughter and William May left that firm to set up on their own in January 1889 they were already known to the Schröder partners, Slaughter having acted on the issues for Erlanger's Alabama Railways in the early 1880s.[61] The late 1880s also saw the beginning of Schröders' special relationship with the stockbroking firm W. Greenwell, which acted as broker to many of the issues of these years, and for half a century thereafter was the firm's principal broker. Walpole Greenwell, the highly-respected senior partner, often served as one of the trustees for bondholders for issues conducted by Schröders.

The issues on behalf of the Chilean railway companies were part of an upsurge in bond issues for Latin American borrowers in the London capital market in the late 1880s, and Schröders took advantage of the favourable climate to raise funds for several other South American clients. In 1888, it brought out a £100,000 loan for the Brazilian city of Santos and issued £250,000 preference shares for the Uruguay Northern Railway Co. The following year it made a further issue for the Uruguay Northern of £450,000 debentures to finance the construction of a link with the Brazilian railway system. The connection with the Uruguay Northern Railway Co. was the chairman, Emanuel Underdown, who was also chairman of the Antofagasta (Chili) and Bolivia Railway Co. and subsequently, perhaps at Schröders' instigation, became chairman of the United Railways of the Havana and Regla Warehouses Co. Underdown was a flamboyant City figure who made a fortune from the promotion of overseas railways. By profession he was a barrister at the Inner Temple, but he spent much of his time away from the Bar promoting his business interests in India, Spain, Egypt, the Straits of Malacca, and in Cuba 'at one of its most exciting times', besides being a friend of the painter James Whistler and giving accomplished operatic performances, counting 'among his happiest memories the days when he sang with the great Grisi and Mario'.[62] Barings took especially active advantage of the bull market for Latin American securities and made

25. Johann Heinrich Schröder as senior partner

26. (*left*) Baron John Henry Schröder

27. (*right*) Alexander Schlüsser,
partner

28. (*right*) Baron William
    Schröder

29. (*left*) Baron Emile d'Erlanger,
    a close business associate

30. Leadenhall Street in the early 1840s

31. Office of J. Henry Schröder & Co., 145 Leadenhall Street, in the 1860s

7 PER CENT COTTON LOAN

OF THE

Confederate States of America.

FOR 3 MILLIONS STERLING OR 75 MILLIONS FRANCS.

Series A   N.º 777

£1000   **F25000**

40,000 lbs. COTTON

THE CONFEDERATE STATES OF AMERICA are indebted to the Holder of this Bond in the Sum of ONE THOUSAND POUNDS Sterling, with Interest at the rate of Seven per Cent. per Annum, payable on the First Day of March and the First Day of September in each Year, in Paris, London, Amsterdam, or Frankfort °/M against delivery of the corresponding Coupon, until redemption of the Principal.

THIS BOND forms part of an issue of Seventy-five Millions of Francs, equal to Three Million Pounds Sterling, with Coupons attached till first September, 1883, inclusive, and redeemable at par in the course of twenty years by means of half-yearly drawings, the first of which takes place first March, 1864, the last first September, 1883.

At each drawing, one-fortieth part of the amount unredeemed by Cotton as indicated below is to be drawn; and all Bonds then drawn will be repaid at the option of the holder, in Paris, London, Amsterdam, or Frankfort °/M.

The Holder of the Bond, however, will have the option of converting the same at its nominal amount into Cotton, at the rate of sixpence sterling per pound—say 40,000 lbs. of Cotton in exchange for a Bond of £1000—at any time not later than six months after the ratification of a Treaty of Peace between the present belligerents. Notice of the intention of converting Bonds into Cotton to be given to the representatives of the Government in Paris or London, and sixty days after such notice the Cotton will be delivered, if peace, at the ports of Charleston, Savannah, Mobile, or New Orleans; if war, at a point in the interior within 10 miles of a railroad or stream navigable to the ocean. The delivery will be made free of all charges and duties, except the existing export duty of one-eighth of a cent per pound. The quality of the Cotton to be the standard of New Orleans middling. If any Cotton is of superior or inferior quality, the difference in value shall be settled by two Brokers, one to be appointed by the Government, the other by the Bondholder: whenever these two Brokers cannot agree on the value, an Umpire is to be chosen, whose decision shall be final.

The said issue and the above conditions are authorised by an Act of Congress, approved 29th January, 1863, a certified copy of which is deposited with Messrs. FRESHFIELDS & NEWMAN, in London, the Solicitors to the Contractors, and the faith of the Confederate States is pledged accordingly.

In Witness whereof, the Agent for the Loan of the Confederate States in Paris, duly authorised, has set his hand, and affixed the Seal of the Treasury Department, in Paris, the first day of June, in the year of Our Lord One Thousand Eight Hundred and Sixty-three.

LES ÉTATS CONFÉDÉRÉS D'AMÉRIQUE doivent au Porteur de cette Obligation la somme de MILLE LIVRES STERLING ou VINGT-CINQ MILLE FRANCS, portant intérêt à raison de Sept pour Cent l'an, payable le premier Mars et le premier Septembre de chaque année à Paris, Londres, Amsterdam et Francfort s/M, contre le Coupon respectif jusqu'à remboursement du Capital.

CETTE OBLIGATION fait partie d'une émission de Soixante-et-Quinze Millions de Francs, égale à Trois Millions de Livres Sterling, avec Coupons jusqu'au premier Septembre 1883 inclus, et remboursable au pair dans l'espace de vingt années moyennant des tirages semestriels, dont le premier aura lieu le premier Mars 1864, et le dernier le premier Septembre 1883.

Chaque tirage comprendra la quarantième partie du capital non-remboursé selon le mode indiqué ci-après, et chaque Obligation sortie sera remboursée au choix du Porteur à Paris, Londres, Amsterdam et Francfort s/M.

Le Porteur de l'Obligation aura le droit de réclamer le remboursement du montant nominal en Coton, au prix de sixpence sterling par livre de Coton, soit 40,000 livres par Obligation de £1000 (Frs. 25,000), et ceci, en tout temps, jusqu'aux six mois qui suivront la ratification d'un Traité de Paix entre les belligérants. La déclaration de convertir l'Obligation en Coton devra être faite aux représentants du Gouvernement à Paris ou à Londres, et soixante jours après le Coton sera délivré, en cas de paix, dans les ports de Charleston, Savannah, Mobile ou de la Nouvelle-Orléans, et, en cas de guerre, dans l'intérieur du pays, à une distance de dix milles au plus d'un chemin de fer ou d'une rivière navigable jusqu'à la mer. La livraison sera faite libre de tous frais et impôts, à l'exception du droit d'exportation actuellement en vigueur de ¼ cent américain par livre. La qualité du Coton devra être le type de "New Orleans middling." Si tout ou partie du Coton est de qualité supérieure ou inférieure, la différence en valeur sera réglée par deux Courtiers, l'un désigné par le Gouvernement et l'autre par le Porteur de l'Obligation. Dans le cas où ces deux Courtiers ne pourraient s'accorder, un Arbitre sera choisi et sa décision sera définitive.

Ladite émission et les conditions ci-dessus indiquées sont autorisées par un Acte du Congrès approuvé le 29 Janvier 1863, dont une copie légalisée est déposée chez Messrs. FRESHFIELDS & NEWMAN, à Londres, Solicitors des Contractants; en conséquence les États Confédérés sont engagés.

En Foi de quoi, l'Agent pour l'Emprunt des États Confédérés à Paris, dûment autorisé, a signé et apposé le Sceau du Trésor à Paris, le premier Juin l'an mil huit cent soixante-et-trois.

CONTRACTORS.   _AGENT FOR THE LOAN._

AGENTS TO THE CONTRACTORS IN LONDON.   (Countersigned.)   _COMMISSIONER._

ON 1st SEPTEMBER, 1883, a further Sum of £35 will be paid by Messrs. J. HENRY SCHRÖDER & Co., London; or Frs. 875 by Messrs. EMILE ERLANGER & Co., Paris; or the equivalents at the Exchange of the day by Mr. RAPHAEL ERLANGER, Frankfort o/M, and Messrs. B. H. SCHRÖDER & Co. Amsterdam; together with the principal Sum of £1000, or Frs. 25,000, on surrender of this BOND and WARRANT.

J. HENRY SCHRÖDER & Cº

ÉMILE ERLANGER & Cⁱᵉ

32.   Confederate Cotton Loan bond, 1863

33 and 34.   Opening of the
Tokyo–Yokohama railway in
1872. J. Henry Schröder & Co.
lead managed Japan's first foreign
loan to finance the line.
Drawing in the *Illustrated London
News* (*above*) and contemporary
Japanese print (*left*)

35. Advertisement for Peruvian Guano, for which J. Henry Schröder & Co. acted as worldwide agent in the 1870s

36. Terminus of the Matanzas and Sabanilla Railroad in Matanzas, Cuba. The first bond issue managed by J. Henry Schröder & Co., in 1853, financed its construction

37.   Baron John Henry Schröder riding with the Bicester Hunt

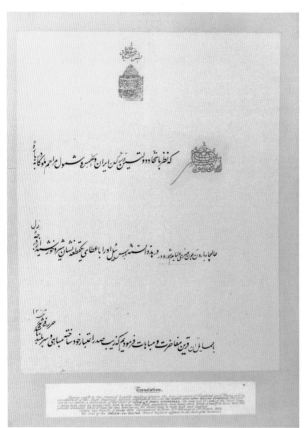

38.   Order of The Lion and
The Sun awarded to
Baron John Henry
Schröder by the Shah of
Persia in 1889

39.　Baron Sir John Henry Schröder Bt. as senior partner in 1900

40.   Henry Tiarks, partner

41. The Dell, Englefield Green, Surrey, home of Baron Sir John Henry Schröder Bt. from 1864

42. Foxbury, Chislehurst, Kent, home of Henry Tiarks from 1877

43. (*above*) Partners' room
    c. 1900

44. (*left*) Banking hall *c*. 1900

45. (*left*) Bruno Schröder as
     a young man

46. (*right*) Frank Tiarks as
     a young man

47. Staff Dinner at the Ship and Turtle, Leadenhall Street, on the occasion of the golden wedding of Baron Sir John Henry Schröder Bt., 19 September 1900

48. State of San Paulo 5 per cent Treasury Bond, 1908, the first of several issues to finance Brazilian coffee price stabilisation schemes

Evening News

AUSTRIAN LOAN SUCCESS

EVENING NEWS

49. (*above*) The City of London in its Edwardian heyday – scene outside the Bank of England (left) and the Royal Exchange

50. (*left*) London evening newspaper's announcement of the £16.5 million loan for Austria in April 1914, which Schröders managed jointly with Rothschilds

256000

App^t. G.R.I.

345895.

264030

Dictated.

RECEIVE

Mr. Secretary McKenna, with his humble duty to

Your Majesty, has the honour to represent to Your Majesty

that Baron Bruno Schröder, partner of the firm of

J. Henry Schröder and Company, Merchants and Bankers,

of No. 145 Leadenhall Street, in the City of London,

being a natural born subject of the Emperor of Germany,

is at the present time, owing to the state of war which

exists between this Country and Germany, unable without

Your Majesty's Licence and permission to reside and

trade here.

Mr. McKenna is satisfied that the case is one in

which such a Licence may properly be granted.

R. A. McKenna

WHITEHALL

7th August, 1914.

51. (*left*) Home Secretary's recommendation to issue a 'Licence to reside and trade' to Baron Bruno Schröder upon the outbreak of the First World War

OWING TO THE OUTCRY AGAINST HIGH-PLACED ALIENS A WEALTHY GERMAN TRIES TO LOOK AS LITTLE HIGH-PLACED AS POSSIBLE.

52. (*right*) *Punch* cartoon published 9 December 1914, two weeks after parliamentary questions about Baron Bruno Schröder's naturalisation

issue after issue for their clients in Argentina. By 1890, investors were becoming concerned about the extent of Argentinian borrowing and more and more of the securities issued by the firm had to be taken on to its own books until its balance sheet became completely illiquid and it had to be rescued by a Guarantee Fund organised by the Bank of England and subscribed by City firms.[63] Naturally, Schröders was a contributor to the fund.

From the outset Schröders' business had been orientated towards northern Europe, especially Hamburg and Russia, and the Americas. Its most significant point of contact with other continents had been the indigo trade, but by the 1880s this was no longer of importance. However, in the issuing boom of the late 1880s and in the early 1890s the firm sponsored issues on behalf of borrowers in parts of the world with which it had no previous contact, a development that should be seen in the context of the drive to develop new business in these years. In 1889, it made an issue of £1 million worth of shares for the Imperial Bank of Persia, a newly formed undertaking to conduct banking operations in the Shah's domain which received its Royal charter during his European tour in 1889.[64] The source of Schröders' introduction to this business is unclear, but there are several possibilities: the promoter Baron Julius de Reuter was of German origin (though he held British nationality); the co-issuer, David Sassoon & Co. was a neighbour in Leadenhall Street and occupied the same building as Ohlendorff & Co.; and the broker was W. Greenwell & Co. The issue was made in September 1889 and proved very popular with the public, being fifteen times over-subscribed.[65] The Persian government was pleased by the scale of support (suggesting that the underpricing was the result of the client's requirements), and as a token of its appreciation John Henry was awarded the Persian Order of the Lion and the Sun. The success of the Imperial Bank issue led to an issue of £350,000 preference shares on behalf of the Persian Bank Mining Rights Corporation in April 1890. This firm was formed to acquire the mining rights granted to the Imperial Bank under its charter in 1889. The issue was successfully executed by the same team of Schröders, Sassoons and Greenwells. In 1885, George Stielow, Schröders' office manager since 1877, left the firm to take up an appointment as a director of the Imperial Bank, which strengthened the relationship between the firms and in the Edwardian era the Imperial Bank was a member of Schröders' underwriting syndicates, often retaining its participations for its own investment portfolio.[66]

South Africa and New Zealand, like Persia, were countries in which Schröders had no acceptance clients and the issues conducted for borrowers there appear to have arisen from City connections. Emile Erlanger plunged with customary gusto into the South African mining boom of 1887–88 and at one time was about to take over the de Beers mine, but the deal fell through. Nevertheless, Erlanger developed considerable interests in South Africa and it may well have been he who introduced Schröders to the National Bank of South Africa. This had recently been established by the South African Republic to act as the state bank, and a concession to conduct its business had been awarded jointly to Labouchère, Oyens & Co. of Amsterdam and the Berliner Handels Gesellschaft. In 1890 Schröders lead-managed a £500,000 share issue on behalf of the National Bank of South Africa, organising the business in London and Pretoria while the concession holders handled the Amsterdam and Berlin tranches. The equity was divided into ordinary and 'founders' shares, the latter carrying special privileges. These were distributed amongst favoured parties who included Schröders' 'friends' Emile Erlanger, Jules Ephrussi, Gebrüder Bethmann, Walpole Greenwell and, of course, the partners themselves. The same year Schröders made an issue of £1.5 million debentures for the Bank of New Zealand Estates Co. Ltd, formed to acquire properties of the Bank of New Zealand in New Zealand, Australia and Fiji. In 1891 it made a £550,000 debenture issue for the New Zealand Loan and Mercantile Agency Co. Ltd, since 1865 the leading Australian wool consignment merchant in London and the colonies and 'regarded as amongst the soundest and most successful of the undertakings of its class'.[67] Again, Schröders' involvement most probably arose through financial rather than commercial contacts, such well-regarded British Empire borrowers taking advantage of the disenchantment of investors with Latin American loans after the Baring Crisis and the cheap cost of money.[68]

The revival of Schröders' activity as an issuing house and the evolution of its role from agent to principal led to yet another important innovation in the conduct of its business in the late 1880s. From 1888 it regularly acted as an underwriter of bonds issued by other firms, extending the same opportunity to those parties when it brought out an issue. The arrival of such underwriting practices may well have been an innovation of the issuing boom of the late 1880s and it appears to have been the development of this system that allowed Barings to go on issuing bonds for which there was no market and so to get into trouble.[69] Amongst the issues for which Schröders was an underwriter were those for the Province of Quebec and the Union Mortgage Co. of Australia in 1888, the Imperial Russian Government Conversion Loan and the San Francisco Northern Pacific Railway Co. in 1889, and the Imperial German Loan of 1891. Such participations generated profits of about £1,000 each and underwritings provided only a small part of issuing revenues in the late 1880s and early 1890s, but it was a beginning and it later became of substantial significance.

Financial Performance and Interests of the Partners

Schröders' profits in the years 1871–92 followed the pattern of the firm's activity and progress: high in 1871–78; low in 1879–84; recovering in 1885–92 (see Figure 4.3). In 1871–78, the years when the Peruvian Department was most active, profits (net of 4 per cent interest on partners' capital) averaged £164,000. In 1879, however, profits fell to a mere £4,000, and in 1879–84, years which saw depressed acceptance credit commissions, declining merchanting revenues and a virtual absence of issuing activity, they averaged only £34,000. The recovery of profits began in 1885, and in 1890, thanks to substantial contributions from issuing revenues, they reached £152,000 – about £7 million in 1990 money. The lower levels of profits in 1891 and 1892 were the result of the fall in issuing activity in the City following the Baring Crisis of 1890. Upsurges of bad debts in the years 1875–80 and 1883–86 contributed to the low levels of profitability in the second half of the 1870s and the first half of the 1880s. In the 1850s and 1860s bad debts had constituted two-thirds of total costs, but in the 1870s and 1880s the proportion fell to less than half, reflecting both the increase in operating costs and the moderate bad debt record over these decades, notwithstanding the losses incurred in 1877–83. In these years bad debts averaged £12,500 per annum and operating costs £14,500 per annum, the latter fluctuating according to the number of staff.

In 1861–70 net interest contributed 9 per cent of Schröders' revenues but in 1871–92 it generated only 3 per cent. The principal reason was the

Figure 4.3   J. Henry Schröder & Co., net profits after interest on partners' capital, 1871–92

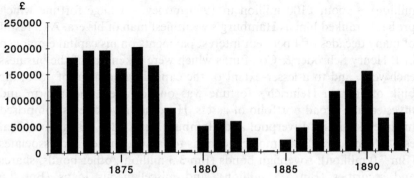

Note: Any liability for income tax was borne by the partners.

prevailing low interest rates, of which the government itself took advantage to convert the national debt to a lower rate of interest in 1888, the coupon on consols being cut from 3 per cent to 2.5 per cent. But another factor was the highly liquid balance sheet maintained by the partners while the threat of the withdrawal of Johann Heinrich's capital hung over the firm. In the 1870s and early 1880s, perhaps 60 per cent of assets consisted of cash and call loans and most of the rest comprised bills of exchange. Immediately after the death of the founder the partners invested £233,000 in securities, representing about a third of the partners' capital, and by 1892 the securities portfolio was £554,000, about half the capital. This shift boosted net interest earnings, while trading the portfolio generated securities dealings profits. Yet call loans continued to constitute a substantial part of balance sheet assets, de Zoete & Gorton, Jourdan & Wylie and, from 1880 onwards, W. Greenwell, featuring prominently amongst the stockbroker clients, and Reeves, Whitburn & Co. and the General Credit Discount Corporation amongst the discount houses. The specialist foreign bill dealers, Bingel & Schumann, of which a partner was a relative of John Henry's private secretary, and Haarbleicher & Schumann, whose office was at 144 Leadenhall Street adjacent to Schröders', also made extensive use of call loan facilities provided by Schröders.

In the years 1871–82, Johann Heinrich's partnership interest declined from 84 per cent to 68 per cent, a consequence of the profit-sharing arrangement with the younger partners and of a partial withdrawal of his capital in 1878. Such rearrangements of partnership interests have been noted of other firms facing similar problems of generational succession, for instance, Brown Shipley and Antony Gibbs.[70] Despite this withdrawal, at the time of his death in June 1883 the founder still owned £1,058,000 of the £1,481,000 capital of J. Henry Schröder & Co. This represented 40 per cent of his total estate of Bancomarks (Bm) 53.5 million (equivalent at the prevailing rate of £1 = Bm 20.25 to £2.64 million) – about £100 million in 1990 money – a huge fortune which probably ranked him as Hamburg's wealthiest man of his era. As a result of many decades of 4 per cent interest payments on his capital employed in J. Henry Schröder & Co., funds which were taken out of the business each year, and to a lesser extent of the capital withdrawal of 1878, the bulk of Johann Heinrich's fortune was outside the London firm and invested in a broad portfolio of assets. His other investments comprised his interests in his Liverpool and Hamburg firms (Bm 7.3 million), real estate (Bm 1.5 million); mortgage loans to family, friends and associates (Bm 7.0 million); sovereign bonds (Bm 3.3 million); other bonds, shares and securities (Bm 7.3 million); and miscellaneous loans (Bm 2.6 million).

After providing Bm 2 million for burial and legal costs, special legacies and, ever cautious, a Bm 0.75 million reserve, Johann Heinrich's remaining estate of Bm 50.7 million was divided equally between his nine children, who were by then aged between 42 and 64, for the benefit of them and their children and even grandchildren, each receiving Bm 5,631,500 (£278,000). In the bourgeois world of the Hamburg merchant, in which each generation was expected to develop his business and build his own wealth, the aristocratic practice of primogeniture to favour the eldest son, or even the favouring of sons over daughters, was frowned

Table 4.4   J. Henry Schröder & Co, balance sheets 1882–83

31 December	Balance Sheet 1882 £	Balance Sheet 1883 £	Difference 1882–83 £
LIABILITIES			
Partners' capital	1 481 000	679 000	(802 000)
Loan: estate of Johann Heinrich Schröder	–	418 000	418 000
Customer balances, etc.	209 000	230 000	21 000
Acceptances	2 128 000	2 299 000	171 000
Total	3 818 000	3 626 000	(192 000)
ASSETS			
Liquid assets – cash, call loans advances etc.[1]	224 000	501 000	277 000
Bill portfolio	673 000	726 000	53 000
Loans: E. Erlanger & Co.	312 000	100 000	(212 000)
Ohlendorff & Co.	243 000	–	(243 000)
Investments: Ohlendorff & Co.	238 000	–	(238 000)
Acceptances	2 128 000	2 299 000	171 000
Total	3 818 000	3 626 000	(192 000)

1. Undifferentiated in balance sheets.
( ) indicates decrease

Source: J. Henry Schröder & Co., balance sheets.

upon. John Henry received Bm 3.6 million (£178,000) on 31 December 1883 and a further Bm 2 million over the subsequent five years. He and his partners were therefore obliged to liquidate some of the firm's assets and to pay £880,000 to the founder's executors. This was achieved principally by the withdrawal from the Ohlendorff & Co. investment – which raised £238,000 through the sale of the firm's 25 per cent interest and £243,000 through the repayment of a loan – and by the repayment by Emile Erlanger & Co. of a £212,000 loan (see Table 4.4). Furthermore, the executors made a loan to the partners of £418,000 and large loans from Johann Heinrich's estate and from William Schröder of Cheshire continued for several years, effectively boosting the firm's capital. In total £1,110,000 was available to pay the £880,000 due to Johann Heinrich's estate, £230,000 more than was necessary. As a result there was no depletion of liquid assets, which in fact grew by £277,000 (see Table 4.4). Moreover, the commercial bill portfolio increased by £53,000 and the scale of the firm's acceptances rose by £171,000. Thus not only was there no disruption of client relationships by the withdrawal of lines of credit or the denial of advances, but business activity expanded in the wake of the withdrawal of Johann Heinrich's capital. The outcome was that despite the reduction in capital by 54 per cent from £1,481,000 to £678,000, the balance sheet shrank by only 5 per cent, from £3,818,000 to £3,626,000. The reduction in partners' capital caused a large rise in the ratio of capital to acceptances; in 1876–82 this ratio averaged 1:1.43, a much lower level than in the 1860s or early 1870s; but in 1883–92, after the withdrawal of Johann Heinrich's capital, it averaged 1:3.9. This adjustment was possible without damage to the firm at a time of underemployed resources, though had Johann Heinrich died at the peak of the guano activity a major withdrawal of capital would have been highly disruptive to business.

Schröders' rate of return on capital – including the partners' 4 per cent interest – in 1871–92 is shown in Figure 4.4. In the years 1871–78, returns averaged 15.3 per cent, a slight improvement on the 1860s, when they averaged 14.5 per cent. In 1879–84, however, the average rate of return was only 6.7 per cent, rather a poor premium for the risks of the business. The rate rose to 12.3 per cent in 1885–92, partly as a result of the growth of profits from 1885 but largely because of the reduction in capital by more than half in 1883. Prices fell in twelve of the twenty-two years from 1871–92, and if the price factor is taken into consideration Schröders' 'real' rate of return was considerably higher than the nominal rate. The cut in capital restored both the capital to acceptances ratio and the rate of return to more accceptable levels. Put another way, in the half dozen or so years prior to 1883, Schröders' was over-capitalised – it had an overabundance of capital relative to commercial opportunities. In

Figure 4.4   J. Henry Schröder & Co., return on capital and annual rate of inflation, 1871–92

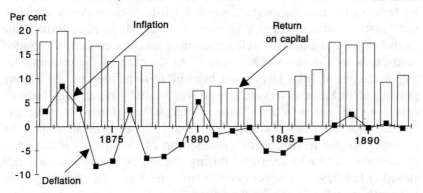

Note: The 'real' return on capital is the difference between the nominal return on capital depicted above and the annual rate of inflation.

fact, the reduction of capital following Johann Heinrich's death should not be seen as a blow to the business, but as an adjustment of the resources employed in the firm to a more appropriate level. Interestingly, two other leading City merchant banks experienced substantial reductions in capital in the mid-1880s: Antony Gibbs, where partners' funds fell from £800,000 in 1882 to £350,000 in 1885; and Kleinworts, where the reduction was from £1 million to £572,000 between 1883 and 1886.[71] Neither appears to have been much harmed by the experience, suggesting, perhaps, that it was not only Schröders that was over-capitalised in the years of the 'Great Depression'.

Business was by no means the only interest of the Schröder partners. By 1883, John Henry was 59 years old and after the death of his father he seems to have devoted more and more of his time to other pursuits. From 1884, freed from the duty of visiting Johann Heinrich in Hamburg every summer to report on business in London, he rented Scottish shoots where he was based each year from the end of July until mid-October.[72] Orchid cultivation had been a pastime of his since the 1860s, but increased application from the 1880s resulted in his plants winning three Royal Horticultural Society gold medals and ten silver medals between 1891 and 1904. John Henry played an active part in the affairs of the Royal Horticultural Society and he contributed handsomely to the Royal Gardeners' Benevolent Institution. He took great pride in the upkeep of the ten acres of grounds surrounding The Dell. Heinrich Schliemann was impressed by the 'large garden cultivated with art and full of camellias, cedars from the Lebanon and other exotic and rare trees'.[73] A staff of fifty was employed to tend the garden and to run the adjacent 150-acre farm. Art was another of John Henry's interests and he built up a considerable collection of pictures, for the most part works by fashionable contemporaries, some English, such as Alma Tadema, but mostly continental genre painters such as Meissonier, though the Barbizon School was also well represented and the collection included landscapes by Corot and Daubigny.[74] At the turn of the century full-length studies of John Henry and his wife were painted by the leading portrait artist Hubert Herkomer, who was a family friend. John Henry's collection of *objets d'art*, Sèvres, English and Oriental porcelain, Renaissance cameos, jewellery and snuff boxes was described by Christies soon after his death as 'made up of the "pick" of the great collections which had been sold during the last 30 years' and their sale raised £138,059.[75] The collection of pictures and statuary was bequeathed to the Hamburg Kunsthalle.

In later life, as earlier, John Henry was a generous benefactor of charitable causes. When the German Hospital in Hackney, of which he continued to be treasurer, got into financial difficulties in the 1870s he paid off its debts, and in 1908 he endowed its new convalescent home at Hitchin in Hertfordshire. Upon his death in 1910 the German Hospital received a bequest of £10,000 and the grateful trustees named the childrens' ward the Baron Schröder Ward in his honour. Numerous other causes beneficial to the welfare of London's German population also enjoyed his financial backing; the Kaiser Wilhelm Stiftung – later called the German Orphanage – which opened in Hackney in 1879; the German Work Colony at Libury Hall in Hertfordshire, established in 1900; the Christus-Kirche built in Knightsbridge in 1904; the German Sailors Home in the London docks, which was erected at his expense and was opened after his death in 1912 by his personal secretary, Carl Albrecht Bingel.[76] 'Baron Schröder,' commented a German quoted by an obituary writer, 'gave more in charity than all the rest of the Germans in this country put together.'[77]

It was not only German charities which benefited from John Henry's generosity. Numerous local causes in the Windsor area also received assistance, most notably the gift of five acres of land to Egham District Council for the erection of an isolation hospital. In recognition of his contributions to the welfare of the locality John Henry was presented with an illuminated address by the Corporation of Windsor on the occasion of his Golden Wedding in 1900. The Schröders became close friends of their neighbours Princess Christian of Schleswig-Holstein, a daughter of Queen Victoria, and her German husband. John Henry and his wife received invitations to Court and to attend important celebrations, such as the Jubilee service in Westminster Abbey in 1887. In 1892, the Queen conferred a baronetcy upon him 'as a mark of personal friendship and esteem, and for the help he had given to the household on matters of finance and accountancy'.[78] He was given a special dispensation to permit him to continue to use his Prussian title and was henceforth known as Baron Sir John Henry Schröder Bt.

Henry Tiarks also pursued a range of interests outside the office. Like his partner, he was a patron of local charities and an enthusiastic horticulturalist. He was president of the Chislehurst and Cray Valley Medical and Surgical Aid Society, which administered the neighbourhood cottage hospital. He was one of the initiators in the early 1880s of plans to build the hospital and was a leading benefactor. His final and most munificent gift to this cause was the children's ward which opened in 1910. His horticultural interest focused upon the chrysanthemum and he was president of the Kent Chrysanthemum Society. A 'staunch Churchman', he was rector's warden at St Nicholas's Parish Church, Chislehurst, for a quarter of a century.[79] He was a member of the various local government bodies that administered the Chislehurst area from the 1880s to 1903 and sat on the board of the Chislehurst and St Paul's Cray Common Conservators. In politics he was a supporter of the Liberal Party, an increasingly unusual allegiance for a leading City man after the 1880s, though one he shared with his Lubbock in-laws.[80]

John Henry Schröder and Henry Tiarks were not alone among the Anglo-German merchants in moving to mansions in the Home Counties after 1860, by which time the development of an extensive railway network enabled the combination of a country residence with daily attendance in the office. For instance, Lewis Huth, the senior partner of Frederick Huth & Co., built Possingworth Manor, Sussex, in 1868–70, and Charles Herman Goschen, the senior partner of Frühling & Goschen, commissioned Ballards, Surrey, in 1873. The Kleinwort brothers remained in Camberwell until the 1890s, but then they too acquired properties outside London, Alexander Kleinwort buying the Bolnore estate in Sussex, and his brother, Hermann, the Wierton estate in Kent.[81] But despite the acquisition of country residences the Anglo-German merchants remained distinct from other merchant banking families such as the Barings, Rothschilds, Sassoons, Gibbs and Hambros, who were socially prominent and politically active, became large country landowners and merged into the English aristocracy. The Anglo-German merchants remained wedded to the values of their continental bourgeois backgrounds and it could be said of them, as it was of their Hamburg cousins by Julius von Eckardt, secretary of the Hamburg Senate in 1874–82, that they 'saw . . . work and the fulfilment of duty as the main preoccupations of life'.[82]

In 1892, the team which had run Schröders in London for the previous two decades was broken up by the retirement of von der Meden upon reaching the age of sixty-five. A new partnership agreement was drawn up between John Henry Schröder and Henry Tiarks, even though the former was sixty-seven and the latter turned sixty that year. In fact, the time had arrived to resolve the question of the future of the firm, which was open because John Henry was childless. There is no record of John Henry's deliberations, but it is not surprising that he wished for the firm to continue, or that he looked to his family in Hamburg for a successor. The leading Schröder family firm in Hamburg was Schröder Gebrüder with which J. Henry Schröder & Co. had developed increasingly close ties since the early 1870s. Rudolph Bruno Schröder, known for most of his life as Baron Bruno, the 25-year-old younger brother of the head of that firm and a nephew of John Henry, was invited to inherit the London firm. John Henry chose wisely and under Baron Bruno's leadership Schröders achieved even greater prominence in the City.

5

High Finance

1892–1914

The two decades from the early 1890s to the outbreak of the First World War saw substantial expansion of the scale and range of the activities of the City of London as an international financial centre. World trade, which was still the bedrock of the City's business, accelerated, the annual rate of growth rising from 2.7 per cent in 1873–92, to 3.1 per cent in 1893–1904, to 4.1 per cent per annum in 1905–13.[1] The result was buoyant demand for the services of the City's ship-broking and marine insurance industries, its commodities markets and for trade finance, which continued to be dominated by the sterling bill of exchange. The issue of sterling securities for overseas borrowers, which had slumped in the wake of the Baring Crisis of 1890, revived in the mid-1890s, such issues totalling £819 million in 1893–1904.[2] The following decade saw a foreign issues boom of unprecedented magnitude and in 1905–14 the total of sterling issues for overseas borrowers was £1,642 million creating buoyant demand for the issuing services provided by the merchant banks. Several new activities also developed rapidly in the City in the 1890s and 1900s, notably foreign exchange dealing, securities arbitrage and commodity futures trading, reflecting the growing complexity of international finance and the increasing interchange with other significant international financial centres, notably New York, Paris and Berlin. Nevertheless, the City maintained its pre-eminence as the world's leading financial centre and the decade or so prior to 1914 was for it a 'golden age'.

The causes of the strong demand for the City's services in the 1890s and 1900s lay in the rapid expansion and development of the international economy, in particular the industrialisation and vigorous economic growth of Germany and the United States. The City boom was divorced from the development of the domestic economy, which in the years 1899–1913 saw growth of little more than 1 per cent per annum, the poorest sustained peacetime performance in Britain's history as an industrial nation.[3] The synchronisation of the City with overseas economic activity derived from the role of sterling in the international economy and the primacy of London's financial markets. Britain's long adherence to the gold standard and the transcendence of the Bank of England amongst central banks made sterling the world's leading reserve currency and made sterling-denominated bills of exchange and sterling denominated long-term securities uniquely negotiable. Moreover, London's short-term and long-term money markets were unrivalled in liquidity and sophistication.

London's leading role as an international financial centre led foreign banks and securities houses to establish representatives and subsidiaries there. The first foreign bank to establish a presence was the French Comptoir National d'Escompte in 1865.[4] In 1885, twenty-two foreign banks had offices in the City, but by the beginning of the twentieth century there were ninety-one.[5] So rapid was the 'foreign invasion' that some City observers reacted with xenophobia and even the sober-minded *Bankers' Magazine* ran an article in 1901 entitled 'Lombard Street Under Foreign Control'.[6] The growing body of foreign firms in the 1890s and 1900s focused upon foreign exchange transactions, securities arbitrage between international financial centres, and the creation of sterling bills of exchange to finance the foreign trade of their own nationals, which were sold in the London discount market. The last was a service which had hitherto been provided by the merchant banks and there was growing rivalry for business between the merchant banks and the foreign banks, particularly the branches of the large German banks. A paper presented to the Institute of Bankers in February 1900 drew attention to this development, the authors commenting that 'while the foreign trader still draws on London, he no longer deems it necessary to make his paper payable at a British bank . . . today the foreign trader or small banking concern is prepared to make his London paper payable with one of his native institutions'.[7] Another threat to the acceptance business of the merchant banks came from the domestic clearing banks. During the nineteenth century the clearing banks left overseas trade finance to the merchant banks, since they lacked the means of making credit appraisals of foreign clients and their staff were without the requisite language skills. These problems were overcome by granting wholesale credit lines to foreign banks which retailed credits to local clients, a system known as 'reimbursement credits' that expanded substantially from the turn of the century. The formation in 1905 of a foreign exchange department by the London City and Midland Bank Ltd (forerunner of the Midland Bank), the first of its kind amongst the clearing banks, was a notable development, but the London County and Westminster Bank, Lloyds Bank and others were also vigorously expanding their activities and in the years immediately preceding the First World War competition for acceptance business was 'acute'.[8]

The developments in the City and beyond in the 1890s and 1900s presented unrivalled opportunities for the development of business, but also mounting competition for the merchant banks. Both factors are discernable as influences upon the development of J. Henry Schröder & Co. in these years. Schröders took full advantage of the opportunities to expand the firm's acceptance and issuing activities, but it also diversified into securities dealing and pursued a strategy of balance sheet management which boosted profits but reduced liquidity. The outcome was the growth of partners' capital from £1,125,000 in 1893 to £3,648,000 by 1913, an increase of almost three times both in nominal and real terms, since inflation was minimal. The larger capital base of 1913 supported a commensurately larger volume of business, but over the same period the number of staff rose not threefold but by a third, from 35 to 46. John Henry's nephew, Bruno, knew not only how to develop new business but also how to control costs, and good profits were the outcome.

Partnership and Staff

Bruno Schröder was born in Hamburg on 14 March 1867, the eighth of the nine children of Johann Rudolph I and Clara Louise Schröder. Both parents were members of the Schröder family by birth: his father, a grandson of Christian Matthias's elder brother Bernhard Hinrich I; his mother, a granddaughter of Christian Matthias and a daughter of Johann Heinrich, the founder of the London firm (see Figure 5.1). Bruno grew up in Hamburg, though some years of his childhood were spent in Lausanne, Switzerland, where his parents took up residence for a while because of his father's outspoken opposition to Hamburg's accession to the German Customs Union and to Bismarck. Upon completing his schooling and his military service, serving in the Second Mecklenburg Dragoons and achieving the rank of captain, he joined the family firm Schröder Gebrüder. In 1888, aged 21, he spent a year at J. Henry Schröder & Co. in London as a volunteer. In 1891, he undertook a tour of the United States and South America, visiting Schröder Gebrüder's clients and learning about their businesses. Upon his return to Hamburg in July 1892 he was made a signatory of the firm and it was anticipated that he would soon become a partner. However, a few months later John Henry invited him to succeed him in J. Henry Schröder & Co. and he accepted 'this exceptional chance of a lifetime'.[9]

Bruno joined Schröders at the beginning of 1893 and on 1 January 1895 he was made a partner, at the age of 27. Under the new partnership agreement John Henry provided four-fifths of the capital and received – after interest on partners' capital – half the profits, the other half being divided between Henry Tiarks and Bruno, taking account of their contributions to capital and seniority. Bruno immediately applied

118

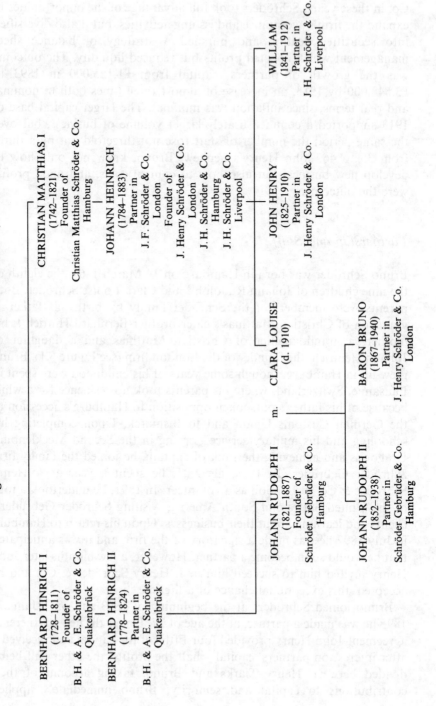

Figure 5.1 Ancestors of Baron Bruno Schröder (1867–1940)

BERNHARD HINRICH I
(1728–1811)
Founder of
B. H. & A. E. Schröder & Co.
Quakenbrück

BERNHARD HINRICH II
(1778–1824)
Partner in
B. H. & A. E. Schröder & Co.
Quakenbrück

CHRISTIAN MATTHIAS I
(1742–1821)
Founder of
Christian Matthias Schröder & Co.
Hamburg

JOHANN HEINRICH
(1784–1883)
Partner in
J. F. Schröder & Co.
London
Founder of
J. Henry Schröder & Co.
London
J. H. Schröder & Co.
Hamburg
J. H. Schröder & Co.
Liverpool

JOHANN RUDOLPH I
(1821–1887)
Founder of
Schröder Gebrüder & Co.
Hamburg

JOHANN RUDOLPH II
(1852–1938)
Partner in
Schröder Gebrüder & Co.
Hamburg

WILLIAM
(1841–1912)
Partner in
J. H. Schröder & Co.
Liverpool

JOHN HENRY
(1825–1910)
Partner in
J. Henry Schröder & Co.
London

CLARA LOUISE
(d. 1910)

m.

BARON BRUNO
(1867–1940)
Partner in
J. Henry Schröder & Co.
London

himself to mastering the acceptance business. A memoir written by one of the firm's executives related that:

> Soon after he had started to work in London he was found examining the bills that had come in for acceptance. When it was pointed out to him that only one or two confidential employees had access to these bills he said that his uncle had given him permission to see them. The bills were of course the very heart of the firm's business and, thus, from the outset he made himself expertly familiar with details and his sense of standards and principles were merged in his sense of form, which expressed itself in everything he did in business.[10]

This command of the business is illustrated by an anecdote which was part of the firm's folklore, that on his first meeting with Caesar Czarnikow the latter was dumbfounded to be told by the young man that he required a larger line of credit than he had arranged because of likely developments in the sugar market; and events proved Bruno right. An immediate effect of his appointment to the partnership was more active securities trading on the firm's account, which went hand-in-hand with a shift in the asset structure towards higher yielding advances and bonds rather than very liquid commercial bills. Another reform was the adoption of systematic annual payments to reserves to cover bad debts, in addition to the traditional practice of *ad hoc* write-offs. Most importantly of all, Bruno's appointment revitalised J. Henry Schröder & Co.'s ties with Hamburg and boosted its business with Schröder Gebrüder and its associates.

Bruno's German ties were also strong at the personal level. In 1894, soon after his settlement in London, he married a German bride, Emma Deichmann, the daughter of a partner in the eminent Cologne private bank, Deichmann & Co. He remained close to his family in Hamburg and kept a house there in the outlying suburb of Othmarschen overlooking the estuary of the River Elbe, which he visited most summers. He was a generous benefactor of Hamburg charities, a magnanimity which was recognised in 1904 when he was created a *Freiherr* by Kaiser Wilhelm II. Moreover, he acted as an adviser to the German Embassy on matters of finance and no senior German figure on a visit to London omitted to call on him; 'the leading German in London' was how Edward Grenfell, the senior partner in Morgan Grenfell, described him.[11] As the historically close relations between the merchants of London and Hamburg became overshadowed by the growing nationalist antagonism between Britain and Germany, Baron Bruno's position as a prominent Anglo-German banker became increasingly difficult.

Bruno and his family, which soon comprised two sons and two daughters, lived in Kensington from the mid-1890s until 1908, when they moved to 35 Park Street, Mayfair. From 1899 he also kept a country residence, Heath Lodge, set in 28 acres adjacent to his uncle's estate at Englefield Green, near Windsor. In 1910, he inherited his uncle's estate and home, The Dell, in which he took up temporary residence while Heath Lodge was rebuilt in 1912–14 as a full-scale country house, which was renamed Dell Park. John Henry was probably the source of inspiration for Bruno's interest in horticulture – he won his first Royal Horticultural Society Medal in 1912 – and in the collection of art. Another feature of the common outlook of uncle and nephew was their sense of responsibility and duty towards their inheritance, the firm of J. Henry Schröder & Co., and each saw himself as a custodian of the Schröder name and its reputation.

On 1 January 1902, Frank Tiarks, the 27-year-old son of Henry Tiarks, was admitted to the Schröder partnership. Frank Cyril Tiarks was born on 9 July 1874 and was initially destined for a career in the Royal Navy. In 1887, aged thirteen, he joined the naval training college HMS *Britannia* and upon being commissioned served as a lieutenant on HMS *Warspite*. In November 1893, his elder brother, who was intended for the Schröder partnership, died of fever while serving with the British Army in India, leading Frank Tiarks to obtain a discharge from the navy and to join the firm early in 1894. Having learnt the routine of the London office he spent a year as a volunteer in Le Havre, another with Conrad Hinrich Donner & Co., a prominent Hamburg merchant bank, and a third with Ladenburg, Thalmann & Co., the New York brokerage house with which Schröders conducted extensive business. In 1899, he married Emmy Brödermann, whose family was of German origin but resident in Mexico. Upon his return to Leadenhall Street, he was an associate partner for two years, as Bruno had been, before being made a full partner. This expansion of the partnership was accompanied by a new partnership agreement by which the older generation, John Henry Schröder and Henry Tiarks, were rewarded for the provision of the firm's capital, and the young men, Bruno Schröder and Frank Tiarks, for their work as executives.

Baron Bruno Schröder and Frank Tiarks conducted the business of J. Henry Schröder & Co. together for the next three decades. They worked well as an effective team, respecting each other's application and judgement, though their personalities were very different. Baron Bruno was quiet and formal, even austere, thoughtful and analytical. He inspired complete confidence and great respect, though always an outsider to the City establishment. Tiarks, on the other hand, was 'pre-eminently practical', brimmed with 'vitality and gaiety', and was very much a City insider.[12] In combination their talents proved complementary, as Schröders' success in the years before the First World War is testimony. The abilities of the younger generation of partners were recognised beyond Schröders' private room, leading to offers of outside directorships. Sir Felix Schuster, for instance, the chairman of the Union Bank, a dynamic clearing bank of the era, approached John Henry to ask for his consent to offer Bruno a seat on the board. Far from being pleased, John Henry became angry and replied 'Certainly not! You are not to mention it to him. Bruno is to work for *me*'.[13] John Henry was even-handed in the application of his veto; when it was suggested that Frank Tiarks should join the Court of the Bank of England he refused to allow it, stating that he wouldn't have his partners 'wasting time on outside business'.[14]

The pair of younger partners almost became a trio. In September 1903, John Henry informed his partners that it was his intention that Henry Bingel, the son of his German-born private secretary, Carl Albrecht Bingel, a distant relation by marriage, should be admitted to the partnership. Henry Bingel was born in London in 1880 and educated at Charterhouse School. He joined J. Henry Schröder & Co. as a volunteer in 1897 and subsequently spent a year at Schröder Gebrüder in Hamburg, two years with Ladenburg, Thalmann in New York, and most of 1903 travelling in Central and South America visiting Schröders' clients.[15] His training complete, he resumed work at Leadenhall Street, but he died of appendicitis in January 1905 before his appointment to the partnership.

The death of Bingel left the partners short-handed to deal with the firm's burgeoning acceptance business. In 1906, Julius Rittershaussen, a clerk of German birth who had joined the firm in 1897, was made an associate partner upon his return from Japan, where he had been sent to explore the development of business following Japan's emergence as a formidable world power by its victory in the Russo-Japanese War of 1905.[16] A shy, modest and meticulous man, he was temperamentally well suited to the task of scrutinising the documents arising from the conduct of accepting. He acted as an intermediary between the full partners and the staff in the highly disciplined and hierarchical Schröder office, being regarded by the clerks as 'a friend at court'.[17]

In 1893, Schröders employed thirty salaried clerks and for the next decade, despite the expansion of activity, there was no increase in permanent staff, temporaries being taken on when necessary. Booming business in the second half of the 1900s necessitated the engagement of additional permanent clerks and between 1908 and 1911 their number increased from thirty-one to forty-one. Nevertheless, the size of Schröders' personnel was considerably smaller than other leading

London merchant banks at the turn of the century: Hambros, 48; Barings, 71; Brandts, 80; and Kleinworts, 60, rising to more than 100 just before the First World War.[18]

In the 1890s, Germans outnumbered Englishmen two to one amongst Schröders' clerks. In the 1900s, for the first time, Englishmen were recruited in greater number than Germans, a shift that reflected the growing importance of US trade to the firm. By the eve of the First World War, English clerks on Schröders' payroll just outnumbered Germans.[19] Another important change amongst the staff was the appearance of women. Typewriting machines began to be used in the City offices around the turn of the century and female 'typewriters', as they were known at the time, were engaged to operate the new technology. Schröders engaged two women prior to the First World War, both of German origin: Miss Luce, in 1906, to handle John Henry's correspondence; and Miss Sommerfeld, in 1908, who worked for Baron Bruno and Frank Tiarks. Another technological innovation which appeared in Schröders' office just after the turn of the century was the telephone. Initially, Schröders' number was omitted from the telephone directory on the instruction of Baron Bruno, in order to avoid the inconvenience of being distracted from business by incoming calls.

The increase in the size of Schröders' staff in the Edwardian era necessitated an enlargement of the firm's premises. In September 1907, at a cost of £55,000, Schröders purchased 4 Crosby Square, a house plus a sizeable garden, some 80 feet by 60 feet, featuring a pond, a summerhouse and a number of picturesque thorn and fig trees, which lay behind the firm's premises at 145 Leadenhall Street. The garden was the last vestige of the grounds of Crosby Hall, a medieval palace that had been the home of Richard Duke of Gloucester, Sir Thomas More and Sir Walter Raleigh, and which soon after was dismantled and moved to its present location on Chelsea Embankment. The garden was covered by a rear extension to Schröders' office while the house was redeveloped as an office by Wallace Brothers, a merchant bank specialising in trade with India, which purchased the premises from Schröders for £36,500.[20] Thus vanished 'the last of the City gardens'.[21]

The process of the withdrawal of capital by the older generation of partners began in 1900 when John Henry removed £211,000 from the firm. Most probably his action was prompted by his intention to retire to the South of France, but the death of his wife led to the permanent postponement of this plan. The withdrawal of Henry Tiarks' capital in the firm, which constituted 19 per cent of the total in 1904, was effected in three equal stages in 1905, 1906 and 1907, the last coinciding with his retirement, and distributed amongst his eleven children. The first decade of the twentieth century also saw a large transfer of funds from John

Henry to Baron Bruno; following the rearrangement of the partnership in 1907 the former owned 52 per cent of the capital, the latter 44 per cent, and Frank Tiarks 4 per cent. Upon John Henry's retirement at the beginning of 1910 he withdrew his capital of £1.4 million from the firm. The timing of this withdrawal was potentially very disruptive to Schröders' business since, in contrast to the withdrawal of Johann Heinrich's capital in 1883, the firm was operating at a high level of activity and the capital was fully committed. Damage was avoided by a £1 million loan by John Henry to his nephew for a period of ten years.[22] Following the retirement of John Henry the partnership was again rearranged; profits were allocated, three-quarters to Baron Bruno, who now provided around 90 per cent of the capital, and a quarter to Frank Tiarks, who furnished the rest of the funds. The older generation did not enjoy lengthy retirements: John Henry died on 20 April 1910, aged 85, and Henry Tiarks on 18 October 1911, aged 79. With the death of John Henry the impediment to Frank Tiarks' appointment to the Court of the Bank of England disappeared, and when the invitation was renewed in 1912 he accepted, a decision that proved vital to the survival of the firm only two years later.

Accepting Business

The years 1893–1913 saw increases in virtually every aspect of Schröders' activities, especially in the decade preceding the war. In 1893–1904, total revenues averaged £137,000, a modest increase on the £105,000 of the years 1885–92, but in 1905–13 they averaged £415,000, three times the level of the preceding decade (see Table 5.1). Taking the years 1893–1913 as a whole, accepting was the most important source of revenues, generating 39 per cent, followed by issuing and underwriting, 33 per cent, net interest 17 per cent and securities dealing 6 per cent. The firm played an active part in the overseas issuing boom of 1905–13 and in these years issuing and underwriting surpassed accepting as a source of revenue, averaging, respectively, £168,000 and £131,000 per annum. Consignment business continued but on a small scale, the firm handling occasional cargoes of Russian wheat for Mahs & Co. or Rafallovich & Co., sugar, and indigo.[23]

Schröders' revenues from accepting expanded throughout the period; slowly during the 1890s and early 1900s; rapidly from 1905, as the rate of growth of world trade accelerated (see Figure 5.2). The geographical location of its acceptance clients in 1894–1912, derived from the conditions book covering these years, is shown in Table 5.2 on page 126. The two major differences to the pattern in these years relative to

Table 5.1   J. Henry Schröder & Co., sources of revenues, 1893–1913

	1893–1904		1905–13	
	Annual average £000	*Per cent*	*Annual average £000*	*Per cent*
Accepting	75	55	131	32
Issuing and underwriting	21	15	168	40
Net interest	18	13	74	18
Securities dealing	13	9	16	4
Other[1]	10	7	26	6
Total	137	99	415	100

1. Consignments, freight, postage, insurance, dealing for clients, paying agency commissions etc.

Source: J. Henry Schröder & Co., profit and loss accounts.

1869–94 were the large increases in the number of clients in Hamburg and in the United States. There were also more modest increases in several northern European cities – St Petersburg, Moscow, Paris, Amsterdam and London, but declines in others – Bremen, Riga, Berlin and Manchester. There were large falls in southern and central Europe, notably in Odessa and Trieste, the latter perhaps a result of the closure of A. & Ch. M. Schröder & Co. in 1898, and in Vienna. There were fewer clients in the West Indies and South America and none at all in Asia.

Figure 5.2   J. Henry Schröder & Co., revenues from accepting, net interest and securities dealing, 1893–1913

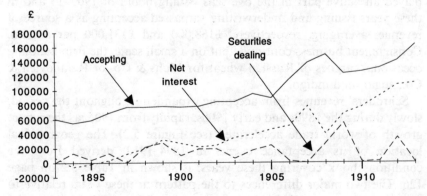

The increase in Hamburg clients, from 158 in 1869–94 to 218 in 1894–1912, reflected the continued expansion of the leading continental port, whose population reached 750,000 at the turn of the century, as a result of the rapid rate of German industrialisation. An important feature of German economic development was the rise of large and powerful banks. They competed aggressively for the acceptance credit business of German firms, not only in Germany but also in London, where the Deutsche Bank established a branch in 1873, the Dresdner Bank in 1895, and the Disconto-Gesellschaft in 1899; and worldwide mostly through consortium banks, such as the Deutsche Asiatische Bank or the Banco Aleman Transatlantico.[24] By 1905 the Deutsche Bank was one of the top five acceptors in the bill portfolio of Gillett Brothers Discount Company Limited, a leading London discount house, the others being Schröders, Kleinworts, Barings and Huths.[25] A few years later, a German economist wrote that 'the time may be said to have passed, at least in the majority of cases, when German exporters . . . and foreign exporters selling goods to Germany, had to draw on London, or when German importers had to settle the credits of their sellers via London'.[26] But despite the vigorous competition from the German banks Schröders' business with Hamburg continued to expand, the reason being its strong ties with Schröder Gebrüder, Baron Bruno's family firm.

Schröder Gebrüder was formed in 1846 by two brothers who were grandsons of Christian Matthias's elder brother, Bernhard Hinrich I, and cousins and contemporaries of John Henry.[27] The elder of the brothers, Bernhard Hinrich III, died in 1849 and it was Johann Rudolph I, Bruno's father, who developed Schröder Gebrüder into a leading Hamburg merchant firm, which after the failure of Christian Matthias Schröder & Co. in 1857 was the foremost Schröder family firm there. J. Henry Schröder & Co. probably acted as London agent for Schröder Gebrüder in the 1850s and 1860s, and in the latter decade it certainly provided acceptance credits of modest proportions, but the close relationship between the firms started in 1871 when the Hamburg house began to use acceptance facilities provided by the London firm on a substantial scale to finance its activities as a distributor of guano in northern Germany. This connection waned with the ending of Schröders' role as central agent for the distribution of Peruvian guano, but revived when Schröder Gebrüder secured the nitrate agency from Gibbs at the start of the 1880s. By 1884, the capital of Schröder Gebrüder was £420,000, about half the size of the London firm (which had recently suffered the withdrawal of Johann Heinrich's funds), though Schröder Gebrüder itself suffered a depletion of capital upon the retirement of Johann Rudolph I at the end of that year.

Table 5.2   Geographical location of the acceptance credit clients of
J. Henry Schröder & Co., 1894–1912

	Number of clients	Per cent
EUROPE AND RUSSIA		
Germany		
Hamburg	218	
Bremen	16	
Altona	1	
Stettin	1	
Total	236	34
Baltic and Northern Russia		
St Petersburg	53	
Moscow	37	
Riga	4	
Total	94	14
Mediterranean, Black Sea and Central Europe		
Odessa	3	
Trieste	4	
Vienna	8	
Total	15	2
Western Europe		
Antwerp	25	
Paris	44	
Amsterdam	11	
Total	80	11
United Kingdom		
Manchester	4	
Liverpool	2	
London	35	
Total	41	6
AMERICAS AND ASIA		
West Indies		
Cuba	5	
Others	2	
Total	7	1

	Number of clients	Per cent
North America		
New York	137	
Others	63	
Total	200	29
South America		
Brazil – Rio de Janeiro	2	
– Bahia	4	
Chile – Valparaiso	5	
Argentina – Buenos Aires	4	
Peru – Lima	3	
Total	18	3
TOTAL	691	100

Source: J. Henry Schröder & Co., conditions book 1894–1912.

From 1884 the senior partner of Schröder Gebrüder was Johann Rudolph II, Bruno's 32-year-old elder brother. Under his leadership the firm dynamically developed its nitrate business and by the beginning of the twentieth century it had the largest distribution network in Germany, France, Belgium and Holland, an achievement that owed much to J. Henry Schröder & Co.'s provision of virtually unlimited acceptance facilities. Schröder Gebrüder itself began to provide acceptance credits for other merchants in the early 1880s, embarking upon the transition from merchant to merchant bank. The development of its acceptance business received a powerful boost in 1890, when the prestigious Cologne private bank Sal. Oppenheim & Cie ceased to conduct this activity in Hamburg and made over its clients to Schröder Gebrüder. In the first decade of the twentieth century it added a securities issuing side to its business, often working in conjunction with J. Henry Schröder & Co.

Johann Rudolph I was one of the founders of the Vereinsbank, a joint stock bank promoted in 1856 by Hamburg's leading merchant families to provide commercial banking services in the city. Its conduct was modelled on the example of English joint stock banks, Schröder Gebrüder's connections with London apparently playing a key role in inspiring its creation.[28] Johann Rudolph I served as a director of the Vereinsbank for twenty-nine years and it was expected that on his retirement in 1885 Johann Rudolph II would succeed to his seat on the board, but his appointment was blocked because of personal animosities amongst the directors.[29] Thereupon Schröder Gebrüder transferred its business to the rival Norddeutsche Bank, of which Johann Rudolph II became a director. When the Norddeutsche Bank was absorbed in 1896 by the Disconto-Gesellschaft of Berlin, one of Germany's major 'universal' banks, Johann Rudolph II joined the board of this leading national institution.

In the couple of decades before the First World War, Schröder Gebrüder's acceptances from J. Henry Schröder & Co. were typically around £200,000. These were large credits, but Hamburg's leading nitrate importers enjoyed even larger facilities; in 1913 Vorwerk Gebrüder and the Norddeutsche Saltpeter Gesellschaft used acceptances of £353,000 and £263,000, respectively, and in 1912 H. Fölsch & Co. had credits of £856,000, a very large sum for a firm with a capital of £3.3 million. There was a wide gulf between the scale of financing provided by Schröders for Schröder Gebrüder and the nitrate importers and for the rest of its Hamburg clients. A handful of leading firms, such as the merchant bank Conrad Hinrich Donner and the coffee importer Theodor Wille, used credits of £50,000–£100,000, but most of Schröders' Hamburg clients were small merchant houses and their credits were commensurately modest, in the range £5,000–£20,000.

The pattern amongst Schröders' acceptance clients in London resembled that of Hamburg, though the number of firms was much smaller. In London there were two clients which used large scale credits of around £200,000, both sugar firms – C. Czarnikow Ltd and the Sena Sugar Estates Ltd. A handful of firms used credits in the range £50,000–£100,000, including the Anglo-Continental Guano Works, Julius Servaes & Co., von der Meden & Co., and the San Paulo Coffee Estates, all of which were closely connected to Schröders in some way, and there was a score or so of smaller scale clients.

The Baltic ports and the cities of northern Russia continued to have important concentrations of merchant clients until the First World War and the list of clients in the conditions books grew from sixty-nine in 1869–94 to ninety-four in 1894–1912. In addition the 1890s and 1900s saw the expansion of the firm's clientele amongst northern Russian banks, which Schröders began to provide with bulk reimbursement credits: in 1893, there were five such clients, though only the Discount Bank used credits of as much as £40,000; in 1903, twelve, of which the largest were the International Commercial Bank of St Petersburg with credits of £200,000, the Discount Bank, £138,000, and the Nordische Bank, £122,000; and in 1913, fourteen. In Odessa too there was a growth of bank clients, offsetting to some extent the decline in merchant clients.

The growth of banks as clients on a reimbursement credit basis was the most important development in Schröders' South American business in the couple of decades before the First World War. Thus although the number of merchant clients recorded in the conditions books fell from thirty-five in 1869–94 to eighteen in 1894–1912, Schröders' presence in the region strengthened through the growth of its business with local banks. In 1893 the Banco de Santiago of Chile was Schröders' only bank client in South America; in 1903 there were five; in 1913, twelve (and some had several branches), the largest user of Schröder credits being the Deutsche Bank associate, the Banco Aleman Transatlantico. which had oustanding availments of £153,000. Amongst the merchant houses Schröders' leading clients were all in the nitrate industry; notably, in 1913, the Amelia Nitrate Co. with outstanding availments of £202,000, and Weber & Co. of Valparaiso £202,000.

The large increase in the number of Schröders' US clients, from eighty-five in 1869–94, to 200 in 1894–1912, was a reflection of the rapid growth of the US economy in the 1890s and 1900s, and the expansion of imports. In these years much US commodity trade was financed in London, both because of the established scale and efficiency of the London discount market and because of the lack of US domestic facilities for international trade finance. Schröders seized the opportunity and greatly expanded its US activities, as did Kleinworts, for which US acceptances generated 45 per cent of acceptance revenues in the first decade of the twentieth century.[30] Most of Schröders' US clients were merchant firms that used credits ranging from £10,000–£40,000. Financing on a much larger scale – in the range £200,000–£500,000 – was provided for the handful of firms which mostly specialised in sugar and coffee trading and sugar refining: notably G. Amsinck & Co., a client since the early 1870s, of which Baron Bruno became a 'special partner' in 1910; the Lewisohn Import Trading Co.; Crossman & Sielcken; the American Sugar Refining Co., and, from 1903, Czarnikow, Macdougall & Co. The last named, the US associate of C. Czarnikow Ltd of London, was established in New York in 1891 to conduct a brokerage and agency business in sugar and other produce. In 1897, Manuel Rionda, a Cuban-born New York based sugar broker, was taken into the partnership thanks to the intercession of Frank Tiarks, who met him on a visit to Cuba while working as a volunteer with Ladenburg, Thalmann.[31] The outcome was a lifelong friendship, which was of enormous significance for the development of Schröders. Following the death of Julius Caesar Czarnikow in 1909 the London firm realised its interest in the New York firm, which became a separate entity controlled by Rionda, renamed the Czarnikow–Rionda Co. Supported by funding from Schröders, Rionda developed the business dynamically and between 1910 and 1913 the scale of credits used by Czarnikow–Rionda rose from £85,000 to £251,000.

Schröders' acceptance activity expanded rapidly under Baron Bruno's direction in the 1890s and 1900s. In these years Kleinworts and Schröders, the sector leaders, established a pre-eminent position in the conduct of acceptance activity amongst the merchant banks. In the early 1890s, Schröders and Kleinworts already conducted the largest acceptance businesses in the City, but there were other firms that were not far behind: Morgan Grenfell; Barings, recovering from the decimation inflicted by the Baring Crisis of 1890; probably Brown, Shipley; and perhaps Huths and Lazards (see Table 5.3). By 1913, however, a great gulf had opened between Schröders and Kleinworts, whose acceptances were £11.7 million and £14.2 million respectively, and the other houses, led by Barings, £6.6 million; Brown, Shipley, £5.1 million; and Hambros, £4.6 million. Moreover, it was only Schröders and Kleinworts that kept abreast of the competition in accepting coming from some British and Continental commercial banks in the 1900s, particularly the large German banks which by 1913 were conducting sterling acceptance business in London on a scale to rival the leading British firms.

There were three reasons for Schröders' and Kleinworts' lead in acceptance business. First, both had well-established connections with Germany and the United States, the most dynamic economies of the era. Second, both firms maintained higher ratios of capital to acceptances than did rival merchant banks. Over the years 1893–1913 Schröders' ratio averaged 1:3.94, just inside the 1:4 ratio which was considered the upper limit to the prudent conduct of the business. Kleinworts' ratio was even higher, averaging 1:4.5. Evidence for other firms, which is fragmentary, suggests considerably lower ratios: 1:2.5 for Morgan Grenfell in 1910–13; 1:2.0 for Hambros in 1905; 1:3.1 for Antony Gibbs in 1893–1912; and 1:0.3 for Rothschilds in 1900. Third, the policy pursued by both houses of granting very large credits to clients prominent in certain commodity trades in the US, Germany and the UK. This practice did not pass unnoticed in the London discount market. In October 1901 the market was buzzing with talk about Schröders' problems in connection with its large credits for Lewisohns, the New York commodity broker, which was believed to have made large losses on its positions in coffee and copper. The rumours reached the ears of Hermann Kleinwort, who wrote to Goldman Sachs, then a New York commercial paper dealer with which Kleinworts conducted joint account securities business, that 'J. H. Schröder & Co., who are reported to have accepted enormous amounts, are giving rise to some little comment. We hear that some of the Banks have lately declined the

Table 5.3 Acceptances of some leading merchant banks and commercial banks, 1893, 1903, 1913

31 December	1893 £ million	1903 £ million	1913 £ million
MERCHANT BANKS			
Kleinwort, Sons & Co.	5.6	8.6	14.2
J. Henry Schröder & Co.	4.8	6.7	11.7
Baring Brothers & Co. Ltd	3.0	3.8	6.6
Brown, Shipley & Co.	n/a	n/a	5.1
C.J. Hambro & Son	1.2	1.9	4.6
Wm Brandt Sons & Co.	0.6	(1902) 1.1	3.3
N.M. Rothschild & Sons	2.8	1.2	3.2
Morgan Grenfell & Co.	4.2	(1901) 5.3	2.8
Antony Gibbs & Sons	0.4	0.9	1.2
BRITISH JOINT STOCK BANKS			
London County & Westminster Bank Ltd		1.6	7.7
Lloyds Bank, Ltd		2.6	7.5
London City & Midland Bank Ltd		2.0	6.1
Parr's Bank Ltd		3.5	5.4
Union of London & Smiths Bank Ltd		2.5	5.0
National Provincial Bank of England Ltd		0.5	0.8
Barclay & Co. Ltd		0.1	0.3
GERMAN BANKS			
Dresdner Bank			14.4
Deutsche Bank	4.6	8.6	13.6
Disconto-Gesellschaft			12.5

Note: Information on other firms unavailable.

Sources: *The Bankers' Magazine*, 1904, 1914; Stanley Chapman, *The Rise of Merchant Banking* (London: George Allen & Unwin, 1984) p. 121; J. Henry Schröder & Co., balance sheets; Kathleen Burk, *Morgan Grenfell 1838–1988* (Oxford University Press, 1989) p. 278; Stephanie Diaper, 'Kleinwort, Sons, & Co. in the History of Merchant Banking, 1855–1966' (unpublished PhD thesis, University of Nottingham, 1983) p. 145; Manfred Pohl, 'Deutsche Bank London Agency Founded 100 Years Ago', *Deutsche Bank Studies* (1973) no. 10, p. 23.

name of Schröder on the ground that the amounts drawn by certain parties on them were too large'.[32] What Kleinwort had in mind when he referred to 'enormous amounts' was made plain in a letter to Brandts on the subject of Schröders and Lewisohns written at the same time. 'Their acceptances on this account surprised me as they were more than their capital,' wrote Kleinwort, commenting, 'the thing is too big for us.'[33] While at one point the credit exposure may indeed have been in excess of the firm's capital of £1.6 million, by the year end it had been reduced to £433,000, still a very large sum, but not dissimilar in scale to the financing being provided by Kleinworts to US clients such as William Ryle & Co., a New York silk importer, or the American Sugar Refining Co.[34]

In summary, the rapid growth and large scale of Schröders' and Kleinworts' acceptances was the outcome of the pursuit of bolder business practices than their rivals. Each of their policies increased their risk exposure: country risk, from the focus on US and German clientele; client risk, from the large scale of individual credits, which breached the traditional conservative canons about the conduct of acceptance activity; and volume risk, from the high ratios of acceptances to capital. But the credit judgement of both firms proved excellent and the rewards for their enterprise were high profits.

Bruno Schröder also took a bold approach to securities dealing on the firm's account. 'They are fond of big deals', commented Hermann Kleinwort, referring to this side of Schröders' business in October 1901, 'and do a lot of speculation (through Greenwells).'[35] In 1893–1904, the firm's revenues from securities dealing averaged £13,000 per annum, which increased to £16,000 in 1905–13 (see Table 5.1 on page 124). Revenues from securities dealing varied widely, as would be expected, ranging from £55,000 in 1909 to nil in 1897, 1907 and 1913.

Under Bruno's direction Schröders' non-accepting banking activities were also profitably expanded, with increases in both client balances and deposits on the one hand, and advances and bond investments on the other. The new policy is reflected in the increase in net interest revenues, which rose from an average of £2,000 per annum in 1883–92, to £18,000 in 1893–1904 and to £74,000 in 1905–13 (see Table 5.1 on page 124). The development of the pattern of assets and liabilities in these decades is shown in Figure 5.3. At the time of Bruno's arrival, Schröders' balance sheet assets were very liquid indeed: 65 per cent commercial bills; perhaps 15–20 per cent cash and call loans; and 15–20 per cent, investments, advances and fixed assets, the accounts not permitting precise identification. Beginning in 1894, a new pattern of assets evolved: commercial bills 30 per cent; cash and call loans 30 per cent; advances 20 per cent; and investments – gilts, debentures and equities – 20 per cent. These changes were accompanied by reforms of Schröders' system of financial control – the commencement of a systematic 10 per cent annual allocation to a bad debts reserve and the preparation of summary balance sheets as a complement to trial balances. Schröders' call-loan clients were a handful of leading Stock Exchange firms, discount houses and foreign exchange specialists. W. Greenwell & Co. was invariably the largest borrower amongst the stockbrokers, though substantial loans were also regularly made to de Zoete & Gorton & Co., A. G. Schiff & Co., and Jourdan, Pawle & Co. From the 1880s to 1904, M. Corgialegno & Co. was much the most important call loan client amongst the discount houses, one of the partners being a Lubbock who was related by marriage to the Tiarks.[36] Other City firms that were regular call loan recipients were the New Zealand Loan and Mercantile Credit Agency, of which Baron Bruno was a director, and B. W. Blydenstein & Co., S. Japhet & Co. and Haarbleicher & Schumann & Co., the firms of German origin which were specialist dealers in foreign bills and currencies, and in international securities arbitrage.[37]

Over the years 1908–13, Schröders' cash and call loans increased from around 30 per cent of assets to 36 per cent, a move which matched the increase in advances, the most illiquid of its assets, from 20 per cent to 24 per cent. The bill portfolio shrank further as a result of these developments. The list of stockbrokers, jobbers, discount houses and other City firms to which Schröders made call loans lengthened greatly in these years. Six-figure sums were loaned to nine stockbrokers or jobbers, including, W. Greenwell, Rowe & Pitman, and de Zoete & Gorton & Co., and to seven discount houses. Much of the increase in advances went to acceptance credit clients, many of whom were German or Austrian, a development that caused problems for the firm on the outbreak of war in 1914.

The shift in the asset portfolio was a consequence of a transformation of the liabilities side of the balance sheet. In the 1870s, 1880s and 1890s the ratio of partners' capital to balances and deposits averaged around 3:1. In the early 1900s this ratio declined to 2:1 as balances and deposits increased faster than partners' capital. In 1907, partners' capital was £2.2 million and balances and deposits were £1.6 million. The following year partners' capital was £2.4 million but balances and deposits had soared to £4.2 million, a ratio of 1:2. This important development, which proved permanent, was initially the result of the placement of large sums with the firm by the Brazilian state of San Paulo and the Russian Banque de l'État, greatly enhancing Schröders' role as a repository for the sterling balances of foreign governments. Another significant move towards the adoption of a more bank-like approach to the conduct of business was the firm's registration with the Inland Revenue as a bank in 1906, because by doing this it was able to take advantage of privileges under legislation covering crossed cheques.[38] Many of its peers in the City did likewise in the first decade of the twentieth century, a

134

Figure 5.3 J. Henry Schröder & Co., balance sheet structures, 1883–1913

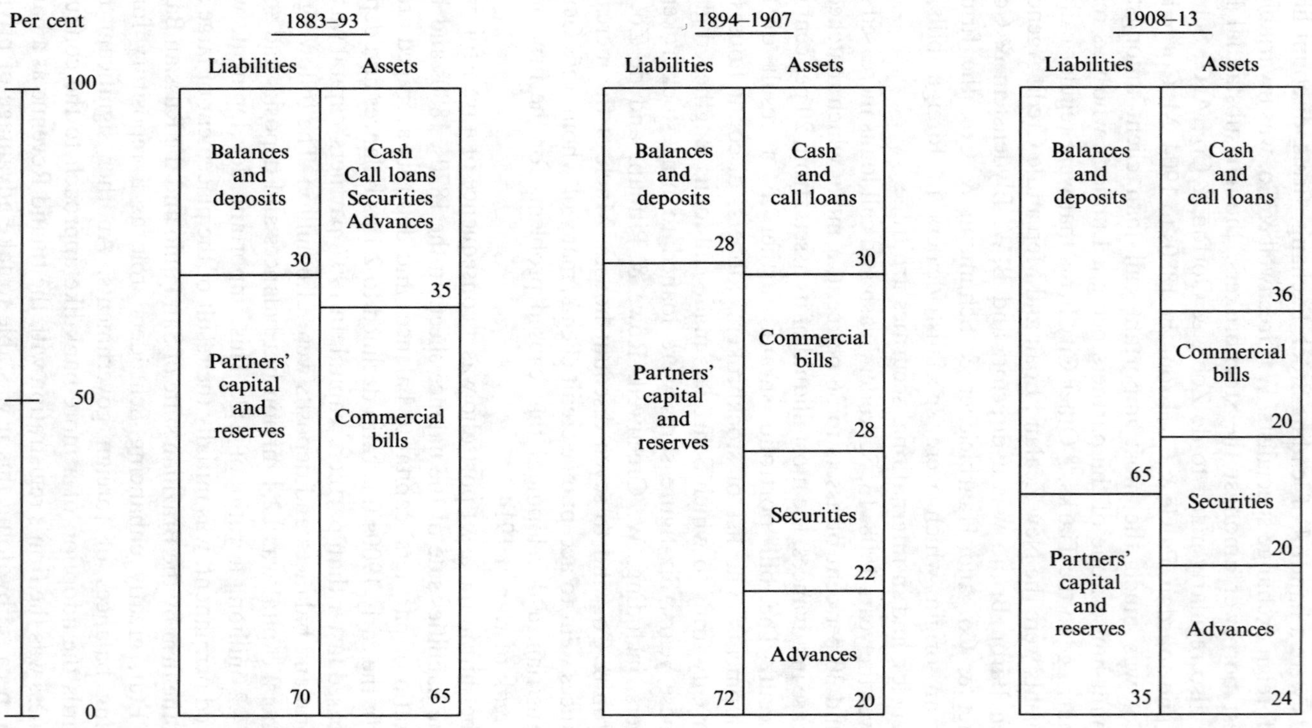

Source: J. Henry Schröder & Co., balance sheets, 1883–1913.

development marked by a semantic watershed – the term 'merchant bankers' came into general usage in the industry.

Issuing and Underwriting

Schröders' revenues from issuing and underwriting varied considerably from year to year in the 1890s and 1900s, ranging from nil in 1893 and 1895, to £301,000 in 1909 (see Figure 5.4). The fluctuations in the firm's activity closely followed the pattern of sterling issues for overseas borrowers, which were modest in the 1890s but buoyant in the decade prior to the outbreak of the First World War: in 1893–1904, Schröders' revenues from issuing and underwriting totalled £246,000; in 1905–14, £1.5 million. The largest borrowers of the latter years were the countries of North and South America[39] and it was the firm's strong connections in both parts of the Western Hemisphere that were the principal, though not the only, reasons for its active participation in the boom. A notable development in the pattern of Schröders' issuing and underwriting activity in the 1890s, and particularly the 1900s, was the increase in the extent to which issues were syndicated amongst consortia of financial houses, more and more of the business arising from such ties.

The imposition of a tariff duty upon Cuban sugar exports to the US in 1894 and the armed uprising of 1895–98, which brought Spanish colonial rule to an end, had a devastating impact upon the island's sugar

Figure 5.4   J. Henry Schröder & Co., issuing and underwriting revenues, and sterling issues for overseas borrowers, 1893–1914

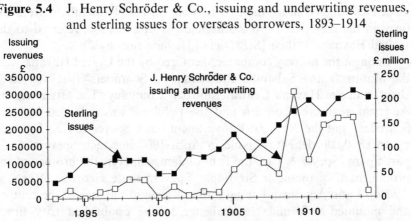

Source: Sterling issues – Mathew Simon, 'The Pattern of British Portfolio Foreign Investment, 1865–1914', in A. R. Hall (ed.), *The Export of Capital from Britain 1870–1914* (London: Methuen, 1968) p. 38.

industry. The United Railways of the Havana and Regla Warehouses Co., the Cuban-registered company whose bonds had been issued by Schröders in 1890 and with whose affairs it was closely concerned, was badly affected by the civil war and was only able to pay the interest on its bonds in 1897 because of a £38,000 advance from the firm. The following year, Schröders organised the acquisition of this company by an English registered company of an identical name formed for the purpose under the chairmanship of Emanuel Underdown – the firm's first cross-border corporate acquisition. To finance the purchase Schröders sponsored a £2 million debenture issue, Bruno Schröder and Frank Tiarks acting as trustees for the bondholders. The Cuban sugar industry revived in the 1900s, following the end of hostilities and the securing of preferential tariff status in the US in 1903, though sugar prices continued to fall because of the rapidly rising output worldwide, particularly of sugar beet in continental Europe. These conditions led to a further rationalisation of the Cuban railway system to provide further integration and lower freight costs. Between 1905 and 1911, the United Havana grew from 390 kilometres to 1,100 kilometres, becoming Cuba's largest railway network and dominating rail transport in the western half of the island (see Map 3.1, page 60). This was accomplished by a series of acquisitions financed by bond issues managed by Schröders in 1905, 1906, 1907 and 1911. Economies of scale led to amalgamations amongst sugar estates, often instigated by new foreign, usually American, owners. One of the leading US firms was the Central Cuba Sugar Company formed in 1911, part of its financing being provided by the United Havana which raised the funds through a £1 million debenture issue conducted by Schröders. Overall, the funds raised by the firm for the United Havana and its associates totalled more than £5 million. So closely identified were the firms in the City that Lord Rothschild, writing in 1906, referred to the United Havana as 'their [Schröders'] Havana railway'.[40]

Amongst the railway companies acquired by the United Havana were the Matanzas and Sabanilla Railroad Co., Schröders' first new issue client, and the Havana Central Railroad Company. The latter was an American-registered concern and the purchase was arranged between Schröders and the New York investment bank Speyer & Co., financed by an £800,000 debenture issue in April 1907 in which Speyers was a participant. Speyer & Co., the firm of James Speyer, the brother of the prominent City financier Sir Edgar Speyer, made vigorous efforts to develop Latin American issuing business around the turn of the century and mounted a formidable challenge to the established City firms. Schröders decided to do a deal with Speyer and immediately after the Havana Central transaction the firms drew up a 10-year agreement whereby each undertook to offer the other 'ground floor participation' of 25 per cent in all Cuban corporate business and 10 per cent in issues for the government, though both firms were free to compete to secure the business covered by the agreement and neither was bound to accept the participations.[41] The 'Speyer Agreement' was an important extension of Schröders' links with Wall Street and soon led to co-operation in business beyond Cuba.

Schröders' close involvement in the Chilean nitrate industry led to further issues on behalf of Chilean borrowers in the 1890s and 1900s. Vorwerk & Co.'s local office appears to have secured for it the issuing business of the municipality of Valparaiso, which raised two loans through Schröders to finance improvements to the city's water supply. In 1894, the firm sponsored an issue of £200,000 bonds, with a 5.5 per cent coupon and a 25-year maturity, which were purchased by the firm at 85.5 and issued at 94, providing a handsome spread for Schröders and a 5.85 per cent yield. The issue of 1912 was for £250,000 bonds with a 5.5 per cent coupon which were priced at 99, trimming the yield to 5.55 per cent. Weber & Co., the merchant house with offices in both Hamburg and Valparaiso, was behind the formation of the Amelia Nitrate Co., which was established to purchase three nitrate works near Pisagua in the province of Tarapaca in northern Chile. The firm was incorporated in England to facilitate access to the London capital market, and in February 1896 an agreement was signed between Weber & Co. and Schröders whereby the latter purchased £73,500 ordinary shares, £15,000 6 per cent preference shares, and £250,000 5.5 per cent debentures. The ordinary shares, which represented 70 per cent of the company's equity, and the preference shares were privately placed by Schröders, some being retained for the firm's account. The debentures were issued to the public at 97.5, redeemable at 105 in 1906, and Henry Tiarks and Walpole Greenwell were appointed trustees for the debenture holders. Bruno Schröder joined the board of the Amelia Nitrate Co. in 1896 and in 1907 became chairman, a position he retained for the following twenty years. Also on the board was the senior partner of Gildemeister & Co., another Hamburg–Latin American merchant house, for which Schröders provided acceptance facilities in London and later New York.

The bulk of Schröders' capital raising on behalf of Chilean clients was to finance railway construction. In 1900, 1904, 1906 and 1907, the firm made debenture issues on behalf of the Antofagasta (Chili) and Bolivia Railway Company, which raised £2.65 million for improvements to the its 600 miles of track and port facilities (see Map 4.1, on page 102). An agreement to incorporate the 223 miles of railway which served the nitrate fields of Aguas Blancas into the Antofagasta system, led to the formation of the Aguas Blancas Railway Company as a subsidiary of the Antofagasta Railway. In March 1909, Schröders issued £900,000 4.5 per cent debentures for this new subsidiary. 'The subscription lists were only opened a few hours,' reported the *South American Journal*, 'and it was promptly announced that the issue had been over applied for, with the result that the stock immediately commanded a substantial premium . . . It is obvious that this issue presents a splendid opportunity for obtaining an investment to give a substantial return, and which is about as secure as anything possibly can be.'[42]

Another promising source of traffic for the Antofagasta Railway was the mineral deposits of Bolivia, which were being actively developed at the turn of the century. In 1906 the Bolivian Government conferred a concession for the construction of railways in Bolivia upon Speyer & Co. and the National City Bank of New York for which purpose they formed the Bolivia Railway Company (see Map 4.1, on page 102). In October 1908, as the Bolivia Railway's first line neared completion, Speyer & Co. came to an agreement with Schröders regarding future issues on behalf of the Antofagasta Railway and the Bolivia Railway, whereby each firm agreed to give the other participations of up to 50 per cent.[43] This was followed in December 1908 by an agreement between the Antofagasta Railway and the Bolivia Railway, whereby the former acquired a lease of the existing and projected lines of the latter which were incorporated into its system. In July 1910, Schröders issued £600,000 debentures for the Bolivia Railway Company, for which the trustees were Baron Bruno, Frank Tiarks and Sir Walpole Greenwell. As a result of the agreement with the Bolivia Railway and the incorporation of the Aguas Blancas Railway's lines the Antofagasta Railway network more than doubled to 1,328 miles. Schröders' expertise in the affairs of the Antofagasta Railway was put to use by actively trading the firm's debentures, which generated dealing profits in most years.

In 1908, the government of Chile decided to construct the Chilean Longitudinal Railway, a line running the length of the country south from Santiago to Puerto Montt, to promote the development of mineral deposits.[44] In London the Howard Syndicate, named after one of its participants, Lord Howard de Walden, was formed to negotiate for the construction contract. Another participant was the Ethelburger Syndicate, a buccaneering Anglo-French consortium which was described by the Controller of Commercial Affairs at the Foreign Office as 'a highly speculative organisation' composed of investors who 'seem to like risky business and can be left to look after themselves'.[45] The Ethelburger Syndicate was especially active in Latin America, securing the Venezuelan salt and match monopolies in 1905, and the Bolivian match monopoly in 1907. All these concessions were negotiated on the Ethelburger Syndicate's behalf by Albert Pam, one of the City's leading authorities on Latin American business, and he was engaged to negotiate for the construction contract for the Longitudinal Railway on behalf of the Howard Syndicate. The Chilean president took a close interest in the project and personally conducted the protracted negotiations with Pam, which were eventually brought to a successful conclusion in May 1910. The £4 million required was raised on the Chilean government's behalf by a financial syndicate led by Schröders, which conducted three issues of Chilean Government 5 per cent bonds in 1912, 1913 and 1914. These were lead-managed by Schröders in London, with Greenwells as brokers, and simultaneously issued by Schröder Gebrüder in Hamburg, by the branches of the Banque de Paris et des Pays Bas in Brussels, Amsterdam and Geneva, and by other banks in Antwerp and Lausanne. The financial syndicate took over the construction contract from the Howard Syndicate, engaging the eminent engineer Sir Norton Griffiths to undertake the work. Inadequate supervision resulted in a final cost far in excess of the agreed price, causing the bankruptcy of the contractor. Pam estimated that the loss to the financial syndicate from this 'very unfortunate contract' was as much as £1 million.

The Peruvian default of 1876 was long remembered by investors, and at Schröders, but by the beginning of the second decade of the twentieth century the country's creditworthiness was restored. In 1910, Schröders sponsored an issue of £1.2 million debentures on behalf of the Lima Light, Power and Tramways Co., which was formed to acquire and amalgamate these utilities in the Peruvian capital. The issue was made simultaneously by Schröders in London, Schröder Gebrüder in Hamburg, and also in Belgium and Switzerland. The following year Schröders sponsored a loan for the government of Peru, which it brought out with a yield of 5.58 per cent, compared to yields of 7.3 per cent in 1870 and 6.45 per cent in 1872, reflecting Peru's rehabilitation as a borrower. The £1.2 million raised was earmarked for the purchase of two small cruisers, and the income of the state salt monopoly was hypothecated to the bondholders to pay the interest on the loan. Simultaneous with the issue by Schröders in London, the loan was brought out by Schröder Gebrüder in Hamburg, and by the Banque de Paris et des Pays-Bas and the Société Genérale in Paris, leading French banks which were often members of Schröders' international syndicates in the Edwardian era.

San Paulo Coffee Valorisation Loans

Schröders' involvement in Brazilian issues had its origin in an inadvertent turn in Schröder Gebrüder's banking business.[46] In 1885, Zerrenner Bulow & Co. of Sao Paulo and Santos, an acceptance client of the Hamburg house, was unable to meet its debts and Schröder Gebrüder was obliged to accept payment in its equity. Zerrenner Bulow & Co. conducted a large import/export business and also owned a number of coffee plantations and the thriving 'Bavaria' brewery in Sao Paulo. The business was soon turned round and Schröder Gebrüder realised its interest, but the legacy was close ties to the Brazilian coffee growers. This led to the sponsorship of a City of Santos loan by J. Henry Schröder & Co. in 1888 and lay behind its appointment as London paying agent for a £787,000 loan issued that year by the London stockbroker Lewis Cohen for the state of San Paulo – in Britain in the early twentieth century the state was known as 'San Paulo' while the city was called 'Sao Paulo'. In 1897, Schröder Gebrüder purchased a large coffee plantation which was for sale on favourable terms, appointing Zerrenner Bulow & Co. its managing agent. A public company, the San Paulo Coffee Estates Co., was formed in London, which purchased the estate from Schröder Gebrüder with funds provided by a public issue, sponsored by Schröders, of £160,000 debentures and £120,000 preference shares. Henry Tiarks became chairman of the board, and Johann Rudolph II, Bruno's elder brother, a director, control of the voting equity being retained by Schröders and Schröder Gebrüder, which thereby became closely involved in the Brazilian coffee industry. These connections led to an issue in 1899 for the state of San Paulo of £1 million bonds to provide funds for improvements to the drainage, sanitation and water supply in the cities of Sao Paulo and Santos, and for the sponsorship of immigration.

Coffee production dominated the economy of the state of San Paulo, and the livelihoods of its inhabitants were heavily dependent upon the crop. Their prosperity fluctuated considerably from year to year because of wide variations in the size of the harvest, which resulted in sharp movements in the price of coffee. It was well established that very large harvests were followed by abnormally small ones, because of soil exhaustion.[47] This suggested the possibility of intervention, termed 'valorisation', to stabilise coffee prices, by the state government making purchases when supplies were abundant and selling stocks when they were short.[48] In 1905, a delegation from San Paulo visited Europe seeking finance for the establishment of an intervention fund. When they visited Rothschilds, the fiscal agent of the Brazilian federal government since the 1820s, they were told that the firm saw the scheme as costly and unworkable. 'Holding these views,' a partner explained to the Finance Minister of the state government, 'we naturally could not give our name to a Loan.'[49]

When Schröders were approached the following year, Baron Bruno took a different view. By then the circumstances of the San Paulo coffee growers was transformed by the enormous size of the impending crop. 'This one is, without question, a bumper,' Naumann, Gepp & Co., coffee merchants of London and Santos, informed Rothschilds.[50] The coffee firm estimated world output for 1906 at 19–20 million bags, of which San Paulo would grow 12 million and other Brazilian producers 3 million, against world consumption of 17 million bags. The shortfall in demand was thus estimated at 2–3 million bags and if the collapse of the price of coffee was to be avoided, the implementation of the valorisation scheme was urgent. The state of San Paulo enlisted the assistance of Baron Bruno and Hermann Sielcken, the German-born head of the leading New York coffee traders Crossman and Sielcken, who put together a syndicate of eleven firms which advanced intervention funds: Schröders and Kleinworts in London; three Hamburg merchants, including, naturally, Schröder Gebrüder; three Le Havre merchants; Crossman and Sielcken and another coffee firm in New York; and Theodor Wille & Co. of Santos, Rio and Hamburg.[51] Purchases began in the autumn of 1906 and by February 1907 the state of San Paulo had acquired a stockpile of 3 million bags. The impact, according to a well-informed contemporary, was that 'it enabled Brazil to sell nearly ten million bags at about 10 per cent more money than they would otherwise have received'.[52]

By the early months of 1907 it was becoming clear that the size of the San Paulo crop of 1906 was not 12 million bags but no less than 16 million bags. Thus the state and the syndicate were faced by the choice of abandoning valorisation, which would lead to the collapse of the price of coffee, ruining many coffee growers and jeopardising repayment of the loans already made, or committing two or perhaps three times as much money to it as originally envisaged. Rothschilds remained deeply hostile to the scheme and to its architects, 'the great house', as Lord Rothschild sarcastically referred to Schröders, and the 'American speculator', as he called Sielcken, but the state of San Paulo and the Schröder syndicate determined to proceed.[53] By May 1908, 8 million bags had been accumulated and there must have been a tense atmosphere in the private room at 145 Leadenhall Street as the partners waited for the smaller harvest of 1907 to be reflected in the market for coffee, which would allow the release of stocks.

Negotiations regarding the issue of a massive £15 million loan – about £660 million in 1990 money – by the state of San Paulo that would enable it to pay off its borrowings from the syndicate got under way with an international group of bankers in the summer of 1908. This group comprised Schröders, Société Genérale of Paris and M. M. Warburg of Hamburg. The terms of the loan were that the state of San Paulo's stockpile of coffee was pledged as collateral for the debt and its realisation was controlled by a valorisation committee, of which Baron Bruno was chairman. Sales were made when conditions were favourable and the proceeds used to purchase bonds in the market. The success of the loan with investors depended crucially upon the bestowal of a guarantee by the Brazilian federal government as to the payment of interest, but this was unlikely without Rothschilds' agreement, and it was decided to send Frank Tiarks to Rothschilds' office at New Court to argue the case. He recalled that he:

> was received by old Lord Rothschild and Mr Leopold and Mr Alfred Rothschild. Old Natty (Nathaniel) as he was called disliked the Valorisation Loan intensely and lived up to his reputation for shall we say bluntness, and replied to my request, 'certainly not for that damned swindle'. I then told him that his plan for holding the Brazilian Exchange would break down at once if the £15 million Valorisation Loan was not carried through. He at once called in his Mr Nauheim, who confirmed to him that this would certainly be the case, and he thereupon agreed to ask for the guarantee at once as a matter of urgency.[54]

On Rothschilds' recommendation the Brazilian government took the necessary measures and the loan went ahead. 'This business which is not ours,' wrote Lord Rothschild to his Parisian cousins in November 1908, 'has given us more trouble than almost any we can recollect, indeed if it had not been for New Court we are quite convinced that it never could have been carried through and no doubt Messrs Schröder fully realise this.'[55]

The prospectus for the £15 million state of San Paulo Coffee Valorisation Loan appeared in December 1908. It was, noted *The Economist*, 'remarkably well received'.[56] In fact, it was many times oversubscribed and Lord Rothschild informed his French cousins that 'the great event of the day in the City had been the success of the San Paulo loan, Messrs Schröder are quite delighted'.[57] After the initial confrontation the Schröders and Rothschild partners worked closely and amicably to ensure the loan's success. Rothschilds' reward was the offer of a £500,000 participation 'practically on bed-rock terms' of the £5 million of bonds offered for sale in London, which Lord Rothschild replied he was 'quite prepared to take'.[58]

Schröders' benefits from its leading role in the coffee valorisation scheme were substantial. There can be no doubt that it was this episode that established the firm as a major financial force in the perceptions of the City and the public. It established Schröders as the leading firm in coffee finance and the firm to which the state of San Paulo turned when it required further large loans, as it did in 1913, 1914 and after the First World War. It was in connection with the coffee loan that Schröders established relations with the Brazilian firm Monteiro Aranha, which became a particularly close and long-standing 'friend'. Moreover, the business was highly profitable. Schröders' profits were earned in a variety of ways: interest was received on the large advances made as a member of the syndicate; the £15 million loan generated commissions and profits far greater than any other single business undertaken by the firm in the first century of its existence; and further commissions were earned for acting as paying agent for the bonds and for handling the sales of coffee. In total, the commissions and profits earned on the San Paulo issuing business alone between 1906 and 1913 amounted to £540,000, a third of the firm's total profits from issues and participations in these years. Lastly, from 1908 the state of San Paulo kept very large sterling balances with the firm in London, boosting net interest revenues and contributing to the jump in balance sheet deposits that year. However, the success of the coffee valorisation scheme should not obscure the gamble which the firm was taking. In December 1907, Schröders' advances to the state of San Paulo exceeded £300,000 – 15 per cent of the firm's capital – of which little would have been recovered had the coffee price collapsed and San Paulo defaulted. The San Paulo story is another example of Baron Bruno's bold approach to business, and again he reaped spectacular rewards.

Argentina was traditionally Barings' territory and Schröders conducted only one issue for an Argentinian client, a £185,000 debenture issue for the Buenos Aires Electric Tramways Co. Ltd in 1903, which was probably introduced by Greenwells. However, other firms were making inroads upon Barings' position in Argentinian finance, and on two occasions Schröders handled the London tranche of issues originated in other centres. The first was an Argentinian government loan issued in 1911 by a consortium of French and Belgian bankers. When Lord Revelstoke, the head of Barings, learned of Schröders' role he was furious: 'If they were a little bigger people,' he wrote to another Barings partner, 'they might have told Bemberg (the associate who had offered the participation to Schröders) to go to blazes and come round here to say they had done so, but the semitic blood which runs so freely through their veins does not seem to permit them to take the course which would have been obvious to a good Englishman.'[59] This outburst, which besides being splenetic and anti-Semitic was inaccurate since none of the Schröder partners was Jewish, was perhaps prompted by a feeling of betrayal, stemming from Barings' invitation to Schröders to join its underwriting syndicates in 1909 following the success of the Valorisation Loan. The most serious challenge to Barings' position in Argentinian finance was mounted by Speyer & Co., though eventually a truce was declared on the basis, explained a Barings partner, 'that they should leave our clients alone and we leave theirs, they keeping out of Argentine government and certain other specified business in that country and we out of Mexico. and Cuba'.[60] Nevertheless, in 1912 Speyer & Co. made a £1.5 million issue of 6 per cent secured notes on behalf of the Argentine Railway Company and Schröders conducted the London end, which perhaps provoked Lord Revelstoke to another fit of ill temper.

In the first decade of the twentieth century Schröders was a participant in several syndicates formed to issue loans for Mexican railway companies. Its involvement in these issues stemmed from its relations with the New York firms Ladenburg, Thalmann and Speyer & Co. In 1902, Schröders placed in London part of the $10 million bond issue brought out by Ladenburg, Thalmann on behalf of the Massachusetts-registered Mexican Central Railway Company. Nationalist resentment of the domination of Mexico's railway system by American companies led to the nationalisation of a large part of the country's mileage between 1906 and 1908.[61] In July 1907, an agreement was reached whereby the Mexican Central Railway was merged with the government's National Railroad Company to form the National Railways of Mexico, a government controlled network comprising some 7,000 miles of track. To finance the formation of the National Railways of Mexico. a powerful syndicate of four New York firms, including Ladenburg, Thalmann, Speyer & Co. and two German banks, was engaged to issue $225 million bonds. In February 1908 the syndicate appointed Schröders and Speyer Brothers (Speyer & Co.'s London associate) to issue £2.8 million of the bonds in London, and a further loan of £4.4 million was brought out in 1909. In 1910, Schröders in London, Schröder Gebrüder in Hamburg and Ladenburg, Thalmann in New York, issued a loan for the United Railways of the Yucatan, another Mexican railway company that had escaped being engulfed by the National Railways of Mexico. Finally, in June 1913, Schröders and Speyer Brothers issued a further loan for the National Railways of Mexico for £5.5 million. The degeneration of Mexico into civil war a few months later caused the National Railways of Mexico to default on the interest payment to bondholders due on 1 January 1914. This development subsequently led to criticism of Schröders and Speyer Brothers, 'than whom there are no more astute financiers', for proceeding with the issue in the summer of 1913.[62] The continued difficulties of the National Railways of Mexico led to the establishment of a bondholders' committee in London in 1917, of which Frank Tiarks was a leading member. In 1922, an international committee representing twenty-six banks, Schröders amongst them, from six countries eventually reached an agreement with the Mexican government for the resumption of payments.

During the 1890s and 1900s Schröders continued to conduct the joint-account business which it had begun in 1885 with Ladenburg, Thalmann, marketing and arbitraging US railway bonds in Europe. In these years it was a participant in numerous selling syndicates organised by Ladenburg, Thalmann: for instance, in February 1911, Schröders handled the London end of a $5 million bond issue for the Kansas City Southern Railway, which was brought out jointly in New York by Ladenburg, Thalmann and the National City Bank. It played a similar role in two issues originated by the New York investment bank Kuhn, Loeb in 1910: a $9.9 million bond issue for the Chicago, Milwaukee and St Paul Railway Co., which was issued simultaneously in Paris by four Parisian banks; and a $25 million bond issue for the Southern Pacific Co., which was also issued in five other European cities and four American ones. In 1911, it organised the London distribution of a £1 million sterling tranche of a $10 million bond issue on behalf of the Chicago, Rock Island & Pacific Railway Co., originated in New York by Speyer & Co. Although US railway bonds were popular with European investors there was little demand for the securities of US industrial corporations in the 1890s. One of the earliest US industrials to find favour was the $75 million share issue by the Amalgamated Copper Co. of New Jersey. It was brought out in New York in April 1899 by the National City Bank and distributed in London and on the Continent by Schröders as a participant in a selling syndicate organised by Lewisohn Brothers.[63] A transformation of the attitude of European investors was effected by the massive $1.2 billion US Steel issue of 1901, which was widely distributed in Europe as well as the US.[64] Schröders played a part in the marketing of US Steel stock as a member of selling syndicates put together by both Greenwells and Ladenburg, Thalmann. In 1902, it joined the Ladenburg, Thalmann selling syndicate handling part of a $35 million Lackawanna Steel Co. issue. Ladenburg, Thalmann was also the origin of the introduction of the Pierce Oil Corporation whose buy-out from the Standard Oil Trust in 1912–13 was partially financed by Schröders – the firm's first buy-out business.[65] The development of strong ties with Wall Street securities houses was complementary to the expansion of Schröders' US acceptance business in the early years of the twentieth century, and served as a springboard for the establishment of a presence in New York after the First World War.

Greenwells continued to be the stockbrokers with whom Schröders worked most closely in the 1890s and 1900s, though this special relationship did not preclude participation in the underwriting syndicates of other brokers, notably R. Nivison and Panmure Gordon.

Membership of Greenwell's underwriting and distribution syndicates led to small participations in issues for British companies, such as: Robinson's Brewery in 1896; Trustees Executors and Securities Corporation in 1897; Frederick's Hotel in 1899; and for Brighton Corporation and the states of Natal, Victoria and Queensland in 1901. Greenwells was also a common factor in the issues made by Schröders for the Pretoria-Pietersburg Railway Co. of South Africa in 1899, and the Manx Electric Railway Co. in 1906. Most likely City connections were also responsible for Schröders' introduction to the Australian Estates and Mortgage Co., for which the firm made debenture issues in 1894 and 1896.

Bruno Schröder's German connections were perhaps behind the issue conducted by Schröders on behalf of the Apollinaris & Johannis Company Ltd in 1897. This was a British-registered concern which was formed to acquire and combine two German mineral water companies, which owned the Apollinaris spring at Bad Neuenahr in the Rhineland and the Johannis spring near Nassau in Hessen. The moving spirit behind this initiative was Frederick Gordon, the chairman of Gordon Hotels, who put together a consortium to buy the companies comprising, somewhat improbably, the London, Brighton and South Coast Railway, the East and West India Dock Company, and Bovril Ltd. The public issue undertaken by Schröders allowed these parties to realise their investments. It comprised 119,000 £10 ordinary shares, the first time that the firm made an equity issue for a manufacturing concern, a further £957,500 in preference shares, and £600,000 in debentures. The Apollinaris & Johannis Company supplied 70,000 addressed envelopes for the despatch of prospectuses, many of them to Germany, and Schröders and Greenwells distributed a further 10,000. Thanks to these efforts the issue was considerably over-subscribed.

In 1909, Schröders and Schröder Gebrüder jointly financed the purchase of an Argentinian sugar plantation and processing plant at Cruz Alta by the Hamburg firm Duhnkrack & Sohn, which had an important subsidiary in Buenos Aires.[66] Schröders advanced £125,000, while Schröder Gebrüder subscribed for 10 per cent of the company that had been formed to own the Cruz Alta interests, Deutsch Argentinische Zucker Plantagen AG, intending to sell the shares to the public through the Hamburg Stock Exchange once a sound trading record had been established. Schröders' interests were represented on the board of the Deutsch Argentinische Zucker by Dr Poelchau, a partner in Poelchau & Schröder, a merchant firm that was appointed as agent for the London firm in Hamburg in 1913, and Johann Rudolph II represented Schröder Gebrüder. The flotation was planned for 1912 but this could not be achieved and the oubreak of the First World War put an end to any hopes of marketing the company, or of Schröders recovering its loans, which by then amounted to £135,000. In 1915, Duhnkrack's Buenos Aires house collapsed with large debts, and the outcome of a complex series of transactions was that the Cruz Alta properties passed into the possession of the Schröder partners. After the war the Deutsch Argentinische Zucker Plantagen AG was wound up, and an Argentinian company, the Ingenio Azucarero Cruz Alta SA, was formed, with its head office in Buenos Aires. This was floated in the early 1920s, though Baron Bruno and Frank Tiarks retained a controlling equity interest.

Schröders' close ties with Schröder Gebrüder in Hamburg, with other German firms, and with banks in Paris, the Low Countries and Switzerland provided the firm with impressive continental placing power for securities issued in London. This ability was attractive to borrowers who wanted an international distribution of their securities, and benefited both the London firm and its associates on the Continent. The relationship also worked in reverse, and the continental connections, especially Schröder Gebrüder, led to the lead-management by Schröders in London of several issues for continental public authorites which would otherwise probably have been made on a continental bourse. In 1909, and again in 1911, there were bond issues for the City of Helsingfors (Helsinki) of £640,000 and £1 million, respectively, and in 1912 £3.8 million was raised for the City of Moscow to finance civic improvements. More significant in terms of Schröders' prestige were the loans which it undertook for continental European sovereign borrowers, the first time it acted for such clients. In 1910, Schröders lead-managed a £3.9 million loan for the Royal Bulgarian Government and in 1913 a £2 million loan for the Royal Romanian Government. On each occasion there was a simultaneous issue by Schröder Gebrüder in Hamburg and by banks in several other European financial centres.

In the final years before the First World War, Schröders' standing as one of the City's leading issuers of foreign loans as well as one of its foremost accepting houses received the recognition of its peers through invitations to join the syndicates that brought out massive loans on behalf of the Russian, Chinese and Austrian governments. In 1909, Barings suggested that Schröders should participate in its Russian syndicate, but the offer was declined, since Baron Bruno was dissatisfied with the terms, writing that 'we could not associate ourselves with any group in London in which our firm played a secondary role . . . however much we should like to be associated with you in such a business we cannot to our great regret waive this principle'.[67] Schröders eventually joined the syndicate on its terms in 1914, though the issue that was in prospect was aborted on the outbreak of war. In December 1912, the firm was made a member of the British group of the China Consortium. This body, which came into being in 1895, was a politically-inspired attempt to order the scramble for concessions in China between European, Russian, American and Japanese interests. The British group invited Schröders to join, to prevent the firm from proceeding with the issue of a Chinese loan in conjunction with Belgian interests.[68] The composition of the British group and the respective interests of the parties at this point were: the Hong Kong and Shanghai Banking Corporation, 33 per cent; Baring Brothers & Co. Ltd, 25 per cent; London County and Westminster Bank Ltd, 14 per cent; Parr's Bank Ltd, 14 per cent; and Schröders, 14 per cent. In 1913, the China Consortium organised a £25 million bond issue for the Chinese government, known as the 'Salt Loan' being secured by the proceeds of the salt tax, which was offered for subscription simultaneously in London, Germany, France, Russia and Belgium, of which the London tranche was £7.4 million. Schröders' Belgian connections led to its participation in large loans originated in Brussels in 1913 for the Lung-Tsing-U-Hai Railway, and in 1914 for the Tung Cheng Railway, which were outside the scope of the China Consortium. An invitation from Rothschilds jointly to lead-manage the syndicate it was putting together to make a £16.5 million treasury note issue for the Imperial Austrian Government arrived in the early months of 1914. The issue took place in April and was a great success. Thus by the eve of the First World War, Schröders had been accepted as an equal partner by the City's leading issuers of sovereign loans, paving the way for the establishment of the Baring–Rothschild–Schröder syndicate, the City's leading issuing syndicate, in the 1920s.

Financial Performance

The two decades before the First World War saw a tenfold increase in Schröders' profits – after deduction of 4 per cent interest on partners' capital – from £44,000 in 1893 to £428,000 in 1913, peaking in 1909 at £495,000, as a result of the state of San Paulo Coffee Valorisation Loan (see Figure 5.5) – £2 million, £18 million and £22 million respectively in 1990 money. The progress of the firm's profits was principally determined by the growth of aggregate operating revenues, costs being relatively stable. The major costs were: staff salaries and office overheads, and bad debt provisions, which averaged £19,000 and £18,000 per annum respectively in 1893–1904, and £33,000 and £37,000 in 1905–13. The introduction in 1895 of a 10 per cent annual payment to a bad debts reserve, in place of the year by year adjustments made

Figure 5.5   J. Henry Schröder & Co., net profits after interest on partners'
capital, 1893–1913

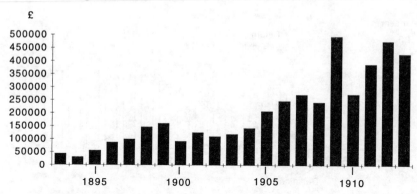

Note: Any liability for income tax was borne by the partners.

previously, reduced the fluctuations in the level of profits. The growth of
profits was moderate in the 1890s and early 1900s, but accelerated in the
years of the overseas issuing boom, averaging £98,000 per annum in
1893–1903 and £318,000 in 1904–13. Aggregate profits in the years 1893–
1913 amounted to £4.3 million most of which was committed to the
business, and financed an increase in capital and reserves of £2.5 million
and the withdrawal of £1 million of capital by Henry Tiarks and John
Henry. Between 1893 and 1903, the partners' capital grew from
£1,125,000 to £1,822,000, a 50 per cent increase. But by 1913 the
capital was £3,544,000, almost double the amount of 1903.

The return on capital earned by Schröders in the 1890s and 1900s
divides into two eras – before and after 1905. In 1893–1904 – including
the partners' 4 per cent interest – it averaged 10.68 per cent; in 1905–13,
16.62 per cent (see Figure 5.6). Prices fluctuated somewhat in the 1890s,
but were stable in the 1900s and the real rates of return were little
different from the nominal rates in these years. Throughout the period
1893–1913 the rates of return achieved by the firm provided the partners
with substantial premiums over the yields available from portfolio
investments – four times the average yield on consols in 1893–1904 and
five times in 1905–13. Moreover, in the latter period Schröders' rate of
return was almost three times the 5.74 per cent estimated average return
for British banking as a whole, the only industry yardstick available.[69]
The sustained high level of performance of the years 1905–13, which
surpassed even the guano era of the early 1870s, propelled the firm to the
forefront of the London merchant banks.

Figure 5.6 J. Henry Schröder & Co., return on capital and annual rate of inflation, 1893–1913

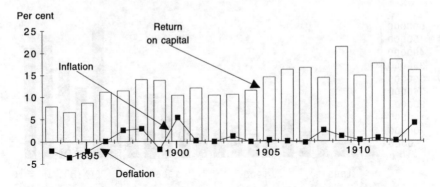

Note: The 'real' return on capital is the difference between the nominal return on capital depicted above and the annual rate of inflation.

Schröders' capital and reserves of £3.65 million in 1913 was the second largest amongst the merchant banks, being surpassed only by Kleinworts' £4.56 million (see Table 5.4). The gulf between the scale of capital of Schröders and Kleinworts and the £1 million or so capital of the other leading firms is a notable feature of Table 5.4. It echoes the gap in the size of the firms' acceptance business, which partly explains the discrepancy, since the larger scale of the leading firms' acceptance business necessitated more capital. However, it also reflected the success of Schröders and Kleinworts and the commitment of their partners to building their businesses. Schröders' success made the firm's partners very rich men. At the time of his death in 1911, Henry Tiarks' estate was in excess of £500,000, while John Henry's was £2,079,000, one of only thirty fortunes in excess of £2 million left in the years 1895–1914.[70]

On the eve of the First World War, J. Henry Schröder & Co. was at the peak of success. In the scale of its capital and its acceptances it was the City's second largest merchant bank. Moreover, in contrast to Kleinworts, which did not undertake issuing business, it was also one of the City's top issuing houses, an activity that conferred a prestige and public profile on a par with Barings, Rothschilds, Morgan Grenfell or Hambros. In combination, these achievements gave Schröders a fair claim to the title of the leading international financial firm in the world's leading international financial centre. Remarkably this role was performed by a team of two partners and forty clerks operating on a capital of £3.5 million – about £150 million in 1990 money. Sustaining

Table 5.4 Capital of some leading merchant banks, c. 1913

Merchant Banks	Year	Capital £ million
Kleinwort, Sons & Co.	1913	4.56
J. Henry Schröder & Co.	1913	3.65
Antony Gibbs & Sons	1913	1.22
Morgan Grenfell & Co.	1913	1.05
Baring Brothers & Co. Ltd	1913	1.03 [1]
C. J. Hambro & Son	1914	c. 1.00
N. M. Rothschild & Sons	c. 1914	c. 1.00
Lazard Brothers & Co.	c. 1914	c. 1.00
Wm Brandt Sons & Co.	c. 1914	c. 1.00
Brown, Shipley & Co.	1914	0.78
Frederick Huth & Co.	1913	0.75

1. Issued share capital excluding inner reserves.
Note: Information on other firms available.

Sources: Stanley Chapman, *The Rise of Merchant Banking* (London: George Allen & Unwin, 1984) p. 55; J. Henry Schröder & Co., balance sheets; Kathleen Burk, *Morgan Grenfell 1838–1988* (Oxford University Press, 1989) p. 268; Stephanie Diaper, 'Kleinwort, Sons & Co. in the History of Merchant Banking, 1855–1966' (unpublished PhD thesis, University of Nottingham, 1983) p. 53.

such a performance would have proved difficult under any circumstances, but the outbreak of hostilities in 1914 threatened not only Schröders' pre-eminence but its very existence.

6

The First World War

1914–18

The declaration of war by Britain on Germany at midnight on 4 August 1914 created a crisis for J. Henry Schröder & Co., since Baron Bruno's German nationality meant that his firm was liable to seizure as enemy property. Immediately, Frank Tiarks set about securing his partner's naturalisation. Tiarks had a public as well as a personal motive for his action, being closely involved as a director of the Bank of England in the endeavours to handle the crisis that had engulfed the City during the preceding week and a half as Central Europe became engulfed in war. More than anyone, Tiarks understood the threat to the position of the City posed by the potential sequestration of Schröders, which would make it impossible for the firm to honour much of its £11 million outstanding acceptances. Tiarks informed Walter Cunliffe, the Governor of the Bank of England, of the seriousness of the situation, who took it up with the Home Secretary, Reginald McKenna, informing him 'that it would be a disaster – no less a word was used – if the doors of Baron Schröder did not open on the following morning'.[1] At the same time representations on Baron Bruno's behalf were apparently also being made by Benjamin Guinness, a partner in Ladenburg, Thalmann & Co., who was a friend of the Prime Minister, Herbert Asquith.[2] The outcome was a promise of immediate naturalisation.

But Tiarks was determined to make doubly sure. Supported by William Slaughter, the senior partner of the City solicitors Slaughter and May, he suggested that Baron Bruno should also be given a royal licence 'to reside and trade in this country so as to avoid any question that might arise as to the legality of the firm's operations in the event of the naturalisation being delayed or irregular'.[3] Such licences had last been granted in 1855 when Queen Victoria had conferred them on seven Russian merchants during the Crimean War. Home Office officials were of the view that no licence was necessary, but Tiarks and Slaughter 'were not satisfied. They said that a different opinion had been given by earlier counsel, and that other counsel might take a different view now. The matter was far too important to leave any room for doubt'. Tiarks got his way and on Friday 7 August 1914 Baron Bruno was issued with both a naturalisation certificate from the Home Secretary and a licence to reside and trade signed by King George V. The threat of sequestration was over, but the commercial problems were only just beginning.

The crisis in the City in late July and early August 1914 had several dimensions, but the most immediately alarming was the prospect of the interruption of remittances on account of acceptance credits outstanding to foreign firms. This created a problem for acceptors of bills, who were obliged to make payment when they matured without being themselves paid by their clients. Most critically affected were the merchant banks; a partner in Brown, Shipley informed an American colleague that 'the Accepting Banks and Houses are in greater or lesser degree insolvent: there is hardly one among them whose cash in hand would permit of Acceptances already falling due being paid'.[4] However, it was not only acceptors, which included the clearing banks, who were in trouble: the holders of bills faced the prospect of being unable to realise their assets, thus making them unable to meet their liabilities. This threatened the wholesale failure of the discount houses and additional difficulties for the merchant banks and clearing banks, which also had considerable holdings of bills. Moreover, the clearing banks had large outstanding call loans to the discount houses, which the latter were unable to repay, presenting a further danger to the soundness of the banking structure. Yet another blow was the closure of the Stock Exchange on 31 July because of a crash in securities prices, which made it impossible to recover call loans to brokers or to gain liquidity by the sale of bonds or shares. By the beginning of August 1914 the whole edifice of the City of London as a financial centre was teetering on collapse. Catastrophe was averted by the government's declaration on 2 August of a month's moratorium on the settlement of outstanding bills, providing a breathing space to address the tangle of problems.

On 5 August, the first day of the war, partners from twenty-one of the City's merchant banks convened in the office of Frederick Huth & Co. to discuss the situation.[5] This unprecedented assembly was itself testimony to their anxieties, particularly on the part of the firms which conducted extensive business with German and Austrian clients, contemporary calculations suggesting £60–70 million outstanding acceptance liabilities by enemy firms to London merchant banks, whose total capital was thought to be only £20 million.[6] Moreover, Frank Tiarks estimated that the amount outstanding from Russia, with which normal commercial communications had been cut, was 'just as bad'.[7] Thus overall no payments could be expected on perhaps £120 million of the estimated £350 million bills in circulation in the London discount market. On 10 August 1914 the merchant banks reconvened and formally constituted themselves as the Accepting Houses Committee, appointing an executive committee to represent the interests of all the firms in negotiations with the government.[8] Frederick Huth Jackson, a very eminent City figure who was a former Governor of the Bank of England and the senior partner of Frederick Huth & Co., became chairman of the new organisation, and an executive committee was formed comprising partners of Brandts, Frühling & Goschen, Hambros, Kleinworts, and Schröders (represented by Tiarks), all houses with large exposures to German clients. Two days later the members of the executive committee appeared on behalf of the accepting houses at a conference at the Treasury chaired by the Chancellor of the Exchequer, David Lloyd George, and attended by eleven government ministers, the Governor of the Bank of England, and representatives of the clearing banks and manufacturing industry 'to think out some method of setting things going again'.[9] The first fruit of the deliberations was the announcement the following day that the Bank of England, supported by the Treasury, would purchase any approved bill accepted before the moratorium. This measure revived the liquidity of the bill market and in the following weeks some £120 million of bills – a sum roughly equivalent to the total outstanding German, Austrian and Russian bills – were converted to cash using this facility.[10] Further measures were taken to solve the problem of the liability of the merchant banks to meet bills for which they had not received remittances.[11] The Bank of England undertook to make advances to acceptors to allow them to pay off outstanding bills, charging 2 per cent above Bank Rate for the loans, which were due for repayment a year after the end of the war, and support was promised from the joint stock banks. These steps successfully restored the workings of the commercial bill market, an achievement that the leading financial journalist Hartley Withers hailed in mid-December 1914 as 'the greatest evidence of London's strength as a financial centre that it could have desired or dreamt of'.[12]

Though the City's resilience in the crisis of 1914 was indeed remarkable, the First World War saw a decline in London's leading position as an international financial centre, for several reasons. First, although in theory Britain remained on the gold standard throughout the war, in practice the plethora of regulations amounted to the abandonment of convertibility, which marked the end of the unrivalled pre-eminence of sterling as the international reserve currency and medium for international financial transactions. Second, by interrupting the flows of credits and remittances the war weakened the City's position as the leading provider of international trade finance, while sterling exchange rate risk made the US dollar a more attractive medium of acceptance finance for foreigners. Third, the City's role as an international capital market came virtually to a halt because of official restrictions on the issuing of securities and stock market transactions, and problems of transfers and remittances. During the war the international capital market moved to New York and the relocation proved permanent. City firms continued to be busy because of the vast war financing requirements of Britain and its allies, but, as Withers wrote in the aftermath of the conflict, 'London, as everyone knows, has been hard hit by the War'.[13]

The Partnership and the Firm in Wartime

Baron Bruno's naturalisation was greeted with outrage by those caught up in the outburst of chauvinistic fervour that swept the country after the declaration of war. In the City, on 24 October 1914 the Court of Aldermen passed a resolution of protest. In Parliament, the matter was raised with McKenna on 16, 19 and 26 November, and on 27 November with Lloyd George, who replied, with some exasperation, 'there is too much nonsense talked about that sort of thing. My Hon. Friend lowers the currency by appeals to the gallery . . . it is unfair and, if I may say so, not very intelligent to appeal to this sort of prejudice against . . . the rather unfortunate name of Schröder'.[14] Expressions of virulent anti-German sentiment appeared in some parts of the press, including *The Times*, but particularly in the pages of the *National Review* which aired 'the problem of the German Plutocrat, of German origin and German proclivities, who enjoys the run of the country at the present time'.[15] Foremost amongst those to whom it referred were Baron Bruno Schröder; Sir Edgar Speyer, the head of the London merchant bank Speyer Brothers and the brother of James Speyer of New York; and Sir Ernest Cassel. Their sponsorship of the Anglo-German Union Club, which was founded in 1905 to improve Anglo-German relations, was portrayed as evidence of treacherous sympathies, as were Baron Bruno's entertainment of a party of English journalists at his Hamburg house in 1907 and his endowment of a Professorship in German at Cambridge University in 1910. Baron Bruno's initiative to make charitable contributions for the relief of German internees and prisoners of war in England as well as for British prisoners of war in Germany was represented as unpatriotic, and Schröders' sponsorship of the Austrian government issue of 1914 was construed as assisting the enemy. But most damning of all was the service of his elder son in the German army. This came about because on the outbreak of war the 19-year-old Rudolph Bruno II, who had recently finished at Eton, was in Hamburg working as a volunteer at Schröder Gebrüder. He was conscripted into his father's old regiment, the Second Mecklenburg Dragoons, given the rank of lieutenant and posted to the Russian front, but the fact that neither he nor his father had any choice in the matter made no difference to Baron Bruno's detractors.

The sinking of the passenger ship *Lusitania* by a German submarine in May 1915, with the loss of 1,198 lives, aroused a new outburst of anti-German feeling, rioting and the sacking of shops owned by Germans, leading to 866 arrests in London alone. In the City the Stock Exchange, the Baltic Exchange and the London Metal Exchange instructed members of German birth not to attend until further notice, and the London Chamber of Commerce required the resignation of German-born members.[16] Once more there were attacks on Baron Bruno in the press and calls in Parliament for his internment.[17] That demand was heard again in the spring of 1916 and the summer of 1917, when there were further upsurges of anti-German sentiment. The attacks were not confined to Baron Bruno; a parliamentary question contained the implication that his wife was a spy;[18] and his younger son, Helmut, was remorselessly taunted at Eton. Challenged to reveal his allegiance in the conflict between Britain and Germany, Baron Bruno is reported to have replied, sadly, 'I feel as if my father and mother have quarrelled'.

Baron Bruno refrained from visiting the City during the war. In fact, he was only occasionally in London, particularly after his home in Park Street was requisitioned by the Ministry of Works in 1917. Most of the four and a half years of war he spent at The Dell, his deceased uncle's country house near Englefield Green. Even living quietly in the country he attracted attacks from anti-German zealots who accused him of hoarding secret stores of coal to heat the Schröder orchid collection, which he had inherited from his uncle.[19] By all accounts he bore the attacks and his enforced idleness stoically, supported by his strong Lutheran faith, and it was in this spirit that he received the news in September 1915 that his son was missing in action. He had been wounded in a skirmish near Vilnius and captured by Russian troops. For the rest of the war the family lived in hope that he was alive and used Russian business friends to try to locate and assist him, but he was never heard of again. Baron Bruno was much marked by his wartime experiences, and in the early 1920s it was remarked that he gave the impression 'of carrying a great slice of life about with him'.[20]

Frank Tiarks, by contrast, was relentlessly busy throughout the war, though not with the affairs of J. Henry Schröder & Co. Even before the beginning of the conflict he was greatly occupied with Bank of England business, informing his brother on 5 August 1914, 'I have been working almost night and day to have laws passed by the Government to keep the City solvent'.[21] In another letter two months later, he wrote 'I can't move from the Bank of England any day this week, not even Saturday, as I have just been put on a Committee with the Governor and Revelstoke [of Barings] to settle the Stock Exchange matters and as far as I can see we shall be in continuous session for some time'.[22] Bank of England business occupied him largely for the following two and a half years, often requiring him to visit the provincial branches.[23] In July 1916, he gave evidence to the committee under the chairmanship of Lord Faringdon to consider 'the best means of meeting the needs of British firms after the War as regards financial facilities for trade'.[24] Tiarks was the first expert witness to appear and was invited by the chairman to state his views. He took issue with the suggestion that trade finance facilities were inadequate, and focused instead upon the shortcomings of the City's mechanism for making issues for manufacturing firms, anticipating the public debate on the subject by a decade. His solution was the establishment of a consortium institution funded by the major clearing banks to undertake industrial issues, a suggestion that foreshadowed the establishment of the Bankers' Industrial Development Corporation in 1930. In May 1917, Tiarks rejoined the Navy. He was seconded to Naval Intelligence and worked in the renowned Room 40, being put in charge of the Direction Finding Section which had responsibility for identifying the location of German submarines by monitoring their radio signals.[25]

The Armistice of November 1918 brought an end to the war, but not to Tiarks' public duties. At the request of Lord Milner at the War Office he consented to act as financial adviser to the British Army of Occupation in Germany, with the title Civil Commissioner, a role for which he was uniquely qualified by virtue of his membership of the Court of the Bank of England and his strong business and personal ties to Germany. Despite the 'considerable personal inconvenience' he took up the post in Cologne in January 1919.[26] He was appalled by the desperate plight of the civilian population and in early March went to Paris, where the Peace Conference was being held, to secure emergency food supplies. 'I completed everything that I wanted by going direct to Lloyd George – Austen Chamberlain – Winston Churchill – Robert Cecil,' he wrote to his wife, adding 'everyone seems to want me and my advice on all and every subject'.[27] His actions earned him the gratitude and friendship of the mayor of Cologne, Dr Konrad Adenauer – the future West German Chancellor. Tiarks also became involved in negotiations about the resumption of Anglo-German trade, a matter of enormous importance to J. Henry Schröder & Co. because of its outstanding credits to German firms, and was able to renew ties with Cologne's private banks, notably Deichmann & Co., the family firm of Baron Bruno's wife, J. H. Stein and Sal. Oppenheim & Cie.

In the absence of both the proprietorial partners it was Julius Rittershaussen, the associate partner, who administered Schröders' day-to-day activities during the war. Rittershaussen was of German birth and was thus a candidate for internment, but his naturalisation was speedily processed and he became a British subject on 28 September 1914. Business was curtailed by the hostilities and the staff employed by the firm fell from forty in 1914 to twenty-eight in 1916. But thereafter activity increased slightly and at the end of 1918 there were thirty-two clerks on the payroll. Twelve of the staff saw active service, five of whom were killed.

Although Baron Bruno and Frank Tiarks were both away from the office during the war, each kept an eye on the business and they met or corresponded over major policy matters. The most fundamental of all the strategic decisions was that the firm should continue to conduct business. In fact, the partnership came close to dissolution in May 1915 following the sinking of the *Lusitania*. A couple of days after the outrage Frank Tiarks wrote to his brother:

> I have been meaning to write to you for some time and tell you what has been in my mind about the future of JHS & Co. Ever since the Germans have been using poison against our troops and sinking women and children with submarines I have felt that no institution with a German name ought to be tolerated in London and on top of all this comes the Lusitania. The wonder is that the country does not turn on the Germans and have them all deported and if things go on like this they will. Anyhow I have decided not to go on with JHS & Co. after the war and to insist on a gradual liquidation and I shall tell Bruno so tomorrow. You know what the destruction of my life's work will mean to me to say nothing of all I feel about what Papa has done to make the firm stand as high as it did till the war broke out. I don't know how much capital I shall be able to save out of the liquidation. It all depends on whether our foreign clients can pay what they owe us when the war is over.[28]

Walter Cunliffe, the Governor of the Bank of England, took a different view and told Tiarks that Schröders' closure would be contrary to the national interest. A week later Frank Tiarks wrote again to his brother in a more sanguine vein:

> No one in the City wants JHS & Co. to be liquidated and Cunliffe has asked one to go on for the present and do nothing towards liquidation. You see JHS & Co. was the greatest House of its kind and one of the institutions which form part of London's great position in the world's trade and finance, so that all the people with brains see that the disappearance of JHS & Co. would be a great loss to the country. Others with less brains only see Bruno's personality in it and would like to loot him, while others see in it personal gain for their own firms at our expense. I am following

Cunliffe's advice and shall peg away in the direction he wants. If JHS & Co. is wanted here for the country's good I shall work with my last breath to keep it.[29]

In the autumn of 1915 Schröders came under pressure from the Bank of England to participate in the £300 million loan for Russia which was organised by the British Treasury. Tiarks put the proposal to Baron Bruno, who wrote in reply:

You know my feelings, right or wrong, as to the future of the finances of *all* the great powers of Europe. Except *perhaps* England, they must all end in bankruptcy and Russia especially as in spite of all her undeveloped wealth, she has the largest pre-war foreign debt of any nation and has in the past only been able to pay her interest through new borrowings in France . . . I am convinced that in the end the whole of the Russian floating debt will have to be funded on very disadvantageous terms and then we shall have a nice lock-up for the rest of our lives.[30]

Baron Bruno's pessimistic view of the prospects for international finance was not the only reason for his opposition to involvement in the Russian loan. Also important were 'conscientious objections' against providing funds that would be used to acquire munitions 'to kill all those who are nearest and dearest to me'. Uppermost in his mind, of course, was his son who had gone missing in action a week or so before he wrote, though it seems unlikely that the news had already reached England. Although reluctant to agree to participation in the loan Baron Bruno was 'acutely' aware of the problems that his stance created for the firm and his partner. 'I don't want to hurt the position of the firm and not offend Cunliffe, for whom I have the greatest esteem,' he wrote, 'but I am sure that he is so large-minded that he will recognise that in a question of conscience it is very difficult to argue and that he might be able to give you a tip how we can honourably escape.' Baron Bruno concluded the letter with an apology: 'I am afraid, my dear Frank, I am giving you a lot of trouble – you are unfortunately connected with a "Hun". But never mind – after rain there must be sunshine and then I hope we shall look back on all this as a bad dream.'

Business in Wartime

The impact of the First World War upon the fortunes of London's merchant banks was mixed. At the outset all were adversely affected by the downturns in issuing and acceptance business. The issuing of loans for foreign borrowers virtually came to a halt because of regulations introduced in January 1915 upon the reopening of the Stock Exchange, requiring Treasury consent for all new issues with the intention of reserving the capital market for the war finance requirements of the British government; in 1914 new overseas issues were £159 million but in the years 1915–18 they were only £142 million in aggregate.[31] 'During the period of actual fighting acceptance business fell very much,' observed a prominent bill broker of the day, 'not only because of the restriction of sea-borne commerce, but because the Government became more and more the principal buyer of everything, and the Government conducted its business on what it described as a cash basis'.[32] For Morgan Grenfell, Barings and some other firms, these adverse developments were outweighed by the bonanza of work on behalf of the British and Allied governments, Morgans acting as the London agent of J. P. Morgan & Co., the British government's financial agent in the US, and Barings on behalf of the Russian government.[33] The firms with large acceptances on behalf of German and Austrian clients had a very different war, suffering the burden of large interest payments on their borrowings from the Bank of England and were not involved in government work because of their associations with German clients. Several of the smaller founder members of the Accepting Houses Committee did not survive the war, and Frühling & Goschen, which in 1919 merged with Cunliffe Brothers (Walter Cunliffe's family firm), and Frederick Huth & Co. never fully recovered. Schröders and Kleinworts, the firms with the largest volumes of frozen credits in 1914, incurred substantial losses but survived.[34]

Schröders' borrowings from the Bank of England under the facility of 5 September 1914, which provided loans to enable firms to remove pre-moratorium acceptances from the market, totalled £5.1 million; £4 million on account of German and Austrian clients, £1.1 million for credits to Russian firms. This was almost half the firm's total volume of acceptance business and one-and-a-half times the partners' capital of £3.5 million. The potentially disastrous magnitude of these ratios indicates that the coming of the war took the Schröder partners by surprise, as it did the City in general, and it seems highly unlikely that the firm could have survived without the special facility provided by the Bank of England for the accepting houses. Yet the rate of interest paid on borrowings from the Bank was expensive and once the immediate emergency was past Schröders took steps to restructure its finances. The reduction of balance sheet assets produced £3.2 million, a sum almost equivalent to the whole of the partners' capital, and a loan from the London County and Westminster Bank (forerunner of the National Westminster Bank) a further £1.5 million to repay its borrowings from the Bank of England. In September 1916 Cunliffe informed Sir John Bradbury, the Joint Permanent Secretary to the Treasury, that 'Messrs Schröder have now paid off all but £397,304 5s. 11d. of the amount of over 5 million pounds advanced in respect of their pre-Moratorium advances'.[35] The outstanding amount was the subject of a dispute between Schröders and the authorities arising from the seizure of a cargo of nitrate financed by Schröders, on behalf of Vorwerk & Co., Weber & Co. and the Banco Aleman Transatlantico, that had been seized by the Royal Navy and appropriated by the British government after designation as enemy property in the Prize Court. 'Schröders are naturally unwilling to pay this sum a second time to the Government who has already received the value of the goods which it represents', continued Cunliffe's letter. 'I daresay it may not be easy to deal rapidly with the appeal, but it seems difficult, does it not, to justify charging 8 per cent interest on a debt which you have already collected, and I would suggest that the fair thing would be to remit interest on that amount from the date when the corresponding goods were realised, pending the result of the appeal'. Despite Cunliffe's intervention the Prize Court cargo dispute was not resolved until 1920 when both principal and interest, which by then totalled £126,000, were settled in Schröders' favour.

Besides the unpaid acceptances, Schröders also had a problem with outstanding advances to German and Austrian clients, which totalled £1.4 million at the outbreak of war. These were not covered by the provisions of 5 September, and although the loans were largely collateralised the sequestration of assets was a slow process. In the meantime Schröders faced a cash crisis. The problem was resolved by a loan from the Bank of England of £1 million, matching the volume of secured but illiquid loans. During 1915 the £1 million secured against assets was recovered by Schröders and the remaining £440,000 was written off by a reduction in partners' capital. However, Schröders did not repay the Bank of England loan in full and the accounts show borrowings from the Bank of £500,000 in 1915, £475,000 in 1916 and £700,000 in 1917, which provided essential liquidity for the firm.

Schröders' operating revenues collapsed during the war years, averaging only £9,000 per annum in total after deductions of large net interest losses compared to £315,000 in 1905–13 (see Table 6.1). Issuing business disappeared in 1915 and 1916, though in 1917 and 1918 the firm secured some underwriting participations in issues made by other houses for domestic and British Empire borrowers. Acceptances continued to be much the largest source of revenues, but the business was much smaller than before the war. In 1913, Schröders' revenues from acceptance commissions were £163,000; in 1917 they were only £21,000. There were three reasons for the sharp fall in Schröders' acceptance activity: the

Table 6.1   J. Henry Schröder & Co., sources of revenues, 1914–18

	1914–18 Annual average £000s
Accepting	50
Issuing and underwriting	18
Net interest	(81)
Other[1]	22
Total	9

( ) indicates loss

1. Consignments, dealing, paying agency commissions, insurance, etc.

Source: J. Henry Schröder & Co., profit and loss accounts.

disappearance of its German, Austrian and Russian business; British regulations against trading with the enemy, which from December 1915 included firms in neutral countries of 'enemy nationality or enemy association', which was much of the client list;[36] and a policy decision on the part of the partners to curtail acceptance activity because of hostility in the market to Schröders' bills.[37]

The bulk of Schröders' acceptance business during the war was conducted with US, South American or UK clients. In the early years of the conflict US sugar and coffee importers continued to make extensive use of facilities provided by Schröders, but by the end of the war firms such as G. Amsinck & Co., Crossman & Sielcken, Lewisohn Importing and Trading Company and A. P. Viela & Brothers had disappeared from the client list, presumably because they had switched to newly available dollar acceptance credits. The notable exception was Czarnikow-Rionda, which became of greater and greater significance to Schröders; by 1918 Czarnikow–Rionda's outstanding acceptances were £648,000, which represented almost the entirety of Schröders' US business and was 50 per cent of the firm's total acceptances. Manuel Rionda's loyalty was of enormous importance to Schröders, but the relationship was mutually beneficial. Schröders' support before and during the war facilitated the emergence of Czarnikow–Rionda as the leading New York sugar broker, handling the entire Cuban crop and the bulk of the Puerto Rican and Dominican crops in the war years.[38] Schröders' business with Latin America was heavily disrupted by the war, which put a stop to financing clients such as Gildemeister & Co., Blohm & Co., Weber & Co. In the war years the Amelia Nitrate Company of Chile, of which Baron Bruno was chairman, was much the most important of Schröders' South American clients, using credits of around £100,000. Amongst UK clients, which more and more sought advances rather than acceptance facilities, the most notable were C. Czarnikow Ltd, the Sena Sugar Estates Ltd, the leading international shipping firm Stein Forbes & Co., and the meat importers Vestey Brothers.

Schröders' acceptances fell from £11.7 million in December 1913 to £5.8 million in December 1914, a fall similar in magnitude to that experienced by all the firms for which information is available (see Table 6.2). The decline continued year by year to 1917 when the volume of acceptances was a mere £600,000, recovering to £1.3 million by December 1918. Barings and Kleinworts, by contrast, managed to emerge from the conflict with acceptance volumes similar in scale to 1914, participating in the recovery of the foreign bill market from 1917 and the growth of domestic acceptance activity during the war. The difference in Schröders' case was discrimination against its bills in the discount market because of the view that Baron Bruno was 'German in sympathy'.[39]

Table 6.2　Balance sheet acceptances of some leading merchant banks, 1913, 1914, 1918

31 December	1913 £ million	1914 £ million	1918 £ million
Kleinwort, Sons & Co.	14.2	8.5	7.8
J. Henry Schröder & Co.	11.7	5.8	1.3
Baring Brothers & Co. Ltd	6.6	3.7	3.1
Brown, Shipley & Co.	5.1	n/a	n/a
C. J. Hambro & Son	4.6	2.3 (1916)	2.3 (1916)
Wm Brandt's Sons & Co.	3.3	0.7	n/a
N. M. Rothschild & Sons	3.2	1.3	n/a
Morgan Grenfell & Co.	2.8	2.0	0.2
Antony Gibbs & Sons	1.2	n/a	4.3

Note: Information on other firms unavailable.

Sources: Stanley Chapman, *The Rise of Merchant Banking* (London: George Allen & Unwin, 1984) p. 121; J. Henry Schröder & Co., balance sheets; Kathleen Burk, *Morgan Grenfell 1838–1988* (Oxford University Press, 1989) p. 278; Stephanie Diaper, 'Kleinwort, Sons & Co. in the History of Merchant Banking, 1855–1966' (unpublished PhD thesis, University of Nottingham, 1983) pp. 145, 210.

Net interest losses after deduction of partners' 4 per cent interest were sustained by Schröders throughout the war. The principal reason was the cost of the interest charges on the funds borrowed to finance the obligations arising from the outstanding German, Austrian and Russian bills, and the German and Austrian advances. On 13 October 1915 the partners held a conference on the interest position at Baron Bruno's house in Park Street with the leading City accountant Ernest Spicer and it was agreed that Baron Bruno would temporarily forgo his 4 per cent interest on capital to ease the firm's financial position.[40] Compensation for his loss of interest was made a priority upon the recovery of bad debts or better trading performance, and the interest charge was reinstated in 1917. The war years saw considerable changes in the pattern of Schröders' assets. In the early years, War Loan became the largest form of liquid asset while Treasury bills supplanted commercial bills in the bill portfolio. Call loans all but ceased in the early years, but lending to discount houses revived in 1917, and in the following year constituted 40 per cent of assets. Another significant development of the final couple of years of the war was the increase in advances to 40 per cent of assets, an unprecedently high proportion.

Schröders' operating costs fell in 1915 and 1916, the reduction in staff in the first two years of the war cutting the salary bill from £18,000 in 1914 to £12,000 in 1916, and office costs were also reduced.[41] Operating costs increased in 1917 and 1918, and by the end of the war the salary bill had risen to £15,000, inflation being a significant reason. Schröders made a loss after deduction of partners' 4 per cent interest in every year of the war. In 1914, as a result of a provision of £395,000 for bad debts, the recorded loss was £379,000. In 1915 and 1916, the deficits were really £69,000 and £77,000 (though because of the waiving of interest on Baron Bruno's capital the accounts prepared for the partners showed profits of £60,000 and £36,000). In 1917 and 1918, the losses were £35,000 and £36,000 respectively after payment of 4 per cent interest to Baron Bruno. Schröders' capital was written down by £440,000 in 1915 and by a further £41,000 in 1916. In 1917 and 1918, however, the firm's capital grew by about £50,000 each year as a result of the retention in the firm of part of the 4 per cent interest on partners' capital.

The First World War cost the Schröder partners in excess of £1 million – at least £25 million in 1990 money; bad debts written off against revenue in 1914, 1920, 1921 and 1922 totalled £800,000; £481,000 was written off against capital, though some of this may have been recovered; plus trading losses of a further £200,000. Over the war years Schröders' capital and reserves fell from £3.54 million in December 1913 to £3.26 million in December 1919, a decline which was less than the aggregate losses and write-offs suggesting the transfer of private funds by the partners to bolster the firm's capital. The war years saw high levels of inflation which reduced the purchasing power of money by about half, and thus in real terms Schröders' capital was considerably smaller at the end of the conflict than at the beginning. However, although the firm was unable to produce profits sufficient to increase the wealth of the partners, it generated earnings enough to pay the interest on the loans from the Bank of England and the London County and Westminster Bank. Most importantly, the firm had survived, though it remained to be seen whether the damage inflicted by the war on its clients and on the standing of the City of London as a financial centre would allow it to rebuild its business with the return of peace.

Part II

London and New York

1919–1959

7

Prosperity Amidst European Instability

1919–31

Disequilibrium was the characteristic feature of the international economy in the years from the end of the First World War in November 1918 to the financial crisis of the summer of 1931. There were several interrelated causes of the imbalances and instability of the 1920s, all of which were attributable to developments since the onset of the conflict and it was widely believed at the time that the solution to the problems of the era lay in a return to the international gold standard, which before the war had provided an automatic international adjustment mechanism. On the outbreak of war the gold standard was effectively suspended by the belligerents and some neutrals to protect gold reserves and to permit the financing of the war by printing money. Inflation was universal during the war years and continued in the immediate post-war period because governments found it politically impossible to slow the printing presses, especially in Central Europe. In the Allied countries there was a post-war boom in 1919–20, in which pent-up purchasing power chased scarce goods, sending prices soaring, followed by a slump in 1920–21, during which prices plummeted and unemployment rocketed. The US dollar was restored to the gold standard in 1919, but in the immediate post-war period all the other currencies were paper-based and fluctuated widely in value, being driven up and down by economic and political developments. This instability was believed to be impeding the conduct of international trade, and currency stabilisation was held to be a vital precondition for post-war economic recovery. By the middle of the decade the international gold standard had been re-established, but under post-war conditions the system proved inoperable and it collapsed after a few years.

Indebtedness was another serious post-war problem. All the belligerent powers emerged from the war with swollen national debts, servicing which caused budgetary problems for post-war governments, fuelling currency instability and prompting the adoption of policies designed to produce budget surpluses that could be used for debt reduction, which were also deflationary and inhibited post-war economic recovery. Inter-Allied war debts totalled about £5.6 billion, of which £2.2

billion was owed to the US, principally by Britain and France. These European powers were both debtors and creditors, Britain having borrowed £1.4 billion and loaned £2.2 billion to its allies, and France having borrowed £1.5 billion and lent £0.7 billion.[1] Germany emerged from the war without overseas assets, which had been either sold or seized by the Allies, and with a reparations bill set initially at £6.9 billion owed in greater part to Britain and France, the US abjuring any claim to reparations. Proposals to cancel the inter-Allied war debts and to scale down reparations came to little because of French intransigence over reparations and the steadfast insistence of the United States upon the duty of the Allied borrowers to honour their debts. Thus all the European belligerents had to make large international transfers, implying the generation of substantial trade surpluses. But the expansion of international trade was impeded by the legacy of wartime disruption and destruction, the currency instability, and the protectionism practised by the United States, the only market in which the debtor nations could possibly earn the required surpluses. Despite this fundamentally flawed structure, the international economy was able to function and grow in the 1920s because of large financial transfers from the United States to other countries, especially Germany, which enabled international remittances to be made. Yet the accumulation of foreign debts increased the German payments burden, and when the flow of funds from the US was curtailed it became impossible to meet the obligations and the system collapsed.

A significant factor in the stability of the pre-1914 international financial system was that there was a single dominant currency, sterling, under the supervision of the Bank of England, the world's foremost central bank, which led to a large proportion of international financial transactions going through London. The emergence of the US dollar as a major international currency and the rise of New York as an important international financial centre from 1914, and Paris too for certain purposes in the 1920s, was destabilising because of shifts of large volumes of short-term balances and securities between the centres, imposing unprecedented strains.[2] A mitigating factor was the co-operation between the central banks of Britain, the United States, France and Germany, but this was inhibited by conflicts between external and domestic policy objectives and the co-operative efforts proved ultimately inadequate to cope with the underlying disequilibria.

Business conditions in the immediate post-war years were rather unfavourable for the London merchant banks and there were several closures and amalgamations. Acceptance business revived in the 1919–20 boom and the volume of foreign-drawn bills in circulation in the London discount market regained the 1913 level of £350 million, though on an inflation-adjusted basis it was only about half the size.[3] In the ensuing slump acceptances fell sharply and at the end of 1922 there were perhaps as few as £175–200 million outstanding. Moreover, the dominant role of the merchant banks in the creation of foreign trade acceptances was increasingly challenged by the major clearing banks, it being estimated in 1923 that whereas before the war the accepting houses were responsible for 85 per cent of these bills their share was only 50 per cent.[4] The revival of the merchant banks' foreign bond issuing business became possible with the lifting of the ban on overseas issues in 1919, though restrictions remained until 1925.[5] There were no official curbs on private placements but this method was suitable only for fund-raising on a modest scale. Foreign exchange dealing boomed as never before in the early 1920s, and although it was the major clearing banks which dominated this activity there was plenty of scope for skilful merchant bank operators to make substantial profits.[6]

The stabilisation of the major European currencies began in 1922 with an issue on behalf of Austria, the first of eleven stabilisation loans sponsored by the League of Nations.[7] In 1923–24, the Netherlands, Sweden, Switzerland, Germany and Hungary stabilised their currencies, and Britain's return to gold in 1925 was accompanied by the British dominions and several other countries. By 1926, thirty-nine countries had stabilised currencies and by the end of 1928 all the major trading nations had accomplished stabilisation by the adoption of the gold standard.[8] The process was interrupted by the French and Belgian military occupation of the Ruhr coalfields in January 1923 to enforce German reparations payments. The Ruhr miners responded by striking, being supported with funds provided by the German government which were obtained simply by printing banknotes. Inflation, which was already high, became hyperinflation and by the summer the German currency had become valueless. In November 1923, the currency was stabilised at the rate of 1 million million old marks to the new mark, the Rentenmark, which soon became the Reichsmark (Rm). At the same time an international committee of bankers and industrialists chaired by General Charles C. Dawes, a Chicago banker (and a future Vice-President of the United States), was appointed to advise on German financial affairs and reparations. These developments were welcomed by a new City publication as providing 'hopes of settlement in Europe' where 'for nine years and more, trade and finance have been chiefly dominated by political influences arising from the War and its consequences. As long as this state of things endures, real recovery is impossible'.[9] The words belong to J. Henry Schröder & Co.'s *Quarterly Review of Business Conditions*, which first appeared in December 1923. Written by Hartley Withers, a prominent financial journalist, who was later assisted by Henry Tiarks, Frank Tiarks' son, the *Quarterly Review* furnished a commentary on important political, economic and financial developments, voicing the views of the Schröder partners on the issues of the day during the inter-war years.

The outcome of the deliberations of the committee of experts was the Dawes Plan of April 1924. This reduced the annual reparations payments to more manageable levels, though not the total amount due, and proposed an international loan of Rm 800 million – £40 million in sterling of the day – to provide the reserves to place the new German currency on the gold standard. In London, reported the *Quarterly Review*, the loan proposal aroused:

a good deal of opposition and apprehension. The joint stock banks have been pelted with letters from customers threatening to withdraw their accounts if the banks give any kind of support to the loan: the Miners' Federation has demanded that the Prime Minister shall receive a deputation, to put before him its views concerning the effect on the coal trade . . . and many industrial bodies have expressed fears concerning the effect on British trade of the restoration of a great and industrious rival, which has, by its policy of currency inflation, wiped out . . . the debt charges of its industry and shipping and the mortgages on its agriculture.

But the main outstanding consideration which should give comfort to those industrialists who are fearing German competition is the general agreement that the derelict state of Germany and Central Europe has been the main cause of trade depression in this country, in our Dominions and in many other lands which used to be our ready customers, but lately have been unable to buy from us, because they have been unable to sell to Central Europe. With world trade reviving . . . England, which since the war has more than retained her former proportion of the world's total exports, ought surely to be able to go forward on the rising tide of prosperity.[10]

In fact, the Dawes Loan proved very popular with the private investors to which it was marketed, the New York tranche, about half the total, being eleven times over-subscribed.

It was generally believed that the turning point for the revival of the international economy, and the British export industries, would be the restoration to the gold standard of sterling, which despite the enhanced role of the dollar was still the leading currency for international trade. There was some debate about the appropriate rate at which restoration should be effected, but in the City it was considered that any rate other than the pre-war rate of \$4.86 to the pound would be a breach of faith with overseas holders of sterling and would damage London's standing as an international financial centre. Since 1919, however, sterling had been trading at a considerable discount to the pre-war parity with the US dollar, reflecting the higher rate of UK price inflation, and the restoration of convertibility into gold had been deferred pending the convergence of the currencies. By the beginning of 1925 it was becoming increasingly difficult to delay the move because sterling was becoming more and more isolated as other countries returned to gold or announced their intention to do so imminently. The decisions by Canada, Australia and South Africa forced the British government's hand, since it was feared that if Britain did not follow suit the dollar would supplant sterling as the normal medium for international financial transactions with 'serious political results on the British Empire as a whole', warned the Governor of the Bank of England, raising the spectre that 'the world centre would shift permanently and completely from London to New York'.[11] Yet there was also a case for delay since the sterling–dollar exchange rate in the market was below \$4.86 and a return to gold at an overvalued rate would lessen the competitiveness of British industry, so leading to an increase in unemployment. The advocates of restoration at the pre-war rate acknowledged the problems that it would cause for British industry, but as Otto Niemeyer of the Treasury put it to the Chancellor, Winston Churchill, 'on the long view the gold standard . . . is likely to do more for British trade than all the efforts of the Unemployment Committee'.[12] Although less than completely happy about the decision, Churchill announced the return to gold in his Budget speech of 28 April 1925. 'It need hardly be said,' commented the *Quarterly Review*, 'that in business this great step towards steadiness in exchange and stable conditions in finance and commerce has been heartily welcomed and approved.'[13]

By the middle of the decade commercial conditions had become considerably more favourable for the merchant banks. In 1925, world trade surpassed the level of 1913 on an inflation-adjusted basis and League of Nations estimates suggest that it grew by almost 20 per cent between 1924 and 1929.[14] In 1926, the volume of international trade bills in circulation in the London market reached a record £415 million.[15] However, profits were blighted by competition from the clearing banks, which cut commissions to win market-share, provoking the eruption of an 'animated controversy' in the City in 1927, between the clearing banks and the merchant banks.[16] In fact, in inflation-adjusted terms, even at its peak in 1926 the volume of international trade bills was lower than in 1913, and the 1920s marked the beginning of the long term decline of the accepting side of the merchant banks' business because of competition from alternative methods of finance and alternative markets, notably New York. While the acceptance credit business of the merchant banks was probably stimulated by the return to gold, the scope for foreign exchange dealing was greatly reduced and this side of their activities was sharply curtailed in the second half of the 1920s.

Following the success of the Dawes Loan in October 1924, international lending resumed on a large scale. Weimar Germany was much the biggest borrower and by the summer of 1930 had accumulated long-term debts of some £590 million and short-term debts of £787 million. German industry responded vigorously to the infusion of credit and capital, labour productivity growing by 25 per cent, industrial production by 40 per cent and exports by 100 per cent, a *Wirtschaftswunder* akin to the period of the Marshall Plan which later followed the Second World War.[17] The bulk of these funds were raised in the United States, partly because of the abundance of capital there but also because, from the autumn of 1924 to November 1925, the British authorities embargoed public issues of foreign loans in London in order to restrict the supply of sterling in order to raise its value against the dollar to facliltate the return to the gold standard. From November 1925 the merchant banks were able to resume making issues for foreign borrowers without official interference, but it was Wall Street which was the leading international capital market in the 1920s. London was surpassed by New York because of the relative cheapness of dollar funds, due to generally lower interest rates and the absence of a 2 per cent stamp duty;[18] the British government's restrictions on the issue of foreign loans; and the energetic approach to business development adopted by Wall Street investment bankers.[19] Mounting pressure on sterling led to the reintroduction of restrictions on foreign issues in the summer of 1929. The problems which the merchant banks encountered in the conduct of their traditional international financial activities persuaded them to turn their attentions to domestic business opportunities, though prior to 1931 the leading firms remained thoroughly internationalist in outlook.

In the spring and summer of 1928 the Federal Reserve raised interest rates to restrain the booming domestic economy. This increased yields on domestic bonds, leading American investors to shun foreign bonds, and between the first and second halves of the year there was a 50 per cent fall in the volume of new foreign issues in the US.[20] Furthermore, noted the *Quarterly Review*:

> with Wall Street chronically rampant, not only had America no money to lend abroad, but the high rates – 8 and 10 per cent and occasionally even 20 per cent – that were to be earned by supplying

money on call to finance the boom, sucked in funds from impoverished Europe. Small wonder that world trade went to pieces and commodity prices collapsed, inflicting embarassment on debtor countries, causing grave anxiety to their creditors and so setting up the usual vicious circle, by making the latter less than ever inclined to lend.[21]

The Wall Street Crash in October 1929 prompted the repatriation of US short-term foreign loans to meet domestic requirements. The combined impact of the boom and bust of the US securities markets of 1928–29 on net capital outflows from the US was a drastic fall from $1,250 million in 1928 to $380 million in 1930, and French gold hoarding and cutbacks by other countries exacerbated the downturn in international lending.[22] But the functioning of the international financial system was now dependent on the continued outflow of funds from the US. Despite a second major international loan for the government of the German Republic, the Young Loan of 1930, German net capital inflows fell from $967 million in 1928, to $482 million in 1929, to $129 million in 1930.[23] And worse was to come. The spring and early summer of 1931 saw a massive wave of capital flight, accelerated by the crisis at the Österreichische Creditanstalt, the principal Austrian commercial bank, and mounting fears of political turmoil, and that year Germany had a net capital outflow of $540 million. In July 1931, its external reserves exhausted, the German government suspended international payments. Sterling came under pressure in the wake of the German financial crisis and in September the pound was forced off the gold standard. It marked, commented *The Economist*, 'the end of an epoch'.[24]

Partners, Executives and Staff

At the end of the war, Baron Bruno was determined to rebuild the business of J. Henry Schröder & Co. and to ensure that the firm should play a full role in the process of post-war reconstruction. Upon the cessation of hostilities he resumed regular attendance at the office and moved back to London, renting a town house in Belgrave Square. Frank Tiarks returned to Leadenhall Street in May 1919, having completed his official duties in Cologne. Two months later a new partnership agreement was drawn up dividing the profits and losses, after interest on partners' capital, between Baron Bruno and Frank Tiarks in a two-thirds/one-third ratio, although their respective contributions to capital were 94 per cent and 6 per cent. The imbalance in rewards was a recognition of Tiarks' role in securing the firm's wartime survival, and Baron Bruno even offered to change its name to Schröder Tiarks & Co., but his partner preferred to continue as before. In 1926, Baron Bruno's son, Helmut, and Frank Tiarks' son, Henry, both aged 25, joined their fathers in the partners' room and each was furnished with a modest amount of capital. Frank Tiarks' share of the capital grew during the 1920s and at the end of 1930 the joint Schröder interest in the firm's capital was 84 per cent, while the Tiarks had 16 per cent.

Baron Bruno and Frank Tiarks, aged respectively 52 and 45 in 1919, were at the peak of their powers in the 1920s. Portraits of them in these years survive in a memoir written by Henry Andrews:

> Baron Schröder was an old fashioned banker, who talked the language of banking and who attached proper importance to the daily work of bread and butter business, out of which would arise naturally and easily the occasional and exceptional great transactions.

> The real point about him was that he was big and that he was substantial . . . he gave the impression of being the senior person in the room at a time when he was in early middle life and there were older men present. What he was interested in was the business, the transaction, was it good, was it right and then was it profitable. He had lots of nice simple expressions such as 'tell him that this is not a very large fish but a sweet one'. His integrity provided an easy artless certainty of what ought not to be done.

> He could be very severe if anyone offended against these fundamentals. I recall that there were technical difficulties in connection with the founding of the J. Henry Schroder Banking Corporation (in New York) and a relative in Switzerland who had some part to play in the matter wrote making a suggestion which involved an untruth and added that it was only a formal matter. The Baron at once replied that many of the most important things in life were formal things.

> He was strongly influenced by Lutheranism and read prayers in German to his family on Sunday mornings and he had something of Victorian high mindedness and also narrowness in matters of conduct. This narrowness made him possibly a little inaccessible.[25]

But formality, and even remoteness, did not mean lack of devotion. At the dinner to celebrate the engagement of Henry Tiarks, which was attended by the whole firm, related Andrews:

the proceedings led up to a speech by the Baron and when it was his turn to speak his speech consisted of the single sentence 'We are one family and one family we shall remain'. His voice broke as he said it and everyone knew that he had listened to the central theme of a great man's life.

Baron Schröder's gift of leadership was of the kind that might be described as ineloquent in the sense that it did not derive from any special gift of words, but seemed to depend upon a power of integrity which was a part of the very essence of his personality.

His impressiveness did not derive from anything that could be singled out as an adjunct or even as a separate part: he had in fact dignity without tricks. He was a personality though with no effort to shine. I do not think that it can ever have occurred to anyone that Baron Schröder could let him down. This sense of dependability was joined to the impression he gave that no confidence would be misused. He was a great gentleman and beyond doubt one of the very small company on whom depended the good name of London in the world of finance and the leadership of London in that world.

Frank Tiarks was, by contrast, the 'happy extrovert and the practical man' who, by virtue of his membership of the Court of the Bank of England from 1912 until 1946, and Baron Bruno's preference for privacy, was the more publicly visible of the two principal partners. Andrews wrote:

Frank Tiarks had a strong personality and no doubt those who did not regularly come in contact with him may have thought he was rather frightening. He was extraordinarily quick and also extraordinarily adroit when it came to solving a practical difficulty or getting out of an awkward situation. He was endowed with unusual physical vitality which expressed itself in a ready and characteristic laugh that infected others with a sense of the enjoyment of work. His laugh had a gay ring and you could watch the images and ideas forming themselves on his face and his thoughts always led to a conclusion. He was gifted with an unusual facility with words and was an exceptionally good business closer.

The partnership of Baron Bruno Schröder and Mr Frank C. Tiarks was a combination of two men with exceptional gifts of leadership, who through the wide differences between them supplemented each other and who understood each other with a

depth of understanding which is only possible when daily association in action continued over many years is built upon a
fundamental sympathy.

The Schröder partners were well-known and highly-regarded figures
in the international banking community in the 1920s. Baron Bruno was a
participant in the Brussels Conference of economic and financial experts
held in the autumn of 1920 which made proposals for the resolution of
the post-war international financial problems, though politicians paid
little heed.[26] His discussions there with the President of the Banque de
France led to a visit to Paris to advise upon the development of the
French discount market. In the early 1920s he acted as one of the 'chief
advisers in the world of banking' to the Governor of the Bank of
England, Montagu Norman, in company with Sir Reginald McKenna,
chairman of the Midland Bank, Sir Harry Goschen of Goschen &
Cunliffe, Sir Robert Kindersley of Lazards, and Lionel Rothschild.[27]
Frank Tiarks was in attendance at the Genoa Conference sponsored by
Britain and France in the spring of 1922 to promote the resumption of
the international gold standard, lending support to Norman's efforts to
secure co-ordinated action amongst the leading central banks.[28]
Norman, the Governor of the Bank of England from March 1920 to
March 1944 and the City's most eminent figure throughout the inter-war
years, was a firm friend of Frank Tiarks, they being of similar age and
both directors of the Bank since before the war, and he was a familiar
face as a weekend house-guest at Foxbury.[29]

In 1921, Baron Bruno and Frank Tiarks facilitated the establishment
of cordial relations between Norman and his counterpart at the German
Reichsbank, Dr Haverstein, Schröders acting as the Reichsbank's
London agent in the early 1920s and the channel for payments whereby
the Bank of England rendered assistance to the Reichsbank in the spring
of 1923.[30] Haverstein's policies were blamed for exacerbating German
inflation in 1922–23, and his succession by Dr Hjalmar Schacht in
November 1923 was welcomed in the City. Schacht, formerly with the
Dresdner Bank, was an old acquaintance of the Schröder partners. His
stewardship of the successful transition from hyperinflation to the stable
gold mark in 1923–24 was much admired in the City, and Baron Bruno's
New Year's greetings of 31 December 1924 exhorted him to:

look back with pride on your activities during the old year, for I
am convinced that had it not been for you the atmosphere would
not have been created in London which was so needed for the
reconstruction of our poor country.[31]

Benjamin Strong, Governor of the Federal Reserve Bank of New York, the most important American central banker of the 1920s, was another friend of the Schröder partners. Tiarks met Strong when he visited Europe in the summer of 1919 and they immediately developed a close rapport. Both had sons on the threshold of a career in banking and they discussed their training. 'Tiarks was good enough to suggest that he would be glad to have Ben [Strong Jnr] in Schröders,' Strong informed Montagu Norman some months later, 'and I told Tiarks that I would be glad to reciprocate with his boy, giving him a little knowledge of banking in this country'.[32] Norman suggested that Ben Strong Jnr should spend a year training in each of New York, Paris and London, and supported the choice of J. Henry Schröder & Co., since it 'is small enough to let Ben easily get the hang of all that is going on and large enough to show him many kinds of business in an adequate volume'.[33] Ben Strong Jnr joined the London firm in June 1922 where he worked until May 1923. The ties with Benjamin Strong were an important factor in the decision to establish a Schröder firm in New York, the J. Henry Schroder Banking Corporation, which was taken during Ben Strong Jnr's sojourn in London.

In the summer of 1919, Major Albert Pam, aged 44, joined the firm as an associate partner. His expertise lay in securities and investment management, complementing the skills of the other partners in trade finance and issuing. Albert Samuel Pam was born in Surrey in 1875, the son of a prosperous Jewish merchant.[34] He was educated at the City of London School and afterwards spent two years in Frankfurt learning German, and a year in Lausanne learning French. His career in the City began with a sugar merchant, coincidentally a client of J. Henry Schröder & Co., and he then became a stockbroker with Vivian Gray, specialising in South American securities. He became an authority on the affairs of that continent, representing the Ethelburger Syndicate and the Howard Syndicate there in the years before the First World War, and, as already related, through their involvement with the Chilean Longitudinal Railway construction contract he got to know the partners of J. Henry Schröder & Co.

In December 1914, Pam was sent to Chile as an agent of British Intelligence to locate the German cruiser *Dresden* which was believed to be hiding in a southern fjord after the Battle of the Falklands. The journey was slow, and upon arrival in Santiago he was greeted with the news of the sinking of the *Dresden* by the British fleet. Upon his return to England he submitted a lengthy report on the German colony in southern Chile which had helped the *Dresden*, 'but I very much doubt whether anyone ever read it'.[35] In addition to his knowledge of South

American finance, Pam was a leading British expert on the flora and fauna of the subcontinent. On the journey back from Santiago he visited the Buenos Aires zoo and collected a consignment of Argentinian flamingos, geese and ducks which travelled with him to England. He was a member of the Zoological Society of London from 1907, serving as treasurer in 1932–45, and he maintained his own menagerie, including a troupe of wallabies, at his home in Hertfordshire. In 1926, on a bulb collecting expedition in Peru he discovered an unknown genus of the Amaryllidaceae which was named *Pamianthe peruviana* in his honour. His eminence as a naturalist was recognised in 1944 by the award of an honorary MA by Oxford University.

In the spring of 1915, Pam joined the British Army and was sent to France, where he served on the headquarters staff of the Third Army until November 1918. He had a distinguished military career, being three times mentioned in despatches, and achieved the rank of major, the title by which he was subsequently known in business, though to friends he was always 'Pamski'. In November 1918, he was appointed to the British Mission to the Permanent International Armistice Commission at Spa in the Rhineland and spent six months as a participant in the negotiations about the details of the German surrender. During his sojourn at Spa he once again met Frank Tiarks, who was based nearby in Cologne and who inquired about his intentions upon demobilisation. On his return to London Pam received an invitation from Baron Bruno to join J. Henry Schröder & Co., 'doing whatever work came along'.[36] The combined talents of Baron Bruno, Frank Tiarks and Major Pam, with support from the diligent and meticulous Julius Rittershaussen, constituted a highly formidable merchant banking team.

Helmut Schröder and Henry Tiarks were carefully groomed for the role of partner and by the time of their appointment each was fluent in German, French and Spanish and had visited most of the firm's important clients. Their fathers considered this traditional form of preparation more important than a university education, with the result that Helmut studied at Corpus Christi College, Oxford, for only one year before being sent to Neuchâtel to learn French, while Henry did not take up his place at Magdalen College, Oxford, but instead took a course in accountancy and worked as a volunteer at the merchant firm Schlubach Behrens in the Hague for a year. In 1922 they were trainees together at the Hamburg merchant and banking firm Schlubach Thiemer & Co., also getting to know the partners of Schröder Gebrüder and other German clients. Helmut then spent three months in Barcelona in 1923, learning Spanish, before going to New York in October to assist with the establishment of the J. Henry Schroder Banking Corporation. This was followed by two years of work in New York and extensive travel in the

United States and Latin America. Henry, after a sojourn in Jerez learning Spanish, spent most of 1924 in Latin America meeting Schröders' clients, and all of 1925 in New York. By the end of that year both were ready to join their fathers in Schröders' private room.

'Helmut's partnership and mine began at Schröders,' wrote Henry Tiarks in his diary for 1 January 1926. New Year's Day was then a working day in the City and it was a busy one for the new partners. That morning Lord Revelstoke of Barings and Douro Hoare, head of Hoare, Miller & Co., 'the well known East India Merchants',[37] both directors of the Bank of England, called at 145 Leadenhall Street 'to congratulate us personally'.[38] Then Frank Tiarks took them to the Westminster Bank, Schröders' clearing bank, where they were introduced to the chairman, Walter Leaf, and to the Midland Bank, then the world's biggest bank, to meet the chairman, Sir Reginald McKenna. At the Bank of England they were received by the deputy governor, Sir Alan Anderson, and signed the signature book. Their final call was at Cunliffe & Goschen where the senior partner, the venerable merchant banker Alexander Goschen (brother of Lord Goschen, the Chancellor of the Exchequer in 1887–92) bestowed wisdom derived from his half-century of experience in the City.[39]

The growth of Schröders' business in the early 1920s led to the recruitment of several executives to assist the partners and associate partners. The first was Ralph Rendell, who joined in 1921, aged 30, with a dozen years' experience in commercial banking. Henry Andrews, who was married to the novelist Rebecca West, joined in 1923, aged 29.[40] He had several years banking experience with Barclays and was fluent in seven European languages. His education began in the Hamburg Gymnasium but he later went to the English public school, Uppingham, and to New College, Oxford, where his studies were interrupted by his internment in Germany for the duration of the First World War, being in Hamburg when the fighting began. His father and uncle worked for Wallace Brothers, a merchant bank whose premises were adjacent to Schröders', and one way or another he met Baron Bruno, who invited him to join the firm. He played an important role in the development of Schröders' continental activities in the 1920s and 1930s, acting as the firm's 'European ambassador'.[41] A substantial inheritance provided financial independence and he left the firm in 1935 following a difference of opinion with Frank Tiarks.

In 1923–24 three patrician young men, Robert Collum, aged 20, Maurice Buckmaster, aged 22, and Toby Caulfeild, aged 22, were recruited as executive trainees in response to the enormous expansion of business at that time. Collum, an Eton school friend of Helmut Schröder, was sent to Schlubach Thiemer in Hamburg for a year to learn

German before taking up a position in the firm. In 1928 he resigned and became assistant to the financier Alfred Loewenstein and later worked on Wall Street, though he maintained close ties with the Schröder family and was Helmut's best man at his wedding in 1930. Buckmaster, also an Etonian, spent a couple of years post-school in France and Germany perfecting his command of the languages. Upon his return he was engaged as a language tutor to one of Frank Tiarks' children, which led to him joining the firm.[42] Working under the direction of Henry Andrews he developed the French side of the business. In 1929 he joined the Ford Motor Company, becoming head of its French and later its European operations, and during the Second World War he ran the French Section of SOE, the Special Operations Executive. Caulfeild, yet another Etonian, joined J. Henry Schröder & Co. upon graduation from New College, Oxford. He spent forty-three years with the firm, the first at Schlubach Thiemer in Hamburg improving his German. A career in the City was still relatively unusual for someone with a university education unless there were strong family connections with a particular firm, and most of his Oxford contemporaries entered the army, the navy, the Church or the law. 'In those days it was considered rather shocking to go into trade,' he recalled. 'The City was very much a world apart, unbelievably so!'[43] In the 1920s Andrews, Collum, Buckmaster and Caulfeild constituted the 'Secretariat', an innovation in the conduct of the firm with the intention of rendering assistance to the partners and relieving them of minor executive responsibilities. It was an important step in the expansion of the executive level of management, a development that distinguishes the twentieth-century firm from its nineteenth-century counterpart.

At the end of the First World War Schröders' staff numbered thirty-two. As business resumed in the early 1920s staff numbers multiplied rapidly: seventy-eight in 1920; 209 in 1922; and a peak of 650 in the summer of 1924. The expansion necessitated additional accommodation, and several buildings were rented in Leadenhall Street. Early in 1924 it was decided to build a much larger modern office on the combined site of 145 and 146 Leadenhall Street, the latter having been purchased in December 1921 for £65,450, and for much of that year the whole firm was housed in temporary rented accommodation. 'Imagine, a rapidly increasing staff, new faces almost every day, and departments scattered over a large stretch of Leadenhall Street,' recalled one of the clerks, 'the result was Bedlam.'[44] The internal audit department, for instance, was split between the 'Duke's Room' over the Ship and Turtle public house, an attic at 140 Leadenhall Street, and two rooms on the top floor of a building in Great St Helens separated by a light well with no way of getting from one to the other save descending to the ground floor and climbing back up. One day, two Germans who were evidently unfamiliar with Schröders' office called to change some currency. 'They were directed up to the Foreign Exchange Department which was then in two rooms in a rather isolated position on the third floor of 140 Leadenhall Street. As these Germans came downstairs after transacting their business, one was overheard to say to the other in tones of disgust 'So! das berühmte Bankhaus Schröder – zwei Zimmer auf dem dritten Stock!' (Well! the famous banking house of Schröders – two rooms on the third floor!)'

The new building at 145 Leadenhall Street was designed by Messrs Joseph, architects and surveyors of Godliman Street, EC4. They did their best with an awkwardly shaped site and earned praise from *The Bankers' Magazine* for producing 'one of the best of our modern banking buildings'.[45] On the ground floor was the banking hall housed in a long corridor which led through to the principal staircase. The partners' panelled room was on the first floor, at the rear, and the conference room, equipped with a comprehensive set of pull-down maps of the world, was at the front. The second floor housed the offices of senior staff and the partners' dining room, and the four further floors accommodated the various departments. The front elevation was in a Georgian style with unadorned Portland stone facings, presenting a sedate and dignified face to the world. But inside, the decoration was sumptuous: the walls of the banking hall and the principal stairway were lined with barley-sugar coloured Siena marble; a Grecian frieze embellished the tiled floor and was echoed along the walnut wood banking counter, which was topped with a polished brass grille; walnut coffering ornamented the tall ceiling, from which was suspended large art deco chandeliers of opaque glass with bronze fittings. The Siena marble was Major Pam's idea, inspired by the decor of the Excelsior Hotel in Rome. Subsequently it was discovered that the Excelsior's marble was a cheap composite – but J. Henry Schröder & Co.'s was the finest to be had.

Pattern of Business Activity

The immediate business outlook for Schröders following the Armistice of November 1918 was gloomy. Issuing business, which had been so highly profitable in the years immediately before the war, was non-existent and the partners held the view that its recovery would take a decade. The prospects for the trade finance side of the firm's activities was not rosy either. In each of the areas of the world in which the firm had specialised before the war there were new and formidable obstacles to revival. In Russia, the 1917 Bolshevik revolution had put an end to acceptance business with Russian clients. In Germany, the political and economic turmoil after the war prompted caution about the renewal of commitments. In the United States and Latin America, the challenge was commercial. During the war there had been a rapid growth in the provision of dollar credits by US banks and the bulk of Western Hemisphere trade finance business was lost to London for ever. So keenly was the shift of business to New York felt at 145 Leadenhall Street that in 1923 the Schröder partners established the J. Henry Schroder Banking Corporation on Wall Street.

In the last year of the war Schröders' revenues totalled £32,000, less than a twentieth of the £729,000 earned in 1913, and on an inflation-adjusted basis only a fortieth as much. The post-war boom in Britain and the US stimulated the recovery of Schröders' business and in 1920 revenues were £226,000 (see Figure 7.1). In 1921, despite the domestic business recession, Schröders' growth accelerated and by 1924 revenues had reached £1 million. After this headlong upsurge, activity subsided somewhat and in the second half of the decade revenues fluctuated around an average level of £735,000. The recovery from the wartime nadir in the early 1920s and the re-establishment of the firm as an important City entity were major achievements. However, it should be realised that, on an inflation-adjusted basis, activity in every year of the 1920s was below the peak of 1913 and only in 1924 did real revenues come near their pre-war level.

Taking the years 1919–31 as a whole, Schröders' revenues, net of the payment of 4 per cent interest on partners' capital, averaged £605,000 per annum (see Table 7.1). Accepting made the largest contribution,

Figure 7.1   J. Henry Schröder & Co., total revenues, revenues from accepting, and from issuing and underwiting 1919–31

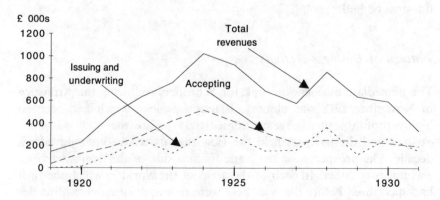

Table 7.1   J. Henry Schröder & Co., sources of revenues, 1919–31

	1919–31 *Annual average* *£000s*	*Per cent*
Accepting	264	44
Issuing and underwriting	177	29
Foreign exchange dealing	24	4
Net interest	141	23
Other[1]	(1)	–
Total	605	100

( ) indicates loss
1. Consignments, insurance, dealing for clients, paying agency commissions, investment and stock account profits, Investment Department.

Source: J. Henry Schröder & Co., profit and loss accounts

generating 44 per cent of revenues. Issuing and underwriting, which in 1905–13 had surpassed accepting as a source of revenue, contributed 29 per cent, a relatively high proportion given the constraints on this side of the business in the 1920s. The Foreign Exchange Department and the Investment Department produced minor revenues compared to the other activities, though this financial yardstick does not fully capture their significance for the firm. Net interest was 23 per cent of revenues, an increase on 1905–13 reflecting the higher post-war interest rates. The deficit on 'other' revenues was the result of losses on securities.

Revenues from accepting rose annually in 1918–24, fell in 1924–27 and reached a plateau in 1927–31. The expansion in the first half of the decade was the result of a substantial increase in the volume of business, balance sheet acceptances increasing from £1.2 million in 1918 to £13.6 million in 1924 (see Figure 7.2). The growth of accepting activity continued in 1925, when acceptances reached £13.9 million, but revenues fell sharply that year and the decline continued until 1927 despite the upturn in acceptances in 1926. The divergence of the acceptance volumes and revenue curves after 1924 in Figure 7.2 was the result of commission-cutting competition from the clearing banks, which J. Henry Schröder & Co. was obliged to match, greatly curtailing the profitability of its accepting activities. The Midland Bank was blamed by the merchant banks for instigating the price war, and when Henry Tiarks was invited to join the Midland board at the end of the decade he refused, telling Sir Reginald McKenna that the behaviour of his bank was not only

Figure 7.2 J. Henry Schröder & Co., acceptances and revenues from
accepting, 1918–30

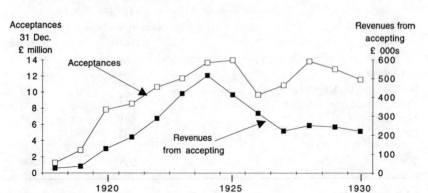

predatory but also unsound.[46] Not long after, as bad debts mounted
because of the economic slump, the clearing banks revised their
commission practices to reflect the true risks of the business.

Revenues from issuing and underwriting fluctuated considerably from
year to year, depending on the requirements of clients, stock market
conditions and official restrictions on fund-raising by foreigners through
public issues (see Figure 7.1 on page 184). The competition from New
York and the increased scale of post-war loans prompted the leading
London firms to co-operate in the conduct of issues for foreign clients.
Schröders' most frequent syndicate partners in the 1920s were Barings
and Rothschilds, with whom sixteen joint issues were made, the alliance
being irreverently referred to in the City as 'the Trinity'.[47] The syndicate
leader on each issue was the firm which originated the business through
its relations with the client. Apparently the initiative for the formation of
the Barings–Rothschilds–Schröders syndicate came from Leadenhall
Street, it being a Schröder client – the state of San Paulo – for which its
first issue was made. Membership of the Trinity did not preclude joint
issues with other firms, each issue being a separate business and the
choice of partners and foreign associates being tailored to requirements.
Besides the large public issues Schröders made numerous private
placements for foreign clients and participated in underwriting
syndicates for domestic issues, thus earning some revenue from the
issuing and underwriting side of the business even when the London
market was closed to public issues for foreign borrowers.

The Produce Department, Schröders' merchanting arm, revived after
the war, though its activities were relatively insignificant in revenue
terms. Hides, coffee and nitrate, followed by bamboo, sheet tin and

bullion were the commodities in which most transactions were undertaken in the 1920s. The conduct of the Produce Department's merchanting activity changed in the course of the decade; at the beginning it was largely consignment business, but by the end it was mostly cable business, simply quoting prices and passing on orders. The arrangement of insurance, earning commissions for the firm, was also a responsibility of the Produce Department. A considerable amount of insurance work was generated by Schröders' merchanting and accepting activities, most of the business being done, as before the war, with the North British and Mercantile Insurance Company of which Helmut Schröder became a director in 1927. The slump in international trade in the early 1930s brought the activities of the Produce Department virtually to a halt, from which only a minimal recovery was made. In 1950, upon the retirement of the last member of staff, it was wound up.

Prior to 1914, foreign exchange dealing was not a major activity in London because most transactions were conducted in sterling, the small amounts of foreign currency or non-sterling denominated bills which Schröders received being sold to specialist brokers at the Royal Exchange. But after the war the volume of foreign exchange dealing increased greatly because of the volatility of sterling and other currencies, the growth of dollar and French franc trade finance, and the increased transfer of balances and securities between international financial centres. In February 1920, in response to the new opportunities, Schröders established a Foreign Exchange Department, recruiting two experienced currency dealers, Neil Adshead and James Gierson, to staff it. Primarily their responsibility was to meet the foreign exchange requirements of the firm arising from the conduct of its other business, but they also took positions in currencies and conducted arbitrage operations in conjunction with firms in Amsterdam and New York. The currency stability which followed Britain's return to the gold standard in 1925 greatly reduced the scope for foreign exchange operations, so much so that in 1927 *The Bankers' Magazine* commented that 'the insignificant profit to be derived (quite incompatible with the risk and time occupied) renders it unworthy of attention as a source of profitable business'.[48] In the early 1920s the Foreign Exchange Department made useful, though never spectacular, contributions to revenues, but after 1925 the sums were much smaller.

In the 1920s, J. Henry Schröder & Co. resumed its leading position in the conduct of accepting amongst the London merchant banks, the volume of its acceptance business being second only to Kleinwort, Sons & Co. (see Table 7.2). The decade saw a widening of Kleinworts' lead, one reason being the transfer of much of Schröders' US and Latin American acceptance business to its New York firm from 1923; if the activity of the

Table 7.2 Acceptances of some leading merchant banks, 1920, 1925, 1930

31 December	1920 £ million	1925 £ million	1930 £ million
Kleinwort, Sons & Co.	15.9	17.6	17.5
J. Henry Schröder & Co.	7.8	13.9	11.5
Hambros Bank Ltd[1]	7.7	10.1	10.9
Baring Brothers & Co. Ltd	3.7	10.0	5.5
S. Japhet & Co. Ltd	n/a	4.8	6.4
Erlangers Ltd	n/a	n/a	4.1
Morgan Grenfell & Co.	1.6	1.6	3.9

1. 31 March following year
n/a = not available
Note: Information on other firms unavailable.

Sources: Stephanie Diaper, 'The History of Kleinwort, Sons & Co. in Merchant Banking, 1858–1966' (unpublished PhD thesis, University of Nottingham, 1983) p. 210; Kathleen Burk, *Morgan Grenfell, 1838–1988* (Oxford University Press, 1989) p. 78; J. Henry Schröder & Co., balance sheets; Barings, Hambros, Japhets, Erlangers – published accounts.

two firms is aggregated, Schröders was the largest of the City's accepting houses in the second half of the 1920s, as at least one contemporary authority guessed it to be.[49] A significant development of the 1920s was the emergence of Hambros as the third largest acceptor amongst the merchant banks, conducting business on only a slightly smaller scale than Schröders by the end of the decade. The growth of Hambros' business was due, it appears, not only to the usual foreign trade financing but also to the development of a substantial domestic clientele, a client base that was the foundation of its emergence as the City's foremost accepting house in the 1930s. The key to the re-establishment of Schröders and Kleinworts as the leading firms in the 1920s was their strong German client base, just as it was the source of their problems from 1931.

Continental European and Japanese Business

As soon as possible at the end of the war ties were re-established with Schröder Gebrüder, where Baron Bruno's brother continued as senior partner, assisted by his partner Ferdinand Peltzer and their sons. Poelchau & Schröder, the partners of which were Werner Poelchau and

Wilhelm Schröder, a cousin of Baron Bruno, was reaffirmed as the firm's Hamburg agent. With their assistance the pre-war debts owed by German clients were recovered and the eventual bad debt losses were small, encouraging the partners to resume business with Germany. Moreover, German firms were desperate for sterling finance and prepared to pay a hefty premium for funds.[50] Between 1920 and 1924, Schröders' acceptances and short-term advances for German clients grew from £823,000 to £5.4 million and again Germany became the most important focus of its banking business (see Figure 7.3). In the early 1920s Hamburg firms accounted for around four fifths of the acceptances and advances provided to German clients, Schlubach Thiemer & Co. and Schröder Gebrüder being the biggest recipients. Other pre-war clients with which business was resumed on a considerable scale included the nitrate merchants H. Fölsch and Ed. Holtzapfel, while amongst the new clients was A. Lüthke, the leading German rice merchant. An important development in the conduct of Schröders' German business in the 1920s was the provision of reimbursement credits on a substantial scale to branches of the Deutsche Bank, the Dresdner Bank and the Disconto-Gesellschaft, the three leading German universal banks. Schröders' closest relations were with the Deutsche Bank, which from 1921 was much the largest of its German clients.

German instability and inflation in the early 1920s made the holding of balances in a stable foreign currency highly desirable, prompting banks, companies and individuals to open current accounts abroad. The seizure by the British government of the London branches of the German banks during the war and the ban on their re-establishment in the City in the early 1920s[51] created an opportunity for firms whose staff could conduct business in German, notably Schröders, Kleinworts and

Figure 7.3   J. Henry Schröder & Co., combined acceptance credits and cash advances for German clients, 1919–30

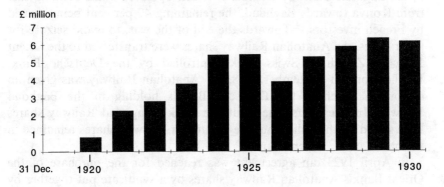

Japhets, to provide clearing services for German clients. Schröders attracted a large amount of this business and developed a substantial clearing operation for German transactions. At the year-end 1921, the first year of operation of this service, German chequing accounts with the firm contained deposits of £1.2 million and overdrafts were £80,000. The acceleration of German inflation in 1922 and the hyperinflation of 1923 led to a large increase in the demand for sterling chequing facilities and by 1924, at the peak, deposits were £4.4 million and overdrafts £320,000. Cheque clearing was a labour-intensive activity and this was the cause of the mushrooming of staff numbers in the early 1920s. Anti-German feeling continued to run high in the City in these years prompting the recruitment of German-speaking Swiss bank clerks, who were eager for employment in London because of the post-war depression in the Swiss banking industry.[52] In 1924, Swiss nationals constituted a sixth of J. Henry Schröder & Co.'s staff. The introduction of the gold-backed Reichsmark in 1924 led to a decline in the scale of Schröders' German clearing operations, though not to their cessation and in 1930 there was still £2 million on deposit with the firm in German chequing accounts. The waning of the clearing business led to the shrinkage of staff numbers, which averaged 315 in the second half of the 1920s. Most of the expatriate Swiss returned home after 1924, but some went to New York and took jobs with the newly established and rapidly expanding J. Henry Schroder Banking Corporation.

The close relations which developed between J. Henry Schröder & Co. and the Deutsche Bank in the aftermath of the First World War led to the firm's involvement in 1923 in an attempted acquisition of the Anatolian Railway Company, an episode that created a 'world-wide sensation'.[53] Before the war the Deutsche Bank was active in the construction of railways in the Ottoman Empire and was the owner of the Anatolian Railway, which connected Constantinople with Ankara and Konya in the heartland of Anatolia. It also had a 60 per cent interest in the Baghdad Railway Company, which operated a line running east from Konya towards Baghdad, the remaining 40 per cent being owned by French investors.[54] Towards the end of the war, to avoid seizure for reparations, the Anatolian Railway shares were transferred to the Orient Bank in Zurich, a Swiss bank controlled by the Deutsche Bank. Furthermore, in September 1918, the Anatolian Railway was given an option to purchase the Deutsche Bank's holding in the Baghdad Railway. In due course the Deutsche Bank's Baghdad Railway shares were seized by the Allies, but the Anatolian Railway shares remained in the hands of the Orient Bank.

In April 1923, an agreement was reached for the purchase of the Orient Bank's Anatolian Railway shares by a syndicate put together by

Schröders, whose other members were Rothschilds, the Westminster Bank, the National Provincial Bank, Lloyds Bank, and the Crédit Suisse.[55] A new private company, the Anglo-Turkish Trust Company (registered address, 147 Leadenhall Street), was formed to act as a holding company for the shares, the plan being to float it in London as a public company, called The National Railways of Turkey 'or some other suitable name', assigning a 37 per cent equity interest to the Orient Bank.[56] These moves would place control of the Anatolian Railway in British hands, though the Deutsche Bank would retain an interest through the Orient Bank. Since the Anatolian Railway would now be a British concern it would be possible to revive the option on the seized Baghdad Railway shares and wrest control from the French. News of the projected sale of the Anatolian Railway Company shares to the Schröder syndicate was obtained by the *Financial News*, a London financial newspaper, which published the story on 8 October 1923. There was a violent reaction in France against the scheme and the Turkish government bowed to French pressure and blocked the transaction, the British Foreign Office adopting its usual non-interventionalist stance in financial affairs. 'We in the FO are children in this game,' commented an official in his briefing note to Lord Curzon, the Foreign Secretary.[57] The Schröder partners were furious about the frustration of their plan, which would have been highly profitable, and when the journalist responsible called at Leadenhall Street shortly afterwards one of them, probably Major Pam, bawled him out of the building.[58]

The hyperinflation of 1922–23 obliterated the financial capital of German companies, necessitating their recapitalisation. Following the stabilisation of the currency and with the prospect of the introduction of the gold-backed Reichsmark, the Deutsche Bank drew up a new balance sheet.[59] This showed share capital and reserves of Rm200 million, comprising 150,000 shares of Rm1,000 each (nominal), of which 110,000 were held by shareholders and 40,000 were unallocated and held in trust, and Rm50 million reserves. The recapitalisation plan required the sale of the 40,000 unallocated shares to expand the capital base, but because of the continuing uncertainties there was no public market for the shares. Baron Bruno was eager to assist the Deutsche Bank in its hour of need and undertook to subscribe for the entire bloc of shares, representing 26.6 per cent of the share capital and a commitment of approximately £2 million – about £50 million in 1990 money – a bold move. On 7 November 1924, ten days after the Dawes Loan, an agreement was signed between the Deutsche Bank and Schröders commiting the syndicate of investors put together by Baron Bruno, comprising Schröders, Rothschilds and General Mining to purchase the shares at Rm1,000 each, with a 10 per cent downpayment. The syndicate undertook to hold the shares and to market them by September 1925, either by public issue or by private placement, probably in London or New York, paying the balance at that future point. The syndicate members received 7 per cent interest on the cash paid amount and were to receive half the profits derived from selling the shares at a premium to the purchase price, the other half accruing to the Deutsche Bank itself, which also retained the voting rights. 'We will consider jointly with you when and at what price the shares are to be sold or introduced in the market' read the contract, but Baron Bruno insisted that 'in case of disagreement, our [Schröders'] views shall prevail'.[60] Subsequently, it was decided to sell the shares through a rights offer to Deutsche Bank shareholders, which was finally effected in July 1926.[61] The commitments of the syndicate meant that the issue was effectively underwritten and the operation went smoothly. On a commitment of £500,000 and a cash payment of £50,000, each of the syndicate members made £75,000 from its participation in the Deutsche Bank business, though the successful outcome should not obscure the considerable risk assumed by Schröders and its partners for twenty months. The Deutsche Bank's directors were fully aware of the significance of the service rendered by Baron Bruno, which reinforced the 'friendship of an especially close and confidential nature' between the firms.[62]

The return of Germany to the gold standard following the success of the Dawes Loan of October 1924 was the cue for an even greater involvement in German finance by J. Henry Schröder & Co. Commercial opportunity was certainly a powerful incentive, but Baron Bruno was also motivated by a strong desire to assist with the economic reconstruction of Germany. Short-term finance by acceptance credits and advances to German clients averaged £5.2 million per annum in 1924–28, almost double the annual average of 1920–23 (see Figure 7.3 on page 189). The clients were much the same as in the early 1920s, predominantly Hamburg merchant firms, Schröder Gebrüder heading the list, and manufacturers and banks elsewhere in Germany. The reversal in the direction of capital flows between the US and Germany in 1928 greatly intensified the demand for working capital from London, and premium rates were paid for funds. There was a significant increase in the number of industrial and utility companies making use of Schröders' facilities on a large scale in 1929–30, notably Allgemeine Elektrizitäts Gesellschaft (AEG), Vereinigte Elecktrizitäts, Eisenwerk-Gesellschaft, and Zucker Raffinerie, Hildesheim. In these years Schröders' acceptances and advances for German clients averaged £6.2 million per annum, more than ever before and almost half of the firm's total. The larger the volume of business conducted with any country, the greater is a bank's exposure to the political risk of a suspension of financial transfers. By increasing the scale of business with Germany in 1929–30 J. Henry Schröder & Co. was assuming additional political risk, but the partners believed that the Young loan negotiations and the creation of the Bank for International Settlements indicated that political action would be taken to solve the reparations question once and for all. It was apparently inconceivable to them that politicians would permit the default of the world's second largest economy in peacetime, with all the damage it would do to international prosperity.

Medium-term finance for German companies was provided by mortgage-loan advances or note issues, for which Schröders acted as agent or syndicate organiser, though few details have survived of these activities. Its role as an accepting house required it to maintain a highly liquid balance sheet, strictly restricting the scale of its own investments in such assets. But the partners' intimate knowledge of German firms and German affairs, which minimised commercial risk, made the high rates of return which could be earned on German financing very attractive. To exploit their expertise profitably an investment trust, the Continental and Industrial Trust Limited (CONTI), was formed in May 1924, the month after the publication of the Dawes Plan, to specialise in making advances to German companies and to underwrite and invest in their securities.[63] William Askew, a leading stockbroker who had recently retired from the Stock Exchange where he had been the confidential jobber of the Bank of England, became chairman, the other directors being Arthur Guinness of Guinness Mahon, John Hugh Smith of Hambros; Major Pam, who acted as managing director; and Henry Andrews, the company secretary. The capital of £1 million was subscribed by Schröders and other City investors, £500,000 being paid-up at the time of formation and the remainder in September, when the first quarter's performance was described as 'so satisfactory'.[64] In 1927, another £1 million was raised, this time from the public by a preference share issue, priced at a 20 per cent premium, and in 1928 a further £1 million from a debenture issue. Baron Bruno became chairman in 1928, the year which also saw the formation of the Second Continental and Industrial Trust Ltd, a wholly-owned subsidiary specialising in medium term advances. In 1930, it was renamed the Tertius Trust Ltd.

The Continental and Industrial Trust's early 'very lucrative' investments came about through a friendship struck up by Frank Tiarks, while taking a cure at Dengler's Sanatorium in Baden-Baden in 1923, with a director of the enormous steel firm Gelsenkirchener Bergwerksgesellschaft and an associate of the leading industrialist Hugo Stinnes.[65] Thereafter the identification of promising investments on CONTI's behalf was undertaken by the German private banks with which J. Henry Schröder & Co. had close ties, notably Schröder

Gebrüder and Poelchau & Schröder in Hamburg, Deichmann & Co. in Cologne, and Hagen & Co. in Berlin. The partner of Hagen & Co. who specialised in Schröders' business was Gustav von Mallinckrodt, who joined the firm in 1919 at the end of the war. He was born in 1892 in Antwerp, where his father, Wilhelm von Mallinckrodt, ran a highly successful trading company and merchant bank. His mother's sister was married to Hermann Kleinwort and thus he had close ties with the Kleinwort family and with the Anglo-German merchant banking community. From 1933, when Hagen & Co. was dissolved, he represented J. Henry Schröder & Co. in Germany, and during the war he looked after the interests of many British companies which had investments or subsidiaries in Germany. After the war he acted as Schröders' representative in Germany until his retirement in 1967.

The Continental and Industrial Trust's investment schedule for 1925 shows shareholdings in about thirty German industrial undertakings, many of them well known enterprises such as Dynamit Nobel; Siemens; AGFA; IG Farbenindustrie; several banks, notably the Deutsche Bank and the Darmstädter und Nationalbank; several Austrian and Hungarian firms, and advances of £50,000–£100,000 to five German companies. By mid-1928 there had been a considerable shift in CONTI's portfolio, 17.5 per cent now being invested in the UK and 27 per cent in the US, riding their booming stock markets. No further details of the pattern of investments survive, but the contrast between 1925 and 1928 suggests a highly active portfolio management policy. At the end of 1930, after six years of trading during which normal levels of dividends had been paid, CONTI's account showed accumulated reserves of £880,000, almost matching the ordinary share capital – an impressive performance.

The London capital market was a significant source of long-term funds for Germany in the 1920s. Public issues for German borrowers between the Dawes Loan of October 1924 and the summer of 1930, when political unrest in Germany scared off investors, raised £50 million, though their counterparts in New York raised £250 million.[66] The German public issues in London in 1924–30 comprised £24 million by the German Republic, through the Dawes Loan and the Young Loan which were issued by a large syndicate of City firms lead-managed by Morgan Grenfell, and £26 million by companies and municipalities. Schröders played the foremost part amongst the London merchant banks in raising the non-sovereign funds, lead-managing six public issues that raised in total £16.5 million. These are summarised in Table 7.3.

The first post-war German corporate issue in London was made in December 1925 on behalf of the German Potash Syndicate. This was a cartel established by statute in 1919 to control the whole German potash

Table 7.3   J. Henry Schröder & Co., German issues, 1925–29

	Borrower	Amount £m	Simple yield %	Yield premium %	Schröders' profit £
7 Dec. 1925	German Potash Syndicate	5	7.4	2.9	122,000
1 May 1926	German Potash Syndicate	3	7.4	2.9	49,000
30 Sept. 1926	City of Hamburg	2	6.4	1.8	17,000
4 Jul. 1927	City of Berlin	3.5	6.1	1.5	26,000
19 Dec. 1928	Hamburg Waterworks Company	1	6.4	1.9	14,000
1 Jul. 1929	German Potash Syndicate	2.25	6.8	2.2	44,000

Source: J. Henry Schröder & Co. bond book.

industry, an enormous undertaking comprising 221 mines and 7 factories, with reserves equivalent to centuries of production. Initially, the intention was to launch the issue in New York, but American lawyers advised that the monopolistic nature of the undertaking might fall foul of US anti-trust legislation. Happily for Schröders, the lifting of the British foreign loan embargo in November 1925 made it possible to proceed in London. The issue comprised £8 million bonds, of which £5 million was made in London by J. Henry Schröder & Co. and Higginson & Co., the London offshoot of the renowned Boston investment bank Lee, Higginson & Co., £1.7 million in Zurich led by Crédit Suisse, £1 million in Amsterdam led by Hope & Co., and £300,000 in Stockholm led by the Stockholms Enskilda Bank. The bonds, which offered investors a 2.9 per cent yield premium over consols, the British government bonds that were used by the market as the risk-free reference point, were very well received and the issue was substantially over-subscribed. J. Henry Schröder & Co.'s profit on the business was £122,000, its largest profit on a new issue in the 1920s. The success of the German Potash Syndicate loan opened the London market for other German borrowers and was hailed by the *Quarterly Review* as 'an event of outstanding importance'.

It was not just the yield of the Potash Loan that appealed to investors but the novel arrangements for the collection of funds to service the debts to foreign bondholders.[67] A large part of the sales of the German Potash Syndicate were exports which generated foreign currency earnings, J. Henry Schröder & Co. being appointed as 'Receiving Bank' for sterling and dollar potash sales receipts. At the end of each month the firm deducted one twelfth of the amount required to service the bonds issued in London from the receipts and remitted the rest to the German Potash Syndicate. Crédit Suisse, Hope & Co. and the Stockholms Enskilda Bank did the same on behalf of the bondholders in their markets. The arrangement worked so well that in the 1930s, when other German corporate bonds were at best receiving partial service, the Potash Loan bondholders received full and punctual payments. Even after the outbreak of war it proved possible to pay interest in London up to January 1941, while payments to bondholders in neutral and German-occupied countries continued throughout the conflict from funds collected by the other Receiving Banks. Private placements by Schröders and its international syndicate raised a further £4 million in May 1926 and £3 million in July 1929 for the German Potash Syndicate.

It was only natural that the City of Hamburg, Baron Bruno's birthplace, should turn to Schröders when it sought funds from abroad. In 1923, the firm conducted a private placement of bonds on its behalf, and in September 1926 the Barings–Rothschilds–Schröders syndicate brought out a £2 million bond issue to finance railway works, harbour improvements and the construction of a bridge over the Elbe. Local connections also led to Schröders appointment as issuer of £1 million bonds on behalf of the Hamburg Waterworks Company in September 1928. Acting without a syndicate, the bonds were issued at a 1.9 per cent premium over consols, but by then investor interest in German bonds had waned and the issue was under-subscribed. Berlin, the German capital, raised funds in New York in July 1925 and in November 1926, but a few months later Schröders trounced the American competition with an offer to raise the £3.5 million required by the City to finance extensions of the underground railway system and the waterworks at a premium of only 1.5 per cent above consols. Acting with Barings and Rothschilds, the issue was brought out in July 1927. In fact, the pricing was too tight and it became necessary to mount a substantial support operation in the market; it was not until two years later that the syndicate finally disposed of its holdings of Berlin bonds at a profit.

There was a handful of clients in Belgium, France and Holland for which Schröders provided credits on a sizable scale in the 1920s, notably the merchant firms Schlubach Behrens of the Hague, an associate of Schlubach Thiemer of Hamburg, and the banks Groupe des Banques Belge of Brussels, Société Générale of Paris and the Österreichische Creditanstalt of Vienna, which received reimbursement credits. Even so, total acceptances and cash advances for clients in continental countries other than Germany were about half the German total in 1921–28 and only a third in 1929–30. But continental countries were of considerable importance as sources of issuing business and as markets for sterling and dollar securities. It was for France's largest railway company, the Paris–Lyons–Marseilles Railway, that Schröders made its first post-war continental issue. In February 1922, with Barings, it issued £5 million bonds in London under French state guarantee. The issue, which gave a 2.3 per cent premium over consols, proved popular with investors and highly profitable for the issuing houses since there was an unusually large 8.5 point spread between the purchase price of 77.5 and the issue price of 86. Schröders' profit on the Paris–Lyons–Marseilles Railway issue was £114,000. In the 1920s Schröders also made issues in London for a number of European companies. For the most part this was through private placements, but the records of this side of the firm's activity are fragmentary. One such client was the Boden-Credit Anstalt, a leading Austrian bank, of which Baron Bruno became a director in the early 1920s. It may well have been this connection which led to an introduction to the Hungarian Commercial Bank of Pesth for which the firm organised a syndicate to place its shares in 1925.[80] The following year it raised £100,000 for the French car manufacturer André Citröen SA. The buoyant stock market of November 1927 provided an opportunity to raise £1.1 million in equity from the public on behalf of the leading Dutch margarine manufacturer, Margarine Union which subsequently merged with Lever Brothers to form Unilever. Finally, in 1929 £110,000 was raised by private placement for Aktiebolaget Separator, a Swedish company which pioneered the manufacture of skimmed milk. To promote the sale of securities to French, Swiss and other continental investors the firm established Major Bill Williams, a British stockbroker, as its resident representative in Paris.

Since the Second World War, such international agencies as the International Money Fund (IMF) have performed the function of assisting nations with financial problems with loans and expertise to put their financial affairs in order, particularly the stabilisation of their currencies. There was no IMF in the 1920s and for guidance and assistance governments turned to the central banks of Britain, the United States and France, and sometimes to the Financial Committee of the League of Nations.[69] But the raising of funds for stabilisation or other purposes was conducted in the international capital market with the sponsorship of merchant banks and investment banks. Naturally, the scale of such sovereign loans was often substantial and in the 1920s it was the usual pattern for them to be issued by syndicates of bankers simultaneously in several financial centres to achieve the widest possible distribution of the bonds.[70]

Schröders was a participant in syndicates which made issues on behalf of five Central European sovereign borrowers for stabilisation and reconstruction purposes (see Table 7.4). In April 1922, the Barings–Rothschilds–Schröders syndicate made issues on behalf of Czechoslovakia, which had come into being as a separate state only in 1919. The 1922 loan was the first post-war issue in London by a Central European country and the Barings partners who negotiated the terms with the Czech representative, no easy matter since he spoke no English and scant French, impressed upon him the difficulties of persuading investors to buy the bonds of a country of which they had never heard.[71] In fact, with the imprimatur of the three leading merchant banks, plus a 4.1 per cent yield premium over consols, the £2.8 million bonds were very well received by investors and were soon trading at a premium. This led to complaints that the pricing had been too generous, prompting the British ambassador to point out that Czechoslovakia had to pay 'for being a fraction of Central Europe – not an encouraging field for the British investor – and for its comic opera name, and so on'.[72] Simultaneous issues were made in New York by a syndicate comprising Kidder Peabody, Kuhn, Loeb and the National City Bank, and in Holland by Hope & Co. A further loan of £1.85 million was brought out in London by the same parties in May 1924.

The Barings–Rothschilds–Schröders syndicate made three issues on behalf of Hungary in the 1920s, lead-managed by Rothschilds. These

Table 7.4   J. Henry Schröder & Co., European sovereign and sovereign guaranteed issues, 1922–30

Date	Borrower	Amount £m	Simple yield %	Yield premium %	Schröders' profit £
27 Feb. 1922	Paris–Lyon–Marseilles Railway Co.	5	7.0	2.3	114,000
5 Apr. 1922	Czechoslovak State	2.8	8.3	4.1	36,000
29 Nov. 1923	Republic of Finland	1	6.7	2.3	28,000
19 May 1924	Czechoslovak State	1.85	8.3	4.0	22,000
1 Jul. 1924	Counties of Hungary	7.9	8.5	4.1	64,000
27 Jul. 1926	Counties of Hungary	1.25	7.7	3.2	9,000
22 Dec. 1926	Kingdom of Bulgaria	2.4	7.6	3.0	13,000
14 Jul. 1927	Counties of Hungary	1	6.8	2.2	6,000
21 Nov. 1928	Kingdom of Bulgaria	1.8	7.8	3.3	12,000
18 Apr. 1930	Industrial Mortgage Bank of Finland	2	6.3	1.8	11,000
15 July 1930	Austrian Government	3	7.4	2.8	13,000

Source: J. Henry Schröder & Co. bond book.

were conducted 'under the auspices' of the League of Nations, meaning that the chairman of the League's Financial Committee acted as trustee for the bondholders. This endorsement, which was generally given to the issues made by the new countries which emerged from the post-war peace settlement, proved a successful marketing device but the implied guarantee proved worthless when put to the test. For the first Hungarian loan in July 1924 it was deemed necessary also to provide a yield premium double the rate on consols. Smaller premiums were offered in 1926 and 1927 by which time the market had become much more familiar with Central European securities. The large 1924 loan was simultaneously issued in the United States, the Netherlands, Sweden, Switzerland, Italy, Czechoslovakia and Hungary, being the most widely syndicated of the issues in which Schröders played a part in the 1920s.

J. Henry Schröder & Co.'s standing in relation to Romanian financial affairs derived from its sponsorship of the loan of 1913. After the war the Romanian government maintained that Article 297B of the Treaty of Versailles entitled it to refuse to honour bonds which had been held by enemy nationals, that is Germans, during the war. The Schröder partners took the view that it would be fraudulent if the antecedence of a bearer bond denied the rights of the current holder, but the Romanians were adamant and despite the involvement of the British Foreign Office, the Treasury and the Bank of England the 'rather complicated' dispute dragged on.[73] By the autumn of 1926 it had become clear that Romania intended to seek a large external stabilisation loan and there was a flurry of activity by all sorts of 'agents' seeking to establish a niche in the business. These manoeuvrings appalled the British embassy in Bucharest, which told the Finance Minister 'that big loans in the City were not negotiated in the hole and corner manner which seemed up to date to have characterised the feelers put out on one side and the other'.[74] The Foreign Office believed that the issue would most probably be led by Schröders and in mid-November 1926 the Bucharest embassy reported that the firm had offered to raise £20 million through an international syndicate.[75] But it was impossible to proceed because of the unresolved dispute over Romania's pre-war bonds, the Schröder partners 'refusing to commit a first class name to a second class borrower'.[76] The partners came under pressure from their prospective syndicate members to weaken their stance. Dr Rudolph Sieghart, head of the Austrian Boden-Credit Anstalt, expressed astonishment, telling Andrews that 'he could not understand how a man of such penetrating understanding as the Baron could fail to see the point of this business', which was, he explained, that 'when the issue has been made we will make an "Arbeit Syndicate", that is a syndicate from whom the great firms like Schneider, Skoda and Vickers will get their contracts for rails and rolling stock, and for the contracts they will pay the Syndicate five per cent. That is an additional profit of three hundred and fifty thousand pounds'.[77] Nevertheless, Baron Bruno held to his principles, remarking 'poor old Sieghart, he always wants to persuade you to do a business by telling you how much money you can make'. Eventually the Schröder partners became so exasperated that they refused to deal further with Romania, and the firm's place was taken by Lazards and Hambros.[78]

Bulgaria, one of Europe's poorest and most undeveloped countries, emerged from the First World War with a reparations bill even heavier than Germany's relative to the country's resources.[79] Ethnic conflicts in the early 1920s created a massive refugee problem, making the economic situation even more desperate and jeopardising the peace of the region. The League of Nations became involved and practically took over the country's financial affairs. In December 1926, a loan was floated in London, New York, Holland and Switzerland under League of Nations auspices to provide funds for refugee settlement. The issue was lead-managed by J. Henry Schröder & Co., its appointment arising from its conduct of the 1909 Bulgarian bond issue, in conjunction with two firms which had a standing of some sort in Bulgarian financial affairs, the Ottoman Bank, an Anglo-French bank which operated in the territories of the former Turkish Empire, and Stern Brothers, an old friend of Schröders' though a very minor house by the mid-1920s. 'We felt that as we were so much the predominant member of the Group we had to treat them exceptionally well', noted a Schröder partner, 'it was the first issue the Ottoman Bank or Stern Brothers had made for many years and they were full of their own importance and very touchy on questions of prestige'.[80] The yield premium over consols was 3 per cent, a rather modest premium given the state of the country, demonstrating the significance of the League of Nations endorsement. In November 1928, the same syndicate brought out a further Bulgarian loan, again under League of Nations auspices, for currency stabilisation. By this time the market for Central European bonds was weaker on both sides of the Atlantic and a 3.3 per cent premium was offered to tempt investors. The issue was successful in London, but in New York, where the issuing syndicate was led by Speyer & Co. and the J. Henry Schroder Banking Corporation, it was a disaster.

Another new country for which Schröders raised a loan was the Republic of Finland, which came into being in 1917. In November 1923, Schröders and Hambros, which had longstanding Scandinavian ties, co-managed a £1 million issue to finance the development of the Finnish timber industry. Evidently investors looked more favourably on Finland than on Czechoslovakia or Hungary and its debut as a borrower was made at a yield premium over consols of only 2.3 per cent. In April 1930 the firms made a £2 million issue for the Industrial Mortgage Bank of Finland, under state guarantee, which was readily absorbed by the market with a premium of only 1.8 per cent over consols. In 1928 Rothschilds signed a contract commiting a syndicate comprising themselves, Schröders, Barings and Hambros, to raise £50 million for the kingdom of the Serbs, Croats and Slovenes, though ultimately Schröders took no part in any such issues. But it did participate in the syndicate lead-managed by Rothschilds, whose other members were Barings and Morgan Grenfell, which in July 1930 brought out a £3 million loan for the Austrian government.

Schröders' ties with Japan were renewed in the 1920s. Following the terrible Tokyo earthquake of September 1923, vast funds were required for reconstruction, and in February 1924 a syndicate led by the Westminster Bank and comprising the Yokohama Specie Bank, the Hong Kong and Shanghai Bank, Barings, Morgan Grenfell, Rothschilds and Schröders successfully raised £25 million for the Imperial Japanese government by an issue of 6 per cent bonds, a simultaneous issue being made in New York. In October 1926 the same syndicate raised a further £6 million for reconstruction purposes through the City of Tokyo 5½ per cent loan. Finally, in May 1930, it brought out a £12.5 million 5½ per cent loan for the Imperial Japanese government, simultaneously with a $71 million issue in New York, raising funds which were used for the conversion and redemption of existing loans. Schröders also pursued Japanese business independently of other firms, for instance raising £1.5 million for Nippon Electric Power in January 1931 through a private placement.

US and Latin American Business

The revival of Schröders' acceptance business in the United States began in 1919. At the end of the war, the only US client making use of its acceptance facilities on any scale was Czarnikow–Rionda, whose £640,000 credit accounted for 84 per cent of total US availments. In 1919–20 the list of US merchants making use of sizeable credits provided by the firm lengthened to about a dozen, and total US credits in the first half of the decade were around £1.5 million. Czarnikow–Rionda continued to be much the most important of the US clients, sometimes accounting for some two-thirds of US business. One reason was its sourcing of supplies of sugar from the British West Indian islands where sterling was the currency. Another was the close friendship between Manuel Rionda and the Schröder partners. The connection was of enormous benefit to Schröders but the scale of the credits occasionally caused problems. Henry Andrews recalled:

> when Prohibition was introduced the price of sugar rose in an unprecedented way and was subjected to violent fluctuations. Mr Rionda required more finance for the transactions of his firm and one fine day a cable was received by Schröders asking if he might draw up to a figure which I have heard was two million pounds, an enormous sum. The Baron and Mr Tiarks agreed that Rionda thoroughly knew his business and that as he was one of their oldest friends this was an occasion when they should stand by him. It goes without saying that it was one of the fundamental principles of the Baron not to put too many eggs into one basket. Mr Arthur Spitzer of Paris told me that he was present on this occasion and that having taken his decision the Baron wrote out the answer to Mr Rionda in the following words: 'Your cable received. Delighted'.

> In due course the acceptances based on this arrangement were discounted and one discount broker closely associated with Schröders took occasion to say to Baron Schröder, 'Baron, there is a very great deal of Rionda's paper in the market, is that all right?' In reply the Baron asked him whether by chance he happened to have one of those bills in his portfolio and on being handed such a bill he asked the broker 'Whose signature is that across the bill?' 'That, Baron, is your firm's signature.' 'Is that all right?' 'Why naturally, Baron, of course it is.' 'Thank you, that is all that I have to say'.[81]

During the First World War the US dollar replaced sterling as the usual medium for international finance in most of the countries of Latin America, and New York supplanted London as their principal source of acceptance credit. In December 1918, J. Henry Schröder & Co.'s acceptances and cash advances on behalf of Latin American clients were £343,000, compared to £1.1 million in 1913. But business revived as regular contract was renewed, and by December 1925 acceptances and advances were £5.3 million. Many of Schröders' pre-war merchant clients complemented their dollar financing with sterling facilities and the client list of the 1920s includes Weber & Co. and H. Fölsch of Valparaiso; Ernesto Tornquist and Staudt & Cia of Buenos Aires; Blohm & Co. of Caracas; Gildemeister & Co. of Valparaiso and Lima; and Theodor Wille & Co. of Sao Paulo. But the most important clients of the 1920s were the various German–South American banks, to which

Schröders provided reimbursement credits on a large scale, especially the Banco Aleman Transatlantico, a subsidiary of the Deutsche Bank, Banco Brasileiro Allemano, Banco de Chile y Alemania, Banco Germanico de America do Sul, and regional banks such as the Banco do Brasil and the Banco Nacional de Commercio. In the second half of the decade the volume of acceptances and cash advances averaged £3.5 million, a reduction that reflected the increasing competition for reimbursement credit business from the British clearing banks and the US commercial banks. The facilities provided by Schröders to the German–South American banks and to regional banks declined somewhat, though in 1929, for instance, both the Banco Aleman Transatlantico and the Banco do Brasil had outstanding credits in excess of £500,000. The familiar set of merchant firms continued to make extensive use of Schröders' facilities until their activities were curtailed by the slump in international trade in the early 1930s.

New York dominated the issue of loans for Latin American borrowers in the 1920s, with the notable exception of the federal government of Brazil and the state of San Paulo, which continued to originate their issues in London, though tranches were issued simultaneously in New York (see Table 7.5). The reason was the coffee valorisation scheme which was denounced in the United States as a trust-like conspiracy to make Americans over-pay for coffee.[82] In 1926, the US Secretary of Commerce even intervened to prevent Wall Street from originating an issue for valorisation purposes.[83] Between 1921 and 1930, Schröders lead-managed four issues on behalf of the state of San Paulo, which were conducted with Barings and Rothschilds. Speyer & Co. undertook the Wall Street issues, working with the J. Henry Schroder Banking Corporation on those of 1926, 1928 and 1930. In March 1922 and October 1927 the Barings–Rothschilds–Schröders syndicate also brought out large issues on behalf of the Brazilian federal government, which were lead-managed by Rothschilds.

The valorisation schemes of the early and mid-1920s were very successful in supporting the price of coffee, stimulating output both in Brazil and in other countries, notably Colombia. By the end of the decade the supply of coffee was outstripping demand to such an extent that the ability of San Paulo to manage the international market was being undermined. The stockpile accumulated in 1927 was intact when there was another bumper crop in 1929, causing the price of coffee to collapse. This led to a Brazilian foreign exchange crisis and the Banco do Brasil, the private bank which acted as the country's central bank, virtually ran out of foreign exchange. J. Henry Schröder & Co. and the J. Henry Schroder Banking Corporation provided an emergency £2 million loan to the Banco do Brasil that enabled it to weather the storm

Table 7.5   J. Henry Schröder & Co., Latin American issues, 1921–31

Date	Borrower	Amount £m	Simple yield %	Yield premium %	Schröders' profit £
1 Mar. 1921	State of San Paolo	2	8.3	3.0	58,000
4 May 1922	United States of Brazil	7	7.7	3.4	105,000
13 Dec. 1922	Peruvian Government	1.25	7.9	3.4	29,000
23 Mar. 1926	State of San Paulo	2.5	7.3	2.7	23,000
13 Oct. 1927	United States of Brazil	8.75	7.1	2.6	48,000
20 Mar. 1928	State of Minas Geraes	1.75	6.7	2.2	13,000
24 Jul. 1928	State of San Paulo	3.5	6.3	1.8	24,000
25 Apr. 1930	State of San Paulo	8	7.3	2.8	116,000
31 Mar. 1931	Compania de Salitre de Chile	3	7.3	2.9	36,000
31 Mar. 1921	Antofagasta Railway Notes	0.6			
31 Mar. 1923	Lima Light, Power & Tramways Co. Debs.	1.5	6.6	2.3	54,000
2 Jul. 1923	Lima Railways Co. Debs.	0.2			
29 Mar. 1927	United Railways of Havana Debs.	1.75	5.9	1.4	19,000

Source: J. Henry Schröder & Co. bond book.

and as reciprocity it thereafter kept a substantial part of its dollar and sterling balances with the Schröder firms in New York and London, which were profitably employed. The £8 million issue of April 1930 was used for valorisation purposes, but the slump in international trade soon rendered the exercise redundant and in 1931 the state of San Paulo ran out of foreign exchange to service its loans and suspended payments. This last of the valorisation loans was eventually paid off nine years late, in 1949.

The antagonism between Schröders and Lazards, a City *cause célèbre* of the 1920s, arose from Lazards' encroachment upon Schröders' lucrative relationship with the state of San Paulo. In 1926, Lazards won the appointment to bring out a £10 million issue on behalf of the San Paulo Coffee Institute to provide further funds for valorisation purposes. The Schröder partners regarded San Paulo as their client and accused Lazards of breaching the unwritten code of gentlemanly behaviour amongst the merchant banks that they did not poach each other's clients. Lazards responded that Schröders' client was the state of San Paulo, not the San Paulo Coffee Institute, fanning the fury at 145 Leadenhall Street, since the Institute was controlled by the state and the loan was backed by a state guarantee. To make matters worse the Coffee Institute loan was followed by a £1.25 million issue by Lazards for the Bank of the State of San Paulo. Moreover, in 1927, Lazards vetoed Schröders' participation in a syndicate that it formed with Barings and Rothschilds to issue a French loan.[84] Cordial relations between the firms were eventually restored at the end of a dinner of the Society of Merchants Trading to the Continent when the Chairman persuaded their partners to drink a toast together – in coffee.[85]

Schröders' close ties with the state of San Paulo led to an introduction to the authorities of the state of Minas Geraes, another coffee-producing state. Hitherto, Minas Geraes had raised external finance in the French market, but Schröders secured the appointment to bring out a loan in the spring of 1928. Schröders was not the only firm chasing the Minas Geraes contract, and an executive of the J. Henry Schroder Banking Corporation who was visiting Rio was astonished to learn that the president of the state of Minas Geraes was negotiating with an American syndicate despite the agreement with Schröders. Hurrying to Belo Horizonte, the state capital, he was able to persuade the president 'that his life would be a lot more pleasant if he respected our preference clause' and it was Schröders which brought out the loan.[86] The Minas Geraes contract was won by bidding a high price, narrowing the spread between the buy and sell prices of the bonds (the source of the firm's gross profits) to 2 per cent, compared, for instance, to the 6.5 per cent spread on the San Paulo loan of 1921. The result was that although the issues were for similar sums their profitability was very different – £58,000 in 1921 but only £13,000 in 1928.

In December 1922, J. Henry Schröder & Co. once again raised a loan for the government of Peru. The £1.25 million issue was conducted with Barings and secured on guano revenues. The following year, acting alone, Schröders made a £1.5 million debenture issue on behalf of the Lima Light, Power & Tramways Company Ltd, a British-registered firm that was the owner of the electric tramways and electrical power supply in the Peruvian cities of Lima and Callao. The public loan, and some additional private placements, financed large extensions of the company's installations and the replacement of overhead power cables by underground transmission. Schroders also sponsored issues for the two Latin American railway companies with which it had very close relations: the Antofagasta (Chili) and Bolivia Railway Co. and the United Railways of the Havana and Regla Warehouses Ltd.

The Chilean nitrate industry with which Schröders had been involved since the 1880s experienced a crisis in the late 1920s due to the falling price of nitrate because of competition from synthetic fertilisers. In response, the Chilean government established the Compania de Salitre de Chile (COSACH) which took control of the whole industry and instigated rationalisation. It came into being in March 1931 owned half by the nitrate producing companies and half by the state. This development was welcomed at 145 Leadenhall Street, the *Quarterly Review* commenting, 'that amalgamation is in the best interests of the shareholders of the existing companies needs little demonstration. From every point of view, the prospects of the nitrate industry, now so drastically reorganised, are highly favourable'.[87] The formation of COSACH was followed by issues in Europe and the United States which sought to raise £10 million working capital for the new undertaking. Schröders lead-managed an issue of £3 million bonds, of which £2 million were brought out in London by a syndicate comprising itself, Barings, Rothschilds and Morgan Grenfell, and the remainder by Mendelsohn & Co. in Amsterdam, Crédit Suisse in Zurich and the Stockholms Enskilda Bank in Stockholm. Investors were offered a 2.9 per cent premium over consols, but the international depression was deepening and the underwriters were obliged to take up 90 per cent of their allocations (though Schröders none the less made a profit of £36,000 on the issue).[88] The public's wariness of the bonds proved to be justified, remittances from COSACH for coupon payments being suspended in April 1932.[89] Early in 1933 the Chilean government annulled the decree by which COSACH had been formed, leaving the bondholders and Schröders in a very uncomfortable position. Litigation by a bondholders' committee commenced late in the year and in October 1934 it was arranged that COSACH bonds would be exchanged for the bonds of a new state corporation, the Corporacion de Ventas de Salitre y Yodo de Chile (Chilean Nitrate and Iodine Sales Corporation), which had a monopoly of nitrate export sales. Schröders was appointed to conduct the conversion operation.

The COSACH Loan of March 1931 was a landmark since it was the last of the series of bond issues conducted by the firm for foreign borrowers which had begun in 1853. Indeed, it was one of the very last such issues conducted in the City before the virtual cessation of primary international capital market activity in London for a generation. But the Schröder partners had anticipated the increased importance of the domestic market and had already begun to focus upon the expansion of their activities in this direction.

Domestic Initiatives

Prior to the First World War Schröders had few British acceptance clients. Immediately after the conflict it began to provide credits of £100,000–£200,000 for a handful of British trading firms, such as the meat shippers Anglo-Argentine Cold Storage and Vestey Brothers, and the Moscow Fur Trading Company. A relationship was developed with the margarine industry and the British subsidiaries of the continental manufacturers Margarine Union and Jürgens were clients, the latter having credits of around £500,000 in the early 1920s. There was also a notable group of a dozen or so Manchester cotton manufacturers which were acceptance clients, though the scale of their facilities was much smaller, being in the range £10,000–£40,000.

From the mid-1920s, Schröders began to become involved in domestic British company finance and issuing business. Its first issue on behalf of a British manufacturing company was in July 1924 when it brought out £550,000 debentures of the Glass, Houghton and Castleford Collieries Ltd. This was a large firm with mining, brick-making and chemical interests in Derbyshire and the West Riding of Yorkshire, and the issue was made in connection with its conversion from a private to a public company. Schröders conducted three further issues for colliery companies in the 1920s: a share issue for the Horton Coal Company in 1926; a £2.1 million debenture issue for Powell Duffryn Steam Coal Ltd in 1928; and a £1.6 million debenture issue for Stevenson Clarke and Associated Companies Ltd also in 1928. As for foreign loans, Schröders' usual professional companions in the conduct of domestic issues in the 1920s, and succeeding decades, were Slaughter and May as solicitors and W. Greenwell & Co. as stockbrokers.

Frank Tiarks provided the introduction to the British Tanker Company, the tanker subsidiary of the Anglo Persian Oil Company (later British Petroleum) of which he had been a director since 1917. In December 1925, in conjunction with Barings, the firm brought out a £4 million debenture issue to finance tanker construction. Barings was the lead-manager on three issues conducted by the Barings-Rothschilds-Schröders syndicate on behalf of London underground railway companies. In 1928 the syndicate raised £4 million for the Underground Electric Railways Company of London, and in 1930 it made debenture issues of £5 million for the London Electric Railway Company and £4.2 million for the Central London Railway Company, which financed suburban extensions of the Piccadilly Line to Cockfosters and North-fields and station improvements including the construction of the long escalator at Holborn. Schröders profits on these issues were respectively

£19,000, £20,000 and £14,000, considerably smaller sums than would usually have been generated by foreign loans of similar size. Finally, in March 1930 the firm conducted its first issue on behalf of a British local authority, Bristol Corporation, for which it raised £2.5 million realising a profit on the business of a mere £7,000.

J. Henry Schröder & Co.'s close connections with the British motor industry began in 1926 when the firm sponsored the introduction to Europe of cold steel body pressing. The previous year Frank Tiarks had been taken on a tour of the Philadelphia pressing plant of the Edward G. Budd Manufacturing Corporation, 'makers of difficult shapes in sheet metal',[90] which had pioneered the production of steel car bodies by hydraulic pressing. He was full of admiration and negotiated the formation of joint ventures with the Budd Company to introduce the technology into Britain and Germany. William Morris, later Lord Nuffield, the chairman of Morris Motors, was persuaded to join the British undertaking, which was registered on 28 April 1926 as the Pressed Steel Company of Great Britain Ltd. The total capital of the new company was £1.6 million, composed of £800,000 7 per cent cumulative participating preference shares, without voting rights, and £800,000 ordinary shares. The agreement between the parties specified that in return for granting to Pressed Steel a 99-year exclusive licence for the exploitation of its patents in Great Britain, the Budd Company was to receive 51 per cent of the £800,000 ordinary capital of the new firm.[91] Morris Motors undertook to use Pressed Steel's products in the manufacture of its automobiles and to provide advice to the new firm. It also agreed to subscribe £300,000 of the £800,000 to be raised by the issue of preference shares and a further £200,000 in debentures. In return it was allocated £200,000 in fully paid ordinary shares. Schröders put together a financial syndicate comprising Baring Brothers, Robert Fleming & Co. and Calouste Gulbenkian which subscribed for £500,000 in preference shares, receiving £192,000 in fully paid ordinary shares (24 per cent of the equity) as a bonus.

The Pressed Steel board was composed of five directors nominated by the Budd Company, two by Morris and two by Schröders – Major Pam, who became the chairman, and Henry Tiarks. Otto Müller, a relative of the chairman of the partner in the German venture, was appointed manager. A plant was erected at Cowley, adjacent to Morris' works,[92] but Morris Motors proved unable to take up all the output of the plant while other manufacturers were reluctant to take supplies from a firm so closely associated with a rival. Nevertheless sales reached £3 million in 1928 and in 1930 turnover for the year was estimated at £3.7 million. Profits, however, were another matter, and five years after the commencement of operations the firm was still unable to meet the dividends due on the preference shares. In May 1930, the ordinary and preference shares allocated to Morris Motors were redeemed so that Pressed Steel should be perceived as an independent concern by other motor manufacturers, though Morris retained the £200,000 debenture holding. The issued ordinary share capital of the firm, after various other minor adjustments, now amounted to £575,570, of which 58 per cent was controlled by the Budd Company and 42 per cent by the Schröder syndicate. So that voting control should remain in British hands for political reasons, £100,000 of Budd's holding was transferred to Schröder Nominees, Schröders' nominee company, and it was agreed that these votes should be cast at Schröders' discretion.[94]

In Germany, Schröders and Budd went into partnership with Ambi-Verwaltung AG of Berlin, whose chairman was Arthur Müller, and formed Ambi-Budd Presswerk GmbH. An ownership structure similar to Pressed Steel was adopted for Ambi Budd, the Budd Company being allocated 51 per cent of equity, Arthur Müller taking 30 per cent, and Schröders 19 per cent, which was divided between the London and New York houses. Again preference shares were used to finance the firm though resort was also made on a large scale to short- and medium-term borrowing from banks, including Schröders, and in 1930 bank credits amounted to twice the preference share capital. Ambi-Budd also quickly established itself as an important concern and by 1930 could boast that 'its customers include practically all of the important German automobile manufacturers and also prominent American manufacturers operating in the field such as the Ford Motor Company, Willys Overland Company, Chrysler Corporation . . . [and] has received large orders from Citröen and Peugeot in France; Steyr in Austria and the Ford Company for the continental requirements'.[93] But again the profits left much to be desired. The German financial crisis of the summer of 1931 locked-up Schröders' interest in the firm for the following two decades.

In 1926, it was decided to develop Schröders' investment management activities and an Investment Department was created. Neil Adshead and Robin Wilson were redeployed from the moribund Foreign Exchange Department to run it, under Major Pam's direction, and henceforth they handled this side of the business. This was apparently a novelty in the City and caused some resentment amongst stockbrokers who were used to dealing with the partners themselves. But the department soon established a strong reputation and flourished, not least because for several years in the mid-1920s J. Henry Schröder & Co. was closely associated with the brilliant and flamboyant Belgian financier Captain Alfred Loewenstein. Loewenstein worked very closely with Major Pam and based himself at 145 Leadenhall Street when he was in London, the office he used being known for many years after his death as the

Loewenstein room. Born in 1877 the son of a Belgian foreign exchange dealer, he made a fortune on the stock exchange before the First World War and yet more money by wartime profiteering.[95] After the war he specialised in the promotion of electrical tramways and electric power generation undertakings, and artificial silk manufacturers. The holding company for his interests in artificial silk companies was the International Holding and Investment Co. formed in 1922 (originally called Cellulose Holdings and Investments Co.). Loewenstein's other important interests were the Barcelona Light and Power Company Ltd, for which Schröders issued £2.8 million bonds in 1926 (making a profit of £60,000), which was the principal asset of Hydro-Electric Securities, a holding company formed in September 1926. Loewenstein was a highly controversial figure and his buccaneering business activities made him many enemies. When he fell to his death from his private aircraft while crossing the English Channel in July 1928 there was much talk of foul play, though the coroner's verdict was misadventure. His sudden and unexpected demise at the age of forty-eight left his business empire bereft of a helmsman. His heirs, the van der Straaten family, turned to Schröders for assistance, and Major Pam assumed a leading role in the management of International Holdings and Hydro-Electric Holdings. The relationship between Schröders and the van der Straaten investment trusts continued for several decades and formed the bedrock of the Investment Department's business.

Financial Performance

Although Schröders' activity revived considerably in the immediate post-war years, net profits in 1919–21 averaged only £65,000 per annum after deduction of interest on partners' capital (see Figure 7.4). In 1922, profits leapt to £245,000, and in the years 1922–25 they averaged £447,000 per annum, peaking in 1924 at £619,000. The reasons for this improvement were the German clearing operations, the revival of issuing and underwriting, the expansion of acceptance activity and the very active foreign exchange market. Profits fell sharply in 1926, partly because of falls in revenues from issuing and accepting and partly because of a £200,000 increase in reserve provisions, and although they subsequently recovered in 1926–30 the annual average was £232,000 per annum – about half the level of 1922–25. The principal reasons were the waning of the German clearing operations and foreign exchange dealing and the increased competition for accepting and issuing business. The onset of the international depression and the financial crises of 1931 affected the firm very badly, explaining the loss sustained that year.

Figure 7.4   J. Henry Schröder & Co., net profits after interest on partners' capital, 1919–31

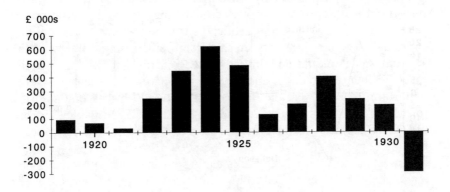

The 1920s saw a fundamentally different relationship between costs and revenues in Schröders' business compared to the pre-war decade. In the years 1903–13 aggregate revenues were £4.1 million, while in 1920–30 they were £7.9 million, which on an inflation-adjusted basis was virtually identical. Aggregate costs, on the other hand, rose from £750,000 in 1903–13 to £4.1 million in 1920–30, a threefold increase on an inflation-adjusted basis. The principal reason for the much higher cost-level of the post-war period was the rise in the number of staff, which in the years 1903–13 averaged 40, while in 1920–30 it was some 285, a sevenfold increase. There were several reasons for the increase. First, the partners of the firm were particularly effective in containing the size of the staff in the Edwardian era, other merchant banks with capitals of similar size having considerably larger staffs. Second, the types of business undertaken in the 1920s, especially the German clearing operations, were more labour-intensive than hitherto. Third, various changes in office administration, the most visible manifestation being the influx of female typists and filing clerks – in 1914 Schröders employed only two women but at the beginning of 1931 there were ninety-five, making up 34 per cent of the staff. Finally, the increasing complexity of operations that necessitated the expansion of the managerial tier of executives. The consequence of the growth of the cost base was a deterioration of the basic profitability of the business compared to the decade before the war.

The partners' capital of J. Henry Schröder & Co. was £3.3 million in 1919 and £3.2 million in 1930; a decrease of £100,000 in an era in which aggregate profits were £3.1 million. The principal reason for this was withdrawals of profits to finance the partners' investments in the J. Henry Schroder Banking Corporation of New York, though write-

Figure 7.5   J. Henry Schröder & Co., return on capital and annual rate of
inflation, 1919–31

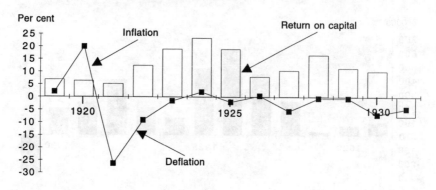

Note: The 'real' return on capital is the difference between the nominal return
depicted above and the annual rate of inflation.

offs of pre-war debts, payments to the estate of Baron Sir John Henry
Schröder and withdrawals for the personal purposes of the partners were
also significant. It was during these years that Baron Bruno and his wife
acquired an extensive collection of paintings, furniture and silver, the
Schroder Silver Collection constituting the finest private collection of
German Renaissance silver.[96] Given the roughly constant capital of the
firm the rate of return on capital was determined by the level of profits.
In 1919–21 the return on capital – including the partners' 4 per cent
interest – averaged 6.12 per cent, a rather inadequate return (see Figure
7.5). But in 1922–25 it averaged 18.4 per cent, a remarkable achievement
given the growth of the cost base. Returns were lower in the second half
of the decade, averaging 11.31 per cent in 1926–30. Over the years 1919–
30 as a whole the annual average return was 12.37 per cent, considerably
short of the 16.62 per cent earned in the golden years 1905–13, but higher
than the 10.68 per cent average of 1893–1904. Apart from the wild
gyrations of 1920–21, the price level over the course of the 1920s was
roughly stable and returns were not undermined by inflation. Thus the
Schröder partners received a real rate of return about three times the
average yield of consols – a very satisfactory performance.

8

The New World Beckons: Schrobanco

1923–35

'From a financial market of hardly more than local importance, New York has developed, almost overnight, into an international financial centre of first rate magnitude,' wrote the financial journalist Paul Einzig in 1931.[1] The vital factor behind this development was the First World War, which turned the United States into the largest international creditor nation, established the dollar as a leading international currency, made New York the principal centre for international capital raising and prompted the rapid rise of the dollar acceptance. Prior to 1900, public offerings of foreign securities were virtually unknown on Wall Street. The decade or so before the First World War saw a marked increase in such issues, principally for Latin American borrowers, but the pre-war peak of new issues for foreign borrowers in the New York market was only a sixth of London's.[2] In 1916, however, foreign securities issues in the US set a new record and thereafter New York was the leading international financial centre for raising long-term capital.[3] In the post-war years 1919–30, total issues of foreign securities in New York were roughly double those in London and it was on Wall Street that the greatest opportunities lay for firms that specialised in that activity.[4]

Just as dramatic was the wartime growth of the New York discount market, which was non-existent in 1913 but by the end of 1919 US bankers' acceptances totalled almost half the volume of commercial bills in the London discount market.[5] The development of the dollar acceptance followed the passage of the Federal Reserve Act of 1913, which permitted banks chartered by the federal government, known as 'national' banks, to create acceptance credits. The principal purpose of the Act was the establishment of the Federal Reserve System as the country's central bank to strengthen the financial infrastructure and the currency, the creation of a discount market being an integral part of the reforms. The outbreak of war in Europe in August 1914 massively boosted demand for dollar acceptances on the part of merchants, who before the war had been accommodated in London, accelerating the development of the New York discount market.[6] Moreover, the war saw a surge in US exports, mainly war materials and foodstuffs purchased by foreign governments, which were financed by dollar acceptances.[7] The

213

rapid expansion of the New York discount market continued in the 1920s, propelled largely by the creation of dollar acceptances for the conduct of foreign trade, and in the latter years of the decade it rivalled the London market in scale.[8]

The development of the dollar acceptance in the war years and after was fostered by the recently established Federal Reserve banks.[9] A leading part was played by Benjamin Strong, Governor of the Federal Reserve Bank of New York from 1913 until 1928, who instigated a variety of measures to promote the growth of the New York discount market.[10] With the return of peace there was the prospect of the revival of international trade financing in London, which threatened to take business away from New York. In response to this competitive challenge the American banks, which had developed international acceptance finance since 1914, formed the American Acceptance Council in the spring of 1919 for the purpose of promoting 'the merits of trade and bankers' acceptances, the method of their use in foreign and domestic merchandising, and for the further purpose of aiding in the establishment of a comprehensive open discount market'.[11] The Council organised a vigorous publicity campaign at the beginning of the 1920s, extolling the dollar acceptance and the New York discount market.

One of Strong's initiatives was to use his friendship with Frank Tiarks to encourage the Schröder partners to establish a firm on Wall Street which could make a significant contribution to the development of the New York discount market.[12] Some of Schröders' American clients, especially Manuel Rionda head of Czarnikow-Rionda, likewise urged them to conduct dollar acceptance business.[13] With this support the Schröder partners decided to proceed, 'looking forward to the time', Tiarks explained, 'possibly ten or fifteen years hence, when they anticipated New York would be more important financially even than it is now and when dollars and dollar credits would be in essential demand in financing overseas trade, especially South American trade'.[14] It was the partners' intention that their New York firm would 'by that time . . . be as well known and occupy as substantially important a position as dollar bankers in Wall Street as they have heretofore enjoyed in London'. Although some other City firms, notably Morgan Grenfell, Brown, Shipley and Lazards, were associates of larger US houses, for many decades Schröders was the only London merchant bank whose partners also owned a major New York firm.

Schröders was not quite the first of the London merchant banks to establish a Wall Street offshoot; in 1917 Frederick Huth & Co. formed Huth & Co. in New York to conduct foreign exchange dealing. At the end of the war Schröders appointed Huth & Co. to act as its New York correspondent, and early in 1920 it was agreed that the Schröder partners should subscribe for an interest in Huth & Co., which would develop an acceptance business in addition to its foreign exchange activities. Following this agreement the firms were approached by Paul Warburg, who had learned of their intentions. Warburg, who was born into the eminent German banking family but had settled permanently in the United States, was a partner in the leading Wall Street investment bank Kuhn, Loeb & Co. and a highly influential figure in American banking, who has been described as the architect of the Federal Reserve Act of 1913.[15] In the summer of 1920 he was in London putting together a consortium of European and American banks to conduct dollar denominated international acceptance business, matching the wholesale credit facilities of the American participants with retail lending opportunities identified by the European firms. The outcome was the International Acceptance Bank (IAB), which became an important Wall Street firm in the 1920s.[16]

Warburg put it to the partners of Schröders and Huths that, 'instead of competing with one another and duplicating an expensive organisation, it might be preferable to join hands'[17] and the IAB's Plan of Organisation, dated 1 November 1920, envisaged that J. Henry Schröder & Co. and Frederick Huth & Co. would each subscribe for 5,000 of the 100,000 common stock, commitments of $250,000 each. Under an agreement with the directors of Huth & Co. its foreign department was to be transferred to the IAB in return for an allocation of 2,000 of the 25,000 IAB Special Stock plus a reserved seat on the board.[18] However, Schröders and Huths evidently had a change of heart, since when the IAB came into being in April 1921 the British subscribers were Rothschilds and the National Provincial and Union Bank.[19] Yet relations with the IAB remained cordial and it undertook to subscribe up to one-third of the capital of the proposed Schröder-Huth undertaking.[20] In fact, the scheme with Huths came to nothing, most probably because of the death of Frederick Huth Jackson, the senior partner, in December 1921, which was followed by the insolvency of the London firm on account of death duties and wartime losses that led the Bank of England to take control of its affairs.[21] Huth & Co. of New York was sold to new proprietors, putting paid to the proposed joint venture. By then, however, J. Henry Schröder & Co. had recovered most of its pre-war debts and was enjoying a rapid revival of business which was generating sufficient profits for Baron Bruno and Frank Tiarks to finance the establishment of a Wall Street firm of their own.

Early in May 1923 Frank Tiarks visited New York for several weeks in order, as he wrote to his wife, to 'lay the foundation stone of the building'.[22] His trip had semi-official status and the night before he departed he saw Montagu Norman to tell him of his plans while on the quayside to welcome him off the ship was Pierre Jay, chairman of the board of directors of the Federal Reserve Bank of New York. 'I was received like a prince on the deck by Mr Jay,' Tiarks reported, 'all the customs formalities were brushed aside and they were all most kind.' Besides reflecting his standing as a director of the Bank of England, the warmth of the reception was also a mark of Benjamin Strong's gratitude for the assistance that Tiarks had given with the training of his son, who had returned to New York a fortnight earlier after a year at J. Henry Schröder & Co.[23] Tiarks turned for assistance with his undertaking to Schröders' pre-war friends, notably Manuel Rionda, but also to the partners of the brokerage house Ladenburg, Thalmann & Co. and to James Speyer, the head of the investment bank Speyer & Co.[24] Another important contact was Herbert Schlubach, a member of the family which owned the Hamburg merchant firm Schlubach Thiemer, and the Hague firm Schlubach Behrens, with which the London firm had close relations. He himself was based in New York and was active in the coffee trade, being a director of the Central American Plantations Corporation, a large grower with plantations in Guatemala. It was Schlubach who suggested that Tiarks should recruit Prentiss Gray as the head of the new firm.[25]

Prentiss Nathaniel Gray was born on 2 July 1884, in Oakland, California. He grew up in comfort, thanks to his father's thriving lumber business which supplied building materials for the rapidly growing city of San Francisco. He attended a local school and in 1902 became a student at the University of California at Berkeley. Upon graduation in 1906 he worked for several lumber and steamship firms on the Pacific coast, becoming manager of the California and Oregon Steamship Company in 1910. From 1914, he was manager of the Fairfax Development Company, a real-estate developer owned by the family firm, Gray & Holt Co., of which he was a partner. A chance encounter on a Berkeley streetcar with a college friend, John Simpson, resulted in an interruption to Gray's business career. Simpson was full of excitement about his appointment to the Commission for Relief in Belgium, a charitable undertaking headed by Herbert Hoover which from November 1914 provided food, medicine and clothing to the ten million people in German occupied Belgium and Northern France.[26] Gray was inspired by Simpson's example and he too volunteered to serve, departing for Belgium in January 1916. In March 1917, aged 33, he was appointed director of the Commission for Relief in Belgium, but the following month America entered the war and Gray was transferred to Washington to work, again under Hoover, for the US Food Administration, whose responsibility was the provision of food for the Allies and neutral countries.[27] The very poor harvest of 1917 in both the US and Europe, and the intensive German submarine campaign, which took a heavy toll of shipping, caused the appearance of 'the spectre of famine', in Hoover's words, in the winter of 1917–18.[28] Gray, the head of the Marine Transport Division of the US Food Administration, played a leading role in the successful resolution of 'the great food crisis'. Subsequently, he was made director of the American Relief Administration, the agency formed early in 1919 to organise the feeding of the starving in Europe.

The outcome of Gray's important war work was that he was highly regarded by an influential group of bankers and businessmen, including the future President of the United States, Herbert Hoover. Moreover, in Europe, his services received public recognition in both Belgium and France, being made an Officier de l'Ordre de la Couronne of Belgium and a Chevalier de la Legion d'Honneur of France. In 1919, he moved to New York and went into grain shipping, trading as P. N. Gray & Co. and specialising in shipment to Europe. He worked closely with John Simpson, the director of the Relief Commission in Paris in 1918–19, who stayed in Europe and formed a firm that handled the distribution of the grain. P. N. Gray & Co. prospered for a few years but fared badly when European demand for American grain fell because of the return to peacetime production and protectionism, and he was delighted to accept the Schröder partners' invitation in the summer of 1923.

Gray's grain merchant background counted greatly in his favour with Baron Bruno and Frank Tiarks, who regarded experience in international trade as an essential qualification for the man who was to lead their New York firm. His lack of experience in banking was not considered a handicap but an advantage, the banking practices of American domestic commercial bankers being held in rather low regard by London merchant bankers.[29] 'Fine, that's just what we want' was Tiarks' reaction when Schlubach outlined Gray's credentials.[30] Tiarks and Gray had much in common in temperament and abilities. Each had a forceful and exuberant personality and was an efficient and effective organiser. Gray's warm-heartedness and forthrightness won the loyalty of his staff, while those he did business with respected his abilities as a deal-maker. At a bankers' dinner in 1929, Ferdinand Eberstadt, a partner in the investment bank Dillon, Read & Co. who was regarded as one of the toughest men on Wall Street, asked John Simpson why Gray was absent. 'He's on safari in Africa,' said Simpson, 'I suppose he's shooting lions.' 'Oh no, he isn't!' responded Eberstadt, 'he's choking them to death with his bare hands.'[31]

Tiarks sailed again for New York on 3 October 1923 to finalise the arrangements for the new firm, the J. Henry Schroder Banking Corporation, which soon became generally known by its cable name 'Schrobanco'. He was accompanied by Baron Bruno's 22-year-old son,

Helmut, to whom he endeavoured to pass on some of his banking experience during the voyage. 'I find Helmut very bright and he has taken a very intelligent interest in everything we discuss,' he wrote to his wife during the crossing, 'it is a pleasure explaining things to him and I think he will take after his father in a good natural instinct for business.' Also aboard was Herr Bauer, a partner in Staudt & Cia, a leading Buenos Aires merchant firm which was a longstanding Schröder client, who provided useful information about the operations of the New York discount market. Characteristically, Tiarks seized the opportunity to make 'great friends' with another passenger, George V. McLaughlin, the Superintendent of Banks in the State of New York, the official responsible for granting charters to Wall Street's state-registered banks, who a month earlier had discussed the proposal to form the J. Henry Schroder Banking Corporation with lawyers representing the London partners.

At the outset it was the intention of the Schröder partners to operate in New York as a partnership, just as in London, but they were persuaded to incorporate for tax reasons.[32] This obliged them to consider what sort of bank charter they should seek, a question that had also exercised the mind of Paul Warburg upon the formation of the IAB three years earlier. Warburg had decided, 'after prolonged study and investigation', as he informed the partners of Rothschilds, to seek incorporation not as a deposit-taking commercial bank but as an 'investment company'.[33] Commercial banks which took deposits from the public were restricted in the employment of their funds in order to safeguard depositors. Investment companies incorporated under Article VII of the Banking Law of the State of New York – Article XII as it later became – had much greater freedom of activity, being able to issue letters of credit in unlimited amounts, make loans of unlimited amounts to clients, invest in any kind of security, and commit up to 10 per cent of their shareholders' funds to a single investment. Moreover, there were no regulatory impediments to undertaking securities underwriting. The forfeit for incorporation under Article VII was that taking deposits, the core business of a commercial bank, was forbidden. It was because investment firms could hazard only the funds of commercially sophisticated parties that the regulations governing the employment of their funds were less stringent than those applying to commercial banks. But the ban on taking deposits raised the question of whether an Article VII corporation could call itself a 'bank'. Warburg took the issue up with the authorities and established that it could. The IAB secured an Article VII Charter and the Schröder partners followed its precedent.

Although Article VII firms were forbidden from taking deposits they were permitted to hold customers' balances, which were defined as 'clients' funds accrued temporarily in the course of transacting business'. The distinction between customer balances and deposits was easier to make in theory than in practice, and lawyers acting for the Schröder partners sought clarification prior to filing Schrobanco's application for an Article VII charter. 'In the course of the proposed company's investment business,' they explained, 'it will expect to receive funds from European banking institutions or business houses, in anticipation of the purchase of acceptances, and of other transactions . . . for the convenience of the customer. How would you regard such a receipt of moneys from the Bank's customers?'[34] 'We would regard the transactions outlined in your letter', replied McLaughlin, 'as within the scope of the powers that an investment company organised under the so-called Investment Article of the Banking Law may exercise.'[35] With this reassurance, an Organisation Certificate was filed on 21 September which declared that the signatories were:

> desiring to form a moneyed corporation pursuant to the provisions of Article VII of the Banking Law of the State of New York, for the purpose of engaging in international and foreign banking . . . and to purchase or otherwise acquire, hold, sell, offer for sale and negotiate shares or stocks and other choses and to possess and exercise such other powers as now are or may hereafter be conferred upon investment companies.[36]

'Everyone here is kind and helpful and I foresee great things for the J. Henry Schroder Banking Corporation,' wrote Tiarks to his wife on 14 October 1923 five days after his arrival in New York. He was particularly impressed by Prentiss Gray, who had made rapid progress with the practical aspects of establishing the firm. 'The more I see of Gray,' wrote Tiarks, 'the more I like him.' The remaining task was to put together the board of directors. Baron Bruno became chairman, and Gray and Tiarks were also appointed, but what was required was 'some really first-class men as non-executive directors', whose presence would impress the American financial and business community and ensure that the firm was properly managed. Naturally, Manuel Rionda agreed to serve, and he also promised that his firm would do substantial business with Schrobanco. 'His support in this way,' wrote Tiarks, 'is quite invaluable.' The other non-executive directors, a remarkably eminent and energetic group, were former colleagues of Gray in the wartime US Food Administration. Julius H. Barnes was president of the Barnes–Ames Co., the largest grain exporting firm in the world. During the war he had served in the US Food Administration and had been the first director of the US Grain Corporation. Barnes was a prominent businessman and at the time he agreed to serve as a Schrobanco director he was president of the Chamber of Commerce of the United States. A senior figure in the Republican Party, he played a leading role in President Hoover's attempts to restore business confidence in the wake of the Wall Street Crash of 1929. George A. Zabriskie was vice-president of the Pillsbury Flour Mills Company, one of the most important American millers and an original subscriber to the IAB. During the war he had served in both the grain and sugar arms of the US Food Administration, and in the early 1920s he became chairman of the US Sugar Association. Gates W. McGarragh was a banker by profession, though during the First World War he too had worked for the US Food Administration and had assisted Barnes with running the US Grain Corporation. It was McGarragh to whom Tiarks referred when he wrote to his wife ten days after his arrival in America that 'at last' he had persuaded 'one of the most important American bankers' to join the Schrobanco board. McGarragh was the chairman of the Mechanics and Metals National Bank of New York. He was also a director of the Federal Reserve Bank of New York and was soon to become the US representative on the Advisory Council of the new German Reichsbank. In 1926, the Mechanics and Metals National Bank merged with the Chase National Bank and McGarragh became chairman of the Chase Executive Committee. Thus began Schrobanco's long and important business association with the Chase Bank and the Rockefeller family. McGarragh resigned from the board of Schrobanco in 1927 when he was made chairman of the board of the Federal Reserve Bank of New York. The apogee of his distinguished career was his appointment in 1930 as president and chairman of the newly created Bank for International Settlements in Basle.[37]

The initial authorised capital of Schrobanco was $2 million. This was divided into 20,000 $100 nominal shares paid up at $125, providing a supplementary surplus of $500,000, which meant that the total shareholders' funds were $2.5 million. Evidently it was soon decided that the capital was inadequate, for the first action of the newly constituted board of directors was to approve the issue of a further 20,000 shares. It was resolved that subscribers should pay $35 for each, representing $10 paid up capital (with a call liability of a further $90), and $25 surplus. Total paid-up capital plus surplus (that is shareholders' funds) at the end of 1923 thus amounted to $3.2 million which at the prevailing exchange rate of £1:$4.57 was £700,000, roughly the combined 1922 and 1923 profits of the London firm. The first 20,000 shares were taken by Baron Bruno and Frank Tiarks in the proportions two-thirds and one-third. The second 20,000 shares went to the Schröder partners, the Schrobanco directors and a number of outside subscribers: Baron

Bruno, Tiarks and Rittershaussen subscribing for a total of 15,401 shares; Schrobanco directors being allocated 199; and a Schröder nominee company, Jean Henrick & Co., taking 1,200. The outside shareholders, which in aggregate subscribed for 3,200 shares, 8 per cent of total equity, comprised four German private banks, Schröder Gebrüder, Gebrüder Bethmann, Deichmann & Co. and J. H. Stein; the Boden-Credit Anstalt and Bankhaus Johann Liebig & Co. of Vienna; the Banque Privee de Glaris of Switzerland and Staudt & Cia.[38]

The Schrobanco board held its first formal meeting on 7 November 1923. Gray reported that the firm had complied with the provisions of the New York State Banking laws and its Organisation Certificate had been approved on 24 October. Operating from the premises of P. N. Gray & Co., the second floor of a warehouse building at 25 South William Street, a few streets south of Wall Street, the firm had begun business on 26 October 1923. Tiarks was still there, having stayed on to help with the 'very difficult' initial work. He was tired but full of elation at what had been achieved. The last letter to his wife before his departure from New York finished with the words 'I have seen a glimpse of the spirit of this great country and it is uplifting. I am glad we are forming a bank here'.

Activities and Management of the Firm

Prentiss Gray was president of Schrobanco from 1923 until his death in a boating accident in February 1935. These dozen years divide into two parts: the prosperous 1920s, when Schrobanco's revenues grew from $990,000 to $4 million in 1929, and the depressed 1930s, which saw revenues decline to $1.3 million in 1934 (see Figure 8.1). Dollar trade finance was the *raison d'être* for the establishment of Schrobanco and was its core activity, generating 80 per cent of revenues in the 1920s. The other sources of revenues in that decade were foreign exchange dealing and securities underwriting, Schrobanco being an active participant in the booming international new issues market on Wall Street. Business conditions were very different in the early 1930s, in the trough of the international slump. Earnings from accepting fell because of the decline in international trade, and revenues from securities underwriting were drastically curtailed following the Wall Street Crash. Gray's response was to focus on the development of specialist foreign exchange dealing and upon marketing US securities in Europe, where there was strong demand for dollar assets. The upturn in Schrobanco's revenues in 1935 was the outcome of these initiatives.

In the 1920s and the early 1930s Schrobanco conducted both accepting, a commercial banking activity, and securities underwriting,

Figure 8.1 J. Henry Schroder Banking Corporation, revenues, 1923–35

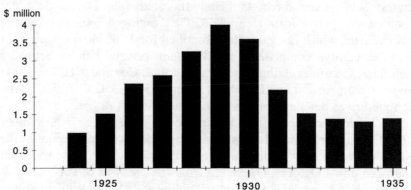

the basic business of investment banking. But this became impossible following the passage of the Federal Banking Act of 1933 – usually called the Glass–Steagall Act – which imposed a strict separation between commercial banking and the underwriting of securities, reflecting the popular conviction that the combination of these activities had stimulated the speculative excesses of the 1920s and was a cause of the depression. Henceforth American banking was to be divided between commercial banks and investment banks. By the time the measure came into effect on 16 June 1934, twenty-one months had elapsed since Schrobanco's last underwriting participation in a bond issue. Thus there was no question of the firm choosing investment bank status and it simply continued to conduct its acceptance credit and other activities under its Article VII charter.

To assist Gray with the development of business the Schröder partners sent two experienced members of the staff of the London firm, F. Seaton Pemberton and Stephen Paul Schluckwarder, to New York in 1923. Schluckwarder – who shortened his name to Stephen Paul upon arrival in New York, at Gray's insistence – was appointed vice-president with responsibility for the conduct of the firm's accepting, banking and foreign exchange activities (see Figure 8.2). Born in Germany in 1886, he worked for the Dresdner Bank until he joined J. Henry Schröder & Co. as the manager of its German accepting business in October 1922. At Schrobanco he was unpopular with the staff because of his curt manner, but also because he was believed to be spying on them on behalf of the London partners. The firm's acceptance business expanded rapidly and profitably under Paul's supervision but he was also behind some costly mistakes and was sacked in August 1930. By then Pemberton, the first company secretary, had also left the firm. It was not until the 1960s that executives from the London firm again played a managerial role at

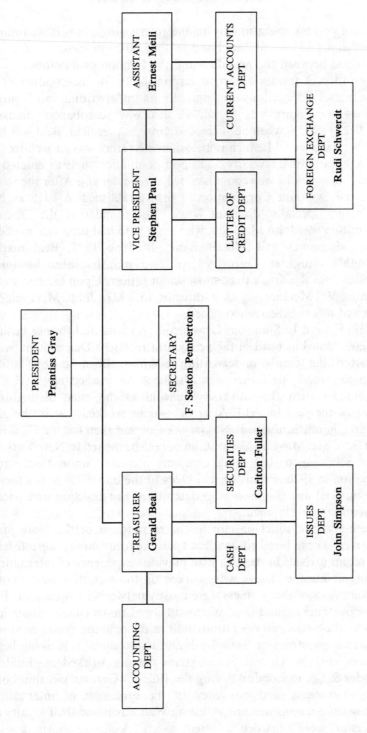

Figure 8.2 Principal officers and departments of the J. Henry Schroder Banking Corporation in the mid-1920s

Source: Information supplied by Henry W. Paul.

Schrobanco, and operationally in the intervening years it was almost entirely independent of the London firm, though close contact was maintained between the president and the London proprietors.

The office of treasurer carried responsibility for the conduct of the firm's treasury operations, and initially its underwriting and securities activities (see Figure 8.2). Gerald F. Beal was Schrobanco's treasurer from 1923 to 1935, when he succeeded Gray as president. Beal was born in 1895 in Hanover, Massachusetts, where his father was an architect. He attended Harvard University and upon graduation in 1917 entered the infantry, in which he was commissioned as a lieutenant. After the war he joined the Discount Corporation, a firm established in 1919 as New York's first specialist discount house. The founder of the Discount Corporation was John McHugh, who since 1915 had been vice-president of the Mechanics and Metals Bank. In June 1923, Beal married McHugh's daughter Dorothy and five months later he joined Schrobanco as the firm's third most senior officer. Upon the resignation of Gates W. McGarragh as a director in 1927, John McHugh was appointed to the Schrobanco board.

In 1925, John L. Simpson, Gray's college friend and former business associate, joined as head of the newly formed Issues Department, which conducted the firm's underwriting business. Born in 1891 in San Francisco, where his father was a teacher, he studied law at UCLA and was awarded the university's medal as the most distinguished scholar of the year in 1913. After the war he worked first in the grain trade in conjunction with P. N. Gray & Co. and then for the California raisin firm, Sun Maid. In the autumn of 1925 he moved to New York and joined Schrobanco, becoming company secretary upon Pemberton's resignation in 1926. From the mid-1920s to the mid-1930s it was the trio of Gray, Beal and Simpson who determined the direction and pace of Schrobanco's development.

There was a distinct pattern to the recruitment of the more junior executives. Those hired to conduct trade finance activity were foreign-born recent arrivals in the US, with previous experience of international banking in Europe. Those who worked on the securities, underwriting and trust sides of the business were mostly native-born Americans from prosperous backgrounds and often with Ivy League college educations. Many of the clerks and operations staff in the banking department were of German, Austrian or Swiss birth and had trained in banking before migration to the United States, some having worked at J. Henry Schröder & Co. in London during the 1922–24 German clearing boom. Their competence and efficiency in the execution of international banking transactions was unrivalled on Wall Street and their loyalty and application were regarded as great assets. A strong *esprit de corps* developed amongst Schrobanco's founding generation, many of whom joined in their mid-twenties and stayed with the firm for the whole of their working lives. There was apparently a boisterous vitality to the organisation in the 1920s, both at work and at play; more than half a century after the event, long-retired members of staff recalled the riotous staff party of 1927 at the Larchmont Yacht Club, which resulted in the suspension of Gray's membership, as the best party under Prohibition.[39]

When Schrobanco opened for business in October 1923 there were sixteen members of staff. By the end of 1924 the personnel numbered over a hundred and the 'loft turned into a bank' at 25 South William Street was becoming rather crowded.[40] In March 1925, the firm moved to more spacious premises at 27 Pine Street, a very convenient location for calling on friends: the International Acceptance Bank was at 29–31; Speyer & Co. at 24–26; and on the other side of the street, behind an exuberant façade featuring terracotta dolphins and seashells, was the Discount Corporation. Soon after the move the senior officers drew up a code of office regulations. Office hours were set as 9.00 am to 5.00 pm and junior officers were charged with keeping staff time sheets. Smoking was forbidden throughout the office until 3.00 pm.[41] The increase in personnel continued during the prosperous years of the second half of the 1920s, and at the end of 1930 the staff numbered 183: 128 men and 55 women.[42] In 1929 the firm moved again, taking occupation of the tenth, eleventh and twelfth floors of the building owned by the Bank of New York on the corner of Wall Street and William Street, which became its home for the next twenty years. Perhaps it was not coincidental that the building at 48 Wall and 46 William also housed Schrobanco's legal adviser, the leading law firm, Sullivan & Cromwell. The connection with Sullivan & Cromwell derived from Gray's close friendship with John Foster Dulles, whom he had met at the Versailles Peace Conference in 1919. Upon his return to the US Dulles joined Sullivan & Cromwell, soon achieving a reputation as a leading international lawyer, and in 1926 he became the firm's senior partner, aged only 38. The business connection began as the result of a disagreement between Gray and Ferdinand Eberstadt of Dillon, Read about the terms of a bond issue the firms were making together, which was amicably resolved by Dulles.[43]

International Accepting and Issuing Activities, 1923–29

'We are equipped to handle all forms of business usual in merchant banking' stated the pamphlet entitled *A Merchant Banking Service* which was issued in 1923 to promote the J. Henry Schroder Banking Corporation. It listed the following services:

1. The opening of accounts current in our books for clients; allowing interest on such accounts when in credit, and charging interest when in debit, at rates and on terms to be agreed. The corporation will issue cheque books for the use of such clients.
2. Dealing in various foreign exchanges.
3. Mail and cable transfers to all parts of the world.
4. Collection of clean and documentary drafts drawn on foreign countries.
5. Letters of credit.
6. Opening of commercial credits to be availed of by sight or long drafts on New York or London.
7. Advances against goods in transit.
8. The execution of orders for purchase or sale of securities on any American or European Stock Exchange, and the safe custody of securities for clients.

Schrobanco rapidly established a substantial acceptance activity (see Figure 8.3). In December 1924, only fifteen months after the beginning of business, its balance sheet acceptances totalled $11.3 million, a volume exceeded by only twelve US banks.[44] There was a further large increase in the second half of the decade, peaking at $34.2 million in 1929 the year that also saw a record volume of total US bankers' acceptances. In 1928, the *Acceptance Bulletin*, the mouthpiece of the American Acceptance Council, commenced publication of a monthly league table, 'The First Forty', ranking the forty leading acceptors. Most of the First Forty banks were large, domestically-orientated, deposit-taking institutions with enormous balance sheets relative to Schrobanco. Nevertheless, in 1928–31 Schrobanco's rank ranged from ninth to fifteenth, averaging a place just outside the top ten, a remarkable performance for a relatively

Figure 8.3   J. Henry Schroder Banking Corporation, acceptances and advances, 1923–35

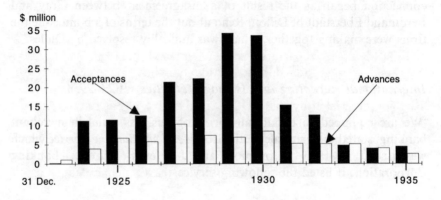

small, foreign-owned and recently-established firm. Fittingly, soon after his appointment as president of Schrobanco, Prentiss Gray was elected to the executive committee of the American Acceptance Council. Schrobanco's banking clientele in the 1920s was predominantly foreign; in 1925–27, the only years for which information is available, European clients, mostly German, were recipients of 70 per cent of credits. and Latin-American firms 10 per cent; US firms, notably Czarnikow-Rionda, received 20 per cent.

Much of the credit for the successful development of Schrobanco's acceptance business in the 1920s belongs to Ernest Meili. Born in Switzerland in 1901, he trained in banking with the Banque Populaire Suisse and in 1920 joined Morgan Harjes & Co., J. P. Morgan's Paris firm. In 1922, he worked at J. Henry Schröder & Co. and early the next year he went to New York, where he became private secretary to the prominent financier, Ivar Kreuger. In November 1923, he joined Schrobanco as Stephen Paul's deputy. By all accounts he was a warm and generous man who was popular with the staff. He was a very gifted singer and it is said that he could have made a career in opera. In July 1927, Paul and Meili were joined by Norbert Bogdan, who was recruited to help with the upsurge in acceptance activity. Bogdan, who was born in 1902 in Abbatisia, Italy, had a cosmopolitan background, being the son of a Russian father – a surgeon who practised in Vienna – and a Hungarian mother. He trained in banking at the Scandinaviska Kredit AB, a leading Swedish commercial bank. Oscar Rydbeck, the head of Scandinaviska Kredit, took a personal interest in Bogdan's career and in 1921 despatched him to King's College, Cambridge, where he was tutored by John Maynard Keynes. Music was a common interest and Bogdan used to play piano duets with Keynes. After a year and a half at Cambridge he enrolled at the London School of Economics, where he spent a further year. Rydbeck then arranged for him to join the IAB, in which the Scandinaviska Kredit AB was a participant, where his fellow juniors were Benjamin Strong's son and Hermann Abs, the future head of the Deutsche Bank. 'Imaginative, and likeable' and abounding with 'contagious vitality' he soon became one of Schrobanco's most senior executives.[45]

Following the departure of Stephen Paul in 1930, Valla Lada-Mocarski was appointed head of the banking side of Schrobanco's business. He was born in Samarkand in 1898, the son of a general of the Russian Imperial army, and in 1910, aged twelve, he entered the Artillery Academy Grand Duke Michael.[46] In the First World War he was wounded in the arm and twice decorated. He fled Russia after the revolution and in 1919 arrived in Paris, by way of Sidi-bel-Abbès in Algeria, where he was briefly enrolled in the French Foreign Legion.

From Paris, where he was reunited with some of the members of his family, he went to Vienna and began his career in banking with the Österreichische Creditanstalt. In 1924 he married an American citizen and moved to the United States, joining Schrobanco upon an introduction to Gray from his wife's uncle. He worked on the securities side of the business until his promotion in 1930. In 1934, at the age of 36, he was appointed to the Schrobanco board.

Schrobanco's peer group of internationally orientated firms amongst the First Forty were the International Acceptance Bank, the French American Banking Corporation, Huth & Co., Brown Brothers & Co., and Lee Higginson & Co. and the Kidder Peabody Acceptance Corporation, both of Boston. A distinctive feature of its conduct of business was that a high proportion of its assets were commercial bills, a practice of the London merchant banks to support the discount market, which was promoted in New York by Schrobanco. Gray's report to shareholders for 1925 stated that 'it is a pleasure to note that throughout the year your institution kept more money in the discount market than any other American institution except one and in the proportion to its resources, it easily led the list'.[47] Another measure to support the discount market inspired by English example was the provision of call loans to the discount houses. Schrobanco's adoption of this London practice appears to have been an innovation in New York. E. R. Kenzal, a deputy governor of the Federal Reserve Bank of New York, informed his opposite number in Cleveland, Ohio, early in 1924 that upon learning of Schrobanco's intentions the as yet inexperienced New York discount houses 'expressed considerable gratification in at last having an important banking firm established here that entertained such views as to the relations which should exist between a banking firm that accepted and the market'.[48]

In addition to providing acceptance credits, Schrobanco also furnished short-term loans to clients; advances peaking in 1927 at $10.4 million, double the firm's capital (see Figure 8.3 on page 226). Banking activities were further developed following the formation of the J. Henry Schroder Trust Company in April 1929 (renamed the Schroder Trust Company in February 1937) and generally known as Schrotrust. This subsidiary, with a capital of $700,000, received a commercial banking charter from the state of New York and became a member of the Federal Reserve System. The trust company was able to take deposits and offered services such as chequing accounts and trusteeships, stock transfer agencies, registrarships and escrows, as well as conducting investment accounts for individuals. In February 1929, in anticipation of the formation of the trust company, Schrobanco's capital was increased by $1 million and the unpaid portion of the second tranche of 20,000 shares was called up. These moves resulted in an increase in subscribed capital from $3.2 million to $5 million, which besides financing the trust company permitted the expansion of Schrobanco's activities.

Foreign exchange operations were a natural complement to the conduct of accepting business. This aspect of activities was energetically developed by Rudi Schwerdt, a bachelor of German birth who had cable links with London and Paris installed in his apartment to enable him to deal with the European markets before New York was awake, arriving in the office each morning with a bundle of instructions for processing. Besides servicing other departments and executing clients' instructions, Japanese banks making much use of Schrobanco's services in the mid-1920s, the department traded actively on own account. In 1926, profits totalled $91,000, but the following year they were a mere $4,000 because of heavy losses from unsuccessful position-taking in Argentine pesos. Schrobanco's senior officers were alarmed at the risks being assumed and decided that henceforth the Foreign Exchange Department should simply service the currency requirements that arose in the course of the conduct of other business. Foreign exchange operations gained a new lease of life from 1933 with the commencement of dealing services in restricted currencies, in which Schrobanco developed an unrivalled expertise. As a result, profits from foreign exchange business soared from $19,000 in 1932 to $395,000 in 1935, constituting a third of the firm's total revenues.

At the outset it was the intention that Schrobanco should confine its business to accepting and related activities, such as foreign exchange dealing, the newspaper advertisements announcing the formation of the new firm even including a protestation that there was no intention of undertaking securities underwriting.[49] But soon there was a change of heart and eighteen months after it opened for business Schrobanco made its first appearance on a prospectus. The reason was the boom in foreign securities issues on Wall Street which began in earnest in 1924 following the success of the Dawes loan for Germany; between 1923 and 1924 the volume of foreign securities issues in the US leapt from $497 million to $1,217 million[50] (see Table 8.1). Once Schrobanco had established itself in the New York financial community through its accepting activity it was very well placed to participate actively in the boom, since J. Henry Schröder & Co.'s extensive international contacts led to approaches from clients who wished to issue dollar loans. Moreover, when J. Henry Schröder & Co. made an issue in London Schrobanco was able to handle a dollar tranche in New York, such dual tranche structures being common because sterling and dollar securities appealed to different investors, and because American investors, who were rather wary of foreign bonds, believed that they carried the quality approval of the City

of London. American investors' reservations were outweighed by the
high yields offered on foreign dollar bonds relative to domestic securities
in the years 1924–28, but when high returns became available from
domestic bonds and equities from mid-1928 it became increasingly
difficult to persuade them to purchase foreign issues and the volume of
foreign securities issues fell sharply[51] (see Table 8.1). There was a revival
of foreign issues in 1930 but the onset of the international slump soon
reduced activity to minimal levels. The pattern of Schrobanco's dollar
bond issuing and sales activities developed with these swings in market
sentiment.

Simpson, with active assistance from Gray and Beal, took the leading
role in the development of Schrobanco's underwriting and securities
activities. His deputy was Carlton P. Fuller, a 29-year-old Harvard
graduate with half a dozen years' experience with Guaranty Trust, who
was recruited in April 1927, at the height of the boom in foreign
securities issues, and was made a director in 1934. The other executives
on the underwriting side were Valla Lada-Mocarski, until his promotion

Table 8.1   J. Henry Schroder Banking Corporation, participations in
issues, 1923–33

	Total US foreign securities issues $ million	Schrobanco foreign securities issues $ million	Schrobanco domestic securities issues $ million	Schrobanco total issues $ million
1923	497	–	–	–
1924	1217	–	–	–
1925	1316	–	–	30
1926	1288	187	10	197
1927	1577	279	11	290
1928	1489	139	10	149
1929	705	27	25	57
1930	1087	114	37	151
1931	285	–	70	70
1932	88	–	19	19
1933	72	–	–	–
Total	9621	746	182	963

Source: Total foreign securities – M. F. Jolliffe, *The United States as a Financial
Centre 1919–1933* (Cardiff: University of Wales Press Board, 1935) p. 106;
Schrobanco – J. Henry Schroder Banking Corporation, Issue Bible.

as head of banking in 1930, Harold A. Sutphen and William A. Tucker. Sutphen, a minister's son who was born in 1897 and educated at Princeton, joined the firm in 1923. He specialised in securities trading and in the 1930s ran a very successful US government bond dealing operation with Beal, who he succeeded as company treasurer in 1935. Tucker, who was born in 1901, was also a Princeton graduate. As a student he became a close friend of Adlai Stevenson, a future Democratic Party presidential candidate, with whom he toured war-torn continental Europe in 1919. Upon graduation he joined Schrobanco, thanks to an introduction to Beal through a Princeton classmate. The Ivy League backgrounds of the senior executives on the investment banking side of Schrobanco's business mirrored the usual recruitment pattern of Wall Street firms.

In the years 1925–30, Schrobanco participated in fifty-seven foreign bond issues, which raised $746 million – about $5.5 billion in 1990 money – 8 per cent of all US foreign issues in the period. Many of the issues were for Central European and Latin American clients who had connections with J. Henry Schröder & Co. Being orientated towards international business, Schrobanco lacked distribution power to US domestic investors and chose syndicate partners who redressed this problem. But through J. Henry Schröder & Co. and its continental connections Schrobanco was able to market bonds in Europe, leading to invitations to join syndicates formed by other firms. The investment banks with which Schrobanco worked most frequently were Speyer & Co., Lee, Higginson & Co., Dillon, Read & Co., Blyth, Witter & Co., and Harris, Forbes & Co., three-quarters of the issues in which it was a participant being led by one of these houses.

In December 1924, Schrobanco teamed up with Lee, Higginson & Co., the Boston associate of the London merchant bank, Higginson & Co., Brown Brothers & Co., an old and very reputable Baltimore investment bank, and Clark, Dodge & Co., a Wall Street brokerage house, to form the Continental Securities Corporation (CSC). This was conceived as an American counterpart to the Continental and Industrial Trust, J. Henry Schröder & Co.'s investment trust, and the intention was to invest in European equities and to make loans with stock options to European companies. Schrobanco, on account of its 'qualifications and facilities for handling work of this character', became the manager of the CSC portfolio, a service for which the firm received 5 per cent of profits distributed to shareholders.[52] Beal became chairman of the board, which comprised partners or directors of Lee, Higginson, Brown Brothers and Clark, Dodge, and his father-in-law, John McHugh of the Mechanics and Metals Bank. Initially the funds at the disposal of the CSC were provided by the four participating firms but in April 1927 $5 million bonds were sold to the public and in May 1928 a further $5.9 million. During the 1920s the CSC paid satisfactory dividends and the value of its investments grew. The stock market crash and the international slump depressed the value of CSC's investments in the early 1930s, though they revived from 1934. In October 1937, control of the CSC was purchased by a Canadian company which took over the management of the fund.

In October 1925, shortly after the establishment of the Continental Securities Corporation, Schrobanco brought in Lee, Higginson to act as joint lead-manager of the $6 million bond issue for the Rhine–Main–Donau AG, which was formed to build and operate a canal connecting the Rhine to the Danube, to permit navigation from the North Sea to the Black Sea. Schrobanco and Lee, Higginson, the 'purchase group' each took $3 million of bonds at a price of 89 $^1/_{16}$ which they sold to a much larger 'banking group' at a price of 92, realising a profit for Schrobanco of $92,500. The firm participated in the banking group, which also included Lee, Higginson and the Mechanics and Metals Bank, to the extent of $2,350,000 of bonds. The banking group sold the bonds to a 'selling group' at a price of 93, realising a further $18,000 for Schrobanco. It took a small part in the selling group, marketing only $300,000 of bonds to private clients at the issue price of 96, upon which it made a profit of $3,500. Promotion expenses and commissions to agents consumed much of the selling group's profits, and $7,500 of the commission paid to the Deutsche Bank, Berlin, was charged to Schrobanco. Total profits from the lead-management of the Rhine–Main–Donau AG issue amounted to an impressive $106,000.

To promote Schrobanco's services as an issuing house to German corporations it was decided to establish a Berlin representative. On the recommendation of the London partners, Dr Endrucks, a friend of the Schröder family and a director of the Rhine–Main–Donau AG, was appointed to this post. Endrucks applied himself to the job with gusto, deluging New York with proposals. Simpson and his colleagues found it impossible to evaluate the merits of Endrucks' schemes and soon became exasperated with their Berlin representative. Nevertheless, Endrucks' presence and Baron Bruno's connections did foster ties with German clients, a notable instance being the issue for the Deutsche Bank of $25 million five-year 6 per cent notes (represented by American Participation Certificates) made by the firm as sole manager in September 1927.

Dillon, Read & Co., led by Clarence Dillon and Ferdinand Eberstadt, was one of the most forceful and successful of the New York investment banks in the 1920s, lead-managing almost $4 billion of securities issues in the years 1918–33. Its greatest strength was its distribution network of 4,000 agents who marketed bonds to American investors.[53] Dillon and

53. Baron Bruno Schröder as senior partner

54. (*left*) Frank Tiarks, partner

55. (*right*) Major Albert Pam,
associate partner

Office of J. Henry Schröder & Co., 145 Leadenhall Street, after rebuilding in 1923

56. Partners' room

57. Banking hall

58. Helmut Schröder (*left*) and Henry Tiarks (*second from right*) while trainees in Hamburg in 1921

59. Dell Park, home of Baron Bruno Schröder in the 1920s

60. (*above*) Helmut Schröder,
Baron Rudolph von Schröder,
senior partner of Schröder
Gebrüder, Hamburg, and Baron
Bruno Schröder in the 1920s

61. (*left*) Alfred Loewenstein, the
flamboyant Belgian financier,
with whom Schröders worked
closely in the 1920s

62. Certificates of German bond issues managed by Schröders in London and New York in the 1920s

63. (*left*) Helmut Schröder and Frank
     Tiarks upon arrival in New York in
     October 1923

64. (*right*) Manuel Rionda of
     Czarnikow-Rionda

65. (*left*) Prentiss Gray, president 1923–35

66. (*right*) Prentiss Gray on a shooting expedition

67.   John Simpson and Ernest Meili

68.   (*above*) Gerald Beal

69.   (*right*) Valla Lada-Mocarski in
      the uniform of the Imperial
      Russian army

70. Gustav von Mallinckrodt, Schröders' representative in Germany

71. (*left*) Frank Tiarks with
Montagu Norman,
Governor of the Bank of
England

72. (*left*) Marga and
Dorothee Schröder,
sisters of Helmut
Schröder, who supported
the firm through the years
of the Standstill lock-up

73. (*below*) Schröder family
at Dell Park, 1938, (*left
to right*) Helmut,
Baroness Bruno,
Charmaine, Meg, Bruno,
Marga and Baron Bruno
Schröder

74. Frank Tiarks and Baron Bruno Schröder prior to the outbreak of the Second World War

Eberstadt developed close ties with German industry and the firm became the most powerful financier for German industry in the 1920s. In January 1926, Schrobanco teamed up with Dillon, Read to lead-manage jointly a $25 million bond issue for the Rheinelbe Union, a major German iron and steel producer, marking the start of a close co-operation between the firms on issues for the German metallurgical, coal and chemical industries. Schrobanco was a participant in the banking and selling syndicates for the three issues lead-managed by Dillon, Read on behalf of the major German steel firm Vereinigte Stahlwerk AG in June 1926, July 1927 and August 1927, which raised $64.2 million in total. In March 1928, it participated in the purchase, banking and selling groups of the $15 million issue lead-managed by Dillon, Read for the coal-mine holding company Gelsenkirchener Bergwerks AG. Later in 1928 Schrobanco took small participations in the Dillon, Read issues of $4 million bonds on behalf of the Ruhrchemie AG, and $12 million for the Ruhrgas AG.

Schrobanco's raising of funds for the new nations that emerged from the Austro-Hungarian empire began, as for Germany, with the creation of an investment corporation. This was the Delaware incorporated European Mortgage and Investment Corporation (EMIC), which was formed in the summer of 1925 by Schrobanco and Lee, Higginson with an equity capital of $250,000 represented by 10,000 shares subscribed equally by the firms. Prentiss Gray became EMIC's first president, and Stephen Paul the vice-president. The Anglo-American board included Baron Bruno Schröder, Sir Guy Granet, an eminent City figure and a partner in Higginson & Co., and a couple of partners of the Boston house. The EMIC made five bond issues between October 1925 and June 1928, raising a total of $22.75 million from the public. These funds were made available to the Austrian General Land Credit Institution and the Hungarian Banks Co-operative Society, which used them to make loans to farmers and estate owners in Austria and Hungary who were in acute need of working capital. The loans were secured against mortgages on the lands of the recipients. Interest payments to EMIC bondholders were stopped with the international financial crisis in 1931, and in March 1933 a receiver was appointed.[54] Soon afterwards a bondholders' protection committee was established, to which Simpson and Tucker were appointed, the Schroder Trust Company becoming the New York depository and J. Henry Schröder & Co. the London sub-depository.[55] The Austrian debts were redeemed at 75 per cent in 1934 but the Hungarian bonds were still in default at the outbreak of war five years later.[56]

Schrobanco brought out the New York tranches of the two issues for Bulgaria lead-managed in London by J. Henry Schröder & Co. Acting with Speyer & Co. and Blair & Co. the $4.5 million bonds of the Kingdom of Bulgaria 7 per cent Settlement Loan were successfully issued in December 1926. In November 1928, the London syndicate organised the issue of a second loan on behalf of the Kingdom of Bulgaria totalling $25 million, of which $13 million was to be issued in New York by a syndicate, again led by Schrobanco and Speyer & Co. Despite the endorsement of the League of Nations, the Wall Street issue was poorly received by investors because of worries about the political stability of Bulgaria and because of the the rival attractions of US equities. Most of the bonds had to be taken up by the underwriters, Schrobanco's share amounting to around $3 million. Their price collapsed with the Wall Street Crash and the value of Schrobanco's holding was written down to $0.5 million. There was a further sharp fall when Bulgaria defaulted on interest payments in 1932, and by 1935 the value of Schrobanco's Bulgarian bonds had fallen to $174,000. The price recovered somewhat thereafter, but a loss of $2 million was sustained when the holding was liquidated in 1938.

During the 1920s Latin American governments and municipalities, and corporations which conducted business there, were large borrowers in the New York market. Schrobanco participated in numerous issues for Latin American clients, the introductions arising both from the London firm's contacts and from relationships developed by its own officers. Foremost amongst the businesses deriving from J. Henry Schröder & Co. were the issues on behalf of the state of San Paulo, which have been described in Chapter 7, for which Schrobanco and Speyer & Co. conducted the New York tranches.

Through an introduction by Herbert Schlubach, Schrobanco became involved in financing the International Railways of Central America (IRCA), a corporation formed in 1904 to build railways in Guatemala and El Salvador. The IRCA's founder, principal owner and chief executive was Minor C. Keith, whose Tropical Trading and Transport Company developed the Costa Rican banana industry and was one half of the merger that formed the United Fruit Company in 1899. It was the IRCA that transported the bananas grown on United Fruit's plantations on the Guatemalan Pacific lowlands to the Atlantic port of Puerto Barrios for export to the United States and Europe. In the mid-1920s, Keith decided to connect the IRCA line in El Salvador to the track running to Puerto Barrios. This required the construction of a further 93 miles of railway, and a loan was raised to finance the work. By the beginning of 1926 it was clear that further funds were required to complete the project and Keith appointed Schrobanco as the IRCA's fiscal agent. Blyth, Witter & Co., the leading San Francisco investment bank, whose management was well known to John Simpson, was invited to act as joint syndicate manager on account of its domestic distribution strength. An agreement was signed in March 1926 whereby the two banks undertook to purchase $3.5 million fifteen-year notes issued by the IRCA at a price of 89½ per cent. The notes were subsequently purchased by a special group, at 91½; a banking group, at 92; a selling group, at 93; and sold to investors at 96. Schrobanco realised a profit of $49,000 upon the issue, three-fifths of which was earned from its purchase group participation. This issue marked the beginning of a close relationship with Blyth, Witter, which in subsequent years invited Schrobanco to participate in its issues and became 'good friends of ours'.[57]

A few months after the successful $3.5 million note issue on behalf of the IRCA, Keith asked Schrobanco to sort out the financial position of his personal corporation, Minor C. Keith Inc. This company had been formed in April 1924 to take over the ownership and management of Keith's securities and property, but by the time Schrobanco took a hand it was on the verge of failure through illiquidity. To pay the creditors Schrobanco brought out $6 million five-year notes, secured against Keith's assets, purchasing the whole of the issue at 86.9. J. Henry Schröder & Co. privately placed $4.2 million of the notes at 89.73 in London, the principal purchaser being the investment trust manager Robert Fleming & Co., and Schrobanco sold the remainder in New York, $500,000 being taken by the American, British and Continental Corporation, an investment trust established by Schrobanco and Blyth, Witter. Schrobanco's profit from this business, in which it assumed all the risk and undertook all the distribution work, was $114,000, the largest sum from any of its underwriting transactions.

Schrobanco led three further issues for the IRCA, all in conjunction with Blyth, Witter. In February 1927, $7.5 million bonds were successfully issued to finance additional construction work, the firm's profits upon its participation in the purchase, banking and selling groups being $110,000. By contrast, the issue of $3 million preference shares in September 1928 was not well received by investors and Schrobanco incurred a loss on the business of $36,000. A further issue of $2 million IRCA notes was made in April 1931. Schrobanco's officers became closely involved in the affairs of the IRCA. Gray joined the board of directors and became a member of the four-man executive committee chaired by Keith. He was succeeded by Simpson, who subsequently became chairman. The connection led to an introduction to the government of Guatemala resulting in an issue of $1.5 million bonds in May 1928 whose proceeds were applied in settlement of debts owed to the IRCA by the government arising out of freight and passenger contracts.

Blyth, Witter's reciprocal favour for its introduction to the first IRCA issue was the inclusion of Schrobanco in its syndicate to make a $2 million bond issue for the Republic of Peru in June 1926. However, Schrobanco was not admitted to the purchasing group but was allowed a 10 per cent participation in the 'special purchase group', which bought the bonds from the purchasing group at 2 points above the ground-floor price. Schrobanco's contribution to the distribution of the bonds was to arrange for the placement of a part of the issue in London through J. Henry Schröder & Co., the issuing house Helbert, Wagg & Co., and the stockbroker, Rowe & Pitman. Its participations in the special and selling groups earned the firm $18,000. Two months later it took small participations in the syndicates formed to issue a further $16 million bonds for the republic of Peru, earning $16,000 from its participations. When the New York investment bank J. & W. Seligman and the National City Bank brought out large Peruvian bond issues totalling $75 million in December 1927 and October 1928, Schrobanco was one of many participants in the selling groups, distributing the securities to its European clients.

Early in 1927, Blyth, Witter, acting in conjunction with the Chatham Phenix National Bank & Trust Company, made a winning bid to make an issue of $3.4 million bonds for the city of Buenos Aires. The firms offered a high price for the bonds in order to establish a position as bankers to Argentina's leading city, with an eye to the large Argentinian refinancings which Chatham Phenix's agent, J. M. de Acosta, a friend of President Irigoyen, advised them would be forthcoming in the near future. Schrobanco agreed to assist with the placement of the Buenos Aires bonds in Europe, J. Henry Schröder & Co. undertaking to market $1,500,000 of them. This 'exceptional service' secured a place in the syndicate for Schrobanco. In April 1930 the Blyth–Chatham–Schrobanco syndicate, plus Continental Illinois, bid successfully for a $50 million Argentinian government treasury note issue. As usual, Schrobanco distributed much of its allocation through J. Henry Schröder & Co. and its continental connections, Major Williams in Paris placing $1.8 million of the notes.

In the spring of 1930 the syndicate also undertook to issue $16 million notes for the city of Buenos Aires. Discussions about this issue had been under way for some time until an approach by a rival syndicate, comprising Baring Brothers, Brown Brothers and J. P. Morgan & Co., prompted action. The Blyth–Chatham–Schrobanco group was concerned about its ability to market so much Argentinian paper, given the post-crash pessimism of American investors, and to boost distribution, Halsey Stuart & Co. was invited to join the syndicate. The Buenos Aires note offering proved successful, Schrobanco earning $4,000 through its participation in the purchasing, banking and selling groups. Again, it was Major Williams in Paris who made it possible for the firm to play a significant part in the selling group by taking $850,000 for placement with French and Swiss clients. It had been hoped at the time of issue that at some point during the six-month life of the notes the New York bond market would recover sufficiently for refunding to be accomplished on a long-term basis, but this did not happen. A few weeks before the maturity of the notes the city of Buenos Aires inquired about the renewal terms. The group replied that it would be possible to renew only $10 million and on more costly terms. An acrimonious exchange of cables ensued and both sides resorted to their lawyers. It became clear that the Spanish translation of the contract had led the city to expect that the loan would be automatically renewed. De Acosta, who had acted for the syndicate, became 'distinctly *persona non grata*' in Buenos Aires, and Chatham Phenix was barred by government and municipal decrees from negotiating for Argentine loans.[58] Neither Blyth, Witter nor Schrobanco was mentioned in the decrees but the firms judged it imprudent to draw attention to themselves by making 'any attempt to dissociate ourselves from the stigma at the time, preferring to await a better occasion when actual business was in sight'.

During the years 1926–32, Schrobanco participated in twenty-six issues for US corporations which in total raised US$ 180 million (see Table 8.1 on page 230). Its first participation was in 1926 but the business really took off in 1928. In that year, a few months prior to his death, Loewenstein visited the United States and acquired an interest in the Standard Gas and Electric Corporation (Stangas), a major utility company serving Pittsburg, Minneapolis, St Paul, Louisville, Oklahoma City, San Diego and San Francisco. Schrobanco was appointed as one of the American bankers to Hydro Electric Securities, which gave it a standing when Stangas made an issue. The next important step in a tortuous story was the formation of the United States Electric Power Corporation (USEPCO) by Hydro Electric Securities and a group of American financiers in September 1929. USEPCO acquired control of the Standard Power and Light Corporation, which in turn took control of Stangas. Schrobanco acted as one of USEPCO's bankers, and Simpson and Baron Bruno joined the board. As a result of these appointments Schrobanco took part in the early 1930s in a series of bond issues led by Harris, Forbes & Co. (a Wall Street investment bank which specialised in utility issues) for a number of Stangas subsidiaries. Despite 'strenuous efforts' on Schrobanco's part the firm was unable to win more than a minor role in these financings, partly because the Wall Street investment bankers were unwilling to relinquish any of the underwriting and partly because of personal friction with the vice-president of Hydro Electric Securities. 'Each issue was a dog-fight all over again,' commented a contemporary report, 'and what little success Schrobanco had was really due to an agreement by Schroder, London, to co-issue in London with Harris, Forbes, Ltd.'[59] Schrobanco's final appearance on a new issue prospectus was in 1932 and by the time that the Glass–Steagall Act came into force in 1934 its activity as a bond underwriter was a thing of the past.

The Wall Street Crash and the German Financial Crisis, 1929–31

Following the downturn in foreign bond issuing activity in 1928, Schrobanco focused upon developing its trade finance activities and sought to expand its European investor base for US dollar securities. It also increased the provision of call loans to brokers who were prepared to pay very high rates for funds during the speculative frenzy which preceeded the Wall Street Crash of October 1929. The outcome of the crash and the German financial crisis of 1931 was a drastic reduction in the scale of Schrobanco's business, and in the first half of the 1930s the themes of the story of the firm are the rebuilding and refocusing of its business. These years also saw an important redefinition of the relationship between the New York and London firms.

Gray was on safari in Africa at the time of the crash and learned of events in a letter from Simpson. 'Just because you have been scampering around among the charging buffalo, you need not think you are the only one who has had any excitement recently,' wrote Simpson. 'Seeing the bottom fall out of the New York Stock Market may not be as exhilarating as tracking the royal Bengal tiger but it certainly does keep time from dragging on one's hands.'[60] Schrobanco's immediate response to the collapse of prices, and that of every other bank, was to require repayment of its 'street loans' – its call loans to brokerage houses which were secured against securities whose value was rapidly diminishing. 'It would be an affectation to say that we had no concern whatever, but the position on our loans was a matter of immense satisfaction,' wrote Simpson. 'We had the best houses in the street, and many others would have had to go before ours could be affected. Furthermore, at no time, even at the low prices of the worst day, were we without full collateral coverage and some margin.'

Only one brokerage house was unable to make repayment, the firm of Prince & Whiteley, to which an advance of $250,000 had been made. Schrobanco foreclosed upon the securities pledged as collateral and sold them for more than the amount owed. But a considerable loss was sustained on a loan that had been made to the Maydor Investment Company, the investment vehicle of Beal's father-in-law, John McHugh. It had borrowed $750,000 from Schrobanco to participate in the booming stock market, pledging the stocks it purchased as security for the loans. When the market collapsed the value of Maydor's investments fell far short of its borrowings. McHugh assumed personal liability for the debt and made over the deeds of two houses as additional collateral. Schrobanco carried the loan in the balance sheet as a fully valued asset until 1942, by which time recoveries through stock sales over the years totalled $223,056 and the houses were estimated to be worth a further $30,000, but the write-off that year totalled $496,944.[61]

In the summer of 1929 Beal had purchased a large 'put' contract on Chase National Bank shares, anticipating a downturn in the market. The 'put' gave Schrobanco the right to sell Chase shares at a price prevailing before the crash, which meant that the contract could be fulfilled at a substantial profit after the collapse of share prices. The firm realised a profit of $345,000 in November 1929 as a result. 'It seems like a dream,' wrote Beal, who was in London when he learned of this silver lining to the cloud enveloping Wall Street. 'I must tell you I spent two absolutely sleepless nights in which I went over the situation ten thousand times trying to find a flaw in it. The Baron is just back from a ten days trip to Hamburg and I am going to have a good deal of pleasure in casually mentioning this matter at lunch today'.[62] Thus overall direct damage to Schrobanco from the Wall Street Crash was slight.

Shortly after the Wall Street Crash, there occurred a dispute between the London proprietors and the New York management over a securities issue on behalf of Ambi-Budd Gmbh which raised important points of principle regarding their relationship. Towards the end of 1929 there was a financial crisis at Ambi Budd, which was 'practically insolvent' and unable to complete its development programme. The Schröder partners were highly alarmed, the firm being a major shareholder, and undertook to raise additional funding through an issue of preference shares of the Budd International Company, Ambi-Budd's biggest shareholder. J. Henry Schröder & Co. undertook to handle the London tranche and committed Schrobanco to do the New York underwriting. Schrobanco's executives learned of this commitment in a letter from Henry Andrews of 30 November 1929 that explained the urgency of the situation and concluded 'the most pressing thing at the moment is to get money for the Budd International Company and it would be difficult to exaggerate the importance of getting that business through'.[63] Nevertheless, Gray was horrified, since it was inconceivable that the New York market would absorb the Budd International paper in the foreseeable future. Furthermore, as he cabled to Beal:

London's decision we must underwrite portion shares raises most serious question principle as this practically means that by decision beyond our control we required lock up portion our banking capital in industrial project STOP This of course first time London has ever made such suggestion and feel such principle if established would be inconsistent with their conception of individual American banking institution STOP[64]

The outcome of the wrangle over 'this painful subject' was a compromise – Schrobanco participated in the underwriting, but the extent of its commitment was reduced from $2 million to $750,000. The fears of Schrobanco's officers were fully justified and it proved impossible to place any of the shares at the time of issue in mid-1930. The Budd International preference shares, with a book value of $750,000 but a much diminished market value, stayed in Schrobanco's securities portfolio for the next five years.

Successive cuts by the Federal Reserve in the aftermath of the crash reduced interest rates by more than half to a level of 2.5 per cent by June 1930, bolstering business confidence. The summer of 1930, however, saw two major policy changes that transformed the international economic environment. Pandering to domestic American opinion, President Hoover signed the Hawley–Smoot Tariff Act, imposing punitive tariffs on imports, and prompting retaliation by other countries which raised their own tariffs. Simultaneously, the Federal Reserve increased interest rates to halt the outflow of gold to Europe. The stock market resumed falling and it was not until mid-1932 that it bottomed out, at one-tenth of its September 1929 peak. These developments exacerbated Germany's economic difficulties, which had been mounting since late 1928, as the international trading system contracted and the supply of money from the United States diminished. Rapidly rising unemployment led to gains by the National Socialists and the Communists in the election of September 1930, further undermining foreign confidence in Germany. The deterioration of Germany's economic position continued, leading to the financial crisis of the summer of 1931.

The international economic depression, but particularly Germany's problems, had a devastating effect on Schrobanco's trade finance business. Between 1929 and 1934, acceptances fell from $34 million to $4 million, a rate of decrease three times faster than aggregate US bankers' acceptances (see Figure 8.3 on page 226). The onset of the German financial crisis in May 1931 led to immediate action to curtail the firm's exposure there; between May and September 1931, credit lines were cut from $74 million to $25 million and acceptance availments were reduced from $33 million to $18 million. Similar actions were taken by every US bank, bringing the German banking system to the brink of collapse and prompting the imposition of moratoria on overseas debt repayments by the German, Austrian and Hungarian governments in July 1931. The declaration of the moratoria posed the danger of a large-scale run on balances by clients worried about the firm's position, but in fact withdrawals were negligible, much to the relief, and surprise, of Schrobanco's senior officers.[65]

The total of Schrobanco's frozen German acceptances and advances in July 1931 was $12.4 million, about $1 million more than the firm's shareholders' funds. A crisis was averted by the 'very neighborly' actions of the Chase National Bank and the National City Bank, which undertook to purchase and hold, respectively, up to $6 million and $4 million of Schrobanco's acceptances to allow the firm time to raise funds to meet its liabilities.[66] The refinancing was accomplished partly by drawing on shareholders' funds and partly by new borrowings. Write-offs and bad debt provisions reduced the sum outstanding by $2.7 million, while the Chase provided an emergency loan of $1 million and subsequently the Federal Reserve Bank of New York advanced $7.5 million secured against securities owned by Schrobanco. The large-scale liquidation of German commercial debts, albeit at a substantial discount to face value, became possible under the terms of the fourth 'Standstill Agreement' which came into effect in February 1933. Schrobanco had a carefully prepared plan for the rapid resolution of the problem and had kept an executive in Berlin for this purpose since July 1931.

In May 1933, Gray visited London to get the proprietors' consent to the implementation of the liquidation plan. Baron Bruno and Frank Tiarks saw the situation differently, having faith in the creditworthiness of German clients, who were mostly longstanding commercial and often also personal friends. Moreover, they were reluctant to accept the losses that liquidation would inflict, being confident of full reimbursement when the German exchange position permitted. But Gray was adamant, and while J. Henry Schröder & Co., like the other London merchant banks, made little use of the liquidation facilities, Schrobanco, in common with most American banks, made very full use. Gray's success in getting his own way was greeted with jubilation by Simpson who, writing from New York, hailed 'your success with London in the matter of German credits which marks a real improvement in our status. We all feel that this has been a most significant week in our history'.[67] In Berlin the process of liquidation was immediately put in hand and by mid-July 1933 outstanding Standstill debts had been reduced from $12.4 million to $8.2 million. By the time of Gray's death in January 1935 the outstanding Standstill debt had been cut to $4.3 million and by the end of the year it was down to $2.8 million. At the outbreak of war between

Germany and the US it stood at $495,000, which was written off against reserves the following year. Surviving records do not permit the calculation of the extent of Schrobanco's losses from liquidation, but Ernest Meili estimated $3 million, about 25 per cent of the initial amount, which he believed compared very favourably with the losses sustained by other banks.[68]

European Offices, 1931–35

The willingness of Baron Bruno Schröder and Frank Tiarks to permit an independent approach by the New York firm was shaped by their deliberate policy of allowing Schrobanco to develop as an indigenous American institution, the management accounting for their actions to the board and consulting the shareholders on major policy matters. Nevertheless, the relationship between the London and New York firms was not without friction. One source of irritation was Dr Endrucks, the friend of the Schröder partners who acted as Schrobanco's Berlin representative. In December 1928, following a highly embarrassing episode in which a large negotiating team from an American vehicle manufacturer returned empty-handed from Germany, complaining bitterly that they had been misled by the firm about investment opportunities, it was decided to station an executive in Berlin 'to bring order out of chaos'.[69] The job was entrusted to Frederick Dolbeare, a former State Department official who had joined the firm on the recommendation of Allen Dulles, brother of John Foster Dulles. Dolbeare soon found himself as confused as his colleagues and advised Simpson that Endrucks' services would have to be dispensed with,[70] but to the frustration of the New York executives it took a year to obtain the agreement of the London partners to his dismissal. Schrobanco's representation in Berlin was then entrusted to J. Henry Schröder & Co.'s representative, Gustav von Mallinckrodt of Hagen & Co.

In 1928, Schrobanco began actively to market foreign dollar bonds to European investors, exploiting the attractive low prices of such securities which were out of favour with American investors, who preferred domestic equities. This was conducted through J. Henry Schröder & Co.'s Investment Department and the firm's Continental representatives, but it also necessitated frequent visits to Europe by the firm's senior officers. Soon they developed ambitions to establish Schrobanco's own securities distribution network in Europe, feeling, as Simpson put it writing from New York, that 'the future of our securities business depends on our being permitted to work ourselves at the business-getting end of it as well as here at the organisation end'.[71] The problem was, that in order to establish the firm's own operations in London, Paris or Berlin it was necessary to break with existing arrangements with J. Henry Schröder & Co. or its representatives which, as the Endrucks episode had demonstrated, was a very touchy matter. The reform of arrangements was most pressing in Paris, where Major Williams' services had long been a source of discontent to Schrobanco's executives, Bogdan's expression of 'feelings of utter indignation and despair at the way our Paris office has once more fallen down on their job' in a letter to Simpson of September 1930 being an example of the comments that passed between them.[72] Discontinuation of the arrangement with Williams was raised by Beal on a visit to London in July 1931, but the proposal was rejected by the London partners who continued to have full confidence in him. However, Baron Bruno and Frank Tiarks did agree to the permanent stationing of Norbert Bogdan in Berlin so that Schrobanco might have its own on-the-spot expert to be ready to take advantage of any opportunity that arose to achieve repayment of its frozen German credits. At the same time Frederick Dolbeare was installed in Leadenhall Street to act, as Simpson wrote, as Schrobanco's 'London Ambassador'.

The break with Williams in Paris was eventually made in the summer of 1932, Schrobanco justifying its termination of payments to support his office on grounds of economy, given the prevailing low level of securities sales through Paris. The Schröder partners accepted this argument, though such was the feeling that Williams was a victim of circumstances beyond his control that Baron Bruno personally lent him the funds to purchase a partnership in the stockbroking firm, Williams de Broe. Under the circumstances it was judged prudent to avoid giving further offence to Leadenhall Street by immediately stationing Lada-Mocarski in Paris, as Schrobanco's executives wished, but to appoint the amiable Dolbeare as a much more junior representative. 'The important thing,' wrote Simpson, upon being informed that London had agreed to this, 'is to reach our end, and if we have to get there by going over a detour instead of the main highway which is under repair, then the only thing to do is to take the detour. The main thing is to avoid any future hook-up with Williams de Broe in Paris and to see our way clear to the promotion of our own interests by our own efforts in that territory.'[73]

The appointment of Dolbeare to Paris also cleared the way to a more dynamic development of business in London. Beal, who happened to be in London at the time of the German financial crisis in July 1931, was astonished by Dolbeare's casual conduct. He reported to Simpson that:

he arrived from Paris the day we arrived and spent the first week here. He was in the office as much as several hours each day, about 11 to 3 on the average. Then on Friday he took Dorothy [Beal's wife] off to Le Touquet. I decided things were so active I had better stay here. Dorothy came back Monday, but Fred went on to Paris and I haven't seen him since. He has just called from Paris to suggest that we go to Le Touquet tonight, take advantage of the French holiday and get back here on Wednesday. I am sure I take business much too seriously.[74]

'In the last analysis,' wrote Simpson after the arrangement to send Dolbeare to Paris had been finalised, 'we can always deal with Fred, and I would much rather wrestle with him as part of our Paris problem than wrestle with Williams who always manages to stage the wrestling bout on the middle of Schröders' lunch table.'[75] The further development of US securities brokerage business in London was raised by Beal with the Schröder partners in the autumn of 1932. He expressed New York's view that, 'in London, just as on the Continent, we are suffering terribly by having no one who gets up every morning, inspired with the idea that his bread and butter depend on producing a little business for Schrobanco between dawn and dusk'.[76] He proposed a new arrangement for profit-pooling between the Securities Department in New York and the Investment Department in London, a plan that received a cool reception, and no action resulted.

The breakthrough in the realisation of Schrobanco's aspirations to develop business in Europe came in 1933. A change in the German regulations governing the liquidation of frozen commercial credits allowed Bogdan to execute the realisation of much of the firm's outstanding debts, an achievement that has already been discussed. Once Schrobanco's own frozen credit situation was in hand, Bogdan marketed his expertise in the tortuous process of liquidation, requiring the collection of innumerable consents from the Reichsbank and the Economics Ministry, to other banks and firms with frozen German credits. There proved to be great demand for his services and thus a Berlin Office, with the status of a department, was established in the summer of 1933.[77] Rooms were rented at 7 Pariser Platz, opposite the office of Gustav von Mallinckrodt, in a building adjacent to the Brandenburg Gate. Bogdan was joined by other executives from the New York office and a lively business trading blocked Reichsmarks was soon under way. 'One of the first large transactions with third parties,' he recalled, 'was the sale of several million dollars worth of registered Reichsmarks offered us by the National City Bank under an outstanding credit to I. G. Farben. Lesson! Never assume that the giants know everything. On the contrary, when things are difficult and complicated the smaller fellow who knows what he is doing and can act fast, will often come home with the bacon.'[78] Many American industrial firms engaged Schrobanco's Berlin Office to extricate whatever could be recovered of their commitments to Germany, leading in some cases to them opening accounts with the firm in New York, an example being International Harvester of Chicago.[79]

The Berlin Office also developed a very active dealing operation in restricted currencies, frozen credits and securities. In collaboration with S. Japhet & Co., the London merchant bank, Bogdan participated in a number of 'Russian conversion schemes'. These transactions involved the exchange of German dollar credits at par for bills issued by the Russian Trade Delegation in Berlin. He recalled that:

Schroders [in London] could not understand why anybody in his right mind would exchange 'good' German claims against Russian paper, but we jumped at the opportunity. I tried to dispose of our Russian bills in order to raise cash. I had been told that Paris was the market for Russian bills so I hot-footed it to Paris but found that no one was willing to pay more than 60 per cent cash for the face value of the Russian bills. All the buyers were Russian emigres who took the position that if the Soviet Government collapsed they would be happy to return to Russia, even at the cost of losing 60 per cent of the face value of the paper they held; and if the Soviet Government stayed in power and continued to meet its obligations, they wouldn't mind making a 40 per cent profit out of the Soviets!!! Anyhow, we hung on to our Russian bills which, of course, were all paid off without a hitch at maturity.[80]

The summer of 1933 also saw the commencement of more active operations in Paris. In May 1933, Gerald Donovan, a graduate of the Harvard Business School who had trained with Goldman Sachs, was installed there to market US securities. Accompanied by Dolbeare, he called on bankers and private clients in Paris and Geneva, acquainting them with the services Schrobanco had to offer. 'It was most gratifying to see that the reception we had was always amiable, and in most instances distinctly cordial,' Dolbeare reported to New York.[81] However, the trip produced little in the way of business since the depreciating dollar and the inflationary policies of the Roosevelt administration meant that Europeans had little interest in purchasing American securities at that moment.

Schrobanco's dissatisfactions with the arrangements for the distribution of US securities in London were again raised by Gray in June 1933,

bringing to the attention of the partners the activities of other Wall
Street houses, such as Iselin & Co. and White Weld & Co., which were
building up substantial US securities brokerage businesses in the City.
To the enormous satisfaction of Schrobanco's senior officers, the
partners agreed, in principle, that Schrobanco could undertake securities
brokerage business in London independently of J. Henry Schröder &
Co.'s Investment Department. Simpson relayed the reaction in New
York to Donovan, who was assisting Bogdan with the development of
the Berlin Office:

> Our feeling here is twofold: first, that we are extremely glad at this
> development and want to take advantage of the opportunity at the
> right time and in the right way. Second, that we are extremely
> anxious to avoid any precipitate action which might be construed
> as an abuse of the privilege . . . It would be penny-wise and
> pound-foolish to an extraordinary degree if we attempted to whip
> up some outside securities business in London with the result of
> irritating everybody.[82]

But the relations between the firms were already strained, and when
Donovan visited Leadenhall Street in August 1933 he met with a hostile
reception. He was accused of employing 'high power salesmanship and
pushing methods', ungentlemanly behaviour that harmed relations with
clients.[83] Dolbeare in Paris was outraged at the 'mass attack' on
Donovan and informed New York that he was doing a 'swell job' in
difficult circumstances.[84] But Simpson understood that the real reason
for the outburst was the culmination of resentment at the intitatives
taken by Schrobanco that disrupted established arrangements and were
redefining the relationship between the firms. In essence, as he put it to
Dolbeare, London was posing the question, 'Why so many of us in
Europe anyway?'.[85]

So successful was the Berlin Office that in the autumn of 1933 Bogdan
was joined there by another senior executive, Ernest Meili. Its
achievements boosted Gray's determination to win the consent of the
Schröder partners to an upgrading of the firm's Paris operation which,
as he put it in February 1934, 'is today costing over $10,000 per annum
and producing practically nothing'.[86] The battle was finally won and in
September 1934 Valla Lada-Mocarski became the resident head of
Schrobanco's Paris Office in premises in the Boulevard Haussmann.[87]
He devoted some attention to US securities brokerage, but in its heyday
in 1934–36 the most successful activity of the Paris Office, like its
counterpart in Berlin, was restricted currency dealing, especially in
Balkan and Latin American currencies. Bogdan handed over control of

the Berlin Office to Meili in October 1934, but briefly that autumn the three most senior executives on the banking side of Schrobanco's business were all stationed in Europe, which provides a measure of the strength of Schrobanco's European orientation in the mid-1930s. Instead of proceeding directly to New York, Bogdan, accompanied by Beal, returned home via Brazil and Argentina, and it was South America that henceforth was the focus of Schrobanco's initiatives to develop business.

Financial Performance

'The last thing Frank Tiarks said to Prentiss Gray and me,' Beal told an audience of staff and friends assembled in 1943 to celebrate Schrobanco's twentieth anniversary, 'just before he got on the boat to go back to London at the end of November 1923 was "Remember, we don't care if you don't make a cent for the first ten years, but just establish Schroders as a first-class name in New York". That made a deep impression upon me.'[88] In fact, Schrobanco's management did much better than Tiarks had anticipated. Not only was the firm's name soon well respected but it also proved profitable from the outset. In 1924 profits after tax were $289,000 and in 1926 they reached $1.0 million – about $7.4 million in 1990 money. The German financial crisis and the international slump hit the firm hard and losses were sustained in 1931 and 1933. Recovery began in 1934, thanks largely to the operations of the Berlin Office, but in the year of Gray's death, profits were only $224,000, which was less than the first year of operations.

It was the policy of the London partners that Schrobanco should retain profits to build up its capital. As a result by 1930 the capital and surplus was $10.3 million – about $81 million in 1990 money – more than double the subscribed capital of $5 million. The losses of the early 1930s led to reductions in capital, principally due to write-offs resulting from the liquidation of the Central European frozen credits, and at the end of 1935 the capital and surplus was $6.8 million.

In the 1920s, Schrobanco's annual post-tax profits produced impressive rates of return on capital. In the years 1924–30, which saw minimal inflation, the rate of return ranged from 8.3 cent to 21.3 per cent and averaged 12.7 per cent (see Figure 8.4). Statistics gathered by the Federal Reserve Board permit a comparison of this rate of return with the return on total capital accounts earned by the federally chartered US national banks. Over the same period the comparable average return for US national banks was 7.3 per cent, roughly half the rate achieved by Schrobanco. Schrobanco's rate of return was negative in 1931 and 1933

Figure 8.4   J. Henry Schroder Banking Corporation, post-tax return on capital and annual rate of inflation, 1923–35

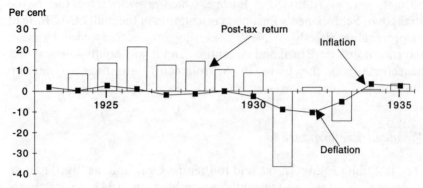

Note: The 'real' return on capital is the difference between the nominal return depicted above and the annual rate of inflation.

and the positive returns of 1932 and 1934 were very low, but it should be realised that the US national banks recorded negative returns throughout 1931–34. In 1935, the US national banks returned to profit and made an average return on capital of 5.1 per cent. That year Schrobanco achieved a return of 3.3 per cent. While modest by the standards of the 1920s, it was indicative that the firm's fortunes were reviving.

9

'Standstill', Depression and War

1931–45

The international financial crisis of the summer of 1931 was a fundamental turning point for London as a financial centre and for the merchant banks. Economic nationalism, which arose from and exacerbated the worldwide slump in the early 1930s, put paid to the liberal international trading environment in which the City of London and the merchant banks had flourished for a century or so. More and more the City became a domestic financial centre and the merchant banks shifted their attentions to the domestic market.[1] The reorientation presented difficulties for every firm, but those such as J. Henry Schröder & Co. which conducted business on a substantial scale with Germany also had to cope with the German suspension of debt repayments in July 1931, a problem that was unresolved for more than two decades.

The slump of the early 1930s saw a drastic drop in international trade; by February 1933 the value of world imports was only a third of the level of April 1929.[2] Naturally, there was a sharp fall in demand for international trade finance, and the decline in the volume of foreign-drawn bills in the London discount market, from £365 million in 1929 to £134 million in 1933, indicates the magnitude of the reduction in the demand for the services of the merchant banks.[3] London's role as a primary international capital market was curtailed by the restrictions on capital exports imposed by the British government; in 1922–28 the UK's annual average net capital export, expressed in US dollars of the day, was $407 million, but in 1931–35 remittances surpassed foreign new issues and there was a net annual average capital import of $74 million.[4] Thus in the early 1930s both aspects of the traditional core activities of the London merchant banks were very depressed.

International trade made a slow and faltering recovery from 1933, but the volume of foreign-drawn bills in London scarcely increased and there was no revival of the trade finance business of the merchant banks. This was because of changes in the ways in which international trade was financed, for instance the growing use of telegraphic transfers and barter arrangements which bypassed the sterling bill of exchange, and increased local financing.[5] As regards foreign securities issues, the London market was even less active in the second half of the decade than in the first, and in the years 1936–38 the annual average net capital import was $212 million. The London merchant banks responded by developing trade finance and issuing services for domestic clients, and pursued new activities such as investment management. The domestic orientation of the merchant banks, and of the City as a whole, was the distinguishing feature of the decades of the 1930s, 1940s and 1950s.

The onset of this new era was heralded by the international financial crisis of the summer of 1931.[6] It began in May when the Österreichische Creditanstalt, Austria's largest commercial bank, revealed difficulties, which undermined confidence in Central European financial institutions and led to massive withdrawals of deposits. By mid-June, the repatriation of short-term loans by foreign, particularly US, banks was inflicting acute pressure on German banks. Alarmed by the mounting financial crisis in Germany, which threatened an intensification of the international economic depression from which the world was already suffering, on 20 June President Hoover declared a one-year moratorium upon the repayment of all inter-governmental debts arising from the First World War. This in practice marked the end of German reparations obligations and Allied war debts to the US, and it was hoped that this 'momentous announcement' would restore confidence in the international financial system.[7] Briefly it did, but political uncertainties persisted and the run on deposits in German banks soon revived. On 13 July, the Darmstädter und Nationalbank, one of the leading German commercial banks, was unable to open because it had run out of funds, and the German government knew that another, the Dresdner Bank, was poised to follow. Fearing the wholesale collapse of the country's banking system, a bank holiday was declared by Presidential decree on 14–15 July, Hungary and Austria taking similar measures. When the German banks reopened on 16 July a comprehensive regime of restrictions on payments was in force, including controls on remittances to overseas creditors. These included the London merchant banks to which some £64 million – as much as £2 billion in 1990 money – was owed on account of outstanding acceptance credits, posing a threat to the City akin to that which it faced at the outbreak of the First World War.[8] Negotiations between creditors and debtors resulted in a six-month 'voluntary' moratorium on payments, known as the Standstill Agreement, which came into effect in mid-September.

Well before then the financial crisis had spread to London. The German freezing of a large volume of credits due to British financial institutions undermined foreign confidence in them and prompted questions about the safety of balances held in London. Moreover, the British budgetary deficit led to reservations about the stability of sterling and there were doubts about the political will of the Labour administration to take the steps regarded as necessary to correct the imbalance. Indeed, on 24 August the Cabinet split over the issue and a new national government was formed comprising a coalition of Labour, Conservative and Liberal Members of Parliament committed to a balanced budget. Far from reassuring foreign holders of sterling, the political crisis further unnerved them, and the news of a protest against pay cuts by British sailors convinced them, in the words of Schröders' *Quarterly Review,* 'that the British Navy was honeycombed with Communism and that all was over with England'.[9] A stampede out of sterling soon exhausted British reserves and on 21 September an Act was passed suspending the convertibility of the pound into gold. Sterling immediately fell in value relative to other currencies, the decline against the US dollar being from \$4.86 under the gold standard to an average of \$3.69 in October–December 1931. 'England inflicted heavy loss on those of her creditors who had believed in and supported the strength of sterling by leaving their funds in London, and has dealt a heavy blow to financial confidence abroad, long accustomed to regard the pound, and the sterling bill, as linch-pins in the wheels of world trade' lamented Schröders' *Quarterly Review.*[10] Further blows to the international business of the merchant banks were delivered by the new policies of tariff protection and restrictions on capital exports that were adopted in the wake of the departure from the gold standard to assist the recovery of domestic manufacturing industry from the slump. Moreover, the low interest rate policy instigated with the same objective, and sustained from 1932 to 1951, reduced interest account earnings. All in all, the 1930s were very difficult years for the merchant banks.

The German financial crisis of 1931 was the greatest calamity in Schröders' history, inflicting substantial losses and freezing a large part of the firm's assets for more than two decades. Two of the most prominent failures of the crisis, Nordwolle, a major textile manufacturer, and Schlubach Thiemer & Co., were major Schröder clients, the firm's exposures being respectively £300,000 and £100,000. Its exposure to the Darmstädter und Nationalbank was £300,000. Schröders' revenues collapsed with the onset of the crisis and there was no substained recovery thereafter; in 1928–30 revenues averaged £697,000 per annum but in 1931 they were £330,000 and in 1934 just £106,000 (see Figure 9.1). By 1936 they had recovered to £460,000, but fell thereafter averaging only £124,000 in 1938–39. The international slump of the early 1930s led to redundancies at Schröders and between 31 December 1930 and 31 December 1932 staff numbers fell from 276 to 157. In the second half of the decade there was renewed recruitment during the short-lived upturn in activity in 1936–37 and at the end of 1937 there were 207 people on the payroll, but by 1939 the staff had fallen to 154 and in 1942 it was 94, with 57 on war service. Survival was

Figure 9.1   J. Henry Schröder & Co., revenues, 1928–45

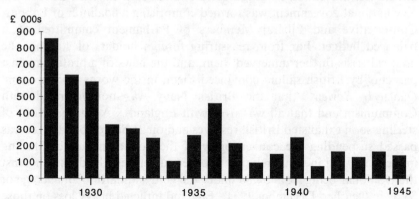

J. Henry Schröder & Co.'s foremost achievement in the years of the depression and the war.

Baron Bruno's German family was hard hit by the financial crisis, and his wife's family firm, Deichmann & Co. of Cologne, went bankrupt. To assist the family in Germany, he established the Baron Bruno Schröder Stiftung in 1931 to provide money for impoverished relations. This was similar to the Rudolph-Clara Schröder Stiftung which he set up at the time of the hyperinflation in 1923 to assist all descendants of his parents.

Frank Tiarks and the German 'Standstill' Agreements, 1931–39

On 10 July 1931, five days before the German suspension of payments, a group of leading London bankers met to discuss 'ways and means of stopping the withdrawal of credits from Germany'.[11] The outcome of the meeting was the appointment of a nine-man 'Joint Committee' to represent the Accepting Houses Committee and the British Bankers' Association in discussions with the Bank of England and the Treasury. For Frank Tiarks, who was one of the nine, the occasion must have evoked memories of the meeting on 5 August 1914 which led to the formation of the Accepting Houses Committee, at which he had also been present.[12] That precedent came into the minds of the members of the Joint Committee when they learned of the closure of the Darmstädter Bank and they informed Montagu Norman that 'it will be necessary to establish some arrangement similar to that established on the outbreak of War in 1914'.[13] But the Governor had no intention of giving any such commitment, which might even precipitate the lock-up he was trying to avoid, though he did contact the chairmen of the major clearing banks to request that 'if applications of a somewhat unusual character were made by Accepting Houses during the course of the next few days, they should be most sympathetically considered'.[14]

Norman hoped that the international conference of world leaders, urgently convened in London by the British Foreign Office, would do away with reparations and the Allied war debts that were the underlying causes of the international financial instability.[15] But the deliberations of the 'most representative and influential body of world statesmen that had assembled since the war', as *The Economist* put it, failed to produce a breakthrough.[16] The London Conference proposed further support for the Reichsbank and recommended that the commercial and private banks should maintain the volume of their credits to Germany. It also suggested the establishment of a committee of experts, nominated by central bank governors, to work under the auspices of the Bank for International Settlements to look at Germany's needs for further foreign credits and the opportunities for the restructuring of its debts. 'Some disappointment has been caused by these recommendations,' commented the *Quarterly Review*, 'as indicating the failure of the Conference to arrive at any solution of the political difficulties, which are the real cause of the lack of confidence which is the root of the mischief.'[17] Arnold Toynbee, Director of the Institute of International Affairs, was more forthright, writing that the London Conference 'resembled nothing so much as a gathering of fashionable physicians, all anxious above all things to preserve their professional reputations, round the bedside of a prominent patient whose malady they have no genuine hope of curing'.[18] The market's verdict on the prospects of a resolution to Germany's financial problems was expressed in the price of the Young Loan bonds, which had fallen from their issue price of 90 in June 1930 to 60 at the end of July 1931.

The outcome of the London Conference was that the politicians 'handed the problem back to the bankers'.[19] They, in turn, handed it to Frank Tiarks, who was made their chief negotiator, with the formal title of Chairman of the German Sub-Committee of the Joint Committee of British Bankers and Accepting Houses, though he was also entrusted to speak on behalf of the short-term creditors of other countries.[20] His task was to strike a 'voluntary' agreement between the short-term creditors and the German debtors, transforming a government decreed default into a payments moratorium by consent. This was a vitally important distinction for the City of London because a default threatened to bankrupt several of the major merchant banks, probably some of the discount houses, and possibly to provoke a crisis in the banking system. Tiarks had many qualifications for the role: 56 years old, he was an eminent City figure and a director of the Bank of England of nineteen years' standing; he spoke fluent German and was personally acquainted with most leading German bankers and many businessmen; he was renowned as a tough negotiator and possessed plentiful reserves of energy; furthermore, he had a great personal interest in a successful resolution of the situation since his own firm was in dire trouble as a result of the German suspension of payments.

On Saturday 25 July, two days after the end of the London Conference, Tiarks and three colleagues from the Joint Committee met with Montagu Norman for a briefing on the views of the Bank of England and the British government.[21] The following day Tiarks went to Berlin to hold preliminary discussions with representatives of the German creditors. James H. Gannon, of whom Norman observed 'fertile mind and brave', a vice-president of the Chase National Bank in London, travelled with him as spokesman for the American banks.[22] Early the next morning, Dr Hjalmar Schacht, now once again a private banker having resigned as Reichsbank President in March 1930, but still one of the most important figures in German finance, called at their hotel and they spent the morning discussing the situation. Tiarks reported back to London that Schacht had told him he believed that Germany had no need for further foreign credits so long as the existing level of short-term credits was maintained, although temporarily it would be necessary for the legal limit of 40 per cent central bank reserve cover for the note issue to be abrogated. Schacht also stated that a further long-term loan was unnecessary so long as the government took appropriate action and cut expenditure on social services. He also provided an 'interesting description of the political background', reassuring the visitors that the advent of a National Socialist government, should it come to pass, would mean domestic economy measures, but that there was no danger to Germany's external liabilities. 'He was sure,' stated Tiarks, 'that such a Government ought to have the confidence of all foreigners, rather than the present Government whose present policy, if persisted in, will ultimately lead to the ruin of Germany.' Tiarks told him that the advent of the Nazis to power 'would create consternation abroad', to which Schacht replied that 'the only way to avoid the overthrow of the present Government and the election of the Nazis was through the formation of a Coalition Cabinet, composed of the best men from all parties, to govern Germany for two years without reference to the Reichstag'.[23]

In the afternoon, Tiarks and Gannon proceeded to the Reichsbank where the President, Dr Luther, introduced the German Bankers Committee, the delegation representing the Standstill debtors, and exhorted his countrymen to find an accommodation with the representatives of the City of London and Wall Street with the least possible delay. Also in attendance were the German government's consultants, Professor Sprague, a Harvard economist who was also an adviser to the Bank of England, and the prominent Swedish businessman Max Wallenberg. Tiarks and Gannon suggested to the Germans that the scheme devised to cope with the problem of the Hungarian frozen credits, to which London and New York bankers had already consented, might serve as a model for their agreement. This established a six-month voluntary moratorium on repayments, and borrowers undertook to deposit collateral for their debts with the Hungarian Central Bank, which acted as trustee for the creditors. The German bankers agreed to spend the afternoon studying the plan and to come up with 'something along similar lines'.

After dinner the delegates got down to detailed discussions. Tiarks and Gannon 'impressed upon the Germans that it was up to them to make us proposals for continuing our credits and deposits which we could pass as probably being acceptable to the London and New York bankers. It seemed to surprise them considerably that we expected to get as much security as possible'. The meeting eventually broke up at 2 am and Tiarks cabled London that progress was being made, though 'necessarily slower than one could wish'. The talks resumed the following morning, Tuesday 28 July, and at 4.30 pm Sprague reported to Montagu Norman by telephone that 'the temper in Berlin is pretty good. They seem to be facing the position quite calmly'. That evening a preliminary draft proposal was prepared and twenty-four hours later the points to be put to Germany's foreign creditors were cabled to the central banks for communication to their respective creditor committees.

The following week was spent gathering the responses of the American, Dutch, Swiss and other creditor committees, answering their queries and formulating a co-ordinated position. It was decided that the best chance for a successful outcome to the negotiations was for them to be conducted under the auspices of the committee of economic experts established at the behest of the London Conference to investigate Germany's credit needs.[24] This body, known as the Wiggin Committee after its chairman Albert Wiggin, President of the Chase National Bank, and comprising ten members representing the principal creditor countries plus Germany, agreed to act as arbitrator in case of irreconcilable differences between Germany and its short-term creditors. Thus the formal negotiations took place in Basle, the home of the Bank for International Settlements.

Tiarks, now referred to in the press as 'the well-known banker', travelled to Basle on Thursday 13 August. He was immediately elected chairman of the representatives of the various creditor committees assembled there, and with this authority, and the back-up of Gannon and William Mortimer, the driving force in the leading City solicitors

Slaughter and May, he began negotiations with the German representatives.[25] By the end of the first day, Saturday 15 August, the differences between the parties had been reduced to six points. On Sunday, 'a second very strenuous day', Tiarks persuaded the Germans to capitulate on three points and a compromise was struck on two more, and by 10 pm there was only one outstanding point of disagreement – the schedule for the release of Reichsmark bank balances to their foreign owners. Tiarks insisted upon the terms set by the creditors' committees – 25 per cent of Reichsmark balances to be freed immediately and the rest paid in monthly instalments of 15 per cent – but the Germans refused to go beyond an initial release of 20 per cent and a six-month moratorium on further releases. Monday's negotiations lasted from 10.30 am to 2 am, but the deadlock continued. The following day members of the Wiggin Committee joined the talks and eventually the issue was resolved, largely to Tiarks' satisfaction. At midnight, Mortimer telephoned London with the news that agreement had been reached.

The first Standstill Agreement was initialled in Basle on Wednesday, 19 August 1931. The draft agreement was then referred back to the various national committees of creditors for ratification and finally it was formally accepted by Germany on 9 September. It applied to Germany's foreign commercial debt, that is the acceptance credits and cash advances outstanding to German banks and companies totalling Rm6,300 million (£307 million), but did not cover similar obligations on the part of the government, the Reichsbank or municipalities. Creditors were to receive all payments of interest in fully convertible form and various forms of supplementary collateral in return for the 'voluntary' extension of their loans.[26] An attempt was made to accommodate the fears of creditors regarding the financial soundness of some debtors by providing that they should receive security in respect of 10 per cent of acceptance credits and 5 per cent of cash advances which were to be assumed by the Golddiskont Bank, a subsidiary of the Reichsbank. Repayment of principal was restricted to these Golddiskont Bank credits. Thereby Germany preserved its foreign exchange reserves and secured the credits which were required for it to continue to conduct international trade, while the foreign banks which provided the credits were safeguarded against 'incurring serious embarassments'.[27]

The successful conclusion of the Standstill Agreement was regarded at the time as an extraordinary achievement, for which Tiarks was given most of the credit. On 10 September he received a telegram from Dr Luther expressing his desire 'to thank you heartily dear Mr Tiarks for the great work you have done from the beginning to the conclusion of the agreement. I should like to express the hope that . . . it will prove to be a suitable instrument to ameliorate the psychological needs of the present time'.[28] 'Unquestionably one of the most remarkable documents in the history of modern banking' was the verdict of an English newspaper, 'its authors deserve to be congratulated on having solved successfully one of the most difficult tasks bankers have ever faced'.[29]

Frank Tiarks and fellow bankers expected the Standstill Agreement to be followed promptly by political initiatives that would resolve the problems of reparations, Allied war debts and the Franco-German antagonism that lay at the root of the worldwide economic depression. Indeed, moves were made towards convening an international conference at Lausanne in January 1932, but electoral considerations in Germany, France and the US led to its postponement until the summer. The Schröder partners were bitterly disappointed by the lack of urgency on the part of the politicians and in February 1932 the *Quarterly Review* gave voice to a plea that 'the Governments must see before their own eyes insistent reasons why affairs should not be allowed to drift. Dwindling revenues, growing unemployment, stagnant trade and drooping prices of commodities and securities should surely have shown them that no time is to be lost'. But as the expiry of the Standstill agreement approached, it was clear that the deterioration in the international economic environment and the Reichsbank's dwindling foreign exchange reserves meant there was no alternative to renewal.

Tiarks' objectives in the renewal negotiations were to ensure that interest payments on the Standstill credits continued to be made in convertible form and on a punctual basis, and to secure some repayment of principal. In October 1931, he informed Montagu Norman that it should be possible to exact a 'substantial reduction' in the level of frozen credits as the price of renewal.[30] However, the decline in Germany's external position meant that repayment of principal was not possible and the 1932 German Credit Agreement (as the Standstill Agreements were now officially called), which came into force for a year in February 1932, provided instead for a reduction in unavailed credit lines. It also introduced mechanisms permitting Standstill creditors to convert cash advances into Reichsmarks which could be invested in securities in Germany. These investments were blocked for five years before they could be converted, at an unfavourable rate of exchange, into foreign currency.

By the summer of 1932, it appeared that a resolution of some of the structural problems affecting the world economy was at hand. On the anniversary of the Hoover Moratorium on payments of war debts and reparations, in early July, governments meeting in Lausanne agreed to cancel all Germany's reparation obligations except for one final payment of Rm3 billion that was due in 1935. Furthermore, indications that the world economy and the German economy were on the verge of recovery

– reflected in a strong rise in the Berlin and other stock exchanges during the autumn of 1932 – and expectations that the National Socialist share of the vote would decline in the November 1932 elections increased confidence that Germany's private external liabilities would be honoured. The improvement in international confidence was reflected in the recovery in the price of Young Loan bonds, which had touched 28 in June 1932 but had climbed to 47 at the time of the Lausanne Conference, and to 60 in early January 1933.

The Standstill Agreement of 1933 resulted in further cuts in unavailed credits and extended the rights to repayments in Reichsmarks to acceptance credits, though a ceiling was imposed upon the proportion of an outstanding debt that could be converted each month. These Reichsmark balances, again blocked for five years, were deposited with the Reichsbank and inscribed in a special register, which led to them being known as 'registered marks'. Registered credit balances could be used by German exporters to subsidise 'additional' exports and were offered at a discount to tourists to stimulate this source of foreign exchange earnings. These registered marks could be transferred between foreigners, both banks and non-banks, and offered an opportunity for Standstill creditors to liquidate their credits, albeit at discounts of up to 50 per cent. It was this liquidation activity in which the Berlin Office of Schrobanco and Anglo-Foreign Securities, the trading firm in which J. Henry Schröder & Co. had a 50 per cent interest, specialised.

The liquidations and other factors, notably the devaluation of sterling and the US dollar relative to the Reichsmark, resulted in the reduction of outstanding Standstill credits from Rm6,300 million in July 1931, to Rm2,600 million in February 1934, and to Rm700 million in February 1939. By the end of the decade the bulk of the remaining Standstill credits were due to British creditors who did not make extensive use of the liquidation facilities, unlike their American counterparts. The behaviour of the London banking firms reflected their longstanding ties with German clients, particularly commercial firms, whereas the recently arrived American banks had conducted business on a wholesale basis with banks and had no such loyalties. Moreover, for the American banks, with the exception of Schrobanco, the frozen German acceptance credits were only a small part of their activities and they had the resources to clear them from their balance sheets, but for many of the much smaller and more specialised London accepting houses the losses from liquidation at a discount would have been ruinous.

Hitler's advent to power in January 1933 led to a more aggressive German stance in international financial affairs and the new President of the Reichsbank, Schacht, determined to take advantage of the currency turmoil that followed the unexpected decision to devalue the dollar in

April 1933.[31] Under the terms of the arrangements made in 1931, interest continued to be paid in foreign currency on all outstanding foreign loans – short-, medium- and long-term – but on 16 May 1933 the Reichsbank cabled the Governor of the Bank of England stating 'we regret to have to inform you that the German foreign exchange position is so unfavourable and the question of the further transfer of funds for the debt service is so seriously affected thereby, that a direct discussion with the creditors is necessary'.[32] Tiarks, accompanied by Robert Brand of Lazards, went immediately to Berlin and impressed on Schacht the importance of the exclusion of the Standstill commercial debts from any additional exchange restrictions. They told him that the suspension of interest payments would make a renewal of the bills impossible and necessitate their withdrawal from the discount market, causing a crisis in the City, which would lead to retaliation from the British government.[33] In this political respect, the London banks were politically better protected than their Wall Street counterparts, for whom President Roosevelt had little sympathy. Indeed, Schacht related in his memoirs that when he visited Roosevelt in Washington in May 1933 to warn him that Germany was running short of foreign exchange, the president 'gave his thigh a resounding smack and exclaimed with a laugh: Serves the Wall Street bankers right'.[34] The lobbying by Tiarks and Brand was successful and the Standstill credits were excluded from the interest transfer moratorium which was declared on 8 June 1933 and applied to all other German external obligations.[35] The following day the price of the Young Loan bonds in London was 46.

Some countries responded to the German suspension of interest payments by instigating a 'clearing', an arrangement whereby the importers of German goods paid a proportion of the sums owed to the exporters into a special 'clearing account' with the central bank, from which the claims of bondholders were met in their own currency.[36] Serious consideration was given to the imposition of a clearing by the British government and in June 1934 legislation was passed to make this possible. The prospect of a British clearing caused consternation amongst the Standstill creditors, since it would mean that the discount market would no longer be willing to handle German bills, and renewal of the Standstill credits would be impossible.[37] Furthermore, the proposal undermined the role of the City as an international financial centre, the *Quarterly Review* expressing the view that the mere threat to German funds was highly detrimental to London as a place of deposit for foreign money and securities.[38] 'I am very much worried,' Tiarks confided in a letter to Gustav von Mallinckrodt on 21 June 1934, 'more so than I have been since the crisis started 3 years ago.'[39] Montagu Norman raised the problem with Neville Chamberlain, the Chancellor of the Exchequer, and reported to Tiarks the following day that 'he is fully alive to the dangers of a German clearing to you Standstill folk and he realises that if there is trouble your blood may fall on his head. I have told him so a dozen times and he accepts it'.[40] The *Quarterly Review* reported 'general relief' in the City of London upon the signature the following month of the Anglo-German Transfer Agreement, which made new arrangements for interest transfers to British creditors.[41] Nevertheless, the imposition of a clearing continued to be a threat to the merchant banks, it being discussed, for instance, in the negotiations for the renewal of the Standstill Agreement in Berlin in November 1934.[42]

The regulation suspending the external transfer of interest payments on medium- and long-term debt in June 1933 stipulated that henceforth the payments were to be made to the Konversionskasse für Deutsche Auslandschulden (Debt Conversion Office), a government body which was given responsibility for settling with the creditors.[43] Creditors received payment partly in cash and the balance in Reichsmark scrip of the Konversionskasse. J. Henry Schröder & Co. assumed a paying agency function in London on behalf of the Konversionskasse for the purpose of receiving matured and drawn bonds of German external loans, holders being given the choice of replacement with a valid security or repayment in 'Amortisation Blocked Reichsmarks'. Under the terms of the Anglo-German Transfer Agreement of July 1934 interest on bonds issued or domiciled in London was settled in 4 per cent Sterling Bonds of the Konversionskasse, and in 1936–38 J. Henry Schröder & Co. conducted five issues of Konversionskasse bonds in London for this purpose.

'Tiarks made up his mind to be on good terms with Schacht because that was the way to get the best results for the Standstill creditors,' stated Henry Andrews, who was privy to Tiarks' thoughts in the early 1930s.[44] His success in persuading Schacht that it would be folly to include short-term commercial debts under the moratorium of June 1933 convinced him that the Reichsbank President was not unamenable to reason, and Schacht's appointment as Economics Minister as well in June 1934 made the maintenance of good relations even more vital. This view was also taken by the British Embassy in Berlin[45] and other international bankers, who saw Schacht as the man who had managed the restoration of sound finance in Germany after the nightmare of the 1923 hyperinflation, rather than as the 'wizard' of Nazi finance, as he later came to be perceived. When rumours reached London in March 1936 that Schacht had fallen into disfavour with Hitler, Tiarks descended upon the German ambassador and informed him that the City would be horrified by 'any loss of position by Schacht [who] . . . is regarded almost as a saving grace'.[46] Tiarks' negotiations with Schacht, his membership of the Council of the Anglo-German Fellowship, a body formed in 1935 to promote goodwill between the two countries,[47] and his speeches, at Schacht's invitation, to the German World Economic Society in Frankfurt in May 1937 and to the Anglo-German Fellowship in March 1939, led to criticism for promoting economic appeasement.[48] But Tiarks believed that by supporting Schacht he was bolstering the sole moderate member of the German government, and the only person who could restore German finances to a sound basis so that its external liabilities could be honoured.[49]

As Germany's foreign policy became more aggressive with the occupation of the Rhineland in 1936, doubts grew about the German government's good faith, and the clearing bank members of the Joint Committee pressed for an insistence on repayment of principal. During the discussions amongst British creditors preliminary to the Standstill Agreement in February 1937 there occurred 'a kind of revolt of the Standstill creditors against his [Tiarks] leadership'.[50] At the instigation of Reginald McKenna, the chairman of the Midland Bank, the clearing bank representatives asked why the Standstill creditors 'should for three years have refrained from pressing for capital repayments. They considered that matters should be brought to a head'.[51] The British negotiators were instructed by the Joint Committee to press for a 10 per cent capital repayment and not to settle for less than 5 per cent. Their resolve was strengthened by the addition to the negotiating team of Charles Lidbury, a director of the Westminster Bank, whose 'fire-eating remarks to the effect that the Germans were working a continuous swindle [and] that he would rather see a clearing imposed than get no cash' made a poor impression on the British Embassy in Berlin.[52] The Germans refused to make repayments of principal, and the British, in the face of a hostile reaction from the other creditors, backed down. The international creditors settled for further cancellation of unavailed credit lines and a small impost on blocked marks sold to tourists, which was to be paid in currency into special accounts for distribution amongst Standstill creditors. Interest continued to paid in convertible form.

Hitler had never entirely trusted Schacht and by 1936 he was convinced that the Reichsbank President and Economics Minister was hindering rearmament. The instigation that year of the Four Year Plan under the direction of Hermann Goering represented a major defeat for Schacht, curtailing his responsibilities and undermining his authority.[53] When in early November 1937 the British negotiators presented a tough set of terms for the renewal of the Standstill Agreement, Schacht responded that they might like to discuss their demands with Goering.[54] Not long after Schacht was relieved of the post of Economics Minister, and although he remained President of the Reichsbank he had less and less influence, and his complaints about the inflationary impact of arms expenditures so exasperated Hitler that he fired Schacht in January 1939. The clearing banks' frustration at the failure to retrieve Standstill debt principal persisted, and in May 1939 McKenna told Lidbury, who was on the point of departure for Berlin for yet another round of standstill talks, that the Midland Bank would not agree to a continuation unless there was a repayment of principal of 10 per cent.[55] But, as ever, the German Credit Agreement of May 1939 effected a renewal of the Standstill without any transfer of principal from Germany. Interest payments came to a halt upon the outbreak of war in September 1939.

Business Activities, 1931–39

At the end of December 1930, the firm's capital of £3,173,000 was owned by the four full partners – Baron Bruno Schröder, Helmut Schröder, Frank Tiarks and Henry Tiarks – as shown in Table 9.1, the Schröder partners having 84 per cent and the Tiarks partners 16 per cent. When the balance sheet was drawn up a year later the partners' capital had fallen to £2,509,000, a write-down of £666,000. In addition, the whole of the bad debt reserve of £550,000 had been written off and the profit and loss account showed a trading loss of £295,000, making total losses of £1.5 million. Under the terms of the 1919 partnership agreement both profits and losses were borne by Baron Bruno and Frank Tiarks in the proportions two-thirds to one-third, which resulted in Frank Tiarks' proprietary interest in the firm virtually being wiped out. A new partnership agreement signed in November 1933 absolved the Tiarks partners from responsibility for future losses and provided them with salaries. The capital losses of 1931 were accompanied by a redistribution of the ownership interest between the Schröder family partners, and henceforth Helmut was the firm's principal proprietor. In March 1932, Veritas Trust Ltd, a company wholly owned by the trustees of Baron Bruno's family trusts, whose beneficiaries were his three children Dorothee, Marga and Helmut, was made a partner. The motives for the introduction of this corporate partner are unknown and the original intentions may well have been unrealised, since until the capital reconstruction during the Second World War it owned only 3 per cent of the capital. Nevertheless, it marked the beginning of the complex entanglement of the affairs of the firm and the whole Schröder family.

Baron Bruno and Frank Tiarks were in their sixties in the 1930s, but both were in regular attendance at the office throughout the decade and continued to direct the affairs of the firm. In his latter years Baron Bruno took a less active role in day-to-day business, being afflicted with

Table 9.1   J. Henry Schröder & Co., ownership of partners' capital 1930, 1931

| | 1930 31 December | | 1931 31 December | |
	£	Per cent	£	Per cent
Baron Bruno Schröder	2,277,978	72	1,082,742	43
Frank Tiarks	450,000	14	4,390	–
Helmut Schröder	394,715	12	1,405,076	56
Henry Tiarks	50,000	2	16,464	1
Total	3,172,693	100	2,508,674	100

Source: J. Henry Schröder & Co., balance sheets.

Parkinson's disease and requiring a wheelchair. Yet he continued to visit Hamburg every summer until the eve of the war, staying at his house on the Elbchaussee, and maintained close ties with his German family. His generous benefactions to the charities of his native city were once more publicly acknowledged on his 70th birthday in March 1937, when he was presented with a doctorate of the Medical Faculty of Hamburg by the German Ambassador in London. He remained a keen horticulturist and a couple of years before his death he carried off the King George V Cup at the Windsor Chrysanthemum Show. Frank Tiarks' role in the annual Standstill negotiations and his position as a director of the Bank of England made him a well-known figure, and not only in the City. He and his son were keen horsemen and many a winter morning was spent with the Pytchley Hunt, though polo at Foxbury was discontinued after the summer of 1931, and in September 1936 the house and estate were sold for development for £170,000.

Helmut Schröder and Henry Tiarks were both in their thirties and eager to make their mark on the firm, but the Standstill lock-up precluded major initiatives. Both were involved in sorting out Standstill derived problems, and Helmut Schröder in particular was active in building the firm's domestic business. He was the first of the Schröder partners of the firm to have an English bride, marrying Meg Darell, the daughter of Colonel Sir Lionel Darell Bt of Saul, Gloucestershire, in 1930. The occasion of their wedding was marked by the presentation of a wireless set to every blind person in the county, a charitable gesture that cost £10,000. Outside the office, Helmut pursued the family pastime of horticulture and began to win major prizes. In 1937 he purchased a large estate on the island of Islay off the west coast of Scotland, to which he became devoted with passionate strength. Henry Tiarks pursued multifarious personal interests, notably astronomy, economics and cinematography, besides a range of sporting activities. In 1936 he married Joan Barry, a well-known West End theatre actress and a star of the early British cinema.

Major Pam and Julius Rittershaussen continued as associate partners. Pam's corporate finance expertise was of enhanced importance because of the shift towards domestic corporate clients. He also developed the firm's investment management activities and supervised the conduct of a new venture capital subsidiary, Leadenhall Securities. Rittershaussen, as ever, kept a close watch on the banking side of the business, a role that assumed an increased importance as Baron Bruno's illness became more pronounced. Assistance to the partners continued to be provided by the Secretariat, comprising Henry Andrews and Toby Caulfeild, but when Andrews left the firm in 1935 there was insufficient work to justify his replacement.

The adverse environment of the 1930s led to a fall in the firm's annual average revenues from £605,000 in 1919–31 to £231,000 in 1932–39 (see Table 9.2). Accepting continued to be the most important source of revenues, generating 48 per cent, an increase on the 40 per cent in the 1920s. Revenues from issuing and underwriting fell steeply and this side of the business contributed only 16 per cent of revenues in the 1930s, compared to 28 per cent in the 1920s. The activities of the Investment Department became of considerably greater importance to the firm, annual average revenues being £42,000 in 1932–39. Net interest generated 7 per cent of the firm's revenues, a much smaller proportion than the 23 per cent in the 1920s.

Although J. Henry Schröder & Co. had begun to curtail the level of its acceptance business in the first half of 1931 – between December 1930 and December 1931 outstanding availments fell from £11.5 million to £6.8 million (see Figure 9.2) – the firm was badly caught by the German suspension of payments. Its frozen debts in July 1931 were £3.7 million acceptances and £1.2 million advances, totalling £4.9 million – about £150 million in 1990 money – which was well in excess of the partners' capital and bad debt reserves of £3.7 million.[56] According to a Bank of England memorandum on the impact of the suspension of payments on City firms Schröders had the second highest amount amongst the eighteen firms, with frozen German credits in excess of £100,000.[57] Top of the table was Kleinworts, with £9.3 million frozen credits, composed of £5.8 million acceptances and £3.5 million cash advances, three times the partners' capital.[58] But virtually every merchant bank in London sustained some losses as a result of the German lock-up, even firms such as Wallace Brothers whose business focused on India and the Pacific

Table 9.2   J. Henry Schröder & Co., sources of revenues, 1932–39

	1932–39 Annual average £000s	Per cent
Accepting	110	48
Issuing and underwriting	37	16
Investment Department	42	18
Net interest	16	7
Other[1]	26	11
Total	231	100

1. European representation fees, sale of assets, appreciation of investments, etc.

Source: J. Henry Schröder & Co., profit and loss accounts.

Basin.[59] A confidential report prepared for the Governor of the Bank of England in June 1936 revealed that six members of the Accepting Houses Committee – Schröders, Kleinworts, Huths, Japhets, Goschen & Cunliffe, and Arbuthnot Latham – were technically insolvent because of their Standstill debts.[60] Schröders and Kleinworts survived by drawing on the private resources of their partners and through the support of the Westminster Bank, which was banker to them both, and Japhets and Arbuthnot Latham also weathered the storm, but Huths and Goschen & Cunliffe which had never fully recovered from the effects of the First World War, disappeared.

Figure 9.2   J. Henry Schröder & Co., acceptances, 1928–45

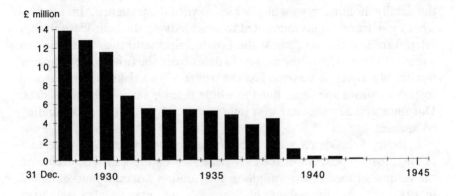

The Bank of England report of June 1936 was a preliminary to the issue of an instruction that 30 per cent of outstanding Standstill bills should be withdrawn from the discount market by repurchase by the firm that had accepted them.[61] This move to boost the quality of the discount market received Frank Tiarks' support in his capacity as a director of the Bank of England, even though it created considerable problems for his firm.[62] J. Henry Schröder & Co. raised the £1 million which it needed to comply with the Bank of England's requirement through a loan from the Westminster Bank, which was repaid from the proceeds of sales of investments and the transfer of funds to the firm by the Schröder family.

The growing likelihood of war with Germany after the occupation of Czechoslovakia in October 1938 quashed any hopes of repayment by German Standstill creditors in the foreseeable future. By December, the Bank of England was receiving informal representations from the discount houses expressing their reluctance to continue to hold Standstill bills. Cater & Co., which held £467,000 of Schröders' Standstill bills, sent word to the Governor requesting him to ask the firm to cut this amount since the firm was 'loath to have to refuse the bills or charge high rates since they have a close relationship with JHS'.[63] Not long afterwards the Bank issued a directive instructing all the accepting houses to reduce their outstanding Standstill bills by a further 40 per cent of the 'basic amount'.[64] To do this, Baron Bruno negotiated a further £1 million loan from the Westminster Bank in February 1939 secured against part of the family's interest in Schrobanco.[65] An incidental result of this fund-raising exercise was the production of the firm's first set of externally audited accounts. When the war broke out seven months later it became necessary to make arrangements for the withdrawal of the firm's remaining £1,017,000 Standstill bills from the discount market. It was accomplished by the realisation of investments and through an advance of £1 million to the Veritas Trust, the firm's corporate partner, by one of the family holding companies which owned Schrobanco. In essence, what these transactions amounted to was pledging the Schröder family's interest in Schrobanco against the London firm, and their effect was to transfer the problem of the Standstill debts from the firm to the Schröder family. Moreover, it was not just the partners who risked their personal fortunes to save the firm, but the whole family, since Helmut's sisters, Dorothee and Marga, were also joint owners of the Schrobanco holding companies.

J. Henry Schröder & Co.'s acceptances in December 1932 were £5.5 million, just 40 per cent of the 1928 peak (see Figure 9.2). The decline in the volume of foreign-drawn bills in the London discount market halted in 1932–33[66] and the volume of Schröders' acceptances also stabilised, averaging £5.2 million per annum in the years 1932–36. The dip in 1937 was a consequence of the removal from the market of 30 per cent of its Standstill bills at the Bank of England's behest, but there was a recovery the following year. The precipitous fall in 1939 was caused by the further withdrawals of Standstill bills from the market and the outbreak of war. During the 1930s the scale of acceptance business conducted by Schröders, Kleinworts and Japhets declined[67] (see Table 9.3). Moreover, much of the volume of acceptances of these firms comprised locked-up German credits. By contrast, other firms such as Barings, Erlangers, Hambros and Morgan Grenfell, whose balance sheets were not clogged with German frozen credits were able to expand their acceptance activities by providing credits for British domestic firms. Thus the 1930s saw a realignment of the acceptance business league table amongst the merchant banks and the end of Kleinworts' and Schröders' long lead over the other firms.

The limited scope for the conduct of acceptance business in the 1930s led J. Henry Schröder & Co. to use its skills in international trade finance in related ways. In 1932, Schröders and Hambros formed Anglo-Foreign Securities Ltd as a joint venture to conduct the liquidation of frozen German credits and to deal in blocked Rm, an activity in which Schrobanco was also very actively involved. Paul Kern, a Jewish Austrian foreign exchange dealer, was engaged to run the firm. A

Table 9.3   Acceptances of some leading merchant banks, 1932, 1938

31 December	1932 £ million	1938 £ million
Kleinwort, Sons & Co.	10.3	7.8
Hambros Bank Ltd[1]	7.8	11.4
J. Henry Schröder & Co.	5.5	4.2
S. Japhet & Co. Ltd	3.5	2.6
Erlangers Ltd	2.8	4.4
Baring Brothers & Co. Ltd	2.5	3.2
Morgan Grenfell & Co.	1.3	2.3

1. 31 March following year
Note: Information for other firms unavailable.

Sources: Stephanie Diaper, 'The History of Kleinwort, Sons & Co. in Merchant Banking, 1858–1966' (unpublished PhD thesis, University of Nottingham, 1983) p. 210; Kathleen Burk, Morgan Grenfell, 1838–1988 (Oxford University Press, 1989) p. 78; J. Henry Schröder & Co., balance sheets; Barings, Hambros, Japhets, Erlangers – published accounts.

description of him by a business acquaintance suggests that he was just the man for the job:

> He was an expert on currency and an even greater expert on the psychology of Continental bankers (especially German) which gave him an enormous advantage over his rivals in estimating the value of a currency. He fully understood the commercial, economic and political policies which dictated business conditions, but long, long before that he would already have decided what to do from his own spy network, based on incessant phone calls made all over Europe . . . Paul Kern was as wily as a monkey. He hedged every single bet: he was never caught short.[68]

Besides Standstill derived work, Anglo-Foreign Securities soon also developed 'constructive business', notably currency and securities arbitrage and the arrangement of credits for first-class continental companies on a strictly secured basis. These ties were forged through a subsidiary, the Axe Trading Company Ltd, for which Anglo-Foreign Securities provided trade credits. Anglo-Foreign Securities proved a highly successful venture and by 1936 its annual trading turnover was £32 million. Employing a capital of £10,000, profits before tax totalled £150,000 in the first five years of trading. 'In spite of opposition in the City,' Kern reported in 1937, 'it proved that the century-old principles of sound commercial banking can even be applied and successfully worked in commercially disturbed times.'[69]

Towards the end of 1936, on the initiative of Paul Kern, another specialist subsidiary, Compensation Brokers Ltd, was formed by Schröders (jointly with Charles Tennant & Son, also a City firm) to conduct barter business between Germany and the British Empire. The object was to organise barter trade, principally in German manufactures and Empire commodities and raw materials, which was otherwise restricted by the Anglo-German Payments Agreement and therefore it was conceived as a brokerage firm rather than as a credit institution. Such business, commented Frank Tiarks, was 'being carried on extensively today in an unregulated manner by all sorts of agents . . . who have extracted extortionate premiums'.[70] Official support for the new venture was sought, but there was concern that it could hurt British exports to the Empire and carried the risk of facilitating German access to war materials.[71] Montagu Norman informed Tiarks that the proposal was viewed unfavourably and the idea was dropped.[72] Compensation Brokers never began trading and Schröders' £1,000 nominal investment was written off.

In the 1930s new issues of foreign loans floated in London 'practically reached the vanishing point', as it was put in 1938.[73] One reason for the low level of activity was the official controls which were imposed towards the end of 1930 and ran throughout the decade.[74] The ban on issues for foreign borrowers was not absolute, but the authorities needed to be persuaded that a loan served the national interest. It was with such dispensations that J. Henry Schröder & Co. conducted the five issues for the Konversionskasse in 1936–38. Although private placements for foreign clients continued it was noted at the time 'that recent years had witnessed a great scarcity of good borrowers, and the long experience of London bankers has rendered them none too anxious to assume doubtful risks'.[75] The low level of Schröders' revenues from issuing and underwriting in the 1930s – annual revenues averaging £177,000 in 1919–31 but only £37,000 in 1932–39 – reflects these factors.

The demise of foreign issues at the start of the 1930s led the merchant banks to focus attention on providing access to the capital market for domestic clients. The firms which made most headway with the development of a domestic clientele were those that had cultivated relationships with British industry in the 1920s, such as Helbert, Wagg and Morgan Grenfell. Schröders, with its strong German and American orientations, had paid little attention to the development of a domestic clientele, and its business suffered accordingly in the 1930s. In the period between the financial crisis of 1931 and the outbreak of war the firm made six issues for British industrial corporations, three for a British local authority, two for British domiciled companies operating overseas, and one for the Continental and Industrial Trust, a total of twelve compared to a fifteen issues for such clients in the years 1919–31. Bristol Corporation, for which £8.1 million was raised through redeemable stock issues in 1932, 1935 and 1936, was the foremost fundraiser. In 1932 the Barings–Rothschilds–Schröders syndicate conducted its last joint business, a £1.5 million debenture issue on behalf of the Metropolitan Railway Co., part of the London underground transport system, which was lead-managed by Barings. Debenture issues were undertaken in 1933 and 1934 for Stevenson Clarke and Associated Companies Ltd, a firm of coal factors which had used Schröders' services in the 1920s, raising £3 million. The Stevenson Clarke connection possibly led to the £800,000 debenture issue for the Great Western Colliery Co. Ltd in 1933, the first of the five new clients of the 1930s. The next was the Argentine Navigation Co. Mihanovich Ltd, which operated passenger boat services on the River Plate, for which £1.5 million was raised in 1934. Major Pam was the link with the Lancashire Steel Corporation Ltd, in whose formation in 1930 he had played a part at the behest of Montagu Norman, for which £1.4 million was raised by a preference share issue in 1935.[76] He was also the tie with Sena Sugar Estates Ltd, an English registered company formed in 1906, with Julius Caesar Czarnikow as chairman until his death in 1909, which had extensive sugar cane interests in Mozambique and operated four refineries in the Portuguese colony and another in Lisbon. Pam was appointed a director of Sena Sugar in the 1920s and thus it was natural for the firm to turn to Schröders for assistance with fund-raising, and in 1936 a £750,000 debenture issue was made. The same year, Schröders conducted its first company flotation by bringing the Pressed Steel Company Ltd to the market. Besides these leading roles, Schröders was also an underwriter of numerous issues, particularly as a participant in the syndicates of the stockbroker W. Greenwell & Co. In total, the revenue from issuing and underwriting in 1931–39 was £447,000, less than a quarter of the £2.1 million in 1919–30 but not far short of the £487,000 apparently earned by sector leader Morgan Grenfell in the same period.[77]

The Pressed Steel Company of Great Britain Ltd was badly hit by the slump of the early 1930s and dividend payments were passed in 1932–35. But as the economy picked up car output grew rapidly and by the summer of 1935 body pressings turnover had trebled since 1932 and sales of the new Prestcold refrigerators were booming. At that point the Budd Company of Philadelphia, the majority shareholder, decided to realise its interest and as a preliminary to the sale the capital was restructured and the company name was changed to the Pressed Steel Company Ltd. Ladenburg, Thalmann & Co. of New York was appointed to find a buyer and a purchase agreement was reached with the British Pacific Trust, a British investment trust, in December 1935. Treasury consent was forthcoming, 'in consideration of the fact that this transaction will place in British hands all the shares of this company'.[78] The buoyant stock market in the spring of 1936 made it possible to float the company on attractive terms and 94.4 per cent of the ordinary shares, including the Schröder syndicate's shareholding, was sold to the public for £2.2 million. The British Pacific Trust's retained shareholding in Pressed Steel was sufficient to provide the managing director, William Stephenson, with ample pretexts for paying visits to its sister company, Ambi Budd, in Germany in the late 1930s. These visits, which always included a courtesy call on Hermann Goering, with whom Stephenson was on good terms because they were both First World War flying aces, enabled him to observe the progress of German rearmament, which he reported to British Intelligence. During the Second World War Stephenson served as one of the heads of British Intelligence.[79] Although Schröders' proprietary interest ended in 1936 it continued to have close ties with Pressed Steel and Stephenson, Major Pam serving as chairman until his death in 1955.

Leadenhall Securities Ltd was formed in July 1935 as a wholly-owned subsidiary of J. Henry Schröder & Co., with a paid-up capital of

£125,000, to undertake 'the provision of medium and long-term capital to industry and to engage in industrial issues, finance and underwriting business'.[80] The press statement announcing its formation made reference to the report of the Macmillan Committee in 1931 which had highlighted the fund-raising problems of medium-sized firms whose scale of operations placed them in a financial limbo, being too big for private resources and too small for the stock market – the 'Macmillan gap'. A suggested solution to the 'Macmillan gap' was the formation of specialist venture capital undertakings, and from 1934 there were several such initiatives, Leadenhall Securities being the most significant response on the part of the merchant banks.[81] 'The news is symptomatic of the changed outlook of many famous houses whose interests are steadily veering from the overseas market, with which they were mainly concerned before the war, to the terrain of home industry', commented The Economist.[82] Perhaps surprisingly, in view of the important support he gave to British industry, Montagu Norman greeted the news with circumspection, noting that J. Henry Schröder & Co. was establishing an 'industrial and possibly speculative business' and he warned the Bank of England's Discount Office, which policed the discount market, that 'JHS are, to some extent, assuming an unliquid commitment in a direction other than banking and accepting'.[83]

Leadenhall Securities' strategy was to invest in established modestly-sized firms with prospects for stock market flotation on a five-year timetable. Normally its investments were partly in ordinary shares and partly in redeemable preference shares. Revenues to pay the running costs were generated by securities dealing, bond washing (then perfectly legal) and participations in underwriting syndicates. The directors of the firm at the outset were Helmut Schröder, who was 'very much the moving force', Henry Tiarks, and Robin Wilson and Neil Adshead of the Investment Department, while Major Pam took an avuncular interest in its affairs.[84] Early in 1936 a Birmingham office was opened to market the firm's services to industry, run by a director of several Midlands engineering companies. Helmut Schröder's Eton school friends provided introductions to two of the firms in which Leadenhall Securities made significant investments in the 1930s: David Allen Ltd, an advertising hoardings firm; and Gambrell Radio Communications Ltd, an aeronautical instrument maker. Robin Wilson was a close friend of John Mallabar, the senior partner of the City accountancy firm J. F. Mallabar & Co., who became an important figure in Leadenhall Securities' affairs.[85] He was the source of introductions to Franco Signs Ltd, another advertising hoardings firm, Vitacream Ltd, a manufacturer of artificial cream; and British Indestructo Glass Ltd, a car windscreen maker. In May 1936, Leadenhall Securities made its debut as an issuing house with the stock market flotation of Franco Signs Ltd. There were three more issues in the years before the war: Vitacream, which was introduced to the market in December 1936; and two in 1937 for Barrow Barnsley Main Collieries Ltd, which raised £700,000.

The Investment Department, under the supervision of Major Pam, with Robin Wilson and Neil Adshead as chief executives, became an important dimension of Schröders' business in the 1930s, generating almost a fifth of the firm's revenues. It was a leading investment trust manager, undertaking the management of the Continental and Industrial Trust (CONTI), International Holdings and Hydro Electric Securities, and the English and International Trust. CONTI's profit and loss account for 1931 shows only a small decline, suggesting that it had largely liquidated its portfolio of German securities well before the German suspension of international transfers.[86] The Investment Department built up a considerable constituency of private clients, many of them continental Europeans who preferred to deal with Schröders than with an English stockbroker since it conducted correspondence in the language of the customer. In the early years of the decade it also conducted a sizable business jointly with Schrobanco, marketing US dollar securities to European investors.

The fall in net interest revenues in the 1930s compared to the 1920s was the outcome of the prevailing low interest rates, which depressed interest earnings from investments, while the partners' charge for the use of capital remained 4 per cent. In fact, to boost interest earnings there was a substantial shift in the pattern of the firm's balance sheet assets away from bills and into bonds and equities, which increased from an average of 2.5 per cent of assets in 1931–32, to 8 per cent in 1933–34, and to 23 per cent in 1935–38. Also underlying this shift in the pattern of assets were the activities of the Investment Department and increased securities trading on the firm's account to compensate for the depressed levels of other activities. Another significant balance sheet development was the growth of balances and deposits in the second half of the decade. In the early 1930s the ratio of partners' capital to balances and deposits fell to 1:1, a cautious relationship last seen during the First World War. But in the years 1936–38, the ratio returned to 1:2, much the same relationship as in the 1920s.

'Bricks and mortar' was a phrase that Baron Bruno was in the habit of using about investments he regarded as unacceptably illiquid, but when in 1934 the estate agent Benjamin Allsop, a friend of Frank Tiarks, showed the partners his plans to build a block of flats on the site of 17–20 Arlington Street, at the rear of the Ritz Hotel, they decided to back the project. A firm called Arlington House Ltd was formed, whose five-man board of directors included Adshead and Wilson, with a registered

Figure 9.3　J. Henry Schröder & Co., net profits after interest on partners' capital, 1931–45

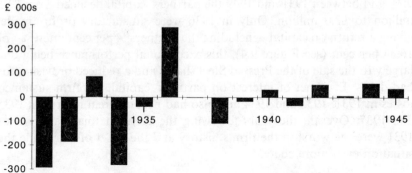

Note: From 1940, 4 per cent interest on partners' capital was discontinued.

office at 146 Leadenhall Street. The architect was Michael Rosenaur, who also designed Kingston House and the Westbury Hotel in Mayfair, and the building's amenities included the fashionable restaurant, Quintos. Neil Adshead and John Mallabar took up residence and for many years Schröders maintained a flat in the building for the accommodation of clients visiting London.

With the onset of the international slump Schröders' revenues fell precipitously, prompting vigorous measures to cut costs: staff numbers were reduced by 40 per cent, and office expenses by 10 per cent.

Figure 9.4　J. Henry Schröder & Co., return on capital and annual rate of inflation, 1931–45

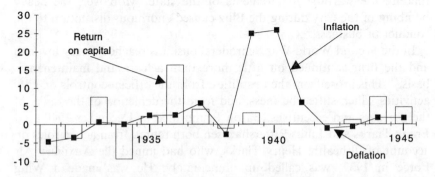

Note: Return on capital for 1940–42 not meaningful; the 'real' return on capital is the difference between the nominal return depicted above and the annual rate of inflation.

Nonetheless, after charging 4 per cent interest on partners' capital, losses were made in 1931, 1932, 1934, 1935, 1937, 1938 and 1939 (see Figure 9.3), and between 1931 and 1939 the partners' capital declined from £2.5 million to £2.0 million. Only in 1936 were satisfactory profits made, giving a return on capital – including the partners' 4 per cent interest – of 16.34 per cent (see Figure 9.4), this exceptional performance being due largely to the sale of the Pressed Steel shares and a reduced provision for bad debts. Even net of interest on partners' capital, the firm sustained losses in 1931, 1932 and 1934 and also had negative real returns in 1935 and 1937. Overall, the years following the German financial crisis of 1931 were the worst in the firm's history and the onset of war made the situation even more acute.

The Second World War

The Second World War led, as the *Financial News* put it in July 1941, to 'an almost catastrophic loss of business' for the merchant banks, since 'almost every change in financial methods resulting from the war seems to have operated to their detriment'.[87] Foreign-drawn bill business disappeared because of the problems of international transfers, while the securing of supplies by government bulk purchasing from the Dominions and through Lend Lease all but eliminated the need for acceptance finance for British trade. Foreign exchange dealing, a significant source of revenue for some merchant banks in the 1930s, disappeared as an activity at the beginning of the war because the accepting houses were omitted from the official list of authorised dealers, but even when they secured recognition there was little business to be done. Issues for private borrowers became rare events as the capital market was reserved for funding the wartime requirements of the state. Moreover, the heavy bombing of the City during the Blitz caused enormous disruption to the conduct of business.

In the Second World War Schroders' business reached a very low ebb and the firm continued on little more than a 'care and maintenance' basis.[88] This arose from the hostilities, from the official controls on City activities which stifled business, and from the depletion of the ranks of the partners and executives. Baron Bruno died in December 1940, and Frank Tiarks and Julius Rittershaussen both retired from active roles on account of ill-health. Henry Tiarks, who had joined the Auxiliary Air Force in 1937, was called up immediately. He was made a Wing Commander and had responsibility for flying barrage balloons until he contracted tuberculosis in August 1943, from which he spent a year recuperating. Toby Caulfeild joined the War Office, and Robin Wilson went into the army and was killed on active service in 1943. On the outbreak of the war Helmut Schroder decided to volunteer for the armed forces but was forbidden from doing so by the Governor of the Bank of England, who informed him that he required a full partner of the firm full-time in the City. Yet there was little business to be done and Helmut found his enforced inactivity difficult to bear, leading to the onset of bouts of depression and illness. The day-to-day affairs of the firm were handled by Major Pam, but he too was restive, making him ill-tempered. The atmosphere in the partners' room at 145 Leadenhall Street was tense and sometimes despondent for much of the war.

In the war years 1940–45 Schroders' revenues averaged £156,000 per annum, compared to £231,000 in 1932–39 (see Figure 9.1 on page 252). In fact, the comparisons are really even more unfavourable since the revenues for 1940–45 are not net of the 4 per cent interest charge on partners' capital, which was waived from 1940, as in 1915–16, and it was not restored at the end of the war. Accepting, issuing and underwriting, and investment management together generated average revenues of a mere £36,000 per annum, and in the war years even the unglamorous Coupons Department was a star performer. To pay the bills, investments were sold and it was such liquidations which generated most of the 'other' revenues. Running costs and overheads were pruned back in the early years of the war to reduce expenditure in line with falling revenues. The salary bill fell by nearly half between 1938 and 1942, mirroring the drop in active staff numbers from some 200 to 100 (those serving in the armed services received payments from the firm to supplement their

Table 9.4   J. Henry Schroder & Co., sources of revenues, 1940–45

	1940–45 Annual average £000s	Per cent
Accepting	9	6
Issuing and underwriting	17	11
Investment Department	10	6
Coupons Department	11	7
Interest	41	26
Other[1]	68	44
Total	156	100

1. European representation fees, sale of assets, appreciation of investments, etc.

Source: J. Henry Schroder & Co., profit and loss accounts.

forces pay, to make up their salaries to pre-war levels). Office administration costs were cut by almost as much as salaries, while 146 Leadenhall Street was let to the Norwegian Shipping and Trade Mission, an agency of the Norwegian government in exile. As a result of these measures the accounts show small profits in the war years, with the exception of 1943, and positive rates of return on the much reduced capital base (see Figure 9.4 on page 273), but the true state of affairs was that the firm was struggling to survive.

It was obvious to John Mallabar that Schroders could not be prospering in the wartime conditions.[89] Amongst his multifarious business interests was a trawler company operating from Fleetwood and Brixham. When war came the supply of imported food was curtailed, the price of fish rose, and soon the trawlers were generating revenues enormously greater than their operating costs, but the introduction of Excess Profits Duty, which levied tax at 100 per cent on any 'excessive' profits, denied the benefits to the operators. But Schroders had overhead costs which could be charged against the revenues earned by the trawlers. Mallabar suggested to Helmut Schroder that the firm should charter some of his boats to relieve its financial problems. After a week in Fleetwood inspecting trawlers with Mallabar, Helmut was convinced and in 1940 the firm chartered two vessels, the 'Toronto' and the 'Dunnet'. For the rest of the war J. Henry Schroder & Co.'s business was a novel combination of merchant banking and trawling.

Baron Bruno's death led the financial affairs of the firm and the Schroder family to become even more intertwined. It was decided in November 1942 that the Schroder family would inject further capital into the firm and assume full liability for the Standstill debts, any future recoveries being credited to the account of the executors of Baron Bruno's estate and the Veritas Trust Ltd. In the spring of 1943, Helmut Schroder undertook the rearrangement of the firm's capital with the purpose, as he wrote to Montagu Norman, of 'cleaning up the balance sheet considerably'.[90] He referred to the curious balance sheet feature shown since 1939 of a negative partners' capital, the result of full provision in respect of the Standstill bills which were withdrawn from the discount market at the Bank of England's instruction. Helmut's restructuring eliminated the negative capital balance of Baron Bruno's estate and the Veritas Trust's interest in the firm was converted from £400,000 in the red to £250,000 in the black. These adjustments were effected by a complex series of steps that transformed the £1 million of securities pledged as collateral for the Westminster Bank's loan into a ten-year interest-free loan to the Veritas Trust, and by the commitment of a further £1 million of the Schroder family's private resources to the recapitalisation of the firm. The new funds, plus Helmut's personal interest, furnished the firm with partners' capital and reserves of £690,000 in December 1943, which by the end of 1945, had become £778,000 – about £13.6 million in 1990 money. This was a sum last seen in Schroders' accounts sixty years earlier, in the 1880s, and on an inflation-ajusted basis it is necessary to return to the 1850s for a comparable level. At the end of the war the impact of the Standstill and the war on the firm amounted potentially to a set-back of almost a century.

In addition to the financial reorganisation of the firm, the form of the partnership when the war ended was on the minds of the partners. Major Pam had his own ideas. Towards the end of 1943 a proposal emerged for a merger with Guinness Mahon, apparently as a result of discussions between Major Pam and his friend, Arthur Guinness. Helmut was unenthusiastic and Montagu Norman 'had not cared for the idea' since it excluded the Tiarks partners in the amalgamated partnership, and the proposal came to nothing.[91] Instead, the deliberations led to the drawing up of a new partnership agreement dated 10 February 1944 which took account of the changed membership of the partnership since Baron Bruno's death, but otherwise reaffirmed existing arrangements between Helmut Schroder, Frank Tiarks, Henry Tiarks and the Veritas Trust. It did not address the asymmetry which had arisen in the standing in the partnership between Helmut Schroder and Henry Tiarks, Helmut having fully assumed his father's position as senior partner, but Henry having no certainty that he would succeed his father in all capacities. But it implicitly recognised that the Tiarks partners had a legitimate interest in the goodwill of the firm, which was of great importance to them. The new partnership agreement stated that the arrangements were of a temporary nature and it was anticipated that a further agreement would be drawn up, 'so soon as practicable after the expiration of the emergency period, namely the present abnormal conditions arising out of Great Britain being in a state of war'.[92] In fact these arrangements lasted until March 1953, when the partnership was fundamentally recast.

The D-Day Allied invasion of France on 6 June 1944 marked the beginning of the final chapter of the war, and in the City planning began for the post-war world. At Schroders it implied the assumption of full responsibility by the younger generation of partners, but the poor health of both of them in the spring and early summer of that year – Helmut Schroder being afflicted by bouts of depression and Henry Tiarks still recovering from tuberculosis – prompted doubts in Helmut's mind about their resolution to shoulder the burden of rebuilding the firm. Replying on 12 June to a letter from Henry, enquiring whether he should take up a non-executive external appointment, Helmut raised fundamental questions about their ambitions:

Your father is very keen to see you and me happily installed in our fathers' and grandfathers' chairs in 145 [Leadenhall Street]. At this juncture in our lives I think it is vitally important to our own happiness that we should make up our minds quite definitely, once and for all, that to run J. H. S. & Co. is what we want to do more than anything in the world. That we want to and can deal with and master awkward folk and awkward unpleasant situations and enjoy doing it. Before you decide to return to 145, do please assure me that you know your own answers convincingly, unswervingly and without regard to what you might conceive would please your father or me. What J. H. S. & Co. wants is partners who know their own minds and enjoy the good struggle of building up J. H. S. & Co., or else we shall just drift.[93]

The following day he received a reply from Henry calling without reservation for the firm's continuation. He argued that it would be a breach of duty for their generation to 'throw away the vantage point of an organisation (however battered) which it has taken our fathers and grandfathers and us 100 years to establish, and which stands for something in the minds of businessmen in nearly every country'.[94] He stated his personal ambition to revive the firm and expressed his impatience 'to get back to a full-sized man's job in the City'. Lastly, he assured Helmut of his faith in his partner's ability to rebuild the firm with the assistance of suitable lieutenants. Helmut was much cheered by this response and warmly thanked Henry for his expressions of confidence and commitment.

The same week that Helmut and Henry were deliberating about the future of the firm, Schroders received an approach from Barings which came about through Major Pam. 'I really have some extremely interesting news for you and see a solution to some of our major problems,' wrote Helmut to Henry on 15 June 1944.[95] Simultaneously, Henry received a letter from his father explaining that:

Barings have sounded us about the possibility of JHS and Barings getting together on very close lines, like those we were discussing with the Guinnesses. They want to link up Schrobanco and Kidder Peabody, also Argentaria and their Argentine connection, and also start something similar in Brazil. They are short of trained young staff and we have good young staff coming along. No details have yet been discussed but my idea is to get Millis as a full partner here as well as at Barings and gradually work out a full amalgamation. Helmut after my talk with him last night is all for it ... I hope and believe something big will come out of this.[96]

The course of the discussions with Barings is not known and may have been interrupted by the death of Helmut's mother five days later on 20 June 1944. Clearly, by the late summer the idea of a merger had passed, for on 8 September 1944 Helmut consulted the new Governor of the Bank of England, Thomas Catto, formerly a partner in Morgan Grenfell, about the introduction of a new partner from outside the firm.[97] This idea also came to nothing and in October 1944 Helmut and Henry, both of whom were now back in the office, began to make preparations for the revitalisation of the firm after the war.

10

Leadership from New York: Schrobanco

1935–62

In New York Gerald Beal succeeded Prentiss Gray as president of
Schrobanco and Schrotrust in January 1935. Beal, who was 39 at the
time of his appointment, ran the firm from 1935 until 1962, his 27-year
presidency constituting an epoch in the history of Schroders' US
operations. He was one of New York's leading international bankers
and an intimate of the inner circle of the city's banking community. By
all accounts he was a modest, kind and genial man, his manner matching
Schrobanco's patrician status: 'very gentle, very fair, incredibly
charming and absolutely part and parcel of the New York establishment'.[1] His personal qualities inspired loyalty amongst the staff and
there was a strong *esprit de corps* in the firm. He was extremely well-
informed on both domestic and international developments and actively
developed Schrobanco as a specialist New York-based international
banking firm.

Beal took a detailed interest in the activities of each department, often
restraining the riskier initiatives of his energetic and enterprising
lieutenants. His cautious conduct of the business not only won the
firm a high standing in the New York financial community but also
fulfilled his brief from the Schroder family to conduct a prestigious and
prudent business during the depression and war years when the London
firm was so vulnerable. His judgement was highly regarded by Helmut
Schroder and they developed a close personal friendship. They
corresponded weekly by letter, by no means only about business
matters, and after the war Beal was a frequent visitor to London. He
became one of Helmut's most trusted advisers on the affairs of the
Schroder firms, and his conservative management of Schrobanco played
a central role in helping to resolve the financial problems faced by the
London house and the Schroder family.

Upon the death of Baron Bruno in 1940, Helmut Schroder became
chairman of the Schrobanco board of directors, but it continued to
develop as an independently-managed US banking firm with the board
of directors predominantly American and the executives responsible to
the board. Manuel Rionda continued to serve in a non-executive
capacity until 1950, being followed by his nephew, George Braga. There
was also a succession of partners of Sullivan & Cromwell, Schrobanco's

legal counsel: Allen Dulles, the brother of John Foster Dulles, 1938–42; De Lano Andrews, 1943–55; and Norris Darrell, 1955–63. The appointment of John Laylin in 1947 meant that henceforth there was also a partner of the leading Washington law firm Covington, Burling, Rublee, Acheson & Shorb on the Schrobanco board. Between the late 1940s and the early 1960s the number of non-executive directors grew from three to seven, the increase resulting from the recruitment of senior figures from leading US corporations with the deliberate intention of strengthening ties with domestic business. Besides Beal, the executive directors were Valla Lada-Mocarski; John Simpson, until his resignation from the firm in 1951 to become finance director of Bechtel (the Californian construction firm run by his old friends Stephen Bechtel and Stribling Snodgrass); Harold Sutphen, from 1942; Ernest Meili, from 1948; and Avery Rockefeller from 1950. In 1962, Helmut Schroder retired as chairman and was succeeded by Beal, who was himself succeeded as president by John Howell.

Schrobanco continued to be owned predominantly by the Schroder family and by the Tiarks family, whose interest was represented by Frank Tiarks until 1945, and thereafter by Henry. During the 1930s the Schroder family increased its interest by buying out many of the original minority shareholders. In 1951, to raise cash, Baring Brothers was invited to take a 10 per cent interest in Schrobanco, paying £528,000 ($1,478,000) for the shares. The choice of Barings was explained by Helmut Schroder thus:

> The two firms have over the past thirty years been on intimate terms and have undertaken together many important business transactions. During this period it has become evident that they have been guided by similar traditions, and have adopted similar methods and lines of conduct. The Partners of the two firms have had the most friendly and close relationship. When, therefore, it was decided to sell shares in the Schrobanco Group, it was evident that Barings should be offered an opportunity to participate.[2]

At the time of Beal's assumption of the presidency in 1935, the initiatives to develop brokerage activities in US securities in Europe, trading in restricted currencies in Europe, and dealing in US government securities were already well underway. Beal further expanded these trading activities, while endeavouring to revive the firm's commercial banking business. The outcome was the recovery of revenues from a trough of $1.3 million in 1934 to $2.8 million in 1939 (see Figure 10.1), but in 1940, as a result of the war, revenues plummetted to $1.4 million and they remained depressed for the duration of the hostilities.

Figure 10.1 J. Henry Schroder Banking Corporation, revenues, 1935–62

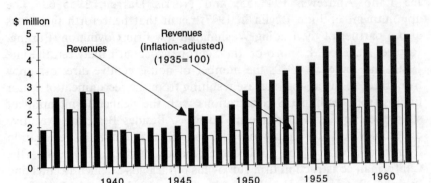

At the end of the Second World War, New York was the world's leading international financial centre and the US dollar the principal currency for international transactions. Having the advantages of an excellent reputation and an experienced and energetic team of executives, Schrobanco was well positioned to take advantage of the new opportunities to develop dollar-based international banking. Its success is reflected in the sustained expansion of revenues from $1.8 million in 1947 to $4.9 million in 1957. In the decade or so following the war Schrobanco had a leading position in international banking in New York, an eminence disproportionate to its size as a firm or the scale of its activities. In the 1930s, the 1940s and for much of the 1950s, the conduct of international business by J. Henry Schroder & Co. in London was hamstrung by the Standstill debts and British official restrictions, but thanks to the activities of Schrobanco its name continued to be known in the market as an international bank. Moreover, in the post-war years, Schrobanco enterprisingly developed business in continental Europe, the Pacific Basin and elsewhere, upon which the London firm was subsequently able to build.

In the 1950s American commercial banks, which had hitherto confined themselves to domestic business, began to conduct international transactions and Schrobanco experienced mounting competition. The fall in the firm's revenues in 1958 to $4.4 million and their stagnation at the end of the 1950s and early 1960s were consequences of the competitive pressures. Schrobanco's officers were well aware of the challenges and responded by vigorously promoting existing activities and pursuing initiatives to develop new business. Yet at the time of Beal's relinquishment of executive responsibilities in 1962, the future direction of the firm was uncertain.

Reorientation from Europe to Latin America, 1935–39

In the mid-1930s Schrobanco's business comprised two principal activities: banking and trading. The core of the banking business was the provision of dollar acceptance credits and advances to US commodity importers and to European merchants. The trading activities, the focus of initiatives since the slump, comprised dealing in foreign exchange and US government bonds, the sale of dollar securities through London and Paris, and restricted currency trading in Berlin and Paris. In 1935 the Berlin office had a staff of twelve, sufficient to warrant the creation of the post of office manager, to which Werner Rabbow, a member of an eminent Hamburg mercantile family with longstanding ties with the Schroder family, was appointed. However, as the Nazi regime became increasingly belligerent, Schrobanco wound down its Berlin activities. Meili left in the spring of 1937 and was replaced by a much more junior executive. By the summer of 1937 the staff had fallen to seven and by the end of 1938 only Rabbow and a secretary were left. Currency trading was discontinued in January 1939, and on 29 April 1940 a cable was received in New York stating that Rabbow had been called up for military service and that the office was closed. In Paris too Schrobanco's operations declined in the second half of the decade. There also the level of Schrobanco's representation was downgraded following Lada-Mocarski's return to New York in 1936. More and more the focus of the firm was shifting away from Europe.

Banking business with European clients saw little revival in the 1930s. Naturally there was no resumption of the provision of funding for German or Austrian clients following the 1931 crisis and the view from New York was that the mounting political uncertainties after Hitler's advent to power made lending to the whole of Europe unattractive. Barter was an alternative means of conducting trade, and from 1935 Schrobanco acted as intermediary in barter deals between German and US importers and exporters which were conducted through Aski Marks, a special currency created for the purpose. Schrobanco was one of four New York banks appointed as Aski Mark agents. The Aski Mark system provided foreign exporters with a premium price for their raw material supplies to Germany, while foreign importers of German manufactures received them at discounted prices. This latter aspect was subsequently deemed to be a form of unfair trade competition by the US authorities. Schrobanco devised a scheme by which a US importer of German goods could pay for them through the sale in Germany of cargoes of cotton, and later copper, by him or in his name. The highly complicated arrangements were handled by the Continental Export and Import Corporation, a firm formed for this purpose in March 1937 by Schrobanco and some German firms. Although the scheme met the letter of the law, some observers regarded it as a form of evasion of US anti-dumping regulations and a contemporary commented that 'many of the new [cotton exporting] firms had no previous connection with the commodity markets, while strong suspicion existed that cotton was never actually shipped by them, or was shipped prior to and independently of the supposed "barter" transaction'.[3] In 1939, the Justice Department, which had previously given a number of favourable judgements on the procedure, ruled that it was in violation of the customs law and the barter operation was closed down. Schrobanco's final foray into German restricted currency business in the 1930s was its participation in the *Rückwanderermark* scheme. By this scheme, five American banks, including Schrobanco, were designated by the Reichsbank as agents for the sale of blocked marks to Germans resident in America, or Americans of German descent. These sales are estimated to have raised perhaps $30 million prior to America's entry into the war.[4]

In the summer of 1934 it was decided to extend Schrobanco's activities to Latin America, where there was ample scope for the exploitation of its expertise in restricted currency transactions. Thus in October 1934 Norbert Bogdan and Gerald Beal, who were both in Berlin, boarded the Graf Zeppelin bound for the subcontinent. The outcome of the trip was the establishment of Argentaria SA de Finanzas in Buenos Aires in October 1935. This was a joint venture between Schrobanco and the Zentral-Europaische Laenderbank of Vienna, the original concept being to develop a triangular business between Buenos Aires, New York and Central Europe. The Laenderbank was represented by Baron Otto Leithner, a colourful and cosmopolitan character who was head of the foreign exchange department of the Laenderbank's Parisian subsidiary, the Banque des Pays de l'Europe Centrale.[5] He was the son of an Austro-Hungarian general, though he held Swedish nationality acquired through his first marriage, and was active in business from the 1930s to the 1950s consecutively in Vienna, Paris, Rio de Janeiro and the United States. He was well known to Valla Lada-Mocarski, Schrobanco's representative in Paris in the mid-1930s, and to Norbert Bogdan, the head of the Berlin office, who reported that his motive was the association of the Laenderbank with the high-standing Schroder name in Latin America, but judged that his energy and abilities were fair recompense.[6] Buenos Aires was chosen as the location for the new firm because it had the most sophisticated financial markets in Latin America and because of its geographical location, giving access to Brazil, Chile, Peru and Uruguay.

At the time of foundation Argentaria had a nominal capital of 1 million pesos (approximately £60,000) which was subscribed 42 per cent each by Schrobanco and the Laenderbank, the remainder being taken by local directors.[7] Evidently the partnership did not work out smoothly, for in April 1936 the Laenderbank sold its interest to Schrobanco, at a 50 per cent premium, and Leithner established himself in Rio de Janeiro. In 1937 the nominal capital was increased to 5 million pesos, and two outside investors, Bemberg Brothers, a leading Argentinian finance house, and the Pacific Railroad, an Argentinian railway controlled by the Lord St Davids investment group in London, each took 7.5 per cent of the equity. Bemberg subsequently withdrew and thereafter Schrobanco's interest exceeded 90 per cent of the equity.[8]

Bogdan moved from Berlin to Buenos Aires in the summer of 1935 and was the driving force behind the expansion of Schrobanco's Latin American activities for the rest of the decade. To assist the development of Argentaria's business, Bogdan recruited several prominent Argentinians as directors, a leading industrialist, Vincente Casares, becoming vice-chairman. Bogdan's endeavours to promote Argentaria included the formation of a Buenos Aires symphony orchestra sponsored by the firm, a remarkable initiative for its day. As managing director he appointed William F. Benkiser, a former manager of the Buenos Aires branch of the First National Bank of Boston, with which Argentaria worked closely in its early years. In 1937, Gilbert van Tienhoven, a young Dutchman who had previously been assistant manager of the local branch of the Hollandsche Bank Unie, joined as submanager. He succeeded Benkiser as managing director and acted as the Schroder firms' representative in Argentina for many years, and also as honorary consul of the Netherlands.

Initially Argentaria focused on restricted currency trading which was conducted successfully by a pair of experienced dealers from the Laenderbank, but this activity waned after a couple of years, since, as Lada-Mocarski informed the Banque des Pays de l'Europe Centrale in August 1937, 'most of the blocked currencies have either been liquidated or frozen so solidly that no ingenuity can bring about their liquidation'.[9] In the meantime Argentaria had developed an acceptance business, using substantial facilities provided by Schrobanco, financing Argentinian exports. By the end of the decade Argentaria had a staff of forty and offered a full range of international banking services 'including the purchase and sale of foreign exchange, foreign collections, remittances, purchases of foreign bills, letters of credit, credit information and other related services'.[10]

Another important development was Argentaria's appointment as agent for the sale of fire and marine insurance policies by the Hanover Fire Insurance Company of New York. This role was further developed during the war when the firm became the agent of American

International Underwriters (AIU), a US-based international insurance company which was rapidly expanding its activities in Latin America by taking over the business formerly conducted by British and German firms. The appointment was secured through Beal's social acquaintance-ship with Cornelius Vander Starr, the founder of AIU (which later became a subsidiary of the American International Group Inc.). This marked the beginning of a close working relationship between Schrobanco and AIU based on the insurance company's large cash flows in Latin American and Asian countries with restricted currencies, which the bank was able to matchup with US companies requiring local financing for their subsidiaries.

In the late 1930s Argentaria also developed a range of securities activities. In 1937 it became affiliated to the Buenos Aires Stock Exchange and subsequently conducted brokerage operations for clients. The same year it established an investment trust, the Sociedad Anonima de Inversiones Sud Americanas (INSA), to take venture capital participations in local industrial and commercial undertakings. The shareholders were Argentaria, which provided the management; J. Henry Schroder & Co.; and a group of private American investors. The board of directors was graced by a couple of former Argentinian ministers of finance. Underwriting was undertaken from the outset, the firm being admitted immediately to the syndicates organised by the three most important Argentinian issuing houses: the Banco Central, the Bembergs' Credito Industrial y Comercial Argentino SA, and Credito Mobiliaro y Financiero Bracht SA. In 1940, Argentaria organised Argentina's first public issue for a private industrial company, a preferred stock issue on behalf of Siam Di Tella Ltda, an important electrical domestic appliance manufacturer. 'This,' commented Bogdan, 'really put Argentaria on the map as far as the financial community was concerned'.[11]

Latin America was the focus of Schrobanco's endeavours to rebuild its banking business after the contraction during the slump. From the summer of 1935 until America's entry into the war in December 1941 Bogdan was ever on the move promoting Schrobanco and Argentaria in the major countries of Latin America, particularly Argentina, Brazil, Chile, Colombia, Cuba, Peru and Venezuela. He was welcomed wherever he went since there were many potential clients for the services Schrobanco had to offer and few other American banks were competing for the business. His exertions established an enduring network of relationships with central banks, commercial banks and local businesses. The central banks were interested in establishing credit lines to serve as standby sources of US dollars in case of temporary shortages of exchange. Though not conventional self-liquidating transactions, the creation of dollar exchange was an approved basis of eligibility for bills in the New York discount market. As reciprocity the central banks left non-interest paying dollar balances with Schrobanco, which the firm put to profitable use. Relationships of this nature were developed with the Banco Central de Venezuela, the Banco Central de Chile, Banco Central de Reserva del Peru, and the Banco de la Republica of Colombia. In Chile and Colombia business was also developed with government corporations, attractive clients on account of the minimal commercial risk. In Chile, Schrobanco provided lines of credit, and occasionally medium-term finance, for the Corporacion de Fomento (the Chilean Development Corporation); the Comercio Exterior SA, an import-export body; and the Chilean Steam Ship Line. In Colombia it financed the supplies of material for agricultural production imported by the Caja de Credito Agraria.

Much the most important of Schrobanco's relationships with Latin American central banks was with the Banco do Brasil, the commercial bank which acted as the government's fiscal agent and performed the functions of a central bank at this time. The Banco do Brasil's dollar balances kept with Schrobanco, which had their origins in the assistance rendered to it by Schroders and Schrobanco in 1930 (see Chapter 7), grew rapidly as economic prosperity returned to Brazil during the Second World War and it has been estimated that they amounted to $30 million by the end of the conflict, which would have constituted more than half the customer balances held by the firm.[12] Naturally Schrobanco provided a large credit line for the Banco do Brasil. So important was the relationship with the Banco do Brasil by the end of the war that in 1946 Schrobanco established a representative office in Rio, headed by Eric Lamb, to ensure its smooth functioning.

Schrobanco's close relations with Latin American central banks led naturally to its appointment as a financial adviser. In 1936–37 Bogdan was closely involved in the preparation of the scheme for the settlement of Chile's suspended external debts, leading to the appointment of Schrotrust as New York paying agent for its bonds, which generated substantial fees and large dollar balances.[13] In February 1939, Schrobanco was appointed financial adviser to the Colombian government, which was endeavouring to reach a settlement with foreign bondholders, to whom payment had been interrupted for many years.[14] Again, the firm acted as paying agent but it also took an active role in the bond market purchasing for cancellation bonds with a nominal value of $42.7 million on behalf of the Banco de la Republica between 1939 and 1946. It was as a result of its appointment as adviser to the Colombian government that Schrobanco began to work with the leading Washington law firm, Covington, Burling, Rublee, Acheson & Shorb.

Hitherto all its legal work had been done by Sullivan & Cromwell, but this firm was unacceptable to the Colombian government on account of its involvement in the separation of Panama from Colombia at the turn of the century.[15]

The bulk of Schrobanco's business with Latin American clients was with local commercial banks on a reimbursement credit basis.[16] Bogdan also established relations with a number of commercial firms, many of which had longstanding ties with J. Henry Schroder & Co. Gildemeister & Co. of Lima, whose connection with Schroders went back to the turn of the century, became a client, and a director acted as Schrobanco's official representative in Peru in the 1930s. Waldemar Schröder, a Peruvian businessman who was a distant cousin of Helmut Schroder, was also active on Schrobanco's behalf from the 1930s to the 1960s. He had close relations with the Gildemeister family and was appointed chairman of the Compania Peruana de Petroleo El Oriente, an important oil company that they formed in 1941. In Chile, Vorwerk & Co. became a Schrobanco client, as did Mauricio Hochschild, a wealthy entrepreneur with interests, particularly in Chile, to whom Baron Bruno provided crucial financial support early in his career. In Brazil, Schrobanco sustained the London firm's close relations with Monteiro Aranha of Rio de Janeiro, and Theodor Wille & Co. of Sao Paulo.

Development of US Domestic Business

The growth in the volume of Schrobanco's acceptances and advances in the second half of the 1930s, shown in Figure 10.2, was largely the outcome of the Latin American initiatives, though the revival of business with US commodity firms, notably Czarnikow-Rionda, also made a contribution. Upon the outbreak of the Second World War both types of banking activity declined because of the curtailment of commercially conducted international trade. The subsequent limited revival was achieved by the development of business with US manufacturing companies engaged in government war work requiring additional working capital to expand their operations. A notable example was the US Time Corporation, a firm established by Norwegian industrialists who fled to the US because of the German military threat and built up a highly successful watchmaking business. Being old friends of J. Henry Schroder & Co. they turned to Schrobanco for financial assistance to develop the firm. Loans to firms engaged in war work – known as 'V-loans' – were guaranteed by the US government, removing the commercial risk, which permitted Schrobanco to make much larger advances to individual clients than would otherwise have been possible

Figure 10.2 J. Henry Schroder Banking Corporation, acceptances and
advances, 1935–62

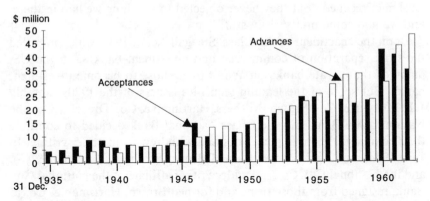

while maintaining prudent banking practices. Schrobanco was thus able
to compete with US commercial banks in the provision of loans to
American corporations, commencing banking relations directly with
domestic US manufacturing firms for the first time.

The second half of the 1930s saw a drive to expand Schrobanco's
investment management activities. John Simpson masterminded the
operation, but its execution was entrusted to Alden B. Cushman, who
joined the firm in 1929, aged 27, after attending MIT and serving an
apprenticeship in the research department of the brokerage house, Paine
Webber. His responsibility was the development of operations in
equities and corporate bonds, Sutphen and Beal continuing their US
government bond dealing activities. The transfer of the management of
the Montreal registered investment trusts International Holdings and
Hydro-Electric Securities from J. Henry Schroder & Co. to New York
upon the outbreak of war provided a major boost to the scale of
Cushman's operations. He was also entrusted with the management of
some of Schrobanco's own funds, including the $1 million realised in
1938 upon the liquidation of the firm's holding of Bulgarian bonds
which had been in its securities portfolio since the failure of the issue in
1928. Rather uncharacteristically, Beal instructed him to invest boldly to
win back the $2 million loss on the Bulgarian bonds. Cushman put the
funds into the defaulted bonds of railroad and property companies
which had gone into receivership in the depression, ' "junk bonds" –
though the phrase wasn't used at the time – which were available at
bargain basement prices. Then the war came and prosperity returned
and soon that fund had built up from $1 million to $10 million'.[17]
Schrobanco was able to invest in such low-grade investments because of
its Article XII charter, which allowed the firm to hold a much wider

range of investments than was permitted for deposit-taking commercial banks. 'Our portfolio was always examined by the Bank Examiners,' Cushman recalled, 'but they never objected to anything we had in there, and we had some pretty risky stuff.'

Upon the enactment of the Glass–Steagall Act of 1933, which imposed the strict separation of commercial and investment banking in the US, many of the private banks on Wall Street chose to become investment banks. But some of the leading securities issuers of the 1920s, notably J. P. Morgan & Co., Brown Brothers, Harriman & Co., Drexel & Co., the National City Bank and the Chase National Bank decided to continue their commercial banking activities and withdrew from underwriting. In June 1934, a number of executives of Brown Brothers, Harriman & Co. and the National City Co., the underwriting affiliate of the National City Bank, resigned from those firms and formed Brown, Harriman & Co. to conduct investment banking business. Three months later, five partners from J. P. Morgan & Co. and Drexel & Co. established Morgan Stanley & Co. for the same purpose. Although both these investment banks were legally independent of the banks from which their directors were drawn, there was some ownership interest on the part of the partners and executives of the commercial banks.[18] The revival of securities issuing business in 1935 led the Schroder partners to consider the establishment of an investment banking firm following the examples of Brown, Harriman and Morgan Stanley. Their minds were made up by the revival of bond issues by the subsidiaries of the Standard Gas and Electric Corporation with whose capital raising they had been closely associated at the beginning of the decade.

On 9 July 1936 it was announced that 'a new investment banking company, to be called Schroder, Rockefeller & Co. Inc, which is to succeed to the underwriting and general securities business formerly done by the J. Henry Schroder Banking Corporation, was formed yesterday'.[19] Schrorock, as the new firm soon became known, was a joint venture between the Schroder partners and Avery Rockefeller, a 33-year-old scion of the Rockefeller dynasty who had joined Schrobanco in 1928.[20] Rockefeller resigned from Schrobanco upon the establishment of the new undertaking, since there could be no overlap of personnel between a commercial bank and an investment bank, taking with him Carlton P. Fuller and Gerald E. Donovan, both alumni of the Harvard Business School, who became Schrorock's leading executives. Rockefeller became a director of Schrobanco in 1950 when regulatory reforms made this possible, and for many years he was one of Helmut Schroder's closest friends and advisers.

Issues on behalf of subsidiary companies of the Standard Gas and Electric Corporation (Stangas) and underwriting syndicate participations were Schrorock's principal activities in the firm's opening years. A cordial and constructive relationship was struck up between Schrorock's officers and Victor Emanuel, the leading figure in the Stangas companies. Emanuel, a business associate of Alfred Lowenstein, was described in a Schrobanco memorandum of 1941 as enjoying 'a friendly relationship with the Schroder people in London for many years, and is regarded by them as an interesting American deal finder. The Schroder people have encouraged Mr Emanuel to bring to them any piece of business which he digs up'.[21] Towards the end of the 1930s the interconnections between J. Henry Schroder & Co., Schrobanco, Schrorock and a handful of Wall Street investment banks, the Lowenstein investment trusts, Victor Emanuel, and the Stangas companies attracted the attention of the Securities and Exchange Commission in Washington which decided to investigate whether there had been any violation of the Public Utility Holding Act of 1935. Hearings were held in 1940 and 1941 which revealed a tangled web of connections between the parties, but no action resulted.

As competition for underwriting business intensified in the late 1930s Schrorock shifted the focus of its activity away from public issues towards private placements and by the early 1950s the firm estimated that it had made placements aggregating $50 million. In May 1944 Schrorock also became a dealer in US government securities, an activity which was of major importance for the rest of the decade. New clients generally came through the personal contacts of the firm's well-connected officers. Some notable clients of the late 1930s and 1940s were Permutit, a producer of water softeners whose chairman was F. Seaton Pemberton, Schrobanco's first company secretary; the General Industries Corporation of Ilyria, Ohio, which made industrial parts and prospered greatly thanks to war contracts, and the Polaroid Corporation. Polaroid was brought to the market by Schrorock and Kuhn, Loeb and for a number of years these two firms each held 10 per cent of the equity. At that point Polaroid produced sunglasses and was developing a system for eliminating glare from car headlamps which was never commercially exploited. The revolutionary instant camera came in the early 1950s, by which time Schrorock had sold its investment. However, it retained close ties with Polaroid, since Fuller joined it as treasurer in 1941.

While endeavouring to develop new business, Schrobanco maintained highly conservative balance sheet ratios in the 1930s and 1940s. In 1924–32 its ratio of capital to lending (advances plus acceptances) had been only a little below the aggregate average for US national banks (see Figure 10.3). Both ratios fell in the early 1930s, but Schrobanco's fell furthest and remained considerably below the industry average.

Figure 10.3 Ratios of capital to loans of the J. Henry Schroder Banking
Corporation and average of US national banks, 1924–62

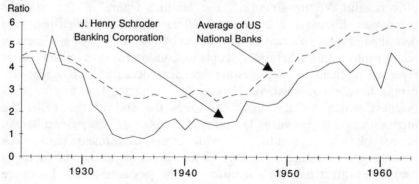

Source: US national banks – US Department of Commerce Bureau of the
Census, *Historical Statistics of the United States: Colonial Times to 1970*
(Washington DC, 1975) Series X, col. 775, p. 1040.

Schrobanco's balance sheet was further strengthened in the late 1930s;
the proportion of highly marketable US Government securities increased
from 26 per cent of total assets in 1931–35 to 49 per cent in 1936–49,
while the proportion of advances and acceptances was reduced.
Schrobanco's prudence impressed the treasurer of the Du Pont
Chemical Company who told the firm that he had decided to open an
account with Schrotrust because it was 'the strongest bank in the city'.[22]
It also made an impression on its landlord, the Bank of New York.
Schrobanco's twenty-year lease on three floors of the Bank of New
York's office building had been signed in 1929 at the peak of the bull
market and some years later the firm appealed to be let out of the
agreement or to have the rent reduced in line with the decline in market
rates. The Bank of New York agreed to reconsider the rent, assuming
that Schrobanco must be in trouble, but when its books were examined
the request was turned down flat because of the strength of the balance
sheet.

The Second World War

The outbreak of war between Britain and Germany in September 1939
put Schrobanco on a war footing some two years before the United
States joined the war. From the outset Schrobanco adopted the policy of
not doing business with any firm whose name appeared on the Statutory
List, the British black-list of firms and individuals from neutral countries

engaged in trade with the Axis, to preclude any possibility of J. Henry Schroder & Co. trading with the enemy through its American affiliate. Since many of Schrobanco's clients and associates were of German origin or had close commercial ties with Germany, the scale of Schrobanco's Latin American business was curtailed, but its precautions did not prevent an episode which drew the attention of State Department officials. In December 1940 the American Embassy in Rio de Janeiro was tipped off by a Brazilian construction contractor that a rival contracting firm, with which Schrobanco and Monteiro Aranha did business, was working with German interests in Brazil.[23] This information was passed on to Schrobanco which investigated the allegations and discovered that a subsidiary of its client, a firm with which the bank had no dealings, was on the Statutory List. After consultations with London, Beal despatched a long letter to Olavo Aranha of Monteiro Aranha instructing him that Schrobanco could have no dealings with the construction firm and requesting him 'to exercise the greatest caution in the future, to the utmost limit of your knowledge and information, to avoid our being brought into relationship of any sort with individuals or concerns whose sympathies, activities, or business affairs link them with Axis interests'.[24]

In August 1941, Bogdan set off from New York on a tour of Latin America, the primary purpose being to ensure that clients were not engaged in compromising activities. He provided a schedule of his itinerary – Miami, Bogota, Caracas, Trinidad, Belem, Rio de Janeiro, Buenos Aires, Santiago, Lima, La Paz, Guayaquil, Cristobal, Mexico City and Los Angeles – to the State Department and a few days later a confidential instruction went out to the US diplomatic offices in the places he proposed to visit instructing them to file reports on his activities.[25] This proved straight forward for the officials, since at every stop Bogdan presented himself at the US Embassy or Consulate and inquired whether any of Schrobanco's clients were suspected of doing business with the Axis powers. Bogdan's probings into this sensitive matter attracted the attention of diplomats, but officials reported that there was no evidence of any contact with firms on the British black-list. His tour was cut short by the Japanese attack on Pearl Harbor on 7 December 1941. He was in Santiago, driving back from the beach when he heard the news on the car radio and was so astonished that he crashed into the vehicle in front.[26]

In the early stages of the war, and particularly in early 1941, there was some concern amongst the London partners that Schrobanco might be sequestrated by the British government and sold to US investors as part of the general effort to raise dollars for the purchase of supplies in America.[27] This risk arose from the terms on which America was willing to help Britain in the early part of the war: in November 1939, the US Neutrality Act was modified to permit Britain to purchase arms but the ban on loans to a country which had defaulted on its First World War debts, introduced by the Johnson Act of 1934, was maintained.[28] Britain was thus obliged to pay for all purchases immediately in cash and in dollars – the so-called 'cash and carry' policy – and throughout 1940 Britain ran down its foreign reserves and sold dollar securities held by its citizens. By December 1940 British reserves were exhausted and Prime Minister Churchill appealed to President Roosevelt for help, receiving the reply that one 'cannot refuse to lend a firehose to a neighbour whose house is on fire'. Yet assistance was not immediately forthcoming and early in 1941 Courtaulds' US subsidiary, the American Viscose Corporation, was sold and the US subsidiaries of many other British companies were reviewed as candidates for sale.

An internal Bank of England memorandum of 17 February 1941, inquiring as to the nature of Schrobanco's business, suggests some degree of official interest in the firm as a candidate for disposal, though there is no evidence that matters were taken any further than this enquiry. The author of the memo discussed the business and also drew attention to the problem of arriving at a reasonable valuation given the close ties between the two firms, commenting – probably mistakenly – that 'even now, if it were to be severed from London, I doubt how much business it would retain or obtain separately'.[29] Furthermore, it was recognised by Montagu Norman that the inclusion of Schrobanco in the 'Roosevelt barrel' would undermine the arrangements to bolster the financial condition of J. Henry Schroder & Co., which was technically insolvent in the wake of having to make full reserves for the Standstill debts, and the risk of the failure of a major accepting house was not an event that the Governor could view with equanimity.[30] As it happened, the threat was averted by Roosevelt's request to Congress on 11 March 1941 to pass the Lend-Lease Act, which permitted the United States technically to lease arms to the British, bringing an end to the fire-sale of British assets in America.

The profits of Schrobanco's wartime banking business were affected both by US money market conditions and by factors particular to it as a British-owned and internationally orientated bank. Like most American banks its principal business became assisting the US Treasury to market bills and bonds, to finance the war, curtailing credit to private-sector businesses and increasing its holdings of government bills and bonds which accounted for 60 per cent of total assets in 1939–45. Interest rates were low, the Treasury bill rate reaching ⅜ per cent in 1939–40, and the Federal Reserve stabilised both short- and long-term rates with a steeply sloped positive yield curve, creating incentives for banks to invest in longer-term Treasury bonds. Throughout the war, Beal and Sutphen conducted a very active bond trading operation which generated much of the firm's profits in these years.

Like many Wall Street bankers and lawyers, a number of the executives contributed to the war effort through service in the intelligence services or by appointment to financial advisory positions. Many Schrobanco executives were particularly well-suited to these assignments, given their European backgrounds and international banking experience. Amongst the senior executives, Valla Lada-Mocarski joined the newly-formed Office of Strategic Studies (OSS) in Cairo and later in Zurich, where he worked with Allen Dulles, the brother of John Foster Dulles and himself a Sullivan & Cromwell partner who had been a non-executive director of Schrobanco from 1938 to 1942. After the war Allen Dulles served as chairman of the Central Intelligence Agency which grew out of the OSS. In 1943 John Simpson became Financial Adviser to the Allied Control Commission in occupied Italy. Marc Gardner and Norbert Bogdan were commissioned in the US Air Force. Bogdan, who reached the rank of major, served on General Dwight Eisenhower's staff in Europe, and following the surrender of Japan he was appointed Financial Adviser to General Douglas MacArthur's US army of occupation and spent ten months in Tokyo doing what he described as 'the most interesting job of my life'.[31]

Simpson's appointment aroused the interest of the radical paper *PM*, which in January 1944 published a lengthy article about Schrobanco presenting a catalogue of its ties with Germany since the 1920s, implicitly suggesting doubts about the loyalties of the firm and its American officers, who were appointed to such positions.[32] Beal chose to ignore the article, taking the view that silence was better than a riposte since 'although there is justification for all Schrobanco's activities and all dealings were in accord with the accepted policies of the United States and with the tacit approval of the State Department, when such approval was necessary, any such explanation is involved, defensive, and is not likely to change many opinions'.[33] In succeeding months articles appeared in other radical publications repeating *PM*'s points. Particular attention was paid to the family connection with Baron Kurt von Schröder, a partner in the Cologne bank J. H. Stein and a notable German banker of the 1920s and 1930s. He played a role in Hitler's rise to Chancellor in January 1933 and later served as one of the German representatives on the board of the Bank for International Settlements.[34] After the war, he was questioned by the investigators preparing the cases against war criminals at the Nuremburg trials, though not himself a defendant.[35] In the course of his testimony, he said that the family connection was distant and that there was no particularly close relationship between J. H. Stein and the Schroder firms. Nevertheless, for years the family connection provoked speculation and considerable confusion, notably the publication by the *New York Times* of Baron Kurt's photograph next to Baron Bruno's obituary notice.[36]

These insinuations, which appeared throughout 1944, a presidential election year, were really targeted at John Foster Dulles, Schrobanco's principal legal counsel for many years. The autumn saw a crescendo of hostile publicity, particularly when US Senator Claude Pepper, a Florida Democrat, accused Schrobanco of being close to Baron Kurt who had supported the Nazi party in the early 1930s.[37] The timing of Pepper's outburst was no accident but was part of the Democratic Party's offensive against the Republicans in the run-up to the presidential election in early November. Dulles played a prominent part in the Republican campaign, being widely tipped as their candidate for Secretary of State, and it was his reputation that the connection was really intended to tarnish. In response, Beal issued a statement describing Senator Pepper's onslaught as unqualifiedly false, and there were no further attacks after polling day.[38]

In February 1947, eighteen months after the end of the war, Schrobanco's reputation as an international firm and its ties with Dulles again attracted some specialist press attention, this time in two articles that appeared in a Soviet publication *New Times*, whose English language edition was aimed at a pro-communist Western readership. These articles entitled the 'International role of the Anglo-American–German Schroder Bank', which appeared under the byline A. Leodinov, claimed that the firm was at the centre of an international capitalist conspiracy 'whose ramifications spread literally to every artery of modern capitalist society; banks and heavy industry, diplomacy and military staff, influential political parties, military and political intelligence services, and occupation authorities in Germany. The outward manifestations of this group's activities are highly diversified and often enough seem to be entirely unconnected; but they are all guided by one purpose and directed from one centre, one headquarters'.[39] The publication of these early Cold War salvoes coincided with Winston Churchill's campaigning for a Western European Federation and with the amalgamation of the American and British occupation zones in Germany into a dual-zone – 'Bizonia' – in early 1947, which was regarded by the Soviet Union as the start of a threatening new Western alliance. In many respects Soviet apprehensions were justified, since it reflected the fundamental change in policy on the part of the US administration which, following the appointment of General George Marshall as US Secretary of State in January 1947, had decided to advocate strengthening Germany economically and politically as a bulwark against the threat of a Soviet invasion of Western Europe. The breakdown of the session of the Four Power Council of Ministers in April 1947 marked the beginning of the freeze in relations between the West and the Soviet Union. On 5 June 1947, Marshall laid out his European recovery programme in a famous speech at Harvard University and a year later the Marshall Plan came into effect. Although Soviet propaganda was absurd, the Schroder firms' pattern of ties in the United States, Britain and Germany and elsewhere was unique and assisted the rapid revival of Schrobanco's business after the war.

Schrobanco's Post-War Expansion, 1945–57

New York was the world's pre-eminent international financial centre in the years following the Second World War. Its position reflected the predominance of the US economy, which in the late 1940s produced half the world output of manufactured goods, and the paramount position of the US dollar as a reserve currency and as a trading currency following the Bretton Woods Agreement of 1944. The post-war years saw the rapid growth of international trade, much of it dollar financed, and large capital flows from the United States, notably in Marshall Aid and direct investments by US multinational corporations. These developments created unprecedented demand for dollar-based international banking services which Schrobanco was ideally positioned to provide, and it was one of the first US banking firms to re-establish business ties with Europe and Japan.

In 1945, Schrobanco had been established in New York for more than two decades and was well known and highly regarded amongst US bankers as a specialist international house. Its overseas contacts, stemming both from its own endeavours and from J. Henry Schroder & Co., were superior to the vast majority of US commercial banks, which hitherto had focused on domestic business. Another advantage derived from its twin charters – Schrobanco's unusual Article XII charter and Schrotrust's commercial banking charter – which permitted it to offer a wider range of services to clients than commercial bank rivals. Finally, it had an experienced, energetic and able team of senior executives who were impatient to rebuild the business. The only factor holding them back was the absence of support from a junior generation of executives, since new recruitment had come almost to a halt in the 1930s and the war years. Recognising this restraint a recruitment campaign was conducted in 1946 that led to the induction of a dozen new men, including Prestley McCaskie, Donald Brown, William Bethune, Howard Gordon, Sherman Gray (the son of Prentiss Gray), and John Howell, each of whom spent all or much of his banking career with the firm and occupied a senior managerial position. The 'Class of '46' were all of American birth and most were graduates of Ivy League colleges and had served in the US armed forces during the war, characteristics which reinforced the American identity of the firm in the post-war era.

The outcome of the combination of the favourable environment and the dynamic response to the new opportunities was the expansion of Schrobanco's revenues from $1.5 million in 1945 to $4.9 million in 1957 (see Figure 10.1 on page 282). Over the same period the combined total assets of Schrobanco and Schrotrust grew from $113 million to $209 million. Staff numbers provide another yardstick of the expansion of the firm, increasing from around 200 in 1945 to 450 in the late 1950s. Soon the office at Wall Street and William Street was becoming very crowded and when the lease expired in 1949 the firm moved to spacious new quarters at 57 Broadway, which it occupied until 1970.

The years after the Second World War saw a third phase in the evolution of Schrobanco's business. In the 1920s and early 1930s the firm had combined the provision of dollar acceptance credits with the issuing and underwriting of dollar securities, a pattern which was a transatlantic echo of the merchant banking business conducted by J. Henry Schröder & Co. in London. In the 1930s and the war years the emphasis was on the conduct of dealing activities and the development of international commercial banking, though opportunities to expand the latter were limited. In the second half of the 1940s and during the 1950s, dealing activities waned in importance while international commercial banking waxed. In these years, Schrobanco acted as New York correspondent for a host of overseas banks and provided international banking services for a long list of US regional banks. Many of the services it offered were also provided by the foreign departments of the major US commercial banks and the analogy between these departments and Schrobanco was frequently drawn. A critical difference was that its rivals had a corporate client base as well as their correspondent relationships, whereas Schrobanco was overwhelmingly a bankers' bank, which proved to be a source of weakness.

The expansion of Schrobanco's banking activity in the years 1935–62 is depicted in Figure 10.4, which shows the combined total assets of the Schrobanco and Schrotrust. The periods 1935–43 and 1955–62 saw slow growth, particularly when inflation is taken into account, but the years 1944–54 saw a relatively rapid rate of increase, and combined total assets rose from $80 million to $220 million (doubling in inflation-adjusted terms). The initiatives which led to this expansion are discussed below, but a general factor was the deliberate development of the banking role

Figure 10.4 J. Henry Schroder Banking Corporation and Schroder Trust Company, combined total assets, 1935–62

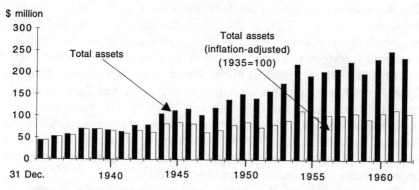

of the Schroder Trust Company, Schrobanco's subsidiary which held a commercial banking charter and was a member of the Federal Reserve System. In the 1930s and the war years, the Schroder Trust Company had focused upon paying agency and stock transfer work but in the post-war years the emphasis shifted to the development of lending, personal trust and investment management activities.

Even before the end of hostilities there was an important development in the conduct of Schrobanco's Latin American activities, which soon grew into a major business. In 1944, it was appointed by the Ford Motor Company to finance the car and truck purchases of their Colombian distribution agents. It was a highly attractive business, since credits carried a 12 per cent interest rate at a time when prime rates were 3 per cent, while commercial risk was eliminated by an insurance policy written by AIU which covered not only normal shipping risks but also non-payment on the part of the automobile dealers, though in fact only twice did dealer-default lead to substantial claims. These arrangements proved highly successful and were extended to Venezuela, Peru, Ecuador and Mexico, and to Chrysler dealers. In 1946, hoping to find further such opportunities, the firm ran advertisements in the *New York Times* and the *Wall Street Journal* publicising its Latin American expertise to US corporations.

Commercial banking business on a reimbursement credit basis with the network of Latin American correspondent banks established by Bogdan in the 1930s continued as before. Additionally, there was the important handful of private firms, such as Monteiro Aranha in Brazil, or Blohm & Co. in Venezuela, which received direct financing, as did certain government agencies, notably the Corporacion de Fomento in Chile. Following Bogdan's departure for the US armed forces in 1942,

William Tucker was given responsibility for Schrobanco's Latin American activities, with the exception of Chile, which was handled by Harold Sutphen because of his local knowledge derived from assisting Bogdan with the Chilean debt negotiations. In the mid-1940s, responsibility for Venezuela, Colombia, Ecuador, Peru, Mexico and Cuba was transferred to Peter Carpenter, an Englishman who had joined the firm in 1931 and worked in the Berlin office before specialising in Latin American affairs. It was Carpenter who developed the motor trade financing business, and in the 1950s and 1960s he was one of the firm's most senior officers. Tucker, Sutphen and Carpenter, in contrast to Bogdan, based themselves in New York, keeping in touch with clients by cable and telephone and through occasional tours, reflecting the improvements in international communications.

The second half of the 1950s saw some unwelcome changes in Schrobanco's Latin American business. Clients increasingly demanded longer-term financing, and although Ernest Meili, the chairman of the Credit Committee, resisted, being adamant that 90 days was sufficient for any genuine trade transaction, more and more the firm found itself obliged to give credits of 180 days or longer to keep abreast of the competition. At the same time there was a widespread increase in the degree of economic and political turmoil in the countries of Latin America, whether it took the form of foreign exchange crises, as in Colombia and Venezuela, nationalism, as in Argentina, or revolution, as in Cuba. All these factors increased the risks of conducting business in the region, and despite the quality of the client list it was decided to retrench on the firm's commitments. The turning point was the Colombian foreign exchange crisis of 1956, which convinced the senior officers that the firm was over-exposed to the region. The motor finance business was wound up and handed over to Ford, which established its own financing subsidiary. 'We were happy enough to get out of it,' Carpenter commented, 'by then the profit margins had greatly narrowed, but basically we just had too many eggs in one basket.'[40] Paradoxically the Colombian exchange crisis had a silver lining for Schrobanco, since the firm was again appointed as adviser to the government and in April 1957 it reassumed the role of New York fiscal agent. Early in May 1957, Beal and Tucker were decorated with the Order of San Carlos by the Colombian Finance Minister at a ceremony in the Metropolitan Club in New York 'in recognition of the important and efficient services which you have given to Colombia'.[41]

In 1957, Schrobanco sold its interest in Argentaria, which for a number of years had been performing poorly, principally because of the difficulties encountered by private business under President Juan Perón's government. Schrobanco's officers envisaged little prospect of any improvement in the foreseeable future, and when an opportunity arose to dispose of the subsidiary it was seized. The purchaser was Deltec, a New York-based finance company which specialised in the provision of working capital for private sector companies in Latin American countries. It also conducted issuing business and it was to expand this activity that it acquired Argentaria. Payment was made in Deltec stock and the transaction forged a close and mutually beneficial relationship between the firms, Schrobanco becoming Deltec's house bank and conducting a large volume of transactions on its behalf. Soon after the sale, van Tienhoven resigned as managing director of Argentaria and opened up a representative office in Buenos Aires for the New York and London Schroder firms.

Post-war Europe offered enormous opportunities, which Schrobanco's officers vigorously pursued. Germany, Austria and Switzerland were the responsibility of Ernest Meili, who as early as 1946 visited the war-torn Continent to restore contact with pre-war clients and to establish new relationships. Because of his determination, Schrobanco was one of the first foreign banks to resume contact with Germany, and a representative office was opened in Frankfurt in 1947 run by Gustav von Mallinckrodt. Meili was the dominant influence on the conduct and development of the firm's commercial banking business in the post-war decade; 'one of the greatest commercial bankers that I have ever known' was Peter Carpenter's assessment, and many others held the same opinion.[42] Scandinavia and the United Kingdom were also under Meili's jurisdiction, but responsibility was delegated to a deputy, R. Canon Clements, a Rhodes Scholar at Oxford University and a Harvard Business School graduate, who joined Schrobanco in 1938 and was soon identified as a high-flier. France, Belgium, Holland, Spain, Portugal, Italy and North Africa were assigned to Valla Lada-Mocarski, and he too was quick off the mark to establish Schrobanco's presence. Lada-Mocarski's leading lieutenant was John Howell, who joined the firm in 1947, aged 30, following war service and a post-college stint in journalism. In the early 1950s, Howell spent a couple of years based in North Africa and the Middle East, extending the geographical spread of Schrobanco's activities. The European clients were commercial banks to which Schrobanco offered correspondent services in New York, notably a very professional foreign exchange dealing operation, developed by Meili and fellow Swiss Emil Kuster, and dollar credit facilities. The Schrobanco officers used their continental tours to promote not only their own services but also those of the London firm, which had no such roving representatives in the 1940s and 1950s.

'Compensating balances' – funds left with a bank by clients and correspondents upon which little or no interest was paid – were crucial to the profitability of Schrobanco's style of banking business, since by the conventions of the day it did not charge fees for many of the services it rendered. Much the most promising sources of dollar balances were central banks, as the massive balances kept with the firm by the Banco do Brasil demonstrated. From the beginning of the post-war era all Schrobanco's senior officers made determined efforts to persuade central banks to place part of their dollar balances with the firm. In return, they provided economic and market intelligence, which was then relatively difficult to obtain, and a highly professional and very discreet foreign exchange service which faciliated quiet intervention in the market. Moreover, the firm offered better rates of return on balances than did the Federal Reserve banks, and assisted the central banks to enhance revenues from their dollar balances, for instance by shifting from dollar time deposits, upon which interest payments were constrained by the Federal Reserve's Regulation Q, into US bankers' acceptances which gave a higher rate of return with almost the same degree of liquidity and security. At its peak in the 1950s, twenty-three central banks were clients of Schrobanco, including every major Western European country save Britain and Greece; most of the nations of Latin America; and Japan, Taiwan and Korea from the Pacific Basin. Lada-Mocarski, by all accounts very well equipped with diplomatic abilities and graceful manners, played a leading role in representing the firm in negotiations with central banks. It was thanks to his negotiating skills that the firm established a relationship with the Vatican, of which it was particularly proud and which was especially valuable. 'It was a very personal service that was rendered to the central banks' commented an executive, its discretion and total confidentiality enabling Schrobanco to retain their clientele for many years.[43]

A new region of activity for Schrobanco in the post-war era, which became of great importance for the firm, was the Pacific Basin. Upon his return to the firm from service as financial adviser to General MacArthur's army of occupation in the summer of 1946, Norbert Bogdan immediately set about developing Japanese business based upon the contacts he had made and his up-to-date knowledge of the country's requirements. He arranged for Beal to be the first American bank president to visit Japan after the war, a gesture which was long remembered by his hosts. In the summer of 1947 he organised the first post-war syndicated credit for Japan, in conjunction with the Bank of America and the Chase National Bank.[44] Bogdan left Schrobanco to join the Ford Motor Co. in 1948 and responsibility for Asian clients was given to Marc Gardner, under Meili's overall control.

Relations with Japanese banks were fostered by Schrobanco's practice of taking trainees from the Bank of Japan and the commercial banks. An especially strong bond was forged with the Bank of Tokyo. Their representative, Yosuki Ono, whose second name impressed Henry Tiarks as ideally suited for their profession, was accommodated by Schrobanco in the early 1950s while he set up his own office in New York.[45] His daughter, Yoko, married John Lennon of the Beatles pop group. Schrobanco's clients in Japan were the commercial banks on whose behalf the firm organised syndicated credits for the finance of foreign trade and provided correspondent services in New York. The scale of Japanese financing requirements rose rapidly in the 1950s, and although Schrobanco itself took only a small part of the syndicated credits it organised, it soon found itself at the upper limit of lending to a single country. In fact, when Japanese outstandings reached $7.5 million the New York State Banking Authority instructed the firm to cut back, on account of country risk exposure. But a New York commercial bank could readily provide a $10 million credit facility for a single client. Inevitably, Schrobanco found it more and more difficult to maintain the early lead it had established in Japan losing out to larger rivals.

During the 1950s and early 1960s, under Marc Gardner and his successor Donald Brown, Schrobanco developed correspondent relationships with banks in other countries of the region, notably Taiwan and Korea, and also Hong Kong, Australia and India. Schroders in London was also interested in developing correspondent business with banks in the region and in 1952 David Forsyth of the Banking Department was sent out to accompany Gardner on a tour of the region, a typical example of the assistance rendered by Schrobanco in the post-war years. In this case, London was able to render a reciprocal service, because after Gardner's premature death in the mid-1950s it was Forsyth who introduced Donald Brown to clients in the region on his first trip.[46]

At the end of the war, Schrobanco endeavoured to restore its business with US import–export firms that had been disrupted by the hostilities. Czarnikow-Rionda continued to be a very important client and notable relationships were also built up with the Atalanta Trading Corporation, the leading importer of Polish hams, and the Pan-American Trade Development Corporation. The latter was the creation of Baron Otto Leithner, Schrobanco's partner in the formation of Argentaria, and Ernest Meili became a director upon his retirement from Schrobanco in the mid-1960s. Nevertheless, Schrobanco's financing of US mercantile firms gradually waned during the 1950s, partly because of the trend towards the direct purchasing of commodities by processors and partly because of mounting competition by US commercial banks for the business.

An exception to the pattern of a gradual loss of position in the commodity trades was the firm's involvement in financing the export of soya bean oil in the late 1950s and early 1960s. The trade, and the preparatory processing, were subsidised by the US government's Food For Peace programme introduced in 1954 for the purpose of distributing surplus US farm produce to hungry people in underdeveloped countries.[47] Schrobanco became involved in financing the stocks of the Scarburgh Company, a subsidiary of the Isbrandtsen Shipping Group. Schrobanco organised a $10 million syndicated credit for Scarburgh, taking $3 million itself, the rest being provided by the United California Bank and the Bank of Montreal. For Schrobanco $3 million was an unusually large commitment, equal to about a quarter of the firm's capital, but it was not judged to be imprudent since the American Express Company was responsible for the issue of the warehouse receipts that provided evidence of the existence and whereabouts of the oil for which the credit was given. Mounting congressional opposition to the continuation of the Food For Peace programme raised the spectre of a soya oil glut, prompting a drastic price fall in November 1962. This led the brokerage houses which had been financing the principal refiner of soya bean oil, the Allied Crude Vegetable Oil Refining Corporation, to make margin calls which Allied could not meet. It was then discovered that Allied was perpetrating fraud on a massive scale and that many of the storage tanks at its New Jersey refinery contained more water than soya-bean oil. Although the settlement of the claims arising from the 'Great Salad Oil Swindle' took several years to achieve, and proved a maddening distraction for the firm's officers, in the end Schrobanco received full payment.[48]

A new source of demand for Schrobanco's services in the post-war era was US regional banks. The great post-war international trade boom led to rapidly rising demand for international banking services from US corporations which the regional banks were unable to meet because they had no international expertise. Many were wary of referring clients to the international departments of the major New York banks, such as Chase or Citibank, for fear of losing their business to such rivals. Schrobanco, however, posed no such threat and many US regional banks used it as New York correspondent for the provision of specialist international services. Notable amongst this clientele were the large Californian banks, the Bank of America and the United California Bank, whose requirements kept some fifty members of staff fully occupied in the early 1950s. The relationship with the Bank of America ended in 1953, when it formed its own international department, as did more and more US regional banks as the decade progressed, and this source of business withered away in the early 1960s.

The banking relationships which Schrobanco had developed with a handful of US manufacturing companies during the war, such as US

Time, continued in the post-war years. However, with the removal of the government guarantee on war production loans the firm was obliged to scale down the size of its commitments to individual clients. 'Our balance sheet just wasn't large enough for us to handle their banking requirements,' Clements explained, 'so the big banks came in and gradually took the business away from us.'[49] Clements, in particular, was convinced that Schrobanco needed to develop a domestic client base, and devoted much effort in the 1950s to promoting the firm to US corporations. To this end a number of leading US businessmen with whom senior officers had personal connections were persuaded to join the Schrobanco board in the late 1940s and the 1950s, causing a rise in the number of non-executive directors from three to seven. The first, Robert P. Patterson, chairman of Patterson, Belknap & Webb, was appointed in 1948. Charles W. Gibson, the president of Air Reduction Inc. joined in 1949; Albert L. Williams, executive vice-president of IBM, in 1952; and Dudley Dowell, executive vice-president of the New York Life Insurance Company, in 1957.[50] These were major US corporations and the presence of such men on Schrobanco's board undoubtedly enhanced the firm's recognition and prestige in the US, though their corporations already had well-established banking relationships and Schrobanco derived little new business as a result of their directorships. None the less, the 1950s did see the development of banking business with US corporate clients, particularly through Schrotrust. Perforce, these were small and often rather risky clients, and in the words of one of those involved, 'we got burned a few times'.[51]

In the immediate post-war years, dealing in US government securities, conducted by Beal and Sutphen, continued to be an important source of revenues. Moreover, the US government securities portfolio, which continued to constitute about 45 per cent of total assets until the late 1950s, generated considerable interest income. The relaxation of official support for the market in March 1951 led to a sharp fall in the price of US government bonds, particularly the long-dated ones of which Schrobanco was a large holder. Instead of incurring large capital losses on the long-dated bonds it was decided to hold them until maturity when they could be redeemed at par, which partly accounts for the persistence of US government securities as almost half the firm's assets for much of the 1950s. The débâcle led to a reprimand from a New York State Banking Commission inspector for 'gambling' which prompted the discontinuation of active dealing in US government securities in the early 1950s.

The post-war years saw a new phase in the development of Schroder, Rockefeller's business. Upon advice from Sullivan & Cromwell following the introduction of new regulations governing the separation of investment banking and commercial banking by the State of New

York, it gave up securities underwriting because of its close association with Schrobanco, though it continued to make private placements and to conduct corporate advisory services.[52] From the late 1940s, Schrorock focused more and more upon venture capital activities. 'We have two chief assets in this area,' explained Schrorock's president, James Madden, at the beginning of the 1960s, 'our money and our experience. Our money is risk money. We provide equity capital to smaller sized, often family owned, companies which we feel are very promising. We want to do everything we can to make the company prosper in the long run. We are patient. We take the long-range attitude.'[53] Notable examples of Schrorock's successful venture capital investments included Capital Car, an East-coast Volkswagen dealership that was secured through Gustav von Mallinckrodt and of which Madden was chairman, and Piggly Wiggly, a chain of supermarkets in the south-eastern US.

Funding Squeeze and Strategic Challenges, 1958–62

In the closing years of the 1950s Schrobanco encountered mounting challenges, leading to the stagnation of revenues and assets that have already been noted, and to a decline in profitability. One reason was the growing competition from US commercial banks which affected every aspect of its operations. The struggle to stay abreast of the competition led to mounting costs, particularly to retain its highly skilled staff, whose services were eagerly sought by rivals. Schrobanco's problem was that the salary bill and other overhead costs of servicing clients were spread over a much smaller volume of business, because of the size of the balance sheet, than the international departments of large commercial banks, which meant higher unit costs and lower profits.

The late 1950s saw an acute 'funding squeeze' in US banking which particularly affected the New York city banks.[54] Inflation and rising interest rates induced the treasurers of US corporations to minimise the balances they kept with banks, causing a widening imbalance between demands for funds and their supply. This led to a search for new sources of funding, prompting the expansion of the inter-bank market, the development of the Certificate of Deposit and recourse to Euro-dollar funding, and also to attempts to develop branch networks, though this was inhibited by regulatory constraints. Central bank balances became more widely recognised as a source of funds and competition for them intensified. Although Schrobanco successfully retained substantial central bank balances in the late 1950s and the early 1960s it became necessary to pay interest on them, and the profits earned from them declined. Schrobanco, like Citibank for instance, responded to the funding squeeze and the booming demand for credit by appropriate adjustments to the pattern of its assets.[55] US government securities fell from 43 per cent of assets in 1950–57 to 22 per cent in 1958–62, while advances increased from 19 per cent to 30 per cent, and acceptances from 17 per cent to 23 per cent.

Even before the problems of overheads and funding became acute, Schrobanco's senior officers had become concerned about the firm's functioning and its future. In November 1956, Beal established a 'study group' comprising R. Canon Clements, chairman; John Howell; Sherman Gray; and an outside management consultant, to consider Schrobanco's organisation and objectives.[56] In particular, they were charged with suggesting ways of streamlining the firm's divisional and committee structures and untangling the responsibilities of individual officers, which had become crossed and complicated as a result of individual initiatives in the post-war period of rapid *ad hoc* expansion. This was an increasingly pressing matter since the firm's founding generation was approaching retirement age and a more clearly defined structure was necessary for a smooth transfer of responsibilities to their successors.

The study group's report – 'The Schroders New York Management Structure and Organisation Plan' – began by stating the assumption that the Schroder interest in the US would remain in American commercial banking. The most promising area for expansion was identified as 'the purely domestic commercial and industrial fields [which] may best be achieved by the extension of loans, solicitation of deposits and increasing contact with American banks, industry and commercial firms'.[57] With this as an objective the study group recommended that the firm's banking operations should be divided into three divisions; 'Domestic', 'Latin America' and 'Eurasia', the last encompassing Europe, the Pacific Basin and the firm's foreign exchange activities. There would also be three further divisions: 'Trust and Investment', which was basically Schrotrust's non-banking undertakings; 'Financial Planning', the money market and treasury activities; and 'Administrative Services', the service functions. The six divisional heads would all report to the president, who would report to the chairman, as would the head of Schroder, Rockefeller. Attention was paid to the function of the chairman and it was reported that 'we believe that the organisation would profit greatly from having an active chairman who would serve as chief executive officer', a suggestion which implied that the firm's existing arrangements were a source of weakness.[58]

The study group's report was considered by Helmut Schroder and his advisers in London and by the senior management in New York, and the result was the reorganisation of the firm into the form shown in Figure

308

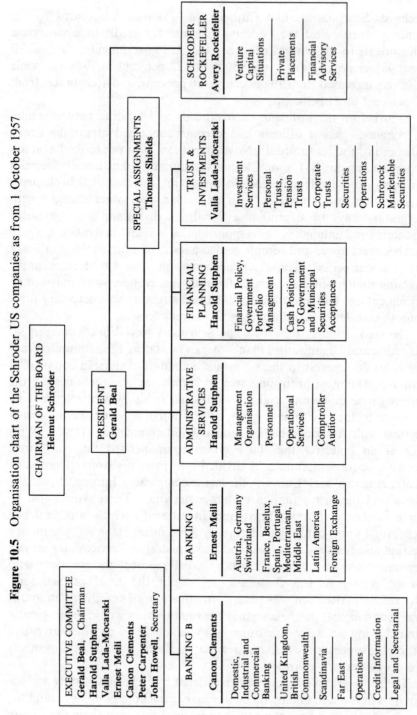

Figure 10.5 Organisation chart of the Schroder US companies as from 1 October 1957

CHAIRMAN OF THE BOARD
Helmut Schroder

PRESIDENT
Gerald Beal

EXECUTIVE COMMITTEE
Gerald Beal, Chairman
Harold Sutphen
Valla Lada-Mocarski
Ernest Meili
Canon Clements
Peter Carpenter
John Howell, Secretary

SPECIAL ASSIGNMENTS
Thomas Shields

SCHRODER
ROCKEFELLER
Avery Rockefeller

Venture Capital Situations

Private Placements

Financial Advisory Services

TRUST &
INVESTMENTS
Valla Lada-Mocarski

Investment Services

Personal Trusts, Pension Trusts

Corporate Trusts

Securities

Operations

Schrorock Marketable Securities

FINANCIAL PLANNING
Harold Sutphen

Financial Policy, Government Portfolio Management

Cash Position, US Government and Municipal Securities Acceptances

ADMINISTRATIVE SERVICES
Harold Sutphen

Management Organisation

Personnel

Operational Services

Comptroller Auditor

BANKING A
Ernest Meili

Austria, Germany Switzerland

France, Benelux, Spain, Portugal, Mediterranean, Middle East

Latin America

Foreign Exchange

BANKING B
Canon Clements

Domestic, Industrial and Commercial Banking

United Kingdom, British Commonwealth

Scandinavia

Far East

Operations

Credit Information

Legal and Secretarial

Source: J. Henry Schroder Banking Corporation organisation plan, 1957.

10.5, which came into effect on 1 October 1957. The new structure effected a major rationalisation of responsibilities and cut the number of executives with the status of divisional head from six to four (Sutphen having responsibility for two divisions). It differed from the blueprint provided by the study group in two significant ways. First, there were two, not three, banking divisions with geographically more hetero-geneous responsibilities, a change which meant the absence of a separate 'Domestic' division, reflecting doubts about this aspect of the study group's development strategy. Second, Helmut Schroder continued as non-resident and non-executive chairman, and played a part in Schrobanco's response to the challenges which confronted it in the late 1950s and the early 1960s. He considered that in view of the increasing competition for banking business, Schrobanco should be redirected more towards investment business, capitalising on its Article XII charter and reflecting the fact that by 1959 $7 million of its $22 million capital was invested outside the banking business, largely in US and Canadian equities. He commented that:

> the tendency in American banks is towards bigger and bigger risks to match the size of the industrial giants. To some extent, Schrobanco is, of course, already an investment trust. I think we have always felt there would have been money to be made in special situations if Schrobanco had had a really outstanding investment man with a nose for special situations. This is difficult to bring about because the top management have since the '30's concentrated on commercial banking. The real money in the United States is made by people like Lazards, Lehmans and Loeb Rhoades. Their stock exchange business is their bread and butter business, but I suspect their big profits are made in special situations where the partners venture their own money. This is due to the fact that the ordinary profits of the business pay about 50% tax whereas capital profits pay only 25%.[59]

But this vision of Schrobanco's development was not pursued and the firm remained principally engaged in commercial banking.

On several occasions in the late 1950s, Beal was approached by other New York City banks to enquire about merger possibilities. Mergers between New York banks were all the rage at the time as they took advantage of new legislation to consolidate domestically and to extend their international activities. Proposals were received from Bankers Trust, Empire Trust and Guaranty Trust to acquire the firm, which they intended as a ready-made foreign department. The idea had considerable appeal to Schrobanco's officers, since the suitors could deliver a domestic corporate client base and their large balance sheets would resolve the problem of the limited scale of credits for individual clients, while overheads could be spread over a greater volume of business, thus cutting unit costs. However, the Schroder family had no interest in becoming a minority shareholder in a US commercial bank and these approaches were politely rebuffed. A merger initiative of a different sort came from Clements in the wake of the passage of the Federal Bank Holding Company Act in 1956, which made it possible to acquire a bank in another state. Being of Texan origin, he was closely in touch with banks in the south-western states, which, unlike their New York counterparts, had large deposit surpluses. He proposed a merger with the Houston-based Bank of the South West, which he argued would solve the funding squeeze and provide the benefits of scale and of access to a client base in the most economically dynamic region of the US economy. Although discussions got underway, his colleagues had little enthusiasm for marriage with a bank 2,000 miles away and Beal soon put an end to the idea with the words 'look Clem, there isn't a soul in this bank who has ever been to Texas but you'.[60]

Financial Performance

From the early 1930s to the end of the 1950s the primary objectives of Schrobanco's management were to manage the business cautiously and to ensure a positive return, however modest, on the firm's capital. Both objectives were achieved successfully. The capital and surplus grew from $6.8 million to $13.3 million over the years 1935–62 (from $11.1 to $20.2 when combined with the Schroder Trust Company), rates of growth which roughly matched the rise in US inflation. From 1931 to 1954 the overriding preoccupation of Schrobanco's proprietors, the partners of J. Henry Schroder & Co., was the extrication of the London house from the consequences of the Standstill and the recovery of the money owed by German debtors. Schrobanco played a vital role in their strategy, serving as the collateral for the loans which were raised to enable the firm to withdraw its Standstill bills from the London discount market at the end of the 1930s. Crucially, Schrobanco avoided making a loss in any of these years, which could have damaged the confidence of the Westminster Bank in the value of its collateral with potentially fatal consequences for the London firm. The deterioration of Helmut Schroder's health at the end of the 1940s reinforced the necessity to safeguard the transatlantic assets which would be required to support the position of the London firm and the Schroder family in the event of his death. Despite the conservative approach to business, the New York firm enjoyed considerable growth in the 1950s and when it became part of the new London-based holding company, Schroders Limited, in 1959, it accounted for 73 per cent of Schroders Limited's total net asset value.

Schrobanco's rate of return on capital in 1935–62 on an unconsolidated basis and excluding Schrotrust, is depicted in Figure 10.6. In 1934–35 Schrobanco's rate of return on capital averaged only 2.1 per cent, but in 1936 it leapt to 10.5 per cent reflecting the revival of the firm's fortunes and in the years 1936–38 its return averaged 9.4 per cent, exceeding the average aggregate rate of return of all US national banks in these years.[61] Schrobanco's strong performance in these years was achieved in spite of cautious balance sheet ratios because the initiatives to develop new business in the mid-1930s focused on 'off-balance sheet' activities, such as restricted currency dealing and investment management, which generated profits or fees rather than interest or acceptance commissions. Its virtuous combination of prudence and profits in 1936–38 was posthumous testimony to the wisdom of Gray's strategy in response to the slump and the Standstill. In 1939–49 Schrobanco's average rate of return was 4.7 per cent, a low figure by comparison with preceeding and succeeding years. It was also less than half the 10 per cent average return earned by all US national banks. The disruptions to Schrobanco's business caused by the war adversely affected the performance of the firm for the duration of the hostilities, and in 1941 the rate of return dropped to 2.5 per cent, the lowest level in the history of the firm save in 1931–34, the trough of the international slump. Furthermore, there were high levels of inflation in the early years of the

Figure 10.6 J. Henry Schroder Banking Corporation, post-tax return on capital and annual rate of US inflation, 1935–62

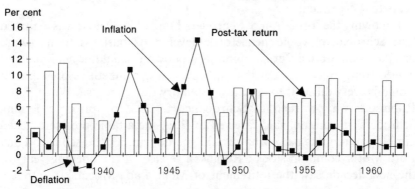

Note: The 'real' return on capital is the difference between the nominal return depicted above and the annual rate of inflation.

US participation in the war and in the immediate post-war years; as a result, in 1941–43 and 1946–48 Schrobanco's real rate of return was negative. None the less, the firm's proprietors were undismayed because it was fulfilling their instruction to conduct a cautious and prestigious business.

The years 1950–57 saw a marked improvement in Schrobanco's performance. The gap between the firm's rate of return and the US national banks narrowed, averaging 7.9 per cent and 8.3 per cent respectively over the period. This improvement was achieved despite continued adherence to highly prudent asset ratios. This was partly the result of renewed vigorous growth in off-balance-sheet activity, particularly foreign exchange dealing. The other important factor was the growth in the size of the firm's balance sheet, which permitted an expansion of banking activities despite the conservative ratios. The increases in advances and acceptances were possible because of the growth of client balances, which rose from $43 million in 1947 to $98 million ten years later. This resulted in a marked shift in the relationship between shareholders' funds and client balances. In 1936–48 the ratio of shareholders' funds to client balances averaged 1:4.0 but in 1949–57 it was 1:7.5. This was the outcome of the endeavours to win the custody of central bank funds. The intensification of competition for these balances led to the stabilisation of the level of Schrobanco's client balances in the late 1950s, and a decline in the ratio of shareholders' funds to client balances to 1:5.1 in 1958–62. Between 1957 and 1958 Schrobanco's rate of return on capital fell from 9.6 per cent to 5.7 per cent, though that of US national banks rose from 8.3 per cent to 9.8 per cent. The following years saw a small recovery for Schrobanco, whose rate of return in 1958–62 averaged 6.5 per cent, while the US national banks averaged 9 per cent. Inflation reduced the firm's average real rate of return in these years to 4.4 per cent.

Following the formation of Schroders Limited in 1959, it was expected that Schrobanco would henceforth develop its business to maximise profits. There were differing opinions on how this could be achieved and indeed some executives felt that, in view of the competitive pressures, it would be very difficult to earn a satisfactory rate of return. When Philip Robinson, who worked at Schrobanco in 1955–61 prior to joining Schroders in London, said farewell to Beal, the affable president asked him 'If you ran this bank what would you do with it?' 'I'd sell it and buy Ford Motor common stock', Robinson replied.[62] The opening years of the new decade saw the retirement of Meili, Lada-Mocarski, Sutphen, Tucker and the other remaining members of the founding generation, including Beal himself. The challenging legacy to the younger generation was to establish a new direction for the firm.

11

Recovery and Growth in London

1945–59

In stark contrast to the opportunities available to New York banks at the end of the war, the recovery of the London merchant banks was beset with problems. Britain had liquidated much of its overseas investments and financially was virtually as weak as the defeated countries. An attempt to make sterling freely convertible in 1947 quickly collapsed, and it was not until 1961 that the pound became fully convertible for trade purposes, while exchange controls remained for capital transactions until 1979. It was New York, the home of the US dollar markets, that played the key role in financing and servicing the rapid growth of international trade and capital flows in the late 1940s and the 1950s. The London merchant banks were largely confined by official controls to conducting international operations in sterling, which more or less restricted their international activities to the 'sterling area' – the British Commonwealth and some other countries that used sterling as the normal means of settlement – or to transactions that benefited the British balance of payments.

The revival of the activity of the London merchant banks in the immediate post-war years was based on the requirements of domestic corporate clients for acceptance credit facilities and for new capital, issues by industrial and commercial companies rising fifteen-fold between 1945 and 1950. Yet the dynamic development of these activities was constrained by the panoply of wartime economic controls which the Labour administration of 1945–51 relinquished slowly and reluctantly. 'Business today,' observed a partner of Hambros in 1948, 'does not only mean selling or buying – that may often be the easiest part – nor financing, but the most intricate and time-wasting labour is in complying with all the various regulations here and abroad.'[1] The pervasive controls created an uncompetitive and introspective environment in the City, whose reputation in these years for stuffiness and complacency was not undeserved.

In reviving its business after the war, J. Henry Schroder & Co. had a great weakness and a great strength. In contrast to many of its peers, it was constrained in terms of both capital resources and managerial attention by the locked-up Standstill credits. On the other hand, uniquely among the London merchant banks, it had in Schrobanco a sister bank in New York that was well-capitalised and a leader in dollar-based international banking, with ties not only in the Americas but also in continental Europe and the Pacific Basin. Contact with many of the London firm's overseas clients was maintained by Schrobanco in the 1940s and 1950s, and its activities sustained Schroders' involvement in international banking. This continuity greatly assisted the re-emergence of the London firm's international financial activities in the 1950s and thereafter.

Helmut Schroder's post-war strategy was for the New York firm to develop the international banking business, while the London firm concentrated on rebuilding its equity base and on developing its domestic British banking and corporate finance clientele. The challenge in London was large, since the firm was virtually moribund at the end of the war – the staff numbered a mere 100; acceptances at year-end in 1945 were just £261,000, the lowest level since surviving records begin in 1850; and the partners' capital was only £778,000, much of it tied up in illiquid real estate investments. The starting point in rebuilding the business was the strengthening of the partnership.

At the end of the war the Schroder partnership comprised Frank Tiarks, aged 71, who was living in semi-retirement in Somerset, and Helmut Schroder and Henry Tiarks, both aged 44. Major Pam, the associate partner who had run the firm during the war, was still playing an indispensable role, though aged 70. Helmut Schroder was the firm's senior partner after his father's death in December 1940. He combined a passionate commitment to the survival and revival of the family firm with a sensitive and even lonely nature, attributed by family tradition to the persecution he suffered because of his German origins while a schoolboy at Eton during the First World War. He found pleasure in literature and was unusually well read. As often as business allowed, he resided on his beloved Scottish estate on the island of Islay, greatly enjoying the roles of laird, farmer, forester and quarryman. He further developed the renowned Schroder orchid collection. He had a strong religious faith – knowing the Bible from cover to cover – and high standards of ethics and integrity. He combined respect for traditional Christian values with a bold nature and support for radical new ideas.

The strain of keeping the business afloat through the war took a toll of Helmut Schroder's health and he became subject to bouts of depression and sickness, particularly after 1948. His poor health and enforced preoccupation with the organisation of the firm's complex financial affairs prevented him from playing an active role in the development and execution of new business, which he largely left to his partners. He called for advice from a group of close confidants, notably Gerald Beal, Avery Rockefeller, Lord Perth, Alexander Abel Smith, Alec Cairns, Henry

Tiarks and Gustav von Mallinckrodt, but retained personal responsibility for all the major decisions about the firm. Sometimes his health led to delays in his decision-making, a state of affairs of which he was fully aware, but once a decision was made he was unwavering in his support and tenacious in the pursuit of its thorough execution. His judgement on policy and people was highly regarded both inside and outside the firm, and almost invariably proved to be sound. 'I look on Helmut as the top banker in the City,' Lord Cobbold, Governor of the Bank of England, remarked to Perth, 'his reaction to problems comes not from his head, but from his guts.'

Henry Tiarks acted as Helmut Schroder's deputy from October 1944, when he returned to the firm from the Air Force, until 1948, but he did not assume a full burden of executive responsibilities as his father and grandfather had done. A highly intelligent and talented man, with great linguistic and sporting abilities, he pursued a wide range of interests in addition to merchant banking. At the beginning of the 1950s he considered moving to New York to assume a senior position in Schrobanco, in which the Tiarks family had a substantial shareholding. But this idea aroused opposition from the American management and was not pursued. He remained in London and made a contribution through the cultivation of client relationships, especially with American clients, and by sitting on outside boards, notably of the Antofagasta Railway, Pressed Steel, Joseph Lucas and Securicor, of which he was a founder, and by representing the firm at home and abroad. He was a director of the Bank of London and South America and was an active ambassador on its behalf. Moreover, at the request of the President of the Board of Trade, he acted as deputy leader of a number of Dollar Export Trade Mission delegations, which promoted British exports to North and South America.

Soon after the war, three new associate partners (known henceforth simply as partners) were appointed. Toby Caulfeild, aged 43, who had been with the firm since 1924, was promoted upon his return from the War Office and assumed responsibility for Latin American clients. Alexander Abel Smith, aged 42, and Lord Strathallan, aged 39, were recruited from outside the firm and brought expertise in securities and investment business which was important for the development of domestic issuing and corporate finance work. Abel Smith was well known at Schroders where he had been a volunteer in 1927–29 after Oxford University.[2] Entering J. P. Morgan & Co. in New York in September 1929, he survived the Wall Street Crash and worked there until 1936. Back in the City he represented the New York stockbroking firm, Spencer Trask, and subsequently joined the Lonsdale Investment Trust. In 1938, he was seconded to the Committee for the Distressed

Areas, of which the chairman was Sir Nigel Campbell of Helbert, Wagg, and conducted several missions to America to encourage US corporations to invest in Britain. After wartime military service he joined Schroders in 1946. He became a director of Pressed Steel in 1950 and chairman in 1955 upon the death of Major Pam. He was also chairman of the Provident Mutual Life Assurance Association and BHD Engineers Ltd, and a director of Hopkinsons Ltd and the Harry Ferguson Group of companies. In 1959, he joined the newly formed Export Council for Europe, becoming deputy chairman in 1964, and he was also a member of the British National Export Council. He received a knighthood for services to export in 1968.

Lord Strathallan, who became the Earl of Perth upon his father's death in December 1951, joined in spring 1946. After Downside and Cambridge he worked in the City for Buckmaster & Moore, a stockbroker, and subsequently on Wall Street for the brokerage firm G. & P. Murphy & Co. In the 1930s he joined Monnet, Murnane & Co., which specialised in raising project finance, especially in China, acting as assistant to Jean Monnet, a French banker and public servant who became well known after the war as one of the leading figures in the formation of the European Community. Perth spent the war in the War Cabinet Office and with the British mission in Washington. Soon after his appointment as a partner Helmut entrusted him with the vital task of preparing a report on the firm's finances, and in September 1947 he was appointed alternate chairman of the daily officers' meeting in the absence of Helmut Schroder, Henry Tiarks or Major Pam. This committee, the firm's first formal executive committee, was an important administrative innovation instigated by Tiarks at the end of the war. In October 1948, a crisis overtook the firm as Helmut's health deteriorated suddenly and alarmingly while both Tiarks and Pam were on prolonged visits to New York.[3] Helmut considered introducing an experienced outsider to take over the running of the firm, but it was Strathallan who took the helm and handled the crisis.[4] For the following decade he was Schroders' chief executive.

In the late 1940s and early 1950s, the partnership expanded further with recruits from both inside and outside the firm. Internal promotions tended to be of those who had banking experience while the external appointments were of men with corporate finance or securities expertise. Ralph Rendell, who had joined in 1921 and had been office manager since 1937, was made a partner in 1949, aged 58, though his tenure was brief since he died in 1952. The vacancy was filled by the promotion of Alec Cairns in April 1953, aged 47. Cairns joined Schroders in 1935, having already gained valuable banking experience with British overseas banks in several parts of the world. He served as Helmut Schroder's private secretary for many years and was one of his closest confidants. The outside recruits were Jonathan Backhouse and Alexander Hood. Backhouse, who joined in June 1950, aged 43, was a stockbroker with Read, Hurst Brown & Co. A man whose exceptional charm was widely recognised, he made a major contribution to the development of Schroders' issuing and investment management activities. He was a long-serving director of the Continental and Industrial Trust and his outside directorships included the Rover Car Co., Lancashire Steel and Sena Sugar. Hood, who had been an adviser to Schroders on American securities since the late 1940s and a director of the Continental Investment Trust since 1951, became a partner in 1957. Educated at Trinity College, Cambridge and the Harvard Business School, he commenced his career with Ladenburg, Thalmann, the New York securities house with which Schroders had had close ties since the late nineteenth century. His outside directorships included Associated Electrical Industries Ltd and the construction firm George Wimpey and Co. The new partners participated in profits, but unlike the full partners had no exposure to losses.

From Partnership to Limited Company

While the recruitment of new partners was relatively straightforward, the financial reorganisation of the firm was complicated and delayed by the outstanding Standstill debts, the financial consequences of Baron Bruno's death in 1940, and post-war tax changes. In the meantime the financial risks of the business were entirely borne by Helmut Schroder and his sisters Dorothee and Marga. It fell to Helmut, the only one of the proprietors who was managerially active in the firm, to organise the family's and the firm's financial affairs to provide sufficient capital for the business, involving endless juggling of its funding and ownership structure. After the war Helmut withdrew from the partners' room and established his own office and staff, devoting much of his attention to this task.

Following the reorganisation of Schroders' finances in 1942–43 (see Chapter 9 on pages 276–7), the proprietary partners were the Veritas Trust, the family trust whose beneficiaries were Helmut Schroder and his two sisters, and Helmut in his own right (see Table 11.1). The immediate post-war priority was to boost the capital of the firm, which was achieved by the injection of capital by the Veritas Trust, raised by realising other investments. This also increased the liquidity of the balance sheet which was further enhanced by the sale of Schroders' interest in Arlington House in 1946 and the sale and lease-back of 145

Table 11.1   J. Henry Schroder & Co., ownership of partners' capital, 1946,
1952, 1954, 1956

31 December	1946 Per cent	1952 Per cent	1954 Per cent	1956 Per cent
Helmut Schroder	32	9	8	4
Veritas Trust Limited	68	91	90	34
Schroder Continuation Limited	–	–	2	–
Schroder Successors Limited	–	–	–	62
Total	100	100	100	100

Source: J. Henry Schroder & Co., balance sheets.

Leadenhall Street to the Prudential in 1949. Finally, in March 1951, further funds were raised by the sale of Schrobanco shares to Barings, and at the end of that year partners' capital was £2.2 million. The spring of 1951 also saw the acceptance in principle by Chancellor Konrad Adenauer of West Germany's liability for its pre-war debts. The prospect of the recovery of the Standstill debts, the benefit of which would accrue to the executors of Baron Bruno Schröder's estate and to the Veritas Trust allowing the Schroder family to repay its loans and unencumbering the capital of the London firm, meant that at last Helmut Schroder was able to proceed with the financial restructuring of the partnership.

In order to be able to include all the partners in a new partnership-like arrangement, it was necessary to resolve the anomalous position of Frank and Henry Tiarks, who had technically remained full partners of the old partnership despite no longer providing any of the firm's capital. In June 1951, discussions began about the purchase by Helmut of the Tiarks partners' interest in the goodwill of J. Henry Schroder & Co. These lasted for about a year, in the course of which Frank Tiarks died. In July 1952, following the mediation of Robert Holland-Martin of Martin's Bank and Sir Edward Peacock of Barings, it was agreed that Henry Tiarks should receive £200,000 in respect of his interest in the goodwill of the London firm. The Tiarks family's shareholdings in Schrobanco were unaffected by this agreement. On 31 March 1953, Henry Tiarks technically withdrew from the old partnership and was thereafter on a par with the other partners, with whom he worked in the private room. His withdrawal enabled the completion of the financial reorganisation of the firm, which was preliminary to its conversion from a partnership to a private limited company.

Most of the merchant banks began as partnerships. Prior to 1945 a few had adopted limited liability as private companies, usually prompted by the need to safeguard capital in turbulent times: Barings in 1890; Helbert, Wagg in 1919; Hambros in 1920; and Morgan Grenfell in 1934. The post-war years saw a wave of conversions because the much-increased levels of personal taxation made the partnership a relatively unattractive form of business organisation: Brown, Shipley in 1945; A. Keyser in 1946; Kleinworts and Rea Brothers in 1947; Grindlays and Antony Gibbs in 1948; Knowles & Foster in 1949; Higginsons in 1950; S. Montagu and Philip Hill in 1951; Brandts in 1952; Sassoons in 1954; Ogilvy and Gillander and N. Bunston in 1955; Leopold Joseph in 1956; and P. P. Rodocanachi and Ullmann in 1962. The incorporation of Schroders in May 1957 was plainly in step with the trend, though the timing was determined by factors particular to the firm. Schroders was one of the last of the merchant banks to adopt limited liability, principally because of the intricate web of the family's and the firm's finances prior to the recovery of the Standstill credits. Moreover, although Helmut recognised the need for change he was, as he explained in a letter to Henry Tiarks just before his withdrawal from the partnership, more concerned to ensure that he made the right decision than to move quickly:

> I want to have plenty of time to reflect before I agree to change a partnership form of business which has served your family and mine so very well in the past into what I conceive to be a more cut and dried, less flexible and to me more impersonal form. To my way of thinking a company, especially a limited one, has many disadvantages. I am proceeding to consider the matter for one main reason only, which is to give as much security for the future as possible to the executives and staff, who are in my opinion at present too dependent on whether I live or die and whether I am in good health or not. The taxation angle is to me a secondary consideration.[5]

As a preliminary step to the conversion a new corporate partner, Schroder Continuation Ltd, was introduced because Helmut was advised that the Veritas Trust, which by 1953 accounted for 92 per cent of the partner's capital (see Table 11.1) was unsuitable to act as sole proprietor in the event of his death. Schroder Continuation Ltd was replaced by Schroder Successors Ltd in April 1955, a change which arose from 'technical legal reasons, and has no bearing on the ordinary business of the firm'.[6] By May 1957, the bulk of the Standstill credits had been recovered and partners' capital was £3.7 million, a considerable increase on the £778,000 at the end of 1945. That month Helmut Schroder and the Veritas Trust technically withdrew from the partnership, leaving Schroder Successors as the sole proprietor of the firm's capital. Schroder Successors Ltd then changed its name to J. Henry Schroder & Co. Ltd and continued the business of the firm, with an initial capital of £2.2 million – £23 million in 1990 money. In this new firm the Schroder family owned the 2 million voting 'A' shares and 500,000 redeemable preference shares, while the senior executives (who continued to be known as 'partners') and certain key members of staff subscribed for 146,000 non-voting 'B' shares. Thus, some twenty-six years after the Standstill calamity, the Schroder family again shared the financial risks of the business with the other partners, albeit in the legal form of a private limited company rather than a partnership.

Recovery of the German Standstill Debts, 1945–54

The timing of the partnership developments was significantly influenced by progress in the recovery of the Standstill debts. In 1945, Schroders' frozen Standstill debts were recorded in the balance sheet at £2.7 million, excluding interest, more than two-and-a-half times partners' funds. Repayment had to wait for a general settlement of Germany's external debts, which was dependent upon international politics and the recovery of the German economy. In the meantime, the Schroder partners pursued some other aspects of the German debt problem. Soon after the end of hostilities, the firm began to endeavour to secure compensation and a resumption of payments for the German Potash Syndicate bondholders, to whom it had responsibilities as the receiving bank. In 1946 and 1947, much of the time of Major Pam, Ralph Rendell and Robin Clutton, the head of the New Issues Department, was absorbed by this work, and Slaughter and May was also heavily involved. It was on behalf of the German Potash Syndicate bondholders that Rendell visited Germany in November 1946, the first post-war visit by a member of the firm. The objectives were to secure the transfer to the bondholders of the remittances made by the German Potash Syndicate, which had been seized by the British authorities since 1941, and to arrange the release of the large sums accumulated on deposit in Holland and Switzerland on behalf of bondholders during the war. Negotiations were also opened with the German Potash Syndicate for the resumption of the service of the loans, though it proved very difficult to reach a settlement.[7] Despite Schroders' endeavours the bondholders had to wait until 1950 for the release of the funds held by the Allied authorities and it was not until August 1956 that an agreement was signed between the bondholders' representatives and the German Potash Syndicate.[8] Under the terms of this treaty Schroders' role as Receiving Bank was confirmed until the redemption of the bonds in 1973, though in fact the arrangement was discontinued in 1959.

The recovery of Schroders' investment in the car body manufacturer Ambi-Budd was another side to the firm's German debt problem. Since the Ambi-Budd works were located in eastern Berlin in a neighbourhood which formed part of the Russian Zone, and a report received in August 1946 suggested that there was little left of the plant, there was no hope of the restitution of the Ambi-Budd shareholders' property. There was, however, the possibility of compensation, and a claim was registered with the Allied authorities. The success of the Committee of British Industrial Interests in Germany in securing the release of blocked marks to the German subsidiaries of British firms, such as Unilever, Shell, Courtaulds and some thirty others, raised hopes at 145 Leadenhall Street in June 1947 that 'we might be able to do something regarding Ambi-Budd in this direction'.[9] William Cavendish-Bentinck, a close friend of Henry Tiarks, had recently become deputy chairman of the Committee and he was asked to pursue Schroders' Ambi-Budd claims. He was unable to do so because his organisation only dealt with restitution cases, but he encouraged the Schroder partners to 'keep badgering the Authorities concerned . . . repeated reminders may be the only way to get anything done'.[10] In August 1947, a senior officer of the other major non-German shareholder, the Budd Company of Philadelphia, called at Leadenhall Street and reported that pressure was also being applied to the State Department regarding compensation. Fortunately for Schroders and the Budd Company, Gustav von Mallinckrodt, their non-executive representative on the Ambi-Budd board since the 1920s, had removed the firm's records during the war for safe-keeping to a farm in Bavaria. Thus they survived the Soviet Army's assault on Berlin and provided the basis for the successful substantiation of the shareholders' claims for compensation in the mid-1950s. Mallinckrodt also provided assistance with the recovery of Schroders' Standstill debts, although the foremost purpose of his appointment as Schrobanco's representative in Frankfurt in 1947 was to promote the New York firm's endeavours to develop German business.

The story of the post-war recovery of Schroders' Standstill debts begins with the currency reform of June 1948, which replaced the valueless Reichsmark with the Deutsche Mark (DM) establishing a possible medium for repayment. The Schroder partners immediately despatched Rendell and S. Podeshwa, a manager in the Banking Department who was one of the firm's technical experts on the Standstill debts, to Germany to discuss the situation with Wilhelm Schröder of

Schröder Gebrüder in Hamburg and Gustav von Mallinckrodt in Frankfurt. They also called on many of the firm's debtors and reported widespread expressions of wishes to repay outstanding Standstill debts, though, of course, the restrictions on transfers made this impossible. Moreover, it was known that the occupation administration regarded post-war debts as taking precedence over pre-war obligations, and that the Americans advocated the priority of the claims of bondholders before banks in the settlement of pre-war debts. Major Pam pessimistically concluded that Schroders was unlikely to see substantial repayments in the foreseeable future and argued that the firm should take advantage of an opportunity to sell its Standstill debts, which could be effected at a 50 per cent discount to their face value.[11] However, his colleagues took the opposite view and it was decided not to liquidate but to await developments.

One reason for optimism was the prominent role in the post-war German financial administration of Dr Hermann J. Abs, who was well known to the pre-war partners since he had been a volunteer in the firm in the 1920s and his wife was related to Helmut Schroder. Moreover, Abs had many dealings with the firm in the 1930s when he was a partner in the prestigious Berlin private bank, Delbrück Schickler, before his appointment as a general manager of the Deutsche Bank in 1937. Since June 1945, Abs had been acting as an adviser on the German financial situation to the British occupation authorities, and his commitment to honouring Germany's pre-war debts and his support for giving precedence to the settlement of the Standstill debts was known in the City of London. The Schroder partners were delighted to learn of his appointment as the president of the Kreditanstalt für Wiederaufbau (Reconstruction Loan Corporation) in April 1948, noting this 'useful' development in the minutes of the officers' meeting.[12]

Preliminary discussions between the Standstill creditors and debtors got under way in the autumn of 1948. The principal participants were Abs for the Germans, and on the British side Sir Edward Reid of Barings, the chairman of the Accepting Houses Committee, supported by Henry Tiarks, thereby continuing the work to recover the Standstill debts begun by his father, and Ernest Kleinwort of Kleinworts. The talks were useful for rebuilding trust between the parties, but the bankers were unable to take action without a general settlement of the German debt problem. Naturally, it was the creditors who were keenest to see an early resolution of the problem, but in the autumn of 1949 Abs too began to press for a German commitment to accept liability for pre-war debts, which ultimately led to Adenauer's undertaking in March 1951.[13]

In the meantime, Schroders began to renew ties with German clients. In April 1949, accounts were opened for six banks, including Schröder

Gebrüder, which had been appointed to act as agents for the Bank deutscher Länder, the institution which became the Bundesbank,[14] and the following December the Bank deutscher Länder itself opened an account and deposited £200,000.[15] The job of re-establishing commercial relations with German clients was entrusted to Henry Tiarks. In February 1950, he toured the country, accompanied by Podeshwa, visiting forty banks in Hamburg, Hanover, Frankfurt, Dusseldorf and Cologne. He assured them that Schroders intended to restore credit facilities when circumstances permitted, a much appreciated commitment. Besides restoring relations with longstanding clients, Tiarks hoped that the prospect of foreign credits would encourage the German banks to exert pressure on the political authorities to expedite the settlement of the German debt problem. Upon his return from Germany, Tiarks wrote reports on his visit for the Governor of the Bank of England and for Sir Edward Reid. Schroders' initiative was applauded by Sir George Bolton, the Executive Director of the Bank of England, who told Tiarks that he welcomed this step, 'which would show some degree of elasticity without showing any weakness, i.e. giving credit facilities on any considerable scale until something was done about the Standstill debts'.[16]

The London Conference on German External Debt eventually opened on 28 February 1952 at Lancaster House in London. Initially, it was expected to last until April but it was not until August that agreement was reached on all points. The Standstill debts, the point of greatest interest to the merchant banks, were but one aspect of the deliberations, which covered the whole of Germany's pre-war debts, both public and private, long-term and short-term, and also took into consideration postwar financial assistance. Intensive negotiations regarding the Standstill debt got under way in May and continued during June. The Standstill creditors lobbied to be given priority in the receipt of repayments since, as *The Economist* put it, 'a satisfactory settlement of their claims is an essential preliminary to the extension of new commercial credits to Germany and that in its turn is necessary to revive Germany's export trade and capacity to meet the service on its pre-war bonded external debts'.[17] The US delegation opposed giving priority to the commercial creditors, which were largely British banks, American claimants being mostly bondholders, but eventually Reid and Tiarks persuaded them.[18] The outcome of the Lancaster House conference was an agreement by which the Standstill creditors were to receive the repayment of principal plus thirteen years' interest at 4 per cent per annum. It came into effect upon ratification in September 1953 and over the following year and a half the Veritas Trust and the executors of Baron Bruno Schröder's estate received repayments amounting to the whole of the outstanding principal plus 50 per cent interest.

Revival of Business in the 1950s

The recovery of the Standstill debts in the mid-1950s coincided with burgeoning opportunities for the merchant banks. The relaxation or abolition of the wartime economic controls was under way by the end of the 1940s, though the process was halted with the outbreak of the Korean War in 1950. Between the summer of 1952 and the end of 1954 the dismantling of the restrictions proceeded apace in fulfilment of the election promises of the Conservative government which came into office in 1951. The abolition of direct controls was accompanied by the resumption of the use of interest rates and credit controls as instruments of economic regulation, which began with the Bank Rate rise of November 1951. Although exchange control, restrictions on foreign lending and the weakness of sterling hampered the revival of the City's international financial activities in the post-war years, some recovery was made, the City's earnings from international banking and foreign exchange trading growing, it has been estimated, from £8 million in the late 1940s to £30 million in 1958.[19]

The end of the 1950s saw a new development in the City which led in the following decade to the restoration of London to the position of the world's leading international financial centre the – advent of the Euro-market, the international money and capital market operating in currencies which are outside their country of origin. From the mid-1950s banks in London and Paris attracted a growing volume of US dollar deposits placed by Communist countries and Arab investors who preferred to keep their funds outside the control of the US government for political reasons. Another important source of dollar balances was US multinational corporations, which kept funds offshore because of US restrictions on interest payments to depositors, notably 'Regulation Q' which forbade American banks from paying interest on demand deposits and placed ceilings on domestic time deposits. Early sources of demand for London's dollar deposits were the merchant banks following the Bank of England's prohibition on the use of sterling to finance non-UK trade, which was a consequence of the sterling crisis of 1957. Furthermore, the restoration of convertibility in the major European economies in 1958 boosted the development of an active interbank market in all the major currencies. Finally, the substantial US balance of payments deficits of the late 1950s and 1960s ensured the continued rapid growth of the Euro-dollar market, which eventually evolved into the broader based Euro-market.

It was not only in international activities that the late 1950s saw stirrings in the City. The abandonment of credit control in 1958, and early in 1959 the elimination of the necessity to obtain Capital Issues

Committee consent for securities issues for UK corporate clients, allowed the merchant banks greater freedom in the conduct of their domestic banking and corporate finance activities. The abolition of these controls was a significant contributory factor to the take-over boom of the late 1950s and early 1960s. The episode that marked the onset of the take-over boom was the struggle for control of the British Aluminium Company in the winter of 1958–59, which is related in Chapter 12 (see pages 407–8). 'The players' was the term used by one of the Schroder partners of the day – for the Warburgs–Helbert, Wagg–Schroders team in that contest – a term derived from the game of cricket which contrasted their professionalism with the gentlemanly amateurism of their opponents. The former team's victory in the British Aluminium contest was the harbinger of the much more dynamic and competitive City environment of the 1960s.

The recovery in Schroders' revenues in the decade and a half following the end of the war is shown in Figure 11.1. Increases were achieved in most years, and overall revenues rose from £143,000 in 1945 to £1 million in 1959. The revival began very promisingly in 1946 when revenues leapt to £414,000, being inflated by the sale of the firm's interest in Arlington House. In 1947, by contrast, revenues were depressed by losses on the gilt portfolio. The advance in 1951–55, from £447,000 to £840,000, was the outcome of the relaxation of British government controls and the buoyant international economy. The years 1957 and 1959 also saw large increases, the former due to thriving accepting activity and the latter on account of the take-over boom and burgeoning Euro-dollar business, a favourable environment that continued into the 1960s. On an inflation-adjusted basis Schroders achieved a fourfold increase in revenues in the years 1945–49. But even by 1959, real revenues had not surpassed the average of the years 1932–39, which themselves were substantially lower than in the 1920s.

Figure 11.1   J. Henry Schroder & Co., revenues, 1945–59

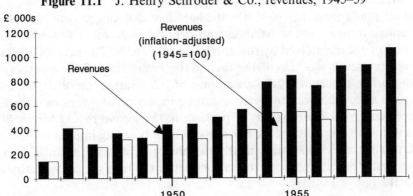

Table 11.2   J. Henry Schroder & Co., sources of revenues, 1946–58

	1946–53		1954–58	
	Annual average £000s	Per cent	Annual average £000s	Per cent
Accepting	128	30	210	25
Issuing and underwriting	20	5	87	10
Interest	61	15	116	14
Investments	70	17	186	22
Other[1]	141	33	233	28
Total	420	100	832	100

1. Recoveries on bad debt reserve, sale of assets, appreciation of assets, foreign exchange dealing, Investment Department, special fees, etc.

The sources of J. Henry Schroder & Co.'s revenues in 1946–53 and 1954–58 are shown in Table 11.2. Accepting generated 30 per cent of revenues in 1946–53 and 25 per cent in 1954–58, proportions similar to the 1930s. Issuing and underwriting contributed 5 per cent in 1946–53 and 10 per cent in 1954–58, considerably less than the 16 per cent in the years 1932–39. Interest from loans constituted around 15 per cent of revenues in the post-war years, a higher proportion than in the 1930s, as might have been expected since the 4 per cent partners' interest charge which had been waived in 1940 was not restored. A new feature of the profit and loss account was the substantial scale of income from investments, mostly British government bonds. It is impossible to identify precisely the earnings of the Investment Department, but it was probably the principal source of 'other' revenues, perhaps 10–15 per cent of total revenues in the 1950s.

The post-war period saw the adoption of considerably bolder balance sheet ratios than the 1930s. On the liabilities side the ratio of partners' capital and reserves to balances and deposits averaged 1:4, double the ratio of 1:2 maintained by the firm in the late 1930s. The ratio of capital to acceptances was also higher than in the 1930s, rising from an average of 1:1.8 in the late 1940s to an average of 1:2.6 during the 1950s. On the assets side, there was an increase in the proportion of advances from 15 per cent in the late 1940s to 35 per cent in the second half of the 1950s, reducing the liquidity of the balance sheet but boosting interest revenues. Overall, the developments in the pattern of Schroders' balance sheets suggest a bolder approach to the conduct of the firm's banking business in the post-war years.

During the war Schroders' acceptance activity virtually ceased, but in the post-war era the firm recovered its position as one of London's leading accepting houses. Acceptance commissions generated average annual revenues of £128,000 in 1946–53 and £210,000 in 1954–58, these figures understating the importance of the activity to the firm since it was the origin of large client balances and deposits which boosted interest revenues. Between 1945 and 1959 Schroders' acceptances grew from £261,000 to £7.9 million as shown in Figure 11.2.

The recovery of the volume of acceptances in the years immediately after the war had two causes – the rapid growth of international trade and the buoyant demand from British companies for acceptances, which were a cheaper source of working capital than bank overdrafts under the low interest rate regime of the post-war Labour administration.[20] The diminished level of Schroders' acceptances in 1952 and 1953 was the result of a concurrence of adverse developments, most notably a waning of demand for facilities from British companies due to higher interest rates after November 1951, which made acceptance finance relatively unattractive, and Bank of England restrictions on access to the London discount market to put an end to the use of commercial bills as a means of speculating against sterling. In the summer of 1953 *The Economist* estimated that the volume of commercial bills in the money market had contracted by 40–50 per cent from its peak eighteen months earlier, though figures published subsequently by the Bank of England of the aggregate acceptances of the members of the Accepting Houses Committee, shown in Figure 11.2, suggest a decline of only 15–20 per cent.[21]

Figure 11.2 J. Henry Schroder & Co., acceptances, and total acceptances of all members of the Accepting Houses Committee, 1945–59

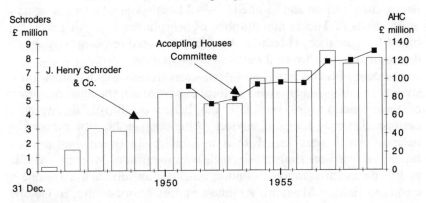

Source: All members of the Accepting Houses Committee – *Bank of England Statistical Abstract* (London: Bank of England, 1970) pp. 54–5.

Underlying the expansion of acceptance business in the rest of the decade was the growth of international trade and British exports. The upsurge in 1954 was the result of interest rate cuts, and that in 1957 was attributable to restrictions on bank lending which led British companies to seek alternative sources of working capital, though the chairman of the Accepting Houses Committee challenged this interpretation, which implied that his members were assisting the evasion of the 'credit squeeze'.[22] The close correspondence in Figure 11.2 between the movements of the level of Schroders' acceptances and the aggregate acceptances of the members of the Accepting Houses Committee indicates that the evolution of Schroders' acceptance activity in the 1950s was heavily influenced by the external economic factors discussed above. But even more fundamental was the development of the firm's relations with clients, of which the minutes of the officers' daily meetings provide a detailed picture.

Banking Business

In the immediate post-war years a special effort was made to develop sterling acceptance business with Latin America, a region which had prospered during the war and was generally believed to have promising prospects for economic expansion.[23] Schroders was well placed to do so because its longstanding ties with clients in the region had been maintained during the war by Schrobanco, giving it an advantage over the other London merchant banks. As soon as the hostilities were over Schrobanco's officers vigorously marketed the services of the London firm, leading Helmut Schroder to comment in March 1946 that 'these efforts to obtain business for London are very highly appreciated'.[24] A few months later he and Caulfeild visited South America, travelling hard on the heels of Tucker and Sutphen of Schrobanco and using their trip report for guidance. Thereafter, Caulfeild assumed responsibility for the development of Schroders' business in the region.

The core of Schroders' Latin American business was its provision of sterling reimbursement credits to local banks. Much the most important of these relationships was with the Banco do Brasil, for which it performed a wide range of services, being compensated by the sterling balances which were kept with it in London. In Brazil, business was rapidly resumed on a substantial scale with the firm of Monteiro Aranha of Rio de Janeiro. Indeed, London quickly built up such a volume of credits to finance Monteiro Aranha's import business, that in October 1946 Beal wrote to Helmut Schroder to alert him to the level of the joint exposure of the Schroder firms to the Brazilian firm.[25] It was decided

75.　Helmut Schroder as senior partner

76. (*left*)
The Earl of Perth

77. (*right*)
Henry Tiarks

78.   (*left to right*) Alec Cairns, Edward (Tommy) Tucker, Lord Perth, Helmut Schroder

79.   (*left to right*) Jonathan Backhouse, Alexander Abel Smith, Henry Tiarks, Alec Cairns

80.   Gerald Beal, president of J. Henry Schroder Banking Corporation, 1935–62

81. Norbert Bogdan, who developed business with Latin America and Japan

82. Avery Rockefeller, president of Schroder, Rockefeller & Co.

83. Some leading officers of J. Henry Schroder Banking Corporation in 1958 (*standing, left to right*) Karl Streeck, John Howell, Mark Gardner, Peter Carpenter, Don Brown, Emil Kuster, Prestley McCaskie (*seated, left to right*) Bob Siegen, Bill Kearns, John Schmid, Canon Clements, John MacNamara

84. Cruz Alta, the Argentinian sugar plantation and refinery owned by the Schroder partners

85. Helmut Schroder (*centre*) with Olavo Egydio de Souza Aranha (*left*) and Joachim Monteiro de Carvalho (*right*), partners of Monteiro Aranha, Schroders' longstanding associates in Brazil

Founders of Helbert, Wagg & Co.

86. (*left*) John Helbert

87. (*below*) John Wagg

88. (*left*) Arthur Wagg, senior partner at the
turn of the century

89. (*right*) Edward Wagg, brother and
partner of Arthur Wagg

90. (*left*) Alfred Wagg, chairman of
    Helbert, Wagg & Co. Ltd, 1919–54

91. (*below*) Albert Palache, partner, with
    his wife

92. Lionel Fraser, chairman of Helbert, Wagg & Co. Ltd, 1954–62

93. (*above*) Office of Helbert, Wagg & Co. Ltd,
    41 Threadneedle Street

94. (*right*) Office of J. Henry Schroder & Co.,
    145 Leadenhall Street

henceforth to offer part of any future sterling credit for Monteiro Aranha to Barings, an arrangement which worked so well that five years later the London firms discussed the establishment of a jointly owned accepting house in Rio, though nothing came of the proposal.[26] Schroders acted as Monteiro Aranha's agent in Britain in negotiations with parties such as the British steel companies which were invited to tender for a Brazilian pipe contract in June 1946, or the engineering firm which was contracted to supply machinery for its bottling subsidiary, when difficulties arose in October 1952. The Schroder partners also provided introductions for Monteiro Aranha to British companies with which it was seeking to do business. In August 1951, for instance, the heads of the firm, Alberto Monteiro de Carvalho and Dr Olavo Egydio de Souza Aranha, were taken round to meet the senior executives of Dunlop, Tube Investments and ICI. Discussions took place on a number of occasions in the early 1950s with British car firms about the establishment of a joint venture to manufacture motor vehicles in Brazil. Since none of the British firms wished to participate a deal was put together with Volkswagen (VW) as a result of discussions conducted on Monteiro Aranha's behalf by Gustav von Mallinckrodt, who was well known to VW's senior management as a director of Ambi-Budd. When Volkswagen do Brazil was established in 1959, Schroders provided Monteiro Arahna with a DM1 million (£85,000) credit which assisted the firm in subscribing for its shareholding.[27]

Monteiro Aranha, in turn, did much more for Schroders than merely making use of its acceptance facilities. The Rio firm provided a constant supply of information about economic and political conditions in Brazil, particularly the coffee harvest that was the crucial determinant of the country's foreign exchange position, and about the creditworthiness of local firms. Brazilian companies such as Brasex, an important Brazilian cotton exporter, became acceptance credit clients on the basis of introductions from Monteiro Aranha. Occasionally the two firms jointly originated new business to their mutual advantage, the foremost example being the sale of the Miranda Estancia Company, a British company which owned a very large cattle ranch in Mato Grosso, to a consortium of Brazilian investors. Schroders and Monteiro Aranha brought the parties together in the summer of 1949 and acted for them in the ensuing negotiations, Miranda Estancia Company shareholders being delighted to receive £1 13s for shares which had recently been almost valueless and had not paid a dividend for years.

Schroders' familiarity with the affairs of the Miranda Estancia Company derived from the friendship of the partners with Brigadier W. H. Crosland, the head of the firm of Parsons & Crosland, a British merchant house specialising in Latin American trade, and a longstanding

Schroder acceptance client. Early in 1950, in the middle of the Miranda Estancia negotiations, the firm decided to revitalise its languishing Brazilian subsidiary, Parsons & Crosland & Cia Ltda, and turned to Schroders for assistance. The partners put them in touch with Eric Lamb, Schrobanco's resident representative in Rio, who agreed to act as an adviser and became a director.[28] With Lamb a member of the board, Schroders was happy to increase credit facilities to the Brazilian subsidiary, which became an important client. The acceptance business ties led on to foreign exchange transactions on behalf of Parsons & Crosland and to a number of new clients on the basis of recommendations to Schroders by the firm. Moreover, Schroders performed services such as presenting the case for awarding Pressed Steel's Brazilian agency to Parsons & Crosland & Cia Ltda. 'An unqualified success' were the words used by Brigadier Crosland to describe the relationship when he lunched with Abel Smith in December 1951.[29]

In the latter years of the 1950s, Brazil's foreign exchange position worsened considerably and credits for Brazilian clients were curtailed as a precaution. The Banco do Brasil was initially an exception, but by December 1959 its account with Schroders was described as 'virtually closed'.[30] In these years the Schroder partners were often asked for expert advice by other City firms and British manufacturers about Brazilian commercial and economic conditions. They themselves relied upon Monteiro Aranha; Schrobanco's old friend Baron Leithner; and particularly Eric Lamb, who was the author of a Chatham House study of the Brazilian capital market and president of the American Chamber of Commerce in Rio, and widely regarded as a leading foreign authority on the Brazilian financial situation. His position *vis-à-vis* the London firm was formalised in February 1956 when he was invited to add to his visiting cards 'Special Correspondent to J. Henry Schroder & Co., London'.[31] Schroders also acted as an adviser on finance for Brazilian firms and participated in the advisory group established by Rothschilds at the request of the new Brazilian Ambassador to Britain in 1957 to counsel him in financial and economic matters.[32]

In Argentina, Schrobanco's subsidiary Argentaria acted as J. Henry Schroder & Co.'s agent, and van Tienhoven kept London regularly informed of local commercial and political developments and of Argentaria's business. Schroders' Argentinian business comprised the provision of a line of credit for Argentaria and reimbursement credits for local banks.[33] Additionally, credit facilities for commercial firms were granted on a single transaction basis to clients, usually the Argentinian subsidiaries of British firms such as Pilkingtons, though the revival of the relationship with the trading firm Staudt & Cia of Buenos Aires also merits mention. Argentaria's wholly-owned subsidiary in Montevideo,

Pena SA Financiera, constituted a Schroder presence in Uruguay, though the London firm did little business with it and apparently some of the partners were even unaware of its existence prior to van Tienhoven's visit to Leadenhall Street in October 1952.[34] Friendly relations with Argentaria persisted after the sale of the company to Deltec in 1957, though requests to increase the size of credits were declined.[35]

The Schroder partners' other interest in Argentina was the Cruz Alta estate in the province of Tucuman, comprising a sugar cane plantation and a substantial mill, which in the early 1950s was producing around 160,000 bags of sugar per annum.[36] After the war the partners sought to realise this asset and discussions were held with several potential purchasers, including the Nawab of Bhopal, Sir Victor Sassoon and Staudt & Cia. However, it proved impossible to come to a satisfactory arrangement on account of problems with exchange controls, and by the summer of 1948 selling was off the agenda. Emilio Eichmann, the Swiss-born manager, travelled to London in September 1948 to discuss the future of Cruz Alta and how to employ the large pesos balances which had been accumulated. It was decided to invest in Argentinian real estate and accordingly 74,000 acres of grazing land and forest, known as Cruz del Norte, were purchased in August 1949. Cruz Alta's business boomed in the early 1950s, and in 1952–53 the firm earned a record profit of 4.3 million pesos, about £110,000 at the contemporary exchange rate.[37] In following years, however, profits and the production of refined sugar declined as Argentina's economic situation deteriorated. The properties were eventually sold in 1969.

In Chile in the decade and a half after the war Schroders' closest business associates were the Banco Mercantil de Santiago, Mariano Puga, head of the Sociedad General de Comercio, and Javier Echeverria of Javier Echeverria y Cia Ltda. The firm acted as Puga's British agent providing a range of services such as gathering tenders for an order for 300 buses in the summer of 1946 or making representations on his behalf to the chairman of the British Overseas Airways Corporation, which Puga hoped to represent in Chile. Puga also did a considerable amount of business with Schrobanco and his American ties led to his appointment as Chilean Ambassador to the United States in 1957. The relationships with Puga and Echeverria were fostered by Henry Tiarks, whose intervention with the chairman of Standard Motors secured the Chilean agency for Echeverria's company in January 1946. Relations also resumed after the war with Cosalitre, the Chilean nitrate monopoly in which Schroders had a considerable bond and equity holding until it was sold in 1948.[38] This followed the settlement of Chile's defaulted external debt, the outcome of negotiations extending from 1946 to 1948, during which Schroders was frequently consulted by the participating parties. Major Pam was outspokenly hostile to the plan agreed between the Chileans and the American negotiators, which he believed was not in the best interests of British bondholders. Fears that Pam's stance would harm Schroders' standing in Chile proved to be unfounded and the Chilean chief negotiator left London in December 1947 expressing 'the greatest admiration and goodwill'.[39] In recognition of the services which the Schroder firms had performed over the years for the Chilean state and its citizens, Helmut Schroder and Henry Tiarks were made members of the Chilean Order of Merit in the early 1950s.[40]

Schroders' ties with the Antofagasta (Chili) and Bolivia Railway Company Ltd went back to the 1880s. Henry Tiarks joined the board in the 1920s and became chairman after the war, being subsequently succeeded by Caulfeild. Schroders provided a variety of financial services for the Antofagasta Railway, particularly foreign exchange transactions, and in return the company kept large sterling balances with it. The Antofagasta Railway's largest clients were the Bolivian tin producers, including Schrobanco's major client, Dr Mauricio Hochschild. In June 1946 he lunched with the Schroder partners, who had been exhorted by Beal to give him a VIP reception, and was offered a £100,000 credit line, increased to £150,000 the following year.[41] Hochschild was an important client of both the London and New York firms in the late 1940s and early 1950s, though business declined from 1952 because the political instability which then overtook Bolivia made the risk unacceptable. Other outstanding Latin American clients with which business revived included Luis Soto & Co. in Colombia; Blohm & Co. in Venezuela; and Gildemeister & Co. in Peru.

The early 1950s saw the nationalisation of the United Railways of Havana by the government of Cuba, and the United Railway of the Yucatan by the government of Mexico. The Schroder partners were deeply involved in the tortuous negotiations that preceded these nationalisations because there were outstanding bonds for which the firm had acted as the issuing house and for which they were the bondholders' trustee. The deterioration of the performance of the Havana railway in the late 1940s was blamed by the company on the 'calculated policy' pursued by the Cuban government against its interests.[42] Schroders devised a scheme which eventually provided the basis for the state purchase of the company for $13 million, though it took from November 1949 to September 1953 to secure agreement.[43] It was also closely involved in the discussions amongst the trustees and the directors about 'the division of the spoils' between the bondholders and shareholders.[44] Trouble between the Yucatan railway and the Mexican government arose on account of an outstanding tax claim which led to a threat to seize the company's assets. Abel Smith visited Mexico in October 1950 and persuaded the administration to stay its hand, but it was not until two years later, when Henry Tiarks attended the World Bank meeting in Mexico City, that Schroders was able to negotiate a settlement of 'this long outstanding matter', salvaging something for the bondholders.[45]

In the decade and a half following the war there was little demand for sterling credits from the countries of continental Europe and while Schrobanco actively developed dollar-based business J. Henry Schroder & Co.'s activities on the Continent were very limited. The exception was Germany, which made substantial sterling-area purchases of raw materials. Schroders resumed the provision of sterling credits to German clients in 1954, and in 1955, to emphasise the firm's commitment to the resumption of business in Germany, Helmut Schroder toured the country, assisted by Gustav von Mallinckrodt and Lord Ogilvy (the future Lord Airlie), a junior executive. 'Of course, the red carpet was laid out everywhere,' recalled Airlie, Helmut's hosts being very gratified by this demonstration that 'Schroders was serious about getting back to business with Germany'.[46] It was decided to grant credits only to German banks, and an upper limit of £800,000 in total was set on these facilities.[47] This presented a dilemma for Tiarks, who was given responsibility for the allocation of the new lines, since he knew that there were 30–40 German banks which were hoping to receive credit lines from Schroders and there was a danger of alienating many longstanding 'friends'. With encouragement from Hermann Abs, then chief executive of the Süd-deutsche Bank AG, he resolved the problem to everyone's satisfaction by offering symbolic 'petty cash' credit lines of around £20,000 to each of the German banks, adding an injunction to telex details of any larger facilities required on an *ad hoc* basis. Thereby Schroders restored friendly relations with most of the leading German banks.

One of the few exceptions to the policy of confining credits to German banks was Norddeutsche Affinerie, the important Hamburg metal-smelting and chemical firm owned by Metallgesellschaft AG and Degussa AG, which had been a major client in the 1920s. In 1949, Ernest Lapierre, the chairman, called at Leadenhall Street and promised full repayment, plus interest, of Norddeutsche Affinerie's Standstill debt whenever exchange controls permitted the transfer, which was accomplished in August 1951.[48] Lapierre was the first Standstill debtor to make such a gesture, and Schroders reciprocated in 1954 by granting the firm a £750,000 credit line. In turn, Norddeutsche Affinerie used Schroders as the depository for its sterling balances and continued to use the London firm's facilities long after it had transferred the rest of its business to German banks.[49]

The post-war years saw the development of strong ties with the Japanese financial authorities and the commencement of the provision of lines of credit to Japanese banks. Within days of the announcement by the occupation authorities in June 1947 that private trade with Japan could resume from 15 August,[50] Norbert Bogdan was in London attempting to organise a syndicate to provide a £6 million credit to finance Japanese imports, a sterling complement to his initiative in New York. Invitations to join were extended to the Hong Kong and Shanghai Bank, the Westminster Bank, Barings, Morgan Grenfell, and Lazards, but only the Hongkong and Shanghai accepted. The British authorities gave the proposal a hostile reception, the Governor of the Bank of England questioning the legality of the provision of finance to nationals of a state with which Britain and forty-one other countries were still officially at war and he was unmoved by the argument that the City would lose out to Wall Street if the scheme was stymied.[51] Although there were several further initiatives, the restrictions imposed by both the British authorities and the Allied army of occupation combined to prevent J. Henry Schroder & Co. becoming actively engaged in the provision of sterling credits to Japan for a further three years. Early in 1950, responsibility for financial administration was transferred from the army of occupation to indigenous institutions[52] and Schroders and the Hongkong and Shanghai Bank immediately revived their scheme, offering their services and a line of credit to the Foreign Exchange Control Board, the body charged with handling Japan's currency reserves. The proposal was gratefully accepted and Schroders thereby established itself as one of only two London merchant banks providing credits to the Japanese authorities.

In the early 1950s practical assistance was provided by Schroders to Japanese officials who visited London, such as the team from the Ministry of Finance who in September 1950 received a thorough introduction to the operation of the City, especially the money market. Moreover, the visitors were briefed on the situation in post-war Germany and were furnished with letters of introduction to the German bankers and Allied administrators who were struggling with problems similar to those facing Japan. When representatives of the Bank of Japan, the central bank, arrived in London in October 1951 to establish an office they turned to Schroders for help and the office manager, Laurance Mackie, helped to find suitable office accommodation and gave guidance in the workings of the City. Official gratitude for this assistance was expressed in December 1951 upon the visit of the Japanese Financial Counsellor to London and J. Henry Schroder & Co. was made one of the nine sterling area firms with which Japanese banks were permitted to open direct correspondent relationships. When

Mackie retired in 1955, after fifty years service with Schroders, he was retained by the Bank of Japan as a consultant, an arrangement that continued for a further three decades until October 1985 when Mackie, aged 97, resigned, since he was finding the journey to the City too arduous.

Schroders' post-war relations with Japanese commercial banks began immediately after the decontrol measure of June 1950 when a letter arrived at Leadenhall Street, to the partners' pleasant surprise, announcing that it had been designated as a correspondent by the Industrial Bank of Japan. The following month the Bank of Tokyo, the successor to the Yokohama Specie Bank, was granted an import letter of credit facility. The visit to Japan made by David Forsyth, a manager in the Banking Department, in the autumn of 1952, mentioned in Chapter 10, resulted in a major expansion of business with Japan. Another important development was the opening by the Bank of Tokyo of a London branch in October 1952, the first Japanese bank to return to the City. This led to an increase of business with Schroders and to the development of closer ties between the firms, and when Yosuki Ono visited London he prudently asked to see Schroders' balance sheet. He was politely informed that as a private partnership Schroders showed its accounts to no one save the Governor of the Bank of England, but Ono was invited to lunch at Dell Park by Helmut Schroder. Evidently the house and gardens reassured him about the resources of the firm and on his departure he told his host, 'I have seen Schroder orchids – no need to see balance sheet'.[53] Subsequently Schroders assisted directly in the establishment of representation in London by the Sumitomo Bank in 1953 and the Sanwa Bank in 1956, both firms taking temporary accommodation at 145 Leadenhall Street while their officers gained experience of the City and searched for premises.

In the early years of the 1950s Japan ran a trading deficit with the sterling area countries and the resulting sterling shortage led to lower levels of compensating balances than was considered adequate by City firms or the Bank of England. Matters began to improve in 1954 when substantial sterling balances were placed in London, and by early 1956 the British authorities were expressing pleasure at the conduct of the Japanese. But simultaneously, Japanese clients began to demand more competitive terms for their credits and in January 1955 it was reported to the officers' meeting that Schroders was making losses on its acceptance business with Japanese banks, though the large balances kept by the Japanese authorities were of sufficient scale to offset them. These balances indicated the close relationship between Schroders and the Japanese financial authorities in the mid-1950s, and when a request was received from them in January 1957 for additional credits to be made to

Japanese banks to relieve a credit shortage it received a positive response.[54]

Schroders also had notably close relations with the Bank of China, the leading Chinese overseas trade and foreign exchange bank, whose London branch was at 147 Leadenhall Street until 1963. Business between the firms had begun in the inter-war years, but broadened with the arrival of K. C. Wu as head of the London office in 1944. The nationalisation of the Bank of China following the Communist revolution in 1949 caused little disruption to the ties between the firms, though henceforth all contacts with the Peoples' Republic of China were dealt with by J. Henry Schroder & Co. while Schrobanco handled any business conducted with Taiwan. Assistance was rendered to several other overseas banks in the early stages of the establishment of a presence in London. In 1951, the Bank of Toronto and the First National Bank of Boston were provided with rooms at 145 Leadenhall Street and conducted their business from there until they were ready to move to their own premises, and the same service was provided for the National Bank of Nigeria in 1955–56. Another form of help was to provide training for the staff of correspondent banks and there were always numerous trainees from overseas around the building.

Prior to the war, Schroders had few clients in the British Empire but in the late 1940s and the 1950s the firm took an interest in developing contacts and business in the sterling area. In March 1948, soon after Indian independence, it opened credit lines for three indigenous banks to finance imports from Britain. The granting of independence to Ghana in 1957 prompted an initiative to foster relations with the newly established central bank, which led to the provision of training for a number of its officers. Relations with Nigerian institutions began in 1955 with the appointment of a former Schroders executive as assistant director of the Marketing and Exports Board.[55] This led to contacts with the administration of the Western Region, and in March 1956 an economic mission headed by the regional prime minister was entertained at Leadenhall Street and there were high hopes of substantial business.[56] Moreover, Schroders undertook to oversee the establishment of a London branch of the National Bank of Nigeria, which placed large balances with the firm. But neither relationship lived up to expectations and by the end of the decade the Nigerian connection had virtually disappeared.

The post-war years saw renewed efforts to expand Schroders' acceptance business with British clients. The leading role in these initiatives was taken by Alec Cairns, who became the foremost figure on the banking side of the business in the 1950s. A new feature of the firm's British acceptance business was the syndication of credits for leading

British companies amongst a group of merchant banks, since the scale of financing required by such firms had outgrown the capacity of individual City houses. David Forsyth recalled the way such credits were arranged in the 1950s:

> the routine was that you went to the head of the Discount Office at the Bank of England and said 'we have been commissioned to form a credit syndicate and we are thinking of asking so-and-so to join us'. In effect you were saying 'do you approve and have you any other names you'd like to chip in?'. Once or twice the Bank of England said 'Oh, do ask so-and-so to come in, they don't seem to have had much business for some time'. Then a partner picked up his bowler hat and went round to see the other firm and said 'would you be kind enough to help us out with this syndicate?' There was never any great discussion because the client was probably Cadburys or Rolls Royce or some such resounding name. It took less than five minutes and to get there you'd walked half way across the City. Bowler hats and all. Gordon Richardson was amazed by it when he joined us.[57]

Schroders' close connections with Pressed Steel and Joseph Lucas Industries led to its leadership of syndicates which provided credits for those firms, but for the most part it was a participant in syndicates led by other merchant banks, reflecting the relatively limited extent of its contacts with British industry, except the motor industry. The major syndicates in which Schroders was a participant during the 1940s and 1950s were those led by Lazards for Rootes and J. Lyons; by Rothschilds for Bowaters and Anglo-African Shipping; by Hambros for Trinidad Leaseholds and Regent Oil; by Kleinworts for BP; by Japhets for Bowmaker; by Barings for the Lancashire Cotton Corporation; by S. Montagu for Cadburys; by Morgan Grenfell for Imperial Tobacco; and by Guinness Mahon for Gallahers. Schroders' participations in these syndicates were generally in the range of £100,000–£300,000, though occasionally they were as much as £500,000 and even more for Pressed Steel. These were large commitments relative to the partners' capital, which averaged £2 million in the decade after the war, and in these years blue chip British corporate clients constituted a large part of Schroders' acceptance business. Government restrictions on lending by banks to curb inflationary pressures in the economy in 1955–57 – the 'credit squeeze' – led to increased demands for acceptance finance from British companies. Schroders responded cautiously to the flood of applications for acceptance facilities, informing one applicant, for instance, that the firm could only meet its request 'so long as we are not put in the position of eluding the "Butler Squeeze" '.[58] Nevertheless, Schroders was able to take advantage of the opportunities to expand its acceptance activity, and balance sheet acceptances increased from £5.8 million in 1954 to £8.4 million in 1957 (see Figure 11.2 on page 327).

A British client of the 1950s which merits special mention is the United Dominions Trust (UDT). This firm was established in the early 1920s, to conduct hire purchase finance, by John Gibson Jarvie who had learnt the business of consumer credit in the United States and pioneered its introduction to Britain. Wartime restictions put a stop to UDT's consumer credit business and it was not until the early 1950s that hire purchase business revived. In the meantime, Gibson Jarvie focused upon venture capital investments in small engineering companies, sometimes using Leadenhall Securities to introduce the firms to the market or to find private investors. Moreover, the Schroder partners provided him with information about investment opportunities that they believed might be attractive to UDT. The revival of the consumer credit side of UDT's business was financed by acceptances and advances provided by the merchant banks and the clearing banks. Schroders was just one of many houses furnishing such facilities, though by July 1952 UDT was already one of Schroders' larger clients, with a line of £200,000, and in April 1955 it was described as one of its 'better customers'.[59] In the meantime relations between the firms had taken several important turns. Early in 1953 Schroders introduced UDT to Pressed Steel, which required consumer credit facilities for purchasers of the Prestcold refrigerators that it was putting into production.[60] When in June 1954 Gibson Jarvie revived UDT's Canadian subsidiary, the United Dominions Corporation (UDC), Schroders and Schrobanco each subscribed 20 per cent of the recapitalised equity and Avery Rockefeller joined the UDC board to monitor these investments. The 'Canadian partnership' continued until 1963 when the Schroder interest was bought out by UDT because of a US regulatory problem. Given the multi-faceted relationship between the firms it was natural that when UDT decided to make a rights issue in August 1954 it was Schroders that acted as the issuing house.[61]

The early 1950s saw much discussion of the problem of the medium-term export finance 'gap'.[62] This was the alleged shortage of appropriate financing for capital goods, which were growing rapidly as a proportion of United Kingdom exports.[63] British firms complained that they were at a disadvantage to foreign competitors, whose financial institutions and governments were more supportive. The Schroder partners took an active interest in the issue and in the summer of 1952 suggested to Rothschilds the establishment of a joint venture to specialise in medium-term export finance, but Rothschilds declined, replying that they regarded the prospects as unpromising.[64] In September 1953 it was announced that Lazards, Erlangers and Morgan Grenfell, in conjunction with the Finance Corporation for Industry, had established Air Finance Limited, a joint venture to provide credits of up to three years for approved export orders for British aircraft. In November came news that another merchant bank had established the Manufacturers Export Finance Company (MEFC) to provide medium-term export finance for engineering firms. The news was received with some dismay at Schroders, since the initiative was almost identical to 'the scheme which we have been studying for so long and in which we have received so little encouragement from the Bank of England or Government Authorities'.[65] As recently as the week before the announcement of the formation of the MEFC Schroders had been trying to persuade the Westminster Bank to back just such a scheme, but without success.[66] Barclays Bank proved more receptive to Schroders' proposals and on Christmas Eve 1953 Abel Smith reported that an understanding had been reached and that Rothschilds, Barings and M. Samuel would probably participate, but this too came to nothing.[67]

The Schroder partners decided to go it alone and early in 1954 established the Westphere Trading Company. Immediately the firm received inquiries regarding medium-term export finance from Pressed Steel, on behalf of a Frankfurt firm that wished to purchase 6,000 Prestcold refrigerators for the German market. Moreover, the Ford Motor Company of Britain, with which fruitless discussions had been held since 1946 regarding the finance of the export of cars manufactured at Dagenham on a similar basis to that which Schrobanco operated so successfully for American car exporters to Latin America, applied for credit for its Cypriot agent. Medium-term export finance was also an issue in the US, and in October 1954 came the news of the establishment of the American Overseas Finance Corporation, an undertaking backed by the Chase National Bank of New York. Norbert Bogdan, who had left Schrobanco several years earlier, was appointed chief executive.

Of all the commodities whose shipment was financed by J. Henry Schroder & Co. in the post-war years, the one most frequently mentioned in the minutes of the officers' meetings was wool. At the end of the war there were large stocks of wool in Britain which the government was eager to have processed and exported to earn foreign exchange. Since British woollen mills were operating at full capacity moves were made to contract foreign plants to process the wool. Schroders became involved in one such scheme organised by the Bradford woollens firm, Andrews & May, which proposed to export raw wool to an Italian mill that would make it into cloth for export to America. The wool was to remain British-owned throughout the manufacturing process, and remuneration for the Italians was to be in wool not sterling.[68] The Schroder partners were taken with the ingenuity of the scheme and sought technical advice on its feasibility from another Bradford firm, S. H. Rawnsley Ltd, who put 'their wool expert friend from Addis Ababa' at Schroders disposal.[69] However, the consultant reported unfavourably on the quality of Italian finished cloth and the proposal was rejected. A similar project was put to the firm a year later by another Bradford firm, the Wool Trading Company Ltd, though this time the processing was to take place in the Soviet Zone of Germany.[70] The Export Credits Guarantee Department furnished 100 per cent support for the business, and Schroders provided a credit of £30,000. Subsequently further processing contracts were entered into by the Wool Trading Company with firms in Belgium and Holland, and Schroders increased its commitment by a further £40,000.[71] For most of the 1950s it provided modestly-sized credits to several Bradford wool merchants and manufacturers but business waned towards the end of the decade due to the decline of the industry because of foreign competition.

In September 1946, Lada-Mocarski telephoned from Paris to alert 145 Leadenhall Street to the discussions which were taking place regarding the finance of French wool imports, the large French woollens industry constituting a quarter of the world's manufacturing capacity and requiring annual imports of raw wool from the British Empire costing £35 million.[72] But it was Lazards which got the business, it being announced in January 1947 that the firm was arranging an anormous £12.5 million revolving credit to finance purchases up to a maximum of £50 million over a twelve-month period. At the time the French wool credit was the largest post-war facility for the supply of Empire raw materials to continental manufacturing industries, being hailed as 'a big step forward in London's efforts to set the wheels of international commerce turning again'.[73] The facility was divided amongst a large syndicate, including Schroders, which received an allocation of £250,000. Participation in the French wool credit continued until the late 1950s, though in the latter years the facility was on a rather smaller scale. Schroders also participated in the large credits arranged to finance purchases of British Empire wool by Lohmann & Co. of Amsterdam for Scandinavia in 1947, by Kleinworts for Poland in 1948, and by Warburgs for Czechoslovakia and Barclays for Italy in 1949.[74]

Schroders' important connection with the Finnish wool industry began in December 1948 when the head of a firm of Bradford export agents, K. Nettl & Co., called to introduce a representative of Yllefabrifernas Inkops Kontor, the central purchasing organisation of the wool spinners of Finland.[75] Three weeks later the firm agreed to give Yllefabrifernas a £300,000 90-day credit, which was arranged on the basis of a 90 per cent ECGD guarantee and a 10 per cent deposit by the

Finns.[76] The following year the line was increased to £700,000 and in 1950 it reached £1 million on a 120-day basis, the longest term the Bank of England would sanction.[77] Remarkably, the whole of the line was provided by Schroders, even though the firm's capital was only £1.9 million. In 1951, the Finns requested that the credit should be increased to £2 million and Schroders successfully obtained the necessary official consents, though not without a tussle with the Treasury. Participations of £250,000 were offered to Barings, Hambros, Lazards and Rothschilds, which were gladly accepted.[78] In return for making these arrangements Schroders suggested that the Bank of Finland, the central bank, should place part of its sterling balances with the firm, and the directors of Yllefabrifernas supported the requests, arguing that 'it was fair that Schroders should have such deposits in view of the credits to the country's wool industry'.[79] Accordingly, in November 1951, £500,000 was transferred from the Bank of Finland's account at the Bank of England to Schroders and a few months later the deposit was increased to £1 million, which amounted to 13 per cent of the firm's total balances and deposits at the end of 1952, though in subsequent years the sums were less substantial.

The large Finnish deposits coincided with the reopening of the London foreign exchange market in December 1951, another reason for the placement of the funds with Schroders, which as an 'authorised dealer' was able to act on behalf of the central bank in the market. J. Henry Schroder & Co. built up its foreign exchange dealing capacity in the 1950s as a matter of deliberate policy in order to be able to offer this service to foreign banks to entice them to establish correspondent relationships, boosting its balances. This strategy was inspired by the example of Schrobanco, and its implementation was assisted by Ernest Meili, who undertook to market the services of the London firm to his important contacts amongst the Swiss banks once the firm had developed 'an excellent FX department'.[80] In 1952, Schroders sent Rudi Weisweiller, a recent recruit who as an Oxford undergraduate had been president of the Union, to Schrobanco for six months to learn the business.[81] In the early 1950s, J. Henry Schroder & Co.'s foreign exchange department comprised only three dealers but it established a very visible presence and strong reputation in the market.

Cairns was quick to recognise the potential of Euro-dollars and Schroders was an early participant in the Euro-dollar market, applying its expertise in forward foreign exchange in the new market. It was one of the first banks to extend offshore deposit-taking to the DM, the Swiss franc, and other currencies. The dynamic development of Schroders' foreign exchange activities in the late 1950s owed much to Ernest Ingold, an experienced Swiss foreign exchange dealer who joined the firm in

1954 and was made head of the team in 1960. In the second half of the 1950s foreign exchange operations made substantial contributions to the profits of J. Henry Schroder & Co.

Corporate Finance and Investment Management

The provision of corporate finance services became a more and more important aspect of Schroders' activities in the late 1940s and the 1950s. In these years Schrobanco and Schrotrust paid the London firm fees of around £20,000 per annum to act as their London representative. They also directed a procession of American businessmen seeking advice on the establishment of European subsidiaries to 145 Leadenhall Street, and J. Henry Schroder & Co. was very actively involved with several US corporations in the late 1940s and early 1950s. One of them was Schrobanco's client the US Time Corporation, whose runaway success with the cheap Timex watch led the firm to decide to establish a British subsidiary, turning to Schroders for guidance through the maze of British regulations, and for assistance with financing the project. Abel Smith conducted the negotiations with the British authorities which resulted in the clearance for the formation of a wholly-owned subsidiary, UK Time, in the early summer of 1946. Funds totalling £130,000 for the construction of a plant at Dundee were advanced to UK Time by Schroders, against the security of a note by US Time endorsed by Schrobanco. In the spring of 1947, with the plant completed and the training of the workforce coming to an end, Schroders and Hambros gave a joint credit of £50,000 to provide working capital. Production began in July, and by November the factory was producing 75,000 watches per month.

Schroders conducted new issues for forty-five British companies between 1946 and 1960. Longstanding ties, whose origins are discussed in other chapters, explain the connections with half a dozen of these clients – Sena Sugar Estates, which made issues in 1945 and 1952; the Continental and Industrial Trust, in 1951 and 1955; British Petroleum, in 1957; David Allen & Sons, in 1946; and Franco Signs, in 1945 and 1958. But the great majority were new clients, personal connections of the partners being the usual source of introduction. For Whitbread, the brewers, Schroders undertook a capital reconstruction prior to a very successful stock market flotation, which enhanced its standing in the City. In all, six issues were made for Whitbread. Other firms for which it conducted several issues were Tube Investments, engineers; Lilley & Skinner, shoe retailers; Lewis Berger, paint manufacturers; F. W. Berk, chemical manufacturers; Consolidated Goldfields; and Asquith Machine

Tool. The funds raised by the Asquith Machine Tool issue of 1955 were used to purchase another company – J. Henry Schroder & Co.'s first experience of managing a corporate acquisition.

In the late 1940s and early 1950s, Schroders organised two or three issues per annum, which generated an average profit of around £6,000 each – about £85,000 in 1990 money – the largest profit from a single deal being the £14,500 made on an issue for the brewers, Fremlins, in 1949. Schroders' participations in the 'Consortium', the syndicate of merchant banks which effected the denationalisation of the steel industry, boosted issuing profits to £69,000 in 1954, in which year the firm made six issues. In the second half of the 1950s Schroders conducted seven to nine new issues per annum, making average profits of £9,000 per issue. In 1957, it made £133,000 on nine issues, including £41,000 on its participation in the £41 million debenture issue for BP undertaken jointly with Morgan Grenfell and Robert Fleming, which at the time was the largest corporate capital-raising exercise ever mounted in the City. In 1958 and 1959 Schroders made numerous small-scale issues, generating profits of around £85,000 per annum. Issuing profits soared to £203,000 – about £2 million in 1990 money – in 1960 when it conducted seventeen issues for British companies, a spectacular start to the new decade.

In the 1930s the name of J. Henry Schroder & Co. had appeared on prospectuses for the issue of fixed interest securities for blue-chip companies and local authorities, but introductions to the market and capital-raising exercises by small firms were conducted by the subsidiary Leadenhall Securities. After the war there was a reallocation of responsibilities, Schroders taking charge of all issues for listed companies and Leadenhall Securities handling listings and sub-underwriting participations. Leadenhall Securities was run by Edward (Tommy) Tucker who had joined Schroders in 1919 as a junior clerk and had been its company secretary since the formation of the firm in 1935. It resumed venture capital activities in the late 1940s, pursuing a policy decided in November 1945 of investment in established private companies that required additional capital, but avoiding start-ups.[82] The usual formula was to take a small equity interest and to provide a large preference share investment, thereby securing, as far as possible, a reliable minimum return and some protection from risk as well as participation in runaway success. A number of successful investments were made in the late 1940s, but in the early 1950s venture capital activity waned and by the middle of the decade sub-underwriting had become the firm's principal business.

A notable venture capital initiative that was conducted independently of Leadenhall Securities, though Tucker was charged with its administration, was English Farms Ltd. This firm was formed in

January 1948 for the purpose of investing in agricultural land. It was the brainchild of Perth and Abel Smith, who brought together a group of affluent individuals attracted by the tax concessions available upon this form of investment.[83] The company had a subscribed capital of £250,000, of which Schroders put up 10 per cent. Land was purchased in Wiltshire and Buckinghamshire during 1948 and 1949, and further properties were acquired in 1952. English Farms took an active interest in the management of its properties and provided funds for agricultural improvement. When Schroders' investment was sold in the early 1970s the shares were worth ten times what had been paid in 1948 – a four-fold increase, on an inflation-adjusted basis.

Much the most important point of contact between Schroders and British manufacturing industry from the 1920s to the 1960s was the Pressed Steel company, of which Major Pam served as chairman from 1930 to 1955, and Abel Smith from 1955 to 1967. During the 1950s the firm went from strength to strength because of booming British car production and strong demand for its railway goods wagons, a new wagon leaving a Pressed Steel plant every eight minutes in 1958. Two new plants were opened and issues to raise capital to finance expansion were made in 1955, 1957 and 1960, conducted by Schroders. Acting together in 1950–51 the firms undertook a rescue operation for the troubled windscreen manufacturer, British Indestructo Glass, reorganising and recapitalising the company and installing John Mallabar as chairman.[84] The Pressed Steel connection was the origin of Schroders' close relations with British motor manufacturers that led to issues on behalf of Rover in 1952 and 1960, and five for Standard Motors.

The relationship with Pressed Steel was in the minds of the Schroder partners when Harry Ferguson, the designer of the revolutionary Ferguson tractor lunched at the firm in June 1945.[85] Ferguson tractors were already in production in the US and Ferguson, who was already lobbying the government for a steel quota, was looking for a partner with which to begin manufacture in his native country.[86] Henry Tiarks was inspired by Ferguson's plans and over the next couple of months he and others acted as advisers to Ferguson, leading to an arrangement with Standard Motors, the Coventry based car-maker run by Sir John Black. In October 1945, Schroders and Helbert, Wagg jointly made an issue for Standard Motors to finance the commencement of the production of Ferguson tractors, the first joint business by the City firms.[87]

Further joint issues on behalf of Standard Motors were conducted in 1948, 1956, 1958 and 1960. In 1950, Helbert, Wagg offered Schroders a participation in an issue on behalf of Tube Investments (TI) on account of advisory services for the TI chairman provided by Perth, though the invitation was presented as a reciprocal gesture for the Standard Motors participation.[88] Schroders protested at being treated as a junior partner and it was on an equal basis that the firms conducted further issues for TI in 1955, 1957, 1958 and 1960, and became comrades in arms during the British Aluminium take-over battle of 1958–59. Through these corporate finance connections the executives of Schroders and Helbert, Wagg became quite well acquainted with each other in the latter years of the 1950s, which assisted their subsequent merger, though the relationship was by no means so special as to make the combination of the firms in 1960 an inevitable development.

The decade and a half after the war saw a considerable development of Schroders' investment management activities. Throughout the period the most important clients remained the Continental and Industrial Trust (CONTI), International Holdings and Hydro-Electric Securities. In the early 1950s Jonathan Backhouse took over the direction of Schroders' investment management activities from Major Pam, though Pam continued to influence decisions until his death in September 1955. The post-war performance of CONTI, where Backhouse succeeded Pam as chairman, was impressive, and further capital was raised in 1951 and 1955. A subsidiary company, Quartius, was formed in March 1950 to conduct short-term finance operations, a replacement for the Tertius Trust that had been sold in 1943 for tax reasons. International Holdings and Hydro-Electric Securities also fared well and an analysis conducted in 1954 showed that their performance matched that of the leading American trusts.[89] London's role in the administration of these investment trusts was limited in the post-war era, since responsibility for managing them had been transferred to Schrobanco in 1941. Nevertheless the provision of services in connection with their European investments generated useful fees.

Immediately after the war, in October 1945, Schroders launched a drive to recruit new clients for the firm's trustee services, which led to an increase in the scale of its private client work, and throughout the 1950s there was an important private client side to its investment management activity. Schroders' entree into institutional investment management was made in June 1947, when Whitbread accepted the Schroder Executor & Trustee Company Ltd's bid to replace Lloyds Bank as trustee and investment adviser. Up to that time, the Whitbread pension fund's investments had been restricted to UK government bonds and it was Schroders' proposals for diversifying into equities that won the business for the firm. Another milestone in the development of Schroders' fund management activities was being entrusted with the portfolio of the Gardeners' Royal Benevolent Institution in March 1950. In the second half of the 1950s Schroders began actively to pitch for pension fund business, with success towards the end of the decade.

Financial Performance

As ever, a variety of yardsticks may be used to measure the progress of J. Henry Schroder & Co. in the decade and a half after the war. In these years staff numbers nearly trebled, rising from around a hundred to 280. Total assets rose almost sixfold, from £5 million to £28 million, an increase of about three-and-a-half times on an inflation-adjusted basis. This was an impressively resilient recovery, the rate of Schroders' growth exceeding that of any of the other leading London merchant banks for which information is available. At the end of the war, when the firm was almost dormant, its total assets were decidedly smaller than its peers: half the size of Morgan Grenfell's; a sixth of Barings'; and a tenth of Hambros', the largest of the accepting houses in the 1940s and 1950s (see Table 11.3). By 1955, with the recovery of the Standstill debts, J. Henry Schroder & Co.'s total assets were £24 million, surpassing Morgan Grenfell's, and the gap with Lazards and Barings was closing, though Hambros remained the sector leader by a large margin. At the end of the decade, Schroders' total assets were £28 million, still a little behind Barings and Lazards and a long way short of Hambros, but substantially

Table 11.3   Total assets[1] of some leading merchant banks 1945, 1955, 1959

31 December	1945 £ million	1955 £ million	1959 £ million
J. Henry Schroder & Co.	5	24	28
Baring Brothers & Co. Ltd	24	30	33
Hambros Bank Ltd†	38	85	108
Lazard Brothers	n/a	27	32
Morgan Grenfell & Co.	11	23	24
S. G. Warburg & Co. Ltd	n/a	n/a	13
All Members of the Accepting Houses Committee	n/a	294	425

1. Including acceptances
† 31 March following year
n/a = not available
Note: Information on other firms unavailable.

Sources: J. Henry Schroder & Co., balance sheets; Hambros, Barings, Lazards, S. G. Warburg – filed accounts, Companies House; Kathleen Burk, *Morgan Grenfell 1838–1988* (Oxford University Press, 1989) p. 281; Accepting Houses Committee – *Bank of England Statistical Abstract*.

ahead of Morgan Grenfell and Warburgs (which had just acquired Seligman Bros). From 1951, statistics of the total assets of all the twenty or so members of the Accepting Houses Committee were published by the Bank of England. That year, J. Henry Schroder & Co.'s balance sheet constituted 6.1 per cent of the total, but it grew in subsequent years, and in 1951–59 overall it averaged 7.8 per cent. Comparisons between Schroders and the other London merchant banks are problematic, because none of the other firms had a large US operation. When the Schrobanco balance sheet is added to J. Henry Schroder & Co. balance sheet a different picture emerges of the respective sizes of the London merchant banks. The combined assets of J. Henry Schroder & Co. and Schrobanco were £33 million in 1945, £93 million in 1955, and £99 million in 1959, similar levels to Hambros.

Salaries and wages constituted about three-quarters of the running costs of the firm in the post-war years. Staff remuneration rose at a rather faster rate than staff numbers over the period, rising from £100,000 to £400,000, a reflection of increased skill levels amongst Schroders' workforce and higher rates of remuneration. Total costs included occasional very large financial adjustments in respect of factors such as charges for losses on securities, depreciation and taxation. These caused erratic variations in total costs from year to year, which led to the fluctuations in net profits that are a feature of Figure 11.3. Although an upward trend is discernable, progress in the years 1945–55 was very uneven and in 1955 the firm even made a loss as a result of capital losses of £395,000 on the gilt portfolio. In these years, net profits averaged

Figure 11.3   J. Henry Schroder & Co., net profits, 1945–58

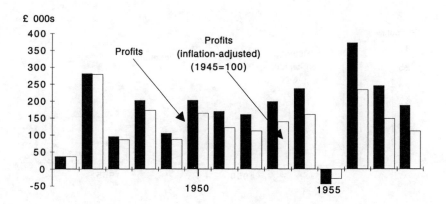

£149,000 per annum. In 1956 net profits leapt to £371,000 – about £4 million in 1990 money – and over the years 1956–58 they averaged £268,000 per annum.

Between December 1945 and April 1957 the partners' capital of J. Henry Schroder & Co. grew from £778,000 to £3.7 million, an increase of £2.9 million. Over the same period, profits totalled approximately £2.3 million. The balance of the increase in partners' capital derived from Standstill debt recoveries, which came back into the firm via the family trust, the Veritas Trust. This process had come to an end by the beginning of 1957, permitting Helmut to complete the conversion of the firm into a private limited company, whose share capital upon incorporation on 1 May 1957, following debt repayments and withdrawals, totalled £2.2 million. By December 1959 through retentions from profits plus some further financial adjustments, the firm's equity was again £3.7 million.

The return on capital (Figure 11.4) fluctuated considerably in 1945–55 because of variations in profits and the fitful growth of partners' capital. In 1945–49 it averaged 11.6 per cent (boosted by the anomalously high level of 1946), providing an 8.6 per cent nominal premium over the 3 per cent average return on consols, and a real rate of return of 7.4 per cent. In 1950–55 the nominal rate of return averaged 6.9 per cent, but interest rates and inflation were also higher in these years, the former climbing to 4 per cent in 1952 and 4.5 per cent in 1955, and the latter averaging 4.4 per cent. Thus the average real return in 1950–55 was 2.3 per cent, a barely satisfactory risk premium. The firm's performance in 1956–58

Figure 11.4 J. Henry Schroder & Co., return on capital and annual rate of inflation, 1945–58

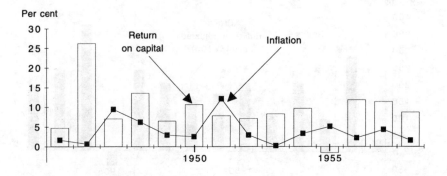

Note: The 'real' return on capital is the difference between the nominal return on capital depicted above and the annual rate of inflation.

surpassed the earlier post-war years, the rate of return being boosted in 1957 by the withdrawal of capital upon the conversion from the partnership to the private company. In these years the nominal rate of return averaged 10.7 per cent, which provided a respectable real rate of return, since inflation averaged only 2 per cent per annum.

Management Changes and Creation of Schroders Limited

Early in 1957, much to his surprise, Lord Perth received an invitation to join Harold Macmillan's cabinet. By coincidence, Helmut Schroder had recently decided that Perth should be given a title in the firm which publicly acknowledged his role as chief executive, though no announcement had been made. Perth consulted the Governor of the Bank of England and Lord Lyttleton, who strongly advised him to seize the opportunity to join the Cabinet, while Helmut left him free to make up his own mind.[90] Leaving the partners with whom he had worked to rebuild Schroders for eleven years was a difficult decision, but he decided to accept the new challenge, and in January 1957 became Minister of State for Colonial Affairs, an appointment resulting from the favourable impression he made as a participant in the conference to determine the future of Malta in 1955. Perth's resignation left the partnership 'rather bare', as Backhouse put it, and immediately a search began to find a suitable replacement.[91] A few weeks later Backhouse met Gordon Richardson at lunch at Helbert, Wagg and invited him to lunch at Schroders, 'and the next thing I knew,' recalled Richardson, 'Helmut was asking me if I would be a partner'.[92] Schroders was not the only City firm eager to acquire Richardson's services, and most of the advice he received spoke in favour of a rival offer. Nevertheless, it was Helmut's invitation he accepted. 'There was something very agreeable about Schroders,' he reflected. 'I talked to the people and they were very nice, and of course it was after the German debt settlement so the agonies, so-to-speak, were over. The situation offered a tremendous challenge.'

Gordon Richardson was born in Nottingham in 1915, the son of a comfortably-off local provision merchant. In 1934 he went to Gonville and Caius College, Cambridge, where he read Law, a subject that appealed to him because of a strong sense of standards imbued by his mother and because it led towards a professional qualification. Upon graduation he worked for a year under articles in a solicitor's office, but being a member of the Territorial Army he was called up immediately the Second World War broke out. In the army he held a series of staff posts which he fulfilled with distinction, being awarded an MBE in 1944. By the time of his demobilisation he had decided to become a barrister and was called to the Bar in 1946, joining the chambers of Montagu Gedge, the pre-eminent company law practitioner of the day, in Lincoln's Inn. Richardson quickly built up a successful practice as counsel specialising in company law, and so highly was he thought of by many of his clients that they subsequently transferred their business to Schroders upon his appointment as a partner, a notable example being Land Securities Investment Trust. In 1955, aged 40, Richardson decided to leave the Bar and pursue a career in the City. At the invitation of the chairman of the Industrial and Commercial Finance Corporation (ICFC), Lord Piercy, he joined the organisation working with Piercy and the general manager, John Kinross. Richardson had been informally led to expect that he would succeed Piercy as chairman of ICFC, but when it became plain that Piercy, despite his 71 years, had no intention of early retirement Richardson began to look for other opportunities, at which point he met Backhouse.

Soon after Richardson's arrival, Helmut Schroder asked him to undertake a fundamental review of the functioning of the firm. Every officer was required to submit a description of his job and to make suggestions to improve the running of the firm; 'writing your own death warrant' was how one of them described the exercise. Richardson, with assistance from Patrick Jerome, a manager in the Banking Department, and David Ogilvy, a manager in the Investment Department, analysed the returns and put together a plan of reform. He also drew on advice from Cooper Brothers, one of the leading City accountancy firms, whose senior partner, Henry Benson, was a personal friend. Cooper Brothers became Schroders' auditors and prepared a report on the financial management of the firm, which identified the need to create the position of financial controller and to appoint a qualified chartered accountant to occupy it. Richardson insisted on advertising the post to ensure the recruitment of the best possible candidate, much to the astonishment of his partners since recruitment to senior positions at merchant banks was never conducted by advertisement. The outcome was the appointment in 1959 of John Bayley, who was very strongly backed by Cooper Brothers and deeply impressed Richardson. Aged 36, Bayley had served in the Navy during the war and trained with the accountants Peat Marwick Mitchell, joining the engineering firm S. Smith & Sons (England) Ltd in 1951 and subsequently the Sperry Gyroscope Co. Ltd as financial controller. Bayley agreed to take the job for a maximum of five years, but in fact stayed with the firm for the rest of his career and was a key figure in the development of Schroders. A complementary step to Bayley's recruitment was the professionalisation of the firm's internal audit function, which was achieved by the appointment of Peter Bulfield, a 29-year-old chartered accountant from a banking family background.

Richardson was also eager to build up the corporate finance side of Schroders' activities and to this end he brought in John Hull, aged 32, who had been with him in chambers. With these professionally qualified, energetic and relatively youthful people in managerial positions the time had come for the retirement of some of the older staff who lacked the skills or outlook fitting to the new times.

Upon Perth's resignation Abel Smith became chairman of the officers' morning meeting. However, his position was not that of chief executive, but *primus inter pares* with Backhouse, his alternate as chairman of the daily assemblies, and the energetic Richardson. This triumverate, with the backing of Helmut Schroder and executive support from Cairns, Caulfeild, Hood and Tucker, who was promoted to the partnership at the same time as Richardson to pre-empt resentment amongst the staff at the introduction of an outsider, ran the firm with great success in 1957–60. The enhanced profitability of these years facilitated another important development, the creation of a publicly quoted holding company in 1959.

By the end of the 1950s the capital position of the firm was secure and unencumbered, and new considerations such as the diversification of assets, the development of liquidity to enable the payment of death duties, and the minimisation of such tax liabilities, became priorities for Helmut Schroder and his sisters. These considerations had already led to the sale by the Schroder and Tiarks families of 10 per cent of the shares of Schrobanco, Schrotrust and Schroroc to Barings in March 1951, to raise cash. In the spring of 1958, Richardson, with assistance internally from Backhouse, Hull and Bernard Knight, a manager on the corporate finance side of the business, and externally from Henry Benson of Cooper Brothers, conducted a thorough review of the situation.[93] Three strategies were considered; the sale of a further portion of Schrobanco shares, which would raise cash and establish a valuation in the over-the-counter market in New York; the sale of an interest in the London firm through a placement with institutions; the sale to the public of shares in a new company formed for the purpose of acting as a holding company for the London and New York interests. It was the last of these options which was adopted, for reasons outlined in an internal report of July 1959:

> We consider that the main source of strength of the Schroder businesses is that their ownership and control are at present in roughly the same hands. It is a major attraction of the holding company proposed that this situation is preserved and, indeed, improved. We consider that if it were necessary to sell shares in Schrobanco and SchroLondon, the time would come when the two businesses would fall apart.[94]

In June 1958, Richardson produced a 'Basic Plan' for the reorganisation of the firms preliminary to a public issue of shares of the new holding company, Schroders Limited (the abbreviation Ltd never being used in this context by the firm). It was to be registered in England and quoted on the London Stock Exchange, and was to own the whole of the capital of J. Henry Schroder & Co. Ltd, the J. Henry Schroder Banking Corporation, the Schroder Trust Company, and Schroder Rockefeller, and would also be available as an entity to own any subsidiaries created in the future. The valuation of the Schroder family's interest in its London and New York firms was a very complex matter that was entrusted to Cooper Brothers. When cross-share-holdings were unravelled the value of the London firm was attributed 83 per cent to the Schroder family and 17 per cent to the 'B' shares held by the senior executives. With respect to the New York firms, the Schroder family owned 81.3 per cent, the Tiarks family 8.4 per cent, and Barings 10.3 per cent. The allocation of shares in the holding company was made on the basis that the New York firms comprised 65 per cent of the value of the new entity and the London firm 35 per cent. 'This apportionment,' explained a report by Cooper Brothers, 'is a compromise between net assets at break-up value, where the relative percentages are 73 per cent American and 27 per cent English, and earnings, where the percentages are 59 per cent and 41 per cent.'[95] The book value of the group was £11.4 million – £120 million in 1990 money – of which the New York firms represented £8.2 million and the London firm £3.2 million.

Schroders Limited was formed in September 1959 for the purpose of acquiring these assets. It was capitalised at a nominal value of £5,000,000 divided into 5 million £1 ordinary shares. As a result of the exchanges of shares, the shareholders of Schroders Limited just prior to the initial public offering were the Schroder family (including its trusts and settlements) 82.5 per cent, the Tiarks family 5.9 per cent, the London executive partners 5.2 per cent, and Barings 6.4 per cent. On 24 September 1959, it was announced that 750,000 shares, 15 per cent of the equity, were to be sold to the public. These were shares held by one of the Schroder family companies, and as a result the family's interest fell to 67.5 per cent of the new holding company. No additional funds were raised for the firm through the public offer, which was motivated not by the need to raise further capital for the business but rather by the family's tax planning and liquidity considerations. The price was 32/6d per share, which put a market capitalisation on the firm of £8,125,000 compared to a book value of £11.4 million, the sale price valuation thus representing a 30 per cent discount to book value. In the prospectus the combined pre-tax profits of the London and New York firms in 1958 was stated as £1,117,000 – £12 million in 1990 money – which meant that the firm was valued at 7.5 times pre-tax profits. The directors forecast a gross dividend of 6 per cent of nominal value and commented that 'it is intended to pursue a conservative dividend policy and to maintain adequate reserves'.[96] At the issue price the shares yielded 3.7 per cent, which was over three times covered by earnings. The broker to the issue was Cazenove & Co. 'Apply Early' was the advice offered to the public by the *Daily Mail*, other press comment being equally positive, and investors rushed to take advantage of the offer which was eighteen times over-subscribed.[97] Applications by the public were drastically scaled down and a ballot was held amongst applicants for less than 1,000 shares. However, staff applications were allocated in full, save for a few very large ones, and the firm made loans to staff to enable them to purchase the shares.

The public offering and the listing of Schroders Limited shares in September 1959 marked the end of an era in the history of the firm. For much of the 1930s, 1940s, and 1950s J. Henry Schroder & Co. was illiquid and it continued only because of the willingness of the family to support the firm with funds secured on their interest in the New York firm. These years spanned the prime of Helmut Schroder's business career and Schroders' survival was due to his determination more than to any other factor, but inevitably this achievement provided less satisfaction than the dynamic expansion of the firm, which was the accomplishment of the preceding and succeeding generations. However, despite the losses of the 1930s, the asset write-offs, inflation, and the high rates of taxation, the £11.4 million book value of Schroders Limited at the time of the public issue was only a third less in inflation-adjusted terms than the £6 million combined book value of J. Henry Schroder & Co., London, and the J. Henry Schroder Banking Corporation, New York, on 31 December 1930. Such was the achievement of Helmut Schroder and his partners in New York and London.

The years 1931–59 saw the supremacy of the J. Henry Schroder Banking Corporation relative to J. Henry Schroder & Co. In 1930 the London firm represented 62 per cent of the combined book value of the firms, but in 1946 it was only 34 per cent. At the time of the public issue the London firm represented just 27 per cent of the book value of Schroders Limited, reflecting the more dynamic expansion of the US interests in the 1950s and the enhanced value of the dollar relative to the pound after the 1949 devaluation of the pound from $4.03 to $2.80. In retrospect it is remarkable that in the 1950s the New York firm was almost three times the size of the London merchant bank with which the Schroder name was associated first and foremost. But in fact it was Schrobanco that sustained Schroders' position as an international merchant bank during the 1930s, 1940s and 1950s. Nevertheless, the establishment of the holding company in New York rather than London was not entertained for several reasons. The regulatory environment in Britain was considerably less restrictive, permitting the London firm to develop investment banking activities in addition to its commercial banking business. If the holding company had been established in New York, by contrast, the Glass–Steagall Act and the Bank Holding Company legislation would have severely restricted the group's development outside the United States as well as within. Furthermore, in the market, Schroders was recognised as a London- based firm with a US associate, not the other way round.

The public offering coincided with the opening of the new era in the City. The 1960s saw the re-establishment of London as the world's leading international financial entrepôt based upon the dynamic development of the new international financial markets and the world economy. Moreover, domestic demand for financial services was also growing fast. The revival measures already undertaken by the firm enabled it to take advantage of the new opportunities, and the acquisition of Helbert, Wagg & Co. at the beginning of the new decade greatly enhanced its position.

12

Helbert, Wagg & Co.

1848–1962

Helbert, Wagg & Co. was formed in 1848 by two London stockbrokers, John Helbert and his nephew John Wagg. For sixty-four years it conducted business as a firm of stockbrokers but this came to an end in 1912 with the resignation of the partners from membership of the London Stock Exchange. Since the 1860s it had been active in the issuing and underwriting of securities and it was on this activity that the partners focused after 1912. Firms such as Schroders, Barings and Rothschilds combined issuing and underwriting with acceptance business, and were called accepting houses or merchant banks on account of the latter activity. Helbert, Wagg, like other firms which conducted issuing and underwriting but which did not have an acceptance activity, was known as an 'issuing house'.

Issuing and underwriting could be highly profitable, but the volume of business varied greatly from year to year and so the issuing houses pursued other activities to generate regular income to meet overheads. Helbert, Wagg developed investment management services from the 1920s and was one of the pioneers of institutional fund management after the Second World War. It was also one of the first firms in the City to develop its issuing and underwriting activities into fully-fledged, recognisably modern corporate finance services. Helbert Wagg's pre-eminence in these activities made it a perfect match for Schroders' strengths in banking, and at the start of the 1960s the firms merged to form Schroder Wagg. The omission of the name Helbert from the name of the new firm is a clue to the identity of the family which played the leading role in the development of Helbert, Wagg & Co., and it is the story of the Wagg family that is the starting point of the history of the firm.

Like many Jewish financial families, the origins of the Wagg family can be traced to Frankfurt-am-Main, which had the largest Jewish community in Germany in the sixteenth and seventeenth centuries. The community there grew and prospered thanks to the absence of anti-Semitic violence and in the eighteenth and nineteenth centuries offshoots of successful Frankfurt Jewish families were established in other cities. In 1565, ancestors of the Wagg family took up residence in Frankfurt and displayed outside their house a sign depicting a pair of golden scales, *Waage*, anglicised in time as Wagg.[1] At the beginning of the eighteenth century members of the family moved to London, though information about them is scant. The first to arrive appears to have been Moses Wagg, who had evidently taken up residence in the City by 1705 for in that year he was fined for refusing to serve as a collector for the poor in the parish of St Catherine Cree, the appointment of Jews and Nonconformists to parish offices being a common contemporary practice by Anglicans for the enrichment of parochial funds. In 1721 Moses achieved the disreputable distinction of being the first person to perpetrate a fraudulent stock transfer at the Bank of England.[2] He fled to Frankfurt and successfully avoided apprehension by the British authorities, though he spent thirteen years in gaol there while his extradition was disputed. Meir Wagg, a younger brother, also moved to London, and family tradition has it that it was thanks to his advice that Sir Robert Walpole, the future Prime Minister, avoided ruin in the South Sea Bubble stock market crash in 1719. Records of the Duke's Place Synagogue reveal that he played an active part in the affairs of the Jewish community in London in the early eighteenth century, serving as treasurer to the congregation in 1712–22.

The first member of the Wagg family to settle permanently in London appears to have been Baruch Wagg, the younger brother of Moses and Meir. His son was another Moses, whose offspring were a daughter and a son named Hyman. All that is known about Hyman Wagg is that he lived in Lamb's Conduit Street, Bloomsbury, outside the City, where he conducted business as a jeweller. He married Mary Israel, the daughter of Israel Israel, a City bullion dealer (see Figure 12.1). Hyman Wagg died in 1803 and Mary in 1806, leaving two orphaned children, Judith and John. They were adopted by their uncle, John Helbert, the brother of Mary Wagg. John Helbert had changed his surname from Israel to Helbert, a name derived from the German town of Halberstadt, the family's place of origin. The Helberts became a distinguished Anglo-Jewish family and by the end of the nineteenth century possessed an English coat of arms.[3] John Helbert married Adeline Cohen, a daughter of Levi Barent Cohen, the 'arch ancestor' of the City's leading Jewish families, whose descendants constituted something of an aristocracy amongst English Jewry.[4] Another of Levi Barent Cohen's daughters married Nathan Mayer Rothschild, the founder of N. M. Rothschild & Sons; another Sir Moses Montefiore, Rothschild's closest business associate; and yet another Samuel Moses Samuel, whose daughters became the wives of leading Jewish financiers. Levi Barent Cohen's second son, Solomon Cohen, married Hannah Samuel, and in 1836 their daughter, Harriet, married John Helbert's nephew, John Wagg. Thus both John Helbert and John Wagg were related to prominent Jewish City families, including the Rothschilds, through marriage.

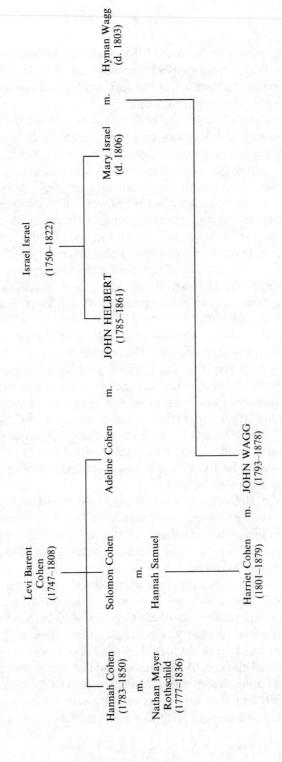

Figure 12.1 Simplified family tree showing connections between the Helbert, Wagg and other leading Jewish families

m. married

Name in capital letters indicates partner of Helbert, Wagg & Co.

Helbert, Wagg & Co., Stockbrokers, 1848–1912

John Helbert, who was born in 1785, was a City stockbroker. His nephew, John Wagg, born in 1793, served as clerk to his uncle and in 1823 himself became a member of the London Stock Exchange, trading as a broker in his own name for a quarter of a century. The only other piece of information about his early life is that in 1816, aged 23, he joined the Moira Lodge, a City freemasons' lodge.[5] John Wagg prospered and became a well-known figure in the Jewish community, being a signatory to the Address in Favour of the Removal of the Civil Disabilities of the Jews, which was presented to the government in 1833.[6] Although uncle and nephew, John Helbert and John Wagg were only eight years apart in age and their careers traced parallel paths, both acting as brokers for Rothschilds. In 1848 they joined forces and formed the firm Helbert, Wagg & Co., apparently to combine their activities on Rothschilds' behalf, and in the second half of the nineteenth century, according to a Wagg family memoir, Helbert, Wagg acted as Rothschilds' principal broker.[7] All applications to the Committee of the Stock Exchange for quotations or special settlements were made through the firm and for many years it also looked after the adjustment of Rothschilds' money position at the end of each account. Despite the family ties, the Helbert, Wagg partners were very much at the mercy of Rothschilds, and Wagg family folklore held many tales of high-handed treatment. 'On the fortnightly settlement days,' related Alfred Wagg, John Wagg's grandson, 'my grandfather or father would go over to New Court (Rothschilds' office) with a statement of the position across which Baron Lionel (the head of the firm) would write 500 or 1,000, being an arbitrary fee which he fixed as our remuneration, varying in amount according to the humour he was in.'[8]

In 1857, John Helbert and John Wagg, aged respectively 72 and 64 years, retired. Helbert, Wagg's new senior partner was Lionel Helbert, the 40-year-old son of John Helbert. All that is known about him is that he became a member of the London Stock Exchange in 1846 and joined the Helbert, Wagg partnership two years later. During the decade in which he directed the firm's affairs he was assisted by William Barley, 'an authorised clerk whose sole job was to go backwards and forwards between the Stock Exchange and New Court, and to keep the partners at New Court informed of what was going on, and to deal for them when they had any orders to give'.[9] Lionel Helbert's death in 1866, at the early age of 49, marked the end of the Helbert side of the partnership and it was the sons of John Wagg who assumed control of the firm.

Between 1866 and the early years of the twentieth century Helbert, Wagg's senior partners were Arthur Wagg and Edward Wagg. Arthur, the elder of the brothers, joined the partnership in 1864, a few months after his admission as a member of the Stock Exchange following his 21st birthday.[10] Thus he was only 23 years old at the time he became Helbert, Wagg's senior partner upon the death of his uncle. Most probably he turned to his father for advice about the conduct of the firm, and a letter written in 1869 demonstrates the latter's continuing interest in its affairs. John Wagg was anxious about the commercial situation and reported to his son the views recently expressed to him by Sir David Salomons, a relative who was one of the most eminent City figures of the day and who in 1855 became the first Jewish Lord Mayor of London. 'Your Uncle David seems to me to take a very gloomy view of the state of money,' wrote John Wagg, 'I think you should act with great caution in your dealings . . . you should select the very best names even if you do not get the highest rate of interest . . . You know how anxious I am for your welfare and at the same time very nervous.'[11]

Arthur Wagg was evidently well endowed with the most important attribute of a successful late nineteenth century stockbroker – excellent social connections. He moved easily amongst City men and in London society and was an acquaintance of the Prince of Wales, the future King Edward VII. But if Helbert, Wagg's business benefited from Arthur Wagg's affability, it may also have suffered on account of his impetuousness. An example which entered family legend was his arrival at Rothschilds to offer unsolicited and misconceived advice upon hearing of the celebrated coup of the purchase of the Khedive's Suez Canal shares on behalf of the British government in 1875. An astonished Baron Lionel Rothschild dismissed him with the words, 'Arthur Wagg, you're a young man and will learn better'.[12]

The driving force in the firm in the late nineteenth century was Edward Wagg, Arthur Wagg's younger brother. He was born in 1843 and practised briefly as a barrister before becoming a member of the Stock Exchange in 1869 and joining the partnership in 1870, the year of William Barley's retirement. Besides being a member of the Helbert, Wagg partnership for half a century he was a director of several companies, including Imperial South Africa Enterprises Ltd. Edward Wagg never married and led a life akin to that of the affluent gentlemen bachelors who do 'something in the City' in the fictional works of Jerome K. Jerome or P. G. Wodehouse. In London he resided close to The Aldwych, a short walk from the Savoy Hotel, where he dined most evenings, and from the Garrick Club to which he repaired for a game of bridge after dinner. He had a country residence near Maidenhead and also rented an extensive shoot at Glenlochay in Scotland. An excellent shot, he was known to his friends as 'The Laird'. According to an obituary, his physical appearance resembled one of the portraits painted by the early-nineteenth-century Scottish painter Henry Raeburn and 'his courteous old-fashioned manners were in keeping', while his personality was 'sturdy and tenacious in character, gentle in disposition, puckish in humour, realistic in judgement'.[13] The last trait was illustrated by his behaviour during the Baring Crisis of 1890 when there was consternation in the City. Edward Wagg was at Glenlochay when Barings' predicament was revealed and received a telegram from his partners requiring his presence at the office. 'If,' he wired back, 'by returning to London I could save Barings I would do so. If not I will remain here.' And on the moors he stayed.[14]

In 1877 the Helbert, Wagg partners achieved the notable coup of persuading Lord Walter Campbell, a younger son of the Duke of Argyll and the brother-in-law of Queen Victoria's daughter, Princess Louise, to join the partnership, the firm henceforth being known as Helbert, Wagg & Campbell. Campbell's appointment drew considerable attention to the firm since it was unusual for members of the aristocracy to join stockbroking firms.[15] It suggests a deliberate move on the part of the Wagg brothers to develop the private client side of their business, most probably to make the firm less dependant upon Rothschilds' favours. The latter years of the nineteenth century saw increasing interest amongst the wealthy in investments other than agricultural land, which earned a miserable rate of return at this time, and there was much scope to develop private client business for those with the right social connections. Campbell left the firm in 1888 in order to make his fortune in South Africa, but he contracted a fever and died in 1889.[16] Campbell's departure prompted the recruitment to the partnership of two more well-born young men, Arthur Haydon and the Hon. Cyril Russell, the latter of whom was the son of Lord Russell of Killowen, the Lord Chief Justice, who was a social acquaintance of Arthur Wagg.

As well as developing broking services for wealthy private clients, Helbert, Wagg was becoming more and more active in the issuing and underwriting of new securities, though the surviving details are fragmentary. In 1864, in conjunction with Cazenove and two Liverpool brokers, it conducted a large issue on behalf of the Australian & Eastern Navigation Company which was formed to provide steamship services to Australia.[17] The issue aroused great interest and the promoters and their associates were able to ensure that dealings opened at a steep premium by cornering the allotment of the issue, for which they were admonished by the Stock Exchange Committee, and the episode became notorious. The practice of dealing in the market prior to allotment, which was at the root of the Australian & Eastern Navigation Company scandal, was probed by the Royal Commission that investigated the Stock Exchange in 1877. Arthur Wagg was summoned as a witness and it was put to him that dealings before allotment were intended to create a false price which would mislead 'outside people', such as 'country investors, country clergymen, widow ladies and the like', for the benefit of insiders.[18] He responded by blaming the press for whipping up exaggerated expectations, a reply which does not seem to have impressed the commissioners. Nevertheless, the episode does not seem to have harmed the firm professionally; in 1881 it acted as broker to a 1 million issue by Barings and Rothschilds for the Bengal & North Western Railway Company, again acting with Cazenove; in 1882, a year which saw a boom in issues on behalf of American railway companies in London, it was a member of a syndicate put together by Matheson & Company, a London merchant bank, of eleven leading City firms to make an issue on behalf of the Mexican National Railway Co.[19] The closing years of the 1890s saw a company promotion boom on the London Stock Exchange, and Helbert, Wagg appeared as broker on eleven prospectuses in 1898 and 1899. These issues included three important shipping companies, and the major shipbuilding firm Furness Withey & Co. The firm also acted as broker to three issues on behalf of businesses established in Egypt. The best-known name amongst its new issue clients in these years was the grocery-chain, Liptons. Helbert, Wagg and Panmure Gordon, Hill acted as joint brokers to the issue of 2 million shares and 500,000 4 per cent debentures in March 1898.[20] The issue was greatly over-subscribed and, according to Alfred Wagg, Sir Thomas Lipton took personal charge of the allocations, which were made on the following basis: 'Dukes and Marquises were allotted in full, Earls, Viscounts and Barons received 50 per cent, Baronets and Honourables 25 per cent, and the general members of the public nil. I believe a certain number of Society beauties were considered as ranking equally with Dukes and Marquises for the purposes of allotment'.[21]

The turn of the century saw the commencement of a new phase in the Helbert, Wagg partnership. In 1899 the firm's name was changed to Helbert, Wagg & Russell, an acknowledgement of the increasingly important part being played by Cyril Russell. Arthur Wagg took a less and less active role in the day-to-day affairs of the firm, which was probably fortunate in view of the impression he made on Henry Gibbs, a partner in the merchant bank Antony Gibbs & Sons, in September 1900. Wagg called on Gibbs to discuss a debenture placement for a Californian mining company by a syndicate to which Helbert, Wagg was acting as broker. Gibbs reported to another partner that 'as I found he (like his clerk) was wholly ignorant of the business, I am forced to believe that the object of his visit was to inspect our private room which he informed me he had never seen . . . He then said . . . that he really didn't understand "latter day finance" '.[22] Nevertheless, around this time Arthur Wagg played a significant role in the promotion of the company that built the London Underground's Central Line, which suggests a continuing command of business matters.[23] Alfred Wagg, Arthur Wagg's son, was brought into the business in 1901. Born in 1877, he attended a preparatory school in Brighton and Eton College. At school he became a practising Anglican, his parents being without strong religious convictions. In 1894–95 he lived in France and Germany learning the languages, though as a student, not as a volunteer in a commercial firm. In 1896 he went up to King's College, Cambridge, where he studied medieval and modern languages without much application and received a Third Class Honours degree. After toying with the idea of a career in the diplomatic service he decided instead to go into the family firm. He became a member of the Stock Exchange in 1901 and was made a partner of Helbert, Wagg in 1903.

The importance of the Rothschild connection waned around the turn of the century because Rothschilds channelled much of their brokerage work through Panmure Gordon, Hill as reprocity for inclusion in the issue syndicates for Chinese and Japanese loans put together by that stockbroker. The loss of Rothschild business was more than compensated for by the development of international securities activities in the Edwardian era. Details are scant but it is known that the firm collaborated with S. Japhet & Co. (a firm that specialised in international securities arbitrage, with branches in London and Frankfurt) upon underwriting $1.5 million United Cigar shares originated by Goldman, Sachs in New York in 1905, and 'a considerable line' of Sears, Roebuck shares the following year.[24] Helbert, Wagg also became substantially and highly remuneratively involved in marketing British and American securities to French investors, and maintained a representative in Paris.

Alfred Wagg recalled that when he joined Helbert, Wagg at the turn of the century it was located in cramped offices on the first floor at 18 Old Broad Street. In addition to the four partners there were three half-commission men, known in the firm as 'the gentlemen', socially well-connected individuals who brought in broking orders from friends and acquaintances. There were also three clerks authorised to deal in the Stock Exchange, two unauthorised clerks, and a general office staff of about a dozen, plus two commissionaires. The expansion of business led to an increase in staff which made the overcrowding unbearable and in 1903 the firm moved to a larger suite of offices at 37 Threadneedle Street. The dynamic development of Helbert, Wagg's activities in the half-dozen years before the First World War owed much to Adolph Schwelm, who joined the firm from Japhets. Schwelm was of German–Jewish origin, his father being a manager of the Rothschild firm in Frankfurt. He made a very favourable impression on Russell when Helbert, Wagg and Japhets jointly introduced the shares of the British North Borneo Co. to the Paris market, and was invited to join the London firm. Arthur Wagg had recently retired from taking an active role in the business and Schwelm was recruited on the understanding that he would join the partnership in due course. 'He was a brilliant businessman,' commented Alfred Wagg, 'and he brought with him valuable connections.'[25]

In the first decade of the twentieth century, Helbert, Wagg acted as broker to a score or so of issues for a mixed bag of British companies, including Clayton & Shuttleworth, agricultural engineers, and the Llandudno and District Electric Tramway Construction Co. More than half of these issues were for companies whose activities were conducted overseas: in Africa, California, China, Brazil and France, the last being the Elysée Palace Hotel Co. Ltd of Paris, the proprietor of 'a magnificent structure combining English and American comforts with luxurious appointments and perfect management'.[26] In addition there was also a group of Canadian registered companies, including the Imperial Paper Mills of Canada, which made issues in 1903 and 1905, and the Atlantic Quebec and Western Railway Co.

In the early years of the twentieth century some members of the Stock Exchange began to complain about the growth of trading practices whereby transactions by-passed the London market. A 'reform' movement emerged which in February 1908 published a manifesto of changes to the regulations of the exchange, intended to return business to the floor.[27] These proposals were opposed by other members, who regarded them as an attempt to stifle competition and the natural evolution of the securities market. The election to the Committee for General Purposes of the Stock Exchange of March 1908 was contested along party lines by 'Reform' candidates who supported the manifesto and 'Independent' candidates who opposed it. The outcome was a victory for the Reformers, and in June 1908 a new set of regulations was promulgated that defined strictly separate roles for brokers and jobbers and banned splitting commissions with non-members.[28] A further objective of the reform campaign was the imposition of fixed commission charges, which, it was argued, were an essential prop for the division between brokers and jobbers. This was the issue at the election to the Committee for General Purposes of March 1912. Arthur Wagg was adamantly opposed to the proposal and was a spokesman for the Independents. The outcome of the poll was a resounding victory for the Reformers, and every Independent candidate, including Arthur Wagg, was defeated.[29]

'Great City Sensation', read the billboards of a London evening newspaper on 6 December 1912. The story behind the headline was the resignation of the partners of Helbert, Wagg and Russell from the Stock Exchange.[30] No explanation of the reasons for this dramatic move survives in the firm's papers, but a well-informed journalist of the day wrote:

> The firm is taking up the business of a finance and issuing house, and this more particularly in connection with certain great Continental interests. We are making these statements quite unofficially, but they represent, we think, the facts of the case. It is thought in the best Stock Exchange circles that dissatisfaction with the working of the new rules has had something to do with influencing the firm in this decision, since the new rules rather hamper this important portion of its business, to the development of which it is now desirous of devoting itself exclusively, and on a more extended scale. There is absolutely no hostility to the Stock Exchange in the action which this important firm has adopted. Rather the reverse, as it will tend to bring business to London.[31]

Prior to the announcement to the press, Alfred Wagg visited Rothschilds out of courtesy to inform the partners of the move. 'On arriving at New Court,' he recalled, 'I asked to see Lord Rothschild privately and he came to see me in a little room at the back of the building. I gave him the letter, the terms of which couldn't have been nicer. He sat down and read it attentively. He then got up saying "Well, you know your own business best", and walked out of the room. Not one word of good wishes or of regret that the hundred year old intimate connection between the two firms was to cease'.[32]

Issuing and Other Activities, 1912–19

The resignations of the Helbert, Wagg & Russell partners from the Stock Exchange took effect on 1 January 1913. On that day the firm ceased to be stockbrokers and became an issuing house. The new status was accompanied by changes in the firm's title and partnership. Cyril Russell retired from the partnership on account of ill-health at the end of 1912 and the name of the firm reverted to Helbert, Wagg & Co.[33] Adolph Schwelm was appointed to the partnership in Russell's place.

The scene in Helbert, Wagg's private room in the early days as an issuing house was described by Lawrence Jones, who joined the firm as a young man in the summer of 1914 just before the outbreak of the First World War:

The Laird [Edward Wagg] and his elder brother, Mr Arthur Wagg, sat side by side at two enormous knee-hole writing tables at one end of the lofty partners' room in Threadneedle Street, facing the door. They shared one characteristic: a capacity for sitting almost motionless. Since they had lately abdicated from active management in favour of the two junior partners, Alfred Wagg and Adolph Schwelm, I, who sat in a corner by the door to pick up what I could by watching and listening, got an impression of two restless, cigarette-smoking figures crossing and re-crossing in front of a pair of benevolent Buddhas. Schwelm in particular, slim and white-faced, with dark, smouldering eyes, was always on the move, endlessly walking and talking. Alfred contradicted everything Schwelm said, and Schwelm contradicted Alfred. The Buddhas said nothing. By the end of the morning the chain of contradictions ended in agreement, the Buddhas nodded, and another step had been taken in the business of the City of Ottawa or that of the Constantinople Trams.[34]

Helbert, Wagg made big profits in its first twelve months as an issuing house.[35] The reason was the boom in new issues for overseas borrowers on the London Stock Exchange in which the firm was an active participant as a lead-manager and as a member of underwriting syndicates. The first issue sponsored by Helbert, Wagg as an issuing house was made in September 1913 for the City of Ottawa, a client which perhaps came from contacts made while acting as broker for the Canadian companies a few years earlier. On Ottawa's behalf, Helbert, Wagg issued £189,000 4½ per cent bonds with maturities over 20–50 years at a price of 98½.[36] The following year the firm was engaged in negotiations about raising funding for the construction of tramways and docks at Constantinople by a consortium led by the British armaments firms Vickers and Armstrongs, but the outbreak of war in August 1914 put paid to the projects.

Helbert, Wagg's underwriting and issuing business came to a halt with the beginning of the war and it became necessary to develop other activities. Rather improbably the partners decided to devote their energies to the promotion of Anglo-Argentinian trade, apparently in response to the government's exhortations to 'capture German trade'. A subsidiary company, the Argentina Agency Corporation, was formed for this purpose and in the late autumn of 1914 Schwelm, who had adopted British nationality, went to Argentina to develop the business. His return to Britain was deferred on account of the great upsurge of anti-German feeling that followed the sinking of the *Lusitania* in the spring of 1915, and he remained in Argentina for the duration of the war, managing the affairs of the Argentine Agency Corporation and playing an important role in running the Argentine railway system. Towards the end of the war Alfred Wagg, who by now was the only partner actively engaged in the firm in London, came to the conclusion that it would be unacceptable in the City for Schwelm to return as a partner of the firm because he had not served in the British Armed Forces. Wagg wrote to Schwelm in August 1918 suggesting that he should take over the business in Argentina and resign from the partnership of Helbert, Wagg, at which Schwelm took great offence and the parting was acrimonious.

At the behest of the Bank of England during the First World War, Helbert, Wagg ventured into the unfamiliar business of acceptance credits, becoming a participant in large City syndicates that provided credits to the banks of allied nations. Helbert, Wagg took £100,000 participations in a series of syndicated credits for Italian and Russian banks, hazardously large commitments for a firm with a capital of £200,000, and when the Russian bills went into default following the revolution there must have been consternation at the firm. After long negotiations the British government assumed responsibility for the Russian bills and the syndicate members received payment in gilts at par. But since the market price of the securities received as compensation was 20 per cent below par, Helbert, Wagg's reward for its accommodation of the Bank of England's entreaties was a £20,000 loss.

In London, from 1916 onwards, Helbert, Wagg developed a substantial business dealing in Treasury bills and gilts, the activity of the discount houses. Between 1915, the first year for which information is available, and 1918, Helbert, Wagg's balance sheet increased from £1.1 million to £4.1 million. In the latter year the holding of Treasury bills and gilts was £3.9 million, constituting 92 per cent of assets. These holdings, which were actively traded, were financed by overnight borrowings from commercial banks and other sources. Alfred Wagg had no experience of conducting this type of business. 'In the early days,' he recalled, 'I used to get rather alarmed at times about the position. By three o'clock each afternoon you had to have balanced your "book", that is to say you had to have found all the money necessary to finance your liabilities, and the amount of money you had borrowed. You might find yourself perhaps half a million short, and that money had to be forth-coming from somewhere between 2.30 and 3 o'clock'.[37] Wagg recruited Henry Fisher from the discount house Reeves, Whitburn & Co. Ltd to manage the bill-book, which he did with great professionalism. Nevertheless, despite the considerable volume of Treasury bill business the firm barely managed to break even during the war years. An audit conducted by Alfred Wagg after the war revealed that for the period as a whole, profits after tax were a mere £19.[38]

During 1919, Helbert, Wagg closed down its discount house activities, causing the volume of Treasury bills in the balance sheet to shrink from £3.9 million at the beginning of the year to £330,000 at the end. This made Fisher and his team of money market specialists superfluous, but instead of making them redundant the paternalistically-minded Alfred Wagg determined to secure alternative employment for them.[39] Early in 1919 he learned of the intention of the partners of Cater Greenwell & Co. to convert the company to limited liability and to expand the capital. An agreement was reached for Helbert, Wagg to subscribe for 33,000 shares, a substantial but not a controlling interest, and for Henry Fisher to become a director of the restructured firm, Cater & Co. Ltd, to which his team transferred en bloc in May 1919. Most probably Wagg also hoped that the establishment of a close relationship with a discount house would assist the conduct of Helbert, Wagg's treasury activities, call loans to the discount houses being an important deployment of liquid assets by issuing houses and accepting houses at the time. To the astonishment of both firms the Bank of England informed Cater & Co. Ltd that it could no longer enjoy rediscount facilities, since an alliance between an accepting house and a discount house compromised the purity of the discount market. Alfred Wagg visited then deputy governor, Montagu Norman, and protested that Helbert, Wagg was an issuing house not an accepting house and the only acceptance business the firm had ever done was its loss-making participations in the Italian and Russian syndicated credits that it had undertaken at the behest of the Bank. But Norman was adamant. Since it would have been impossible for a discount house to operate without recourse to the Bank, Helbert, Wagg sold its Cater & Co. Ltd shares early in June 1919.[40]

Emergence as a Major Issuing House, 1919–31

In July 1919 the partnership Helbert, Wagg & Co. became the private company Helbert, Wagg & Co. Ltd. The event that triggered this change was the death of Arthur Wagg in April 1919 and the withdrawal of his capital from the partnership. This necessitated the recapitalisation of the firm and the opportunity was taken to adopt a form of ownership which gave future protection to the capital, doubtless taking into consideration that Edward Wagg was 76 years old. The principal owners of Helbert, Wagg & Co. Ltd were Alfred Wagg, who financed his shareholding from his share of his father's £400,000 estate, Edward Wagg, the first chairman, and other members of the Wagg family.[41] Despite his age, Edward Wagg was 'still fond of a flutter' and the gyrating post-war market offered plenty of scope for speculation, which Wagg appears to have conducted on an impressive scale since the firm's accounts show an advance to him of £150,000 on his personal account in 1920 and 1921.[42] He retired as chairman in 1922 and there after played no part in Helbert, Wagg's business, though he remained a director until his death in 1933.

Alfred Wagg, the chairman from 1922 to 1954, was the leading figure in the history of Helbert, Wagg in the inter-war years. 'A tall, pale man, of ascetic appearance, with the kindest pair of eyes I have ever seen, and a delicious sense of humour,' was how a colleague described him.[43] Alfred Wagg left the executive conduct of business to his colleagues, himself focusing upon the recruitment and motivation of personnel, believing that the key to success lay in the morale of the staff. His approach made sound business sense, but his concern for the staff was also a reflection of personal circumstance; he was unmarried and the staff of the firm were his surrogate family. Wagg was uncommonly magnanimous about salaries, which were reputed to be the best in the City, and pioneered benefits such as generous contributions to a pension scheme run by the Prudential Assurance Company; three weeks summer holiday and a week in winter; Wimbledon and Test match tickets; house purchase loans; a house magazine, the *Wagtail*; an annual dinner; and a summer garden party. In return he received genuine gratitude and loyalty from the staff at all levels. Upon his retirement as chairman, a former colleague wrote that he was 'Father and Mother and Uncle and Godfather and Confessor and Money-lender and Universal Aunt and SOUL of H. W. & Co.'.[44] Many charitable causes were also beneficiaries of Alfred Wagg's philanthropy, especially the Eton Manor Boys Club, an Eton 'mission' in London's poor East End, of which he was an active supporter from 1907.[45]

Alfred Wagg was a well-known City figure with many outside directorships, mostly of financial firms, notably the Provident Mutual Life Assurance Association. His personality and standing in the Square Mile helped him to attract able men to Helbert, Wagg, but another important factor was the novel profit participation scheme he devised, which much resembled a partnership arrangement. It proved wonderfully effective in motivating his colleagues, and from the outset Helbert, Wagg's directors behaved with a professionalism and drive which was absent from many other City firms until the 1960s. 'They were all executive, and on duty every day, except normal holidays; no odd days off to hunt, shoot or fish, or to poodle-fake at a race meeting or such like; no dilettante approach,' wrote one of them about his colleagues. 'There was an alertness, a tautness, which kept us all at our desks whenever it was necessary for the good of the business . . . Yet there was a camaraderie and underlying happiness which were our encouragement and our incentive.'[46]

Within a couple of years of the formation of Helbert, Wagg & Co. Ltd, Alfred Wagg had put together one of the most talented executive teams in the City. It had two distinct components, a trio of public-school-educated patrician Englishmen, Nigel Campbell, Bernard Barrington and Lawrence Jones, and Albert Palache and Max Bonn, who were foreign-born and Jewish and had extensive experience of dealing and a sophisticated grasp of the operation of markets. Wagg himself had something of both backgrounds and under his overall guidance their respective strengths complemented each other and the firm made remarkable strides.

Nigel Leslie Campbell was born in 1878 and educated at Eton, where he was a friend of Alfred Wagg.[47] At the turn of the century he went to North America and after a spell prospecting in the Rockies he became a door-to-door bond salesman for the Wall Street investment bank William A. Read & Co. (the forerunner of Dillon, Read & Co.). He married an American bride in 1905 and in 1913 was made a partner of William A. Read & Co. where he worked during the war. The resumption of international financial transactions at the end of the hostilities presented profitable opportunities for securities arbitrage between the City and Wall Street, and Campbell returned to London. When he joined Helbert, Wagg the firm became the London agent for the arbitrage operations of William A. Read & Co., providing a useful initial boost to business. Nigel Campbell's principal contribution to the firm in the 1920s and the 1930s were the close ties that he developed with British manufacturing industry. 'He had the imagination to foresee broad combinations, and the ingenuity to make them practical,' commented a colleague, 'his simplicity and integrity made him trusted and he achieved many notable successes.'[48]

The Hon. Walter Bernard Louis Barrington, the second son of the 9th Viscount Barrington, was born in 1876. He was educated at Charter-house and trained as a solicitor, being admitted to the profession in 1900. In 1904, he became a partner in the leading City law firm Norton, Rose, Barrington & Co., serving as a member of the Council of the Law Society in 1909–11. Alfred Wagg met him in 1914 during the negotiations for the Constantinople docks issue when he was acting for the National Bank of Turkey, Helbert, Wagg being represented by Sir William Slaughter. Upon the death of Slaughter in March 1917, Wagg engaged Barrington to act for Helbert, Wagg, and two years later persuaded him to retire from the legal profession and to join the issuing house as a director, one of the first City solicitors to make such a move. Barrington was cautious by nature and saw his role as tempering the wilder enthusiasms of his colleagues. 'He always said his main job was to keep us out of the Old Bailey,' one of them recalled.[49] He was the personification of the City gentleman: tall, patrician-featured and soft-spoken; a keen sportsman, staunch Tory and ever meticulously attired in wing collar, bow tie and spats. He was well known and well liked in the City and was appointed to the board of numerous financial companies, for instance the Loch Lomond Investment Trust, the Gresham Life Assurance Society, and the Legal and General Assurance Society, of which he was a director from 1914 and chairman in 1945-58. When the Legal and General financed the construction of a major office development in Gresham Street, which was completed in 1957, the building was called Barrington House.

Lawrence Evelyn Jones, who became a director on 1 January 1923, was born in 1885, the second son of Sir Lawrence John Jones, fourth baronet; he succeeded to the title in 1952. Educated at Eton and Balliol College, Oxford, he was called to the Bar in 1909 and practised as a barrister until his engagement to marry required him to take up more immediately lucrative employment in the City. He joined Helbert, Wagg in 1914 and returned to the firm upon demobilisation in 1919. Jones worked in the mainstream issuing business as a member of the team that conducted that activity. 'Gifts for accuracy, research, and a sure instinct for the quality of a fellow-creature are not always found in the same person,' he wrote, reflecting on the work. 'Hence the advantage, in an issuing house, of team-work, and it was as a team that the firm I served achieved success and even prominence.'[50] Jones was a popular man with his colleagues, who enjoyed his charm and wit. In retirement from 1945, he wrote several volumes of autobiography which, in the words of his obituary in *The Times*, 'established him as an author of some merit'.[51]

The success of the securities arbitrage operations with New York in 1919 led the partners to seek to develop this activity with continental financial centres. Albert Palache, a Belgian with extensive pre-war experience of continental securities, was engaged as manager of the new operation in January 1920 and was made a director three years later. Palache was with the firm for almost four decades and played a vital part in its achievements, and yet remained an enigma to even his closest colleagues. Wrote one of them:

> It is difficult to give a true portrayal of him for he was utterly unusual and conformed to no pattern at all. He was a Jew and often told me he had Dutch, Spanish, Portuguese and Turkish blood in him . . . He was an international banker to his finger-tips – nobody could mistake him for any other profession. He spoke the major Continental languages with equal ease. He was an artist in business – it was the pure accomplishment of a deal which gave him real pleasure – not the financial gain. A vain man, yet so naive

in his vanity as to make those of us who knew him well disregard it. Wherever he went, business came to him. People from all over the world sought his advice – business was instinctive in him, morning noon and night . . . Palache was a special article – a giant amongst arbitrageurs – an international figure, at home as well in a banking parlour as a casino.[52]

Palache was the driving force behind Helbert, Wagg's financial operations on behalf of continental clients in the 1920s. As a result he accumulated a long list of directorships of foreign banks, including Labouchère & Co. NV, a leading Dutch merchant bank, and the Österreichische Creditanstalt, Austria's largest commercial bank.[53]

Dealing in foreign exchange was a complementary activity to international securities arbitrage. In May 1921, the firm acquired a fully-fledged foreign exchange operation by the purchase of Bonn & Co. This firm was formed in 1910 by Max Bonn and an uncle and cousin, Leo Bonn and Walter Bonn. Before the war it conducted international banking business on a small scale and after the end of the hostilities it specialised in foreign exchange transactions. When Leo and Walter Bonn retired on account of ill health early in 1921 Max Bonn decided to amalgamate with a larger and financially stronger partner, choosing Helbert, Wagg, of which he became a director and shareholder. Max Bonn was born in New York in 1877 into a German–Jewish family and was educated in the United States and at the University of Munich, where he distinguished himself in economics and statistics. Upon his move to London he adopted British nationality by naturalisation. Although a director of Helbert, Wagg from 1921 to 1938 he rarely attended board meetings, having many outside interests, especially the United Glass Bottle Manufacturers Ltd, of which he was chairman from the mid-1920s to 1943.[54] He was also a director of the Underground Electric Railways Company of London Ltd, the Bank of London and South America, and the Brazilian Trust and Loan Corporation. He was very active for charitable causes, notably those concerned with juvenile welfare, and was knighted in 1926 in recognition of his work.

Helbert, Wagg's foreign exchange dealing activities in the 1920s were conducted by an uncommonly able pair of young men, Lionel Fraser and George Bolton, both of whom became major City figures in later life. William Lionel Fraser was born in 1895, the son of the butler to Gordon Selfridge, the founder of Selfridges department store. At the age of thirteen he won a scholarship which allowed him to attend Pitman's School where he learned bookkeeping, shorthand and typing, and French, German, and Spanish in preparation for a commercial career, joining Bonn & Co. in 1911, aged sixteen, as a clerk. He rejoined the firm after military service during the First World War and in 1921, aged 25, became head of Helbert, Wagg's foreign exchange operations. George Lewis French Bolton, who was born in 1900, started work in the City before he was seventeen and trained as a foreign exchange dealer with the French bank Société Générale de Paris.[55] He joined Helbert, Wagg's bookkeeping department in 1920, from whence he was plucked by Fraser to act as his deputy. 'A brilliant, forceful and creative banker,' was Fraser's assessment, 'the original of the now much used adjective "dynamic", pouring out new ideas incessantly'.[56] The activities of Fraser and Bolton made Helbert, Wagg one of the top half-dozen firms in the London foreign exchange market in the early 1920s, vitally promoting its standing. 'It made the name prominent in all the leading banking circles,' commented Fraser proudly.[57] Bolton's reputation as a foreign exchange expert led to his recruitment by the Bank of England in January 1933 and not long afterwards he was put in charge of the management of sterling. He was made an executive director of the Bank of England in 1948. In 1957 he left the Bank to become chairman of the Bank of London & South America, in which capacity he played a leading part in the development of the Euro-dollar market in London.[58] Another member of staff who made his mark was Douglas Jardine, who worked for the firm in 1928–31. His fame, however, came from cricket not merchant banking and shortly after leaving Helbert, Wagg he captained the England team on a tour of Australia which provoked heated and notorious controversy.

The progress of Helbert, Wagg's overall activity in the years 1915–31 is reflected in the ups and downs of the firm's gross revenues, which are shown in Figure 12.2. In the war years, when its business was akin to that of a discount house, gross revenues averaged £34,000 per annum. In 1919–21, the years when securities arbitrage and foreign exchange

Figure 12.2   Helbert, Wagg & Co. Ltd, revenues, 1915–31

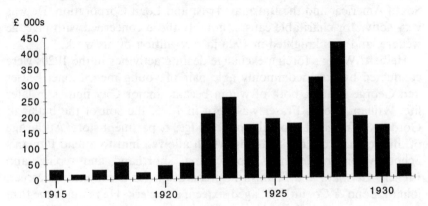

dealing were its principal activities, revenues rose to an annual average of £57,000, though inflation accounted for much of the increase. In 1922 business accelerated dramatically and revenues leapt fourfold to £221,000. Between 1922 and 1930 they averaged £239,000 each year and in the peak years 1927 and 1928 reached £318,000 and £428,000. The much higher level of revenue from 1922 reflected the revival of issuing and underwriting activity. The resulting expansion of staff necessitated more office space, and in 1925 the firm moved to 41 Threadneedle Street, which was its home until the acquisition by Schroders. The onset of the international economic crisis in 1929 led to sharp falls in Helbert, Wagg's revenues from all sources, and in 1931 they totalled only £41,000, a mere 10 per cent of the level of 1928.

Issuing securities was much the most important of Helbert, Wagg's various activities in the 1920s. Between 1919 and 1930, issuing profits, including underwriting commissions, produced almost two thirds of the firm's gross revenues. In these years the firm made issues on behalf of both continental European and British clients. The largest and most prestigious of the issues were big bond issues for European governments and public authorities, and it was the conduct of these that established Helbert, Wagg as a leading City issuing house. Continental European corporations, particularly German ones, also used its services to raise funds in the London market in the 1920s. The British clients were mostly manufacturing companies, though there was also a noteworthy number of financial trusts. In general, the issues for continental European clients were much more profitable than those for British clients, the accounts suggesting that they generated probably three-quarters of the profits from issuing in 1919–30.

In the boom of 1919–20 British manufacturing companies sought funds to expand capacity to meet the surge in orders and to augment working capital as prices soared. Helbert, Wagg made several issues for corporate clients during the boom, its first post-war issue being for A. G. Mumford Ltd, an engineering firm for which it issued 100,000 ordinary shares in December 1919. A feature of the fund-raising of 1919–20 was the issue of notes rather than bonds, with shorter maturities and higher yields than was typical before the war. This was because borrowers wished to avoid long-term commitments to payment of the high interest rates then prevailing, but notes were also popular with investors, since their redemption in the relatively near future protected purchasers against capital loss. Helbert, Wagg made three corporate note issues during 1920. The largest was 3 million 8 per cent seven–year notes priced at 96.5 per cent, giving a yield of 8.29 per cent, for Explosive Trades Ltd, which soon after changed its name to Nobel Industries and was subsequently one of the firms that combined to form Imperial Chemical

Industries (ICI). The *Financial Times* commented 'even in these days of high yields this issue strikes us as exceptionally attractive' and the offer was quickly over-subscribed.[59] Helbert, Wagg arranged the underwriting, working jointly with the British Overseas Bank, a consortium bank established in 1919 by the Union Bank of Scotland, Williams Deacon's Bank, and the Prudential Assurance Co. The British Overseas Bank soon emerged as a leading City issuing house, specialising in issues for Central European clients, and was a very active participant in the foreign exchange markets. This was a pattern of business similar to Helbert, Wagg's and the firms collaborated on many issues in the 1920s. A strong friendship developed between the leading executives of the firms from the Explosives Trades issue, following which Arthur Gairdener, the British Overseas Bank chairman, wrote to Alfred Wagg, 'I trust you will not think it out of place for me to congratulate you on the manner in which you have handled the issue of the Explosive Trades. It has been a great pleasure to be associated with you in this business.'[60]

The post-war boom collapsed during 1920 and a recession ensued. In this depressed business environment few British manufacturers required additional funds from the capital market, and Helbert, Wagg made only a single issue for a British firm during 1921. But market conditions were right for long-term fund-raising by public authorities, and the relaxation of the wartime restrictions on access to the London capital market by overseas borrowers was followed by an upsurge in bond issues for continental European governments and municipalities. Most were conducted by prestigious accepting houses which had long specialised in such loans, notably the Barings – Rothschilds – Schroders consortium, but remarkably the newcomer Helbert, Wagg managed to win appointments to bring out half a dozen foreign sovereign or municipal clients in the 1920s. These large, highly publicised issues won the firm much prestige. Moreover, as the lead-manager to the issue it was usually appointed paying agent for the bonds, generating useful fees in subsequent years.

The first of Helbert, Wagg's sovereign issues was for the Kingdom of Iceland in August 1921. The Icelandic government was seeking long-term funds for the settlement of outstanding debts to British firms, and Helbert, Wagg was encouraged to assist by the Foreign Office, which informed the firm 'this department is prepared to afford you all the support it properly can in regard to the execution of the contract'.[61] Palache visited Iceland to negotiate the loan and his hosts recorded confidentially that he made 'a genial and intelligent impression'.[62] Helbert, Wagg, in conjunction with Higginson & Co., contracted to purchase £500,000 thirty-year 7 per cent sterling bonds at 85, to be sold to investors at 91. The Prudential Assurance Company was brought in to underwrite £200,000 of the issue, which it agreed to take at 90 if they could not be retailed at 91. The Icelandic loan marked the beginning of a close relationship with London's leading insurance company, which was of crucial importance to Helbert, Wagg over the next four decades. The successful issue of the loan despite 'the extremely adverse financial conditions prevailing' was hailed as a triumph by the Icelandic government, which undertook to give Helbert, Wagg and Higginsons first refusal of any future external funding either in the UK or the US.[63] Further proof of the client's satisfaction was the award to Alfred Wagg of Iceland's Order of the Falcon.

The Icelandic loan of 1921 enhanced Helbert, Wagg's reputation, but it produced only £4,000 profit. The foreign bond issues which the firm conducted in 1922 on behalf of the department of the Seine, the city of Prague and the Kingdom of Romania were prestigious and much more remunerative. After the war it was decided to make major improvements to the public transport of the city of Paris, which was administered by the department of the Seine. A fierce and highly political contest for the appointment as issuing house began in the summer of 1921 amongst financial firms in London, and between London and New York. Schröders made vigorous efforts to secure the contract on behalf of the Barings–Rothschilds–Schröders syndicate and 'animosity' was expressed when their bid was beaten by Helbert, Wagg's.[64] The Wagg team, led by Bonn, pulled off this coup through superior intelligence work, which made them aware that the department of the Seine worked its Sinking Fund calculations on different tables from those used in Britain and made due allowance.

Helbert, Wagg contracted to bring out £3 million 7 per cent thirty-year bonds in London at a price of 95, while Kuhn, Loeb & Co. undertook to issue $25 million in New York. Helbert, Wagg, which had a capital of only £500,000, needed a powerful partner to assist with the execution of the operation and turned to the Prudential, which agreed to take the whole of the issue at the purchase price of 90. Helbert, Wagg retained an option to repurchase 1 million from the Prudential near to the time of the public offering, which was duly exercised, and to charge a 1.5 per cent commission to the Prudential for the organisation of the issue. The recruitment of the Prudential as a partner was vital not only because of its vast financial resources but because of its clout when the Bank of England attempted to halt the issue because it claimed that it violated the Treasury's voluntary guidelines on foreign loans, Alfred Wagg having the disconcerting experience of being told by Montagu Norman, now Governor, that he would incur his undying displeasure if the loan went ahead. Wagg replied that he had given his word to the client and would proceed accordingly. Sir George May, the head of the Prudential, and Reginald McKenna, the chairman of the Midland Bank, 'took up the cudgels on Helbert, Wagg's behalf' and the matter was resolved at the cost of a few weeks' delay.[65] The issue eventually took place in early February 1922 and was oversubscribed. The Seine loan, described by Fraser as 'the greatest coup of all', not only enormously enhanced the firm's reputation, but it generated a profit of £30,000. Moreover, there was an unexpected epilogue. Unbeknown to Alfred Wagg, his principled refusal to bow to the Bank of England's pressure had much impressed Norman, and a few weeks after the issue he was summoned to the Bank of England and informed by the Governor, to Wagg's astonishment, that he wished Helbert, Wagg to manage his personal investments henceforth.[66]

The loan to the state of Czechoslovakia issued by the Barings–Rothschilds–Schröders syndicate early in April 1922 established confidence on the part of foreign investors in the creditworthiness of Czech public authorities. The same day as the publication of the prospectus a delegation from the municipal authority of Prague arrived in London to negotiate a loan to provide funds for improvements to the Czech capital's gas, electricity and water supplies.[67] A week later, on 13 April 1922, Barrington made an offer to the Czechs on behalf of Helbert, Wagg to purchase £1.5 million thirty-year 7.5 per cent bonds at 86, to be sold to investors at 91.5. An important condition of the contract was that preference was to be shown for British tenders for any ensuing orders of equipment placed outside Czechoslovakia. The Czech delegation agreed to these terms and Palache was despatched to Prague to sort out the details.[68] While this was being done the price of the State of Czechoslovakia bonds began to slide in the market, which threatened to undermine the terms upon which the Prague loan could be issued. Cable upon cable was despatched to Palache instructing him to impress upon the Czechs the necessity of instructing Barings to intervene in the market to support the price of the bonds. Palache did his utmost, but to no avail, and complained to London 'you constantly omit to wire me the price, which makes it difficult for me to argue the point with the minister'.[69] In fact, Barings was not displeased by the situation, hoping that the decline would temper unrealistic Czech expectations and refused to take action.[70] The dollar tranche of the Prague loan was brought out by Kuhn, Loeb in early June and was well received by investors. The London issue was made only a few days later but by then the market was experiencing 'a moment of reaction' and *The Time* reported that the underwriters were left with 87.5 per cent of the bonds.[71] Evidently the securities subsequently proved popular with investors, for Helbert, Wagg's year end accounts showed a profit on the business.

While Palache was in Prague, Jones was sent to Bucharest to settle the terms of an issue for the kingdom of Romania. In the summer of 1922 Romanian public finance was in a mess; revenues fell far short of government spending and the country's ability to borrow externally was blocked by defaulted pre-war bonds and a large volume of outstanding Treasury bills (denominated in ten currencies) issued immediately after the war to raise funds to purchase food for the starving population. Helbert, Wagg and the British Overseas Bank were appointed to assist the Romanian authorities with the disentanglement of the national finances and the restoration of the country's international creditworthiness. Upon his arrival in Bucharest, Jones called on the finance minister and asked to see the text of the law authorising the loan. 'The big, bearded man pulled out a pencil,' he recalled, 'and, after a moment's consideration, scrawled a couple of lines in French on a piece of blotting paper. He tore it off and pushed it across to me. "Will that do?" he asked'.[72] Satisfactory terms were eventually agreed and the outcome was an issue of £35 million forty-year 4 per cent Consolidation Bonds, issued to the holders of outstanding Romanian Government Treasury bills and bonds; and a further issue of £2.5 million twenty-year 4 per cent External Loan bonds to meet the costs of the consolidation and to provide funds for the initial coupon payments.[73] The latter bonds, which were secured by a prior charge on a new export tax, were privately placed by a group of British banks led by Helbert, Wagg and the British Overseas Bank. Helbert, Wagg's total revenues from its involvement in the Romanian financial reconstruction was a very handsome £135,000 – about £3.4 million in 1990 money.

Helbert, Wagg and the British Overseas Bank made two joint issues under the auspices of the League of Nations on behalf of Danzig, which had been established as a free city-state by the Treaty of Versailles at the end of the First World War. The first, in April 1925, was an issue of £1.5 million 7 per cent twenty-year bonds to provide funds for improvements to utility services, the harbour and the opening-up of a new industrial district and residential suburbs, the bankers purchasing the bonds from the city at 86 and selling them to the public at 90, offering investors a yield of 7.8 per cent. The second, in June 1927, was for £1.5 million 6.5 per cent twenty-year bonds priced at 90, a yield of 7.2 per cent, the drop reflecting the additional guarantee of the receipts from the Tobacco Monopoly concession which comfortably covered the loan's service charge. When the Danziger Elecktrische Strassenbahn AG, the Danzig tramway company, required funds for extensions and working capital in 1928 it turned to Helbert, Wagg and the British Overseas Bank. The bankers contracted to issue £225,000 7 per cent twenty-year sterling mortgage bonds which they privately placed with investors at 95 per cent, their reward being a 4 per cent commission.

The first half of the 1920s saw several issues of securities for British companies by Helbert, Wagg. The largest were the issues for the Marconi Wireless Telegraph Company in November 1922 and for the English Electric Company in June 1923. Marconi pioneered the development of radio and the fund-raising coincided with the boom in demand that followed the creation of the British Broadcasting Corporation (BBC). Helbert, Wagg organised a syndicate that purchased the £1.5 million 6.5 per cent ten–year convertible debentures at 94 and sold them to the public at 97. 'Much is expected from the company's "broadcasting" developments,' commented the *Financial Times*, 'the debentures are an attractive proposition, especially when the possibilities of the conversion rights are taken into consideration and will probably be readily subscribed.'[74] In fact, so great was public demand for prospectuses that the City police had to be called to control the crowds.[75] The issue for English Electric in June 1923 was for the conversion of £1,250,000 8 per cent notes issued during the post-war boom into debentures bearing a 6.5 per cent coupon. Helbert, Wagg and Higginsons put together a syndicate, of which the Prudential was an important member, which purchased the debentures from the English Electric Company at 95.25 and offered them to note-holders at 97, thus assuming the risk that the note-holders would decline to convert. In fact, applications to convert were received for the whole of the issue.

Helbert, Wagg's closeness to its British corporate clientele during the 1920s may be illustrated by two examples: the Borneo Company Ltd and the United Glass Bottle Manufacturers Ltd. In July 1922, Helbert, Wagg sponsored the issue of £400,000 7.5 per cent cumulative convertible preference shares for the Borneo Company, though only on condition that one of its directors was appointed to the Borneo board. 'Many thanks for the loan, it has been most valuable to us,' wrote the chairman chirpily nine months later, though he then complained at length about the conservatism of Helbert, Wagg's profits projection at the time of the issue.[76] The United Glass Bottle Manufacturers Ltd, formed in 1913 to amalgamate and rationalise the British bottle-making industry, experienced problems in the early 1920s. In 1925 control was acquired by a consortium headed by Helbert, Wagg, which imposed 'drastic modifications' upon the capital structure and revitalised the management, installing Max Bonn as chairman.[77] It was then sold through a private placement, Helbert, Wagg retaining a modest equity interest. The firm prospered under Bonn's leadership and he became absorbed in its affairs, continuing as chairman until his death in 1943.[78]

During the 1920s, Helbert, Wagg developed an important relationship with the highly regarded Amsterdam merchant bank Labouchère & Co. The firm took a small shareholding in Labouchère, and Palache joined the board of directors, of which he remained a member until 1947. Labouchère and Helbert, Wagg acted as joint issuers of guilder-denominated securities on the Amsterdam bourse, the latter's role being the distribution of part of the issue in London. Their first joint undertaking was the issue of 3 million guilder 6 per cent mortgage bonds for the Van Niefelt Goudriaan Steamship Company of Rotterdam in August 1923. The following year, the firms purchased jointly a 10-million-guilder issue of ordinary shares by the Rotterdamsche Bank-vereeniging, which were then sold to the Prudential. In January 1925, Helbert, Wagg organised the placement of 2.25 million 6 per cent convertible debentures of the "Hollandia" Anglo-Dutch Milk & Food Company in London out of a 3 million issue in Amsterdam. In March 1927, Helbert, Wagg and Labouchère collaborated on two fund-raising exercises on behalf of the Dutch 'artificial silk' (rayon) manufacturing company ENKA which sought cash resources to enable it to expand by acquisition. The next year Helbert, Wagg acquired ordinary and preference shares of ENKA on behalf of Cazenove, acting for Schröders, which in turn was acting for the financier Alfred Loewenstein, who was highly active in the continental European rayon industry. Yet more guilder-denominated issues were made by Helbert, Wagg for Wm H. Mueller & Co. of the Hague, a shipping company, in 1928; Hegl-Beringer AG of Berlin, a manufacturer of dyestuffs, in 1929; and AKU, another Dutch rayon concern, in 1930.

Palache's Dutch connections were the origin of Helbert, Wagg's important ties with the sugar industry. The production of sugar from beet was introduced to Britain in 1912 at a pioneer factory at Cantley in Norfolk financed by Dutch capital.[79] The Sugar Subsidy Act of 1925 stimulated the cultivation of beet in Britain, prompting an increase in beet sugar refining capacity. In 1927, Helbert, Wagg made issues on behalf of four beet sugar refineries which were owned by Anglo-Dutch interests and known as the Van Rossum group.[80] In 1936, these firms and many others were amalgamated as the British Sugar Corporation, of which Palache served as a director for many years.

Palache was also behind Helbert, Wagg's participations in various financial transactions for corporate clients in the countries of Central and Eastern Europe. In 1923, it organised a syndicate to purchase 100,000 ordinary shares of the British and Hungarian Bank of Budapest. It undertook further capital raising exercises for this client in 1927 and 1929, in conjunction with Labouchère & Co. In 1927, in conjunction with the Prudential and the British Overseas Bank, Helbert, Wagg purchased and placed 200,000 new shares of the Österreichische Creditanstalt, Austria's leading commercial bank, a deal which included the condition 'that this purchase is made on the explicit understanding that you [Creditanstalt] will henceforth give a reasonable proportion of your London business to the British Overseas Bank'.[81] This connection led to Helbert, Wagg organising, in 1929, a £220,000 mortgage bond issue for the leading Austrian manufacturer of electrical engineering products. Amongst the very last of Helbert, Wagg's fund-raising activities for foreign firms was its orchestration of the syndicates formed in the spring of 1931 to purchase securities issued by the International Bodenkreditbank of Basel, and the Union International de Placements, the first French investment trust. The Prudential was a participant in both syndicates, as was Helbert, Wagg's own investment trust, the British & German Trust, and Labouchère & Co. was closely involved in the latter business.

Helbert, Wagg, like Schröders, played a significant role in raising funds for German industry in the 1920s, Palache and Bonn having extensive contacts amongst German bankers and industrialists. In the years 1924–28 it made nine issues for German corporate clients, by the private placement of bonds secured by mortgages. The usual pattern for these mortgage loans was that Helbert, Wagg negotiated the terms of the loan and verified the security; the British Overseas Bank acted as trustee; and the Prudential headed the list of subscribers. The prototype was the £1,125,000 6.5 per cent First Mortgage Loan for the Bremen-based shipping company Norddeutscher Lloyd AG which was contracted in April 1924. Once all the paperwork was completed, Helbert, Wagg transferred its rights under the loan agreement to the Prudential, which took over the funding of the loan. Besides receiving interest on the loan, the Prudential received Norddeutscher Lloyd's fire insurance business, and the firm's sterling balances were transferred to the British Overseas Bank. To justify the provision of sterling funds for German industry to the authorities and the public, attention was drawn to the large extent of Norddeutscher Lloyd's purchases of coal and stores from British suppliers and it was predicted that 'both these figures will increase considerably this year since the company has every intention to continue to make purchases in the United Kingdom'.[82] Helbert, Wagg's remuneration 'for your mediation' was a 3 per cent commission on the nominal amount.[83] The full list of loans raised for German corporate clients on a mortgage loan basis is shown in Table 12.1.

In June 1924, Helbert, Wagg organised the placement of 2.5 million Gold Mark ordinary shares for the Metallbank AG, the banking associate of the Metallgesellschaft AG, one of Germany's leading metallurgical firms. Perhaps it was family ties that led to this business, since Alfred Wagg's mother was a Merton, the founding family of the Metallgesellschaft. In June 1925 and again in August 1928, Helbert, Wagg placed ordinary shares of the Disconto-Gesellschaft, the major

Table 12.1 Loans for German corporate clients secured by mortgages issued by private placement by Helbert, Wagg & Co. Ltd, 1924–28

Date	Borrower	Activity	Amount
May 1924	Norddeutche Lloyd AG, Bremen	Shipping	£1,125,000
Nov. 1924	Oberschlesiche Kokswerke und Chemische Fabriken AG, Berlin	Coal mines	£400,000
Dec. 1924	Rombacher Huttenwerke AG	Coal mines	£350,000
Jan. 1925	Woermann Linie AG, Hamburg	Shipping	£330,000
Jan. 1926	Zellstoffabrik Waldhof AG, Mannheim	Pulp & Paper	£750,000
May 1926	Feldmuehle Papier AG, Stettin	Paper	£350,000
Aug. 1927	Gebrüder Korting AG, Hanover	Diesel motors	£175,000
Dec. 1927	Woermann Linie AG, Hamburg	Shipping	£655,000
Nov. 1928	Zellstoffabrik Waldhof AG, (Finland)	Pulp & Paper	£498,000

German bank with which it had a close relationship, amongst British insurance companies and investment trusts. The only public issue undertaken by Helbert, Wagg for a German client was in December 1925 on behalf of the Bank für Textilindustrie AG of Berlin, a holding company for eleven large and well-established German textile undertakings. The issue of £1 million 7 per cent twenty–year bonds was bought by a syndicate formed by Helbert, Wagg, which included the Prudential and the British Overseas Bank, for 86 and sold to the public for 93. Prominent publicity was given to the client's purchases of British textile machinery and yarn and the prospectus included an undertaking that the firm would spend £3 million in the United Kingdom in the following year if the loan went ahead. 'The high yield, the excellent security and the fact that subscription will aid British trade represent a combination that should ensure the prompt subscription of the issue' commented the *Financial Times*.[84]

Helbert, Wagg's expertise in continental securities led to its entree into investment management. In May 1926, it formed the British & German Trust Ltd, an investment trust that specialised in the provision of sterling finance for medium-sized German industrial firms, an initiative with many similarities to Schröders' Continental and Industrial Trust. The British & German board comprised Alfred Wagg, chairman; Palache; Sir George May of the Prudential; Lord Ashfield, a prominent business figure who dominated passenger transportation in London in the inter-

war years; and four German bankers representing the German partners –
the Reichskredit AG, the Deutsche Bank, the Berliner Handelsgesell-
schaft and the Commerz-und Privat-Bank – which provided guidance on
investment opportunities. Ordinary share capital of £1 million was raised
in May 1926 and a further £750,000 by a debenture issue in February
1928.

The formula of combining British and foreign investment expertise to
run a specialist investment trust was repeated in January 1928, when the
Trans-Oceanic Trust was formed to participate in the booming Wall
Street stock market. Helbert, Wagg became managers of the fund,
though Barings and Robert Benson were also involved at the London
end, while the American participants were recruited from Campbell's
extensive Wall Street contacts. The new trust got off to a strong start and
such was the confidence in the prospects for Anglo-American business
that in February 1929 a US subsidiary, Helbert, Wagg & Co. (New
York) Inc., was established. This initiative was overtaken by the Wall
Street Crash of October 1929 and never became more than a nameplate,
though it proved quite a useful one for booking international
transactions, particularly during the Second World War. It became
inoperative in 1946. The Trans-Oceanic Trust was badly mauled by the
crash and took several years to recover. A better-timed undertaking was
the formation of the Westpool Investment Trust in April 1931, which
was able to enter the market at almost its lowest point and to enjoy the
recovery of prices. Westpool's capital was subscribed one-third by
Thomas Tilling, the road transport firm with which Helbert, Wagg had
close connections for many years; one-third by Lewis's, a northern
multiple retailer, and the remainder by insurance companies. Besides
managing the investment trusts Helbert, Wagg also developed a sizable
volume of private client work in the 1920s.

During the final years of the partnership, Helbert, Wagg operated on
a capital base of approximately £225,000. This was more than doubled in
1919 upon the incorporation of the firm. The new capital structure was
300,000 5.5 per cent cumulative preference shares of £1 each, subscribed
at par, and 91,000 cumulative ordinary shares of £1 each, subscribed at
£2. This resulted in a paid-in capital of £391,000 plus a general reserve
(or share premium account) of £91,000, totalling £482,000 – about £10
million in 1990 money. At the end of 1930 the paid-in capital totalled
£560,000, an increase of £78,000, of which £58,000 derived from the issue
of additional shares to new directors. Thus during a decade when the
firm's operating profits amounted to £1.4 million only £20,000 was
retained, virtually the whole profit being paid out to shareholders and
management each year, a continuation of its practice as a stockbroker.
Issuing houses did not need substantial capital, since their business was

that of intermediaries, not principals. When a large sum was required for the purchase or underwriting of a large issue, subunderwriters, such as the Prudential, were called upon. Nor was it necessary to accumulate capital to expand activities, since issues were distributed quickly and in practice the scale of operations was not constrained by balance sheet size.

The shifts in the scale and pattern of Helbert, Wagg's balance sheet in the years 1915–31 reflect the changes in the firm's business activities. During the war years balance sheet total assets averaged £2.5 million, reaching £4.1 million in 1918, on account of the large holdings of government securities. The liquidation of the Treasury bill portfolio in 1919 led to a sharp fall in the size of the balance sheet, total assets averaging £780,000 in 1919–21. In these years, when securities arbitrage and foreign exchange dealing were the leading activities, the ratio of partners' capital to deposits and client balances was 2:1, a very un-bank-like ratio. The development of the firm's issuing and investment management business during the 1920s led to increases in the provision of interim financing for clients and holdings of securities, and in 1922–28 balance sheet assets averaged £2 million per annum. The increase was financed by the expansion of deposits and client balances, and the ratio of capital to deposits and client balances became 1:2, still a remarkably conservative one in banking terms. The difficult business conditions of 1929–31 led to reductions in clients' balances, which caused a contraction of Helbert, Wagg's balance sheet, assets averaging £1.5 million per annum in these years.

Helbert, Wagg's revenues were closely related to issuing volume and stockmarket levels, while the firm's overheads, of which the most important component was staff salaries, varied little from year to year. Thus, in bull market conditions huge profits could be made, while in bear market years a mere break-even was not unusual. In the war years, despite the large volume of dealing in government securities, pre-tax operating profits were small and averaged only £8,000 per annum in 1915–18 (see Figure 12.3). The immediate post-war years saw an improvement and in 1919–21 they averaged £16,000 a year. In 1922 they leapt to £140,000, and in 1922–26 averaged £138,000 per annum. Securities prices climbed steeply in 1927–28 and Helbert, Wagg was a vigorous participant in the accompanying domestic issuing boom, operating profits soaring to £255,000 in 1927 and to £345,000 in 1928, the firm's all-time record in real terms – about £9.4 million in 1990 money. Over the years 1922–28, issuing generated approximately two-thirds of total revenues, securities dealing being the other important source of earnings. The end of the bull market led to a steep fall in new issues, and Helbert, Wagg's operating profits dropped to £131,000 in

Figure 12.3   Helbert, Wagg & Co. Ltd, pre-tax operating profits, 1915–31

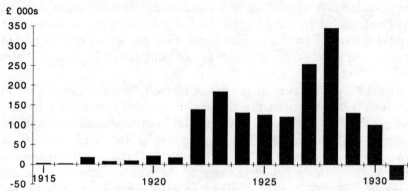

1929 and £101,000 in 1930. In 1931, with the economy deep in recession, the firm made a loss of £38,000, because of both lower revenues and write-downs in the value of investments.

Helbert, Wagg & Co. Ltd's operating profits for each year were distributed amongst the shareholders, directors and members of staff in a set manner following an arrangement devised by Alfred Wagg in 1919. First, the preference shareholders, who provided approximately three-quarters of the capital, were paid a fixed cumulative preferential dividend of 5.5 per cent, which was in principle equivalent to the 4 per cent interest paid on partners' capital in the Schröder partnership. Second, the ordinary shareholders, who provided approximately a quarter of the capital, were paid a dividend at a rate of 12 per cent on the nominal value of their shareholding, a charge which could be waived in difficult years, but the cumulative liabilities had to be discharged before any bonus was paid to the management. Thereafter, the remaining operating profit was divided between bonuses for the directors and staff and a supplementary dividend for the ordinary shareholders. These arrangements ensured that all providers of capital received a basic return in good and bad years alike, while the management and the ordinary shareholders had a powerful incentive to maximise profits.

Analysis of the rates of return achieved by Helbert, Wagg is complicated by the pay-out arrangements outlined above. Figure 12.4 shows two measures of returns: the 'operating return' and the 'return on equity'. The operating return is the operating profit, before payments for capital or bonuses, relative to paid-in capital. The return on equity is a 'blended' return of payments on both preference shares and ordinary shares, most shareholders having both categories, relative to paid-in capital. Since virtually all profits were distributed and the capital base (or book value) did not grow, the dividend stream constituted the

Figure 12.4 Helbert, Wagg & Co. Ltd, pre-tax operating return, pre-tax return on equity and annual rate of inflation, 1915–31

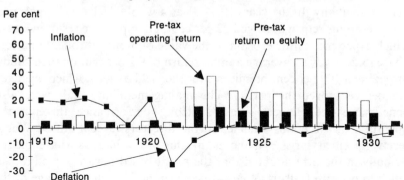

Note: The 'real' return on capital is the difference between the nominal returns on capital depicted above and the annual rate of inflation.

entirety of the shareholders' return on their investment. Furthermore, since the operating profits were virtually fully distributed as dividends or bonus payments to staff, tax was paid by the recipients and not by Helbert, Wagg, whose net profits under these arrangements were negligible, and thus all the figures for operating profit and rates of return are pre-tax.

The low level of profits during the First World War led to miserable returns which fell well short of the 18 per cent per annum average price inflation (see Figure 12.4). In 1920 and 1921 the operating return averaged 4 per cent, enough to honour the preference share dividends but not to pay a dividend on the ordinary shares or a bonus to management. Prices were volatile in these years, distorting the performance picture, but for the rest of the decade they were essentially stable, and nominal returns and real returns were very similar. The profits upturn in 1922 led to a great improvement in performance, and in the years 1922–26 the pre-tax operating return averaged 28 per cent per annum and the return to shareholders 12 per cent. Helbert, Wagg's results for the years 1927 and 1928 were the best in its history: in 1927, operating returns were 48 per cent and the return on equity was 17 per cent; and in 1928, 62 per cent and 20 per cent respectively. In these two boom years the bonus distributed amongst the directors and staff averaged £188,000 per annum compared to £56,000 in 1920–26 and £34,000 in 1929–47. In 1929 and 1930 the operating return fell back to 23 per cent and 18 per cent, remarkably good results in the context of the deteriorating economic position. The operating losses incurred by the firm in 1931 led to a negative return on capital and a suspension of the ordinary dividend, though the payment upon the preference shares was made punctually. In the years 1919–31 as a whole, Helbert, Wagg's pre-tax, pre-bonus return averaged 22 per cent, an impressive result in an era which experienced little erosion of the value of money through inflation. Shareholders saw an average annual return of 9.2 per cent on their funds, providing a 100 per cent premium over the yield on gilts, which averaged 4.6 per cent over the period. The management and staff were also beneficiaries of Helbert, Wagg's strong performance through the operation of the bonus scheme, all the directors (except Alfred Wagg) receiving much larger payments in this way than as shareholders. Nobody in the firm doubted that the profit-based reward structure had much to do with Helbert, Wagg's success in taking full advantage of the opportunities which arose in the bull market of the 1920s.

The Depression and the Second World War, 1931–45

Helbert, Wagg's revenues plummeted with the onset of the depression, falling from £428,000 in 1928 to £40,000 in 1931. The British economy's recovery began in 1932 and Helbert, Wagg's fortunes revived with it. By 1933 revenues had grown to £208,000 and in the years 1933–36 the firm was almost as busy as in the mid 1920s, revenues averaging £247,000 per annum in these years (see Figure 12.5). The slowdown in British economic activity in 1937 and the increasing likelihood of war led to a sharp downturn in Helbert, Wagg's activity and revenues fell to £114,000. There was a further abrupt fall in the firm's revenues following the outbreak of war and in 1940 they were £64,000, but with that exception the years 1937–44 saw a remarkably steady level of

Figure 12.5   Helbert, Wagg & Co. Ltd, revenues, 1931–47

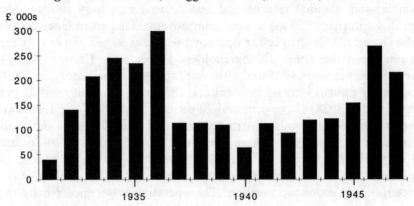

revenues, which averaged £107,000 per annum. The end of hostilities brought a revival of activity and revenues soared to £269,000 in 1946, though they fell back to £216,000 in 1947.

The team that directed Helbert, Wagg in the 1930s and during the war was basically the same as in the 1920s. Alfred Wagg remained chairman and principal proprietor. His uncle, Edward Wagg, who had taken little part in the affairs of the firm in the 1920s, died in 1933, aged 90. Campbell, Barrington and Palache continued to be the most important of the managing directors. Sir Max Bonn and Lawrence Jones played less active parts and retired in 1938 and 1944 respectively. As business picked up in the mid-1930s there was need for additional active directors, which led to the appointment of Gordon Munro in 1933 and Lionel Fraser in 1934. Munro, who was born in 1895 and educated at Wellington and Sandhurst, joined Helbert, Wagg in 1923 after five years in the cavalry and three in Whitehall. His first wife was the eldest daughter of Stanley Baldwin, the Conservative prime minister, and he entered the firm because the Baldwins were close friends of the Waggs. Munro married again in 1934, this time to the daughter of the South African diamond multi-millionaire, Sir Otto Beit. As an incidental result his brother-in-law, Sir Alfred Beit, used 41 Threadneedle Street as his London base in the 1930s and 1940s. Fraser's promotion was a recognition of his hardwork and exceptional talents, qualities that eventually took him to the top of the firm.

The 1930s saw some fundamental changes in the conduct of Helbert, Wagg's issuing and underwriting activities. Fund-raising for foreign clients came to a halt in 1931 and did not resume because of the official restrictions imposed in 1932 on issues for borrowers outside the British Empire. This posed fewer problems for Helbert, Wagg than for many other City firms because of the efforts to develop ties with domestic companies that had been made during the 1920s. Campbell and Munro played leading parts in forging these links, though the other directors also assisted, particularly Barrington and Wagg, who had extensive social contacts. During the 1920s Campbell worked closely with the Governor of the Bank of England upon the rationalisation of the troubled iron and steel and cotton industries. Both he and Wagg served as directors of the Bankers' Industrial Development Corporation and Campbell acted as Montagu Norman's alternate as chairman in the 1930s. Campbell's industrial expertise led to his appointment as chairman of the Nuffield Fund for the Distressed Areas and as chairman of the Development Areas Treasury Advisory Committee. He was also a director of the iron and steel firms Stewarts & Lloyds, Richard Thomas and Baldwins, and Stanton Ironworks, and of Short Brothers, the Belfast aircraft manufacturer, and a member of the Bacon

Development Board. Munro's role was to tour the country marketing Helbert, Wagg's services, an uncommonly dynamic approach to business development on the part of a City merchant bank in the inter-war years. 'Every week he was off round the provinces seeing industrialists and trying to get their financial requirements met by Helbert, Wagg,' recalled a colleague. 'We rather scooped the pool because everybody else was trying to do foreign business, so we had little competition for British business.'

For almost two years, from April 1931 to February 1933, Helbert, Wagg made no public issues at all. This was due initially to the slump and then to the restrictions imposed by the government on access to the London capital market by private borrowers during the massive operation to convert the British national debt to a lower rate of interest. But private placements continued and one of these was of particular significance for the firm. In July 1932, Barrington organised the orderly disposal of the shareholding of the late Colonel Whitburn in the family firm, Reeves, Whitburn & Co., Ltd, a prominent London discount house. The Prudential purchased 70,000 of Whitburn's 102,000 ordinary shares, and the remainder went to the British & German Trust and other investment trusts. Helbert, Wagg's role in the placement of the securities bestowed a trusteeship duty upon the firm on behalf of the new shareholders, and Reeves, Whitburn agreed that Helbert, Wagg had the right to appoint a director. However, an alternative arrangement was made whereby 'one or two of their partners once a month (or more frequently if occasion arises) would come over to our office and tell us something about their position and about things in general in the discount market'.[85] By this roundabout route Helbert, Wagg secured the closeness to the money market that it had been seeking though the investment in Cater & Co. a decade earlier.

The revival of the firm's issuing business began with the Chancellor of the Exchequer's announcement on 13 January 1933 of a relaxation of the embargo on new capital issues following the completion of another stage in the national debt conversion operations.[86] Helbert, Wagg had been waiting for this moment and four days later a rights issue was made on behalf of the important paper manufacturer Albert E. Reed & Co., which raised £825,000, doubling the firm's capital. The following month it conducted a large £5 million – £160 million in 1990 money – debenture issue on behalf of the Gaumont British Picture Corporation, owners of the largest chain of cinemas in the country, with more than 300 picture houses. The funds were required to retire outstanding debentures, effecting an annual saving of £165,000 in interest charges, to increase the firm's holdings in subsidiaries, and to boost capital. A sub-underwriting agreement for the whole of the issue was arranged through Cazenove, who were also brokers to the Reed issue, at the rate of 1.75 per cent on the £5 million debenture stock and a fee of £2,000.[87] The *Financial Times* was favourably impressed by the company's prospects and by the yield on the debentures, and deemed them 'a good investment'.[88] Unfortunately, investors took a less sanguine view of the securities and *The Times* reported that the underwriters had to take up 'an appreciable proportion of the issue'.[89]

The dispute that developed between Helbert, Wagg and the British Gaumont management in the wake of the issue of February 1933 illustrates an inter-war issuing house's view of its relationship with corporate clients and its responsibilities for the securities with which it was 'associated'. At a meeting between representatives of the parties in January 1934, a Helbert, Wagg spokesman explained that 'as they had been associated in the issue of Debenture Stock of the Gaumont British Picture Corporation . . . when individuals or Institutions in the City wished to make enquiries as to the Gaumont British Picture Corporation it was natural for them to approach Messrs Helbert, Wagg & Company Limited. In consequence, Messrs, Helbert, Wagg & Company Ltd felt that it was in the interest of the Gaumont British Picture Corporation, and only right according to usage, that they should be in a position to deal diplomatically with persons and Institutions approaching them'.[90] Helbert, Wagg's complaint was that Gaumont British was failing to provide the information that was required to discharge its duties. The dispute was resolved through the mediation of Claud Serocold, a Cazenove partner, but Helbert, Wagg was from that time wary of the film industry. When it was approached to make an issue on behalf of Ealing Studios in April 1947 the board declined 'as a matter of principle' because it was 'a cinema proposition'.[91]

From the spring of 1933 to the opening months of 1937 the price of the shares of British companies sustained a more-or-less continuous advance, while retail prices were stable and interest rates remained low due to government policy. These were favourable circumstances for the issue of securities by British firms, and Helbert, Wagg was very active on their behalf, both as lead-manager and as a participant in underwriting syndicates put together by other firms. During the 1920s many issues for British companies had been made by stockbrokers, but with the demise of foreign issues in the early 1930s the merchant banks focused upon the origination and underwriting of issues for domestic corporate clients, and stockbroking firms were relegated to broking and placing roles. An example of this process is provided by the issue undertaken by Helbert, Wagg in January 1935 on behalf of the International Tea Company's Stores Ltd of 1.2 million 4.25 per cent preference shares, which raised £1.25 million. Previous issues had been made by Cazenove, which evidently bridled at being demoted: 'Owing to our intimate relations in the last few years with the company, we feel it only right that we should make it clear to you that we cannot regard the fact of our being one of the brokers to the issue as altering in any way our personal relations with the company; that is to say we must be free on future occasions, as in the past, to do business direct with the company,' ran Cazenove's letter accepting the appointment. 'We feel sure that you will appreciate our reason for writing this letter is to avoid any possible misunderstanding in the future.'[92]

Helbert, Wagg's introduction to International Tea came through the Lonsdale Investment Trust and the outcome of this collaboration was the establishment of close relations between the firms.[93] Leopold Lonsdale, the driving force behind the Lonsdale Investment Trust, wanted to forge closer ties with an issuing house for the same reasons as issuing houses created investment trusts. In April 1935, Lonsdale, purchased a minority shareholding in Helbert, Wagg by agreement and henceforth was a regular participant in Helbert, Wagg's underwriting syndicates and placements lists. This arrangement, described by Fraser as 'most happy and friendly', came to an end in 1948 when the Lonsdale Investment Trust and the issuing house Robert Benson & Co. Ltd executed a fully-fledged merger to form Robert Benson, Lonsdale & Co. Ltd, which in 1961 combined with Kleinworts to form Kleinwort, Benson. Lonsdale's shareholding in Helbert, Wagg was purchased in roughly equal parts by the directors, the Australian Mercantile Land and Finance Company, the Prudential, and the Pearl, which strengthened the firm's ties with these important City institutions.

Amongst Helbert, Wagg's corporate clients in the 1930s were major iron and steel companies with which Alfred Wagg, Munro and Campbell had strong personal ties. The firm had already made issues for Richard Thomas and Baldwins, in 1923 and 1928, raising £200,000 and £1 million respectively, and conducted further issues in 1934 and 1936, which raised £1.2 million and £1.5 million. In 1935, £2.25 million was raised for Guest, Keen & Baldwins. For Stewarts & Lloyds, £2 million was raised in 1934, £350,000 in July 1935 and a further £350,000 in January 1938. For firms in the newer industries the scale of issues was much smaller and the funds were usually raised by the placement of securities with institutional investors rather than by public issue. Examples are £200,000 for S. Smith & Sons, clockmakers; £80,000 for Sangamo Western electrical switchmakers; and £350,000 for Revo Electric. Similar sized placements, raising sums in the range of £100,000–£300,000, were made for firms conducting sundry sorts of activities, such as the Eastern Counties Omnibus Co.; Express Supply Concrete; and L. Rose & Co., manufacturers of lime juice cordial. In 1936, Helbert, Wagg sponsored issues by the property companies, Site Improvements and Finsbury Circus Estates, which required funds to take advantage of the favourable climate for major real estate development projects. Palache became closely involved in the affairs of these property companies, of which he was a director for many years.

Helbert, Wagg's relationship with Marks & Spencer began in 1930 with the issue of £1 million preference shares and £1 million debentures. The firm was introduced to the business by the Prudential, which had a close relationship with Marks & Spencer, underwrote the issue and was obliged to take up practically all the securities when it was shunned by investors. 'I had to look after the market on their behalf,' recalled Fraser, 'and strangely enough, although the public issue had been so poorly received, a demand soon arose on the Stock Exchange. By feeding it gently and carefully, the whole of both blocks were sold at a satisfactory profit within a fairly brief space of time, thus fully justifying the confidence of the sponsors.'[94] Three years later, Helbert, Wagg was approached by a Dutch multiple retailer (unidentified in the records, but presumably C & A) for advice on the finance of a chain store undertaking in Britain. Palache informed the Dutch that he would have to consult Marks & Spencer prior to agreeing to advise them and was given leave to do so. 'Mr Marks greatly appreciated our courtesy in this direction,' Palache reported, 'and asked me a great many questions about the intentions of the new combination. During the conversation he put it to me that it was difficult for Helbert, Wagg & Co. to "run with the hare and hunt with the hounds", and that from their point of view they would not like to see us associated with another chain store proposition . . . I had a strong impression that Marks & Spencer have taken a moral obligation upon themselves and cannot after this interview ignore us in any future finance.'[95] Marks & Spencer honoured their 'moral obligation' and in 1936 Helbert, Wagg brought out a £2.5 million debenture issue for the firm, a sum exceeded only by the British Gaumont issue. 'We were very proud of our early connection with Marks & Spencer,' commented Fraser, 'even in those days, it was obvious to us that this concern had genius behind it.'

'Horlicks, the manufacturer of Horlick's Malted Milk, needs no introduction to the general public' commented the *Financial Times* in January 1937 upon the publication of a prospectus for a public issue of 550,000 ordinary shares, a quarter of the equity capital.[96] The sale came about as a result of the death of the former chairman, who was a major shareholder in the family firm, and the introduction of the business to Helbert, Wagg through Kenneth Wagg, a nephew of Alfred Wagg who worked at 41 Threadneedle Street in the 1930s but did not return to a permanent position after the war. 'The excellent earnings yield, combined with expanding trade and the financial strength of the company,' continued the *Financial Times*, 'indicates that a very satisfactory return on the money invested should be forthcoming.' The issue caught the imagination of the investing public and Fraser recalled that 'the queues of people seeking prospectuses were almost frightening in their determination. Some were paying a premium for application forms'.[97] When the list was closed it was found that the issue was thirty times over-subscribed and members of the public were scaled down to twenty shares each. It was a fitting finale for Helbert, Wagg to the bull market of the mid-1930s.

Share prices declined in 1937, reflecting the economic recession of that year. The increasing likelihood of war was another factor discouraging investors, which accounts for the continued decline of share prices in 1938, despite an upturn in economic activity, and the acceleration of their fall in 1939. This was a market environment in which it was very difficult to sell new issues of securities by public issue, and Helbert, Wagg's name appeared on only a single prospectus between the Horlicks issue of January 1937 and the outbreak of war in September 1939. The exception was the £2 million 4.5 per cent debentures issued in February 1939 jointly by Helbert, Wagg and Morgan Grenfell on behalf of the steel company, John Summers & Sons, to finance the completion of a slip mill.[98]

In these bear market conditions, corporate fund-raising from the capital market was accomplished by the private placement of securities with insurance companies and investment trusts. The close contacts that Wagg and Barrington maintained with the insurance industry were of vital importance to the firm's placing power, the Prudential and the Pearl Assurance Company featuring prominently on most of the placement lists. Helbert, Wagg conducted placements on behalf of two dozen or so clients in these years, both quoted companies and private ones. Their activities were very varied – brewing, building, clockmaking, coal, electrical equipment, iron and steel, mining finance, paint, paper, sugar and an investment trust. The sums raised were mostly in the range £100,000–£300,000, though £750,000 4 per cent debentures were placed for the brewers, Barclay Perkins, in 1937. An example of this form of fund-raising in the late 1930s is provided by the West Indies Sugar Co., which was formed in May 1937 by Tate & Lyle and a number of other leading sugar interests to develop sugar cultivation in Jamaica and to modernise sugar refining on the island.[99] Palache was recruited to the board of directors, because of his sugar industry expertise, and Helbert, Wagg raised £1 million for the company and an associate in four separate modestly-sized placements of ordinary and preference shares in 1937 and 1938. The bulk of the securities were taken by insurance companies, notably the Provident Mutual and the Pearl, and the sugar companies represented on the board were also substantial subscribers. Around 10 per cent of these securities were placed with investment vehicles within Helbert, Wagg's direct ambit – the British & German Trust, the Manor Charitable Trust, the Lonsdale Investment Trust – and some were taken for the firm's own investment account.

Rising security prices on the London and New York stockmarkets from 1932 restored the values of the investment portfolios of the Trans-Oceanic Trust and the Westpool Investment Trust. The success of these trusts in the mid-1930s led to the launch of yet another in December 1937: the Ashdown Investment Trust. The British & German Trust had a very different fortune. At the time of the German financial crisis of July 1931 its German loans and investments amounted to £895,000, constituting 40 per cent of the total value of assets of £2.3 million.[100] It was thereafter impossible to recover the principal of the loans which were gradually written down, being valued at £755,000 in December 1932 and £486,000 at the start of the war.[101] Although some interest on the German loans was received in the 1930s, the need to make provisions against their possible loss caused the cessation of the payment of dividends on the ordinary shares from 1931. Upon the outbreak of the Second World War it was considered inappropriate for the word 'German' to form part of the name and in December 1939 it was renamed the Broadstone Investment Trust. The hostilities led to the end of remittances from Germany and other problems for Broadstone, and in 1942 pay-outs to the preference shareholders were suspended.

Helbert, Wagg's high reputation for investment management skills caused it to be called upon to assist in the rescue of the Independent Investment Trust in July 1932.[102] The formation of the Independent Investment Trust in 1924 caused 'quite a stir' in the City because its three-man board of directors comprised John Maynard Keynes, the most controversial economist of the day, who was already credited with making a fortune for his Cambridge College through his investment skills; Oswald Falk, a City-based economist with the stockbroker Buckmaster & Moore, and a leading adviser to the Scottish investment trusts; and Ian Macpherson, a well-known stockbroker. The new trust was nicknamed the 'Brains Trust' because of the academic reputations of the directors, who announced that it was their intention to apply economic theory in the service of investment management, then a novel approach. Unfortunately, differences of opinion arose between Keynes and Falk, and the performance of the Independent Investment Trust was lamentable. In the wake of the crash and the slump in which much of the capital was lost it was decided to resort to conventional investment management. Helbert, Wagg was appointed 'managers and secretaries' to the trust and Barrington joined the board of directors. Under Helbert,

Wagg's 'low brow and common sense' management the losses were recovered and the Independent Investment Trust prospered.[103] Helbert, Wagg continued to manage the Independent Investment Trust until November 1958, when it was acquired by John Sheffield, the chairman of Norcros, the industrial holding company.

With the onset of the slump there was little scope for Helbert, Wagg to conduct international financial transactions, but when an opportunity arose in the mid-1930s the directors responded enthusiastically. Towards the end of 1936 the firm was approached by three Argentinian bankers who were seeking European backing for the establishment of a firm in Buenos Aires specialising in foreign exchange, security business, interim financing, acting as agent for opening special credits both in the Argentine and abroad, and also to act as agent for Government, Municipalities, Corporations and private individuals both in the Argentine and abroad. For this last purpose the firm counts on the active co-operation of its European friends'.[104] Palache attended a series of meetings in Paris whose outcome was that Helbert, Wagg and the Australian Mercantile Land and Finance Co. Ltd, of London; the Nederlandishe Standards Bank, of Amsterdam; the Banque Suisse, of Geneva, and the Societé Anonyme Hersent, of Paris, each subscribed 400,000 pesos towards the capital of the firm and the Argentinian partners 500,000 pesos, making a total capital of 2.5 million pesos. Palache visited Buenos Aires in April 1937 on behalf of the European partners and assisted with the establishment of Shaw, Strupp & Co., as it was named after the local managing partners. This undertaking had many similarities with Argentaria, Schrobanco's Argentinian subsidiary, and the staff included Ernest Borchardt, who had previously worked at Argentaria. In 1940, the Australian Mercantile Land and Finance Company's shareholding was acquired by the Lonsdale Investment Trust, which was introduced to the consortium by Helbert, Wagg. Shaw, Strupp had a difficult start but by 1941 the losses of the early years had been recovered and profits were 200,000 pesos. The following year profits of 620,000 pesos gave a highly satisfactory 25 per cent return on capital and a 'maiden dividend' of 8 per cent was declared. The success was short-lived, however, and in the summer of 1943 Palache reported to the Helbert, Wagg board that 'the personal relationships between the partners in this firm have deteriorated to the point where the most desirable solution would be liquidation'.[105] Wartime restrictions complicated and delayed the recovery of Helbert, Wagg's investment, but eventually in August 1946 the firm received £21,000, which gave a profit of £6,000 on the original investment.

The looming likelihood of war led to the establishment in October 1938 of a working party under Palache to make preparations. Business was blighted well before the outbreak of hostilities and in January 1939 the Helbert, Wagg board minuted that 'there is very little going on'.[106] A few days after the declaration of war in September 1939 Fraser called upon Helbert, Wagg's clearing bank, the National Provincial, and was assured that 'war or no war' they would 'always be prepared to satisfy Helbert, Wagg & Co.'s reasonable requirements' as they regarded the firm as 'amongst our best and most intimate friends'.[107] The National Provincial's promise of support was an important encouragement, since by 1940 there was a 'complete stagnation of business'.[108] Strict controls on the raising of capital by firms during the war drastically curtailed issuing activity and in the five-and-a-half years of hostilities Helbert, Wagg made only six placements and two rights issues. From 1941, Helbert, Wagg's most remunerative activity was dealing in government securities, which was conducted by the Bond Trading Department headed by the doyen of City bond dealers, George Wood, whose team were the only members of staff to earn bonuses during the conflict. Another reason for the low level of Helbert, Wagg's activity during the war was the engagement of the most dynamic of the directors upon government war work: Campbell at the Board of Trade and the Ministry of Production; Fraser at the Treasury; and Munro in the War Office and from 1941 to 1946 as financial adviser to the United Kingdom Commission to Canada.

Helbert, Wagg's profits in the 1930s and 1940s fluctuated to the rhythm of the general political and economic environment (see Figure 12.6). In 1931, the firm made a loss of £38,000 due to the drop in revenues and a £64,000 write-down on securities valuations. The loss plus the cost of the preference share dividend consumed the whole of the accumulated undistributed profits and there was a charge of £34,000 to the General Reserve. An operating profit of £51,000 in 1932 permitted payment of the preference dividends and a rebuilding of the General Reserve. In both these years, however, there was no profit available for dividends to ordinary shareholders or directors' bonuses. The return to significant profits in 1933–36, which averaged £172,000 per annum in these years – about £5.5 million in 1990 money – permitted the cumulative dividend liability on the ordinary shares for 1931–32 to be honoured, and enabled the management and staff again to receive significant bonuses. Operating profits slumped in 1937 and in the years 1937–42 averaged only £29,000, just covering the preference and minimum ordinary dividends (except in 1940). No bonuses were paid in these years, the directors receiving salaries of approximately £2,000 per annum each. From 1943 to the end of the war operating profits averaged £66,000, an improvement which permitted the resumption of modest bonus payments. There was a big rise in profits in 1946 but a

Figure 12.6   Helbert, Wagg & Co. Ltd, pre-tax operating profits, 1931–47

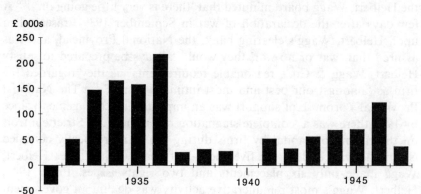

sharp fall in 1947, and the surge in inflation the latter year also weakened performance.

The years 1931–47 saw a continuation of the policy of the total distribution of operating profits amongst the shareholders, management and staff, and thus the capital of the firm remained virtually unchanged. Given the constant capital base, the operating return shown in Figure 12.7 mirrors the profile of operating profits: in 1931 the return was negative; in 1932 it recovered to 9 per cent; in 1933–36 it averaged 31 per cent per annum, a remarkably impressive performance at a time of negligible inflation; in 1937–42, however, it averaged only 5 per cent per annum; but in 1943–47 the annual average was 13 per cent, which was a great improvement on the firm's performance in the First World War and an acceptable return in an era of great uncertainty. For most of the period price inflation was negligible and real returns were almost identical to nominal returns, the exception being the years 1939–40 which saw inflation in excess of 20 per cent per annum, turning the real returns for these years negative. Shareholders participated in the prosperity of the mid-1930s through supplementary dividends on their ordinary shares, the return on equity averaging 13 percent in 1933–36. The annual average return on equity fell to 5.9 per cent in the decade 1937–47, which though a deterioration in performance was almost double the yield on gilts, which averaged 3.1 per cent over the period. Overall, the years 1931–47 demonstrated the volatility of the investment banking business and the durability of the rewards structure created by Alfred Wagg in 1919 which provided shareholders with consistently satisfactory returns and permitted management to participate substantially in profits in prosperous years but did not compensate them in lean years.

Figure 12.7 Helbert, Wagg & Co. Ltd, pre-tax operating return, pre-tax return on equity and annual rate of inflation, 1931–47

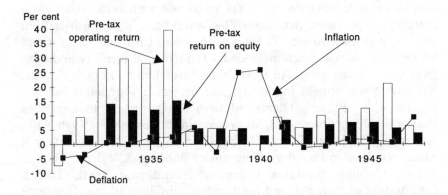

Note: The 'real' return on capital is the difference between the nominal returns on capital depicted above and the annual rate of inflation.

In the middle years of the 1930s, Helbert, Wagg's balance sheets resembled those of the prosperous years of the 1920s. Loans made up three-fifths of assets, resulting from the commitment of funds to underwriting and to meeting the requirements of new issue clients, which were funded by an expansion of deposits and balances. In the war years there was a contraction of loans and of deposits and balances, reflecting the low level of issuing business, while the holdings of Treasury bills and gilts increased because of George Wood's trading activities. During the war years, highly liquid assets comprised 36 per cent of the total, twice the proportion of the mid-1930s, while capital constituted 44 per cent of liabilities, very conservative ratios which reflected the hazards of the times and the prudence of the management. This pattern was maintained in the immediate post-war years and it was not until 1948 that the strategic emphasis shifted from risk avoidance to profit maximisation.

Lionel Fraser and his Team, 1946–62

In the decade and a half following the end of the Second World War the pre-eminent figure in the history of Helbert, Wagg was Lionel Fraser, who became deputy chairman in 1946, aged 50, and succeeded Alfred Wagg as chairman in 1954. Fraser had none of the advantages of birth and education enjoyed by most of his colleagues and his rise to the top of Helbert, Wagg was entirely attributable to his abilities and character.

Described in the late 1950s, when he was at the peak of his career, as a 'tall, straightbacked, handsome, commanding figure',[109] he had a forceful and energetic personality and a strong will to win, which sometimes made him enemies.[110] Yet his friends, such as the writer of his obituary in *The Times*, remembered his 'warm heart, a gift for friendship and a gay attitude to life . . . He was an ardent Christian Scientist and his deep religious convictions added a fundamental integrity and deep seriousness of character. All these things made him an inspiring leader. His advice was sought intimately, and he was a formidable but fair negotiator'.[111] Fraser's talents led to his appointment to numerous boards, including Spicers Ltd, his first outside directorship in 1940; Atlas Assurance; Brighton, Hove & District Omnibus; and Tube Investments. Moreover, he also served as chairman of Babcock & Wilcox; Thomas Tilling; Cornhill Insurance Company; Scandinvest Trust; Triarch Corporation of Toronto; and the London subsidiary of the Banque de Paris et des Pays-Bas. In the City he was a highly regarded figure: for instance, his services were called upon when a neutral chairman was needed for negotiations between the parties in the bitterly acrimonious take-over bid by Sears for Watneys in 1959.[112] During the war, thanks to the support of Montagu Norman, he worked at the Treasury as liaison officer between the British financial authorities and the Allied Governments based in London and was awarded the CMG in 1945 for his services. These connections led to his appointment in 1945 as the Bank of England's representative to the State Bank of Morocco. Fraser's wish to continue to undertake public work led him to serve as a Conservative member of Chelsea Borough Council in 1945–50 and as a trustee of the Tate Gallery, he and his wife being avid collectors of abstract art. He was a keen club-man and was a member of half-a-dozen clubs including the Garrick, the Travellers' and the aristocratic Whites, some of whose more elderly members might well have recalled his father in the capacity of a 'gentleman's gentleman'.

At the time of Fraser's appointment as deputy chairman in 1946 the founding generation of Helbert, Wagg's directors were in their sixties, and Bonn and Jones had already left the firm. Campbell died in 1948 and although Palache continued on the board until 1957, and Wagg and Barrington until 1958, by the 1950s they were playing less and less of a part in the day-to-day business of the firm. Munro, who was Fraser's age and his rival for the post of chief executive, resigned in 1946 and took up the post of representative of H. M. Treasury at the British Embassy in Washington and subsequently held a number of other important public service positions. The revival of business at the end of the war necessitated the appointment of new directors, which led to the promotion of Gordon Gunson and James O'Brien, who were of

Fraser's generation, and Alan Russell, Michael Verey and Charles Villiers, all aged around 35–36 when they joined the board. They were supported by a group of younger executives who were in their late twenties when they joined the firm after the war, including Robert Hollond, David Murison and Ashley Ponsonby, each of whom was 35 when he was made a director in 1956. The outcome of the retirements of the older generation and new appointments was that the average age of Helbert, Wagg's directors fell from 61 in 1945 to 47 in 1958. The directors appointed in the late 1940s and mid-1950s were all of English birth and most had public-school educations. These characteristics mirrored those of the senior management of the firm's clients of the era, which were major British companies and financial institutions. Gunson, Hollond, Murison, Russell and Villiers worked on the corporate finance side of the business, while O'Brien, Ponsonby and Verey developed the investment management side, though specialisation was not as rigid as it was to become and each could turn his hand to any aspect of the firm's business when necessary.

Statistics of Helbert, Wagg's revenues are unavailable from 1948 because of changes in the firm's accounting procedures following the Companies Act of that year. Instead it is the pre-tax operating profit which is shown in Figure 12.8 to illustrate the growth of business in the years 1948–61. The post-war expansion of Helbert, Wagg's operating profits occurred in three phases. In 1948–53, operating profits averaged £130,000 per annum, much higher than the £48,000 per annum average of the years 1937–47, but considerably less than the profits of 1933–36, which averaged £172,000 per annum. The mid-1950s saw an increase on the immediate post-war years, and in 1954–58 Helbert, Wagg's operating profit averaged £224,000. The third phase opened in 1959, when

Figure 12.8 Helbert, Wagg & Co. Ltd, pre-tax operating profits, 1948–61

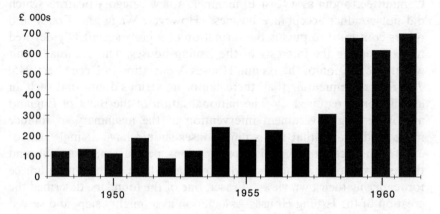

operating profit leapt to £677,000 – £6.9 million in 1990 money – and it was following this record result that the decision was taken to sell the business to Schroders. In 1960 and 1961, years when Schroders already had a 70 per cent interest in the firm, operating profits were £617,000 and £697,000 respectively. Making allowance for the depreciation in the value of money, the profits of 1959–61 were similar in magnitude to those earned by the firm in 1927, though in real terms the result for 1928 was a third higher still.

Towards the end of the war the focus of Helbert, Wagg's directors shifted from survival to revival. The change was marked by boardroom discussions about the firm's strategy and identity, and after one of these 'it was unanimously agreed that the style of the firm in future should be that of INVESTMENT BANKERS, and that in all advertisements, reference books, etc, this description should be inserted instead of the present one [Issuing House]'.[113] Helbert, Wagg was in the forefront of the usage of this Wall Street term in London, which presumably was adopted to convey an up-to-date image, since New York was now unquestionably the world's leading financial centre. A clear under-standing of the realities of the post-war world by the Helbert, Wagg board is also suggested by the decision to send, unbidden and for the first time, a copy of the firm's balance sheet to the Governor of the newly nationalised Bank of England in April 1946.[114]

During the war it was decided that Helbert, Wagg should become a member of an association of financial firms 'in view of the growing tendency on the part of the authorities to put City firms into categories'.[115] In October 1944, following a 'discreet enquiry' about joining the British Bankers' Association, which evidently received an unsatisfactory answer, Alfred Wagg entered discussions with the Bank of England about the formation of an association of issuing houses.[116] In May 1945 the firm accepted an invitation from the Accepting Houses Committee to join as a 'List B' member, a new category of firms which did not conduct acceptance business. However, Wagg and Fraser and others continued to pursue the formation of a body specifically devoted to representing the interests of the issuing houses. The eventual result was the formation of the Issuing Houses Association in December 1945, *The Times* commenting that' there can be no serious doubt that such an association is required'.[117] The nationalisation of the Bank of England and increasing government intervention in the machinery of finance made it 'desirable that the issuing houses should have a single pair of ears for the reception of advice, explanations, persuasion, directions, and the rest from official sources and should also have a single mouthpiece for tendering their own views'. Fraser, one of the founders, described the creation of the Issuing Houses Association as a 'mighty step' and served as the first deputy chairman and as chairman from October 1946 to 1948.[118]

The formation of the Issuing Houses Association proved timely, since the volume of new capital issues in the United Kingdom soared in the years directly after the war – in 1944 they totalled only £9.4 million, but rose to £24 million in 1945 and £278 million in 1948.[119] Helbert, Wagg's issuing business revived with the market: in 1945, it raised £6 million for clients; in 1946, £10 million; in 1947, £24 million (but this includes the whole of the massive £15 million issue on behalf of the Steel Company of Wales by the 'Consortium', the syndicate of eight leading City houses of which Helbert, Wagg was a member and which from 1953 conducted the denationalisation of the steel industry); and in 1948, £8 million. Its first post-war business was to secure a quotation of the ordinary shares of the iron and steel company, J. Stone Ltd in September 1945. The bulk of these securities had been placed with institutional investors by the firm two years earlier. The arrangement of an 'introduction' was a method of creating a market in securities, not for raising new money *per se*, although introductions were often combined with new issues. This was the first time that Helbert, Wagg conducted an introduction, but there after they became a standard feature of its activities. Three months later, in December 1945 it had the distinction of making the City's first 'normal' post-war issue.[120] The client was John Summers & Co. and the issue of preference shares, conducted, as before, jointly with Morgan Grenfell, raised £2 million. December 1945 also saw the Standard Motors issue to finance the production of Ferguson tractors, which was conducted jointly with Schröders, the first collaborative effort between the firms.

The immediate post-war years saw a vigorous and highly successful drive to recruit new British corporate clients, thirty-two of the fourty-six firms for which Helbert, Wagg conducted issues in 1945–49 being first-time clients. Most of the credit for this achievement belongs to Fraser, though he would not have made so much headway without the assistance of introductions from Barrington, Campbell, Palache and Wagg. Many of the new clients were leading blue-chip companies such as Leyland Motors, Standard Motors, H. J. Heinz, Babcock & Wilcox, and City of London Real Properties, the doyen of British property companies, and the post-war recruitment drive was one of the reasons for Helbert, Wagg's impressive client roster in the 1950s. Fraser was also happy to raise funds for much smaller firms so long as they were well managed. These included John Reddihough Ltd, a Bradford wool-comber, for which Helbert, Wagg raised £350,000 in 1948;[121] and L. H. Lavery & Co. Ltd, a manufacturer of 'slab cakes, Swiss Rolls, sponges and Christmas puddings', for which it made an issue which raised £500,000 in July 1947, the first offer-for-sale conducted by the firm.[122] Although the issue was over-subscribed the shares soon languished at a discount to the offer price, and with hindsight Fraser noted that they had charged too much for the 'good will'.[123] A débâcle of these years was the offer-for-sale in February 1948 of 900,000 ordinary shares of the Hulton Press Ltd, the publisher of the best-selling magazine *Picture Post* and a host of specialist publications such as *Farmers' Weekly*. Hulton Press' recent earnings growth had been 'dynamic', and even better results were predicted with the imminent ending of paper rationing.[124] Unfortunately the day before the subscription list opened the Chancellor made some gloomy remarks about the economy, upon which 'the public took fright and abstained' leaving the underwriters awash with shares.[125]

The economic problems that caused investors to shy away from the Hulton Press issue led to the collapse of share and bond prices in the first half of 1949. The bear market was accompanied by a slump in new issues, which fell from £278 million in 1948 to £157 million in 1949, and for most issuing houses 1949 was a lean year. However, Helbert, Wagg's issues actually increased from £8 million to £11.3 million and the firm's postwar resurgence continued. The reason was the energetic development of business by the five new directors: Gunson, O'Brien, Russell, Verey and Villiers. Amongst the new clients of 1949 was the Municipal Council of Nairobi, Kenya, for which Helbert, Wagg and Morgan Grenfell jointly raised £1.5 million by the sale of 3.25 per cent sterling registered stock 1970–74 at 98. 'This is the first time,' noted *The Times*, 'on which these famous merchant banking names have been associated with the raising of funds on behalf of a crown colony. Extension of their activities to the colonial market is a natural sequel to the change in market conditions since the war.'[126] The issue was over-subscribed in both London and Nairobi. But despite the precedent set by the issue, Helbert, Wagg did not develop a clientele amongst crown colony municipalities, though it did conduct two further issues for Nairobi in 1951 and 1954.

The stock market's slide came to a halt in the summer of 1949, and issuing activity, which was virtually at a standstill in the first half of the year, began a tentative revival. Helbert, Wagg boldly made several issues in the summer months but investors proved unenthusiastic about the offerings. The shareholders of Albert E. Reed, a longstanding client, proved unwilling to take up their rights in July 1949, and the underwriters, led by Helbert, Wagg, were left with half of a £1 million share issue.[127] An almost simultaneous issue to raise £4 million on behalf of Babcock & Wilcox, a leading boilermaker and heavy engineering group, proved even more of a headache for the underwriters, who had to take up 37 per cent of the ordinary shares and 82 per cent of the preference shares.[128] Helbert, Wagg's engagement to conduct this issue arose from Fraser's friendship with Babcock director, Air Chief Marshal Sir Wilfred Freeman, a fellow member of the board of British European Airways and a director of Courtaulds. The Babcock directors were much impressed by Fraser's conduct and a few months after the problematic issue invited him to become chairman upon the unexpected death of the previous incumbent. He fulfilled this role for almost a decade, devoting as much as a third of his time to Babcock's affairs. Naturally, Helbert, Wagg acted as Babcock's issuing house during the 1950s, and raised a further £6.5 million for the firm through issues in 1951, 1953 and 1958.

Share prices rallied in 1950 and began an advance which continued, despite a set-back in 1952, until 1955. The same period also saw new issues in the UK rise from £157 million in 1949 to £635 million in 1955. Helbert, Wagg's directors seized the opportunities presented by this favourable environment and in 1950–55 the firm conducted 93 issues, twice as many as in the preceding five years. In 1950, and again in 1951, issues in which the firm was a participant raised £24 million for clients. The temporary downturn in share prices in 1952 was reflected in exaggerated form in Helbert, Wagg's new issues, which slumped to £2 million, but the resumption of the upward movement of stockmarket prices was matched by a revival of business to £7 million in 1953, £16 million in 1954, and £21 million in 1955, excluding its participations in joint issues in connection with the denationalisation of the steel industry.

The early 1950s saw the addition of yet more leading industrial firms to the roster of Helbert, Wagg's new issue clients. Thomas Tilling and Tube Investments used the firm to raise funds because of the presence of Helbert, Wagg directors on their boards. Alfred Wagg became a director of Thomas Tilling, a large bus operator, in the 1930s, while Sir Frederick Heaton, the Tilling chairman, joined the board of the Westpool Investment Trust. In July 1942, Wagg was joined in the Tilling boardroom by Fraser, who soon became deputy chairman. The post-war Labour administration earmarked road transport as an industry for nationalisation, and in 1948, to forestall forcible acquisition, Heaton negotiated the sale of Tilling's bus services to the government's Transport Commission. Heaton died in April 1949, and in May, Fraser was appointed chairman of Thomas Tilling, a post he held until 1965. Under his leadership, Tilling developed into an industrial holding company using the proceeds of the sale of the buses to finance the acquisition of a diversified portfolio of undertakings. Fraser explained that 'our companies . . . retain their own sense of identity and their freedom to manage. . . . Our Headquarters Executive Staff consisting of engineers, accountants, lawyers, surveyors, marketing experts etc. are constantly available to our companies for advice and guidance'.[129] In the early 1950s this was a novel strategy, and some observers were sceptical about the likelihood of success, but doubts were soon laid to rest by Tilling's performance, Fraser proudly reporting a five-and-a-half times increase in the share price between 1949 and 1962. Helbert, Wagg assisted the expansion of Tilling by conducting a rights issue for the firm in 1955, and two more in 1961, which together raised £8 million.

Fraser was also the tie between Helbert, Wagg and Tube Investments (TI). In January 1948, he accepted an invitation from Ivan Stedeford, the TI chairman, to become joint deputy-chairman of this important British engineering firm. Under Stedeford's forceful leadership, TI expanded rapidly during the 1950s and Helbert, Wagg made nine issues for the firm, raising £100 million to finance investments and acquisitions. Four of the issues were conducted jointly with Schroders, which was appointed co-issuing house in 1955. A noteworthy feature of the first joint issue for TI were the 'novel arrangements' to safeguard shareholders who did not take up their rights, which was accomplished by the issuing houses subscribing for such shares, selling them in the market and distributing the net proceeds to the shareholders.[130]

In the post-war years many American corporations established subsidiaries in Britain. Often a minority equity interest was sold to British investors, with the intention of forging a bond between the new undertaking and the host country. The services of firms such as Helbert, Wagg were engaged to place such shares amongst British institutional investors and subsequently to raise additional capital. Helbert, Wagg's relationship with H. J. Heinz Ltd began in November 1948, when it raised £1 million for this British subsidiary of the American food manufacturer by placing 600,000 preference shares and 100,000 ordinary shares.[131] Heinz' 57 varieties proved popular in Britain, and further issues, underwritten by Helbert, Wagg, were made in February 1951, July 1952 and September 1954, which produced a further £3 million to finance expansion. In November 1954, Helbert, Wagg secured a Stock Exchange quotation for the firm's £3 million 4.5 per cent redeemable preference shares.[132] Even more important was the securing of the business of IBM United Kingdom, the British subsidiary of the American computer manufacturer. This arose from a chance meeting in London in June 1951 between Fraser and an acquaintance who informed him that Thomas J. Watson, the chairman of IBM, was in town to find financing for a British offshoot.[133] On the following day, much to his disappointment, Fraser learned that IBM was having discussions with Morgan Grenfell. However, Morgan Grenfell declined to act because of a conflict of interest, and Fraser secured the business. In November 1951, Helbert, Wagg placed 40 per cent of the equity of IBM United Kingdom amongst British institutional and private investors, raising £800,000 for the company, and in 1955, 1956 and 1958 organised rights issues which raised a further £5 million to finance growth.

The 1950s saw vigorous expansion in British industry, and many of Helbert, Wagg's established manufacturing clients sought additional investment funds. The firm acted on eight occasions to make issues for Albert E. Reed, raising £14 million to finance the investment and acquisition programme of Reed's ambitious management. Babcock & Wilcox, Leyland Motors and Standard Motors each made three issues through Helbert, Wagg during the decade. Horlicks, whose flotation had been conducted by the firm in January 1937, made use of its services again in December 1951 to conduct a £1.25 million rights issue. As in many contemporary issues, debentures and equities were offered simultaneously, but they received a 'contrasting reception' from shareholders, who subscribed for all the 500,000 ordinary shares but only 6 per cent of the 750,000 debentures.[134] The strong preference of the Horlicks shareholders for equities over debentures was an early manifestation of the phenomenon which came to be known later in the 1950s as 'the cult of the equity'. Equities were preferred by investors in these years, partly because inflation eroded the value of bonds and partly because, for much of the decade, they appeared cheap when compared with pre-war valuations.[135] The pattern of Helbert, Wagg's issues reflected this preference and in the post-war years the proportion of equity issues was much higher than in the 1930s.

The offer-for-sale on behalf of United Steel Companies in October 1953 was the first step in the denationalisation of the steel industry.[136] The return of the industry to the private sector was effected by the sale of the pre-nationalisation steel firms to the public. These issues were conducted jointly by the Consortium which, as already noted, first came together to make the £15 million debenture issue for the Steel Company of Wales in July 1947. Helbert, Wagg was the joint lead-manager with Morgan Grenfell for the issues made by the Consortium for Stewarts & Lloyds in June 1954 and John Summers in October 1954, and a participant in the Consortium issues for Lancashire Steel Corporation in January 1954; Dorman Long in November 1954; Colvilles in January 1955; Whitehead Iron & Steel in February 1955; and the Steel Company of Wales in March 1957. Back in the private sector , Stewarts & Lloyds and John Summers returned to the list of Helbert, Wagg's clients, the latter on joint account with Morgan Grenfell.

The bull market of the early 1950s peaked in the summer of 1955 and it was not until the spring of 1958 that share prices resumed an upward trend. New issues in the UK mirrored the pattern of share prices, falling back from the peak of £630 million in 1955 and maintaining a constant

£360 million in 1956, 1957 and 1958. Helbert, Wagg's issuing activity followed the market, totalling £21 million in 1956, £23 million in 1957 and £22 million in 1958, excluding its participations in joint issues by the Consortium. Most of the fifty-nine issues conducted by the firm in the years 1956–58 were for firms that had joined Helbert, Wagg's client list in previous years, such as Albert E. Reed, Tube Investments, Leyland Motors, IBM United Kingdom, City of London Real Properties and Babcock & Wilcox. The new clients of these years were small and obscure by comparison and had modest fund-raising requirements, with the notable exception of Raleigh Industries, bicycle manufacturers, for which £3.3 million was raised in November 1957, the company's first recourse to external financing since 1934.[137]

The 1950s saw the commencement of the modern corporate finance function of City firms. Previously, companies had contacted their financial advisers if and when they wanted to raise funds through the issue of securities. The new pattern was for much more frequent contact and for the provision of a wider range of financial advisory services by the City houses. Helbert, Wagg was in the forefront of the professionalisation of corporate finance services. In the late 1940s, Russell and Gunson (himself a Scottish chartered accountant) recruited a team of qualified chartered accountants to provide in-house assistance to the directors with corporate finance work. This constituted the first modern corporate finance department in the City, though soon there were others.

There were several reasons for the development of the corporate finance function in the 1950s. First, there was the need to obtain the consent of the Capital Issues Committee for any sizable issue, which meant that it was essential to have cases expertly presented. Second, inflation caused companies to review their financial structures, and capital reorganisations became a feature of Helbert, Wagg's corporate finance services in the post-war period. A third factor pushing companies closer to their financial advisers was the increase in merger and acquisition activity during the 1950s, expenditure on acquisitions growing from £735 million to £2.5 billion between 1949 and 1960.[138] The companies involved turned to their merchant banks for counsel upon the terms of the transactions and for assistance with the funding of the deals. More and more of the issues which Helbert, Wagg conducted in the 1950s were to finance mergers and acquisitions, either by borrowing or through the exchange of shares. But the development which more than any other impelled companies to develop close ties with City advisers was the advent of the 'take-over' – the acquisition of a firm against the wishes of the incumbent management through an offer direct to shareholders. Take-overs began in the early 1950s, when Charles

Clore and other pioneers realised that the prevailing share price of many firms fell short of the value of their assets. The Bank of England disapproved of this development, fearing that it jeopardised dividend restraint and other government policies, and directed banks and insurance companies not to finance hostile bids. This curbed take-over activity, though it by no means ceased.[139] City firms, acting in accordance with the wishes of the Bank, refused to act on behalf of the predators, though they conducted defensive actions on behalf of the victims. The relaxation of controls on bank lending in July 1958 and a change of view on the part of the authorities, which now regarded the threat of a take-over bid as a useful spur to management to increase the efficiency of British industry, created the conditions for the take-over boom of the late 1950s and early 1960s. Most City men continued to disapprove of take-overs, believing that the directors of a company knew what was in the best interest of the shareholders and the workforce better than marauding financiers motivated by profit. Yet a few, such as Lionel Fraser and Siegmund Warburg (the founder and chairman of the merchant bank S. G. Warburg) who were close friends, held the view that the owner that put the highest valuation on assets was most likely to manage them most effectively. In 1958, Warburg and Fraser, both outsiders by birth to the City Establishment, broke ranks and led a hostile bid for the British Aluminium Company, an episode that was an important turning point in the history of the City.

'The Great Aluminium War', as Fleet Street called it, had its origins in the ambitions of American Metal, a US aluminium company, to expand overseas because of the saturation of the domestic market.[140] It decided to attempt to purchase the British Aluminium Company, the leading British aluminium producer, whose troubles were reflected in the recent halving of its share price. American Metal engaged Warburgs as its advisers, who picked up 10 per cent of British Aluminium shares in the market, there being no restrictions on such purchases at the time, as a preliminary to negotiations.[141] However, the directors of British Aluminium, led by the Establishment figures Lord Portal, former Chief of Staff of the Royal Air Force, and Geoffrey Cunliffe, son of a Governor of the Bank of England, refused to recommend a foreign purchaser to shareholders, and the rebuff put an end to American Metal's acquisition plans. Another American aluminium firm, Reynolds Metals of Virginia, was also interested in acquiring British Aluminium, and at Warburg's instigation it formed an alliance with Tube Investments (TI) to launch a joint bid in which the British firm had a 51 per cent interest to overcome the British Aluminium board's objection to foreign control. Tube Investments' City advisers were Helbert, Wagg and Schroders, which thus joined forces with Warburgs. In September

1958, Warburg and Fraser sought the agreement of the British Aluminium board to an offer by TI–Reynolds to acquire the company at 78 shillings per share. While the British Aluminium directors were pondering this proposal, the advisers to TI–Reynolds were discreetly buying shares in the market and by mid-October controlled 15 per cent of their target. The British Aluminium board decided to thwart the bid and came to an agreement with the Aluminium Company of America (Alcoa) for Alcoa to acquire one-third of the capital of the firm at 60s. per share. The move alienated shareholders, who resented the dilution of their interests by sale of shares at a bargain price to secure the continued control of the incumbent management. The announcement was followed by a deluge of selling orders to take advantage of the prices which the brokers to TI–Reynolds were prepared to pay.

By December the British Aluminium board had become alarmed by the size of the TI–Reynolds stake, and its advisers, Hambros and Lazards, organised fourteen of the foremost City firms, including the merchant banks Morgan Grenfell, Samuel Montagu, Philip Hill, Higginson, Erlanger, Brown, Shipley and Guinness Mahon, and the leading brokers Cazenove and Rowe & Pitman, into a buying consortium to deny control to the hostile bidders and their advisers. Fraser's reaction to the grand alliance was that it 'smacks of fear' and he condemned the attitude of the opposing City firms as 'unprogressive'.[142] In the first week of January 1959 the struggle was resolved in the market in favour of TI–Reynolds. The reward of Helbert, Wagg and Schroders for their contributions to the victory was a fee of 50,000 guineas which was divided between them. 'The merchant bankers are more on their toes,' wrote Fraser in the aftermath of the struggle. 'They vie with one another to give a better service to industry and their clients; there has been a girding of loins, resulting in more enterprise and competitiveness and less reliance on the "old boy" idea.'[143]

The background to the British Aluminium take-over battle was a vigorous upsurge in share prices which began in the summer of 1958 and continued until the spring of 1961. The bull market was accompanied by an issuing boom and a merger boom. Between 1958 and 1961 new issues in the United Kingdom grew from £360 million to £670 million, while the volume of mergers and acquisitions rose from £1.2 billion to £2.2 billion. Helbert, Wagg's business mushroomed in this favourable environment: in 1958 the value of issues in which it was a participant leapt to £72 million; in 1959, £68 million; in 1960, £71 million; and in 1961, £143 million, seven times the level of the mid-1950s. Market conditions were an important factor, but Helbert, Wagg's participation in the British Aluminium battle also gave a boost to business, since it led to an influx of new corporate clients eager to retain the services of one of the houses on the winning side. Additions to Helbert, Wagg's client list at the start of the 1960s included English Sewing Cotton, Smiths Potato Crisps, Goldfields Mining and Industrial, and Tate & Lyle. Another new client was City Centre Properties, a dynamic property company run by Jack Cotton, to whom Charles Villiers acted as financial adviser.[144] Helbert, Wagg made two issues for City Centre Properties to finance take-overs in 1959, and in 1960 it assisted with the ill-fated merger between City Centre Properties and Charles Clore's City & Central Investments.

Amongst the hundred or so issues conducted by Helbert, Wagg in the years 1959–61, the one that really caught the public's imagination was that for Penguin Books undertaken in April 1961. Not only was the new issue boom in full flight, but Penguin Books enjoyed 'the benefit of building up a brand-image for 25 years on every bookstall in the country, and as several recent offers-for-sale have shown, a well-known name is an added attraction when a company becomes public'.[145] Applications to invest in the firm that had recently caused massive controversy by publishing the D. H. Lawrence novel, *Lady Chatterley's Lover*, poured in from the public, greatly exceeding all expectations. Despite closing the list after only one minute the issue was 150 times over-subscribed, which *The Times* reckoned was probably an all-time record. Another business which requires special mention is the operation conducted by Helbert, Wagg in November 1959 on behalf of the American parent company to buy back the shares in IBM United Kingdom which it had placed in 1951 with British investors. The explanation given for this change of policy was that 'it is difficult to reconcile the interests of the minority shareholders with the necessity to integrate the business with a world-wide organisation'.[146] The repurchase price was 165s. for each share which had been sold in 1951 for 40s. Helbert, Wagg had taken a considerable number of IBM United Kingdom shares for the firm's account and the buy-back made a substantial contribution to the spectacular profits of 1959.

Helbert, Wagg was deeply involved in one of the more controversial take-over bids of the early 1960s: the 'Battle of Long Acre' for control of Odhams Press, Britain's largest magazine publisher and an important newspaper publisher whose titles included the *People* and the *Daily Herald*, the voice of the Labour Party.[147] The episode began in December 1960 with a chance meeting at a Christmas party between Cecil King, head of the Mirror Group, the publisher of the *Daily Mirror* and also a major magazine publisher, and Sir Christopher Chancellor, the chairman of Odhams.[148] King suggested the pooling of their magazine publishing interests to halt the cut-throat competition between the groups in the womens' weekly market that was causing them both to lose money. Chancellor, who had no intention of forming an association with the buccaneering King, hastily arranged for a merger with Thomson Newspapers, publisher of the *Sunday Times*. The Mirror Group responded to the proposed Odhams–Thomson merger by launching a take-over bid that offered much better terms to Odhams shareholders. The Mirror Group's City advisers were Warburgs and Helbert, Wagg, the latter's involvement arising from the close ties between the Mirror Group and the firm's longstanding client, Albert E. Reed; while Odhams was advised by Rothschilds, and Thomson Newspapers by Philip Hill, Higginson, Erlangers. An acrimonious bid battle, with a highly charged political dimension because of the *Daily Herald*, developed 'and soon,' wrote Fraser, 'blood was spilt, financial blood, newspaper blood and labour blood'.[149] The outcome was another victory for the formidable combined expertise of Helbert, Wagg and Warburgs.

In the post-war years Helbert, Wagg emerged as one of the City's leading firms of investment managers. In the late 1940s, principally at the instigation of Alan Russell, the firm made a deliberate and determined bid to develop a clientele of institutional investors. Russell was one of the first in the City to foresee the post-war expansion of pension funds, and his appointment to the Helbert, Wagg board in 1946 was followed by the adoption of a new strategy. Michael Verey, who became head of the Investment Department in the 1950s, recalled that:

> from then on we were going for pension funds and shedding private clients. Over four or five years we collected almost one a month and we recruited a very considerable pension fund business, far in excess of Morgans or Barings or anybody else. Private clients, on the other hand, were a perfect nuisance. They took an awful lot of time and trouble and you couldn't charge them. We just got 1/4 per cent return commission, whereas with pension funds you both got the return commission and charged a fee. The business in those days was very profitable.[150]

Helbert, Wagg's first pension fund client was the Suez Canal Company, which built up a fund of £6 million in the decade after the war.[151] In May 1946, Palache secured appointment as joint manager with the Centre d'Etudes des Placements of Paris, estimating that it would generate £1,500 per annum in fees for the following 10–20 years. The next milestone in the development of Helbert, Wagg's institutional investment management business was the firm's appointment as manager to the newly established pension fund of the BBC. In May 1947, a BBC director, John Adamson, an accountant and 'a great admirer of the firm', wrote inviting Helbert, Wagg to apply for the appointment. Eventually they were made joint managers with Eagle Star Insurance Co., though Helbert, Wagg did most of the work and received the bulk of the fees. The prestige bestowed by the BBC account was of great benefit in marketing the firm's services to other institutional clients, such as Boots, IBM United Kingdom, and Heinz, not forgetting the Fishmongers' Livery Company. There was a great deal of overlap between the clientele of the Investment Department and the Corporate Finance Department, one service often leading to the other. There were many advantages to the firm and its clients from the combination of strengths in corporate finance and institutional fund management when it came to making securities issues. It gave Helbert, Wagg considerable placing power, which facilitated the distribution of an issue, but also meant that clients obtained securities on advantageous terms. 'When we were doing a placing or an underwriting,' explained Verey, 'it was recognised that the house would take at least a quarter for its investment clients, which was very much to their advantage, although it was also to our advantage. On those transactions we kept the commission which would otherwise have been paid to a stockbroker. Stockbrokers, of course, did not particularly like this, but we saw no reasons why our clients shouldn't benefit from our transactions.'[152]

The £750,000 debenture issue in August 1954 on behalf of the Broadstone Investment Trust, the successor to the British & German Trust, marked the beginning of a drive to build up the investment trust side of the investment management activity. In the 1940s and early 1950s, under Palache's guidance, Broadstone achieved a complete recovery of capital, despite writing down the value of its continental investments from £702,000 to £183,000, and paid off arrears of the preference dividend.[153] The large issue of August 1954 drew public attention to Broadstone's achievements, attracting favourable press comment upon Helbert, Wagg's abilities in investment management. It was followed by further fund-raising issues for the firm's various investment trusts, and in 1954–58 the capital of Broadstone was increased by £1.25 million, Trans-Oceanic by £1 million, Ashdown by £675,000 and Westpool by £150,000.

The share price boom of 1959–61 saw further and larger increases in the capital of Helbert, Wagg's investment trusts. In these years Ashdown raised £2.9 million, Trans-Oceanic £2.1 million, Broadstone £480,000 and Westpool £428,000. The big increase in Ashdown's capital was a result of the adoption in May 1959 of an innovative strategy of promoting the trust to small investors. It was, commented *The Times*, 'the first attempt in the City to combine the advantages of investment and unit trusts. Briefly Ashdown's scheme will offer the public the capital gearing and retained earnings cushion of investment trusts while giving the marketability which is a feature of unit trusts'.[154] In the event, only half of the 2.5 million shares on offer were subscribed for, an outcome that was attributed to 'the novelty of the scheme – from the simple fact that the managers have pioneered this form of investment trust offer' and because it was 'rather too sophisticated for small investors'.[155] Nevertheless, Helbert, Wagg persevered with the new approach and the second issue in January 1960 was over-subscribed. Supported by the financial press, which pronounced that 'the widening of the market in investment trust shares is a most desirable end' and described the initiative as 'a most significant move', Ashdown made three further issues in 1960 and 1961.[156]

The outcomes of the highly successful development of Helbert, Wagg's corporate finance and investment management activities in the years 1948–61 were increasing profits and rising operating returns. In 1948–53, pre-tax operating returns averaged 20 per cent per annum; in 1954–58, 27 per cent; and in 1959–61, 45 per cent (see Figure 12.9). For the period as a whole the average pre-tax operating return was 28 per cent, which surpassed the performance of earlier eras of the firm's history, the annual average of 1919–30 being 25 per cent and 1931–47 being 13 per cent. Inflation averaged 3.5 per cent in the years 1948–61, though in 1951 it hit 12 per cent as a result of the Korean War, which meant a real pre-tax operating return of about 24 per cent over the period as a whole, an impressive achievement, particularly since in these

Figure 12.9 Helbert, Wagg & Co. Ltd, pre-tax operating return, post-tax return on equity and annual rate of inflation, 1948–61

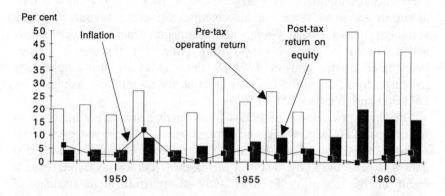

Note: The 'real' return on capital is the difference between the nominal returns on capital depicted above and the annual rate of inflation.

years the aggregate capital and reserves grew from £617,000 to £1.6 million – £9.2 million to £15.7 million in 1990 money.

From 1948 Helbert, Wagg abandoned the practice of paying out virtually the whole of pre-tax operating profits in bonuses and dividends. The result was the growth of reserves from £29,000 in 1947 to £1.2 million in 1961. One reason was the rapidly expanding volume of business, which necessitated a larger capital base. Another was the high rates of taxation on income introduced during the war and retained afterwards by the Labour government of 1945–51, which discouraged the distribution of profits. Moreover, the growth of the capital made the shares more valuable and since there was no capital gains tax at the time this was the most advantageous way for the shareholders and directors to benefit from the strong performance of the firm.

The larger capital base of the firm permitted a steady growth of the balance sheet, total assets expanding from the wartime average of £1.2 million, to £2.2 million in 1948, £3.9 million in 1957, and £6.6 million in 1961. The profile of liabilities and assets also changed. Capital and reserves increased more slowly than deposits and client balances, and by the late 1950s the ratio between them was 1:4. On the assets side, the notable changes were the disappearance of overnight loans to the money market and the bill portfolio, and instead the expansion of term loans, advances and investments, from 30 per cent of the total in 1939–47 to 80 per cent in 1948–59.

In 1948, as a result of the Companies Act of that year, there was a change in the presentation of the firm's accounts. Hitherto, dividend payments had been made gross, tax being paid by the recipients. Henceforth, in the annual returns now required by the Registrar of Companies, post-tax profits were reported – that is, net of bonuses and tax but before the payment of dividends. The post-tax profits relative to the total capital and reserves are shown as the 'post-tax return on equity' in Figure 12.9. Again, the firm's performance measured by this yardstick has three phases. In 1948–52, the post-tax return on equity averaged 5.3 per cent per annum, though the real rate was much lower, with inflation running ahead of returns in 1948 and 1951. In 1953–58, the post-tax return on equity averaged 8.6 per cent, which provided a more acceptable margin over inflation. The extraordinary levels of operating profits in 1959–61 resulted in post-tax profits totalling £780,000, which yielded an average post-tax return on equity of 17.7 per cent, a remarkable result in view of the prevailing rates of taxation.

The taxation bias against the distribution of dividends and in favour of capital gains rather than income meant that the way for the shareholders to achieve the full cash benefit of their success was, ironically, to sell the firm. Helbert, Wagg's performance at the end of the

1950s meant a valuation of the business which was unlikely to be exceeded in the forseeable future. Furthermore, there were willing buyers prepared to pay good prices for the firm, since amalgamations between accepting houses and issuing houses were proceeding apace in the City. Yet Fraser had another reason to sell. He was approaching his midsixties and although he was not contemplating immediate retirement, the identification of a successor was becoming a pressing matter. His dilemma was not a shortage of talented candidates, but the difficulty of choosing between Russell, Verey and Villiers, all of whom were much the same age. The elevation of one of them to chairman posed the danger that the others would look elsewhere for promotion, breaking up the team so carefully constructed over the previous couple of decades. What was needed was a bigger entity within which each could develop his career. The creation of Schroder Wagg solved Fraser's succession problem.

Part III

The International Firm

Since 1960

13

Schroder Wagg

1960–73

The eight months from September 1959 to May 1960 saw several developments which together constitute a major turning point in the history of Schroders. The first of these was the public offering in September 1959, which has already been discussed in Chapter 11. The reorganisation undertaken prior to the public offering brought together the London and New York firms into a single entity for the first time. Thereafter, Schroders was a multinational company, of which the London merchant bank was but a part, albeit a very important one. However, it should be recalled that at the time of the public offering the New York firm constituted some three-quarters of the book value of the group and the London firm only a quarter, a radically different pattern from any other merchant bank. During the 1960s and early 1970s Schroders' worldwide presence expanded rapidly and it evolved from a London/New York-based firm into a broader international one. These developments and the changing role of Schroders Limited, the holding company, are discussed in Chapter 14. The present chapter focuses on the conduct of the business in London.

The appointment of Gordon Richardson as deputy chairman of J. Henry Schroder & Co. in March 1960 was the second important development. Thereby he became chief executive of the London firm and was the driving force behind its achievements in the 1960s. The appointment was doubly significant since it prompted the opening of the negotiations that led to the agreement in May 1960 for Schroders to purchase Helbert, Wagg & Co., the third critical development of 1959–60. The combined company in London, J. Henry Schroder Wagg & Co. Ltd, was highly successful, its performance surpassing what the firms might have achieved as separate entities. Richardson became chairman of Schroder Wagg in 1962, and in 1965, upon Helmut Schroder's retirement, he was also appointed chairman of Schroders Limited, a post which he occupied until July 1973 when he became Governor of the Bank of England.

The decade and a half from the late 1950s to the early 1970s, the years in which Richardson was Schroders' leading figure, was a dynamic era in the City. The rapid expansion of the Euro-markets in these years led to London's resurgence as the leading international financial centre. The

417

major merchant banks were active participants in this development, which provided the basis for the revival of their international banking activities. Further factors boosting the expansion of their banking business were the growth of international trade and the burgeoning foreign exchange market in London. Moreover, corporate finance services were in heavy demand due to the restructuring of British industry, which was in full swing, leading to mergers, acquisitions and capital raising for expansion. The rapid growth of the funds of institutional investors – pension funds, insurance companies, investment trusts and unit trusts – generated strong demand for the merchant banks' investment management expertise. Finally, these years saw the development by the merchant banks of a range of ancilliary financial services, such as hire purchase, leasing, factoring and insurance broking. The quadrupling of oil prices in 1973, leading to inflation and recession, and the onset of the secondary banking crisis, marked the arrival of a harsher economic environment and the opening of a new and more problematic period for the merchant banks whose difficulties mirrored the turmoil of the international economy.

The Acquisition of Helbert, Wagg & Co. by Schroders Ltd

The late 1950s and early 1960s saw a spate of mergers amongst City firms with the objective of creating entities with strengths in all three of the merchant banks' core activities – banking, corporate finance and investment management – which were increasingly complementary. Schroder Wagg, Kleinwort Benson, Hill Samuel and Charterhouse Japhet emerged from unions between accepting houses and issuing houses, while Warburgs and Lazards made strategic acquisitions without changing their names. 'The marriage is a very natural one', commented the *Financial Times* on 20 May 1960 upon the announcement of the agreement to amalgamate the businesses of J. Henry Schroder & Co. and Helbert, Wagg & Co. 'It is a case of the almost classic link-up between the predominantly "banking" bank [Schroders] and the predominantly "industrial" bank [Helbert, Wagg]'.[1]

The suggestion of closer co-operation culminating in a possible combination of the activities of J. Henry Schroder & Co. and Helbert, Wagg was first mooted by Richardson, who saw in it a potential for synergy. His thoughts, which were fully supported by Helmut Schroder and by Gerald Beal in New York, were considered intriguing at 41 Threadneedle Street since, besides the operational benefits of amalgamation, purchase by Schroders presented the partners of Helbert, Wagg with a possible means of realising their locked-up interests in the firm. However, no formal discussions on a combination had been held when Lionel Fraser, the chairman, who was on holiday in Antibes, learned of Richardson's appointment as deputy chairman of J. Henry Schroder & Co.[2] He immediately notified his fellow directors and added his thoughts to the memorandum:

> Helmut Schroder sent me an advance message about Gordon R's appointment as Deputy Chairman. Terrific and surprising, but I think farsighted.

> It set me thinking about a tie-up with them. G R has touched on it once or twice in conversation, skated over it, but I imagine he is keen. I feel we have much to offer one another – they are all delightful, if not great, people, and would be pleasant partners in every way, well-behaved and all that. At first sight, there wou'd seem to be vast scope to develop in Europe – it would make us straightaway a force in international banking, both merchant and investment.

> They think somewhat like us. I mean they are not grabbing, acquisitive people. They have a sense of service, to use a ripe old cliché, and could be relied upon to play the game.[3]

Negotiations soon resulted in an agreement for Schroders Limited to acquire Helbert, Wagg through the purchase of its entire share capital: a simple concept, though its accomplishment to the satisfaction of all the parties was by no means straightforward. Richardson's plan was to execute the acquisition in two stages, the first of which was enacted in May 1960. A new company, Helbert, Wagg Holdings Ltd, was formed, whose purpose was to act as a holding company for Helbert, Wagg & Co. Ltd, the existing operating company. Schroders Limited acquired a controlling interest of 70 per cent of the equity of Helbert, Wagg Holdings for £241,500, the remaining 30 per cent being subscribed by the partners of Helbert, Wagg & Co. for £103,500. Helbert, Wagg Holdings then purchased the entire share capital of Helbert, Wagg & Co. which became a wholly-owned subsidiary, for £2,086,000. This effected the buy-out of the shareholdings of members of the Wagg family and the institutional shareholders. It was largely financed by a £1.8 million loan from Schroders Limited to Helbert, Wagg Holdings. The price paid by Helbert, Wagg Holdings for Helbert, Wagg & Co. was eight times the net earnings in respect of 1959, which equated to 1.9 times the £1,124,000 book value (shareholders' funds). Schroders provided £2,041,500 of the purchase price (the £241,500 paid for the equity plus the £1.8 million loan), which it raised by the private placement of £2,500,000 6 per cent unsecured loan stock 1980/85 at a price of £99 per cent.

The second stage of the acquisition became effective on 16 April 1962. Schroders Limited acquired the outstanding 30 per cent of Helbert, Wagg Holdings through the issue to the Helbert, Wagg directors of 198,000 ordinary shares at a value of £4 per share, which was approximately the average price of the Schroders Limited shares on the London Stock Exchange in the three months ended 31st December 1961, thus paying a further £792,000 for complete control. In total, Schroders paid £2,833,500 for the Helbert, Wagg business – about £28 million in 1990 money. The purchase price was ten times the net income (after tax) of £266,516, which was equivalent to twice the book equity at end 1961 of £1,420,932. While Schroders paid quite a full price for Helbert, Wagg, it proved to be a successful investment, not only because of the operational synergy between the firms but also because of the structure of the financing of the acquisition by Schroders Limited. The bulk of the funds were raised by the issue of the unsecured loan stock, which proved to be a cost-effective form of financing when inflation accelerated and eroded the value of fixed-income sterling securities. Moreover, because the Schroders Limited share price was firm at the time, the 198,000 additional shares issued by Schroders Limited represented a dilution of shareholders' equity of only 4 per cent. Nevertheless, the Helbert, Wagg acquisition was a very major investment for Schroders Limited – equivalent to some 20 per cent of its net worth of £12 million. It involved assuming a substantial amount of long-term debt for the first time in the firm's history, and a considerable part of the price was 'goodwill' which had no realisable value and had to be written off.

The news of the amalgamation was greeted with dismay by many of the staff of both firms, who feared that redundancies would result. Worry was greatest in Leadenhall Street because of Helbert, Wagg's formidable reputation in the City; 'they're going to swamp us, they'll eat us' were the words of one of Schroders' senior managers on hearing the news.[4] A few of the older members of Schroders' staff were obliged to retire following the merger, but for most it was unexpectedly advantageous. Thanks to Alfred Wagg's paternalism and determination to attract and retain highly skilled personnel, Helbert, Wagg's staff enjoyed some of the most generous terms of employment in the City, and remuneration and benefits rose in Leadenhall Street to bring the firms into line.

The operational integration of the firms was implemented gradually and cautiously. The process began with an exchange of directors: Fraser became deputy chairman of Schroders Limited; Richardson, Abel Smith and Backhouse joined the board of Helbert, Wagg; and Fraser, Russell, and Verey that of J. Henry Schroder & Co. Senior executives were seconded in both directions, but for more than a year after the agreement to combine each firm continued to deal with its own clients and conducted business much as before. Russell was given responsibility for the physical amalgamation of the firms. After detailed consideration he came to the conclusion that the integration of the departments of the two firms in the existing unsatisfactory buildings would cause such disruption that it would outweigh any advantages, and recommended postponement until the whole firm was accommodated in the same building.[5] However, this was unacceptable to the other directors and the integration of the departments proceeded, banking and company finance being located in Leadenhall Street and investment management, trading and new issues in Threadneedle Street.

The reorganisation of accommodation was just the beginning of the process of integration. The experience of company finance illustrates the practical problems encountered. A report prepared in March 1962 detailed how virtually every practice of the two company finance departments was different.[6] For instance, J. Henry Schroder & Co. had a centralised filing system whereas at Helbert, Wagg each executive kept his own files; J. Henry Schroder & Co. published a weekly work list, giving details of each current operation, whereas Helbert, Wagg maintained a card index recording similar information; at Helbert, Wagg it was the practice to circulate duplicates of all letters written by members of the department in a daily file but there was no such arrangement at J. Henry Schroder & Co. A set of standardised procedures, which seemed to owe rather more to previous practice at Helbert, Wagg than at J. Henry Schroder & Co., was issued in May 1962, but the immediate disruption was considerable.[7]

The quest for suitable premises for the combined firm began soon after the agreement to the acquisition. Initially, the search was confined to the immediate environs of the Bank of England, the traditional location of the merchant banks. It was considered that 'it is better to wait for the right building than to accept something just outside the vital limits, which we might live to regret for a long time to come'.[8] Serious consideration was given to the redevelopment of the Leadenhall Street site but this proved impractical and both buildings were sold, 145 Leadenhall Street to Barings, which turned the banking hall into a staff recreation area where table tennis was played against the back-drop of Major Pam's ochre-coloured marble, and 41 Threadneedle Street to the Westminster Bank. As mentioned in Chapter 11, J. Henry Schroder & Co. had sold the freehold of its building to the Prudential Assurance Company in 1949 for £520,000 in order to increase the liquidity of the balance sheet, but the contract contained an option to repurchase at the sale price. This option was exercised in 1964, by which time the value of the premises had risen substantially. The sale of the two premises generated a capital profit of £1.5 million, which was added to the inner reserves of Schroder Wagg.[9]

Leslie Murphy, who had recently been recruited by Richardson, was given charge of the search for new premises. At the St Paul's Cathedral end of Cheapside, outside the traditional merchant banking quarter of the City but still only a few minutes' walk from the Bank of England, he found what was required – a large office development at the drawing-board stage which could be completed to the firm's specifications. The negotiations took place in October 1964 in the run-up to a general election, with the Labour Party threatening rent controls and interference in the property sector, making the landlord eager to find a tenant, and Murphy secured highly favourable terms – a 70-year lease at £2.50 per square foot with rent reviews at 21, 35 and 56 years, at a time when commercial lettings usually had seven-year rent reviews. The staff magazine, called the *Schroder Wagtail*, welcomed the prospect of modern accommodation with enthusiasm: 'Air conditioning and double glazing throughout will insulate us effectively from London's increasing noise and dirt so that it will no longer be necessary to blow the soot off papers before starting work in the morning or to shut a window before having a telephone conversation.'[10] The move to the new building at 120 Cheapside in August 1965 boosted staff morale and completed the process of forging a Schroder Wagg identity.

The Senior Management

Gordon Richardson ranks as one of the leading figures in the history of Schroders. The testimony of his contemporaries indicates some of the reasons for his success. 'First class brain, moral courage, persistence, strong personality, a very shrewd man, a very nice man, but he could be hard as nails', were the words used by John Kinross to describe his colleague at ICFC.[11] A Schroder Wagg client who knew him well has written:

When he was appointed in 1957 at the age of forty-one, it caused a great stir in the City: a complete outsider, a lawyer, no title, no money, not even an Etonian; it was without precedent. He had no banking experience and to cap it all he was coming in at the top. It was an incredible appointment and as it turned out, once he was appointed Chairman a few years later, possibly the best top banking appointment made by anyone at any time in the City of

London. Under Gordon Richardson, Schroders undoubtedly became one of the smoothest, best-operated merchant banks in the City: general overall expansion, little publicity, less fanfare, superb results. A natural leader and a natural banker.[12]

Richardson enjoyed the total confidence of Helmut Schroder, a shrewd judge of character, who had selected and promoted him. The two men developed a close friendship and mutual respect based on similar views of fundamental human values, ethics, integrity and the need for a high-quality, low-key approach to business. From Helmut Schroder, Richardson learned the unwritten rules of international merchant banking and the essentials of Schroders' particular culture; in Richardson, Helmut Schroder had found someone with the talents, energy, judgement and ambition to develop the firm and lead it into the future.

Colleagues at Schroders particularly recall the high standards of effort and accomplishment Richardson set himself and expected of others. His example impressed and inspired the executives and generated a strong commitment to the firm. 'Excellence' was his watchword long before it was made fashionable by American business school writers. 'The struggle for excellence was a very dominant part of what I wanted to do,' he explained; 'the best people, the best business, the best execution. I think it was probably some instinct that this might be possible at Schroders that made me go there in the first place. I think excellence is the only thing that is interesting. In more practical terms it has its own reward – the reputation of being best is itself a powerful draw.'[13] He developed a detailed understanding of every aspect of Schroder Wagg's activities and kept the operations of the firm under close scrutiny. The head of the Banking Division, for instance, recalled that Richardson would turn up unannounced at routine Credit Committee meetings, following the proceedings closely but never interfering.[14] Richardson's active interest was much appreciated by managers and executives, who were unaccustomed to being able to explain their day-to-day difficulties before such a senior figure. It won him loyalty from the staff and engendered a strong *ésprit de corps* at Schroder Wagg that was an important element in the firm's success in the 1960s.

Some of Richardson's more senior colleagues, particularly those in company finance, his own field of expertise, who were used to operating with a considerable degree of independence at Helbert, Wagg, regarded the close interest shown by Richardson as meddlesome. Sir Charles Villiers, a senior figure on the corporate finance side, observed that Richardson wanted to know the details of everything the company financial directors were doing, 'and if you didn't take him with you you might find the rug was pulled out'. He recalled an occasion when he was representing Schroder Wagg on a joint issue in New York, and when the business was at an advanced stage he received a telegram from Richardson saying 'Schroders will not participate in this deal at all'. It was not, said Villiers, that there was anything wrong with the deal. It was simply that 'Richardson felt that other people shouldn't take positions without his being a party to them. And in a business as risk-bearing as merchant banking I think there is a lot to be said for that. To have one person at the centre who takes the decision. I didn't like it much at the time, but Richardson was right'.[15]

The establishment of a rigorous system of internal managerial controls was one of Richardson's achievements as chairman of Schroder Wagg. The executives chiefly responsible for the development of the firm's internal disciplines were John Bayley and Leslie Murphy, both of whom had worked for American multinational industrial corporations – Sperry Rand and Mobil Oil respectively – and were thereby familiar with the science as well as the art of creating effective managerial structures. Bayley, in particular, devised and implemented modern systems of financial controls, efficient tax planning (which took the firm further into the leasing business), and efficient computerisation of the back office (which led to its involvement in computer services). Thoroughness was also a hallmark of Richardson's approach to strategic decision-making, doubtless reflecting his legal training and background. He endeavoured to consider every aspect of a problem and every solution before coming to a conclusion, an approach to policy-making which sometimes exasperated colleagues. 'My only reservation about Richardson,' said one of them, 'was his tendency to study things to death. There was never a major issue in the Schroder Wagg board meetings that got an immediate decision or a quick decision. We missed opportunities because of our tendency to over-study things. Other institutions moved on the basis of intuition and instinct based on their exposure in the field.' On the other hand, his professional and prudent approach enabled Schroder Wagg to avoid some of the pitfalls of acting on impulse. Overall, the rigorous and disciplined managerial style stamped upon the firm in its early years under Richardson was highly advantageous and it had a lasting legacy.

Richardson took a very close interest in recruitment, interviewing all who were considered for executive posts. 'Merchant banking is primarily a service business,' he once explained, 'in such a business you must have the best talent and employ it in the best way. This means we have to recruit the right sort of people and see that they have, or acquire, the requisite skills.'[16] He required that new recruits had a university degree or membership of a professional body, qualifications possessed, he estimated, by 60 per cent of the firm's decision-takers in the mid-1960s. In 1966, Schroder Wagg instituted a systematic graduate recruitment and training programme, one of the first merchant banks to do so. Numerous highly talented men and women – the first female graduate was recruited in 1967 – began their merchant banking careers at Schroder Wagg in Richardson's era. Many stayed with the firm and moved into executive positions, though for some Schroders was a stepping-stone to senior posts elsewhere. The latter included Anthony Loehnis, who moved to the Bank of England as overseas executive director and later became a vice-chairman of Warburgs; Geoffrey Bell, who also had experience at the Treasury and as an academic economist, who formed his own highly regarded firm in the US; John Cooper, who joined Singer & Friedlander; and Peter Rona, who became head of IBJ–Schroder in New York upon the sale of the J. Henry Schroder Bank & Trust Company to the Industrial Bank of Japan in 1985.[17]

In addition to a full workload at Schroders, Richardson assumed a series of public service responsibilities in the 1960s and early 1970s. The first invitation to serve on a public enquiry arrived even before his appointment to the deputy chairmanship of J. Henry Schroder & Co. This was the Jenkins Committee, established at the end of 1959 to review company law in the wake of the controversy over take-over bids, which had been an issue in the general election of October 1959. The Jenkins Committee reported in 1962, and the following year Richardson was appointed chairman of the committee established to inquire into value added tax, which reported in 1964. From 1967 he was a member of the Court of the Bank of England and served on the National Economic Development Council in 1971–73. In 1972, he was appointed chairman of the Industrial Development Advisory Board, a body established to assist the government with the allocation of funds made available under the 1972 Budget to aid the rationalisation of British industry. Besides these public responsibilities, Richardson was also a director of ICI, Lloyds Bank, the Legal and General Assurance Co., and Rolls Royce after the government rescue in 1971.

Upon Richardson's appointment as chairman of Schroder Wagg in May 1962, Helmut Schroder focused on his role as chairman of the holding company, Schroders Limited. Lionel Fraser, who had hoped to become the first chairman of Schroder Wagg, left at the end of the year to start up a new London subsidiary of Paribas and to devote more time to the Thomas Tilling Group, of which he was chairman. Richardson acquired additional responsibilities upon his appointment as chairman of Schroders Limited in 1965, and thereafter he directed the development of the firm both in London and internationally. In June 1972, he relinquished the chairmanship of Schroder Wagg, which was taken on by Michael Verey, the deputy chairman since 1965. Verey, a graduate of Trinity College, Cambridge, joined Helbert, Wagg in 1934. After wartime military service, attaining the rank of Lieutenant Colonel, he returned to the firm, specialising in investment management, and became a partner in 1948. At the time of his appointment as deputy chairman he was head of Schroder Wagg's Investment Division and held a score of directorships including Boots, and Northern and Employers Assurance, of which he was deputy chairman. He was a member of the advisory panels of the Local Authorities Mutual Investment Trust and the Charities Official Investment Fund as well as an investment adviser to Eton, his school, and his Cambridge college. 'A tall, slender, elegant and patrician figure, very much the beautifully mannered Etonian merchant banker' was a journalist's thumbnail sketch at the time of his promotion.[18]

Schroder Wagg's leading executives in the years immediately following the merger were the directors of the two predecessor firms, but in the second half of the decade many of them retired or left the firm. Amongst the former J. Henry Schroder & Co. directors, Helmut Schroder, Henry Tiarks and Edward Tucker retired in 1965; Toby Caulfeild and Alexander Abel Smith in 1967; and Jonathan Backhouse in 1970; while Alec Cairns moved to Edinburgh to take up a senior position with National Commercial & Schroders, a newly established joint venture, in 1964. Amongst the former Helbert, Wagg directors, Gordon Gunson retired in 1967 and Alan Russell in 1970, while Charles Villiers left in 1968. These departures and over thirty new appointments to the Schroder Wagg board in 1962–73 meant that by the time of Richardson's departure the firm's senior management had undergone a wholesale change of generations, three-quarters of the directors in 1973 being post-acquisition appointments. The new directors were mostly internal promotions, men who had been with J. Henry Schroder & Co. or Helbert, Wagg since the start of their City careers. A minority were recruited from outside the firm, mostly from the legal or accountancy professions, but some from industry and the civil service too. Richardson's deliberate purpose in making these external appointments was to deepen Schroders' in-house professional expertise and generally to broaden the collective perspective of the senior executives. A number of the outside appointees made especially important contributions to the development and smooth functioning of the firm's managerial disciplines.

Between 1962 and 1973 the Schroder Wagg board increased in number from 20 to 33 members. Moreover, in December 1968 the new rank of 'assistant director' was introduced and a dozen executives were given this status. The multiplication of directors was a phenomenon common to the merchant banks in the 1960s (at Morgan Grenfell the rank of 'assistant director' was introduced in 1967).[19] Richardson, addressing an audience at the London School of Economics in January 1966, attributed the expansion to several causes: the growth in the size of firms, particularly when accomplished through amalgamation; the extension of the range of their activities; the increasing professionalism and specialisation of directors – the days when each partner could handle every aspect of a firm's affairs were over; the expectation on the part of corporate clients that their financial adviser was someone of director status whose judgement and knowledge commanded respect. The growth in the number of directors was an aspect of a more general increase in the proportion of staff who were 'decision takers' in the merchant banks in the 1960s. Richardson identified a fifth of Schroder Wagg's staff as decision takers – directors, managers and junior executives numbering about 100 in 1966. 'It is a predominantly young team,' he commented, 'I think that some of our alertness and enterprise springs from the fact that about two-thirds of the people who are directly engaged upon handling the problems of our customers and clients are under the age of 40.'[20]

The Schroder Wagg directors held a weekly board meeting at which they heard reports on operational activities and considered proposals from a smaller executive committee which was the key policy-making body. In 1962–67 this was the Chairman's Committee, comprising Richardson, the heads of the three main operating divisions – banking, company finance and investment management – and five further directors. Its functions were to act as a steering committee for the board of Schroder Wagg; to resolve problems of policy referred to it by the operating departments; and to review the activities of the bank as a whole with a view to exercising overall control of its general policy and operations.[21] In April 1967 the weekly Chairman's Committee was replaced by the Business Management Committee, a smaller, five-man body which met every morning at 9.45 am. This arrangement, which had similarities to the J. Henry Schroder & Co.'s officers' meetings scrapped in 1962, allowed faster responses to operational requirements. Moreover, it cleared the way for the transfer of major policy decisions to Schroders Limited, the holding company, which was eventually achieved by the creation of the Group Management Committee in the summer of 1970. The operational orientation of the Business Management Committee led to the formation of four further committees to handle other aspects of the business. These were a Senior Advisory Committee, which included a number of retired members of the board; an Appeals Committee, to advise on subscriptions to charities; a Staff and Administrative Committee, to consider matters relating to the staff and internal administration, all of which met on a regular basis; and an *ad hoc* Investment Committee. The new structure worked well and proved enduring.

Investment Committee. The new structure worked well and proved enduring.

In its first decade Schroder Wagg's disclosed post-tax profits rose fourfold, from £373,000 in 1962 to £1.4 million in 1972 (see Figure 13.1).[22] There was considerable price inflation in Britain in these years and on an inflation-adjusted basis the increase was about twofold. In the early years after the amalgamation disclosed profits were flat on account of substantial transfers to inner reserves. From 1966 the benefits of the acquisition were reflected in the upsurge of disclosed profits and in the standing of the firm in the City. 'Top of the form' was Schroder Wagg's 'end of term report' for 1968 from Andreas Whittam Smith, then financial editor of the *Daily Telegraph*, and in 1970 the *Investors' Chronicle* called it 'the most conspicuously successful' merchant bank of the year.[23] Sir Charles Villiers – no mean authority on such matters – described it as 'the most successful merger that I'm aware of'.[24]

Between 1962 and the end of the decade Schroder Wagg's gross revenues grew by two-and-a-half times, each of the firm's divisions contributing to the increase.[25] The Banking Division was much the most important source of revenues, generating 40 per cent of total revenues for the period as a whole, derived from acceptance commissions, net interest, foreign exchange and money market dealing. The Investment Division contributed around 30 per cent, from management fees, commissions and securities dealing. Company Finance produced about 20 per cent, and some 10 per cent came from investments and miscellaneous activities. By the late 1960s the latter included modest sums generated by the sale of services by the Operations Division, which was formed in 1966 and encompassed the staff conducting administrative and clerical duties, some 200 people in all, under John Bayley, the finance director.

Figure 13.1 J. Henry Schroder Wagg and Co. Ltd, disclosed profits (after tax), 1962–73

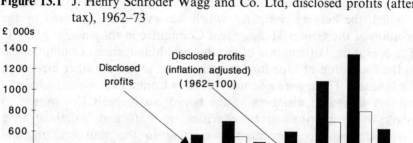

The pre-eminence of banking revenues reflects Schroder Wagg's vigorous and substantial participation in the interbank and Euro-currency markets, and its profitable foreign exchange activities. However, it was also the result of the growing strength of its corporate client list, since balances placed by corporate clients continued to be an important part of the remuneration for the provision of company finance services and banking facilities. Moreover, banking facilities, such as bridging funds for firms waiting to make an issue or arranging take-over financing, were part of the package of services offered by the firm. Investment management advice was another service offered to corporate clients. In the 1960s, Schroder Wagg's three core activities were increasingly complementary and although earnings were booked by one division or another they derived from broadly-based relationships. With the pattern of business evolving in this way the key to success was the length and quality of the corporate client list. Richardson worked assiduously to develop it, building on the foundation provided by both Helbert, Wagg and J. Henry Schroder & Co. 'We had,' he recalled with pride, 'the best client list of big manufacturing firms of any of the merchant banks.'[26]

Corporate Finance

Although the revenues generated by the Company Finance Division were smaller than those from the Banking or Investment Divisions, corporate finance services were the key to the development of Schroder Wagg's corporate client list, and hence to the firm's success in the 1960s. Richardson himself acted as head of the Company Finance Division immediately following the formation of Schroder Wagg, but after a couple of years he handed over to John Hull, with whom he had worked for more than a decade. Hull, who was educated at Downside and Cambridge, followed his father to the Bar, and in 1954, aged 29, joined the chambers of Montagu Gedge where Richardson was already a junior. Upon Gedge's retirement Hull accepted Richardson's invitation to join J. Henry Schroder & Co.'s small corporate finance operation and was appointed a director in 1961, just prior to the full merger with Helbert, Wagg. In 1969 he was made a director of Schroders Limited, appointed Group Planning Officer and became concerned with the affairs of the holding company. In 1972–74 he served as full-time Director General of the Take-over Panel, returning to the firm at the end of his period of office.

The majority of the leading executives of the Company Finance Division in the 1960s came from Helbert, Wagg – Gordon Gunson, Alan

Russell and Charles Villiers were the senior figures, and Francis Cator, Leslie Fletcher, Robert Hollond, David Murison and William Wiltshire a younger contingent. Their common characteristics were professionalism and all-round competence in investment banking, reflecting the rigour of their training and experience at Helbert, Wagg. Besides Richardson and Hull, the leading executives in the Corporate Finance Division in the 1960s from J. Henry Schroder & Co. were Jonathan Backhouse and Philip Robinson.

There were two important outside appointments amongst the senior corporate finance executives, Leslie Murphy and Geoffrey Williams. Murphy began his career in the Civil Service where he reached the position of Assistant Secretary at the Ministry of Fuel and Power and was Private Secretary to the Minister, Hugh Gaitskell. In 1952, he joined Mobil Oil and subsequently became finance director of the Iraq Petroleum Company, being lured to Schroder Wagg by Richardson in 1964. He made a speciality of raising finance for the UK subsidiaries of US multinationals. Towards the end of the 1960s he became closely involved in the development of the role of the holding company, and in 1970 was appointed a director of Schroders Limited. Williams read law at Cambridge and was articled to Slaughter and May in 1952, becoming a partner in 1961. He was closely involved with the affairs of J. Henry Schroder & Co. from the mid-1950s, and in 1966 he accepted Richardson's invitation to join Schroder Wagg. His was one of a spate of resignations by partners of leading City solicitors to join the management of merchant banks in the mid-1960s, which were endeavouring to broaden the scope of their corporate finance services to keep abreast of growing competition.[27] He succeeded Hull as head of the Company Finance Division in 1968. A further figure recruited by Richardson from outside the firm was Sir Leslie Robinson, a former senior official at the Board of Trade, who acted as 'Industrial Adviser' in 1964–74. All the leading executives held non-executive directorships of major British public companies, including Rolls-Royce, Boots, Scottish and Newcastle Breweries, Powell Duffryn, Unigate, Bass Charrington, the British Sugar Corporation, Wimpey, and Harland & Wolff, and at the start of the 1970s the thirty-four Schroder Wagg directors sat on a total of 201 boards, averaging 5.9 directorships per head.[28]

The company law expertise of Richardson and Hull, reinforced by the recruitment of Williams, allowed Schroder Wagg's Company Finance Division to make an important innovation in the conduct of its work. 'We were the first firm to do the whole thing ourselves,' said Hull. 'Other houses having done a deal would simply fling the paperwork at Slaughter and May, or whoever. We decided to provide the whole service – negotiate the deal, do the documentation, provide the underwriting if necessary – rather than just being the people who did a few sums on the back of an envelope.'[29] This approach gave Schroder Wagg important competitive and cost advantages, allowing a rapid response, which pleased clients, while controlling legal expenses. Moreover, when several firms were involved in a deal, as was often the case, Schroder Wagg's ability to execute from start to finish often ensured its appointment as lead adviser.

Schroder Wagg acted as an adviser in several hundred mergers or take-overs during the 1960s and 1970s. The years of most intense activity were those of the merger boom of the late 1960s and early 1970s. In 1967 the Company Finance Division did three times the level of business of the previous year, and in 1968 it was involved in fifty-four completed take-overs, seventeen of which were in excess of £10 million – £75 million in 1990 money – a record level of activity for these years. The great majority of the mergers were negotiated between the parties and recommended by the board of the bid-for-company, the role of the merchant bankers being to advise on terms and assist with the negotiations. The diplomatic skills of Schroder Wagg's executives were tested to the full in the negotiations in 1963–4 to unravel the interests of ICI and Courtaulds in their British Nylon Spinners joint venture.[30] They were conducted in an acrimonious atmosphere because of ICI's unsuccessful take-over bid for Courtaulds two years earlier. That failure caused ICI to become disenchanted with its financial advisers, providing an opening for Schroder Wagg, Richardson's acquaintance with Paul Chambers, the ICI chairman, being a helpful factor. Schroder Wagg's tactful handling of the British Nylon Spinners negotiations confirmed its position as adviser to Britain's leading industrial company.

The negotiated mergers in which Schroder Wagg played a part in the 1960s and early 1970s are too numerous for comprehensive mention, though a few warrant individual notice on account of their scale or novelty. The merger between the *Daily Mirror* and the *Sunday Pictorial*, which was announced in November 1962, was reported at the time to be the largest newspaper merger ever carried out. In 1968, which saw a very high level of merger activity, Schroder Wagg was an adviser in the merger between Typhoo Tea (Holdings) and Schweppes, to form one of Britain's largest food firms; the three-way amalgamation of Tarmac, Derbyshire Stone and Withain Briggs into the country's biggest roadmaking group; the £65 million merger between Land Securities Investment Trust and City Centre Properties to form the largest British property company with a portfolio worth around £300 million; the acquisition of Northern and Employers Assurance Company, of which Verey was deputy chairman, by Commercial Union Assurance Company, creating a firm with a capitalisation of £264 million, which rivalled the size of the Royal Insurance Company, the industry leader. In 1971 Schroder Wagg acted for Trust Houses in its negotiations with Forte Holdings, which resulted in the formation of Trust House Forte; and for Penguin Publishing when it was acquired by Longman Holdings.

'The merchant bankers' merchant bank' was a contemporary comment that reflected the esteem in which Schroder Wagg was held by fellow bankers in the late 1960s.[31] In May 1969, Standard Bank engaged its services to assist in its discussions with The Chartered Bank which led ultimately to the formation in 1971 of the Standard and Chartered Banking Group in London. The formation of a joint venture in Hong Kong, Schroders & Chartered, related in Chapter 14, was a by-product of the relationship. National and Grindlays, a British bank operating principally in Africa and the Middle East, was advised by Schroder Wagg in the negotiations which led to the acquisition of a 40 per cent interest by Citibank, advised by Hill Samuel, in the winter of 1968. Hill Samuel itself had been a bidder some months earlier when it had taken over Lambert Brothers, a firm of insurance brokers and underwriting agents, which was advised by Schroder Wagg. Two years later, Schroder Wagg was again called in to advise on a merger involving Hill Samuel. With the active encouragement of the Hill Samuel chairman, Kenneth Keith, the Metropolitan Estate and Property Corporation (MEPC), the United Kingdom's second largest property company, launched a bid for the merchant bank with the ambition of forming a large financial services and property conglomerate. It was a proposal that horrified conservative City opinion, for whom a liquid and low-risk balance sheet was the foremost necessity for a merchant bank. Three weeks later Commercial Union, the large insurance company, announced a bid for MEPC, a move which was widely interpreted as the City establishment's response to the reckless proposal to merge Hill Samuel and MEPC. This led to Schroder Wagg's resignation as adviser to MEPC, since there were two Schroder Wagg directors on the Commercial Union board. The outcome of the bids was stalemate and both were abandoned.[32]

Schroder Wagg was closely involved in the restructuring of the British motor industry in the 1960s.[33] It acted twice for Rover in 1965, in June upon a merger with Alvis, and again at the end of the year when it was acquired by the Leyland Motor Company. British Motor Holdings (BMH), another major car firm, used Schroder Wagg's services in its merger with Jaguar in the summer of 1965 and its acquisition of Pressed Steel two years later. When the Pressed Steel purchase was referred to the Monopolies Commission, Schroder Wagg presented BMH's case, which it was able to argue with special authority because Alexander Abel Smith was the Pressed Steel chairman and Schroders had been closely associated with the firm ever since its establishment in 1926. The application was successful, the Monopolies Commission consenting on the grounds of the promotion of industrial efficiency.[34] The culmination of the amalgamations in the British motor industry was the merger in January 1968 of BMH and the Leyland Motor Company, to form the British Leyland Motor Corporation, in which Schroder Wagg acted as adviser to BMH.

The formation of British Leyland was the brainchild of the Industrial Reorganisation Corporation (IRC), an agency established by the Labour Government in 1966 to promote the rationalisation of British manufacturing industry through mergers. The IRC was much resented in the City because it seemed to be usurping the corporate finance function of the merchant banks and was suspected of being a covert route to further nationalisation. Upon the resignation of the IRC's first managing director after only two years in the job a search was mounted to find a successor, which led to the appointment of Charles Villiers to this highly controversial 'hot seat'.[35]

Soon after Villiers' appointment, Schroder Wagg and the IRC both became embroiled in another notable exercise in industrial restructuring, the 'Great Ball-Bearing Affair' of 1968–69.[36] The episode began when it was learned by the IRC that a British firm, the Ransome and Marles Bearing Company, a Schroder Wagg client, had been holding discussions about a merger with Skefko, the British subsidiary of the Swedish firm SKF that dominated the European ball-bearing industry.[37] Then it became known that the two other British owned ball-bearing manufacturers, the Pollard Roller Bearing Company, another Schroder Wagg client, and the Hoffman Manufacturing Company, were also talking to foreign firms. Faced by the prospect of the whole industry passing into foreign control, the IRC determined to effect the amalgamation of the British firms into a single entity of sufficient size to be internationally competitive. It began by launching a 'surprise bid' on its own behalf in January 1969 for Hoffman's parent company, an independent steel company, a successful but highly controversial step that was condemned by some as 'back door' nationalisation.[38] In May 1969, Ransome & Marles made a bid for Pollard. Since both firms were Schroder Wagg clients, Pollard's defence was 'handed over' to Kleinworts.[39] The Pollard board was dissatisfied by the terms of the bid and complained about its treatment by Schroder Wagg. It urged its shareholders to reject the Ransome & Marles offer, itself favouring a merger with Skefko. The IRC then again took a direct hand, underwriting a revised higher offer from Ransome & Marles and revealing that a merger had been negotiated between Ransome & Marles and its subsidiary Hoffmann. The outcome was the amalgamation of the three British firms into a new entity, the Ransome Hoffmann Pollard Company, whose capacity amounted to half the domestic ball-bearing market.

Simultaneously with the ball-bearing industry bid battles, Schroder Wagg conducted a successful defence of the British confectionery company, Rowntree, against a hostile bid from a foreign predator. In January 1969 General Foods of the US offered £39 million for the firm, which, after consulting Schroder Wagg, rejected the bid, cheekily offering to provide General Foods with envelopes addressed to Rowntree's shareholders, so confident was it of their support. Contemporary commentators were much impressed by this gesture, being unaware that three Rowntree trusts controlled 56 per cent of the equity. Seizing the initiative, Rowntree itself announced a bid for John Mackintosh, another British confectionary manufacturer, with the blessings of the IRC and the Mackintosh board. General Foods, whose first offer had received few acceptances, increased its bid for Rowntree to £49 million. This was again rejected by the Rowntree board, and General Foods retired from the field. The merger between the British firms proceeded smoothly and the new company adopted the name Rowntree Mackintosh Ltd. When this company became the target of hostile bids by the Swiss food companies Jacobs Suchard and Nestlé in 1988, Schroder Wagg again conducted its defence, which led Nestlé to pay £2.6 billion for the acquisition.

Schroder Wagg acquired a formidable reputation for defence work in hostile take-overs in the 1960s. A notable episode was its defeat of the Rank Organisation's bid for De La Rue – a firm best known for its banknote printing – which was announced in November 1968. De La Rue's management, a team that had recently turned in record profits and had their own plans for the development of the firm, rejected the bid out of hand and called in Schroder Wagg as adviser. Together they conducted a remarkable defence which caught Rank off-guard in every round. The financial press was won over from the start by the argument that 'there is simply no industrial logic in the move', and remained sympathetic to De La Rue throughout the struggle.[40] The City was unimpressed by the 57s. 9d. per share which Rank proposed to pay, and when De La Rue produced a profits forecast for 1968–69 of £1.8 million the shares rose to around 68s., comfortably beyond Rank's offer. Rank came back with a revised offer of 69s. 9d. per share, and to rally the support of its shareholders produced a forecast of its own profits for 1968–69. To the astonishment of observers its predictions of its own performance fell well short of market expectations, which did nothing to strengthen Rank's share price or to inspire confidence in the judgement of the firm's management or their advisers.

In response to Rank's revised offer De La Rue produced a profits forecast for the year 1969–70 of £2.75 million, a 50 per cent rise on the figure predicted for 1968–69. This forecast, which was endorsed by Schroder Wagg, ruled out the revised Rank bid as effectively as the earlier one and the *Investor's Chronicle*, for instance, advised shareholders to hang on to their holdings.[41] 'There are precedents for Rank's bidding three times for a company,' commented *The Times*, 'but De La Rue's will to survive may well scare them off.'[42] Then came the news that the bid had been referred to the Monopolies Commission, which was a notable coup for the defence team, since it marked an unprecedented extension of the basis for referral.[43] At this point, trounced at every turn, Rank bowed out of the contest. There was a somewhat embarassing epilogue nine months later when the De La Rue chairman announced a revised profits forecast for 1969–70 of £1.7 million, the downward revision being explained by an explosion at the firm's chipboard factory and 'a number of acts of God, Government and omission'.[44] Schroder Wagg went to the Take-over Panel to explain the discrepancy between the two forecasts and the firms were absolved of any charge of deliberate misrepresentation.

Richardson was reluctant to allow Schroder Wagg to act for bidders in hostile take-overs, unless there were exceptional reasons for making an offer direct to shareholders without winning the consent of the board. One such occasion was the bid by Consolidated Goldfields for Amalgamated Roadstone in August 1968, in which the hostile board was won over by a skilfully timed cash alternative made possible by a £7 million underwriting commitment organised by Schroder Wagg. The victory further strengthened the relationship between Consolidated Goldfields and Schroder Wagg. In January 1969, a bid battle developed for City of London Real Property (CLRP), in which Schroder Wagg became involved as adviser to Land Securities. Already in the ring were Trafalgar House, which had started the contest with a bid of 102s. per share, and the Metropolitan Estate and Property Corporation at 160s. per share, when Land Securities offered 177s. per share. All were paper bids, and a sharp drop in property share prices caused their values to fall. Land Securities remained the front-runner and a tiny increase in price was sufficient to persuade the CLRP directors to commit their holdings and to advise shareholders to do likewise. This 'considerable coup' resulted in the creation of the largest property company in the world, with properties valued at some £550 million. Later that year Schroder Wagg also helped Glynwed Ltd to victory in a bid battle for Allied Iron Founders, marking the beginning of a close relationship between the firms. This was cemented by the recruitment of Schroder Wagg director Leslie Fletcher as chairman in 1971, serving in that capacity until 1986.

Schroder Wagg's association with ICI commended its advisory services to textile firms which were recipients of bids by its rival Courtaulds, and the firm twice negotiated acceptable terms for such targets.[45] The board of English Calico, which received an offer from Courtaulds in January 1969, was determined to maintain its independence and, advised by Schroder Wagg, successfully repulsed the takeover. The episode led the government to declare a moratorium on amalgamations in the textile industry in June 1969, blocking ICI's plan to bid for Viyella, which it intended to merge with Carrington & Dewhurst, in which it held a controlling interest.[46] Undaunted, on Christmas Eve 1969, ICI launched a 'shock £50 million bid' for Viyella which took the government completely by surprise, there even being uncertainty about which department had responsibility for the enforcement of the moratorium,[47] and in May 1970 ICI took control. The really taxing task for Schroder Wagg, ICI's adviser on the bid, was devising a scheme to combine the profitable Viyella with the loss-making Carrington & Dewhurst which maintained Carrington & Dewhurst's public quotation and provided ICI with control of the combined company. These objectives were secured by a share exchange, though commentators complained that such was the complexity of the deal that valuation of the reconstructed Carrington & Dewhurst amounted, in the words of the contemporary Beatles pop song, to a 'magical mystery tour'.[48]

As Schroder Wagg's client list lengthened, so did the likelihood of finding itself with divided loyalties. The firm's dilemma at the time of Ransome & Marles' bid for Pollard has already been mentioned. Another instance was the bid battle for Horlicks, which manufactured milk products, foods and pharmaceuticals, early in 1969. Horlicks, whose advisor was Schroder Wagg, received a bid from Beecham of 50s. per share, which was rejected by the board. Boots then entered the fray with a bid of 57s. per share. This development was described by a Schroder Wagg spokesman as 'mildly embarrassing', since Boots was a longstanding client of the firm, which thus found itself advising both the predator and the prey.[49] Verey's membership of the Boots board determined where the firm's loyalty lay, and it thus resigned as adviser to Horlicks, whose board was obliged 'to take themselves off' to Barings in the middle of the bid. 'It all feels a little like being in the auction room,' stated a rather bewildered-sounding spokesman for Horlicks, 'basically we would far rather continue on our own.' Boots was considered a more compatible partner than Beecham, and Horlicks recommended acceptance of its offer. But when Beecham came back with an offer of 68s. per share Boots decided to withdraw from the bidding, leaving the outcome to be decided by others.

On several occasions in the 1960s Schroder Wagg acted for American firms in negotiations for the acquisition of British companies. These included the purchase of Presswork Hydraulics by Parker Hannafin, an American manufacturer of hydraulic and aerospace equipment in 1964; Mountain Copper by Stauffer Chemical in 1965; and Smiths Crisps by General Mills in 1966. The influx of US multinationals caused alarm in Europe, as expressed in Jean Jacques Servan-Schreiber's best-seller, *Le Defi Americain*, published in 1968. The purchase of complete control of the Ford Motor Company of Britain by the Ford Motor Company of the US in 1960, and the acquisition of an interest in Rootes by Chrysler in 1964 aroused anxieties about American economic domination in Britain. Such was the strength of feeling in the wake of the Rootes deal that even the bid to buy out the minority UK interest in the UK affiliate of the US film processor Technicolor, which was handled by Schroder Wagg, led to calls in Parliament for a halt to the 'sell-out' of British industry.

The transatlantic take-over struggle for control of Pergamon Press filled the headlines in 1969.[50] In the early part of the year, Robert Maxwell, Pergamon's founder, chairman and principal shareholder with 28 per cent of the equity, agreed to a merger with Leasco Data Processing Equipment Corp. of the US, of which Saul Steinberg was chairman. As a result, Leasco purchased a 38 per cent interest in Pergamon. Then the merger agreement broke down, leaving a residue of mistrust between Maxwell and Steinberg, neither of whom owned a controlling interest in the company. In September 1969, Steinberg announced that he proposed to ask a meeting of Pergamon shareholders to dismiss the existing board of directors and to replace it with one nominated by Leasco. Maxwell was generally believed to be popular with the small shareholders who held 19 per cent of Pergamon's equity, and it appeared unlikely that Steinberg would receive much assistance from them. However, their support was insufficient to guarantee Maxwell victory, and thus the control of Pergamon turned on the 15 per cent of shares held by a group of nineteen institutional investors. These shareholders decided that 'a powerful member of the City establishment was needed to bat for them' and appointed Schroder Wagg to advise them. The firm held discussions with Brandts, the adviser to Pergamon; Rothschilds, which was acting for Leasco; and the director-general of the Take-over Panel. 'Maxwell must go say City bankers Schroder Wagg', was how the *Daily Telegraph* announced its judgement in favour of Steinberg. The Extraordinary General Meeting of Pergamon shareholders held on 10 October 1969 fully lived up to its title. Maxwell railed against the 'Schroder Plan', which he claimed would bring about 'disastrous losses', and showered abuse on Rothschilds and the Take-over Panel. Despite his robust performance he was outvoted by 2 to 1 and removed from the Pergamon chairmanship. 'We've never seen anything like it in the States', observed Steinberg afterwards, and the *Spectator* commented that 'there has been no bloodier battle since Bosworth'.[51]

Throughout the 1960s and early 1970s Schroder Wagg ranked amongst the City's leading issuers of securities for corporate clients, its peer group in this activity being Warburgs, Hill Samuel, Lazards and Kleinworts. In 1962–73 the Company Finance Division handled on average fifty-one such issues per annum. Issuing activity measured by the number of issues peaked in 1969, when Schroder Wagg completed sixty-nine issues, which raised £112 million. The size of issues rose continuously, and in 1972 funds raised totalled £234 million of which £67 million was found outside the UK.[52] The most noteworthy event on the capital-raising side of the business was the £50 million – about £430 million in 1990 money – unsecured loan stock issue for ICI underwritten by Schroder Wagg in 1965, at the time the largest single industrial loan ever made in the City. 'It was a landmark,' recalled a senior executive of the day, 'everybody in the City sat up and thought, so now they have ICI too as a client.'[53] This advertisement of ICI's presence on Schroder Wagg's corporate client list was the best possible promotion for its corporate finance services and was followed by a flood of new business. Schroder Wagg conducted further ICI loan stock issues for £60 million in 1966; £26 million in 1969; and £40 million in 1970, and also organised smaller Euro-issues, denominated in dollars and Swiss francs. Property companies were avid for funds in the late 1960s and early 1970s, and Schroder Wagg sponsored issues for several of them, of which the largest was the £30 million convertible loan stock issued by Land Securities in 1970.

Schroder Wagg also expanded international issuing activities, stimulated by the beginning of the Euro-bond market in 1963. The pattern of Schroder Wagg's participations in this market reflected the fact that its principal clients were corporations rather than governments or banks. UK corporations used Schroder Wagg's issuing services to raise foreign currency financing for overseas expansion because of exchange control restrictions. A concerted effort was made to develop Euro-market services – Euro-dollar banking services, Euro-dollar issuing services, international cash management, and cross-border mergers and acquisitions – for international clients. Charles Villiers was the driving force behind these initiatives until 1968. Upon his departure, Leslie Murphy was given overall responsibility for the expansion of international business and James Wolfensohn was put in charge of international issues. He was succeeded by Geoffrey Williams in 1970, and in 1972 George Mallinckrodt was given overall responsibility for international issues. Schroder Wagg pioneered a significant innovation in the international capital market of the late 1960s, the sterling–dollar convertible loan stock. This product was tailored to the requirements of the UK subsidiaries of US multinational corporations that wished to meet their capital requirements by sterling borrowings, but at rates which reflected the strength of their overseas parents. It was also believed that sterling–dollar convertibles would be popular with British investors, since overseas investment opportunities were severely limited by exchange controls. But the authorities took the view that sterling–dollar convertibles were a device for evading the hefty dollar conversion premium to which purchases of dollar securities were liable under British exchange control regulations, and refused to allow their issue. The breakthrough came when Murphy persuaded them to allow Schroder Wagg to act as the conversion agent for the sterling–dollar convertibles which it issued, thus guaranteeing payment of the dollar conversion premium and overcoming their objections for the first time. The new form of security proved popular with clients, including Ford, Continental Oil, Cummings Engine, and Burroughs.

Most of the firms seeking Stock Exchange quotations in the 1960s were recently formed, fast growing concerns requiring capital to continue their expansion, but occasionally long established and well-known privately owned family firms converted to public company status. In 1970 Schroder Wagg created a stir when it brought two such firms to the market within weeks of each other: Pilkington Brothers, the leading glass maker and the second largest British private company, and H. P. Bulmer, the world's largest cider maker. The appointment as adviser to Pilkington Brothers was secured on the recommendation of Henry Benson of Cooper Brothers, an example of an extension of the corporate client list deriving from Richardson's contacts. An original feature of the issue, which attracted great interest, was that it was the first time that a prospectus had been produced in colour. This led to another novelty – the cost. 'The Pilkington Brothers offer for sale may not be raising a record amount of money,' commented *The Times* Business Diary, 'but it must rank as one of the most expensive. The costs, charges and expenses are estimated at £560,000 and this does not include Schroder Wagg's fee which it will get from its turn on buying the 5.7 million shares at 33s. and selling them at 34s., less underwriting commission fees and legal expenses.'[54] The money proved to be well spent. On 28 November 1970 it was announced that the offer was more than three times over-subscribed, despite being priced at the top end of market expectations. The Bulmer issue too came to the market on terms pitched on the high side. On 11 December 1970 it was announced that the 3.5 million shares offered at 13s. 6d. were also comfortably over-subscribed. 'Very satisfactory if you are a vendor and the issuing house can get away with it,' remarked a financial commentator, 'top marks then to merchant bank J. Henry Schroder Wagg.'[55]

Banking Activities

Schroder Wagg's corporate finance services were the bedrock of the firm's superb corporate client list and its high-profile image in the 1960s and the early 1970s, but the Banking Division made twice as much money as the Company Finance Division. All the senior executives on the banking side of the firm had trained with J. Henry Schroder & Co., Helbert, Wagg having conducted virtually no banking business. The first head of Schroder Wagg's Banking Division was Alec Cairns, a continuation of the position he held at J. Henry Schroder & Co. It was he who established the conservative lending policies, focusing on the top-tier companies, that became a hallmark of the firm in subsequent years. Cairns was succeeded in 1964 by David Forsyth, who had been divisional manager since 1960 and a Schroder Wagg director since October 1963. Forsyth's banking career began in 1937 when he joined Martins Bank, aged 16, transferring to the Hong Kong and Shanghai Bank early in 1939. After the war he rejoined the Hong Kong and Shanghai and spent four years working in Asia before joining J. Henry Schroder & Co. in 1951, aged 32. After little more than a year's service he was sent to Japan to develop business with Japanese banks, and thereafter Japan was one of his regional specialisations. Another was South America, which he first visited in 1957 when he accompanied Caulfeild there. Under the direction of Cairns and Forsyth, Schroder Wagg took full advantage of the new opportunities to develop banking business, with highly successful results.

Forsyth's leading lieutenants in the 1960s were Peter Bulfield, who had responsibility for UK and Japanese clients; John Hall, who joined J. Henry Schroder & Co. in 1955 after studying modern languages at Oxford, and handled Latin America and Scandinavia, and George Mallinckrodt, who was responsible for continental and US clients. Mallinckrodt, a nephew of Gustav von Mallinckrodt, had joined Schrobanco in 1954, and in 1960 moved to London with his wife, Charmaine, Helmut Schroder's daughter, to develop the business of the London firm with continental European clients. Bulfield, Hall and Mallinckrodt were appointed directors of Schroder Wagg simultaneously in April 1967. Under the direction of Ernest Ingold, 'a foreign exchange magician' in the words of a colleague, Schroder Wagg's foreign exchange and money market activities expanded rapidly and the firm's commercial banking and loan business became heavily influenced and driven by the growth of the Euro-currency markets.

Between 1962 and 1973 Schroder Wagg's deposits and customer balances expanded sixfold, from £58 million to £376 million, an increase of three-and-a-half times on an inflation-adjusted basis (see Figure 13.2). Up to 1969 the rate of increase was much the same as that of the aggregate deposits of the Accepting Houses Committee, though thereafter they grew rather slower. The fast growth of the merchant banks' deposits was possible only because of the rapid expansion of the inter-bank market in the 1960s, which allowed banks to expand their balance sheets, and hence their lending, by purchasing wholesale deposits from other banks. Schroder Wagg's first inter-bank lending arrangement was with the Netherlands Bank of South Africa, whose manager was a friend of Cairns. By the mid-1960s there was a long list of approved banks from which the Banking Division acquired deposits or to which it made advances, the Credit Committee keeping a careful watch on the latter since all transactions in the inter-bank market were unsecured.

There were three principal sources of demand for funds which were serviced by Schroder Wagg's Banking Division: first, there were the sterling requirements of corporate clients; second, the burgeoning market in local authority short-term paper, which developed parallel to the discount market in the 1960s with much the same characteristics; and third, clients' Euro-currency requirements. Euro-currency lending became an increasingly important aspect of the merchant banks' banking

Figure 13.2 Deposits of J. Henry Schroder Wagg & Co. Ltd and all members of the Accepting Houses Committee, 1962–73

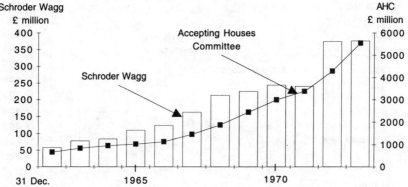

Note: All members of the Accepting Houses Committee – *Bank of England Statistical Abstract* (London: Bank of England, 1970) pp. 54–5.

business, the proportion of non-sterling deposits on the aggregate balance sheets of members of the Accepting Houses Committee rising from 45 per cent in 1962 to 54 per cent in 1973.[56] Ernest Ingold and George Mallinckrodt pioneered and developed Schroder Wagg's Euro-currency lending, most of which in the early days was conducted with continental European clients. Just as deposit-taking had gone over to a wholesale basis through the development of the inter-bank market, so did Schroder Wagg's lending and accepting operations. It was simply not economical for the small staff of a merchant bank to administer small lines of credit, so business in this field became limited to clients wanting £100,000 or more.

The accepting side of Schroder Wagg's banking business grew much more slowly than the lending side in the 1960s, acceptances less than doubling in the years 1962–71, in which advances increased sixteen-fold. The slow rate of growth of Schroder Wagg's acceptance business mirrored that of the Accepting Houses in general in these years (see Figure 13.3). The merchant banks lost market share of acceptance business to other British banks and to the overseas banks which flocked to London in the 1960s, because of their adherence to the cartel commission rate of 1.25 per cent which was undercut by the other firms. It was not until 1972, following the death of Sir Edward Reid, the Baring Brothers partner who was chairman of the Accepting Houses Committee throughout the period 1946–66, that the cartel rate was abandoned. Another constraining factor was the extension of official quantitative controls on credit, which had hitherto applied only to the clearing banks.

Figure 13.3 Acceptances of J. Henry Schroder Wagg & Co. Ltd and all members of the Accepting Houses Committee, 1962–73

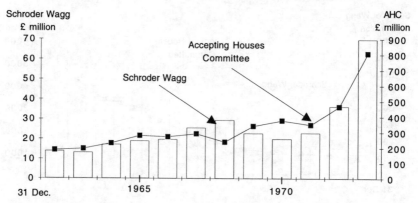

Note: All members of the Accepting Houses Committee – *Bank of England Statistical Abstract* (London: Bank of England, 1970) pp. 54–5.

This was effected as an emergency measure in May 1965 by the new Labour administration in response to balance of payments problems and anxiety over inflation. All banks were 'requested' to set a ceiling upon the increase of credit to the private sector of 5 per cent of the amount provided during the financial year which ended in March 1965. In order to forestall circumvention through the use of acceptance credits, the Bank of England decreed that the limit applied to advances and acceptances in aggregate. This produced a howl of protest from the merchant banks, arguing that the stipulation would restrict trade finance and hence harm exports, but to no avail. 'This directive,' Richardson explained to shareholders, 'compelled us to exercise considerable restraint in our lending and credit operations.'[57] Quantitative limits proved to be a permanent feature of Labour's regime of regulations, curtailing the growth of Schroder Wagg's acceptances and sterling advances for the rest of the decade, though Euro-market activity, being unrestricted, continued to expand rapidly.

Many of the merchant banks diversified into hire-purchase finance and leasing finance in the 1960s on the basis of their banking expertise. In January 1960, J. Henry Schroder & Co. and Pressed Steel formed Prestcold Finance Limited, owned 60 per cent by Schroders, to provide hire-purchase finance to buyers of commercial refrigerators manufactured by Pressed Steel. Farmers who required instalment finance for the purchase of refrigerated bulk milk tanks were typical clients. In May 1961, Prestcold formed a subsidiary, Beagle Aviation Finance, to finance sales of the Beagle aircraft, which were also made by Pressed Steel. This formula of 'same name finance companies' was employed when further developments of the business were made.[58] Prestcold was one of the first finance companies to offer leasing as an alternative to hire-purchase to its clients, an idea imported from the United States. This met with an enthusiastic response, since with the benefit of investment allowances Prestcold was able to offer the facilities at nominal charges. The expansion of leasing activities was constrained by the ownership structure, which meant that Prestcold was unable to take full advantage of tax provisions. Thus in August 1965 Schroder Wagg acquired the whole of the Prestcold equity and the following year the name was changed to Schroder Finance Ltd. Ownership was transferred to Schroders Limited in 1967 in order to develop leasing activity independently. By the early 1970s Schroder Finance was trading profitably, with ten subsidiary companies and 18,000 accounts and employing a staff of 35 at its new headquarters in Harrow. In 1977 it was renamed Schroder Leasing.

The return of a Conservative Government at the election in June 1970 bolstered spirits in the City and gave rise to hopes at the merchant banks of a relaxation of the constraints on their banking business. The new Chancellor favoured deregulation and in September 1971 a new framework called 'Competition and Credit Control', which in practice virtually removed official constraints on bank lending, came into operation. It was greeted enthusiastically by Richardson, who told shareholders 'we welcome the liberalisation of sterling lending. We believe we are well placed in the new conditions to compete for further sterling business both in terms of the quality of our staff and the sound basis on which our banking business is founded'.[59] To allow Schroder Wagg to take advantage of the new opportunities it was allocated additional resources on a major scale by the holding company, Schroders Limited, in 1972. The outcome was the surge in deposits shown in Figure 13.2 (see page 441) and acceptances in Figure 13.3 (see page 442). Other firms took similar expansionary steps and the aggregate scale of banking business conducted by members of the Accepting Houses Committee soared in 1971–73.

The property sector was a prime beneficiary of the credit boom that followed the introduction of the new policy of Competition and Credit Control. Between 1971 and 1973, direct lending to property companies increased from £447 million to £2.1 billion, two-thirds of which was provided by the merchant banks and the 'secondary' banks.[60] The secondary banks, or fringe banks, so-called because they operated on the fringe of the banking sector under licence from the Department of Trade but not under the supervision of the Bank of England, expanded dramatically in these years. They used short-term funds from the inter-bank market to finance medium-term or long-term loans to property companies, which were prepared to pay high rates of interest because of rapidly rising real estate values. Schroder Wagg, like most of the accepting houses, was very wary of lending against such illiquid collateral and made only very modest advances to property companies. It also avoided entering the ship mortgage market, another hot market at the time. 'What I wanted,' said Richardson, 'was to have the best merchant bank in the City and we didn't think mucking about with that sort of stuff fell within that vision.'[61] This prudence was fully vindicated in the ensuing property slump of 1973–75, when Schroder Wagg sustained only a single small property sector bad debt.

Investment Management

Schroder Wagg was one of London's leading investment managers in the 1960s and the early 1970s. The Investment Division was headed by Michael Verey until his appointment as deputy chairman in 1965. His successor was Lord Ogilvy, who became the Earl of Airlie in 1968. After Eton and a commission in the Scots Guards, Airlie joined J. Henry Schroder & Co. in 1953, becoming a manager in the Investment Department a few years later. He assisted Helmut Schroder and Gordon Richardson with special assignments in the 1950s, and in 1961 was made a director, shortly before the merger with Helbert, Wagg. During the 1960s he also sat on the boards of a number of other companies. His interests included the Scout movement in Scotland, of which he was Chief Commissioner in 1960–62. He was appointed to the Schroders Limited board in 1970 and became deputy chairman of Schroder Wagg in 1972. His successor as head of the Investment Division was Gordon Popham, who joined Helbert, Wagg in 1951 after Cambridge and was made a director of Schroder Wagg in 1967. 'One of the shrewdest investors I've ever known,' commented Airlie, 'with a real feel for the market.'[62] The other senior executives of the Investment Division in the 1960s and early 1970s were Sir Ashley Ponsonby from Helbert, Wagg; the Hon Alexander Hood from J. Henry Schroder & Co.; and David Hunter Johnston, a civil servant who was recruited by Verey to develop investment research in 1965.

Total funds under management by Schroder Wagg grew from £266 million at the end of 1962 to £992 million at the end of 1973 – £2.7 billion to £5.2 billion in 1990 money. Much of the increase was the result of the growth of pension funds under management, which rose from £103 million to £539 million over these years. Underlying the increase was the expansion of occupational pension schemes and the shift by larger firms to self-administered schemes managed by professional advisers, an activity dominated by the merchant banks.[63] Dozens of new, high-quality institutional clients were taken on, many of them companies which were clients of the firm's corporate finance services, the others ranging from the Marylebone Cricket Club to the Nuffield Foundation. Between 1963 and 1968 the rate of accrual of new institutional funds under Schroder Wagg's management rose from £500,000 per week to £750,000. In 1969, it leapt to £1.25 million per week with the firm's appointment, in conjunction with Warburgs, as managers of the massive, newly-established Post Office Pension Fund, which was investing £60 million per annum. By the beginning of the 1970s Schroder Wagg's institutional funds under management were second only to Flemings', the long-established industry leader. Institutional funds constituted a larger and larger proportion of total funds under management each year, the rest comprising Schroder Wagg's investment trusts, unit trusts, charities and private clients.

The expansion of the merchant banks' business as investment managers on behalf of institutional investors led to mounting discontent with the size of stockbrokers' commissions. The merchant banks argued that prevailing commission rates were unreasonably high for their clients' large-scale transactions. The grievance was taken up with the Stock Exchange by the Accepting Houses Committee, with Verey, who became chairman of that body in 1974, playing a leading part in the negotiations. 'We had some fairly uncomfortable meetings,' he recalled. 'I remember Graham Greenwell [senior partner of the stockbroker Greenwells] complaining to the Committee, "What Michael Verey wants is to share in our profits" '.[64] The merchant banks' response to the Stock Exchange's intransigence was to establish the Automated Real-time Investments Exchange Limited (ARIEL), a computer-based block-trading system to transact large deals between subscribers bypassing the Stock Exchange. The first managing director of ARIEL, Colin Leech, was recruited from Schroder Wagg,[65] but even before it began operations in 1974 the Stock Exchange capitulated and drastically reduced commission rates.

The Schroder Wagg Investment Division inherited responsibility for five investment trusts, which in 1964 had total assets of £58 million.[66] Much the largest was the Continental and Industrial, ranking 36th in the industry with assets of £19.8 million at market value. The others were Trans Oceanic, £11.9 million; Broadstone, £10.3 million; Ashdown, £9.3 million; and Westpool, £6.6 million. Two new investment trusts were launched by Schroder Wagg in 1962. European investment opportunities were much in favour at the time, and the Anglo-Spanish Investment Trust and the Trans-European Investment Trust specialised in continental securities, particularly Spanish banks and utilities. Neither was very successful; the Anglo-Spanish was wound up in October 1967 and the Trans-European was converted into a unit trust early in 1971. Australia was a focus of investment interest in the late 1960s, and in July 1968 Schroder Wagg launched the Trans-Australia Investment Trust, which in its early days was closely identified with Broken Hill Proprietary and Western Mining.

The unit trust industry grew spectacularly in the 1960s, the total value of funds invested in them rising from £200 million in 1960 to £1.5 billion in 1968.[67] Schroder Wagg entered unit trust management in January 1968 when it was appointed investment manager to the Trustee Savings Bank's (TSB) new and highly publicised unit trust, which was trumpeted as 'probably one of the most significant steps the unit trust movement has made towards its objective of bringing the benefits of equity investment to the ordinary man'.[68] It was called the only unit trust with 1,400 branches and the *Scotsman* declared that 'the TSB has brought the Stock Exchange to the people'.[69] The public response was very gratifying and in 1968 nearly 47 million units were sold, making a fund of £15.5

million. Even in 1969, a terrible year for equities and equity investment vehicles, a further 14 million units were sold, raising the fund to £18.5 million. In its first year, the TSB unit trust ranked 29th amongst the hundreds of funds in operation, and Schroder Wagg's skilful management was praised by *The Times*.[70]

In October 1968, Schroder Wagg launched its own unit trusts, the Schroder Income Fund and the Schroder Capital Fund. 'The Capital Fund aims at capital growth – but without inviting a "go-go" label,' reported the *Daily Telegraph*, 'while the other aims at income with enough growth at least to maintain the original value of the investment.'[71] The 'middling rich' were the target of these funds, which had minimum subscriptions of £2,500, amongst the highest in the industry.[72] A golden apple was adopted as the trade-mark of the new trusts – a confusing choice, since members of the public apparently assumed that it signified a connection between Schroder Wagg and the Beatles' Apple Organisation. A film explaining how to get 'a bigger bite of the money apple' was produced, and Investment Division executives took to the road with portable desk-top projectors, the first time that the firm had undertaken such a retailing exercise. The publicity campaign marked a new departure for Schroder Wagg in terms of the conduct of self-promotion. 'Though it handles investments worth more than £600 million,' observed the *Investors' Chronicle* in 1968, 'Schroder Wagg have been remarkably publicity shy up to this point. This week, however, the merchant bank emerges from its shell. There is nothing shy about the film. It boasts quite openly of the success of the bank in handling investments. Mr. Michael Verey claimed that Schroders were "rather good at investment, having done it for a long time, and not a bit ashamed of it".'[73] This campaign, which brought in subscriptions of £15 million, much outstripping expectations, was symptomatic of the transformation of the attitude of the merchant banks to publicity in the 1960s. The increase in competition led to rivalry to market their services, and the promotion of unit trusts served as a 'shop window for their investment expertise'.[74] Schroder Wagg took advantage of the revival of the stock market towards the end of 1969 to launch another unit trust. This was the General Fund, which was aimed at the small investors having a low minimum subscription of £250. The General Fund was promoted by a television advertising campaign, a marketing initiative which had been tried only once before.[75] Sales in the first four months were £1.4 million, which more than recouped the expenditure on London Weekend Television air-time. By the end of 1970 unit trust funds under management totalled about £45 million. 'For a group less than two years old to be already the 13th largest force in the industry is quite an achievement,' commented *The Times*.[76]

In February 1970, Schroder Wagg established Schroder Life Assurance Limited (initially called Cheapside Assurance) to market its unit trusts through the sale of unit-linked life assurance policies. The insurance risks incurred were reinsured with the Dominion–Lincoln Assurance Company, a British subsidiary of the Lincoln National Life Insurance Company of the United States. In 1973, Schroder Wagg purchased Dominion–Lincoln to acquire a direct sales force to develop its unit-linked life assurance business. Intermediary originated business was boosted by the acquisition in 1975 of the Individual Life Assurance Company at a cost of £2.35 million. The launch in 1972 of a managed bond with a life assurance component, the Schroder Flexible Fund, was a significant further development of the business. Managed bonds were a recent innovation which permitted maximum discretion for managers to shift funds between a wide range of investments and included a life assurance contract.[77] The flexibility of this form of fund was highly appropriate to the turbulent market conditions of 1972 and 1973, and so many managed bonds were launched that commentators wondered whether they would supplant unit trusts in the affections of investors.[78] The Schroder Flexible Fund proved very popular, sums assured totalling £11 million in its first three months. The opening years of the 1970s also saw the launch of a number of specialist Schroder Wagg investment products: the Schroder Recovery Fund was started in 1970; and the Schroder Property Fund and Schroder Europe Fund in 1971, the latter being the former Trans-Europe Investment Trust, which was converted into a unit trust because of the excessive discount between the quoted price and the net asset value of the fund.

Schroder Wagg's corporate finance and investment management executives co-operated closely on new issues, the former devising securities appropriate to their clients' requirements, while the latter assisted with pricing, underwriting and placing. The Investment Division also marketed securities which were not issued by Schroder Wagg but were bulk-purchased by the firm; for instance, blocks of the shares of Hidroelectricia de Cataluna, a large Spanish electricity utility; Ready Mixed Concrete (Australia); and Ferranti. Although Schroder Wagg was not a member of the Stock Exchange it had a small but active securities trading operation which was conducted by a team inherited from Helbert, Wagg. This was headed by George Wood, the son of a printer who had entered the City as an office boy in 1918 and joined Helbert, Wagg as a dealer in 1934, of whom it was said that he never made a loss. It was estimated that in the mid-1960s his activities, specialising in South African securities, generated several hundred thousand pounds in trading revenues per annum for Schroder Wagg. A personal profile that appeared in *The Times* in 1968 portrayed him as one of the City's living legends.[79]

The 1960s and early 1970s saw new levels of professionalism and rapid technical innovation in Schroder Wagg's Investment Division. In 1965, a Research Department was established to provide detailed analysis of companies and sectors. Computerisation began in 1969, initially simply for drawing up contract notes and compiling the 'business sheet', but by 1971 machines had replaced men in the production of portfolio valuations for pension funds. Closed-circuit television screens displaying London and Wall Street securities prices appeared in the Investment Division for the first time in 1969, and the same year saw the installation of Datastream and Telecomp facilities for the research team. The innovation of 1972 was the interconnection of the officers of the department by 'intercom' to facilitate more rapid consultation. The following year saw yet another significant development – the appointment of the first two female investment managers.

Diversification

Competition in merchant banking increased markedly in the 1960s. In part this was the result of a more dynamic and aggressive approach to business amongst the merchant banks themselves – it was in these years that the longstanding taboo against 'poaching' each other's clients disappeared. It was also the product of the encroachment of other firms into the activities conducted by the merchant banks. On one flank there were the foreign banks, on the other the new domestic 'secondary banks', plus the giant British clearing banks, which began to bestir themselves in ways which suggested forthcoming challenges. The competitive pressures, coupled with restrictions on credit provision, encouraged the merchant banks both to be innovative and to diversify their domestic activities.

Rivalry for corporate finance clients led to the opening of regional offices by many merchant banks in the 1960s, the idea being to take their services to industry rather than waiting for clients to turn up in the metropolis.[80] The first was opened by Singer & Friedlander in Leeds in 1960 and by the end of the decade that firm had five regional offices, while the ICFC had nineteen; Hill Samuel, five; Samuel Montagu, five; and Rothschilds, three. Schroder Wagg established a presence in Scotland and Ireland through the formation of joint ventures with leading local banks, its favoured strategy when entering new markets. The inspiration for the Scottish joint venture was the Toothill Report of 1964, which drew attention to the absence of merchant banking services north of the border.[81] In December 1964, Schroder Wagg and the National Commercial Bank of Scotland each subscribed 50 per cent of the capital of National Commercial and Schroders Ltd (NCS), and Alec Cairns returned to his native Scotland to strengthen the NCS management team in Edinburgh. The business grew rapidly and in 1967 it was reported that it 'has so far stopped £20 to £25 million of Scottish money going to London for investment . . . This has been an important addition to the Scottish economy'.[82] Schroder Wagg realised its interest in NCS in February 1969 following the merger between the National Commercial Bank and the Royal Bank of Scotland, which already had a merchant banking arm.

The Investment Bank of Ireland Ltd was a joint venture with the Bank of Ireland and Morgan Grenfell, Schroder Wagg subscribing £100,000 for 20 per cent of the equity in August 1966. The enterprise also prospered and the report and accounts for 1967 revealed that total assets were already £12.8 million and demand for company finance services was described as 'very heavy'.[83] In 1972, when additional resources were being sought to back the expansion of Schroder Wagg's banking business, the shareholding in the Investment Bank of Ireland was sold.

The most obvious direction of diversification for the merchant banks was into related financial services. Their development of leasing and unit trust business, for example, have already been mentioned. Another financial activity in which several of the merchant banks became involved was insurance broking:[84] Hill Samuel purchased Lambert Brothers, Noble Lowndes and Partners, Hamilton Smith & Co., and L. Hammond & Co., and by 1973 insurance broking operations contributed 38 per cent of the profits of the Hill Samuel Group; Montagu Trust, the parent of Samuel Montagu, acquired Bland Welch and E. W. Payne, one of the largest insurance brokers; and Kleinwort Benson and Morgan Grenfell purchased shareholdings in insurance broking firms. In the case of Singer & Friedlander the link-up was achieved from the other direction when the firm was acquired by the insurance broker C. T. Bowring in 1973. Consideration was given at Schroder Wagg to the purchase of an insurance broker, but it was decided not to move into this sector because the firm acted as financial adviser to a large number of quoted brokers whose business it was likely to lose if it went into competition with them. In fact, its neutral stance enabled it to act as adviser to many of the mergers and acquisitions in that field.

Schroder Computer Services Ltd was formed as a subsidiary on the initiative of John Bayley in July 1969 to provide computer consultancy services for the financial services industry and to market Schroder Wagg's spare computer capacity. Its origins lay in the merchant bank's endeavours to computerise its own operations, which began in September 1965 when the Hoskyns Group was engaged as a consultant.[85] In May 1966, Schroder Wagg appointed a Data Systems

Manager and a year later the Operations Division took delivery of an IBM mainframe. Despite the careful preparation, progress was far from smooth, but by the end of the 1960s the bulk of routine operations had been computerised. This enabled the containment of overhead costs, despite the continued expansion of the volume of operations. In fact, so much progress had been made that Schroder Wagg found itself in the forefront of the application of computers in the financial services industry, which suggested profitable opportunities for marketing its expertise. Three months prior to the establishment of Schroder Computer Services, Schroder Wagg purchased a 26 per cent shareholding in the Hoskyns Group at a cost of £160,000, cementing the relationship between the firms.[86] Accommodation was rented in Holborn for the rapidly expanding computer staff and for a second IBM machine, which was installed in 1970. Hopes for the new business ran high, a report prepared by the Hoskyns Group in October 1969 predicting an annual rate of increase in demand for computer services of 29 per cent during the 1970s.[87] But Schroder Wagg was not the only firm developing computer services for the financial services industry, and soon there was over-capacity. By mid-1971 Schroder Computer Services' expected profits of £115,000 had turned into projected losses of £180,000, upsetting the finances of the firm, which in the expectation of immediate profitability had deliberately been provided with a capital of a mere £100 so as not to tie up funds that could be used in Schroder Wagg's banking business. In April 1972, it was reluctantly judged necessary to increase the capital to £100,000. Yet Schroder Wagg's directors remained convinced of the rosy prospects for the computer industry, and in September 1973 the bank provided a £725,000 loan to the Hoskyns Group for the purchase of Datasolve, a software house, and increased its shareholding from 26 per cent to 35 per cent. At the end of the year the financial performance of Schroder Computer Services was reported to be improving, though there was no immediate prospect of profits.

Another potentially profitable form of diversification for Schroder Wagg in the view of Richardson and Bayley was taking equity stakes in ailing or fledgling enterprises, whose performance could be radically improved through the application of the merchant bank's expertise in corporate finance and its financial support. Once the transformation had been effected, Schroder Wagg would be able to realise its investment, making a capital gain that would far exceed any fees it might receive for performing the same services for other proprietors. Of course, the strategy was inherently riskier than acting as an adviser or lender, since it necessitated the commitment of equity, but Schroder Wagg's own outstandingly successful performance was taken as proof of its managerial capabilities and in July 1968 a new operational entity, the Industrial Department, was formed to execute this entrepreneurial initiative.

Richardson recruited William Hyde, a 48-year-old accountant and expert on management organisation who had made his career with the nationalised West Midlands Gas Board, a somewhat unlikely sector of origin, as head of the Industrial Department.[88] Naturally, the gas industry was the first sector on which he focused, purchasing three firms that were amalgamated as Whitaker Ellis Bullock Ltd, which conducted activities such as pipe-laying and pipe maintenance, and whose development plans included a training school for gas industry operatives. 'Clearly,' concluded a profile in *Gas World*, 'the place is going places.'[89] Another acquisition was Michael Birch, a manufacturer of spectacles, and there were several other purchases. The Industrial Department also took over Schroder Wagg's large shareholding in R. Willett Ltd, which was an investment made many years earlier by Leadenhall Securities, the now inactive venture capital subsidiary of J. Henry Schroder & Co.[90] Willett, a successful, Croydon-based manufacturer of machines for packaging supermarket foodstuffs, with a growing business, was merged with G. D. Peters Ltd, a 'struggling' engineering firm with plenty of spare capacity, in which Schroder Wagg purchased a majority shareholding in February 1969.[91] The prospects for G. D. Peters were transformed and the share price raced upwards, registering a rise of 238 per cent, making it the best performing share in the first half of 1969.[92] This was just the sort of alchemy that the Industrial Department had been established to conduct, and financial commentators were much impressed, but in fact it marked the high point of its fortunes.

Schroder Wagg had greatly underestimated the problems of the industrial firms it had acquired and massively overestimated the abilities of merchant bankers to run industrial enterprises. G. D. Peters, the largest of the stable, proved the biggest headache, and in the summer of 1971 Schroder Wagg felt obliged to buy out the minority shareholders at £1 per share (little more than a quarter of the price of two years earlier) in order to safeguard its good name.[93] By then the problems of G. D. Peters and the other protégés of the Industrial Department were occupying a third of the time of the senior executives of the Corporate Finance Division, an enormous opportunity cost.[94] Hyde left in January 1972 and the Industrial Department was wound up, though the realisation of the assets took several years, during which they continued to take a heavy and unprofitable toll of managerial energies. 'One of the less happy examples of merchant banking in industry,' commented the *Financial Times*, but every Schroder Wagg director used the word 'disaster'.[95] With hindsight, the notion that merchant bankers could miraculously improve the performance of manufacturing industry was seen to be flawed. As Leslie Murphy later observed, 'it was a very amateur, ill-conceived idea, a disaster for the very good reason that the people involved didn't know what they were doing'.[96]

The Industrial Department was not the firm's only foray into unfamiliar territory which came unstuck in the early 1970s. Schroders' association with the property developer, Dick Dusseldorp, the managing director and later chairman of the Lend Lease Corporation in Australia, began in the early 1960s, when the firm put together a consortium in London to finance the Australia Square Development in Sydney, the city's tallest building. Despite large cost overruns the project proved profitable because rents rose faster than anticipated and thus the yield remained roughly as projected. When Dusseldorp decided to extend his operations to the United States, Schroders joined him, forming a jointly-owned company, Property Holdings International (PHI), in Bermuda in 1970 for the purpose. Another, though much smaller-scale property joint venture, Queensborough Property Finance Ltd, was established in association with the Percy Bilton Group Ltd on a 50–50 basis to undertake commercial and residential property development in the UK. PHI and Queensborough were hit hard by the slump in property prices on both sides of the Atlantic in the mid-1970s and were closed down after sustaining substantial losses.

The post-mortem assessments upon the Industrial Department and the PHI and Queensborough investments drew the conclusion that it was the basis of the firm's participations that were misconceived. Some years later, Schroders profitably re-entered the venture capital and real estate businesses, but at that time as professional portfolio managers and financial advisers backing high quality industrialists and entrepreneurs.

The early 1970s saw several indications of a slackening of the rapid growth that had characterised Schroder Wagg in the 1960s. One was the size of the staff. In 1962–71 Schroder Wagg's staff increased from 425 to 775, but by 1973 the number had fallen to 735. Another was a slippage in the firm's ranking in the league tables for several of its activities.[97] Balance sheet size is the conventional yardstick for comparisons between banks, though in the case of merchant banks it has the drawback of shedding little light on the scale of their corporate finance or investment management activities. By this measure Schroder Wagg ranked second amongst the London merchant banks in 1962, third in 1967 and fourth in 1973 (see Table 13.1). But if Schroders Limited is regarded as the appropriate entity for comparative purposes, its consolidated balance sheet was the largest of the merchant banks for most of the 1960s. Towards the end of the decade and in the early 1970s other firms

Table 13.1   Total assets[1] of some leading merchant banks, 1962, 1967, 1973

31 December			
	1962 £ *million*	*1967* £ *million*	*1973* £ *million*
Schroders Limited	137	293	706
J. Henry Schroder Wagg	68	174	397
Baring Brothers	53	93	222
Hambros Bank†	129	270	1,226
Hill Samuel[2]	48	216	1,141
Kleinwort Benson	67	173	836
Morgan Grenfell	39	125	281
S. G. Warburg†	29	84	329
All Members Accepting Houses Committee	753	1,545	6,030

† 31 March, following year.
1. Excluding acceptances.
2. Philip Hill, Higginson, Erlangers, 31 March 1963.
Note: Information on other firms unavailable.

Sources: J. Henry Schroder Wagg – balance sheets; other firms – *Times 500*; Accepting Houses Committee – Bank of England Statistical Abstract.

expanded their UK banking activities very rapidly and by 1973 Hambros, Hill Samuel and Kleinwort Benson had larger balance sheets than Schroders Limited. In part this was a consequence of Schroder Wagg's conservative lending policies, but it was also a reflection of the allocation of resources to international expansion. It is the development of Schroders as an international group of companies and the evolution of the role of Schroders Limited that is the subject of the next chapter.

14

International Expansion

1960–73

The formation of Schroders Limited and the public offering in September 1959 were motivated by the Schroder family's desire for a public quotation for their investments in the firms in London and New York, as discussed in Chapter 11. Financially, the advantage of having a common holding company was immediately demonstrated, since the strength of the consolidated equity of the holding company permitted the acquisition of Helbert, Wagg & Co. to be financed principally by unsecured debt, with only a 4 per cent increase in shareholders' equity. Operationally, the creation of the holding company initially made no difference, since the London and New York firms were managed independently, but gradually the holding company became of greater and greater significance and the evolution of its strategic and managerial roles is one of the themes of this chapter. The other theme is the creation of an international group of Schroder companies through the formation of subsidiaries and associates.

Helmut Schroder was the chairman of Schroders Limited from September 1959 until the end of December 1965. Initially, there were only three other directors: Gordon Richardson, Gerald Beal and Norris Darrell. In 1960, upon the acquisition of the 70 per cent interest in Helbert, Wagg, Lionel Fraser joined the board as deputy chairman. Following the full merger in 1962, the board of Schroders Limited was expanded by the appointment of Jonathan Backhouse and Alan Russell, senior Schroder Wagg executives; Lord Perth and Henry Tiarks in non-executive capacities; and Bruno Schroder, representing the Schroder family interest. Under Helmut's chairmanship, the board received periodic summaries of assets and liabilities, prepared on a consolidated basis by John Bayley, the financial controller, who thereby began to play a key role in the holding company. However, decisions about both day-to-day operations and vital policy issues continued to be made by the operating companies, and in reality Schroders Limited performed only a supervisory role as a holding company with accountability to shareholders.

Gordon Richardson became deputy chairman of Schroders Limited in October 1964 and succeeded Helmut as chairman on 30 December 1965. At the same board meeting, Helmut Schroder and Henry Tiarks retired as directors, though the former was given the honorific title of president and retained an office at the firm, which he attended most days until his death in 1969. At the same time John Howell, the president of Schrobanco, Michael Verey, the newly appointed deputy chairman of Schroder Wagg, and John Bayley were appointed directors of Schroders Limited.

Richardson succeeded Beal as chairman of Schrobanco in June 1967. For three years, from June 1967 to October 1970, Richardson held the executive chairmanships of the London and New York operating companies and the group holding company. With this remarkable concentration of authority he promoted the development of the role of the holding company and the subordination of the operating companies to it. He was assisted with the formulation and implementation of these changes by John Bayley, and by John Hull, Leslie Murphy and James Wolfensohn, who became directors in 1969–70; 'Richardson's Court' was the collective term used by a former Helbert, Wagg director. The late 1960s also saw a strengthening of the non-executive element of the Schroders Limited board. Lord Franks, originally an Oxford philosophy don, a highly distinguished former British Ambassador to Washington and chairman of Lloyds Bank, joined the board in 1968. The following year, Dr Harold Brown, an eminent scientist who served as Secretary of the US Air Force in 1965–69 and then became president of the California Institute of Technology, and Paul Nitze, who served as US Deputy Secretary of Defence under President Johnson, also became non-executive directors. Besides the prestige bestowed by the presence of these eminent public figures, they proved very supportive of Richardson's endeavours to develop the strategic role of Schroders Limited. Once the new structures had been implemented, Richardson relinquished the Schrobanco chairmanship to John Howell in 1970 and the Schroder Wagg chairmanship to Michael Verey in 1972. The following year he resigned from the chairmanship of Schroders Limited to become Governor of the Bank of England.

The reorganisation at the time of the public offering in 1959 brought together the London and New York firms on a formal corporate basis for the first time. At that point the New York firm constituted 73 per cent of the total book value. The acquisition of Helbert, Wagg augmented the relative size of the London firm, though this was partly offset by the devaluation of sterling from $2.80 to $2.40 in 1967 which boosted the value of the US assets, and in 1973 the book value of the New York firm was still in excess of half of the book value of Schroders Limited. By then, Schroders Limited had become an international group of companies, which besides its major interests in Britain and the US had a growing subsidiary in Switzerland, associates in Australia, Brazil, France and Hong Kong, and representative offices in Argentina, the

95.   Gordon Richardson, later Lord Richardson of Duntisbourne

96. (*left*) Michael Verey

97. (*right*) John Howell

98. (*right*) James Wolfensohn

99. (*left*) John Hull

100. (*right*) The Earl of Airlie

101. (*left*) John Connor

102. (*left*) George Mallinckrodt

103. (*right*) Win Bischoff

104. (*left*) Bruno Schroder

105. (*right*) Laurance Mackie on the
      occasion of his 100th birthday in
      1988 with portrait of Baron Sir
      John Henry Schröder Bt, the
      senior partner when he joined
      the firm in 1905. The lives of
      these two men span the history
      of Schroders

106. The Board of Schroders plc, 1992. Standing (*back row*) William Turner, Nicholas MacAndrew, Alva Way, William Slee, Charles Sinclair; (*middle row*) James Harmon, Peter Sedgwick, Adam Broadbent, Jean Solandt, Sir Ralph Robins; (*seated*) Win Bischoff, George Mallinckrodt, Bruno Schroder; (*absent overseas*) Baron Daniel Janssen

107.   The Coat of Arms of Schroders plc

Bahamas, Bermuda, the Cayman Islands, Colombia, Germany and Japan. Other merchant banks also pursued a strategy of international expansion in the 1960s, but Schroders had a long lead because of Schrobanco and Richardson's determination to make the most of the opportunities that arose from its international ties.

Continental Europe and the Middle East

The early 1960s saw an upsurge of interest at both Schrobanco and Schroder Wagg in opportunities for expansion in continental Europe. One reason was the move to convertibility of European currencies in 1958 and the development of the Euro-dollar market. Another was the growing interest in Britain in membership of the European Economic Community, which resulted in the unsuccessful British applications of 1963 and 1967. Indeed, other merchant banks, for instance Morgan Grenfell and Warburgs, were also pursuing continental connections in these years.[1] A further reason, particular to Schroders, was the personal commitment of Helmut Schroder to the re-establishment of the London firm's continental ties, and he was the 'driving force' behind the initiatives of the early 1960s.[2] In February 1962, he told Schroders Limited's shareholders that 'we especially welcome the challenge offered by the proposed entry of this country into the Common Market where we have old and valued connections. We have taken steps to see that these relationships are kept fresh and active so that we can play our part in furthering the development of business between the United Kingdom and the Continent'.[3]

The initiative for an expansion of continental European business came from Schrobanco, which provided dollar-based banking services for its European clientele. In the late 1950s, as it became increasingly clear that Schrobanco's international activities on behalf of US domestic clients were being adversely affected by the overseas push of the American banks, Ernest Meili advocated an aggressive expansion of business with European clients. He recognised that in view of the emergence of the nascent Euro-dollar market this initiative required the full co-operation of Schroders in London and he was gradually able to persuade the London management to act: foreign exchange business in both New York and London was expanded; Euro-dollar market activities were commenced; and staff were relocated. In 1960, George Mallinckrodt was sent to London from New York to promote business with continental European clients, and Max Zeller, a Schrobanco officer of Swiss birth, established a representative office in Zurich to develop business with Swiss industry and banks, including the placement and trading of Latin

American promissory notes. In 1962, Valla Lada-Mocarski, who had run Schrobanco's Paris office in the 1930s, again opened a representative office there, this time in the prestigious Place Vendôme. All the while the Frankfurt representative office continued to foster relations with German clients. While all three offices were clearly perceived in the market as offshoots of Schrobanco, they represented both the London and New York firms. At the instigation of Lada-Mocarski, Schroders joined a consortium comprising the Banco Urquijo of Madrid, the Banque de Paris et des Pays-Bas of Paris, and Lehman Brothers of New York, which in 1962 established the Corporacion Espanola de Financiacion International, SA (CEFISA) in Madrid.

The Zurich, Paris and Madrid initiatives were aspects of the drive to develop business in continental Europe referred to by Helmut Schroder in 1963 as 'our European effort'.[4] Charles Villiers, who was the most enthusiastic of the senior Schroder Wagg directors about the prospects for business in continental Europe, was put in charge of the programme in London, working closely with Ernest Meili in New York. Senior officers were given responsibility for different countries and a secretariat was established to support them. These efforts enjoyed some success and Schrobanco became an important banker to additional European clients, particularly German and Swiss companies, assisting them to finance new investments in the United States. Schroder Wagg also established new relationships and expanded its business base on the Continent. The election of a Labour administration in Britain in October 1964 raised anxieties in the City that government restrictions would lead to the transfer of the Euro-market from London to European financial centres. These fears gave a renewed impulse to the development of a presence in the major continental centres. In response to the imposition by the government of physical controls on credit in May 1965, Richardson instructed an internal team to draw up a plan for Schroders' expansion into continental Europe. However, no action was taken to implement their report since the Euro-market in London continued to grow, and foreign banks continued to flock to the City. 'One reason that not much happened,' said the team leader, Philip Robinson, 'was that London was becoming more and more the international financial entrepôt, so if you wanted to make money in Europe it was easiest to do it in London.'[5] Furthermore, the expected development of a single capital market in the Common Market, as envisaged, for instance, by the group of experts that presented an influential report to the EEC Commission in 1966, did not materialise – exchange, capital and financing controls being maintained by many European countries until the 1980s.[6]

Continuing concern about the future of London as an international financial centre and frustration with UK exchange controls led to the commissioning of a further report on continental expansion, drawn up by Martin Witschi, of Schrobanco, and George Mallinckrodt. This identified Zurich as the most promising location for the conduct of banking activities complementary to those of the London and New York firms. Coincidentally, Ernest Ingold, the head of Schroder Wagg's foreign exchange and money market operations, informed Richardson of his wish to return to his native Switzerland following his marriage. Ingold's expertise permitted the desired expansion of Schroders' activities in Zurich. Thus in February 1967 a subsidiary finance company, Schroders AG, was formed with a capital of 5 million Swiss francs subscribed by Schroders Limited. Building on the work of Max Zeller, who had already transformed the Zurich office from a cost centre to a profit centre, Schroders AG was highly active from the outset. In 1969, the capital was raised to 20 million Swiss francs (£2 million) and in March 1970 a full banking licence was granted and the company was renamed J. Henry Schroder Bank AG. A new chief executive, Dr Erik Gasser, aged 42, an experienced Swiss banker, was appointed chief executive in 1971, by which time the staff had grown from three to ten. Under Gasser's direction the business continued to expand, supplementing its banking activities with the development of investment management and related services in the early 1970s.

Schroders' presence in Frankfurt and Paris remained at the representative office level but the firms in London and New York increased their business with German and French clients. In Frankfurt, Gustav von Mallinckrodt retired in 1967, aged 75, though continuing as a consultant until 1982, and was succeeded by Ulf Sudeck. Around this time, consideration was given to the expansion of Schroders' presence in Germany, either through the acquisition of an interest in Schröder Gebrüder, which was owned by two of Helmut's cousins, Hans Rudolph and Manfred von Schröder and continued to be one of Hamburg's leading merchant banks, or in B. Metzler seel. Sohn & Co., a leading Frankfurt-based private bank with strength in the investment management business. The initial idea was to persuade these two firms to merge, thus combining their respective commercial and investment banking strengths, and for Schroders Limited to take a significant interest in the merged bank. Discussions were held, but Schröder Gebrüder decided instead to join up with the Hamburg merchant bank, Münchmeyer & Co. and the Frankfurt bank, Friedrich Hengst & Co., which led to the formation of Schröder, Münchmeyer, Hengst & Co. in 1968. Subsequent talks were also held with Metzlers alone about the acquisition by Schroders of an interest in the firm, or the establishment of a joint venture to undertake investment management and company finance activities along the lines of a London merchant bank, but nothing came of these proposals. The Frankfurt representative office remained Schroders' only presence in Germany, though J. Henry Schroder Bank AG of Zurich became increasingly active in investment management for German clients.

In Paris, Lada-Mocarski was succeeded by Peter Wahl and business developments included participation in 'our first big hotly contested take-over battle' in France in 1967.[7] In the mid-1960s Schroders assisted Charles Clore and Jack Cotton with their endeavours to promote City Centre Properties in the continental European real estate market. This followed the successful establishment of a $25 million letter of credit to raise the financing on behalf of City Centre Properties for the construction of the Pan-Am Building in New York, acting jointly with Hambros. The revival of Britain's aspirations to EEC membership in 1970 again focused Schroders' attention on opportunities in France.[8] Discussions were held with Crédit Commercial de France about the establishment of a joint venture, but these came to nothing. Soon afterwards it became known that a 14 per cent shareholding in the Société Privée de Gestion Financière (SPGF), a Parisian merchant bank, was for sale. In a paper presented to the Schroders Limited board in April 1972, it was argued that the purchase of this interest would give access to French franc finance, which could be made available to non-French clients and provide an opportunity to market Schroder Wagg's services to French clients: 'the advantages of participation in SPGF are advantages we urgently need to acquire if we are to establish ourselves as providers of European-wide financial services to corporate clients in the crucial next five years as Britain joins the EEC and the barriers to capital movements come down between Britain and Continental Europe'.[9] Hitherto it had been Schroders' policy to have majority ownership or management control of new ventures and to avoid passive minority investments. However, it was felt that this was a unique opportunity to enter the French market, and the management of SPGF was well regarded by the Paris representative. The board was impressed by the case and in June 1972, having obtained Bank of England consent, Schroders Limited acquired 14 per cent of SPGF at a cost of £338,000.

Beirut became increasingly important as a regional financial centre in the 1960s, intermediating financial flows between the Middle East, London and New York. Murphy, an expert on the region through his work in the oil industry, pressed for the establishment of a Schroder presence in Beirut, and in December 1965, having obtained Bank of England exchange control consent, Schroders took a 25 per cent interest in Rifbank SAL at a cost of £100,000, being the first London merchant bank to make such an equity investment.[10] Rifbank's principal sponsors were the National Bank of Kuwait and Commerzbank, and it was anticipated that the participation in the Beirut venture would foster closer ties with the Kuwaitis. Business began promisingly and by the winter of 1966 the firm had a staff of 25, but its activity was largely of a Lebanese domestic nature and its development of international business was upset by the Intra Bank collapse, that undermined international confidence in Beirut as a banking centre. Since Rifbank had not fulfilled Schroders' objectives in the region, the other shareholders agreed in 1973 to buy out its interest, realising a handsome capital gain. This cleared the way for the establishment of a subsidiary in Beirut the following year in conjunction with the Asseilys, a prominent Lebanese merchant family.

United States

In New York, as in London, 1962 saw a change of generation of management. With the elevation of Gerald Beal to chairman and the retirement soon after of Ernest Meili, Valla Lada-Mocarski and Harold Sutphen, a younger generation of officers took executive control of the firm. The new president was John I. Howell, aged 45, who held this post until 1970. He was very much in the Beal mould, a quiet spoken, graceful mannered, patrician East Coast American, who joined the firm in 1947 thanks to a social introduction to Beal.[11] Initially he worked on the development of the firm's business in Asia, but from the beginning of the 1950s he acted as Lada-Mocarski's principal lieutenant on the Southern European side. His deputy, the new executive vice-president, was Canon R. Clements, aged 47, an energetic Texan who worked hard and played hard. Although by no means lacking an international outlook, he was more enthusiastic than most of his colleagues about pursuing domestic opportunities.

Despite the common ownership of both J. Henry Schroder & Co. and Schrobanco by Schroders Limited from 1959, the two firms continued to operate independently, and prior to 1967 they in fact grew further apart rather than closer. Whereas the acquisition of Helbert, Wagg orientated the London firm more towards providing investment banking services for a domestic British corporate client base, Schrobanco was prevented by both regulatory and competitive hurdles from developing in the same manner in the American domestic market. Instead, under the cautious leadership of John Howell, Schrobanco maintained its traditional profile as a specialist New York firm providing dollar-based international banking services to its predominantly European, Latin American and Asian clientele, taking advantage of its Article XII charter, while Schrotrust continued to provide trust banking services to the US clientele, and Schrorock focused on venture capital business.

In these years Schrobanco responded to the increasing competition from the US commercial banks, which had the advantages of cheaper deposits and larger balance sheets, by concentrating on providing specialist services to an international clientele. It retained close connections with its central bank clients, although the volume of deposits from these sources diminished because of increasing competition from the new certificate of deposit market, and expanded correspondent banking business through letters of credit and foreign exchange activities. Arising from business generated by the Frankfurt, Paris and Zurich representative offices, Schrobanco held the dollar cash and custody accounts of many prominent European banks which did not have branches in New York during the 1960s. It was also banker to many leading European corporations, assisting them in the establishment and financing of their US subsidiaries. It was a US banker to most of the large German companies, such as Volkswagen and Daimler-Benz, and many Swiss companies, for instance Ciba-Geigy and Brown Boveri. A similar strategy was pursued with respect to its Japanese clientele, and the firm began to do business with the trading companies as well as the banks as trade between the US and Japan increased. In Latin America, by contrast, its clients remained predominantly the banks.

In the US the client base comprised regional banks, corporations which required the benefits of its expertise to do business in Latin America and Europe, and a few commodity import-export firms. In contrast to its prime overseas clientele, Schrobanco's US domestic clients were second-tier and it proved almost impossible to win the business of top-tier US corporations since it could offer only limited facilities compared to the much larger commercial banks. The consequence, commented Howell, was that 'we would make more bad loans domestically than in the foreign field. That was because we didn't understand it as well, and because we had to take second and third class credit risks as we couldn't get the others. We were scarcely known west of the Hudson'.[12] Howell and Clements identified East Coast US corporations as the most promising domestic market for Schrobanco's services, and in the spring of 1963 a carefully targeted advertising campaign was launched in the business pages of the *New York Times* around the slogan 'Schroder? What's that?'. The rationale behind the move was explained at the time thus:

For many years, Schrobanco was able to do nicely without advertising, except for annual statements of condition. Its connections with foreign banking and its strength among a small and powerful group of export-import specialists contributed to consistent growth.

But a change has come over banking in recent years. More and more American banks have expanded their own foreign banking services. More and more American manufacturers have developed export divisions, thus bypassing the specialists.

In both instances, Schrobanco executives felt that Schrobanco was suffering in this new era of banking because of its relative anonymity. It was clear that the Schroder name must be made better known and its services brought to the attention of the greatest possible number of business prospects.[13]

The response was encouraging and in the autumn of 1965 the exercise was repeated. This time the campaign focused upon the range of services offered by the firm and the specialist knowledge and experience of its executives, featuring a series of group portraits of the various officers' committees. Again the response was positive, but there was no follow-up because advertising was expensive and the publicity budget was axed in a cost-cutting exercise. 'Like many of the things we tried,' commented Clements, 'we just didn't have the business to support the overheads.'[14]

In the 1960s, Schrobanco's nominal return on equity averaged around 6 per cent after tax, giving a real return of only about 2 per cent in the second half of the decade, since US inflation averaged 4 per cent per annum. This modest rate of return was the consequence of the high overhead costs of offering a full range of international services to a geographically diverse client base without the volume of business or margins that could provide a better return. The continuing erosion of Schrobanco's competitive position led both the New York management and Richardson in London to consider more radical solutions to reposition the bank. While there was general agreement on the nature of the problems, there were widely differing proposals for their solution, reflecting varying visions of Schrobanco's future.

Clements, who was the strongest proponent of developing the firm domestically, saw Schrobanco's future in the context of the changing regulatory and competitive environment of New York commercial banking. By the early 1960s the opportunity of merging Schrobanco with a prominent US commercial bank to form its international department, which had existed in 1958–59 when those banks felt a strong impulse to 'go international', had passed, since most had developed their international activities organically. But the passage of the Omnibus Banking Bill by New York State in 1960, which permitted New York city banks to merge with suburban and upstate banks, led to a new vogue for taking over such banks to obtain access to cheap retail deposits. When Clements learned that the Meadow Brook National Bank, a publicly-quoted Long Island bank with some thirty branches, was for sale he pushed for a merger. Howell, however, had reservations, believing that a move into suburban retail banking was not the answer. 'If Meadow Brook is having difficulties, we are going to buy a lot of trouble,' he told Clements. 'I feel totally incapable of sorting out a retail suburban bank. I don't know anything about that business and I don't know how much you know about it either.'[15]

Clements' concept was to form a US holding company which would own Schrobanco and Meadow Brook. It would have two operating arms: the merged Schroder Trust Company/Meadow Brook National Bank to conduct domestic business; and Schrobanco, which would retain its special charter, to undertake foreign business. Schroders Limited would be allocated 25–30 per cent of the holding company equity, enough, Clements believed, to give Schroders control, since Meadow Brook's shares were widely dispersed. Nevertheless, anticipating objections to the idea of a minority shareholding, he suggested that some European banks with which Schroders had close relations but which did not have a significant presence in New York, such as Deutsche Bank and Lloyds Bank, should invest in the new holding company. The Europeans could thereby attain a 51 per cent stake and the extra capital could be used to acquire further upstate banks. Despite 'very fruitful' discussions with the management of Lloyds Bank, of which Gordon Richardson was non-executive deputy chairman, nothing came of these proposals.[16] The proposal did not appeal to Richardson and others in London who did not wish to move into consortium banking and who doubted the wisdom of developing the US business further in the direction of domestic commercial banking, particularly suburban banking. When Clements was offered the post of president of Meadow Brook by its new owners in 1966 he accepted and left Schrobanco.

As chairman of Schrobanco in 1967–70, Richardson took a very active role in its affairs, basing himself jointly in London and New York. His vision of Schrobanco's future was as a provider of specialist wholesale banking services, a Wall Street complement to Schroder Wagg. His intention was to change Schrobanco's business profile and increase profitability by developing its corporate finance and investment management activities, so that it more closely resembled Schroder Wagg. While aware that Schrobanco's US corporate client base was limited and that the Glass–Steagall Act prevented it from engaging in bond and equity underwriting business, he was determined to transform the business within these constraints. In 1966 he sent John Bayley to New York to explore the possibilities, and upon becoming Schrobanco chairman he commissioned a review of its business and its prospects. The Schrobanco Management Report of February 1968 was an impressively thorough and analytically incisive document, though there was nothing new about its account of the causes and nature of Schrobanco's problems – competition from US commercial banks putting pressure on margins; high overheads and the relatively small scale of operations; and the lack of a domestic client base. The report recommended moving towards investment banking, making much more of the opportunities Schrobanco enjoyed to conduct non-banking activities by virtue of its unusual Article XII charter from the state of New York, which allowed greater leeway than was available to banks with normal banking licences. Its conclusion was that Schroders in the US should become an 'Investment Bank of Deposit – a unique concept made possible by our status under New York State Banking Law and our membership in the international Schroder Group'.[17]

In November 1968 a holding company, Schroders Incorporated, a wholly-owned subsidiary of Schroders Limited, was established in the state of Delaware to own the various New York operating entities. Richardson became chairman of the new US holding company, the other directors being John I. Howell and John Bayley and four non-executives, Norris Darrell of Sullivan & Cromwell, Ragnar Naess, the senior partner of Naess & Thomas, Dr Harold Brown and Paul Nitze. In the latter half of 1969, Richardson and Bayley introduced a new managerial structure whose principal innovation was the formation of a management committee, comprising the chairman and chief executive of Schroders Inc., the chief executives of the operating divisions or subsidiaries, and four vice-presidents with responsibilities for finance, administration, planning and marketing.

Richardson's ambition was to develop a US corporate client base through the provision of specific services or banking products which would differentiate Schrobanco from other banks. Following the retirement of Avery Rockefeller in 1968, Schroder Rockefeller (Schrorock) was renamed Schroder Capital Corporation, and under the new leadership of Stephen Petschek it was repositioned to act more as a corporate finance advisory unit than as a venture capital firm. It achieved modest success, but found it difficult to obtain business from the largest US corporations, and for regulatory reasons was unable to engage in the lucrative corporate bond underwriting business which was the preserve of the domestic investment banks. The introduction of government restrictions on foreign investment by US corporations in 1968, which was monitored by the Office of Foreign Direct Investment (OFDI), created an opportunity for Schroder Wagg to market the London firm's international issuing and banking services to US corporations. The marketing was undertaken by Leslie Murphy, James Wolfensohn and George Mallinckrodt, who travelled regularly to the

United States. They enjoyed considerable success in arousing the interest of the finance officers of the firms they visited in the services that Schroder Wagg was able to offer. For instance, it managed Euro-dollar bond issues and cross-border merger and acquisition assignments for General Electric, including the sale of its interest in AEG of Germany and the provision of additional finance to its joint venture with Bull of France. Some of Schrobanco's European clients also used Schroder Capital Corporation to conduct acquisitions in the US.[18]

A core element of the blueprint for Schrobanco's development as an 'investment bank of deposit' was the creation of an institutional investment management activity. In July 1968, Schroders agreed to purchase a leading investment counselling firm, Naess & Thomas, for US$3.8 million from its founder, Ragnar Naess, who was near retirement, and his partners. The firm was highly regarded, having been founded in 1939 by Naess, formerly Goldman Sachs' chief economist. The price was about nineteen times the net earnings of $200,000, but this was considered justified by its impressive trading record, averaging an annual compound growth of 14.5 per cent in 1958–67.

The Schroder Trust Company's investment management activities were merged with Naess & Thomas and the new entity, a subsidiary of Schroders Inc., was called Schroder Naess & Thomas. Its performance did not live up to expectations. It made a loss in 1969, the first year of operation, and further losses in 1970 and 1971. These were attributed to the withdrawal of institutional accounts as a result of the firm's loss of independence and to the depressed stock market of 1970. The response of the management was to redouble efforts to attract new clients, opening a sales office in Atlanta in November 1970 which helped to bring the firm into profit in 1972. But the following year, despite a buoyant stock market, Schroder Naess & Thomas again sustained losses and it became clear that Ragnar Naess's personal contribution to its success had been greatly underestimated.

To increase the profitability of the commercial and trust banking activities, a branch office was opened in Nassau, Bahamas, in April 1969 to attract Euro-dollar deposits. Also that year a money-market fund, the Cheapside Dollar Fund, was established by Schrobanco and marketed to British fund managers by Schroder Wagg with great success. In September 1969, the Schroder Leasing Corporation was established to conduct leasing business, and in 1970 a Canadian subsidiary was formed. In addition, a Real Estate Department was opened to provide property management services, in 1975 becoming the separately constituted Schroder Real Estate Corporation.

Having reorganised and reorientated Schroders' US activities, Richardson administered yet another shock – he appointed James

Wolfensohn to the post of president of Schrobanco. The energetic new chief executive was a 36-year-old Australian, a qualified lawyer who had practised as a solicitor in Sydney and subsequently taken an MBA at the Harvard Business School. Returning to Australia, he became a partner in the Sydney stockbroker Ord, Minnett, T. J. Thompson & Partners. Ord, Minnett was a shareholder in Schroders' Australian associate company, Darling & Co., of which Wolfensohn became a managing director in 1965. Three years later he joined Schroder Wagg in London to head its international bond-issuing business. Besides his business activities, Wolfensohn was a member of the Australian fencing team in the 1956 Olympic Games, a commissioned officer of the Royal Australian Air Force and an accomplished musician. He took control in New York on 1 October 1970, while Howell became chairman and Richardson returned to London. His appointment astonished Schrobanco's senior officers, who resented further interference from London and felt that Wolfensohn was neither experienced in commercial banking nor fundamentally interested in developing a commercial banking firm. For a couple of weeks wholesale resignations seemed likely, but in fact all stayed on.

One of Wolfensohn's priorities was to assess the implications of the newly passed US Bank Holding Company Act of 1970. This measure was enacted to curtail the growth of the 'one-bank holding company', a device by which US commercial banks could escape from federal restrictions upon the scope of their activities.[19] The act placed one-bank holding companies, like multi-bank holding companies, under the control of the Federal Reserve Board, which was charged with determining what were proper activities for bank holding companies. The results of the Federal Reserve Board's deliberations, which were published in the spring of 1971, were alarming, Wolfensohn reporting to the Schroders Limited board that:

> he had received two papers from the Federal Reserve Board regarding the one-bank holding company legislation, the contents of which were far more disturbing than the legislation itself in that they widened the scope of the powers of the Federal Reserve and presented even more stringent restrictions on the activities of one-bank holding companies. For example if 50 per cent of the revenue and capital reserves of the Schroder Group were in the New York companies, then all the activities of the Schroder Group, in and out of the United States, would come under American Law which would result in restricting the Group's activities to pure banking operations.[20]

Despite the acquisition of Helbert, Wagg and the rapid expansion of operations in London and elsewhere, Schroders Inc. still accounted for over 50 per cent of the capital and reserves of Schroders Limited and thus it seemed likely that Schroders Limited would be caught by the legislation. But there was a slim chance that Schroders Inc. fell outside the definition of a bank for the purposes of the Bank Holding Company Act, and a ruling was sought from the Federal Reserve Board. Privately, the management had little confidence in a favourable judgement because they were advised that the Schroder Trust Company's membership of the Federal Reserve System brought the American companies, and the Schroder group, squarely within the legislation. This prompted consideration of the sale of the Schrotrust which led, in turn, to a re-examination of the whole future of Schroders' activities in the United States. 'The question to be answered,' stated a resolution of the Schroders Limited board in October 1972, 'was "what are the Group's overall policy objectives regarding the United States, bearing in mind the restrictive legislation imposed on our activities by the recent amendment to the Bank Holding Company Act and by the Federal and New York State Glass-Steagall Acts?"'[21] While the ruling on Schrobanco was awaited no action was taken to dispose of Schrotrust, which turned out to be fortunate since consideration of Schrobanco's case was overtaken by the Federal Reserve Board's decision to reform the legislation governing the activities of the subsidiaries of foreign banks in the United States. This new development led to yet another 're-examining of the question of the future direction of the business in the US' in June 1973.[22] The outcome was the 'major policy paper' that was presented to the Schroders Limited board on 3 October 1973, which confirmed the strategy of the Schrobanco Management Report and recommended further expansion of non-banking activities in the United States.

Wolfensohn, in his four years as president of Schrobanco from October 1970 to November 1974, took many new business initiatives, but was unable to establish an overall direction for the firm because of the shifting regulatory environment. Schrobanco and Schrotrust expanded their activities and product range, including services to the regional banks and to selected US industrial clients. The firm maintained its 'mystique' (the term used in-house at the time) as a specialist international banking firm, and its reputation with its European, Latin American and Asian clientele continued to be high.[23] To increase profitability, Wolfensohn reduced the staff, and the rental outgoing was cut by letting two of the eleven floors at the smart new 'Schroder Building' at One State Street, adjacent to Battery Park at the southernmost tip of Manhattan, to which the firm had moved in June 1971 upon the expiry of the lease at 57 Broadway. He also looked for ways of expanding non-banking activities. In October 1972, he reported to the Schroders Limited Board that he had been holding discussions with E. F. Hutton, a leading Wall Street brokerage firm, with a view to establishing a joint undertaking between Schroder Naess & Thomas and a team of US government securities specialists who were looking for a backer for a bond-trading business.[24] The board expressed interest in both initiatives, though members questioned the high risk nature of the latter. Wolfensohn countered that the only way to improve, or even to maintain, the profitability of the New York operation, given the diminishing margins in commercial banking business due to competitive pressures, was to expand trading activities which carried higher risks.[25]

Wolfensohn was concerned that generally Schrobanco was not perceived by US corporations as an international bank because it did not have an international network of branches and representative offices. 'To be recognised as an international bank, we had to have something on the ground,' he stated.[26] But in Argentina and Brazil it did have established representative offices, and its historic ties the length and breadth of the continent made Latin America appear the most promising place to start to develop a physical presence. Schrobanco's appointment as financial adviser and lead-manager for a $23 million loan for the state of Minas Gerais in 1972 fired Wolfensohn's enthusiasm and in October 1972 he presented a plan to the Schroders Limited board to expand the group's activities in Brazil. The following month Richardson visited the country to assess the situation for himself. The outcome was the formation of a joint enterprise with Monteiro Aranha in June 1973, J. Henry Schroder do Brasil (Consultores) S/C Ltda. The new firm, which was established under the guidance of Schrobanco's Latin American expert, Frederick D. Seeley, provided advice on mergers and acquisitions, and fund-raising to Brazilian firms and Brazilian subsidiaries of multinationals, and an international financial consultancy service to federal and state bodies. Initially, Monteiro Aranha took a minority interest, but in 1974 it became a full partner and the new firm was subsequently renamed Schroder–Monteiro Aranha Participacoes Administracao e Consultaria Limitada. Schroders and Monteiro Aranha established a second joint venture in 1974. This was Schroder–Monteiro Aranha Distribuidora de Titulos e Valores Mobiliarios S.A., a discount house which operated very successfully in the Brazilian money market until 1991.

A radically different potential strategy for Schroders in the US was the development of a comprehensive domestic investment banking business. Richardson and other colleagues in London were in principle attracted to this course of action since the corporate advisory and underwriting business undertaken by US investment banks was similar to that conducted by Schroder Wagg in London. But there were drawbacks. The

Glass–Steagall legislation would have obliged the sale of the US commercial banking subsidiaries, while the opportunities to break into the investment banking business were limited since these activities were dominated by a small oligarchic group of old partnerships, which were traditionally very close to American industry. 'We would have had no basis to build on,' commented Wolfensohn; the few remaining executives 'would just have been a bunch of guys, none of whom really knew about US investment banking, with forty or fifty million dollars trying to become an investment bank. Gordon Richardson and I thought that it was a pretty negative plan.'[27] One proposal was to use the proceeds of any sale of the banking interests to acquire a substantial interest in First Boston Corporation, a publicly quoted company whose chairman, Paul Miller, was a friend of Richardson. Some discussions took place but this suggestion was not pursued, since Schroders was not in a position to secure either majority ownership or managerial control. A major concern was how any such joint venture or tie-up would function and as Richardson put it, 'if you've got a living, working entity in the United States do you really want to let it go?'.[28] The outcome was that Schroders pursued the remoulding of Schrobanco under its own ownership.

Pacific Basin

As in continental Europe, much of the initiative for the development of Schroders' business in the Pacific Basin region was taken by Schrobanco, which had established relationships with many of the central banks and local banks. Its relations were particularly close with Japan, Korea, Taiwan, Thailand and the Phillipines, which were within the US sphere of interest and conducted their trade in US dollars. Its strong ties with the US Commodity Credit Corporation and American International Underwriters, which were very active in the region, led local Asian banks to open accounts with Schrobanco. Schroders' business with Japan continued to be the most important feature of its activities in the region. An indication of the strength of Schroder Wagg's business with Japanese banks was the distinction in 1962 of being one of the first banks to lend unsecured Euro-dollars to four Japanese banks – half a million dollars each to the Bank of Tokyo, the Sumitomo Bank, the Sanwa Bank and the Mitsui Bank, which led to warm thanks from the Japanese 'for evidencing the trust we had in Japan'.[29] In 1963, Schroder Wagg co-managed the Japanese government's first bond issue in the Euro-dollar bond market, and in 1964 sponsored with Nomura Securities an international bond issue for the leading engineering firm Komatsu, one of the first Euro-market issues for a Japanese company.

During the 1960s and 1970s Schroders seized the opportunities that arose to develop domestic merchant banking business in Australia and in the emergent Asian financial centres. On each occasion it pursued the strategy of entering the market with a prominent local bank or family. It was British ties that led to the establishment of firms in Australia, Hong Kong and Singapore. The first such undertaking was the joint venture in Australia formed by Helbert, Wagg in 1960. Charles Villiers was the initiator of this development, choosing John Darling, the scion of a famous Australian business dynasty whose father had been chairman of Broken Hill Proprietary, as his principal local partner, though there were several other local participants: the Bank of New South Wales; Ord, Minnett, T. J. Thompson & Partners; Binder Hamlyn & Co.; and Jardine Matheson & Co. The new firm, in which Helbert, Wagg, and subsequently Schroders Limited, had a 23.5 per cent interest, was called Darling and Company Ltd and opened in Sydney in 1960, one of the first Australian merchant banks.[30] At the outset the joint managing directors were John Darling and Rupert Burge, who spent some months with Helbert, Wagg before taking up his position. Burge was succeeded by John Broinowski, supported by David Murison on a three-year secondment from Schroder Wagg, while the leading business-getters were James Wolfensohn and Michael Gleeson-White. In 1965, a branch was opened in Melbourne, and another in Perth in December 1972. Looking back on the first decade of the firm, Darling characterised the first five years as a period of apprenticeship which had seen the achievement of a high level of professionalism, providing the basis for the 'tremendous growth in business and achievements' which were reflected in the 25 per cent return on capital for 1970–71.[31] By then the staff numbered 105 and it was reported that it had an impressive 12 per cent market share of the banking and money-broking business conducted by Australia's merchant banks. The close ties developed with Australian companies, such as Alcoa of Australia, also benefited Schroder Wagg and Schrobanco, which provided regular banking as well as specialised project finance services for them. The closer integration of the firm into the Schroder group led to it being renamed Schroder, Darling & Co. in 1975.

Schroders' presence in Asia took a leap forward with the establishment of Schroders & Chartered in Hong Kong. The initiative in fact came from The Chartered Bank, Hong Kong's second largest bank, which decided in the spring of 1970 to found one of the Crown Colony's earliest merchant banks to undertake investment management, securities underwriting and corporate advisory work. Schroders' advisory work on the merger with the Standard Bank had impressed the Chartered's directors, who invited it to be their partner in the new venture.[32]

Schroders responded positively and subscribed 40 per cent of the new venture, The Chartered Bank taking 40 per cent and Dr Lawrence Kadoorie, the major shareholder of the China Light and Power Company, Hong Kong's second largest public company, 20 per cent. Kadoorie, one of Hong Kong's leading businessmen, became non-executive chairman. *The Economist* was impressed by the prospects for the new firm and envisaged strong demand for its services from international companies which favoured Hong Kong as a base in the Pacific Basin region, because of low taxes and excellent communications with London, New York and Sydney.[33] The commencement of business coincided with a new issues boom that got the firm off to a flying start, and under the direction of Win Bischoff, a 29-year-old Schroder Wagg corporate finance executive, it made rapid progress. Richardson visited Hong Kong at the beginning of 1973 and reported back to the Schroders Limited board that Schroders & Chartered was already an 'outstanding success'.[34]

The achievements in Hong Kong led to plans to expand Schroders' activities to Singapore and Tokyo. The initiatives began during Richardson's chairmanship but the execution of the moves was conducted subsequently. In February 1971, the Schroders board commissioned a study of opportunities in these centres, which reported favourably. In July, during a visit to Hong Kong, Murphy suggested to the management of The Chartered Bank that Schroders & Chartered should extend its activities to Singapore. His plan was for Schroders & Chartered to acquire Chartered Merchant Bankers Limited, an established joint venture between The Chartered Bank, Arbuthnot Latham, and Sime Darby in Singapore, whose performance was lacklustre when compared to the Hong Kong firm. Chartered put the proposal to its partners but was unable to get their agreement, deferring Schroders' entry to Singapore for five years.

While the report to the Schroders board on the prospects for business in Singapore and Tokyo was being prepared in the spring of 1971, the firm was approached by the Sanwa Bank with a proposal that Schroders, Sanwa and Nomura Securities should establish a joint venture to undertake investment banking business in Japan. This led to the despatch of Leslie Murphy, James Wolfensohn and John Darling, representing respectively Schroder Wagg, Schrobanco and Darling & Co., on a fact-finding mission to Tokyo. They reported unfavourably on the joint venture proposal because of the disparity in size between Schroders and the suggested partners but they were enthusiastic about the establishment of a Schroder presence in Japan in an appropriate form. In January 1973, Gordon Richardson and David Forsyth visited Japan and held discussions with leading bankers about the establishment of a Schroder presence in Tokyo. They were much impressed by the hospitality shown to them, and reported to the Schroders board that 'there was no doubt that the Schroder name was regarded as important in the financial sector'. This convinced them that it was feasible for Schroders to develop business through its own representative office rather than through a joint venture. Burgis Coates, Schrobanco's expert on Pacific Basin business, came to London to work out a detailed proposal which was finally approved by the Schroders board in June 1973, and the new office opened in February 1974.

Evolution of Schroders Limited

The development of the key policy and strategy-making role of Schroders Limited began soon after Richardson's appointment as chairman in December 1965. In May 1966, John Bayley presented the board with the first 'Group Report', a statistical and analytical account of the finances of the subsidiary companies in much greater detail than hitherto, marking a major advance in the monitoring of the operating companies.[35] The following month the board received notification of the establishment of a Group Investments Control Committee, whose purpose was to co-ordinate the commitment of capital on a group-wide basis, taking account of group-wide objectives. Initially, the writ of the Group Investments Control Committee covered only the London subsidiaries, but when Richardson became chairman of Schrobanco in June 1967 it was extended to New York.

A new phase in the evolution of the role of Schroders Limited began in June 1969, when Bayley presented a paper to the board entitled 'Schroder Group Management Structure'. He summarised the position thus:

> During the past decade, the Schroder Group has grown from a group comprising two relatively small and unintegrated banking operations into a large, complex, integrated group of companies engaged in a relatively wide range of activities.

> While the number and quality of the individuals comprising the group management has increased to meet the demands of the expansion, the structure in which they operate has not.

> This failure to develop the Group Management structure has created stress in the present structure which is due to three main weaknesses:-

1. A failure to identify the functions which management has to discharge.
2. A failure to set up a 'strategic' long term plan and to co-ordinate efforts towards achieving group aims.
3. An over concentration of responsibility and initiative on the group chief executive.[36]

On Richardson's instruction, John Hull prepared a report on the means to redress these shortcomings, the principal proposals being to establish a Group Management Committee and to appoint a Group Planning Director.[37] The Group Management Committee, which was to meet monthly, was to comprise seven or eight senior executives and its functions would be to monitor the performance of the operating sub-sidiaries and to formulate policies for the attainment of group objectives. In addition, there would be three specialist advisory sub-committees on Group Resources, Group Co-ordination and Group Management. The Group Planning Director would act as the executive officer of the Group Management Committee under the direction of the Group Chief Executive (the chairman of Schroders Limited). The Schroders Limited board accepted these recommendations and proposed that Hull should be appointed the Group Planning Director. Implementation, however, was deferred on account of Richardson's preoccupation with matters in New York and it was not until the summer of 1970 that action was taken. In July 1970, the formation of a Group Management Committee was confirmed by the Schroders Limited board and immediately implemen-ted. But no more was heard of the Group Planning Director, since the role had effectively been assumed by Leslie Murphy, who had been appointed head of a new International Committee which had been formed in October 1969 to co-ordinate the business of the non-UK subsidiaries. At this point, in recognition of the international nature of the firm's activities, it was decided to hold meetings of the Schroders Limited board alternately in London and New York.

In February 1971, the Group Planning Committee, a sub-committee of the Group Management Committee, consisting of Murphy, Bayley and Sir Henry Fisher, was appointed to draw up long-term plans for the development of the Schroder group of companies. The sub-committee undertook a thorough review of the firm and its future, with assistance from Cooper Brothers in an advisory capacity. Its foremost finding was 'the overriding importance of banking profits to total Group earnings'. This led to the conclusion that the firm's performance would be enhanced by the expansion of banking activity, which meant increasing its capital.[38] The report confirmed the contention that had been put forward several times at Schroder Wagg board meetings that the firm was hindered from taking advantage of opportunities arising in the UK as a result of the introduction of the policy of Competition and Credit Control by a shortage of capital. The outcome was a substantial capital-raising exercise in 1972. In January, Schroders Limited issued £10 million 8.75 per cent unsecured loan stock 1997/2002 at £99.5 per cent, and later that year it borrowed from Sanwa Bank $15 million for 15 years at 7.9 per cent; £7.5 million and $12.4 million of these funds were used to strengthen Schroder Wagg's capital base and $2.6 million was allocated to J. Henry Schroder Bank AG of Zurich. Following the increases in the resources available to the London and Zurich subsidiaries, the Group Management Committee focused upon the challenges facing the rest of the Schroder group.

In June 1973, it recommended that 'in order to develop the international activities of the group, it was necessary to create a management structure within the Group to plan, supervise and co-ordinate the Group's international expansion'.[39] The outcome was the formation in October 1973 of Schroder International Ltd, a separate holding company for the Schroder group's non-UK subsidiary and associate companies with Murphy, chairman; Bayley, deputy chairman; Wolfensohn, president; and Mallinckrodt and Gasser, executive vice-presidents. Although at the time this appeared to be a significant management development, it did not assume an important role, not least due to resistance from the Schroder Wagg operating management, and was only continued in a passive form as a holding company for most of the overseas assets.

The expansion of the scale and scope of Schroders Limited's activities in the 1960s and early 1970s is reflected in the growth of total assets from £99 million in 1959 to £792 million in 1973 (see Figure 14.1). Prices were

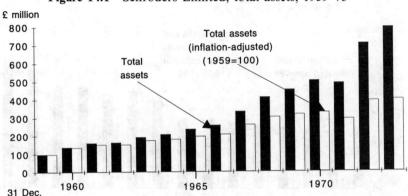

Figure 14.1   Schroders Limited, total assets, 1959–73

rising more and more rapidly in these years and on an inflation-adjusted basis the increase was threefold, which was still a substantial advance. The upturn in 1967 was a consequence of the devaluation of the pound, which increased the value of the firm's dollar and Swiss franc assets when reported in sterling. In fact, this currency factor created a capital adequacy problem for Schroder Wagg because of the appreciation of its substantial non-sterling assets, which derived from its active Euro-currency lending business, relative to its sterling-denominated capital, necessitating additional capital. The even more marked upsurge in assets in 1972 was the result of the injection of loan capital and the expansion of Schroder Wagg's banking business. During the 1960s and early 1970s the post-war trend towards a more 'bank-like' balance sheet continued, and by 1973 deposits and balances constituted 90 per cent of liabilities. On the asset side the notable feature was the proliferation of the variety of types of lending, a notable development being the growth of term-lending necessitating increased attention to the matching of the maturities of liabilities and assets.

After the formation of Schroders Limited a major priority was the creation of inner reserves and thus in the 1960s both disclosed reserves and disclosed profits were substantially understated. Between 1959 and 1973 the equity capital and disclosed reserves of Schroders Limited grew from £12.5 million to £25.9 million, an increase which exactly kept pace with inflation (see Figure 14.2). Disclosed profits, on the other hand, expanded from £496,000 in 1960 to £2.8 million in 1972, a two-and-a-half times increase on an inflation-adjusted basis (see Figure 14.3) – from £6 million to £14.6 million in 1990 money.

The growth of profits at a more rapid rate than shareholders' funds led to the rising disclosed returns on equity shown in Figure 14.4, which

Figure 14.2 Schroders Limited, consolidated equity capital and disclosed reserves, 1959–73

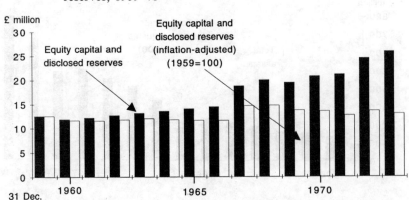

Figure 14.3 Schroders Limited, disclosed profits (after tax), 1959–73

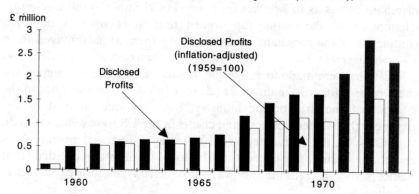

increased from 4.2 per cent in 1960 to 11.6 per cent in 1972. However, inflation was also rising, cancelling out the increase in real terms: in 1960–66 the average disclosed real return on equity was 1.6 per cent; in 1967–72, 2.4 per cent; and in 1973, as inflation soared and crisis overtook the City, it was minus 1.5 per cent.

Schroders' real returns in the 1960s and early 1970s appear to compare unfavourably with those achieved by both J. Henry Schroder & Co. and Helbert, Wagg & Co. in the 1950s, but the practice of publicly-quoted merchant banks making only partial disclosure of profits, reserves, and additions to reserves, creates considerable uncertainty about statistics of rates of return. The abandonment of partial disclosure by the clearing

Figure 14.4 Schroders Limited, disclosed return on equity and annual rate of inflation, 1959–73

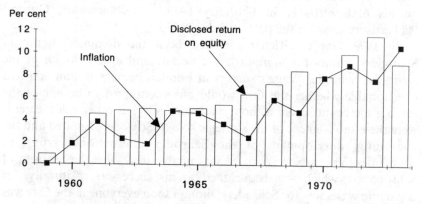

Note: The 'real' return on capital is the difference between the nominal return depicted above and the annual rate of inflation

banks at the beginning of the 1970s provoked debate amongst the merchant banks as to whether they too should move to full disclosure. Champions of the status quo argued that inner reserves bolstered confidence in the merchant banks and gave them an advantaged them *vis-à-vis* overseas rivals.[40] The issue was discussed at Schroders and calculations were made to gauge the impact of full disclosure upon the share price. Most of the directors felt that full disclosure was not in the interests of the firm or the industry, but they were swayed by the argument that sometimes potential clients in the US were reluctant to do business with the subsidiary of a firm whose financial position was uncertain. When the Accepting Houses Committee decided that members should continue the practice of partial disclosure, Schroders complied.

The special relationship between the merchant banks and the Bank of England arose in the nineteenth century because of their pivotal role in the City. In the second half of the nineteenth century and the first half of the twentieth century most of the governors of the Bank of England were drawn from the ranks of the partners of the merchant banks, including Lord Norman, from Brown, Shipley, who held the post for a record 24-year term (1920–44), and his successor, Lord Catto, from Morgan Grenfell, who was governor in 1944–49. Catto's successor was Lord Cobbold, the first career central banker to hold the post. He was followed in 1961 by the Earl of Cromer, from Barings, who was succeeded in 1966 by Lord O'Brien, another Bank of England official. Well before O'Brien's first five-year term of office drew to a close, speculation began regarding his successor. Inside candidates were considered to be the favourites, though several outsiders were also believed to be in the running, including Richardson.[41] In the event, O'Brien was reappointed for a further term in mid-1971, but much to the surprise of the City he tendered his resignation on his 65th birthday in February 1973.[42] His successor, Gordon Richardson, took up the post on 1 July 1973.

By 1973 Gordon Richardson had been the dominant figure in Schroders' affairs for more-or-less a decade and a half. Much of the credit for Schroder Wagg's success in London belongs to him and it is questionable whether the firm would have continued to be one of the leading merchant banks without his leadership. His other achievements were the establishment of the strategic role of Schroders Limited and the continuing development of the Schroder international group of companies. Yet in New York he was unable to resolve the problem of Schrobanco, which was bequeathed to his successors. Naturally, his departure was a loss for Schroders, though soon everyone in the City was thankful to have him in charge at the Bank of England, as the secondary banking crisis and property crash overtook the Square Mile.

15

Schroders

Since 1973

The decades of the 1970s and 1980s are too recent for historical perspective. This chapter presents an account of Schroders in these years which reflects contemporary perspectives focusing particularly upon strategic developments and overall financial performance.

International transactions have always been a significant part of Schroders' activities and the evolution of the firm has mirrored the development of the international economy and international finance. In the nineteenth and early twentieth centuries it provided services that facilitated international trade and capital movements from a base in London, which was possible because of the pre-eminence of the City and sterling in international finance. After the First World War, when New York emerged as an important international financial centre, the Schroder partners established a firm on Wall Street to conduct international financial business in US dollars. Since the 1960s, significant new financial centres have emerged and there has been an acceleration in international financial flows, to which Schroders responded by the establishment of numerous subsidiaries, associates and representative offices. By 1992, the firm had offices in Europe in the Channel Islands, Cyprus, Denmark, France, Germany, Italy, Liechtenstein, Spain, Switzerland and the United Kingdom; in the Americas in Bermuda, Brazil, Canada, the Cayman Islands, United States and Venezuela; in the Pacific Basin in Australia, Hong Kong, Indonesia, Japan, Korea, Malaysia, Singapore and Taiwan; and in the Middle East in Lebanon. The geographic expansion of the firm and important developments in communications technology required a new form of corporate organisation, and the 1980s and early 1990s saw increasing integration of Schroders' subsidiary and associate companies to form a single international merchant and investment banking firm.

The year 1973 marked a fundamental turning point in the development of the international economy. The quadrupling of the price of oil at the end of that year led to inflation and recession in the industrial nations in 1974–75. The recovery in the latter half of the decade was generally slow and faltering, and a second round of oil price rises in 1979 resulted in the onset of another bout of recession at the start of the 1980s. These years also saw greater volatility in exchange rates (following the abandonment of the Bretton Woods system of fixed parities at the beginning of the 1970s), interest rates, commodity prices and stock markets, which made the conduct of international lending more difficult and more hazardous. In the mid-1970s, the commercial banks of the industrial economies found themselves awash with deposits from the surplus earnings of the oil-exporting nations, and competitive pressures led to the relaxation of prudent credit criteria. Simultaneously, developing countries and the Central European states were making insistent demands for funds to bridge trade deficits or to fulfil ambitious development plans, and amassed enormous and unsupportable external debts. Mexico's announcement in August 1982 that it could no longer service its foreign currency debt heralded the end of the era of 'recycling' and the beginning of a decade or more of 'debt crisis' problems for international bankers.

For the United Kingdom, the 1970s were a nadir in the country's long-term economic decline relative to the other industrial nations. Inflation, strikes, stagnation and rising unemployment were the hallmarks of the domestic economy. The secondary banking crisis of 1973–75, though skilfully handled, cast a pall over the Square Mile, and the collapse of property and share prices caused harm and hardship to City firms. The sterling crisis of 1976 was a reflection of the loss of foreign confidence in the UK economy and the UK government. Yet, despite the domestic difficulties, foreign banks continued to flock to London to participate in the thriving Euro-markets that were centred there. The strategic response of Schroders, and other leading London merchant banks, to the economic environment of the 1970s was to extend its involvement in the international financial markets as far as possible and to look overseas for opportunities to develop business.

By 1982 the industrial economies were moving out of recession and entering a period of growth accompanied by lower inflation, which lasted until the end of the decade. In Britain in the early 1980s inflation was brought under control and industrial militancy died down, though the price was a rash of bankruptcies and a sharp increase in unemployment. In the City, confidence in the UK economy returned as people became convinced of the government's resolution and as corporate profitability began to revive. At the same time, the major securities markets of the world set off on what was to become the most sustained bull market of the century. This came to an end with the worldwide stock market crash in October 1987, which caused apprehension about the international economy, but co-ordinated measures by the authorities of the leading industrial nations ensured that there was no repetition of the slump that followed the 1929 crash.

The 1980s saw rapid and radical changes in the international financial services industry, stemming from the acceleration of trends that had begun in the previous decade or before – notably 'deregulation', 'globalisation' and 'securitisation'. The most prominent milestones in the process of deregulation were the suspension of the Federal Reserve Board's Regulation Q, which restricted interest paid on deposits and thus curbed competition among US banks, in June 1970, and the reform of the securities industry in New York in 1975 and London in 1986. But the process encompassed all aspects of financial services and was adopted in many countries. The abolition of many of the traditional boundaries in financial services and a wave of technological and product innovation greatly enhanced the range of activities of both investment banks and commercial banks. Globalisation – that is, the organisation of markets and trading on a worldwide basis – was another long-term trend. This was made possible by developments in computers and electronic communications equipment. It gave an additional impetus to the internationalisation of firms in the financial services industry. The advances in communications technology assisted the emergence of new financial centres, notably in the Pacific Basin. Finally, there was the trend towards the securitisation of lending – that is, the shift away from balance-sheet-based lending by banks to the issue of tradeable securities on behalf of borrowers. Banks encouraged this development because it allowed them to curtail their lending activities and thus strengthen their balance sheets, while earning fees from servicing clients' financing requirements. Borrowers benefited by obtaining funds directly from the money market at lower interest rates than from banking intermediaries. All these developments presented new opportunities for London's merchant banks. However, they were also accompanied by increased competition from the merchant banking subsidiaries of commercial banks from around the world, from New York investment banks and from Japanese securities houses. The merchant banks adopted a variety of strategies to meet the challenges and opportunities of the 1970s and the 1980s, resulting in an increasing diversity in the patterns of their activities.

Schroders' fortunes fluctuated from year to year according to conditions in the international economy, but taking the period as a whole, the 1970s and 1980s saw substantial expansion in the scale and scope of the firm's activities. Between 1973 and 1991 the consolidated equity capital and disclosed reserves of Schroders plc (as Schroders Limited was renamed in 1982) increased from £25.8 million to £360.6 million, almost trebling on an inflation-adjusted basis (see Figure 15.1). The growth of capital was mirrored by the expansion in the Schroder group's personnel, which more than doubled from 1,500 in the early

Figure 15.1 Schroders plc, consolidated equity capital and disclosed reserves, 1973–91

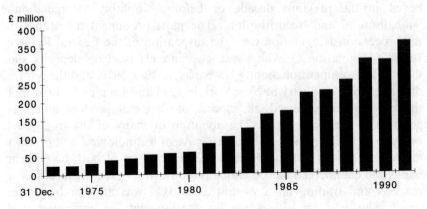

1970s to 3,400 in 1991. In the UK, the increase was from 715 in 1973 to 1,500 in 1991, reflecting both the expansion and diversification of the business, especially in the 1980s. Outside the UK, the rate of growth was even faster, and by 1991 more than half of the Schroder group's personnel worked in North or South America, the Pacific Basin or continental Europe (see Table 15.1). The expansion of Schroders' worldwide presence in the 1970s and 1980s was a dynamic response to the changing nature of the firm's business, building on its international culture and orientation.

Table 15.1 Schroder group employees, 1991

31 December	Employees
United Kingdom	1474
Continental Europe	202
North America	1065
Japan	180
South-East Asia	364
Australia	144
Total	3429

Source: Schroders plc Annual Report and Accounts, 1991.

Senior Management, 1973–84

Michael Verey, the new chairman of Schroders Limited, took office on 1 July 1973. Aged 60, he had four decades of business experience behind him and was a highly-respected figure in the City, serving as chairman of the Accepting Houses Committee in 1974–77. His many outside directorships included BP, Boots and Commercial Union, and he was chairman of the Charities Official Investment Fund. Interviewed soon after his appointment as chairman of Schroders, he told a correspondent of *The Banker* that the firm's strategy was to promote its development as an international group and he drew attention to its already extensive international capability. He identified Europe, the Middle East, the Far East and Australia as the areas to which Schroders was looking and stressed the pragmatism and creativity of its approach to the development of new business, 'so it will be behaving round the world like merchant banks have always behaved in London itself'.

The leading executives during Verey's chairmanship from 1973 to 1977 were the Earl of Airlie, James Wolfensohn, John Hull, John Bayley, Leslie Murphy and Mark Maged. The energetic and ebullient Murphy was appointed deputy chairman of Schroders Limited in July 1973, and in October assumed the additional role of chairman of Schroder International Limited. In 1974, he was appointed a member of the Royal Commission on the Distribution of Income and Wealth established by the recently elected Labour Government, and the following year he left Schroders to take up the position of deputy chairman of the newly-created National Enterprise Board, a public service for which he received a knighthood in 1978. Bayley continued to occupy the position of group finance director as he had under Richardson and to conduct his influential role in a low-key manner. In London, Airlie succeeded Verey as chairman of Schroder Wagg, and Hull became deputy chairman in November 1974. Assuming office on the eve of the property crash and the secondary banking crisis, Airlie steered the firm safely through the difficult years of the mid-1970s.

In New York, Schroders' leading figure was Wolfensohn, who continued as president of Schroders Incorporated, the holding company for the firm's US interests, and chief executive of Schrobanco and Schrotrust. In October 1973, he was given operational responsibility for the implementation of Schroders' international strategy by his appointment to the post of president of Schroder International in addition to his US positions. In November 1974, he was appointed to the newly-created position of group chief executive, a role defined as 'to direct, control and supervise the activities of Schroders Limited in all parts of the world and to co-ordinate the activities of the executive directors of Schroders

Limited'. Upon assuming this position he also became chairman of
Schroders Incorporated. Mark Maged, Schrobanco's legal counsel,
succeeded him as president. Wolfensohn's group-wide responsibilities
required continual travel, and in the first eight months of the new job he
estimated that he crossed the Atlantic twenty times in addition to trips to
Venezuela, Nigeria, Iran and Australia. 'The urge to travel is not just to
see the sights,' he told the house magazine; 'today the problems of the
international money markets and the speed of change in the world
economy and in our business has made it essential that one keeps in first
hand touch with what is going on. This is not only to supervise and co-
ordinate the work of our operating companies, but much more
importantly to plan with management where we as a Group should go
in the next five to ten years. I would hope that members of the Schroder
Group will see themselves not working only for a London company but
as part of a much broader international group from which we can all
derive strength and which we will continue to build' .

Verey retired as chairman of Schroders in May 1977 upon reaching
the age of 65. The two candidates for the succession were Airlie and
Wolfensohn. Both were exceptional men who were well qualified for the
chairmanship, and the choice between them was as much a strategic
decision about the direction of development and future nature of
Schroders as a judgement on the individuals. Wolfensohn, the
multifariously talented, intellectually brilliant internationalist was the
embodiment of dynamism, and above all promised challenges to
cherished assumptions. Airlie, the Scottish earl and 'Establishment'
figure personified integrity and prudence, and he stood for continuity.
He was renowned for his courtesy and charm, which made him popular
with colleagues and staff, and with clients: 'merchant banking is very
much a people's business,' he told an interviewer following his
appointment as chairman of Schroder Wagg. His judgement, affability
and dedication to the firm were qualities that were highly regarded and
he was the preferred candidate of the majority of the London
management. The Schroders board appointed Airlie chairman, hoping
that Wolfensohn would continue as executive deputy chairman.
However, early in 1977 Wolfensohn resigned to join Salomon Brothers
in New York. Following the take-over of Salomon Brothers by the
commodity firm Philips Brothers (Phibro) in 1981 he opened his own
investment banking boutique on Wall Street, James D. Wolfensohn Inc.

The Earl of Airlie, the new chairman, was 51 years old and had been
with the firm since 1953. A director of Schroder Wagg from 1961, he had
worked closely with Michael Verey in the 1960s to develop the
investment management side of the business. In 1966 he succeeded
Verey as head of the Investment Department and subsequently as

chairman of Schroder Wagg and chairman of Schroders Limited. Airlie's outside directorships included the Royal Bank of Scotland Group, Scottish & Newcastle Breweries and General Accident, of which he was deputy chairman. He was also Treasurer of the Scouts Association and performed a variety of public services, mostly connected with Scotland. He was devoted to his family and to his ancestral home in Scotland: Cortachy Castle, Angus, the management of his Scottish estate being both a matter of business and a pastime.

Airlie's promotion to the chairmanship and Wolfensohn's departure from the firm led to a rearrangement of responsibilities amongst the senior executives. From 1977 until the summer of 1983, John Hull was chairman of Schroder Wagg in London while Mark Maged continued to be chief executive officer of Schrobanco in New York. Hull was a well-known figure in the City, having served as director-general of the Panel on Take-overs and Mergers in 1972–74, his outside directorships including the Legal & General Group, Lucas Industries and Land Securities. He was assisted by Geoffrey Williams, the new deputy chairman of Schroder Wagg. Williams had a formidable reputation as a corporate financier, and in 1979–81 served as chairman of the Issuing Houses Association. A cultured man and a cinema enthusiast, he was appointed to the board of the National Film Finance Corporation in 1970, becoming its chairman in 1976. Other outside responsibilities included membership of the Bank of England's Capital Markets Committee and the board of Bass Charrington. John Bayley succeeded Wolfensohn as chairman of Schroders Incorporated, and at the same time he and John Hull were made joint deputy chairmen of Schroders Limited. Bayley was succeeded as chairman of Schroders Incorporated in 1980 by John T. Connor, a distinguished American businessman who had made his career in the chemical industry with Merck and subsequently with the Allied Chemical Corporation, of which he became chairman. He had served as Secretary of State for Commerce under President Johnson in the 1960s, and he was a director of major US corporations including Chase Manhattan Bank and General Motors. Maged's principal colleague in these years was Martin Witschi, a Swiss-born banker who had joined Schrobanco in the 1950s.

The other leading executive directors of Schroders Limited in the years 1977–82 were David Forsyth, Gordon Popham and Jean Solandt, all of whom had responsibility for the business in London, and George Mallinckrodt and Michael Bentley on the international side. Mallinckrodt assisted Airlie with Schrobanco's business development and was also the senior executive for continental Europe and the Middle East. Bentley, who joined Schroders from Lazards in 1980, had responsibility for transatlantic investment banking, and he played a particularly important role in developing the group's existing venture capital activities and expanding them into new fields.

Richardson and his successors proved adept at persuading eminent and influential figures to join the board of Schroders plc as non-executive directors. At the time of Verey's appointment, the outside directors were the Britons Lord Franks and Lord Perth, and the Americans Dr Harold Brown and Paul Nitze. Perth and Nitze retired as directors in 1975, and Brown resigned in 1976, following his appointment as US Secretary of Defense. The new non-executive directors were Sir Ernest Woodroofe, a former chairman of Unilever; Sir Leslie Murphy, who resumed his seat in a non-executive capacity in 1979 after the end of his work for the National Enterprise Board; and Baron Daniel Janssen, a leading Belgian industrialist who was chairman of the Executive Committee of the chemical company Solvay.

The other key member of the board of Schroders Limited was Bruno Schroder. He was born in 1933 and educated at Eton, University College, Oxford, and the Harvard Business School. While he was a student at Harvard his father, Helmut, suffered a heart attack and so upon graduation as an MBA in 1960 he returned from the US and joined Schroders, being appointed to the board of Schroders Limited in 1963 and Schroder Wagg in 1966. Although he worked on both the banking and corporate finance sides of the business, his most significant achievement was the organisation of the Schroder family interests in such a way as to ensure the continued independence of the firm.

Schroder Wagg, 1973–84

The mettle of Schroders' management following Richardson's departure was soon severely tested by the secondary banking crisis of 1973–75. This saw the collapse of property and share prices and the failure of many property companies and secondary banks, which were closely involved with the property sector. There were many contributory causes to the crisis, the foremost being the macroeconomic mismanagement of the British economy and the OPEC-induced inflation and consequent international recession. In the City, the onset of the crisis was marked by the failure of London and County Securities in December 1973. The problems of this firm, and the others, stemmed from the conjunction of soaring interest rates in the second half of 1973 – minimum lending rate rising from 7.5 per cent in July to 13 per cent by November – with tumbling asset values. The short-term funds upon which so many property companies and secondary banks had relied became not just expensive but unavailable, and the rash of failures was the outcome. Verey and the Schroders board gave strong support to the initiatives undertaken by the Governor of the Bank of England, their recently departed chairman, Gordon Richardson, to organise a 'Lifeboat' to save the situation. Moreover, Schroder Wagg, and in particular Geoffrey Williams in his capacity as head of the Corporate Finance Division, played a leading part in the conduct of some of the major corporate rescues that were the outcome of the Lifeboat.

Schroder Wagg suffered negligible bad debt losses arising from the secondary banking crisis and the recession of the mid-1970s, a remarkable achievement which is testimony to the wisdom of its credit judgement under the leadership of David Forsyth. However, it did not escape from the crisis unscathed, being caught out by the rapid rise in interest rates, which led to large losses on treasury operations. These arose from its substantial holdings of sterling and dollar certificates of deposit, medium-term assets which were funded by short-term borrowing in the inter-bank market. The cost of funding soared due to the surge in interest rates and simultaneously the certificate of deposit market became illiquid, making it impossible to unwind the position. 'If you're earning 10 per cent and financing at a cost of 22 per cent you're losing a hell of a lot of money,' commented a senior executive, 'and we did.' 'It was a very, very dangerous situation,' recalled Lord Airlie, who had just taken over as chairman of Schroder Wagg. Airlie entrusted the resolution of the crisis to Jean Solandt, the youngest director in the Banking Division, which he accomplished with such skill that he was appointed head of the division in 1977 when Forsyth retired.

In the 1970s and early 1980s Schroder Wagg's business continued to be a mixture of corporate finance, banking and investment management, the classic pattern of the London merchant banks. Schroder Wagg entered the 1970s with probably the most impressive client list of UK companies of all the merchant banks, and throughout the decade it retained a leading position in both mergers and acquisitions and equity underwriting. The mid-1970s saw corporate finance activity in the City at a low ebb and this side of Schroder Wagg's business was depressed by the downturn. The low volume of merger and acquisition and issuing activity caused Schroder Wagg both to expand its range of services and to extend its geographical coverage. In 1979, the Schroder Strategy Group was established in London to provide advisory services on long-term financial and economic strategy. By the end of Airlie's chairmanship it had clients in the UK, the US and Asia, including central banks and government institutions as well as private corporations, but its activities proved less profitable than had been hoped and it was disbanded. Schroder Wagg also developed its underwriting of equity and equity-linked issues for international companies, notably its Japanese clients; in 1982, for instance, it participated in ninety of these international issues.

Overall, in the 1970s, Schroder Wagg's core banking business – that is, treasury, accepting and lending – generated around three-fifths of revenues. But from the middle of the decade lending margins began to fall, because of the abundance of petro-dollar deposits seeking borrowers, and international lending became an increasingly unremunerative activity. Schroder Wagg resisted the temptation to boost lending margins by granting loans to less creditworthy borrowers, the consequence being declining profitability. Banking profits were also curtailed by the firm's implementation in the mid-1970s of a system of prudential capital allocation not dissimilar to the subsequent Bank for International Settlement capital adequacy rules, which came into force in the late 1980s. Yet another factor that adversely affected the return from lending was increasing competition from several sources: the British clearing banks and their merchant banking subsidiaries; a new set of consortium banks; and foreign banks, whose London subsidiaries and branches increased from 267 in 1973 to 449 in 1982. The volume of acceptance business conducted in London grew substantially in the late 1970s and early 1980s, stimulated by measures taken by the Bank of England in 1978 to restrain bank lending which led companies to resort to funding by acceptance credits. Schroder Wagg seized the opportunity and total acceptances rose from £152 million in 1978 to £347 million in 1982. However, the profitability of acceptance activity was declining because of growing competition, which intensified following the Bank of England's decision in the summer of 1981 to extend the list of banks whose bills were automatically eligible for rediscount.

Schroders' response to the competitive pressures in lending and accepting was to focus upon specialised forms of banking activity. Leasing is a notable example. Changes in the tax position of capital allowances introduced in 1974 led to a leasing boom. Schroder Finance, the specialist leasing subsidiary which in 1975 changed its name to Schroder Leasing, was a vigorous participant in the boom and its business grew rapidly. Half a dozen regional offices were opened, and to permit expansion the head office was moved to Harrow, which has continued to be its base. Volatile interest and exchange rates presented opportunities for profitable treasury management, which became an increasingly important source of banking profits. High interest rates boosted the return on the firm's capital and Schroders used its expertise to lock in high yields. Volatility also created profitable trading opportunities and Schroder Wagg expanded its trading operations in the money and currency markets in the 1970s. It also formed a joint venture with Czarnikow, the leading commodities house with which the firm had done business for a century, to trade gas oil futures.

In international banking, lending was increasingly supplemented by fee-earning advisory services. A team was created in the Schroder Wagg Banking Division, which specialised in the provision of highly sophisticated export and project finance services. The expansion of the size and breadth of its activities led to the formation of a separate Project Finance Division in 1975 and subsequently to the establishment of satellite offices in Hong Kong, Singapore, Sydney and Caracas. A breakthrough in the development of its business was its appointment to arrange the financing of the China Light & Power Company's Castle Peak electricity generating station in Hong Kong. This was secured in the face of powerful competition because of the close relationship between Schroders' senior personnel and Sir Lawrence Kadoorie, the chairman of China Light & Power, which had developed through their partnership in Schroders & Chartered. Over the years 1977–81, Schroder Wagg arranged a series of multi-currency financings totalling approximately $3 billion for the Castle Peak project, much the largest project finance operation ever conducted in the City. The Castle Peak financings boosted Schroder Wagg's reputation for project finance work with the British government and major British companies and in the 1980s the firm was one of the two top City firms in this business. It successfully maintained its pre-eminence through manifold product innovation, its ability to find creative solutions tailor-made to the needs of clients constituting its competitive advantage over the large commercial banks and other rivals. Schroders also developed a specialist service for advice on asset and liability management for central banks, public authorities and corporations: the Reserve Asset Management Programme (RAMP). This got off to a flying start with an appointment by the Venezuelan government in 1973 to advise on the management of its booming oil revenues.

Both Verey and Airlie made their careers predominantly in investment management, and during the decade of their chairmanships this important activity expanded substantially. The growth of UK pension funds and unit trusts under management were the keys to the success of Schroder Wagg's Investment Division, though the management of investment trusts, insurance company funds, charities and private clients' portfolios were also important. At the start of the 1970s Schroder Wagg was already a leading firm in pension fund management, on account of the rapid growth of this side of the business in the 1960s. By the end of 1984, Schroder Wagg had £4.6 billion funds under management in the UK, mostly pension funds, and it was consistently one of the three largest pension fund managers in the City. There was also a major expansion of unit trust funds under management, particularly after the transfer of the promotion and management of the firm's unit trust business to Schroder Life, the life assurance subsidiary, in 1980.

Zurich's importance as an international financial centre grew in the 1970s since, like London, it played an important role in handling the huge balances of the Middle Eastern oil producers. Under the direction of Dr Erik Gasser, the scale and scope of J. Henry Schroder Bank AG's activities expanded substantially, the staff growing from ten in the early 1970s to fifty in 1983. Gasser was an active member of the Swiss banking community, being a founder and chairman of the Association of Foreign Bankers in Switzerland and the foreign banks' representative on the board of the Swiss Bankers' Association, enhancing Schroders' standing in Switzerland. The Zurich firm played an important role in Schroders' international new issues business and privately placed securities with Swiss investors, particularly on behalf of Japanese borrowers. Switzerland as a financial centre had long played a leading role in international private banking; that is, investment management and related fiduciary and banking services for private clients from all over the world. From the outset, J. Henry Schroder Bank AG actively developed portfolio management and other private banking activities for an international clientele seeking a high level of personal service. In 1984, a branch was opened in Geneva which made an important contribution to the expansion of the Bank's private banking business.

With an entirely Swiss management, J. Henry Schroder Bank AG enjoyed a great deal of autonomy within the Schroder group of companies. Thanks to conservative policies, Schroders in Switzerland had only a very small lending exposure in 'problem' countries and it successfully avoided any other serious setbacks. Having well diversified revenues from investment management, lending, treasury, trading and capital market activities, the bank generated good profits. It pursued a long-term policy of disclosing only moderate, though steadily increasing, net profits, in line with prudent Swiss banking practices, the rest being channelled into undisclosed inner reserves. The growth of inner reserves widened the firm's capital base far beyond Swiss regulatory and practical requirements, though in conformity with the very strong capitalisation prevailing in the Swiss banking industry. In spite of the surplus of capital funds, the bank was able to achieve by Swiss standards (and expressed in Swiss francs) an above-average return. With the additional benefit of the appreciation of the Swiss franc versus sterling, the Swiss subsidiary proved to be a very rewarding investment for Schroders plc.

Despite Britain's entry into the European Economic Community in 1973, Schroders did not vigorously pursue the development of a presence in Common Market financial centres. In contrast to London and Zurich, the continental financial centres (with the exception of Frankfurt) played only marginal roles in servicing international money flows, and the pattern of the 1970s and the early 1980s was for the banks of the continental countries to establish a presence in the dynamic international financial market in London, and not vice versa. Moreover, their highly regulated domestic money and capital markets and the dominant position of the local universal banks restricted opportunities for outsiders. Schroder Wagg continued to service its continental clients from London, though the representative office in Frankfurt was maintained to stay close to German clients. The Paris representative office, on the other hand, was closed in 1980. It was believed that the shareholding in the Parisian merchant bank, Société Privée de Gestion Financière, which became the Banque Privée de Gestion Financière SA (BPGF), was the most promising means of developing business in France, though tangible results were modest. BPGF survived the 1981 nationalisation of banks, but in 1982 it suffered large losses on property loans which resulted in Schroders being obliged to write off its investment, valued at £2.8 million. In the 1970s, it was anticipated that Brussels, the home of most of the European Community's institutions, would emerge as an important international financial centre. This consideration prompted Schroders and the Mitsubishi Trust and Banking Corporation (MTBC) to establish a joint venture there in 1976 to undertake syndicated loans and to provide company finance services. By the beginning of the 1980s the MTBC & Schroder Bank was well established and proving profitable, and in 1981 it was decided to increase the capital substantially to allow the bank to take advantage of opportunities that it was being obliged to turn down because of the size of its balance sheet. Schroders decided against subscribing to the increase in capital, in conformity with a policy decision to reduce its lending activities, with the result that its shareholding interest fell from 50 per cent to 14 per cent and the Schroder name was withdrawn. The remaining interest was sold to MTBC in 1984.

The importance of the Middle East as a source of deposits and business following the oil price rises of 1973 led to the establishment of a Schroder presence in the Lebanon and in Saudi Arabia. In 1975, Schroders formed J. Henry Schroder & Co. SAL in Beirut, the leading regional financial centre. This was a joint venture with the Asseilys, a prominent Lebanese industrial and commercial family. Anthony Asseily, the managing director, an Oxford graduate with a doctorate in economics, had worked at Schroder Wagg since 1967, so the parties were well known to each other and the relationship worked very smoothly. At the outset, the new firm concentrated on money market operations and corporate finance activity. The outbreak of intercommunal fighting later that year eventually made it impossible to operate from Beirut and in 1981 a new firm, Schroder Asseily & Co. Ltd, was established in London with a small back office in Cyprus. This firm developed a comprehensive range of private banking, investment management and corporate finance services to meet the needs of Schroders' Middle Eastern clients.

Schroders' other initiative to develop business in the Middle East was a participation in the Saudi Investment Banking Corporation, a consortium bank established in Saudi Arabia in July 1976 to conduct investment banking business. Saudi interests contributed 65 per cent of the capital of the new undertaking; the Chase Manhattan Bank, 20 per cent; and Commerzbank, The Industrial Bank of Japan and Schroders, 5 per cent each. Schroders provided practical assistance with the setting-up of the Riyadh-based bank, which opened for business in April 1977. Generally, Schroders preferred joint ventures to consortium arrangements but the opportunity to develop contacts in Saudi Arabia with the government, public institutions and the private sector was not to be missed, and indeed significant relationships stemmed from it.

Schrobanco, 1973–84

Schrobanco and the other US interests represented the largest part of the capital of Schroders' Limited in 1973 and, as the dollar appreciated against sterling during the decade, the proportion rose. Dollar assets were highly prized at a time when investment in the UK or continental Europe was believed to incur higher commercial or political risks. Even so, Schrobanco's nominal return on equity of around 8 per cent in the early 1970s was low, and an improvement in profitability remained a priority of the group's senior management. Wolfensohn, as deputy chairman of Schroders Limited with responsibility for all international activities, and as chairman of Schroders Incorporated, concentrated on developing a clear direction for the New York firm. The idea of selling the commercial bank and becoming a US investment bank had already been rejected, as described in Chapter 14. Furthermore, the immediate future of the investment banking and securities industry in the US was uncertain, with the onset of deregulation in 1975, which led to increased competition in the US securities industry and diminished profitability. Besides, UK Stock Exchange regulations prevented Schroder Wagg from undertaking broking and market-making business in securities, so there was no synergystic advantage to a US involvement in this activity. Wolfensohn came up with the novel idea of forging a close working relationship with a major US insurance company, which would enable Schrobanco to enlarge its capital and to expand the range of its banking and financing services. The outcome of his deliberations upon the future of Schroders' US interests in the mid-1970s was a dual strategy – to move decisively to expand the US domestic client base through the provision of commercial banking services while simultaneously developing, as far as the regulatory framework allowed, specialist investment banking and investment management services, drawing on the Schroder group's international strengths.

A preliminary to the revitalisation of Schrobanco's banking business was the expansion of the balance sheet which, because of its small size, was believed to be a hindrance to the development of a domestic US corporate clientele. This expansion was achieved in the summer of 1977 in two steps known by the codename Jaguar: the merger of the J. Henry Schroder Banking Corporation and the Schroder Trust Company to form the J. Henry Schroder Bank & Trust Company; and the doubling of the capital of the merged entity. The capital in Schroders Incorporated, the US holding company, was increased from $46 million to approximately $80 million; Schroders provided $13.5 million in additional equity; the Equitable Life Assurance Society of the United States, a New York based insurance company, also provided $13.5 million, in the form of a $3.5 million equity injection and a $10 million long-term loan to Schroders Inc.; and Allianz of America Inc., the US subsidiary of the leading German insurance company, and the Bank of Nova Scotia of Toronto, Canada, also subscribed $3.5 million each of equity. Besides their interests as investors, it was hoped that the new minority shareholders would generate new business for Schrobanco that would be beneficial to all the parties. The Jaguar exercise was followed by an expansion of deposits during 1978 from some $600 million to $1 billion, and during the next four years Schrobanco, as the J. Henry Schroder Bank & Trust Company continued to be known, grew rapidly and total assets reached about $2 billion.

The drive to develop US domestic banking activities in the late 1970s achieved some notable successes, particularly on the trust side of the business, Schrobanco becoming the leading adviser and trust bank on the 'demutualisation' of savings and loans associations, the US equivalent of UK building societies. On the lending side, however, the conduct of business with leading US corporations made little headway, since even with the additional capital Schrobanco was below the size of banks with which the Fortune 500 companies did business, and fierce competition made lending to corporate clients inadequately profitable. Schrobanco's loan officers thus sought other opportunities to employ the bank's resources, targeting medium-sized companies and Latin American borrowers. Schrobanco's long association with Latin America gave it a head start in building up business in the region. During the 1970s, the long established representative offices in Rio de Janeiro and Buenos Aires were supplemented by the opening of new ones in Bogota in 1973, where Luis Soto y Compania Ltda acted on Schroders' behalf; Sao Paolo in 1975; and Caracas in 1978. In 1980, Schrobanco used some of its increased capital to establish a Miami subsidiary under the Edge Act, a measure which authorised the formation of specialist internationally orientated banking subsidiaries, to finance trade between the United States and its Latin American neighbours, and it also opened a branch in the Cayman Islands. In fact, the actual evolution of Schrobanco's banking business in the late 1970s and early 1980s was different from the pattern anticipated at the time of the Jaguar exercise. US domestic lending made little headway and the firm found itself heavily exposed to Latin America when the debt crisis blew-up in the summer of 1982, even though it had been significantly cutting back on its lending since early 1981 anticipating a deterioration in Mexico's finances.

The other part of the strategy for Schrobanco was the development of investment banking activities focusing on cross-border business and drawing on the Schroder group's international connections. Schroders in New York enjoyed considerable success in developing specialist corporate finance and investment management subsidiaries, which serviced flows of funds into and out of the United States. Schroders' US corporate finance subsidiary, known until 1977 as the Schroder Capital Corporation and thereafter as the J. Henry Schroder Corporation, assisted successfully a number of Schroders' UK, continental European and Latin American clients to make acquisitions in the US. In addition, the existing venture capital activities were significantly expanded, particularly in the biotechnology area. The Schroder Oil Financing and Investment Company (SOFI), formed in 1974 in Houston, Texas, provided financial advisory services to the oil and gas industry and acted as an intermediary in arranging participations by international investment institutions in US exploration projects. In the late 1970s the managers of US pension trusts were developing a growing interest in adding foreign securities to their portfolios. To take advantage of this trend Schroder Naess & Thomas formed Schroder Naess & Thomas International in 1979. This subsidiary offered an international securities service that drew upon the Schroder group's worldwide investment management expertise. In 1980, Schroder Naess & Thomas was renamed Schroder Capital Management Incorporated. Schroder Real Estate successfully turned to advantage the crash in US property in the mid-1970s by promoting the low US real estate prices as a buying opportunity for foreigners. An important milestone in the development of its business was its appointment as adviser to the North American Property Unit Trust (NAPUT), a new unit trust established in 1975 by forty-nine UK institutions to invest in US commercial property. Demand from foreign investors for US commercial property grew in the late 1970s and Schroder Real Estate's business expanded with it. Sarakreek, a small Dutch quoted company through which continental and Middle Eastern investors made substantial investments in the US, was acquired. Agency services were developed and by the early 1980s the firm was responsible for the administration of substantial portfolios of US properties amounting to over $1 billion on behalf of European and Middle Eastern clients.

Growth in the Pacific Basin, 1973–84

In the 1970s and early 1980s many of the economies of the Pacific Basin region enjoyed very rapid economic growth. Recognising this, Schroders devoted a lot of attention to the development of its presence in that part of the world. The Tokyo representative office was established in February 1974. It enjoyed a very busy first year because of the relaxation by the Japanese authorities of restrictions on overseas borrowings by Japanese companies. In the following years, more and more Japanese companies looked overseas for funds and the Tokyo office's banking activity expanded rapidly. In addition, Schroder Wagg acted as manager for Japanese bond issues in the Euro-dollar market and commenced portfolio investment management services. However, because of regulatory impediments the office did not develop domestic merchant banking services in Japan, and in 1983 it still employed only seven people.

Schroders & Chartered, the Hong Kong joint venture with The Chartered Bank and the Kadoorie family, in which Schroders had a 40 per cent interest, also grew rapidly during the 1970s. Under Win Bischoff's leadership from 1970 to 1982, it expanded from 'managing just my secretary and myself', as he put it, to a staff of sixty-five. In these years it developed significant underwriting, corporate finance, and mergers and acquisitions activities. Subsequently, a banking and treasury business was added and the investment management activity, which had been nurtured with faith for a decade, became highly profitable. Returns on capital were consistently high and Hong Kong proved to be an excellent training ground for several of Schroders' senior management.

Schroders' entry into Singapore was achieved in 1976 through the purchase of a 24.5 per cent shareholding in Singapore International

Merchant Bankers Limited (SIMBL), an established enterprise which was one of Singapore's first merchant banks, founded in 1970. The other shareholders were the Oversea–Chinese Banking Corporation, a local bank in which the prominent Lee family was the major shareholder which, along with its associates, controlled 51 per cent, and the Continental Illinois Bank of Chicago with 24.5 per cent. In 1980, Schroders raised its participation to 49 per cent by purchasing Continental Bank's interest. At the time of the acquisition of the shareholding, SIMBL provided banking, company finance and investment management services, and held a substantial equity interest in one of Singapore's largest discount houses. In the following half-dozen years, its investment management business grew rapidly and it became the leading equity issuing house for Singapore companies on the local market.

Schroder Darling & Co. Ltd, as the Australian associate was known from 1975, expanded its operations substantially under the direction of Michael Gleeson-White, who became chairman and chief executive in September 1972. He was a former senior partner of Ord, Minnett, a well-known figure in Australian financial circles and was a founding director of Darling and Company. It conducted the full range of merchant banking activities and also had significant interests in a wool broker, a leasing firm and an Indonesian venture capital undertaking.

The success of the undertakings in Australia, Hong Kong and Singapore fully vindicated the strategy of entering new markets through joint ventures with prominent local partners, Schroders supplying the managerial expertise and international links while the indigenous party provided business introductions and understanding of local conditions.

Figure 15.2   Schroders plc, total assets, 1973–91

Figure 15.3　Schroders plc, disclosed profits (after tax), 1973–91

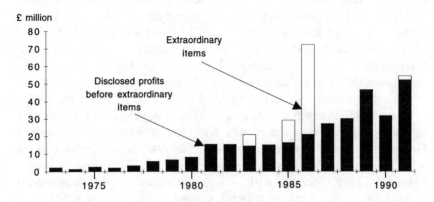

In each case, Schroders' joint venture became a leading firm in the domestic market and together they established a strong presence for the Schroder group in the Pacific Basin. Other helpful factors were the strong British ties and traditions in all these markets and the absence of established indigenous universal banks, while the dynamic economic expansion of the region fostered their rapid growth.

Between 31 December 1973 and 31 December 1983, the consolidated equity capital and disclosed reserves of Schroders plc grew from £25.8 million to £124.8 million, an increase of 40 per cent on an inflation-adjusted basis (see Figure 15.1 on page 482). This was achieved partly through low dividend payouts and therefore relatively high retention of net profits, which grew from £2.3 million to £14.4 million (see Figure 15.2), but also significantly from the higher values of Schroders' subsidiaries in New York and Zurich when translated into sterling. In these difficult times of high inflation and high corporate tax rates the augmentation of the real value of the capital without any recourse to shareholders was a considerable achievement. In the same period, the firm's total assets grew from £792 million to £3,385 million, a fourfold increase in nominal terms and a 22 per cent increase on an inflation-adjusted basis (see Figure 15.3).

Strategic Developments

The years 1983–86 saw far-reaching changes at Schroders. These began under the leadership of Lord Airlie, but in June 1984 it was announced that he had accepted the Queen's invitation to become Lord

Chamberlain, the head of the Royal household. He was succeeded as executive chairman of Schroders plc by George Mallinckrodt, while Win Bischoff was appointed group chief executive. A year earlier, Mallinckrodt and Bischoff had succeeded Maged and Hull as chairmen of the New York and London firms respectively. Mallinckrodt and Bischoff had much in common; both were of German origin and internationalist in experience and outlook. They made an effective team, which led Schroders through the rest of the decade and into the 1990s.

George Mallinckrodt was born in Germany in 1930 and, having spent his early childhood in Paris, was educated at Salem, the renowned German school, from which he graduated in 1948. Before embarking on a banking career, he qualified as a precision mechanic, undertaking a 2½-year apprenticeship with Agfa, the photographic equipment manufacturer. His banking training started at Münchmeyer & Co., a leading Hamburg merchant bank, and he passed his German National Banking Exam with distinction. He was sent to London in June 1953 to gain experience working at Kleinworts and a year later he joined Schrobanco in New York as a trainee. He spent the following six years in New York, with the exception of a nine-month interlude in Geneva in 1955 with the Union Bank of Switzerland. In July 1958, he married Charmaine Schroder, Helmut's daughter. During his years with Schrobanco and upon joining Schroder Wagg in London in 1960, he specialised in banking business with clients in continental Europe. He was made a director of Schroder Wagg and of the J. Henry Schroder Bank AG of Zurich in 1967. During the mid-1970s he was very active in the development of Schroders' Middle Eastern business. In 1977, he was appointed to the board of Schroders Limited, with responsibility for the firm's activities in continental Europe, the Middle East and the United States. He was a founder member of the German Chamber of Industry and Commerce in the UK in 1971, and was appointed its president in 1992. His charitable activities included serving as president of the German YMCA, and as a trustee of the Kaiser Wilhelm II Fund and several other charities associated with the German Lutheran churches in the UK, and of the University of Cambridge Kurt Hahn Trust.

Win Bischoff was born in 1941 in Germany. His family moved to South Africa in 1955 where he completed his schooling and studied Economics at the University of Witwatersrand in Johannesburg. In 1962, he went to New York to work at the Chase Manhattan Bank and to study law at the New York University School of Law. He joined Schroder Wagg in 1966, working in the Corporate Finance Division in London. In 1970, he was appointed the first managing director of Schroders & Chartered, the new joint venture in Hong Kong, which over the next twelve years he built into one of Hong Kong's leading merchant banks. Bischoff's energy and achievements led to his promotion as head of Schroder Wagg's Corporate Finance Division upon his return to London in 1982, and the following year he was appointed chairman of Schroder Wagg, aged just 42.

The change in the senior executive management at Schroders coincided with, and was largely prompted by, an acute awareness that a far-reaching and fast-moving transformation of the economic and banking environment was under way, which would oblige all banking firms to make harsh choices about their future direction. The strongly disinflationary policies of the US authorities under the leadership of Paul Volcker, chairman of the Federal Reserve Board, led to similar tight monetary policies elsewhere in the world and a shift in international financial flows from the developing countries back to the industrialised world. The advent of this fundamental change was highlighted by the events of the summer of 1982, when Mexico announced that it was unable to pay the interest on its external obligations, and the US bond and equity markets set off on the boom of the 1980s. These years also saw an acceleration of the trend towards financial deregulation, not only in the US but also in Europe and Japan, which permitted a substantial increase in international capital flows and ever closer ties between capital markets.

Against this background, the board of Schroders plc – principally at the instigation of the US and UK non-executive directors with industrial backgrounds and the Schroder family, the major shareholders – decided to conduct a fundamental review of the group's activities and future direction. Early in 1983 the Management Analysis Centre (MAC), a Boston-based management consultant, was commissioned to assist in this exercise. The outcome was the Strategic Review, completed early in 1984, which provided a basic framework for the development of the firm for the rest of the 1980s. The broad scope of the review led management to make choices primarily with reference to the international financial environment and regulatory changes in the major capital markets.

The Strategic Review recommended that Schroders should be developed as an integrated international business undertaking a balanced mix of activities. It suggested a curtailment of capital intensive activities, especially commercial banking, and a shift of emphasis from credit-risk business to market-risk business. Every effort was to be made to achieve the potential benefits of conducting corporate finance, credit and capital markets, treasury and trading, and investment management activities on a global basis. The Schroder group was potentially well-placed to benefit from enhanced cohesiveness because of its established presence in the principal financial centres of the world. What was needed was a managerial structure that would promote the conduct of the firm's activities on an integrated worldwide basis. This was effected through the creation of the Group Executive Committee, which replaced the Group Management Committee. It was chaired by the chairman of Schroders plc and comprised the two chief executives in London and New York, three other senior executives of the Schroder group, and six managing directors with functional group-wide responsibilities. In addition to Mallinckrodt and Bischoff, the senior executive members of the Group Executive Committee in 1984–92 were: Geoffrey Williams of Schroder Wagg; Martin Witschi of Schrobanco and later James Harmon of Wertheim Schroder; and Erik Gasser of J. Henry Schroder Bank AG. The functional managing directors were: Bischoff and subsequently Adam Broadbent for corporate finance; William Slee for credit and capital markets; Jean Solandt for treasury and trading; Richard Watkins for equities; Gordon Popham and then Peter Sedgwick for investment management; and Benjamin Strickland followed by Nicholas MacAndrew for finance, information technology and strategic planning.

The latter half of the 1980s and early 1990s saw changes amongst the non-executive directors of Schroders plc. Lord Franks retired in 1984, John T. Connor in 1987, and Sir Ernest Woodroofe and Sir Leslie Murphy in 1989. The new members were: William I. M. Turner Jr, a Canadian citizen who was chairman and chief executive of Consolidated Bathurst Inc., Montreal; Alva O. Way, a US citizen who was formerly chief financial officer of General Electric and then president of American Express Company; Sir Ralph Robins, chief executive of Rolls-Royce plc; and Charles Sinclair, chief executive of the parent company of the Associated Newspapers Group. The responsibilities of the non-executive directors were considerably enhanced through their full involvement in the audit and compensation committees. In addition, all large lending limits, market and liquidity risks, annual budget reviews, strategic reviews and capital allocations were subject to the authorisation of the board. A noteworthy feature of the composition of the Schroders plc board was its cosmopolitan nature, more than half the members being non-British.

Between the summer of 1983 and the summer of 1986, the principal decisions were taken which permitted Schroders to thrive in subsequent years. In these years, Schroders switched from commercial to investment banking in the United States by selling Schrobanco and acquiring a 50 per cent interest in Wertheim & Co. It developed investment banking activities in London and continental Europe by enhancing its corporate finance and securities capabilities, though it avoiding buying a UK broker or jobber. Moreover, unlike most of its peers, it decided against becoming a primary UK gilt dealer. The sale of Schroder Life, the life assurance subsidiary, greatly strengthened the capital base of the firm. Furthermore, these years saw rapid expansion of its business in Japan and elsewhere in the Pacific Basin region. By the end of 1986, the firm had gone through three of the most dramatic years of change in its history and was positioned as a London-based international merchant banking and investment management firm.

Change on Wall Street

The process of change began in New York. While the rest of Schroders' worldwide organisation was concentrating ever more on investment banking and investment management activities, the commercial banking business conducted by Schrobanco continued to represent the bulk of Schroders' business in the US. The strategic review concluded that this was inappropriate and it was decided to refocus Schrobanco with a greater emphasis on investment-banking-type business. This view was endorsed by the board of the J. Henry Schroder Bank & Trust Company, and Schroders Inc., notably by the US non-executive directors. In October 1983, George Mallinckrodt was appointed chairman and chief executive officer of the bank, and president and chief executive officer of Schroders Inc., and given responsibility for executing the required transformation.

The review of US banking legislation being undertaken at the time by the Senate Banking Committee under the chairmanship of Senator Jake Garn raised hopes that the Glass–Steagall Act would be overturned, thus enabling Schrobanco to engage in underwriting and securities activities, as it had done prior to 1933. However, the near collapse of the Continental Illinois Bank in May 1984 persuaded Mallinckrodt that such fundamental changes in US banking legislation would be delayed for a protracted period, perhaps for up to ten years. He thus explored alternative solutions to the New York problems, seeking ways of developing the business in co-ordination with the rest of the group, but soon came to the conclusion that this would continue to be impossible under the existing ownership structure, given the US regulatory environment. In order to be free to develop its investment banking business Schroders would have to reduce its equity interest in Schrobanco to 24.9 per cent or less, for technical regulatory reasons. Various approaches to acquire Schrobanco had been received from both within the US and overseas, but none was regarded as meeting Schroders' overall requirements, or to be in the best interests of the employees. The ideal solution was identified as being a partnership with a larger bank which would acquire the majority of Schrobanco's equity and support the development of its commercial banking activities. On account of Schroders' aspirations for expansion in the Pacific Basin, Japan was regarded as the most promising source of such a partner.

The Industrial Bank of Japan (IBJ), one of the largest Japanese banks, which enjoyed very close ties with Japanese industry arising from its leading position in the provision of long-term finance, was identified as the ideal partner. The senior management of IBJ were well known to Mallinckrodt through the Saudi Investment Banking Corporation, in which both Schroders and IBJ were minority shareholders, and they responded positively to his invitation. IBJ already had a branch in New York but saw the acquisition of a long-established bank, particularly one with Schrobanco's standing in the New York banking industry and with the American banking authorities, as a means to achieving an indigenous presence. IBJ also appreciated the potential for improving Schrobanco's profit performance from increased productivity on a larger volume of business and by cheaper funding. Informal talks began between Schroders and IBJ in the latter part of 1984, and in June 1985 it was decided that IBJ would acquire initially a 50.1 per cent shareholding in Schrobanco, proceeding later with the acquisition of a further 25 per cent. Alva O. Way, who joined the board of Schroders plc in May 1985, was appointed non-executive chairman of the renamed IBJ Schroder Bank & Trust Company on 1 January 1986, while Peter Rona, who had made his career with Schrobanco since 1969, was made president and chief executive officer.

The sale of 50.1 per cent of Schrobanco's equity generated about $80 million for Schroders Inc., Schroders' US holding company, with which it was intended to develop investment banking activities. The transaction excluded the subsidiaries and associates that conducted corporate finance, venture capital, investment management, real estate and energy resource development activities, which remained wholly-owned subsidiaries of Schroders Inc. But they amounted to no more than a toehold in investment banking on Wall Street, which would take years to develop into a substantial business. Schroders therefore considered possible candidates amongst the Wall Street investment banks for cooperation or for acquisition, identifying Wertheim & Co. as the best candidate on account of its reputation, range of activities and size. Through the fortunate coincidence of a personal friendship between Alva O. Way and James Harmon, a senior partner of Wertheim & Co., Way learned that Frederick Klingenstein, the senior partner in Wertheim & Co., was contemplating the sale of his family's interest in the firm. Serious discussions got under way in April 1986, and in June it was announced that Schroders was to acquire 50 per cent of the equity of Wertheim & Co. for a total consideration (including a subordinated loan) of $100 million, and the firm was to be renamed Wertheim Schroder & Co. The acquisition obliged Schroders to reduce its interest in IBJ Schroder to 24.9 per cent, comprising 4.9 per cent voting shares and 20 per cent non-voting shares. Schroders intended to retain this level of holding, but later in 1986 IBJ Schroder decided to purchase the US government bond trading firm Aubrey Lanston for $240 million. This presented a potential conflict with Wertheim Schroder, which was also involved in US government bond trading, and also necessitated an increase in the capital of IBJ Schroder. Schroders declined to participate in the capital increase and sold its holding of non-voting shares, maintaining its 4.9 per cent holding of voting shares.

Wertheim & Co. was founded in 1927 by Maurice Wertheim, a partner in the Wall Street investment bank Hallgarten & Co., and Joseph Klingenstein, a broker in Hallgarten, who decided to start their own business. Wertheim furnished the capital for the new firm and undertook the corporate finance side of its activities, while Klingenstein ran the firm's trading operations. Wertheim was a man of diverse activities and interests: the founder of the New York Theatre Guild; a member of the War Production Board; the proprietor of *The Nation* magazine; and the author of a book on fly fishing. He married the daughter of Henry Morgenthau, Secretary of the Treasury under Franklin D. Roosevelt. He was a graduate of Harvard and his notable collection of French Impressionist paintings is on display at the university's Fogg Museum. Upon Wertheim's death in 1950, at the early age of 65, his capital in the firm was withdrawn and Joseph Klingenstein became the principal proprietor, though there were always other partners with minor interests. Klingenstein was born in 1889 of German-Jewish immigrant parents, his father running a dry goods store on New York's Lower East Side. He attended Columbia University, joining Hallgarten & Co. in 1911. His three great interests were family, finance (he served two terms as a governor of the New York Stock Exchange) and charitable causes, most notably the activities of the Mount Sinai Hospital, of which he was president in 1956–62. He died in 1976, aged 85. Frederick Klingenstein, the son of Joseph Klingenstein, was educated at Yale and the Harvard Business School, and spent two years in the army and one with a specialist broker before coming into the family firm in 1956, aged 25. In 1962 he was made a partner and in the late 1960s assumed the role of managing partner. Following the retirement of his father and uncle in quick succession at the beginning of the 1970s he became the senior partner of the firm, the role he fulfilled until the sale of his interest to Schroders a decade and a half later.

Wertheim & Co. came into being during the great Wall Street bull market of the 1920s and throughout its history securities trading was an important activity. During the 1930s and 1940s the firm was particularly active in foreign securities trading and arbitrage, and in commercial real estate. In the 1950s and 1960s, under Joseph Klingenstein's conservative leadership, it built up equity services focusing on high quality research on US corporations. This expertise provided the basis for making venture capital investments in private firms, in whose growth or recovery Wertheim proceeded to play a very active part. In the post-war decades Wertheim became an important underwriter through its close relationships with Goldman Sachs and Kidder Peabody. It also built up a substantial business in investment management services under the direction of Joseph Klingenstein and continued to be active in foreign securities but lost market position due to competition from larger rivals. During the 1970s and the early 1980s the firm made an entrée into the businesses of risk arbitrage and trading US government securities, and built up trading in OTC stocks and corporate bonds, and corporate finance activities. It opened branch offices in Philadelphia in 1972, San Francisco in 1979, London in 1982, Boston in 1983 and Geneva in 1984. In 1973, Wertheim and Lehman Brothers formed LEWCO, a joint venture to provide back-office services for securities firms. It was an initiative that proved highly successful and provided steady profits. At the time of the deal with Schroders, Wertheim had a staff of around 1,000, of which 600 worked for the investment bank and 400 for LEWCO, which by then was under Wertheim's sole management.

Klingenstein was looking for a means of withdrawing the bulk of his family's capital from Wertheim in a way that would not harm the firm he and his father had built up. The replacement of the Klingenstein interest by the Schroder investment permitted the preservation of the private-firm culture that was an important element in Wertheim's success. It was also consistent with Schroders' strategy of entering new markets with a leading local partner, in this case the Wertheim management. The tie-up with Schroders provided Wertheim with major new business openings in Europe and, even more importantly, in the Pacific Basin, where it had no presence. For both firms there arose possibilities of expanding cross-border corporate finance and international securities business. For Schroders, the opportunity to market its worldwide investment banking services in the US through Wertheim was a valuable complement to its existing activities.

Schroders' commercial banking activities in Latin America were curtailed during the 1980s, partly on account of the economic and financial difficulties experienced by many countries of that region and partly because of the deliberate retrenchment in the group's commercial banking activities. The reduction of Schroders' overall exposure to Latin America was achieved promptly from 1982, through a combination of curtailments of credit lines, asset sales and write-offs by both the New York and London firms. The sale of Schrobanco led to a further fall in Latin American loans and a much lower volume of business with that continent. But the Brazilian joint enterprises with Monteiro Aranha continued and the Sao Paulo and Caracas representative offices were maintained, preserving Schroders' presence in the region. The outbreak of the Falklands War between Britain and Argentina in 1982 led to the closure of the Buenos Aires representative office, though Schroders' retained the services of Jan Stuijt, their representative since 1966, who continued to advise the firm.

Growth in the UK and Continental Europe

Shortly before Bischoff's appointment as chairman of Schroder Wagg, the London Stock Exchange announced its intention to deregulate its activities. This applied principally to the sales and trading of domestic securities, since international securities trading, in both bonds and equities, was already liberalised. In the three years from July 1983 until 'Big Bang' day on 27 October 1986, there was a rapid change in the structure and size of merchant banking and securities firms in London. In many firms securities capabilities were added to existing corporate finance and banking activities, while the investment management business was physically separated from the others to avoid conflicts of interest and to comply with the new regulatory regime introduced by the 1986 Financial Services Act. It was decided that Schroder Wagg should emphasise corporate advisory, financing and treasury activities, while also developing selectively a securities business as a complement to capital-raising, and that the investment management business should be expanded.

Bischoff led the initiative to strengthen and enhance Schroder Wagg's corporate finance activities. This enabled it to regain its position as one of the leading firms specialising in providing advice and procuring financing for mergers, acquisitions, divestitures and other forms of corporate reorganisations, in both the UK and continental European marketplaces from the mid-1980s. The quality of service provided proved an enticing lure to new clients. Schroders also expanded its continental European business, conducting significant levels of transactions for German, French, Spanish, Italian and Dutch clients, in particular. From 1988 onwards there was a considerable increase in continental European activity as companies took advantage of opportunities stimulated by the European Community's Single Market 1992 programme. The adoption of the group management structure in

1984 enabled Schroders to give its merger and acquisition business a global focus and led to a large increase in the number of cross-border transactions conducted by Schroders' corporate finance teams around the world. Schroders entered the 1990s at or near the top of the league tables for UK corporate finance work, and a leader in cross-border mergers and acquisitions.

Schroder Wagg's expertise and reputation led to its appointment to undertake government advisory and financing business, particularly in the field of privatisation. It was closely involved in the UK government's privatisation programme from 1982, acting that year as adviser to the government in connection with the staff buy-out of the National Freight Company. Subsequently, it also played a leading part in the privatisation of Associated British Ports, the VSEL Consortium, Jaguar, Cable and Wireless, the British Airports Authority and the Water Authorities. In continental Europe, it advised DSM, the Dutch state-owned chemicals group, on its privatisation. Following the collapse of Communism in Central and Eastern Europe, Schroders immediately began to pursue privatisation opportunities and was soon appointed to advise on privatisations in Czechoslovakia, Hungary and Poland, thus re-entering a region where it had been active in reconstruction finance in the 1920s. Its privatisation expertise was also deployed in other parts of the world, notably the Pacific Basin.

Schroders concentrated its financing activity upon equity and equity-linked underwritings, structured project and leasing finance, and private placements and syndicated loans. It developed its capabilities in the underwriting and distribution of equities and equity-linked securities such as convertible bonds or bonds with warrants, not only for its UK clients but also increasingly its Japanese, US, continental European and Asian clientele. It developed structured private placements using its contacts with Japanese investors. More complex forms of financing were provided by the Project Finance Department, which took a leading role in export finance as well as structuring and advising on large project loans, particularly in the power generation sector. Leasing was another financing medium in which Schroders was active, specialising in 'small ticket' leasing, in which it had a significant market share. At the same time, direct lending was reorientated towards medium-sized companies and private clients.

Schroders' banking business diversified from traditional lending to the provision of liability management services for its clients. The operations of the Treasury and Trading Division, which executed Schroder Wagg's business in treasury, money market, foreign exchange, swaps and arbitrage business, grew successfully, its activity being spurred by the development of the markets in derivative products. Consideration was given to becoming a primary dealer in UK government bonds at the time of the market reforms in 1986 and an application was made, but the requirement to commit at least £25 million of capital and the large number of licences granted led Schroders to conclude that the returns would be insufficient and thus the firm decided against proceeding.

As a result of the Big Bang deregulation, Schroder Wagg had the option of purchasing a jobber or a broker and making a major strategic push into domestic securities trading. This was considered but explicitly rejected because of reluctance to pay large sums for 'goodwill' at a time when deregulation was likely to lead to overcapacity and poor returns from domestic securities business. Instead, in July 1984 Schroders formed a new member firm of the London Stock Exchange called Helbert, Wagg & Co., Anderson, Bryce, Villiers, a mouthful which combined the name of Schroder Wagg's stockbroking forerunner and the individuals recruited from the stockbroker, Panmure Gordon, to run this business. Initially, Schroders' shareholding was restricted by Stock Exchange regulations to 29.9 per cent, but when the regulations were relaxed in 1986 it took complete control and the firm was renamed Schroder Securities. From the outset, the equities sales and trading business was developed on a group-wide basis. The acquisition of Wertheim added a significant broking business in US securities, while Schroder Securities (Japan) became a broker in Japanese equities, thus giving Schroders a presence in the world's two largest equity markets. In Europe, Schroder Securities focused on smaller UK companies and developed its expertise in the continental European markets, particularly those of Southern Europe, complementing its capital-raising activities in these regions.

The investment management side of Schroders' business in London continued to expand rapidly and rewardingly during the 1980s. In April 1985, in anticipation of more stringent requirements regarding the separation of corporate finance and investment management, Schroder Wagg's Investment Division became a separate company, Schroder Investment Management Ltd (SIM). In 1988, SIM became a directly-held subsidiary of Schroders plc. Total funds under management in London rose from £4.6 billion at the end of 1984 to £20.9 billion by the end of 1991, the preponderance being UK pension funds. The 1980s was a decade of increasing sophistication and specialisation in institutional investment management; SIM's long-term emphasis on building up an in-house research capability of the highest quality, both at home and overseas, played an important part in establishing its impressive performance record which provided the essential basis for gaining new business.

Unit trust funds under management expanded particularly rapidly in the mid-1980s, rising from £240 million at the end of 1982 to £1.2 billion at the end of 1986, by which time Schroder Life employed a staff of 700 and had become the fourth largest unit-linked life assurance business in Britain. In order to develop Schroder Life to its full potential it became clear that it needed further capital, better distribution, better product development and international insurance linkage. It was evident that Schroder Life had outgrown the synergistic benefits possible from a merchant bank and needed the backing of an international insurance company. Mallinckrodt thus proposed to sell Schroder Life and to apply the capital released to the development of the Schroder group's other activities. There was no shortage of interested buyers because of the promising outlook for the unit-linked life assurance business in the UK. In September 1986, Schroders secured a price of £99 million, compared to an investment of £12 million, from the National Mutual Life Association of Australia (the preferred suitor from Schroder Life's point of view), and the firm was renamed N. M. Schroder Financial Management. Under the terms of the sale agreement, the investment management of nearly all of the unit trusts stayed with SIM for three years during which time it was debarred from developing its own unit trust retail business. The re-entry of SIM into the unit trust retail business in 1989 was assisted by the timely publication of an analysis which identified the firm as the best-performing unit trust manager of the 1980s. Although 1990 and 1991 were relatively subdued years for the unit trust industry, Schroder Unit Trusts was able to build up a considerable volume of new business. Combined with the existing institutional unit trust business, by the end of 1991 Schroder Unit Trusts Ltd had £2.1 billion under management, making it the sixth largest manager in the UK.

The second half of the 1980s saw a determined thrust to expand Schroders' investment management business by strengthening the co-ordination of this activity in London, Zurich, Tokyo, Hong Kong, Singapore and Sydney. US Employee Retirement Income Security Act (ERISA) funds were targeted as promising clients for Schroders' services because they were busily adding foreign securities to their portfolios and, by the end of 1990, Schroder Capital Management had £3 billion ERISA funds under management, making it one of the largest active international equity managers of US ERISA funds. Schroders was well placed to benefit from the rapid internationalisation of investment management in the 1980s because of its presence in all the major international financial centres. By the beginning of the 1990s it had established a strong position in the Pacific Basin region, being the largest merchant bank investment manager in Singapore, the second largest foreign fund manager in Japan, and one of the top three fund managers in Hong Kong. Continental Europe offered promising opportunities for the application of Schroders' expertise, and the closing years of the 1980s and the early 1990s saw a drive to develop business there. At the end of 1991, total funds under management by the Schroder group amounted to £27.7 billion.

Another recommendation of the Strategic Review was to expand Schroders' venture capital fund management activities. The first independent venture fund with capital subscribed by outside investors was launched in September 1983 by Schroder Rockefeller's successor company, the J. Henry Schroder Corporation of New York. Schroders decided to build an international network of specialists who would act as investment advisers to dedicated funds raised from third-party investors. The first step was the establishment of a UK operation, Schroder Ventures, early in 1985. Within a year this had raised £100 million for a venture capital fund and a buy-out fund, the latter being the first independent fund raised in the UK specifically for investment in management buy-outs. With the launch of successor funds the volume of Schroder Ventures' UK funds grew rapidly, totalling £420 million by 1991. In 1986–92, further venture capital firms were formed in France, Germany, Italy, Spain, Canada and Japan. Each operation was staffed by nationals of the country concerned, many of the 60 executives in the group having had experience at a senior level in industry, no less than eighteen of them at chief executive or managing director level. By 1991, $1.5 billion had been raised for sixteen funds – nine buy-out funds and seven venture funds – making Schroder Ventures the largest manager of such funds outside the US.

As almost every element of Schroders' business in continental Europe expanded, it developed its presence in the principal financial centres. By 1992, the Schroder group had offices in Amsterdam, Copenhagen, Frankfurt, Madrid, Milan and Paris, which were engaged in a mixture of investment banking, securities sales, investment management and venture capital activities. J. Henry Schroder Bank AG reduced its commercial lending activities and concentrated on investment management and related private banking services, as well as on capital markets, treasury, foreign exchange and securities business. By 1991, the staff in Zurich and Geneva numbered 110, and the total number of employees in continental Europe exceeded 200.

Expansion in the Pacific Basin

In the second half of the 1980s and the early 1990s, the economies of Japan and the newly industrialised economies of the Pacific Basin, particularly Hong Kong, Korea, Singapore and Taiwan – the 'Four

Tigers' – continued to grow rapidly. Schroders benefited because of its established presence in the region as a result of its initiatives of the 1970s and the early 1980s. The increase in global capital flows and the deregulation of local financial markets meant that it was important both to develop these businesses and to integrate them fully with the rest of the Schroder group of companies.

Japan was the market of greatest change. Having developed as an industrial powerhouse, Japan became the world's leading capital exporter in the 1980s and developed a symbiotic economic relationship with the United States. Following the Plaza Agreement of September 1985 to reflate the Japanese domestic economy to assist the devaluation of the US dollar, Japanese economic activity grew rapidly and the Tokyo Stock Exchange became the largest and most active equity market in the world. Capital-raising activity, both in Japan and in the Euro-markets, and secondary market volumes expanded dramatically. Against this background, access to Japan's financial market was gradually liberalised. Schroders responded with initiatives to develop further its close business links with the Japanese government, companies, banks, securities firms and investors. It increased its Euro-currency capital market activities on behalf of Japanese corporate clients in London and Zurich, while in Tokyo it developed a growing range of services through a variety of specialist subsidiaries. Schroder Securities (Japan) was formed in 1985 following the granting of a licence to conduct securities business in Japan by the Ministry of Finance in December 1985 and became a member of the Tokyo Stock Exchange in June 1988, one of the first six British firms to be granted membership. Schroder Investment Management KK was formed in 1985 to provide investment advisory services to Japanese investors and to act as representative in Japan for the Schroder group's investment management services. In 1991, Schroder Investment Trust Management was established, with Schroders owning 80.5 per cent and the other 19.5 per cent held by eleven Japanese securities firms, to distribute mutual funds in Japan. Schroder PTV Partners KK was formed to engage in venture capital activities and to manage the Schroder Japan Venture Fund. In 1989, Schroders added a corporate finance capability and entered the merger and acquisition advisory business to meet the overseas and domestic requirements of Japanese corporations. At the beginning of 1990, a Japanese executive chairman was appointed to direct Schroders' expanding activities in Japan, signifying the firm's strong commitment to the further development of its presence there.

As recommended by the Strategic Review, it was decided that Schroders' shareholdings in associate companies in the region should be increased, if the opportunity arose, to achieve greater integration with the rest of the group. In 1984, the firm's interest in its Hong Kong associate was raised from 40 per cent to 75 per cent, and the Kadoorie family's interest from 20 per cent to 25 per cent, by the purchase of The Chartered Bank's shareholding, and Schroders & Chartered was renamed Schroders Asia Ltd. It continued to be one of the leading merchant banks in Hong Kong and also began to develop business with mainland China. Moreover, in 1982, Schroder Securities became a stock exchange member in Hong Kong. In 1985, the Australian associate, by then called Schroders Australia Ltd, became a fully-owned subsidiary through the acquisition of the interests of the other shareholders. At the same time, Schroders Australia sold its commercial banking book, focusing thereafter on corporate finance, capital market, treasury, real estate and investment management activities. Singapore International Merchant Bankers Ltd continued to thrive as a prominent Singapore-based merchant bank, particularly developing investment management and capital market activities. In 1989, Schroders increased its interest from 49 per cent to 100 per cent by buying out the Oversea–Chinese Banking Corporation and other shareholders and the firm was renamed Schroder International Merchant Bankers Limited.

Schroders took advantage of the growing opportunities to develop business in other countries of the Pacific Basin. In South Korea, it opened a representative office in Seoul in 1987 and the same year it was appointed manager of the Korea Europe Fund. Late in 1991, Schroder Securities applied to become one of the first foreign firms with a Korean securities licence. In Taiwan, it established a representative office in 1989. In Malaysia, Schroders advised on the government's privatisation masterplan, and in 1991 an office was opened in Kuala Lumpur and an investment management joint venture was established with Seacorp, a leading government-owned financial services company. Schroder International Merchant Bankers had long been close to many Indonesian banks and companies, and in 1991 a new joint venture named PT Schroders Indonesia was established in conjunction with the Soeryadjaya family, the principal shareholders in one of Indonesia's largest quoted companies, the PT Astra group. Once again, Schroders entered a new market with a well-established local partner.

Performance and Perspectives

Schroders' financial results of the mid-1980s were greatly affected by the major structural changes of these years, including the cost of provisions against Latin American loans, the gain on the sale of Schrobanco, the acquisition of 50 per cent of Wertheim & Co., including the cost of the goodwill, and the capital gain realised through the sale of Schroder Life. By contrast, in the years 1987–91, the results were principally determined by the operating performance of the firm. Net profits before extraordinary items advanced from £15.1 million in 1984 to £52.1 million in 1991 (see Figure 15.2 on page 496). Moreover, in some years there were large 'extraordinary profits', notably in 1986 from the sale of Schroder Life. Consolidated equity capital and disclosed reserves grew from £124.8 million at the end of 1983 to £221.1 million in 1986, and £360.6 million at the end of 1991 (see Figure 15.1 on page 482). Schroders plc's total assets almost halved in 1984 with the sale of Schrobanco, whose commercial banking business was highly balance-sheet based (see Figure 15.3 on page 497). Total assets recovered rapidly in the second half of the 1980s, and by 1991 were £4.1 billion, but on an inflation-adjusted basis the balance sheet was still smaller than in 1983.

In the early 1970s, the firms which comprised the top tier of London's merchant banks had many common traits: all were long-established City houses and members of the Accepting Houses Committee; all were British-owned and most were independent of commercial banks or other firms; all conducted acceptance finance and most were active in corporate finance and investment management business. Many also undertook ancilliary financial activities such as bullion and commodity trading and insurance, but none did domestic securities business, which the rules of the London Stock Exchange reserved for stockbrokers and jobbers. Schroders conformed to the general pattern in each respect, though the scale of its overseas operations, notably in New York, was a distinctive feature. By the beginning of the 1990s, the business of international merchant and investment banking had been transformed. There was a host of new competitors from home and abroad and the business was now conducted on a worldwide basis. The London merchant banks adopted a variety of strategies in response to the deregulation of financial services in the 1980s and became much more diverse in the pattern of their activities. Many were acquired by British or overseas banks, but most of the highly regarded firms remained independent. Schroders, which enjoyed a head start on account of its US interests, pushed the internationalisation of its business further than most of the other London merchant banks. The establishment of the international Schroder group of companies in the 1960s, 1970s and early 1980s was the first stage in this process. The second stage, which was achieved in the latter half of the 1980s, was the integration of the conduct of operations on a worldwide basis. In these years, the international Schroder group of companies became a single entity – Schroders.

Appendices

Contents

514

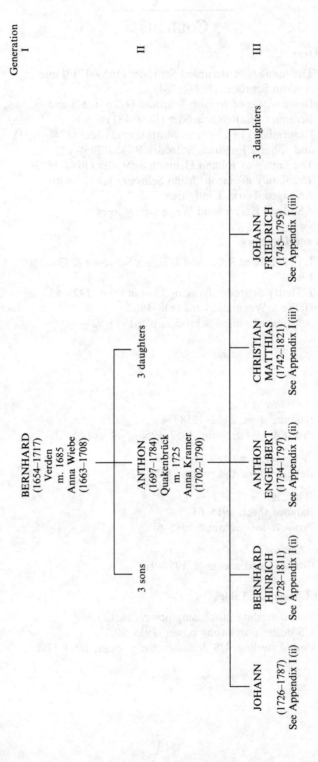

Appendix I (i)   The families of Bernhard Schröder (1654–1717) and Anthon Schröder (1697–1784)

Generation

I

II

III

BERNHARD
(1654–1717)
Verden
m. 1685
Anna Wiebe
(1663–1708)

ANTHON
(1697–1784)
Quakenbrück
m. 1725
Anna Kramer
(1702–1790)

3 daughters

3 sons

JOHANN
(1726–1787)
See Appendix I (ii)

BERNHARD
HINRICH
(1728–1811)
See Appendix I (ii)

ANTHON
ENGELBERT
(1734–1797)
See Appendix I (ii)

CHRISTIAN
MATTHIAS
(1742–1821)
See Appendix I (iii)

JOHANN
FRIEDRICH
(1745–1795)
See Appendix I (iii)

3 daughters

Appendix I (ii)   Descendants of Johann Schröder (1726–1787) and Bernard Hinrich Schröder (1728–1811)

Generation

Appendix I (iii)

III

IV

V

VI

JOHANN
(1726–1787)

Johann Schröder & Co.
Bremen

BERNHARD
HINRICH I
(1728–1811)

B. H. & A. E. Schröder
Quakenbrück

ANTHON
ENGELBERT
(1734–1797)

B. H. & A. E. Schröder
Quakenbrück

PETER
(1755–1829)

Johann Schröder & Co.
Bremen

GERHARD
(1765–1829)

Christ. Matthias
Schröder & Co.
Hamburg

ANTHON
(1783–1865)

B. H. & A. E. Schröder
Quakenbrück

BERNHARD HINRICH II
(1778–1824)

B. H. & A. E. Schröder
Quakenbrück

BERNHARD
HINRICH
(1794–1868)
Bremen

GOTTFRIED
HEINRICH
(1797–1851)

G. H. &
P. D. Schröder
Bremen

PETER
DANIEL
(1800–1885)

G. H. &
P. D. Schröder
Bremen

BERNHARD
HINRICH
(1807–1889)

B. H. Schröder & Co.
Quakenbrück

JOHANN
HEINRICH
(1815–1890)

B. H. Schröder & Co.
Amsterdam

BERNHARD
HINRICH III
(1816–1849)

Schröder
Gebrüder & Co.
Hamburg

ANTHON
CHRISTIAN
(1818–1891)

B. H. & A. E.
Schröder & Co.
Quakenbrück

JOHANN
RUDOLPH I
(1821–1887)

Schröder
Gebrüder & Co.
Hamburg

JOHANN
FRIEDRICH
(1831–1888)

B. H. Schröder Söhne
Bremen

ANTHON
(1833–1909)

B. H. & A. E.
Schröder & Co.
Quakenbrück
Schröder Böninger
London

JOHANN
HERMAN
(1834–1902)

B. H. Schröder & Co.
J. Herm. Schröder
Amsterdam

BERNHARD
HINRICH
(1837–1901)

Schröder Böninger
London

JOHANN
RUDOLPH II
(1852–1938)

Schröder
Gebrüder & Co.
Hamburg

BRUNO
(1867–1940)

J. Henry Schröder & Co.
London

See Appendix I (v)

516

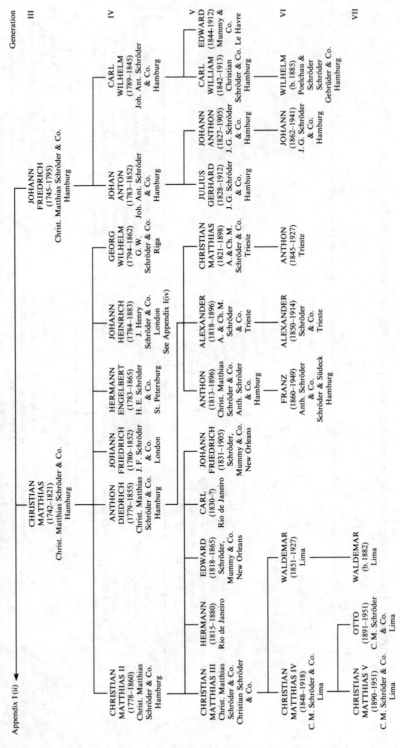

Appendix I(iii) Descendants of Christian Matthias Schröder (1742–1821) and Johann Friedrich Schröder (1745–1795)

Appendix I(ii)

Generation

III

CHRISTIAN MATTHIAS II
(1778–1860)
Christ. Matthias Schröder & Co.
Hamburg

CHRISTIAN MATTHIAS
(1742–1821)
Christ. Matthias Schröder & Co.
Hamburg

JOHANN FRIEDRICH
(1745–1795)
Christ. Matthias Schröder & Co.
Hamburg

IV

ANTHON DIEDRICH
(1779–1855)
Christ. Matthias Schröder & Co.
Hamburg

JOHANN FRIEDRICH
(1780–1852)
J. F. Schröder & Co.
London

HERMANN ENGELBERT
(1783–1865)
H. E. Schröder & Co.
St. Petersburg

JOHANN HEINRICH
(1784–1883)
J. Henry Schröder & Co.
London
See Appendix I(iv)

GEORG WILHELM
(1794–1862)
G. W. Schröder & Co.
Riga

JOHAN ANTON
(1783–1852)
Joh. Ant. Schröder & Co.
Hamburg

CARL WILHELM
(1789–1845)
Joh. Ant. Schröder & Co.
Hamburg

V

CHRISTIAN MATTHIAS III
(1848–1918)
Christ. Matthias Schröder & Co.
Christian Schröder & Co.

HERMANN
(1815–1880)
Rio de Janeiro

EDWARD
(1818–1865)
Schröder, Mummy & Co.
New Orleans

CARL
(1830–?)
Rio de Janeiro

JOHANN FRIEDRICH
(1831–1905)
Schröder, Mummy & Co.
New Orleans

ANTHON
(1813–1896)
Christ. Matthias Schröder & Co.
Anth. Schröder & Co.
Hamburg

ALEXANDER
(1818–1896)
A. & Ch. M. Schröder & Co.
Trieste

CHRISTIAN MATTHIAS
(1821–1898)
A. & Ch. M. Schröder & Co.
Trieste

JULIUS GERHARD
(1828–1912)
J. G. Schröder & Co.
Hamburg

JOHANN ANTHON
(1827–1905)
J. G. Schröder & Co.
Hamburg

CARL WILLIAM
(1842–1913)
Schröder & Co. Le Havre

EDWARD
(1844–1912)
Mummy & Co.

VI

CHRISTIAN MATTHIAS IV
(1848–1918)
C. M. Schröder & Co.
Lima

WALDEMAR
(1851–1927)
Lima

FRANZ
(1860–1949)
Anth. Schröder & Co.
Schröder & Südeck
Hamburg

ALEXANDER
(1850–1914)
Schröder & Co.
Trieste

ANTHON
(1845–1927)
Trieste

JOHANN
(1862–1941)
J. G. Schröder & Co.
Hamburg

WILHELM
(b. 1885)
Poelchau & Schröder
Schröder Gebrüder & Co.
Hamburg

VII

CHRISTIAN MATTHIAS V
(1890–1951)
C. M. Schröder & Co.
Lima

OTTO
(1891–1951)
C. M. Schröder & Co.
Lima

WALDEMAR
(b. 1882)
Lima

517

Appendix I (iv) The family of Johann Heinrich Schröder (1784–1883)

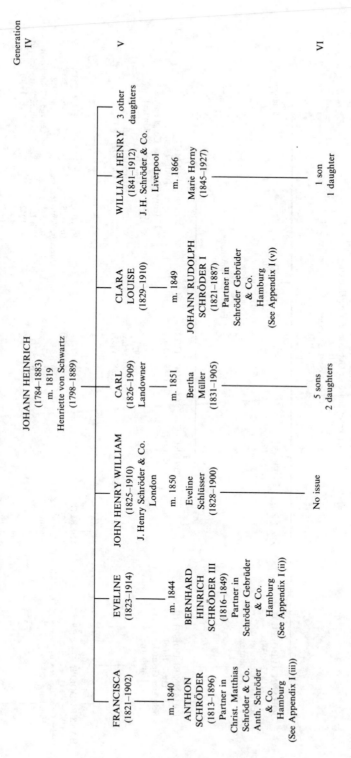

518

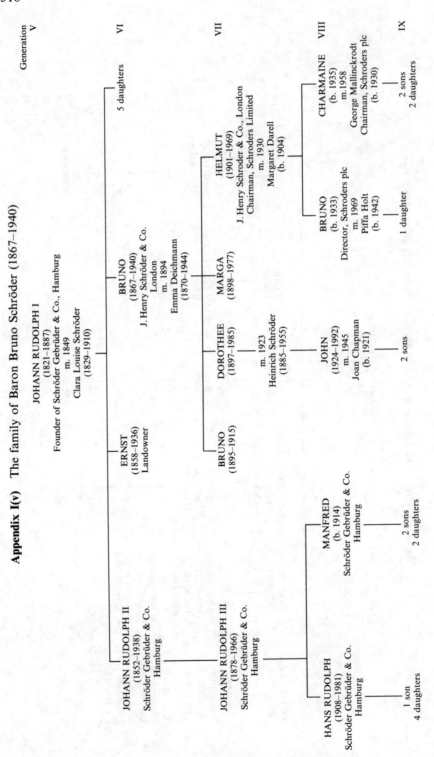

Appendix I(v) The family of Baron Bruno Schröder (1867–1940)

Appendix I(vi)   Abridged Tiarks family tree

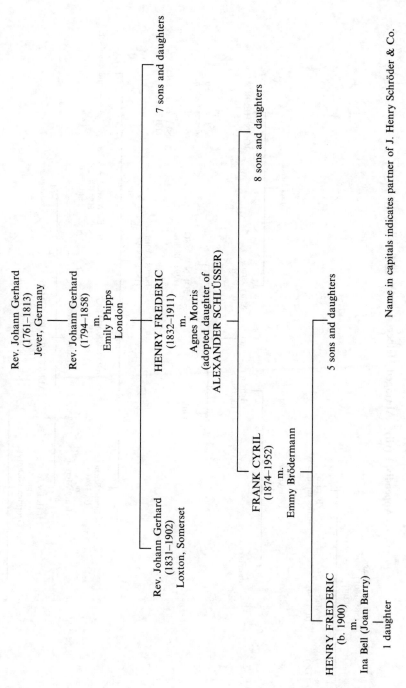

Rev. Johann Gerhard
(1761–1813)
Jever, Germany

Rev. Johann Gerhard
(1794–1858)
m.
Emily Phipps
London

Rev. Johann Gerhard
(1831–1902)
Loxton, Somerset

HENRY FREDERIC
(1832–1911)
m.
Agnes Morris
(adopted daughter of
ALEXANDER SCHLÜSSER)

7 sons and daughters

FRANK CYRIL
(1874–1952)
m.
Emmy Brödermann

8 sons and daughters

HENRY FREDERIC
(b. 1900)
m.
Ina Bell (Joan Barry)

5 sons and daughters

1 daughter

Name in capitals indicates partner of J. Henry Schröder & Co.

520

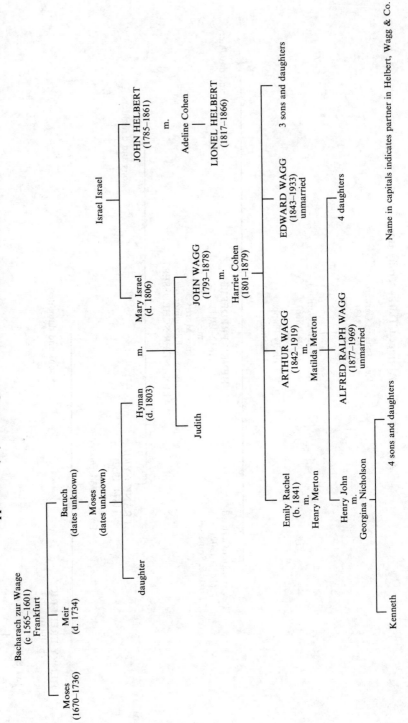

Appendix I (vii)   Abridged Helbert and Wagg family trees

Bacharach zur Waage
(c 1565–1601)
Frankfurt

Moses
(1670–1736)

Meir
(d. 1734)

Baruch
(dates unknown)

Moses
(dates unknown)

daughter

Hyman
(d. 1803)

m.

Israel Israel

Mary Israel
(d. 1806)

JOHN HELBERT
(1785–1861)

m.

Adeline Cohen

LIONEL HELBERT
(1817–1866)

Judith

JOHN WAGG
(1793–1878)

m.

Harriet Cohen
(1801–1879)

Emily Rachel
(b. 1841)
m.
Henry Merton

ARTHUR WAGG
(1842–1919)
m.
Matilda Merton

EDWARD WAGG
(1843–1933)
unmarried

3 sons and daughters

Henry John
m.
Georgina Nicholson

ALFRED RALPH WAGG
(1877–1969)
unmarried

4 daughters

Kenneth

4 sons and daughters

Name in capitals indicates partner in Helbert, Wagg & Co.

Appendix II (i)   J. F. Schröder & Co. and J. Henry Schröder & Co.,
1800–1962

J. F. Schröder & Co., 1800–33

Partners

1800 – 1833	Johann Friedrich Schröder
1804 – 1817	Johann Heinrich Schröder

J. Henry Schröder & Co., 1818–1962

Trading Names

1818 – 1957	J. Henry Schröder & Co.
1957 – 1962	J. Henry Schroder & Co. Ltd

Partners (1918–1957)		Partnership Status
1818 – 1883	Johann Heinrich Schröder (Baron from 1868)	– Full
1818 – 1824	Francis Gill	– Associate
1824 – 1849	Hermann Otto von Post	– Associate
1849 – 1910	John Henry William Schröder (Baron from 1868)	– Full
1849 – 1870	Alexander Schlüsser	– Full
1862 – 1870/92	Otto von der Meden	– Associate/Full
1870 – 1907	Henry Frederic Tiarks	– Full
1895 – 1940	Rudolph Bruno Schröder (Baron from 1904)	– Full
1902 – 1952	Frank Cyril Tiarks	– Full
1906 – 1940	Julius Rittershaussen	– Associate
1919 – 1955	Albert Pam	– Associate
1926 – 1957	Helmut William Bruno Schroder	– Full
1926 – 1953/62	Henry Frederic Tiarks	– Full/Associate
1932 – 1956	Veritas Trust Ltd	– Corporate
1946 – 1957	Toby Caulfeild	– Associate
1946 – 1957	Lord Strathallan (Perth from 1951)	– Associate
1946 – 1957	Alexander Abel Smith	– Associate
1949 – 1952	Ralph Rendell	– Associate
1950 – 1957	Jonathan Backhouse	– Associate
1953 – 1957	Alec Cairns	– Associate
1953 – 1957	Schroder Successors Ltd	– Corporate
1957 – 1957	Alexander Hood	– Associate
1957 – 1957	Gordon Richardson	– Associate
1957 – 1957	Edward Tucker	– Associate

Directors (1957–1962)

1957 – 1962	Helmut Schroder (Chairman)
1957 – 1962	Gordon Richardson (Deputy Chairman from 1960)
1957 – 1962	Alexander Abel Smith
1957 – 1962	Jonathan Backhouse
1957 – 1962	Alec Cairns
1957 – 1962	Toby Caulfeild
1957 – 1962	Alexander Hood
1957 – 1962	Edward Tucker

Appendix II (ii)   J. Henry Schroder Banking Corporation, 1923–85

Directors

1923 – 1940	Baron Bruno Schröder (Chairman 1923–40)
1923 – 1945	Frank Tiarks
1940 – 1962	Helmut Schroder (Chairman 1940–62)
1945 – 1962	Henry Tiarks

Executive Directors

1923 – 1935	Prentiss Gray
1923 – 1930	Stephen Paul
1923 – 1926	F. Seaton Pemberton
1929 – 1971	Gerald Beal (Chairman 1962–67)
1931 – 1951	John Simpson
1934 – 1936	Carlton Fuller
1934 – 1968	Valla Lada-Mocarski
1942 – 1968	Harold Sutphen
1948 – 1973	Ernest Meili
1950 – 1970	Avery Rockefeller
1962 – 1985	John Howell (Chairman 1970–77)
1962 – 1966	R. Canon Clements
1967 – 1970	Gordon Richardson (Chairman 1967–70)
1969 – 1973	Peter Carpenter
1970 – 1973	Hermann Schwab
1970 – 1976	James Wolfensohn
1973 – 1979	Ramsay Wilson
1973 – 1985	Martin Witschi
1973 – 1983	Mark Maged (Chairman 1977–83)
1980 – 1986	John Connor
1984 – 1986	George Mallinckrodt (Chairman 1984–86)
1984 –	Colin Browning
1984 –	Peter Rona
1984 – 1984	Earl of Airlie
1984 – 1986	Jean Solandt
1984 – 1987	Michael Magdol

1984 – 1986	William Slee
1985 – 1990	Takeo Kani
1985 – 1988	Hiroshi Nakamura
1985 -	Norihide Yoshioka

Non-Executive Directors

1923 – 1950	Manuel Rionda
1923 – 1927	Gates McGarragh
1923 – 1933	Julius Barnes
1923 – 1935	George Zabriskie
1925 – 1932	Herbert Deans
1927 – 1933	John McHugh
1937 – 1942	Allen Dulles
1943 – 1955	DeLano Andrews
1947 – 1973	John Laylin
1948 – 1950	Robert Patterson
1949 – 1965	Charles Gibson
1950 – 1983	George Braga
1952 – 1966	Albert Williams
1955 – 1963	Norris Darrell
1958 – 1968	Dudley Dowell
1963 – 1978	Malcolm MacIntyre
1965 – 1973	Royal Firman Jr.
1966 – 1976	Bertram Witham
1969 – 1992	Charles Meares
1973 –	Norris Darrell Jr.
1973 – 1977	Winthrop Knowlton
1973 – 1986	William Turner Jr
1973 – 1979	Dr Hugo Uyterhoeven
1974 – 1976	Dr Richard Cooper
1974 –	Bayless Manning
1978 – 1989	Edward Michaelsen
1981 – 1990	Alonzo McDonald
1986 -	Alva Way (Chairman 1986 –)

Appendix II (iii)   Helbert, Wagg & Co., 1848–1962

Trading Names

1848 – 1857	Helbert, Wagg & Co.
1857 – 1870	Helbert & Wagg
1870 – 1877	Helbert, Wagg & Co.
1877 – 1888	Helbert, Wagg & Campbell
1888 – 1899	Helbert, Wagg & Co.
1899 – 1912	Helbert, Wagg & Russell
1913 – 1919	Helbert, Wagg & Co.
1919 – 1962	Helbert, Wagg & Co. Ltd

Partners (1848–1919)

1848 – 1857	John Helbert
1848 – 1857	John Wagg
1848 – 1866	Lionel Helbert
1857 – 1870	William Barley
1864 – 1919	Arthur Wagg
1870 – 1919	Edward Wagg
1877 – 1888	Lord Walter Campbell
1888 – 1902	Arthur Haydon
1888 – 1912	Hon. Cyril Russell
1903 – 1919	Alfred Wagg
1913 – 1919	Adolph Schwelm

Directors (1919–1962)

1919 – 1958	Alfred Wagg (Chairman 1923–53)
1919 – 1933	Edward Wagg
1919 – 1958	Walter Barrington
1919 – 1947	Nigel Campbell
1921 – 1938	Max Bonn
1923 – 1944	Lawrence Jones
1923 – 1957	Albert Palache
1933 – 1946	Gordon Munro, MC
1934 – 1962	Lionel Fraser, CMG (Deputy Chairman 1946–54, Chairman from 1954)
1946 – 1962	Alan Russell
1948 – 1962	Gordon Gunson, CA
1948 – 1957	James O'Brien, MC
1948 – 1962	Michael Verey, TD
1949 – 1962	Charles Villiers, MC
1956 – 1962	Robert Hollond
1956 – 1962	Ashley Ponsonby, MC
1956 – 1962	David Murison, MBE

Appendix II (iv) Schroders Limited/Schroders plc, 1959–92

Executive Directors

1959 – 1965	Helmut Schroder (Chairman 1959 – 1965)
1959 – 1973	Gordon Richardson (Deputy Chairman 1964–1965; Chairman 1965 – 1973)
1959 – 1967	Gerald Beal
1960 – 1963	Lionel Fraser
1962 – 1965	Henry Tiarks
1963 – 1970	Jonathan Backhouse
1963 – 1970	Alan Russell
1966 – 1982	John Howell

1966 – 1983	John Bayley (Joint Deputy Chairman 1977–83)
1966 – 1977	Michael Verey (Chairman 1973–77)
1969–72/1974–85	John Hull (Joint Deputy Chairman 1977–85)
1970 – 1984	Earl of Airlie (Chairman 1977–84)
1970 – 1975	Leslie Murphy (Deputy Chairman 1973–75)
1970 – 1977	James Wolfensohn (Executive Deputy Chairman 1974–77)
1974 – 1978	David Forsyth
1975 – 1983	Mark Maged
1976 – 1990	Geoffrey Williams
1977 –	George Mallinckrodt (Chairman 1984–)
1980 – 1987	John Connor
1980 – 1985	Michael Bentley
1982 – 1986	Gordon Popham
1982 –	Jean Solandt
1983 –	Win Bischoff (Group Chief Executive 1984–)
1983 – 1991	Benjamin Strickland
1984 –	William Slee
1986 – 1989	Frederick Klingenstein
1986 – 1987	Robert Shapiro
1986 –	James Harmon
1987 –	Peter Sedgwick
1990 –	Adam Broadbent
1991 –	Hon Nicholas MacAndrew

Non-Executive Directors

1959 – 1970	Norris Darrell
1962 – 1976	Earl of Perth
1963 –	Bruno Schroder
1968 – 1984	Lord Franks
1969 – 1976	Paul Nitze
1970 – 1977	Dr Harold Brown
1974 – 1989	Sir Ernest Woodroofe
1979 –	Baron Daniel Janssen
1980 – 1989	Sir Leslie Murphy
1984 –	William Turner Jr.
1985–86/1991 –	Alva Way
1987 – 1989	Sir John Bremridge
1990 –	Sir Ralph Robins
1990 –	Charles Sinclair

Appendix III: Staff

J. Henry Schröder & Co., 1830 – 1960

	Staff (excluding partners)
1830	7
1840	7
1850	16
1860	21
1870	30
1880	35
1890	36
1900	35
1910	40
1920	83
1924	c 650
1930	282
1940	c 115
1950	191
1960	281

J. Henry Schroder Wagg & Co. Ltd and other UK Companies, 1965–90

1965	500
1970	725
1975	798
1980	909
1985	1,471
1990	1,494

Schroder Group Employees Worldwide, 1990

1990	3,311

Appendix IV (i) J. Henry Schröder & Co., Balance Sheet, 1852–1958

31 December
£

1852–93

	Liabilities				Assets			
	Partners' Capital	*Acceptances*	*Deposits & Client Balances*	*Total*	*Commercial Bills*	*Cash, Securities, Advances, Other Assets*	*Customers' Liabilities for Acceptances*	*Total*
1852	261,000			n/a				n/a
1853	285,000			n/a				n/a
1854	306,000			n/a				n/a
1855	328,000			n/a				n/a
1856	357,000			n/a				n/a
1857	n/a			n/a				n/a
1858	n/a			n/a				n/a
1859	n/a			n/a				n/a
1860	453,000			n/a				n/a
1861	484,000	1,387,000	146,000	2,017,000	472,000	158,000	1,387,000	2,017,000
1862	523,000	1,037,000	121,000	1,681,000	387,000	257,000	1,037,000	1,681,000
1863	589,000	983,000	321,000	1,893,000	655,000	255,000	983,000	1,893,000
1864	600,000	1,329,000	221,000	2,150,000	510,000	311,000	1,329,000	2,150,000
1865	655,000	1,491,000	45,000	2,191,000	534,000	166,000	1,491,000	2,191,000
1866	699,000	1,871,000	155,000	2,725,000	732,000	122,000	1,871,000	2,725,000
1867	721,000	1,714,000	102,000	2,537,000	727,000	96,000	1,714,000	2,537,000
1868	779,000	2,102,000	735,000	3,616,000	943,000	571,000	2,102,000	3,616,000
1869	821,000	2,585,000	355,000	3,761,000	729,000	447,000	2,585,000	3,761,000

	Liabilities				Assets			
	Partners' Capital	Acceptances	Deposits & Client Balances	Total	Commercial Bills	Cash, Securities, Advances, Other Assets	Customers' Liabilities for Acceptances	Total
1870	891,000	3,219,000	1,103,000	5,213,000	1,190,000	804,000	3,219,000	5,213,000
1871	947,000	2,821,000	646,000	4,414,000	776,000	817,000	2,821,000	4,414,000
1872	1,145,000	4,187,000	511,000	5,843,000	1,297,000	359,000	4,187,000	5,843,000
1873	1,346,000	4,079,000	1,089,000	6,514,000	1,183,000	1,252,000	4,079,000	6,514,000
1874	1,533,000	3,732,000	563,000	5,828,000	972,000	1,124,000	3,732,000	5,828,000
1875	1,686,000	4,553,000	441,000	6,680,000	995,000	1,132,000	4,553,000	6,680,000
1876	1,892,000	3,352,000	327,000	5,571,000	950,000	1,269,000	3,352,000	5,571,000
1877	1,914,000	2,441,000	458,000	4,813,000	763,000	1,609,000	2,441,000	4,813,000
1878	1,612,000	1,784,000	259,000	3,655,000	827,000	1,044,000	1,784,000	3,655,000
1879	1,429,000	2,051,000	225,000	3,705,000	675,000	979,000	2,051,000	3,705,000
1880	1,423,000	1,973,000	180,000	3,576,000	474,000	1,129,000	1,973,000	3,576,000
1881	1,383,000	2,256,000	287,000	3,926,000	784,000	886,000	2,256,000	3,926,000
1882	1,481,000	2,128,000	209,000	3,818,000	673,000	1,017,000	2,128,000	3,818,000
1883	679,000	2,299,000	648,000	3,626,000	736,000	591,000	2,299,000	3,626,000
1884	718,000	2,325,000	483,000	3,526,000	586,000	615,000	2,325,000	3,526,000
1885	672,000	2,472,000	389,000	3,533,000	695,000	366,000	2,472,000	3,533,000
1886	701,000	2,661,000	380,000	3,742,000	569,000	512,000	2,661,000	3,742,000
1887	770,000	3,748,000	548,000	5,066,000	659,000	659,000	3,748,000	5,066,000
1888	845,000	4,443,000	614,000	5,902,000	794,000	665,000	4,443,000	5,902,000
1889	1,038,000	3,773,000	492,000	5,303,000	833,000	697,000	3,773,000	5,303,000
1890	1,149,000	4,256,000	406,000	5,811,000	1,068,000	487,000	4,256,000	5,811,000
1891	1,195,000	4,313,000	310,000	5,818,000	887,000	618,000	4,313,000	5,818,000
1892	1,095,000	3,960,000	203,000	5,258,000	878,000	420,000	3,960,000	5,258,000
1893	1,125,000	4,783,000	185,000	6,092,000	1,253,000	56,000	4,783,000	6,092,000

1894–1958

	Liabilities				Assets			
	Partners' Capital	Acceptances	Deposits & Client Balances	Total	Cash, Call Loans, Bills	Securities, Advances, Other Assets	Customers' Liabilities for Acceptances	Total
1894	1,172,000	4,779,000	636,000	6,587,000	604,000	1,204,000	4,779,000	6,587,000
1895	1,174,000	4,957,000	214,000	6,345,000	663,000	725,000	4,957,000	6,345,000
1896	1,238,000	5,087,000	218,000	6,543,000	644,000	812,000	5,087,000	6,543,000
1897	1,339,000	4,472,000	606,000	6,417,000	528,000	1,147,000	4,742,000	6,417,000
1898	1,466,000	5,777,000	427,000	7,670,000	680,000	1,213,000	5,777,000	7,670,000
1899	1,636,000	5,652,000	427,000	7,715,000	672,000	1,391,000	5,652,000	7,715,000
1900	1,435,000	6,055,000	828,000	8,318,000	817,000	1,446,000	6,055,000	8,318,000
1901	1,565,000	6,199,000	617,000	8,381,000	671,000	1,511,000	6,199,000	8,381,000
1902	1,709,000	6,048,000	671,000	8,428,000	545,000	1,835,000	6,048,000	8,428,000
1903	1,822,000	6,724,000	1,777,000	10,323,000	796,000	2,803,000	6,724,000	10,323,000
1904	1,922,000	6,837,000	1,117,000	9,876,000	637,000	2,402,000	6,837,000	9,876,000
1905	1,979,000	8,776,000	1,244,000	11,999,000	304,000	2,919,000	8,776,000	11,999,000
1906	2,031,000	10,284,000	1,458,000	13,773,000	575,000	2,914,000	10,284,000	13,773,000
1907	2,153,000	11,736,000	1,624,000	15,513,000	1,139,000	2,638,000	11,736,000	15,513,000
1908	2,359,000	9,328,000	4,307,000	15,994,000	1,194,000	5,472,000	9,328,000	15,994,000
1909	2,857,000	10,182,000	4,730,000	17,769,000	1,608,000	5,979,000	10,182,000	17,769,000
1910	2,530,000	10,632,000	5,485,000	18,647,000	1,854,000	6,161,000	10,632,000	18,647,000
1911	2,879,000	11,295,000	6,653,000	20,827,000	1,276,000	8,256,000	11,295,000	20,827,000
1912	3,301,000	11,948,000	5,557,000	20,806,000	2,450,000	6,408,000	11,948,000	20,806,000
1913	3,544,000	11,663,000	3,902,000	19,109,000	1,862,000	5,584,000	11,663,000	19,109,000
1914	3,535,000	5,825,000	3,766,000	13,126,000	2,375,000	4,926,000	5,825,000	13,126,000
1915	3,095,000	3,867,000	3,862,000	10,824,000	2,081,000	4,876,000	3,867,000	10,824,000
1916	3,054,000	1,637,000	5,597,000	10,288,000	989,000	7,662,000	1,637,000	10,288,000

| | Liabilities | | | | Assets | | | |
	Partners' Capital	Acceptances	Deposits & Client Balances	Total	Cash, Call Loans, Bills	Securities, Advances, Other Assets	Customers' Liabilities for Acceptances	Total
1917	3,104,000	634,000	7,737,000	11,475,000	2,813,000	8,028,000	634,000	11,475,000
1918	3,159,000	1,255,000	8,265,000	12,679,000	3,501,000	7,923,000	1,255,000	12,679,000
1919	3,259,000	2,844,000	5,640,000	11,743,000	1,696,000	7,203,000	2,844,000	11,743,000
1920	2,938,000	7,808,000	4,623,000	15,369,000	3,408,000	4,153,000	7,808,000	15,369,000
1921	2,717,000	8,558,000	7,771,000	19,046,000	5,667,000	4,821,000	8,558,000	19,046,000
1922	2,880,000	10,622,000	10,023,000	23,525,000	7,819,000	5,084,000	10,622,000	23,525,000
1923	2,971,000	11,707,000	13,113,000	27,791,000	8,798,000	7,286,000	11,707,000	27,791,000
1924	3,208,000	13,654,000	13,480,000	30,342,000	11,044,000	5,644,000	13,654,000	30,342,000
1925	3,224,000	13,972,000	11,325,000	28,521,000	8,773,000	5,776,000	13,972,000	28,521,000
1926	3,212,000	9,651,000	9,853,000	22,716,000	7,472,000	5,593,000	9,651,000	22,716,000
1927	3,131,000	10,832,000	9,328,000	23,291,000	6,394,000	6,065,000	10,832,000	23,291,000
1928	3,158,000	13,821,000	10,450,000	27,429,000	7,000,000	6,608,000	13,821,000	27,429,000
1929	3,202,000	12,829,000	9,954,000	25,985,000	6,010,000	7,146,000	12,829,000	25,985,000
1930	3,173,000	11,547,000	8,759,000	23,479,000	5,584,000	6,348,000	11,547,000	23,479,000
1931	2,509,000	6,858,000	4,396,000	13,763,000	2,396,000	4,509,000	6,858,000	13,763,000
1932	2,391,000	5,503,000	3,303,000	11,197,000	2,212,000	3,482,000	5,503,000	11,197,000
1933	2,424,000	5,343,000	4,765,000	12,532,000	2,350,000	4,839,000	5,343,000	12,532,000
1934	2,111,000	5,375,000	4,697,000	12,183,000	2,134,000	4,674,000	5,375,000	12,183,000
1935	2,192,000	5,227,000	5,465,000	12,884,000	1,692,000	5,965,000	5,227,000	12,884,000
1936	2,358,000	4,784,000	6,961,000	14,103,000	1,916,000	7,403,000	4,784,000	14,103,000
1937	2,269,000	3,731,000	6,745,000	12,745,000	1,344,000	7,670,000	3,731,000	12,745,000
1938	2,090,000	4,368,000	5,337,000	11,795,000	1,673,000	5,754,000	4,368,000	11,795,000
1939	2,047,000	1,151,000	6,889,000	10,087,000	262,000	8,674,000	1,151,000	10,087,000

	Liabilities				Assets			
	Partners' Capital	Acceptances	Deposits & Client Balances	Total	Cash, Call Loans, Bills	Securities, Advances, Other Assets	Customers' Liabilities for Acceptances	Total
1940	495,000	362,000	2,238,000	3,095,000	160,000	2,573,000	362,000	3,095,000
1941	352,000	301,000	2,691,000	3,344,000	214,000	2,829,000	301,000	3,344,000
1942	72,000	121,000	4,309,000	4,502,000	1,200,000	3,181,000	121,000	4,502,000
1943	643,000	300,000	2,835,000	3,778,000	347,000	3,131,000	300,000	3,778,000
1944	774,000	157,000	3,776,000	4,707,000	1,319,000	3,231,000	157,000	4,707,000
1945	778,000	261,000	3,954,000	4,993,000	1,282,000	3,450,000	261,000	4,993,000
1946	1,071,000	1,510,000	4,599,000	7,180,000	1,168,000	4,502,000	1,510,000	7,180,000
1947	1,349,000	3,057,000	5,624,000	10,030,000	2,242,000	4,731,000	3,057,000	10,030,000
1948	1,491,000	2,768,000	4,608,000	8,867,000	1,454,000	4,645,000	2,768,000	8,867,000
1949	1,616,000	3,387,000	4,647,000	9,650,000	1,987,000	4,276,000	3,387,000	9,650,000
1950	1,903,000	5,275,000	7,825,000	15,003,000	6,808,000	2,920,000	5,275,000	15,003,000
1951	2,156,000	5,440,000	8,504,000	16,100,000	7,343,000	3,317,000	5,440,000	16,100,000
1952	2,241,000	4,683,000	8,219,000	15,143,000	7,560,000	2,900,000	4,683,000	15,143,000
1953	2,401,000	4,747,000	16,283,000	23,431,000	12,536,000	6,148,000	4,747,000	23,431,000
1954	2,451,000	5,755,000	17,077,000	25,283,000	5,521,000	14,007,000	5,755,000	25,283,000
1955	2,888,000	7,176,000	14,267,000	24,331,000	6,165,000	10,990,000	7,176,000	24,331,000
1956	3,133,000	6,366,000	13,103,000	22,602,000	5,948,000	10,288,000	6,366,000	22,602,000
1957	2,146,000	8,403,000	12,447,000	22,996,000	6,921,000	7,672,000	8,403,000	22,996,000
1958	2,146,000	7,749,000	16,886,000	26,781,000	9,504,000	9,528,000	7,749,000	26,781,000

n/a not available

Appendix IV (ii) J. Henry Schröder & Co., Profit & Loss Account, 1852–1958

£	Revenues						Costs		Profits
	Acceptances	Consignments	Issuing & Underwriting	Net Interest	Other	Total	Administration	Bad Debts	
1852	24,000		—	5,000	n/a	n/a	n/a	n/a	31,000
1853	34,000		—	5,000	n/a	n/a	n/a	n/a	39,000
1854	35,000		—	6,000	n/a	n/a	n/a	n/a	35,000
1855	38,000		—	—	n/a	n/a	n/a	n/a	43,000
1856	45,000		—	—	n/a	n/a	n/a	n/a	48,000
1857	51,000		—	—	n/a	n/a	n/a	n/a	n/a
1858	44,000		—	—	n/a	n/a	n/a	n/a	n/a
1859	50,000		—	—	n/a	n/a	n/a	n/a	45,000
1860	48,000		—	—	n/a	n/a	n/a	n/a	n/a
1861	79,000		—	6,000	6,000	91,000	6,000	51,000	32,000
1862	60,000		—	8,000	4,000	72,000	7,000	9,000	56,000
1863	48,000		54,000	10,000	8,000	120,000	8,000	6,000	106,000
1864	43,000		7,000	13,000	8,000	71,000	12,000	9,000	50,000
1865	73,000		—	9,000	9,000	91,000	8,000	23,000	60,000
1866	71,000		—	12,000	9,000	92,000	8,000	19,000	65,000
1867	82,000		—	5,000	5,000	92,000	14,000	12,000	66,000
1868	76,000		6,000	4,000	7,000	93,000	10,000	11,000	72,000
1869	88,000		1,000	9,000	12,000	110,000	11,000	32,000	67,000
1870	96,000		47,000	17,000	5,000	165,000	11,000	28,000	126,000
1871	77,000	44,000	4,000	10,000	*10,000	145,000	16,000	—	129,000
1872	88,000	39,000	23,000	15,000	*34,000	199,000	15,000	2,000	182,000
1873	80,000	25,000	32,000	17,000	*55,000	209,000	14,000	—	195,000
1874	76,000	27,000	37,000	8,000	*61,000	209,000	14,000	—	195,000
1875	75,000	30,000	31,000	6,000	*64,000	206,000	14,000	31,000	161,000

£	Revenues						Costs		Profits
	Acceptances	Consignments	Issuing & Underwriting	Net Interest	Other	Total	Administration	Bad Debts	
1876	64,000	45,000	—	4,000	*115,000	228,000	14,000	13,000	201,000
1877	47,000	29,000	—	(1,000)	*157,000	232,000	15,000	51,000	166,000
1878	42,000	30,000	—	12,000	*55,000	139,000	14,000	41,000	84,000
1879	35,000	23,000	—	1,000	*6,000	65,000	15,000	46,000	4,000
1880	36,000	18,000	17,000	2,000	*9,000	65,000	13,000	3,000	49,000
1881	34,000	12,000	—	7,000	*6,000	76,000	14,000	—	62,000
1882	39,000	18,000	—	10,000	*4,000	71,000	13,000	—	58,000
1883	36,000	12,000	—	—	3,000	51,000	14,000	11,000	26,000
1884	34,000	11,000	—	(10,000)	6,000	41,000	15,000	24,000	2,000
1885	36,000	12,000	—	(10,000)	5,000	43,000	13,000	8,000	22,000
1886	41,000	11,000	16,000	—	5,000	73,000	13,000	15,000	45,000
1887	42,000	9,000	13,000	2,000	7,000	73,000	13,000	—	60,000
1888	51,000	19,000	52,000	9,000	10,000	141,000	15,000	12,000	114,000
1889	48,000	13,000	69,000	8,000	11,000	149,000	16,000	—	133,000
1890	43,000	8,000	115,000	10,000	8,000	184,000	16,000	16,000	152,000
1891	51,000	5,000	17,000	(1,000)	6,000	78,000	16,000	—	62,000
1892	52,000	2,000	36,000	(6,000)	6,000	90,000	16,000	3,000	72,000
1893	61,000	—	—	7,000	12,000	80,000	16,000	20,000	44,000
1894	55,000	13,000	23,000	(6,000)	12,000	97,000	17,000	49,000	31,000
1895	59,000	4,000	—	(2,000)	15,000	76,000	14,000	6,000	56,000
1896	69,000	13,000	18,000	3,000	10,000	113,000	15,000	10,000	88,000
1897	77,000	—	28,000	12,000	8,000	125,000	14,000	11,000	100,000
1898	77,000	22,000	53,000	20,000	6,000	178,000	15,000	16,000	147,000
1899	78,000	28,000	52,000	32,000	6,000	196,000	17,000	18,000	161,000
1900	77,000	10,000	1,000	27,000	7,000	122,000	20,000	10,000	92,000
1901	78,000	19,000	32,000	22,000	11,000	162,000	22,000	14,000	126,000

£	Revenues						Costs		Profits
	Acceptances	Consignments	Issuing & Underwriting	Net Interest	Other	Total	Administration	Bad Debts	
1902	84,000	19,000	7,000	24,000	11,000	145,000	22,000	12,000	111,000
1903	84,000	6,000	18,000	35,000	8,000	151,000	18,000	13,000	120,000
1904	95,000	17,000	15,000	39,000	14,000	180,000	21,000	16,000	143,000
1905	89,000	24,000	80,000	46,000	13,000	252,000	21,000	23,000	208,000
1906	115,000	2,000	118,000	51,000	14,000	300,000	25,000	27,000	248,000
1907	138,000	–	99,000	78,000	12,000	327,000	25,000	30,000	272,000
1908	149,000	27,000	67,000	40,000	16,000	299,000	29,000	27,000	243,000
1909	123,000	55,000	301,000	68,000	17,000	564,000	54,000	15,000	495,000
1910	126,000	1,000	107,000	77,000	32,000	343,000	39,000	30,000	274,000
1911	131,000	2,000	206,000	92,000	43,000	474,000	42,000	43,000	389,000
1912	141,000	35,000	255,000	107,000	39,000	577,000	47,000	53,000	477,000
1913	163,000	–	277,000	110,000	47,000	597,000	46,000	123,000	428,000

Appendix IV (ii)

	Revenues					Costs	Reserves	Profits
	Acceptances	Issuing & Underwriting	Net Interest	Other	Total	Administration		
1914	117,000	18,000	90,000	15,000	60,000	46,000	395,000	(379,000)
1915	52,000	–	(111,000)	30,000	(28,000)	41,000	–	(69,000)
1916	32,000	2,000	(86,000)	14,000	(38,000)	39,000	–	(77,000)
1917	21,000	29,000	(60,000)	24,000	14,000	49,000	–	(35,000)
1918	26,000	39,000	(58,000)	25,000	32,000	68,000	–	(36,000)
1919	36,000	–	48,000	61,000	145,000	51,000	–	94,000
1920	129,000	11,000	53,000	33,000	226,000	76,000	81,000	69,000
1921	190,000	117,000	115,000	46,000	468,000	104,000	333,000	31,000
1922	288,000	249,000	73,000	27,000	637,000	155,000	237,000	245,000
1923	420,000	133,000	223,000	(12,000)	764,000	252,000	69,000	443,000
1924	517,000	293,000	215,000	(1,000)	1024,000	356,000	49,000	619,000
1925	413,000	280,000	179,000	51,000	923,000	385,000	57,000	481,000
1926	315,000	154,000	166,000	52,000	687,000	314,000	246,000	127,000
1927	222,000	161,000	147,000	47,000	577,000	256,000	118,000	203,000
1928	251,000	363,000	164,000	81,000	859,000	257,000	203,000	399,000
1929	243,000	122,000	212,000	58,000	635,000	266,000	132,000	237,000
1930	221,000	266,000	118,000	(12,000)	593,000	257,000	142,000	194,000
1931	193,000	153,000	123,000	(139,000)	330,000	188,000	437,000	(295,000)
1932	147,000	31,000	(38,000)	166,000	306,000	151,000	342,000	(187,000)
1933	117,000	20,000	(13,000)	124,000	248,000	137,000	25,000	86,000
1934	123,000	61,000	–	(78,000)	106,000	171,000	218,000	(283,000)
1935	108,000	38,000	(8,000)	128,000	266,000	148,000	158,000	(40,000)
1936	92,000	96,000	45,000	227,000	460,000	147,000	22,000	291,000
1937	99,000	12,000	78,000	27,000	216,000	218,000	–	(2,000)
1938	96,000	19,000	50,000	(68,000)	97,000	184,000	21,000	(108,000)

	Revenues					Costs		
	Acceptances	Issuing & Underwriting	Net Interest	Other	Total	Administration	Reserves	Profits
1939	99,000	17,000	10,000	24,000	150,000	155,000	13,000	(18,000)
1940	10,000	16,000	61,000	166,000	253,000	147,000	73,000	33,0000
1941	11,000	44,000	24,000	(3,000)	76,000	101,000	9,000	(34,000)
1942	10,000	7,000	35,000	115,000	167,000	102,000	12,000	53,000
1943	7,000	12,000	30,000	83,000	132,000	108,000	16,000	8,000
1944	11,000	1,000	47,000	107,000	166,000	104,000	3,000	59,000
1945	5,000	19,000	48,000	71,000	143,000	105,000	1,000	37,000
1946	61,000	21,000	25,000	307,000	414,000	128,000	5,000	281,000
1947	74,000	14,000	12,000	180,000	280,000	146,000	39,000	95,000
1948	104,000	24,000	19,000	223,000	370,000	165,000	3,000	202,000
1949	108,000	29,000	17,000	177,000	331,000	193,000	33,000	105,000
1950	151,000	21,000	38,000	231,000	441,000	220,000	18,000	203,000
1951	188,000	28,000	79,000	152,000	447,000	253,000	25,000	169,000
1952	186,000	18,000	132,000	167,000	503,000	290,000	52,000	160,000
1953	148,000	6,000	164,000	247,000	565,000	301,000	65,000	199,000
1954	181,000	69,000	117,000	420,000	787,000	338,000	212,000	237,000
1955	184,000	63,000	46,000	499,000	792,000	373,000	464,000	(45,000)
1956	186,000	62,000	116,000	390,000	754,000	380,000	3,000	371,000
1957	288,000	137,000	145,000	344,000	914,000	411,000	258,000	245,000
1958	211,000	102,000	158,000	444,000	915,000	461,000	267,000	187,000

n/a not available

Appendix IV (iii) J. Henry Schroder Banking Corporation and Schroder Trust Company, Balance Sheet and Profits, 1923–62

$ million
31 December

	J. Henry Schroder Banking Corporation				Schroder Trust Company
	Capital and Surplus (1)	Acceptances	Total Liabilities/Assets	Profits After Tax (1)	Total Liabilities/Assets
1923	3.2	.2	10.7	—	—
1924	3.5	11.3	27.9	.3	—
1925	4.0	11.5	31.3	.5	—
1926	5.0	12.6	35.3	1.1	—
1927	5.7	21.4	49.2	.7	—
1928	6.6	22.3	55.7	1.0	—
1929	9.4	34.2	71.8	1.0	—
1930	10.3	33.5	76.6	.9	4.6
1931	7.5	15.3	39.6	(2.8)	5.5
1932	7.7	12.7	35.0	.1	5.8
1933	6.6	4.8	24.0	(1.0)	8.4
1934	6.7	3.9	25.9	—	11.4
1935	6.8	4.4	29.5	.2	14.7
1936	7.0	4.9	33.9	.7	19.0
1937	7.3	6.3	37.8	.8	20.3
1938	7.5	8.7	46.8	.5	24.0
1939	7.5	8.9	45.1	.3	25.7
1940	7.6	5.6	41.6	.3	25.4
1941	7.6	6.7	37.8	.2	25.9
1942	7.6	6.1	48.7	.3	29.3
1943	7.6	5.8	46.6	.4	32.2

	J. Henry Schroder Banking Corporation				Schroder Trust Company
	Capital and Surplus (1)	Acceptances	Total Liabilities/Assets	Profits After Tax (1)	Total Liabilities/Assets
1944	7.7	6.4	60.4	.5	44.4
1945	8.2	8.5	65.6	.4	46.4
1946	8.3	14.8	79.3	.4	35.4
1947	8.3	9.7	63.1	.4	37.9
1948	8.3	8.6	79.9	.4	38.4
1949	8.5	11.3	95.7	.5	41.9
1950	9.0	14.1	106.1	.8	42.3
1951	9.0	17.5	93.9	.7	45.3
1952	9.2	18.1	103.7	.7	50.3
1953	9.5	18.9	103.4	.7	69.8
1954	9.8	24.5	131.1	.6	86.5
1955	10.0	24.3	118.4	.7	71.6
1956	10.3	19.8	131.7	.9	68.5
1957	10.6	23.2	133.2	1.0	74.4
1958	11.0	21.8	121.2	.6	97.7
1959	12.2	23.0	119.2	.7	70.3
1960	12.3	42.0	144.8	.6	76.7
1961	12.4	40.2	154.5	1.2	87.2
1962	13.3	34.6	143.8	.9	87.9

(1) These figures are prepared on an unconsolidated basis and do not include the accumulated reserves or profits of subsidiaries of J. Henry Schroder Banking Corporation, notably the Schroder Trust Company.

Appendix IV (iv)   Helbert, Wagg & Co., Balance Sheet, 1915–61

£
31 December

31 December	Capital and Reserves	Total Liabilities/Assets	31 December	Capital and Reserves	Total Liabilities/Assets
1915	272,000	1,064,000	1939	572,000	1,290,000
1916	200,000	1,767,000	1940	555,000	1,062,000
1917	200,000	3,209,000	1941	561,000	1,040,000
1918	225,000	4,073,000	1942	563,000	1,265,000
1919	492,000	722,000	1943	563,000	1,027,000
1920	492,000	828,000	1944	563,000	1,155,000
1921	491,000	780,000	1945	564,000	1,745,000
1922	490,000	2,095,000	1946	582,000	2,114,000
1923	513,000	1,255,000	1947	583,000	2,538,000
1924	517,000	1,582,000	1948	617,000	2,231,000
1925	518,000	2,235,000	1949	623,000	2,353,000
1926	520,000	1,974,000	1950	636,000	2,654,000
1927	530,000	2,258,000	1951	695,000	2,533,000
1928	555,000	1,942,000	1952	662,000	2,390,000
1929	565,000	1,574,000	1953	676,000	2,387,000
1930	560,000	1,506,000	1954	749,000	3,038,000
1931	506,000	1,499,000	1955	789,000	3,040,000
1932	540,000	1,482,000	1956	847,000	2,755,000
1933	557,000	2,759,000	1957	844,000	3,962,000
1934	560,000	2,976,000	1958	971,000	4,998,000
1935	562,000	2,107,000	1959	1,355,000	7,013,000
1936	577,000	2,775,000	1960	1,452,000	5,102,000
1937	575,000	2,095,000	1961	1,646,000	6,509,000
1938	576,000	1,479,000			

Appendix IV (v) Helbert, Wagg & Co., Profit & Loss Account, 1915–61

£	Revenues Issuing	Stocks & Shares Trading and other Revenues	Total Revenues	Costs Operating and Other Expenses	Profits Operating Profits	Preference/ Ordinary Dividends and Bonuses	Retained Earnings for year
1915	–	32,000	32,000	29,000	3,000	–	(10,000)
1916	–	17,000	17,000	15,000	2,000	–	(8,000)
1917	–	31,000	31,000	13,000	18,000	–	8,000
1918	–	54,000	54,000	46,000	8,000	–	(1,000)
1919	–	21,000	21,000	11,000	10,000	–	–
1920	21,000	17,000	44,000	22,000	22,000	25,000	(3,000)
1921	18,000	34,000	52,000	34,000	18,000	17,000	1,000
1922	116,000	89,000	205,000	65,000	140,000	141,000	(1,000)
1923	140,000	117,000	257,000	72,000	185,000	185,000	–
1924	68,000	103,000	171,000	39,000	132,000	133,000	(1,000)
1925	112,000	77,000	189,000	63,000	126,000	126,000	–
1926	79,000	96,000	175,000	54,000	121,000	121,000	–
1927	193,000	125,000	318,000	63,000	255,000	249,000	6,000
1928	246,000	182,000	428,000	83,000	345,000	331,000	14,000
1929	100,000	95,000	195,000	64,000	131,000	127,000	4,000
1930	132,000	34,000	166,000	65,000	101,000	106,000	(5,000)
1931	34,000	6,000	40,000	78,000	(38,000)	17,000	(51,000)
1932	30,000	111,000	141,000	90,000	51,000	17,000	34,000
1933	114,000	94,000	208,000	61,000	147,000	130,000	17,000
1934	91,000	155,000	246,000	80,000	166,000	163,000	3,000
1935	101,000	134,000	235,000	77,000	158,000	158,000	–
1936	112,000	188,000	300,000	82,000	218,000	212,000	6,000
1937	71,000	43,000	114,000	88,000	26,000	32,000	(6,000)

Year	Operating Profits	Investment Income	Total Profits	Directors' & Auditors' Fees	Taxation	Net Income	Dividends
1938	58,000	56,000	114,000	82,000	32,000	32,000	—
1939	41,000	69,000	110,000	82,000	28,000	32,000	(4,000)
1940	4,000	60,000	64,000	64,000	—	17,000	(17,000)
1941	27,000	86,000	113,000	60,000	53,000	47,000	6,000
1942	9,000	85,000	94,000	61,000	33,000	32,000	1,000
1943	36,000	75,000	111,000	54,000	57,000	58,000	1,000
1944	13,000	107,000	120,000	50,000	70,000	71,000	1,000
1945	7,000	138,000	145,000	74,000	71,000	71,000	—
1946	—	269,000	269,000	153,000	116,000	98,000	18,000
1947	57,000	87,000	144,000	106,000	38,000	38,000	—

Year	Operating Profits	Investment Income	Total Profits	Directors' & Auditors' Fees	Taxation	Net Income	Dividends
1948	103,000	21,000	124,000	49,000	48,000	27,000	10,000
1949	111,000	24,000	135,000	51,000	56,000	28,000	26,000
1950	93,000	20,000	113,000	23,000	62,000	28,000	26,000
1951	163,000	26,000	189,000	28,000	98,000	63,000	28,000
1952	64,000	26,000	89,000	17,000	43,000	29,000	25,000
1953	108,000	19,000	127,000	17,000	68,000	41,000	27,000
1954	220,000	23,000	243,000	22,000	127,000	99,000	30,000
1955	157,000	25,000	182,000	28,000	92,000	62,000	31,000
1956	196,000	33,000	229,000	30,000	120,000	80,000	34,000
1957	126,000	36,000	162,000	40,000	77,000	44,000	34,000
1958	271,000	37,000	308,000	53,000	161,000	94,000	38,000
1959	622,000	55,000	677,000	69,000	332,000	275,000	49,000
1960	550,000	67,000	617,000	87,000	291,000	239,000	119,000
1961	632,000	67,000	699,000	90,000	342,000	267,000	89,000

Appendix IV (vi) Schroders Limited/Schroders plc, Consolidated Accounts, 1959–91

£ million

	Equity Capital and Disclosed Reserves	Total Liabilities/ Assets	Disclosed Profits Before Extraordinary Items	Extraordinary Items	Total Disclosed Profits After Tax
	31 Dec	31 Dec			
1959	12.5	98.7	.1	—	.1
1960	11.9	137.2	.5	—	.5
1961	12.2	160.3	.6	—	.6
1962	12.7	162.8	.6	—	.6
1963	13.2	191.5	.8	—	.8
1964	13.6	208.1	.7	—	.7
1965	14.0	236.2	.8	—	.8
1966	14.5	257.7	.8	—	.8
1967	18.7	333.1	1.3	—	1.3
1968	20.0	409.9	1.8	—	1.8
1969	19.4	450.6	1.6	—	1.6
1970	20.7	501.1	1.6	—	1.6
1971	21.1	486.0	2.0	—	2.0
1972	24.4	698.4	2.8	—	2.8
1973	25.8	773.4	2.6	—	2.6
1974	26.4	761.1	1.6	—	1.6
1975	32.0	823.8	3.2	—	3.2
1976	40.7	971.9	2.2	—	2.2
1977	44.9	1,132.3	4.0	—	4.0
1978	55.0	1,485.9	6.0	—	6.0

£ million

	Equity Capital and Disclosed Reserves 31 Dec	Total Liabilities/ Assets 31 Dec	Disclosed Profits Before Extraordinary Items	Extraordinary Items	Total Disclosed Profits After Tax
1979	57.9	1,748.8	6.8	–	6.8
1980	60.9	2,106.3	8.2	–	8.2
1981	83.7	2,767.1	15.6	–	15.6
1982	102.9	3,139.8	15.4	–	15.4
1983	124.8	3,395.0	14.4	6.5	20.9
1984	164.0	3,920.2	15.1	–	15.1
1985	171.6	2,161.7	16.3	12.9	29.2
1986	221.1	2,673.2	20.9	51.3	72.2
1987	227.4	2,816.7	27.1	–	27.1
1988	254.7	3,060.5	30.1	–	30.1
1989	313.1	3,675.2	46.6	–	46.6
1990	310.3	3,972.1	31.6	–	31.6
1991	360.6	4,142.5	52.1	2.3	54.4

Appendix V (i) Pound Sterling Purchasing Power, 1850–1990[1]

Year	Retail Price Index 1990 = 100	Multiple for Conversion of Contemporary Prices to 1990 Values	Annual Rate of Inflation per cent
1850	2.42	41.29	−5.25
1851	2.37	42.26	−2.30
1852	2.46	40.67	3.91
1853	3.05	32.79	24.03
1854	3.46	28.94	13.30
1855	3.52	28.40	1.92
1856	3.39	29.49	−3.71
1857	3.16	31.62	−6.75
1858	2.65	37.67	−16.05
1859	2.68	37.26	1.11
1860	3.00	33.32	11.83
1861	3.10	32.30	3.15
1862	2.96	33.81	−4.48
1863	2.79	35.90	−5.83
1864	2.77	36.16	−0.70
1865	2.78	35.91	0.69
1866	3.00	33.30	7.81
1867	3.37	29.64	12.37
1868	3.24	30.83	−3.87
1869	2.80	35.66	−13.53
1870	2.83	35.35	0.87
1871	2.92	34.26	3.19
1872	3.16	31.62	8.33
1873	3.28	30.50	3.68
1874	3.01	33.26	−8.30
1875	2.79	35.85	−7.23
1876	2.89	34.65	3.46
1877	2.69	37.11	−6.61
1878	2.53	39.58	−6.24
1879	2.43	41.12	−3.76
1880	2.56	39.12	5.12
1881	2.51	39.80	−1.70
1882	2.49	40.17	−0.93
1883	2.48	40.28	−0.28
1884	2.35	42.48	−5.18
1885	2.22	44.97	−5.53
1886	2.16	46.24	−2.75
1887	2.11	47.42	−2.49
1888	2.11	47.32	0.22

Year	Retail Price Index 1990 = 100	Multiple for Conversion of Contemporary Prices to 1990 Values	Annual Rate of Inflation per cent
1889	2.16	46.21	2.40
1890	2.16	46.37	−0.34
1891	2.17	46.11	0.56
1892	2.16	46.33	−0.46
1893	2.11	47.31	−2.08
1894	2.04	49.09	−3.63
1895	1.99	50.18	−2.16
1896	1.99	50.15	0.05
1897	2.04	48.91	2.54
1898	2.10	47.53	2.88
1899	2.07	48.41	−1.80
1900	2.18	45.95	5.35
1901	2.18	45.87	0.16
1902	2.18	45.89	−0.04
1903	2.20	45.38	1.14
1904	2.20	45.41	−0.07
1905	2.21	45.30	0.24
1906	2.21	45.30	0.00
1907	2.20	45.42	−0.27
1908	2.26	44.31	2.51
1909	2.28	43.80	1.17
1910	2.29	43.68	0.28
1911	2.31	43.45	0.74
1912	2.31	43.30	0.13
1913	2.40	41.61	4.05
1914	2.43	41.20	1.00
1915	2.91	34.39	19.80
1916	3.44	29.10	18.18
1917	4.16	24.05	20.98
1918	4.78	20.91	15.03
1919	4.88	20.50	2.00
1920	5.85	17.08	20.00
1921	4.31	23.18	−26.31
1922	3.92	25.50	−9.09
1923	3.86	25.88	−1.46
1924	3.94	25.38	1.98
1925	3.86	25.88	−1.94
1926	3.88	25.75	0.50
1927	3.67	27.26	−5.54
1928	3.65	27.40	−0.52
1929	3.63	27.55	−0.52

Appendix V

Year	Retail Price Index 1990 = 100	Multiple for Conversion of Contemporary Prices to 1990 Values	Annual Rate of Inflation per cent
1930	3.38	29.62	–6.98
1931	3.22	31.07	–4.67
1932	3.10	32.22	–3.57
1933	3.12	32.02	0.62
1934	3.12	32.02	0.00
1935	3.20	31.26	2.45
1936	3.28	30.48	2.54
1937	3.47	28.80	5.83
1938	3.38	29.62	–2.75
1939	4.22	23.71	24.93
1940	5.31	18.84	25.85
1941	5.62	17.78	10.06
1942	5.56	17.98	–1.11
1943	5.52	18.10	–0.69
1944	5.62	17.78	1.82
1945	5.72	17.48	1.70
1946	5.76	17.37	0.67
1947	6.30	15.86	9.47
1948	6.70	14.94	6.22
1949	6.89	14.51	2.93
1950	7.07	14.15	2.57
1951	7.92	12.62	12.11
1952	8.16	12.26	2.96
1953	8.18	12.23	0.23
1954	8.45	11.83	3.33
1955	8.88	11.26	5.09
1956	9.08	11.02	2.21
1957	9.47	10.56	4.32
1958	9.62	10.39	1.62
1959	9.62	10.39	0.00
1960	9.80	10.20	1.84
1961	10.17	9.83	3.81
1962	10.41	9.61	2.30
1963	10.60	9.44	1.84
1964	11.10	9.01	4.78
1965	11.62	8.61	4.61
1966	12.04	8.30	3.66
1967	12.34	8.10	2.46
1968	13.06	7.66	5.85
1969	13.68	7.31	4.76
1970	14.76	6.78	7.86

Year	Retail Price Index 1990 = 100	Multiple for Conversion of Contemporary Prices to 1990 Values	Annual Rate of Inflation per cent
1971	16.08	6.22	8.98
1972	17.31	5.78	7.64
1973	19.15	5.22	10.61
1974	22.82	4.38	19.16
1975	28.50	3.51	24.90
1976	32.79	3.05	15.07
1977	36.78	2.72	12.15
1978	39.86	2.51	8.39
1979	46.73	2.14	17.23
1980	53.80	1.86	15.13
1981	60.28	1.66	12.05
1982	63.54	1.57	5.41
1983	66.91	1.49	5.31
1984	69.98	1.43	4.58
1985	73.96	1.35	5.69
1986	76.71	1.30	3.72
1987	79.54	1.26	3.69
1988	84.95	1.18	6.80
1989	91.49	1.09	7.70
1990	100.00	1.00	9.30

Sources: J. Williamson, 'Did Capitalism Breed Inequality', *Journal of Economic History*, vol. 45 (1985) p. 220; C. H. Feinstein, *National Income, Expenditure and Output of the United Kingdom, 1865–1965* (Cambridge: Cambridge University Press, 1972) Table 65; Central Statistical Office, *Annual Abstract of Statistics*

[1] See preface p. xviii for comments on usage of conversion tables.

Appendix V (ii)   US Dollar Purchasing Power, 1914–90[1]

Year	Retail Price Index 1990 = 100	Multiple for Conversion of Contemporary Prices to 1990 Values	Annual Rate of Inflation per cent
1914	7.68	13.02	1.35
1915	7.76	12.89	1.00
1916	8.35	11.98	7.57
1917	9.80	10.20	17.43
1918	11.51	8.69	17.45
1919	13.22	7.56	14.86
1920	15.32	6.53	15.83
1921	13.68	7.31	−10.67
1922	12.81	7.80	−6.34
1923	13.04	7.67	1.79
1924	13.07	7.65	0.20
1925	13.40	7.46	2.54
1926	13.53	7.39	0.95
1927	13.27	7.53	−1.89
1928	13.09	7.64	−1.35
1929	13.09	7.64	0.00
1930	12.76	7.84	−2.35
1931	11.64	8.59	−8.80
1932	10.44	9.58	−10.31
1933	9.90	10.10	−5.13
1934	10.24	9.77	3.35
1935	10.49	9.53	2.49
1936	10.59	9.44	0.97
1937	10.98	9.11	3.61
1938	10.77	9.28	−1.86
1939	10.62	9.42	−1.42
1940	10.72	9.33	0.96
1941	11.26	8.88	5.00
1942	12.46	8.03	10.66
1943	13.22	7.56	6.15
1944	13.45	7.43	1.74
1945	13.76	7.27	2.28
1946	14.93	6.70	8.53
1947	17.08	5.86	14.36
1948	18.40	5.43	7.77
1949	18.23	5.49	−0.97
1950	18.40	5.43	0.98
1951	19.86	5.04	7.91
1952	20.29	4.93	2.19

Year	Retail Price Index 1990 = 100	Multiple for Conversion of Contemporary Prices to 1990 Values	Annual Rate of Inflation per cent
1953	20.45	4.89	0.75
1954	20.55	4.87	0.50
1955	20.47	4.88	−0.37
1956	20.78	4.81	1.50
1957	21.52	4.65	3.56
1958	22.11	4.52	2.73
1959	22.28	4.49	0.81
1960	22.64	4.42	1.60
1961	22.87	4.37	1.01
1962	23.13	4.32	1.12
1963	23.41	4.27	1.21
1964	23.59	4.24	0.76
1965	24.12	4.15	2.27
1966	24.81	4.03	2.86
1967	25.53	3.92	2.88
1968	26.60	3.76	4.20
1969	28.03	3.57	5.37
1970	29.69	3.37	5.92
1971	30.99	3.23	4.38
1972	31.98	3.13	3.21
1973	33.97	2.94	6.22
1974	37.72	2.65	11.04
1975	41.16	2.43	9.13
1976	43.53	2.30	5.76
1977	46.37	2.16	6.50
1978	49.89	2.00	7.59
1979	55.55	1.80	11.35
1980	63.05	1.59	13.50
1981	69.55	1.44	10.32
1982	73.83	1.35	6.16
1983	76.21	1.31	3.21
1984	79.50	1.26	4.32
1985	82.33	1.21	3.56
1986	83.86	1.19	1.86
1987	86.92	1.15	3.65
1988	90.51	1.10	4.14
1989	94.87	1.05	4.82
1990	100.00	1.00	5.40

Sources: US Department of Commerce Bureau of the Census, *Historical Statistics of the US: Colonial times to 1970* (Washington DC: US Department of Commerce, 1975) Series E 135; *US Economic Indicators* (Washington DC, monthly).

[1] See preface p. xviii for comments on usage of conversion tables.

Appendix V (iii)   Pound Sterling: US Dollar Exchange Rates, 1860–1990

Year	Dollars per £1 New York	Year	Dollars per £1 New York
1860	5.31	1952	2.81
1870	5.32	1953	2.81
1880	4.83	1954	2.79
1890	4.82	1955	2.80
1900	4.87	1956	2.79
1910	4.87	1957	2.81
1920	3.67	1958	2.81
1921	3.85	1959	2.81
1922	4.43	1960	2.81
1923	4.57	1961	2.80
1924	4.42	1962	2.81
1925	4.83	1963	2.80
1926	4.86	1964	2.79
1927	4.86	1965	2.80
1928	4.87	1966	2.79
1929	4.86	1967	2.76
1930	4.86	1968	2.39
1931	4.86 (a)	1969	2.39
	3.69 (b)	1970	2.40
1932	3.50	1971	2.45
1933	4.22	1972	2.50
1934	5.00	1973	2.45
1935	4.90	1974	2.34
1936	4.97	1975	2.22
1937	4.94	1976	1.80
1938	4.89	1977	1.75
1939	4.46	1978	1.92
1940	4.03	1979	2.12
1941	4.03	1980	2.33
1942	4.03	1981	2.03
1943	4.03	1982	1.75
1944	4.03	1983	1.52
1945	4.03	1984	1.34
1946	4.03	1985	1.30
1947	4.03	1986	1.47
1948	3.68	1987	1.64
1949	2.80	1988	1.78
1950	2.80	1989	1.64
1951	2.79	1990	1.78

(a) Before leaving the gold standard in September 1931.
(b) After leaving the gold standard in September 1931.

Sources: B. R. Mitchell, *British Historical Statistics* (Cambridge: Cambridge University Press, 1988) pp. 702–3; *Financial Statistics* (HMSO).

Note on Sources

Foremost amongst the sources upon which this history of Schroders is based are the firm's own records. Although efforts had been made to preserve papers considered to be of historical significance, no organised archive existed at the time that it was decided to write the history of the firm. Thus a preliminary task, which proved to be a major undertaking, was to locate and catalogue the records of the London and New York firms. These records were complemented by research in other archives, a large number of interviews (see Acknowledgements), and by the financial press and secondary literature (see Notes and References).

The surviving records of J. Henry Schröder & Co. prior to 1945 mostly comprise various forms of financial accounts and these form the bedrock of the story of the firm in the nineteenth century and the first half of the twentieth century. The accounts are presented in simplified form in Appendix IV and are the data source of the graphs which appear in the text. The absence of other records is the result of a zealous response to the government's appeal for paper during the Second World War which led to the pulping of the letter books (with a single exception) and many other papers. From the end of the war the archival situation is reversed and instead of a dearth of material there is an abundance, notably the voluminous unindexed minutes of the executives' daily morning meetings. The formation of Schroders Limited in 1959 led to the production, for the first time, of a set of significant board minutes and supporting papers. Moreover, some divisions also have rich records of their operational activities.

Family papers were also an important source of information. The Schröder'sches Familienarchiv, the collection of documents pertaining to the history of the Schröder family assembled by Eduard Eggers and housed in the Staats Archiv, Hamburg, was especially useful. Archives of other banks in which research was conducted into the development of Schroders were those of the Bank of England, Baring Brothers, Kleinwort Benson (at the Guildhall Library), the Midland Bank, Morgan Grenfell (at the Guildhall Library) and Rothschilds. Foreign Office, Home Office, Treasury and Board of Trade papers were consulted in the Public Record Office. Other records consulted were those of the Accepting Houses Committee (at the British Merchant Bankers Association), the German Church, Camberwell, Lloyds of London, the Peruvian Corporation (at University College, London), the Russia Company (at the Guildhall Library) and papers held by the Port of London Authority Library and the Stratford Reference Library.

Board minutes and published accounts provide a basic framework for the account of the development of the J. Henry Schroder Banking Corporation of New York. Happily, a substantial cache of lively correspondence between senior officers in the 1920s and 1930s was discovered providing insights into their activities and ambitions. Archival research was conducted in the United States at the National Archives, Washington DC, the Federal Reserve Bank of New York, the New York Stock Exchange, the Chase Manhattan Bank, and at Yale University on the papers of Paul Warburg.

No records survive of Helbert, Wagg's stockbroking days, though there are several unpublished memoirs which permit an outline of these years to be written. The records of the Stock Exchange (at the Guildhall Library) provided a few additional details. A much fuller account of the development of the firm as an issuing house is possible because of the survival of financial accounts from 1915, board minutes from 1919 and files on particular transactions from the early 1920s. Moreover, amongst City firms Helbert, Wagg is unusual in that two of the partners, Lawrence Jones and Lionel Fraser, published colourful autobiographies. Additional archival research was undertaken on the Gibbs manuscripts (at the Guildhall Library) and the papers of the Issuing Houses Association (at the British Merchant Bankers Association).

The most directly relevant works of secondary literature are Stanley Chapman, *The Rise of Merchant Banking*; Philip Ziegler, *The Sixth Great Power: Barings 1762–1929*; Kathleen Burk, *Morgan Grenfell 1838–1988*; Jacques Attali, *A Man of Influence: Sir Siegmund Warburg 1902–82*; Vincent Carosso, *Investment Banking in America*; Ron Chernow, *The House of Morgan*.

Notes and References

Abbreviations

1 Origins in Quakenbrück and Hamburg: 1654–1821

1. Genealogical information about the early history of the Schröder family is derived from Schröder'sches Familienarchiv which comprises documents relating to the history of the Schröder family collected by Eduard Eggers and deposited in Staats Archiv, Hamburg.
2. Hildegard von Marchtaler und Eduard Eggers, *Genealogie der Familie Schröder* (Hamburg: Kruger & Nienstedt, 1955) p. 3.
3. P. Dollinger, *The German Hansa* (London: Macmillan, 1970) pp. 362–6.
4. Eleanor von Schwabach, *Erinnerungen an die Familie Schröder* (Hamburg: Hans Christian Verlag, 1957) p. 7.
5. Philip Ziegler, *The Sixth Great Power: Barings 1762–1929* (London: Collins, 1988) p. 14
6. I am grateful to Frau Magnus of the Stadtmuseum Quakenbrück for drawing this to my attention.
7. Eduard R. Eggers, *Die Schröder-Hauser in Quakenbrück und ihre Besitzer (1725–1904)* (Hamburg: privately printed, 1977/78) p. 13.
8. Interview with Herr Behre, C. Kruse & Co, Quakenbrück.
9. The letters are held by the Schröder'sches Familienarchiv (SFA) in the Staats Archiv, Hamburg.
10. John Burnett, *A History of the Cost of Living* (London: Penguin Books, 1969) p. 155.

11. See, Joachim Whaley, *Religious Toleration and Social Change in Hamburg, 1529–1819* (Cambridge University Press, 1985)

12. K. Liebel, 'Laissez-faire vs mercantilism: the rise of Hamburg and the Hamburg bourgeoisie vs Frederick the Great in the crisis of 1763', *Vierteljahrschrift für Social und Wirtschaftgeschichte*, (1965) vol. lii, pp. 207–38.

13. SFA Stammbuch der Familie Schröder.

14. SFA Letter from Johann Friedrich Schröder to Anthon Schröder, 29 September 1767.

15. See, Walter Kresse, *Materialien zur Entwicklungsgeschichte der Hamburger Handelsflotte, 1765–1823* (Hamburg: Museum fur Hamburgische Geschichte, 1966).

16. Eckart Klessmann, *Geschichte der Stadt Hamburg* (Hamburg: Hoffmann und Campe, 1981) p. 329.

17. SFA Note by Eduard R. Eggers on Christian Matthias Schröder.

18. Schroder ships called at London in 1781, Newcastle in 1782 and Liverpool in 1783, but made no further visits until 1797.

19. Whaley, *Religious Toleration* pp. 19–22.

20. SA Letter from Christian Matthias Schröder to 'My Children', 7 November 1779.

21. See, François Crouzet, *L'Economie Britannique et le Blocus Continental 1806–1813* (Paris: PUF, 1958) vol. I; Erwin Wiskmann, *Hamburg und die Welthandels Politik* (Hamburg, 1929) pp. 128–33.

22. David Macpherson, *Annals of Commerce, Manufacturing, Fisheries and Navigation* (London, 1805) vol. IV, p. 463.

23. Arthur D. Gayer, W.W. Rostow, Anna J. Schwartz, *The Growth and Fluctuations of the British Economy 1790–1850* (Oxford: Clarendon Press, 1953) p. 33.

24. Sir F.M. Eden, *Eight Letters on the Peace and the Commerce and Manufactures of Great Britain* 2nd ed. (London, 1802) p. 133.

25. Ian Blanchard, *Russia in the 'Age of Silver'* (London: Routledge & Kegan Paul, 1989) p. 274.

26. J.B. von Spix and C.F.P. von Martius, quoted in Leslie Bethell, 'The Independence of Brazil', in Leslie Bethell (ed.), *The Cambridge History of Latin America* (Cambridge University Press, 1985) vol. III, p. 161.

27. Eduard Rosenbaum, 'MM Warburg & Co. Merchant Bankers of Hamburg', *Leo Baeck Institute Yearbook* vol. vii (1962) p. 122.

28. Herbert A.L. Fisher, *Studies in Napoleonic Statemanship: Germany* (Oxford: Clarendon Press, 1903) p. 62.

29. Fisher, *Studies* pp. 336–7.

30. 'As sound as Christian Matthias' was a saying amongst Hamburg merchants according to the Hamburg paper *Reform*, 21 April 1858.

31. Schwabach, *Erinnerungen* p. 40.

32. Schwabach, *Erinnerungen* p. 40; Burnett, *Cost of Living* p. 140.

33. J. Mistler, 'Hambourg sous l'Occupation Francaise', *Francia*, (1973) vol. i, pp. 445–6; Georges Servieres, *L'Allemagne Francaise sous Napoleon ler* (Paris, 1904) pp. 186–213.

34. Fisher, *Studies* p. 343.
35. G. J. Marcus, *A Naval History of England: the Age of Nelson* (London: George Allen & Unwin, 1971) vol. 2 p. 442; H. R. C. Wright, *Free Trade and Protection in The Netherlands, 1816–1830* (Cambridge University Press, 1955) p. 24.
36. Klessman, *Stadt Hamburg* p. 325.
37. Ibid.
38. SA Hildegard von Marchtaler, 'The Firm of J. H. Schr.öder & Co in Hamburg 1819–1903' (unpublished typescript, 1951).
39. Raymond de Roover, 'New interpretations of the history of banking', *Cahiers d'Histoire Mondiale* (1954) vol. ii, pp. 44–6
40. Stanley Chapman, 'The International Houses: the Continental contribution to British commerce, 1800–1860', *Journal of European Economic History*, (1977) vol. vi, pp. 5–23; Stanley Chapman, *The Rise of Merchant Banking* (London: George Allen & Unwin, 1984) pp. 3–4.
41. SA G. Ahrens, 'The Collapse of the Firm of C. M. Schr.oder & Co, Hamburg' (Unpublished typescript, 1977).
42. D. Morier Evans, *The History of the Commercial Crisis 1857–1858* (London: Groombridge & Sons, 1859) pp. 39–40.

2 Johann Heinrich Schröder in London, Hamburg and Liverpool: 1800–49

1. See, Norman Sydney Buck, *The Development of the Organisation of Anglo-American Trade 1800–1850* (New Haven, Conn.: Yale University Press, 1925) pp. 4–29; Edwin J. Perkins, *Financing Anglo-American Trade: the House of Brown, 1800–1880* (Cambridge, Mass.: Harvard University Press, 1975) pp. 93–103.
2. J. H. Clapham, *An Economic History of Modern Britain: Free Trade and Steel 1850–1886* (Cambridge University Press, 1932) p. 315; Perkins, *House of Brown* pp. 7–8.
3. See, Perkins, *House of Brown* pp. 4–15; Ralph W. Hidy, *The House of Baring in American Trade and Finance: English merchant bankers at work 1763–1861* (Cambridge, Mass.: Harvard University Press, 1949) p. 131–53; Gillett Brothers Discount Company Ltd, *The Bill on London* (London: Chapman & Hall, 1976); Henry Harfield, *Bank Credits and Acceptances* 5th edn (New York: Ronald Press Co., 1974) pp. 25–7.
4. Macpherson, *Annals* p. 463.
5. Select Committee on the expediency of removing the charter of the Bank of England, and the system on which banks of issue in England and Wales are conducted. BPP 1831–2 (vi) cap. 4799, 4802, 4866.
6. Arthur D. Gayer, W. W. Rostow and Anna J. Schwartz, *The Growth and Fluctuation of the British Economy 1790–1850* (Oxford: Clarendon Press, 1953) p. 52. The increase was in 'official values' – which were not necessarily by any means identical with market values.

7. I am grateful to Major Malcolm Morris of Pilgrim Lodge for bringing the membership of these members of the Schröder family to my attention and for making the membership records available.

8. *Kent's London Directory 1801.*

9. Lloyds of London. Membership Roll, 1790–1930.

10. *Gentleman's Magazine* (1802) vol. lxxii, part 2, p. 685.

11. 'Sugar merchant' was given as Johann Friedrich Schröder's occupation on the death certificate of his widow Isabella Schröder who died on 26 May 1868 at Bentley, Hampshire.

12. PLAA West India Dock Company Ledger 1 1805 and Ledger 2 1805. These are the only early ledgers which survive.

13. RA MS I/218/35. Letter from N. M. Rothschild to John Frederick Schröder, 30 April 1802; see S. D. Chapman, 'The Foundation of the English Rothschilds: N. M. Rothschild as a textile merchant, 1799–1811', *Textile History*, (1977) vol. vii, p. 102.

14. GL MS 11,741 Russia Company Court Minutes, 6 November 1807.

15. Susan Fairlie, 'The Anglo-Russian grain trade 1815–1861' (unpublished Ph.D thesis, University of London, 1959) p. 247

16. GL MS 11,741 Russia Company Court Minutes, 12 February 1808.

17. See, A. N. Ryan, 'The Defence of British Trade with the Baltic, 1808–1813', *Economic History Review*, (1959) 2nd Series vol. xii, pp. 443–66

18. Matilda Edgar (ed.), *Ten Years of Upper Canada in Peace and War, 1805–1815; being the Ridout letters [edited] with annotations by M. E.* (London: T. Fisher Unwin, 1891) pp. 52, 58.

19. J. B. Williams, *British Commercial Policy and Trade Expansion 1750–1850* (Oxford: Clarendon Press, 1972) p. 356.

20. SFA, Bill of Exchange dated 10 July 1814.

21. RA MS I/112/IB. Letter from J. F. Schröder to N. M. Rothschild & Sons, 21 January 1831; Georg Wilhelm Schröder joined the Riga guild of timber merchants and was a member of the town council, Anders Henriksson, *The Tsar's Loyal Germans: the Riga German com-munity, 1885–1905* (New York: Columbia University Press, 1983) p. 170.

22. Lloyds of London. Membership Roll, 1790–1930.

23. Marchtaler und Eggers, *Genealogie der Familie Schröder*; Dulwich College, *History of Ellison Lodge* (no date); William Young, *History of Dulwich College* vol. I (London: T. B. Bumpus, 1889).

24. SA Correspondence between J. F. Schröder & Co. and F. W. Karthaus Reinicke & Co., 1817.

25. BBA Confidential Credit Report Book 1835. Report no. 49.

26. *The London Gazette*, 3 January 1818, p.21.

27. J. Schröder, *Das Elternhaus in Eimsbuttel* (Hamburg, 1883) p. 30; RA. MSXI/126/9B. Letter from J. Henry Schröder & Co. to N. M. Rothschild & Sons, 30 June 1846.

28. SA Letter from Rudolph Schröder, Hamburg, to Helmut Schroder, London, 26 September 1951, enclosing 'Reminiscences of Baron Sir John Henry William Schröder by Evelina D. Bingel, 7 November 1909'.

29. Leo Deuel, *Memoirs of Heinrich Schliemann* (London: Hutchinson, 1978) p. 60.

30. Royal Commission on the Port of London. Appendix 6, p. 348. BPP 1902 (lxiii).

31. Julius von Eckardt, quoted in Richard J. Evans, *Death in Hamburg* (Oxford: Clarendon Press, 1987) p. 4.

32. Hanse Towns – Hamburg, p. 303. BPP 1851 (iv).

33. SA Hildegard von Marchtaler, 'The firm of J. H. Schröder & Co. in Hamburg, 1819–1903' (unpublished typescript, 1951).

34. RA MS XI/112/61. Letter from J. Henry Schröder & Co. to N. M. Rothschild Esq., 29 August 1832.

35. Gayer, Rostow and Schwartz, *Growth and Fluctuation* p. 426.

36. Shizuga Nishimura, *The Decline of the Inland Bill of Exchange in the London Money Market, 1855–1913* (Cambridge University Press, 1971) pp. 13–14.

37. GL MS 11,741 Russia Company Court Minutes, 23 July 1819; Fairlie, 'Anglo-Russian grain trade' p. 247.

38. BBA Credit Report Book, 1835. Report no. 49.

39. RA MS XI/126/8B. Letter from J. Henry Schröder & Co. to N. M. Rothschild & Sons, 14 October 1844.

40. David Morier Evans, *City Men and City Manners* (London: Groombridge & Sons, 1852) pp. 136–8; Ziegler, *Sixth Great Power* pp. 131–2; Hugh Barty-King, *The Baltic Exchange: the history of a unique Market* (London: Hutchinson Benham, 1977) pp. 50–60.

41. Hermann Otto von Post is listed in the Post Office Directory of London in 1822 as a merchant. He died in Brighton on 13 February 1866, aged 76.

42. Baron Sir John Henry Schröder described the building as 'a mansion house over a pickle factory'. SA 'Reminiscences of Baron Sir John Henry Schöder by Evelina D. Bingel, 7 November 1909'. The night-time residents recorded by the 1841 census were two Scottish clerks and a housekeeper, Mary Rabbit, and her five children. Census of 1841. PRO HO 107 721.11.

43. Chapman, *Rise of Merchant Banking* p. 13.

44. SA Circular announcing formation of J. H. Schröder & Co, Liverpool, 1 July 1839.

45. Chapman, *Rise of Merchant Banking* p. 40.

46. BoEA Liverpool Branch Letter Book no. 1, 1840, p. 137.

47. BoEA Liverpool Private Letter Books, 3 May 1842, 5 May 1842.

48. Ziegler, *Sixth Great Power* pp. 148–9; Aytoun Ellis, *Heir of Adventure: the story of Brown, Shipley & Co. merchant bankers 1810–1960* (London: Brown, Shipley & Co., 1960) pp. 36–51.

49. J. R. Freedman, 'A London merchant banker in Anglo-American trade and finance 1835–1850' (unpublished Ph.D thesis, University of London, 1969) p. 68.

50. W. Maude, *Antony Gibbs & Sons Limited, Merchants and Bankers 1808–1958* (London: A. Gibbs & Sons, 1958) pp. 11, 132; Hidy, *House of Baring* p. 107; Stephanie Diaper, 'The History of Kleinwort, Sons & Co. in

Merchant Banking, 1855–1966' (unpublished Ph D Thesis, University of Nottingham, 1983) p. 302.
51. SA 'Reminiscences of Baron John Henry Schröder by Evelina D. Bingel, 7 November 1909'.
52. BBA Credit Report Book, 1835.
53. See, A. J. Murray, *Home From The Hill: a biography of Frederick Huth 'Napoleon of the City'* (London: Hamish Hamilton, 1970)
54. See, Diaper, 'History of Kleinwort, Sons & Co.
55. SA Erbschaftsrechnung [Inheritance Valuation] über John Henry Schröder, 28 June 1883.

3   Emergence as Leading Merchant Bankers: 1849–71

1. Arthur Lewis, 'The Rate of Growth of World Trade, 1830–1973', in Sven Grassman and Erik Lundberg (eds), *The World Economic Order: past and prospects* (London: Macmillan, 1981) pp. 62–3.
2. SA Marriage Certificate of John Henry William Schröder, 19 September 1850; Marylebone Reference Library. Census Emmerator's Book 1851. Adolphus Klockmann is recorded as the head of household at 41 Acacia Road, Marylebone. He was a 40-year-old 'merchant (colonial produce)' of German birth.
3. *The Bankers' Magazine* (1866) vol. xxvi, p. 639.
4. BoEA Mem GL 11,621. Liverpool Private Letter Books, vol. 12, p. 190. Letter from Bank of England, London, to Bank of England, Liverpool, 19 July 1866.
5. Diaper, 'History of Kleinwort, Sons & Co., p. 78.
6. The analysis of J. Henry Schröder & Co.'s conditions books was undertaken by Dr Roger Alford in the early 1950s. The documents are no longer present in the Schroders Archive.
7. Ralph W. Hidy, 'The Organisation and Functions of Anglo-American Merchant Bankers, 1815–1860', *Journal of Economic History* (1941) vol. i, Supplement, p. 65.
8. Royal Commission on the Port of London. Appendix 6, p. 348. BPP 1902 (lxiii).
9. Deuel, *Memoirs of Heinrich Schliemann* p. 60.
10. SA Letter Heinrich Schliemann, Wurzburg, Bavaria, to Johann Heinrich Schröder, Hamburg, 4 November 1864.
11. Deuel, *Memoirs of Heinrich Schliemann* pp. 169, 292.
12. Patricia Herlihy, *Odessa: a history, 1794–1914* (Cambridge, Mass.: Harvard University Press, 1986) pp. 88–108.
13. *History and Activities of the Ralli Trading Group* (London: Ralli Brothers (Trading), 1978).
14. Barty-King, *Baltic Exchange* pp. 97–8.
15. Barty-King, *Baltic Exchange* pp. 114.
16. BBA Baring Brothers, Liverpool, to Baring Brothers, London, 20 April 1860. House correspondence – English HC 3.35; D. M. Williams,

'Liverpool Merchants and the Cotton Trade 1820–1850', in J. R. Harris (ed.), *Liverpool and Merseyside, Essays in the Economic and Social History of the Port and its Hinterland* (London: Frank Cass & Co., 1969) p. 209.

17. SA J. Henry Schröder & Co. letter book, 1858–79. This is the only surviving letter book.

18. *The House of Brandt* (London: privately printed, 1956).

19. Brown, Shipley & Co.'s partners' capital in 1875 was £1.2 million while that of J. Henry Schröder & Co. was £1.6 million. J. S. Morgan & Co.'s commission income in 1870 was £73,000 compared to J. Henry Schröder & Co.'s £96,000.

20. Estimates based on calculations from *Fenn's Compendium on the English and Foreign Funds* (various editions). See also, A. K. Cairncross, *Home and Foreign Investment* (Cambridge University Press, 1953) pp. 222–35; John J. Madden, *British Investment in the United States, 1860–1880* (New York: Garland Publishing Inc., 1985) p. 242.

21. David Williams, 'The Evolution of the Sterling System', in C. R. Whittlesey and J. S. G. Wilson (eds), *Essays in Money and Banking* (Oxford: Clarendon Press, 1968) pp. 266–8.

22. *Journal of the Royal Statistical Society*, (1909) vol. lxxii, p. 484; see also, D. C. M. Platt, *Britain's Investment Overseas on the Eve of the First World War* (London: Macmillan, 1986) pp. 31–6.

23. Matthew Simon, 'The Pattern of New British Portfolio Foreign Investment, 1865–1914', in J. H. Alder (ed.), *Capital Movements and Economic Development* (London: Macmillan, 1967) pp. 24, 38–39. Simon estimates 'creations of New British Portfolio Foreign Investment' in the years 1865–1914 to be £4,180.8 million.

24. Hugh Thomas, *Cuba: or the Pursuit of Freedom* (London: Eyre & Spottiswoode, 1971) p. 123.

25. Merl E. Reed, *New Orleans and the Railroads* (Louisiana: Louisiana State University Press, 1966) pp. 90–107.

26. Hidy, *House of Baring* pp. 430–1.

27. SA Agreement between William Simpson Campbell for the New Orleans, Jackson and Great Northern Railroad and J. Henry Schröder & Co., 27 November 1854; Reed, *New Orleans and the Railroads* p. 151, note 30.

28. SA Agreement between James Robb of New Orleans in the United States of America, Esquire, the duly authorised agent in London and Messrs J. Henry Schröder & Co. of the City of London, Merchants, represented by Alexander Schlüsser, 11 August 1856. There was a simultaneous issue of bonds with a nominal value of £225,000 in New York.

29. 'John Slidell', *Dictionary of American Biography*, vol. 17 (New York: Scribner, 1935) pp. 209–11.

30. For biographical information about Emile Erlanger, see Baron E. B. d'Erlanger, *Quelques Souvenirs de France: My Souvenirs* (London: privately printed, 1978); Obituary of Emile Erlanger, *The Times*, 25 May 1911.

31. Letter from Charles Prioleau, Liverpool partner of Fraser Trenholm & Co. to Trenholm, 21 October 1863. Quoted in Chapman, *Rise of Merchant Banking* p. 85.

32. See Philip L. Cottrell, 'Anglo-French Financial Co-operation, 1850–1880', *Journal of European Economic History* (1974) vol. 3, pp. 54–86.
33. 'A Sketch of the History of Foreign Loans', *The Bankers' Magazine*, (1876) vol. xxxvi, p. 425.
34. David S. Landes, *Bankers and Pashas: International Finance and Economic Imperialism in Egypt* (Cambridge, Mass.: Harvard University Press, 1958) p. 117.
35. W. O. Henderson, *The Lancashire Cotton Famine 1861–1865* (Manchester University Press, 1934) p. 35.
36. Paul Pecquet du Bellet, *Diplomacy of the Confederate Cabinet of Richmond and its Agents Abroad: being memorandum notes taken in Paris during the Rebellion of the Southern States from 1861 to 1865* (Tuscaloosa, Ala.: Confederate Publishing Co., 1963) pp. 53, 123.
37. There are several accounts of the Confederate Cotton Loan by historians. See, Richard I. Lester, 'Confederate Finance and Purchasing in Great Britain during the American Civil War' (unpublished PhD thesis, University of Manchester, 1961); Richard Cecil Todd, *Confederate Finance* (Athens, Georgia, 1954); Judith Fenner Gentry, 'A Confederate Success in Europe: the Erlanger Loan', *Journal of Southern History* (1970) vol. xxxvi, pp. 157–88.
38. *The Economist*, 21 March 1863.
39. USNA RG 365/Entry 8. Letter from Emile Erlanger, 145 Leadenhall Street, to Christopher G. Memminger, Richmond, Virginia, 28 March 1863.
40. *Official Records of the Union and Confederate Navies in the War of the Rebellion* (Washington, DC: Government Printing Office, 1921) Series II, vol. 3, p. 714. Letter from L. Q. C. Lamar, Confederate States Commission, London, to Hon. J. P. Benjamin, Secretary of State, Confederate States of America, Richmond, Virginia, 19 March 1863.
41. USNA RG 365/Entry 8. Letter from Emile Erlanger, 145 Leadenhall Street, to Christopher G. Memminger, Richmond, Virginia, 28 March 1863.
42. RA MS RAL II/10/30. Letter from N. M. Rothschild & Sons, London, to August Belmont & Co., New York, 24 March 1863.
43. USNA RG 365/Entry 8. Letter from Emile Erlanger, Paris, to Christopher G. Memminger, Richmond, Virginia, 28 April 1863.
44. USNA RG 365/Entry 320. Letter from Emile Erlanger, Paris, to Christopher G. Memminger, Richmond, Virginia, 11 February 1864.
45. Stephen R. Wise, *Lifeline of the Confederacy – Blockade Running During the Civil War* (Columbia, S.C.: University of South Carolina Press, 1988) p. 176. I am grateful to Frank Hughes for drawing my attention to the operations of the Denbigh.
46. Larry Schweikart, *Banking in the American South from the Age of Jackson to Reconstruction* (Baton Rouge La.: Louisiana State University Press, 1987) p. 296.
47. *The Times*, 15 July 1863.
48. Gentry, 'A Confederate Success', p. 171.

49. Baron E. B. d'Erlanger, *Quelques Souvenirs de France: My Souvenirs* (London: privately printed, 1978) p. 9.
50. Gentry, 'A Confederate Success', p. 169.
51. USNA RG 365/Entry 320. Letter from Emile Erlanger, Paris, to Christopher G. Memminger, Richmond, Virginia, 11 February 1864.
52. *The Times*, 5 April 1864.
53. SA Swedish Government Loan 1864. Prospectus.
54. *The Times*, 9 December 1864; Deuel, *Memoirs of Heinrich Schliemann* p. 105.
55. *The Times*, 28 October 1868.
56. *The Times*, 27 November 1868.
57. James F. Doser, *Railroads in Alabama Politics, 1875–1914* (University of Alabama Press, 1957) pp. 46–8; Cleona Lewis, *America's Stake in International Investments* (Washington, DC: Bookings Institution, 1938) pp. 57–62.
58. *Morning Post*, 6 September 1887. The committee of advisers appointed by the liquidator included Henry Tiarks, Emile Erlanger and Walpole Greenwell. *The Times*, 23 June 1888.
59. Grace Fox, *Britain and Japan, 1858–1883* (Oxford University Press, 1969) pp. 386–93.
60. PRO FO 46/126. Sir Harry Parkes, British Legation, Yokohama, to the Earl of Clarendon, Foreign Office, London, 31 July 1870.
61. Obituary of Horatio Nelson Lay, *The Times*, 6 May 1898.
62. *The Times*, 26 February 1873.
63. PRO FO 46/126. Sir Harry Parkes, British Legation, Yokohama, to the Earl of Clarendon, Foreign Office, London, 31 July 1870.
64. Lay lost the case which came to court in 1873. See *The Times*, 26 February 1873.
65. SA Letter from Prince Matsukata Masoyoshi, Tokyo, to Joseph Foreman, J. Henry Schröder & Co., 1 October 1882.
66. Select Committee on Loans to Foreign States. Minutes of Evidence, cap 3719–4006. BPP 1875 (xl).
67. 'Bread and butter business' was a favourite phrase of Baron Bruno Schröder to describe the acceptance business of J. Henry Schröder & Co.
68. Michael Edelstein, 'Realised Rates of Return on UK Home and Overseas Portfolio Investment in the Age of High Imperialism', *Explorations in Economic History*, (1976) vol. 13, p. 291.
69. SA Agreement between A. Schlüsser and E. Ellice, 15 May 1854.
70. See John Summerson, 'The Victorian Rebuilding of the City of London', *London Journal* (1977) vol. 3, pp. 163–85.
71. *Building News*, 15 July 1859, p. 654.
72. *Building News*, 25 May 1860, p. 416.
73. SA Agreement between A. Schlüsser and E. H. and M. Moser, 2 July 1859.
74. SA Salary books 1851 onwards.
75. George Kitson Clark, *The Making of Victorian England* (London: Methuen, 1962) p. 119.
76. Burnett, *Cost of Living* p. 241.

77. Burnett, *Cost of Living* p. 234.
78. SA Notes on Interview with E. L. Cheese conducted by R. F. G Alford, 6 May 1954.
79. Diaper, 'History of Kleinwort, Sons & Co.' p. 352.
80. *The London Telegraph*, 1880, quoted in Gregory Anderson, 'German Clerks in England, 1870–1914; Another Aspect of the Great Depression Debate', in Kenneth Lunn, *Hosts, Immigrants and Minorities* (London: Dawson, 1980) p. 204; Gregory Anderson, *Victorian Clerks* (Manchester University Press, 1976) pp. 60–5.
81. Francis Sheppard, *London 1808–1870: the infernal wen* (London: Secker, 1971) p. 107.
82. See *List of the Inhabitants of the Parish of Clapham* (London, 1844); H. N. Batten, *Plan of Clapham* (London, 1858).
83. Hurford Janes and H. J. Sayers, *The Story of Czarnikow* (London: Harley Publishing Co., 1963) pp. 20–3.
84. Agnes Tiarks' diary, which she kept from 1859 to 1923, details the family world of the partner of a merchant bank but there are few references to business affairs. It was made available by her grandson, Henry Tiarks.
85. William Harnett Blanch, *Ye Parish of Camberwell* (London: E. W. Allen, 1875) p. 238; Records of the German Evengelical Church, Denmark Hill, Verhandlungen Protokolle, 1853–68, 8 vols.
86. *German Hospital, Dalston, Established 1845* (London, 1846) pp. 70–88.
87. SA See J. Puschel, *Die Geschichte des German Hospitals in London 1845 bis 1948* (unpublished typescript, no date).
88. GL MS 8, 358 Vellum Book, 1702–1875. The surviving records of the Hamburg Lutheran Church are held by the GL: *Die Deutsche Kolonie in England* (London: Anglo-German Publishing Co., 1913) pp. 17–18.

4   Boom, Recession and Recovery: 1871–92

1. Quoted in W. O. Henderson, *The Rise of German Industrial Power, 1834–1914* (London: Maurice Temple Smith, 1975) p. 161.
2. S. Japhet, *Recollections From My Business Life* (London: privately printed, 1931) p. 15.
3. Calculated from world exports data in Lewis, 'World Trade', pp. 62–5.
4. Nishimura, *Bills of Exchange* p. 25.
5. Gerard van de Linde, *Book-keeping and Other Papers* (London: Blades East & Blades, 1904) pp. 127–8 (the paper was written in 1887). See also Chapman, *Rise of Merchant Banking* pp. 126–49; Jeffrey Kieve, *The Electric Telegraph: a Social and Economic History* (Newton Abbot: David & Charles, 1973) p. 237; R. C. Michie, *The London and New York Stock Exchanges 1850–1914* (London: George Allen & Unwin, 1987) p. 42.
6. Philip Ziegler, *Sixth Great Power* p. 376; Kathleen Burk, *Morgan Grenfell, 1838–1988: the biography of a merchant bank* (Oxford University Press, 1989) p. 264; Diaper, 'History of Kleinwort, Sons & Co.' p. 399.

7. W. Arthur Lewis, *Growth and Fluctuations 1870–1913* (London: George Allen & Unwin, 1978) pp. 41–2.

8. Simon, 'New British Portfolio Foreign Investment', p. 40

9. A. R. Hall, T*he London Capital Market and Australia 1870–1914* (Canberra: Australia National University, 1963) pp. 71–5; P. L. Cottrell, *British Overseas Investment in the Nineteenth Century* (London: Macmillan, 1975) pp. 36–7.

10. SA The letter was sent from Brown, Shipley & Co. to Wm Brandt Sons & Co. and was quoted in information supplied by Walter Brandt to Helmut Schroder, 28 February 1958.

11. SA Baron John Henry William Schröders Hunting Journals, 1872–81. In possession of Bruno L. Schroder.

12. Jose Harris and Pat Thane, 'British and European Bankers 1880–1914: an "aristocratic bourgeoisie?"', in Pat Thane, Geoffrey Crossick and Roderick Floud (eds), *The Power of the Past* (Cambridge University Press, 1984) p. 227.

13. BBA Credit Report Book, 1835. Report no. 24.

14. Agnes Morris (1841–1923) was a relation of Alexander Schlüsser's wife. The details of the Tiarks family's domestic life are derived from her diary.

15. D. Ware, *A Short Dictionary of British Architects* (London: George Allen & Unwin, 1967) p. 45.

16. *Who Was Who 1897–1916*, p. 440; P. Eynon Smart, 'John Lubbock, 1st Lord Avebury', in *Dictionary of Business Biography* (London: Butterworths, 1985) vol. 3 pp. 873–6.

17. SA Announcement of Office Reorganisation June 1871.

18. Heraclio Bonilla, 'Peru and Bolivia from Independence to the War of the Pacific', in Leslie Bethell (ed.), *The Cambridge History of Latin America*, vol. III (Cambridge University Press, 1985) p. 551: Some historians have questioned the validity of the criticisms of the consignment system: Bill Albert, *South America and the World Economy from Independence to 1930* (London: Macmillan, 1983) p. 71–2.

19. W. Stewart, *Henry Meiggs: Yankee Pizarro* (Durham, N.C.: Duke University Press, 1946) p. 267–8.

20. Stewart, *Meiggs* p. 269.

21. SA Contract between Dreyfus Frères & Cie and J. Henry Schröder & Co., 7 April 1870.

22. *The Economist*, 11 June 1870.

23. SA Contract between Dreyfus Frères & Cie and J. Henry Schröder & Co., 2 February 1871.

24. BoEA Mem GL 13, 065. Liverpool Private Letter Books, vol. 12 (1864–72). Letter from Bank of England, London, to Bank of England, Liverpool, 9 March 1871.

25. *The Bankers' Magazine* (1876) vol. xxxvi, pp. 517–8.

26. SA Agreement between Dreyfus Frères and J. Henry Schröder & Co., Société Genérale, Stern Bros and Mr B. Premsel, 12 March 1872.

27. *The Economist*, 23 March 1872; *South Pacific Times*, supplement, October 1873, p. 3.

28. Bonilla, 'Peru and Bolivia' p. 554.
29. Fisons Archive. 'The Anglo–Continental Guano Works Ltd' (unpublished typescript, no date). I am grateful to Michael Moss and Alison Turton for providing a copy of this paper.
30. SRL W. A. Parks, 'The Development of the Heavy Chemical Industries of West Ham and District' (Typescript, no date).
31. SA Contract between Dr Augustus Voelcker and J. Henry Schröder & Co., 1 January 1873.
32. E. Ballard, *Report in Respect of the Inquiries as to Effluvium Nuisances Arising in Connexion with Various Manufacturing and Other Branches of Industry* (London, 1882) pp. 148–57.
33. SRL West Ham Local Board of Health, Minute Book, vol. 11, 10 March 1874.
34. SRL West Ham Local Board of Health, Minute Book, vol. 12, 12 January 1875; 12 February 1875.
35. SA Circular announcing the transfer of the guano and chemical manure works of Ohlendorff & Co. in London, Hamburg, Antwerp and Enmerick-on-the-Rhine to the Anglo–Continental Guano Works Company, 15 December 1883.
36. W. A. Parks and G. A. Rudge, 'London's Chemical Industry II', *The Chemical Age* (10 August 1946) pp. 167–8.
37. PLAA London & St Katherine's Dock Company, Committee of Treasury Minute Book no. 13, 11 June 1872.
38. PRO FO 61/304. J Twycross, *To the Holders of Peruvian Bonds* (London, 1876) p. 14.
39. PLAA London & St Katherine's Dock Company, Committee of Treasury Minute Book no. 15, 9 March 1876; Court of Directors Minute Book no. 3, 13 March 1876.
40. *The Economist*, 2 June 1883.
41. Archive of the Peruvian Corporation. University College London, Manuscript Library. MS G2/A. Anon, 'The First Forty Years of the Peruvian Corporation 1890–1930' pp. 2–3.
42. SA Obituary in unidentified local newspaper, 15 January 1912.
43. J. H. Galloway, *The Sugar Cane Industry: An Historical Geography From Its Origins to 1914* (Cambridge University Press, 1989) pp. 162–8.
44. Royal Commission on the Port of London. Appendix 6, p. 349. BPP 1902 (lxiii).
45. Evans, *Death in Hamburg* p. 31.
46. Fritz Stern, *Gold and Iron: Bismarck, Bleichröder and the Building of the German Empire* (New York: Vintage Books, 1977) p. 396.
47. SA Johann Rudolf Schröder, 'Geschichte der Firma Schröder Gebrüder' (unpublished typescript, 1956); Maude, *Antony Gibbs & Sons Limited* pp 29, 31.
48. Thomas, *Cuba* p. 274.
49. SA Schröder, 'Schröder Gebrüder' (unpublished typescript, 1956).
50. Janes and Sayers, *Story of Czarnikow* p. 40.
51. Diaper, 'History of Kleinwort, Sons & Co.' p. 144.

52. Michie, *Stock Exchanges* pp. 64–6.
53. Edward Liveing, *A Century of Insurance: the Commercial Union Insurance Group, 1861–1961* (London: Witherby, 1961).
54. Lloyds of London. Membership Roll, 1790–1930.
55. PLAA West India Dock Company board minutes, 13 July 1888.
56. Barry Supple, *The Royal Exchange Assurance* (Cambridge University Press, 1970) pp. 260–1, 351.
57. Thomas F. O'Brien, 'The Antofagasta Company: a Case Study of Peripheral Capitalism', *Hispanic American Historical Review* (1980) vol. 60, pp. 24–7.
58. d'Erlanger, *Quelques Souvenirs* p. 118.
59. Harold Blakemore, 'Chile from the War of the Pacific to the world depression, 1880–1930', in Leslie Bethell (ed.), *The Cambridge History of Latin America*, vol. V (Cambridge University Press, 1986) p. 506.
60. See, Harold Blakemore, *British Nitrates and Chilean Politics, 1886–1896: Balmaceda and North* (London: Athlone Press, 1974).
61. Laurie Dennett, *Slaughter and May: A Century in the City* (Cambridge: Granta Editions, 1989) pp. 30–1
62. Obituary of Emanuel Underdown, *The Times*, 14 April 1913. The singers referred to were the soprano Giulia Grisi (1811–69) and the tenor Giovanni Mario (1810–83).
63. Ziegler, *Sixth Great Power* pp. 244–66.
64. Herbert Feis, *Europe the World's Banker, 1870–1914* (New Haven, Conn.: Yale University Press, 1930) pp. 361–3.
65. Geoffrey Jones, *Banking and Empire in Iran: the History of the British Bank of the Middle East*, vol. I (Cambridge University Press, 1986) pp. 25–31.
66. Jones, *Banking and Empire* p. 111.
67. *The Economist*, 12 May 1894. The possession of a board of directors composed of 'public men of prominent position and repute', including the President of the Board of Trade, did not prevent the failure of the firm through fraud in 1894.
68. Hall, *London Capital Market* p. 171.
69. *The Bankers' Magazine* (1892) vol. liii, pp. 46–7.
70. Perkins, *House of Brown* pp. 66–7, 242; M. J. Daunton, 'Inheritance and Succession in the City of London in the Nineteenth Century', *Business History* (1988) vol. xxx, p. 276–82.
71. Diaper, 'History of Kleinwort, Sons & Co.' pp. 52, 62.
72. SA Baron Sir John Henry William Schröder's Game Books, 1884–1900. In possession of Bruno L. Schroder. He took Ben Alder Deer Forest from 1884 to 1890 and Glen Feshie Forest from 1892 to 1900.
73. SA Diary of Heinrich Schliemann, January 1866. Extracts from the diaries of Heinrich Schliemann collected and translated by Eduard Eggers.
74. H. R. Leppien (ed.), *Ein Hamburger Sammelt in London, die Freiherr J. H. von Schröder – Stiftung 1910* (Hamburg, 1984). Catalogue of exhibition of pictures and sculptures bequeathed by Baron Sir John Henry William Schröder to the Hamburg Kunsthalle held 11 May to 29 July 1984.

75. *The Times*, 10 June 1910.
76. *Die Deutsche Kolonie in England* (London: Anglo-German Publishing Co., 1913) pp. 25, 44, 47, 49, 50, 53.
77. *Surrey & Middlesex Journal*, 30 April 1910.
78. SA Memorandum from Helmut Schroder to Roger Alford c. 1953.
79. Obituary of Henry Tiarks, *Chislehurst District Times*, 20 October 1911.
80. Harris and Thane, 'British and European Bankers', p. 224.
81. Diaper, 'History of Kleinwort, Sons & Co.' pp. 69–70.
82. Evans, *Death in Hamburg* pp. 34–5.

5   High Finance: 1892–1914

1. Calculated from world exports data in Lewis, 'World Trade', pp. 62–5.
2. Simon, 'New Portfolio Foreign Investment', pp. 38–9.
3. C. H. Feinstein, R. O. C. Matthews and J. C. Odling-Smee, 'The Timing of the Climacteric and its Sectoral Influence in the UK, 1873–1913', in Charles P. Kindleberger and Guido di Tella (eds), *Economics in the Long View* vol. 2 (London: Macmillan, 1982) pp. 169–74.
4. R. J. Truptil, *British Banks and the London Money Market* (London: Jonathan Cape, 1936) p. 179.
5. 'Colonial and Foreign Banks: their position in this country', *The Bankers' Magazine*, (1904) vol. lxxvii, p. 356.
6. W. R. Lawson, 'Lombard Street Under Foreign Control', *The Bankers' Magazine* (1901) vol. lxxi, pp. 376–89.
7. Frederick J. Fuller and H. D. Rowan, 'Foreign Competition in its Relation to Banking', *Journal of the Institute of Banking* (1900) vol. xxi, p. 52.
8. A. R. Holmes and Edwin Green, *Midland: 150 Years of Banking Business* (London: Batsford, 1986) pp. 134–5; Sir Robert Kindersley's evidence to the Committee on Finance and Industry, 23 January 1930. Cmd 3897, 1931, p. 73.
9. SA Johann Rudolph Schröder, 'Geschichte der Firma Schröder Gebrüder' (unpublished typescript, 1956). This account of the history of Schröder Gebrüder was written by the founder's grandson.
10. SA Henry Andrews, 'Memoir' (unpublished typescript, 9 March 1955).
11. GL Morgan Grenfell Papers. Grenfell Correspondence 1900–36, fo. 108, MS 21, 799, EC Grenfell, 1914.
12. SA Letter describing Baron Bruno Schröder and Frank Tiarks written by Henry Andrews who was an executive with the firm 1923–35, 1 November 1954.
13. Ibid.
14. Interview with Henry Tiarks.
15. SA H. Bingel, *Leaves From My Tree* (London: privately published, c. 1910) preface by Evelina D. Bingel.
16. Interview with Laurance Mackie.

17. SA Laurance Mackie memoir; upon joining the staff of Barings at the turn of the century, a clerk commented in his diary on how undisciplined the office was compared to Schroders. Quoted in Ziegler, *Sixth Great Power* p. 295.

18. Diaper, 'History of Kleinwort Sons & Co.' p. 350. Schröders' accounts suggest that the firm employed temporary staff in some of these years in addition to the permanent clerks and volunteers; Chapman, *Rise of Merchant Banking* p. 33.

19. On the basis of the surnames in the years 1902 to 1914, J. Henry Schröder & Co. recruited 27 British and 19 German permanent clerks and accepted 13 German and 4 British volunteers. SA List of Staff 1829–1922.

20. A. C. Pointon, *Wallace Brothers* (London: privately published, 1974) p. 52.

21. Philip Norman, *Crosby Place* (London: London County Council, 1908) survey of London, vol. 9, p. 38.

22. SA Letter from Baron Bruno Schröder to Baron Sir John Henry Schröder, 1 January 1910. Interest was charged at 4 per cent on the loan.

23. SA Interview with E. L. Cheese conducted by Roger Alford, 6 May 1954.

24. Manfred Pohl, 'Deutsche Bank London Agency Founded 100 Years Ago', in *Deutsche Bank Studies in Economic and Monetary Problems and on Banking History* (1973) no. 10, pp. 17–28.

25. R. S. Sayers, *Gilletts in the London Money Market 1867–1967* (Oxford University Press, 1968) p. 46.

26. Jacob Riesser, *The German Great Banks and their Concentration in Connection with the Economic Development of Germany* (Washington DC: Government Printing Office, 1911) pp. 431–2.

27. SA Schröder, 'Schröder Gebrüder' (unpublished typescript, 1956).

28. Manfred Pohl, *Hamburger Bankengeschichte* (Mainz: V. Hase & Koehler, 1986) pp. 80–1.

29. SA Schröder, 'Schröder Gebrüder' (unpublished typescript, 1956)

30. Diaper, 'History of Kleinwort Sons & Co.' p. 164.

31. Interview with Henry Tiarks. Rionda was with J. M. Ceballos & Co. of New York before joining Czarnikow, Macdougall & Co.; Hurford James and Sayers, *Story of Czarnikow* p. 44; Manuel Moreno Fraginals, 'Plantation Economies and Societies in the Spanish Caribbean, 1860–1930', in *The Cambridge History of Latin America*, vol. IV (Cambridge University Press, 1986) p. 196.

32. GL Kleinwort Benson Papers, MS 22,033, vol. 1. Report to Goldman Sachs, 8 October 1901.

33. SA Letter from Walter A. Brandt to Helmut Schroder, 11 March 1958.

34. Diaper, 'History of Kleinwort Sons & Co.' pp. 165–6.

35. SA Letter from Walter A. Brandt to Helmut Schroder, 11 March 1958, citing letter from Kleinworts to Brandts written in October 1901.

36. The discount house M. Corialegno & Co. was founded in 1876 and went out of business around 1904.

37. Japhets were admitted to the client list of J. Henry Schröder & Co. upon an introduction from the Darmstädter und Nationalbank of Berlin. Japhet, *Recollections* p. 77.

38. The first appearance of J. Henry Schröder & Co. in the *London Gazette*, as a firm making returns to the Inland Revenue as a bank, was in 1906.
39. Simon, 'New British Portfolio Foreign Investment', p. 29.
40. RA MS XI/130A.0. Letter from Lord Rothschild, London, to Rothschild partners, Paris, 3 December 1906.
41. SA Letter from J. Henry Schröder & Co., London, to Speyer & Co., New York, 22 March 1907.
42. *South American Journal*, 13 March 1909.
43. SA Letter from J. Henry Schröder & Co., London, to Speyer & Co., New York, 15 October 1908.
44. Albert Pam, *Adventures and Recollections* (Oxford University Press, 1945) pp. 38–51.
45. Quoted in R. P. T. Davenport-Hines, 'Albert Samuel Pam', *Dictionary of Business Biography*, vol. IV (London: Butterworth, 1985) pp. 526–7.
46. SA Schröder, 'Schröder Gebrüder' (unpublished typescript, 1956).
47. *The Economist*, 15 December 1906.
48. Leon F. Sensabaugh, 'The Coffee Trust Question in United States – Brazilian Relations: 1912–1913', *Hispanic American Historical Review* (1946) vol. xxvi, p. 480.
49. RA MS XI/111/37. Telegram from N. M. Rothschild & Sons, London, to The Minister of Finance, Rio, early February 1906.
50. RA MS XI/111/37. Letter from Naumann Gepp & Co. Ltd, 130 Fenchurch Street, London, to N. M. Rothschild & Sons, London, no date (*c.* February 1907).
51. RA MS XI/111/37. Letter from Landsberg & Co., 29 Mincing Lane, London, to N. M. Rothschild & Sons, London, 31 January 1907; Siegfried Zimmermann, *Theodor Wille 1844–1969* (Hamburg: Verlag Hanseatischer Merkur, 1969) pp. 130–4.
52. RA MS XI/111/37. Letter from Landsberg & Co., 29 Mincing Lane, London, to N. M. Rothschild & Sons, London, 12 February 1907.
53. RA MS XI/130A/0. Letter from Lord Rothschild, London, to Rothschild partners, Paris, 3 December 1906; MS XI/130A.1. Letter from Lord Rothschild, London, to Rothschild partners, Paris, 3 April 1907.
54. SA 'Recollections of Frank C. Tiarks', 22 August 1939.
55. RA MS XI/130A.2. Letter from Lord Rothschild, London, to Rothschild partners, Paris, 8 November 1908.
56. 'The End of Valorisation', *The Economist*, 19 December 1908.
57. RA MS XI/130A/2. Letter from Lord Rothschild, London, to Rothschild partners, Paris, 15 December 1908.
58. RA MS XI/130A/2. Letter from Lord Rothschild, London, to Rothschild partners, Paris, 2 November 1908.
59. Ziegler, *Sixth Great Power* p. 309.
60. Ziegler, *Sixth Great Power* p. 304.
61. Lewis, *America's Stake* p. 316.
62. *Financial Mail*, 13 June 1915.
63. SA Note on Amalgamated Copper Co. issue.
64. Michie, *Stock Exchanges* p. 56.

65. The Pierce Oil Co. was formed to acquire the Waters Pierce Oil Corporation, a petroleum products distribution firm, whose divestiture from the Standard Oil Trust was necessitated by anti-trust legislation.
66. SA Memorandum on Cruz Alta (c. 1924).
67. BBA MS COF 05/06/09. Letter from Baron Bruno Schröder to Mr Farrer, 23 November 1909.
68. SA Memorandum. The China Consortium, 23 June 1937.
69. Calculated from estimates in Forrest Capie and Alan Webber, 'Profits and Profitability in British Banking, 1870–1939', SRRC Research Project Monetary History of the UK 1870–1970. Discussion Paper no. 18 (1985) p. 44.
70. W. D. Rubinstein, *Men of Property* (London: Croom Helm, 1981) p. 41; *The Times*, 19 July 1910; William Schröder, John Henry's younger brother, who had retired from business 30 years earlier to pursue the life of a gentleman of leisure, left £645,000 at his death in 1912 – half of which he had recently inherited from his elder brother, *The Times*, 3 April 1912.

6   The First World War: 1914–18

1. Hansard 26 November, 1914, col 1392.
2. Obituary of Baron Bruno Schröder, *Daily Telegraph*, 11 December 1940.
3. PRO HO45/10745/264030(2). Note entitled 'Licence to reside and trade granted to Baron Bruno Schröder', 8 August 1914.
4. Letter from Montagu Norman, London, to James Brown, New York, 12 August 1914. Quoted in Sir Henry Clay, *Lord Norman* (London: Macmillan, 1957) p. 82.
5. BMBA Minute of meeting held 5 August 1914.
6. PRO T172/134. Conference between the Chancellor of the Exchequer, Members of the Cabinet and Representatives of Accepting Houses, 12 August 1914, p. 12.
7. PRO T172/134. Conference between the Chancellor of the Exchequer, Members of the Cabinet and Representatives of Accepting Houses, 12 August 1914, p. 12.
8. BMBA Statement signed by the Chairman of the Accepting Houses Committee, Frederick Huth Jackson, 11 August 1914.
9. PRO T172/134. Conference between the Chancellor of the Exchequer, Members of the Cabinet and Representatives of Accepting Houses, 12 August 1914, p. 12.
10. R. S. Sayers, *The Bank of England 1891 to 1944* (Cambridge: Cambridge University Press, 1976) p. 78.
11. BMBA Statement of the Treasury Published 5 September 1914.
12. Hartley Withers, *War and Lombard Street* (London: Smith, Elder & Co., 1915) p. 99.
13. Hartley Withers, 'The City's Lead in Finance and Trade', in *The City of London* (London: Times Publishing Company, 1927) p. 160.

14. Hansard. Commons, 27 November 1914 col. 1531–2. See also, Commons, 16 November 1914, col. 226; Commons, 19 November 1914, col. 540; Commons, 26 November 1914, col. 1386.

15. 'The Problem of the Speyer', *The National Review* (September 1914–February 1915) vol. 64, p. 441.

16. Panikos Panayi, 'German Business Interests in Britain during the First World War', *Business History* (1990) vol. xxxii, p. 249.

17. Hansard. Lords, 18 May 1915, col. 1027; Commons, 19 May 1915, col. 2360; Commons 17, June 1915, col. 870.

18. Hansard. Commons, 27 July 1915, col. 2136.

19. Obituary of Baron Bruno Schröder, *The Star*, 11 December 1940.

20. SA Henry Andrews 'Memoir' (unpublished typescript, 9 March 1955).

21. SA Letter from Frank Tiarks to Herman Tiarks, 5 August 1914.

22. SA Letter from Frank Tiarks to Herman Tiarks, 26 October 1914.

23. SA Agnes Tiarks' diaries, 1914–17. Frank Tiarks' mother recorded his comings and goings but the diaries contain few details of his business activities.

24. PRO BT 55/32. Minutes of Evidence taken before the Financial Facilities Committee, 5 July 1916, p. 2.

25. Patrick Beesley, *Room 40: British Naval Intelligence 1914–1918* (New York: Harcourt Brace Jovanovich, 1982) pp. 174, 265.

26. SA Letter from Lord Alfred Milner, War Office, to Frank Tiarks, 9 January 1919.

27. SA Letters from Frank Tiarks to his wife while Civil Commissioner, January–April 1919. See also, David Williamson, *The British in Germany 1918–1930: the reluctant occupiers* (Oxford: Berg Publishers, 1991)

28. SA Letter from Frank Tiarks to Herman Tiarks, 9 May 1915.

29. SA Letter from Frank Tiarks to Herman Tiarks, 15 May 1915.

30. SA Letter from Baron Bruno Schröder to Frank Tiarks (no date – early October 1915).

31. John Atkin, 'Official Regulation of British Overseas Investment, 1914–1931', *Economic History Review* (1970) vol. xxiii, pp. 325, 335.

32. Leland Rex Robinson, *Foreign Credit Facilities in the United Kingdom* (New York: Columbia University Press, 1923) p. 21.

33. Burk, *Morgan Grenfell* pp. 125–34; Ziegler, *Sixth Great Power* pp. 320–32.

34. Kleinwort's borrowings from the Bank of England on account of pre-moratorium loans were £6.7 million in 1914 and over the war years borrowings averaged £2.8 million, which must have precluded profits. Diaper, 'History of Kleinwort Sons & Co.' pp. 209, 213.

35. BoEA C47/237. Letter from Walter Cunliffe, Governor, to Sir John Bradbury, Treasury, 21 September 1916.

36. Panayi, 'German Business Interests', p. 250.

37. SA Letter from Baron Bruno Schroder to Frank Tiarks (no date – early October 1915).

38. SA Henry Andrews 'Memoir'.

39. GL Morgan Grenfell Papers. Grenfell Correspondence 1900–36 fo 120, MS 21, 799. E. C. Grenfell, September 1915.

40. SA Partnership Documents. Memorandum of Agreement, 2 November 1915.
41. The military salaries of staff serving with the armed forces were supplemented by the firm to maintain their pre-war levels.

7 Prosperity Amidst European Instability: 1919–31

1. Stephen A. Schucker, *The End of French Predominance in Europe: The Financial Crisis of 1924 and the Adoption of the Dawes Plan* (Chapel Hill, NC: University of North Carolina Press, 1976) p. 9.
2. William Adams Brown, *The International Gold Standard Reinterpreted, 1914–1934* (New York: Ams Press, 1940) pp. 138–61.
3. 'The Money Market Since the War', *The Bankers' Magazine* (March 1923) vol. cxv, pp. 427–8. See Appendix V(i) for basis of inflation adjustment.
4. Robinson, *Foreign Credit Facilities* p. 21.
5. Atkin, 'Official Regulation', pp. 325–7.
6. See, Joseph S. Davis, 'Recent Developments in World Finance', *Review of Economic Statistics* (1922) vol. iv, pp. 3–87; Robert Z. Aliber, 'Speculation in the Foreign Exchanges: the European Experience, 1919–1926', *Yale Economic Essays* (1962) vol. 2, pp. 171–245.
7. Sir Henry Strakosckh, 'The Monetary Tangle of the Post-War Period', in A. D. Gayer (ed.), *Essays in Honour of Irving Fischer* (London: George Allen & Unwin, 1937) p. 157.
8. Derek H. Aldcroft, *From Versailles to Wall Street 1919–1929* (London: Allen Lane, 1977) p. 127.
9. J. Henry Schröder & Co., *Quarterly Review of Business Conditions*, December 1923.
10. *Quarterly Review*, October 1924; See also, *The Bankers' Magazine* (1924) vol. cxviii, pp. 579–80.
11. Quoted in Frank C. Costigliola, 'Anglo-American Financial Rivalry in the 1920s', *Journal of Economic History* (1977) vol. xxxvii, pp. 926–7.
12. Otto Niemeyer, Treasury, to Winston Churchill, Chancellor, 2 February 1925. Quoted in Costigliola, 'Financial Rivalry' p. 926.
13. *Quarterly Review*, July 1925.
14. League of Nations, *Review of World Trade 1938* (Geneva: League of Nations, 1939) p. 60.
15. Thomas Balogh, *Studies in Financial Organisation* (Cambridge University Press, 1947) p. 167.
16. Truptil, *British Banks* p. 137; 'Acceptance Commissions', *The Bankers' Magazine* (February 1927) vol. cxxiii, p. 243; see also evidence of Sir Robert Kindersley to the Committee on Finance and Industry, cap 1223, Cmd 3897, 1931.
17. Brendan Brown, *Monetary Chaos in Europe* (London: Croom Helm, 1988) p. 212.
18. John Atkin, *British Overseas Investment, 1918–1931* (New York: Arno Press, 1977) pp. 147–55.

19. Brown, *Monetary Chaos* p. 217.
20. Derek H. Aldcroft, *Versailles to Wall Street* p. 263.
21. *Quarterly Review*, May 1931.
22. United Nations, *International Capital Movements During the Inter-War Period* (New York: United Nations, 1949) p. 10.
23. United Nations, *International Capital Movements* pp. 11–12.
24. *The Economist*, 26 September 1931.
25. SA Henry Andrews, 'Memoir'.
26. SA Henry Andrews, 'Memoir'.
27. Clay, *Norman* pp. 199, 201.
28. Lord D'Abernon, *An Ambassador of Peace: Pages from the Diary of Viscount D'Abernon*, vol. I (London: Hodder & Stoughton, 1929) p. 315.
29. Interview with Henry Tiarks.
30. Sayers, *Bank of England* pp. 175–6.
31. Hjalmar Schacht, *My First Seventy Six Years* (London: Allan Wingate, 1955) p. 217.
32. FRBNYA Strong Papers 1116.1. Letter from Benjamin Strong to Montagu Norman, 11 December 1919.
33. FRBNYA Strong Papers 1116.1. Letter from Montagu Norman to Benjamin Strong, 8 January 1920.
34. See, Pam, *Adventures*; SA 'Notes by A. Pam' (unpublished typescript, 1955); Davenport Hines, 'Albert Samuel Pam' pp. 526–34.
35. Pam, *Adventures* p. 56.
36. SA 'Notes by A. Pam' (unpublished typescript, 1955).
37. Obituary of William Douro Hoare, *The Times*, 11 April 1928.
38. SA Henry Tiarks' diary, 1 January 1926.
39. Obituary of Alexander Goschen, *The Bankers' Magazine* (August 1928) vol. cxxvi, p. 209.
40. I am grateful to Victoria Glendinning, biographer of Rebecca West, for biographical details of Henry Andrews.
41. Interview with Justin Lowinsky. Henry Andrews and Rebecca West were friends of Justin Lowinsky's mother and upon her death took a close interest in his upbringing.
42. Interview with Maurice Buckmaster.
43. Interview with Toby Caulfeild.
44. SA Fritz Dingle, 'Recollections' (unpublished typescript, 5 May 1955)
45. *The Bankers' Magazine* (May 1926) vol. cxxi, p. 741.
46. Interview with Henry Tiarks.
47. Paul Einzig, 'The Jews in International Banking', *The Banker* (October 1933) vol. xxviii, p. 31.
48. F. R. Acheson Shortis, 'Some aspects of the future of foreign banking in London' *The Bankers' Magazine* (November 1927) vol. cxxiv, p. 623.
49. Truptil, *British Banks* p. 147.
50. Sir Robert Kindersley of Lazards estimated that German borrowers had to pay 2–2½ per cent premiums over their British counterparts since 'no-one had much confidence in Germany and her need was very great'.

Evidence of Sir Robert Kindersley to the Committee on Finance and Industry, cap. 1596, Cmd. 3897, 1931.

51. 'German Banks in London', *The Bankers' Magazine* (January 1925) vol. cxix, p. 49.
52. Max Ikle, *Switzerland: an International Banking and Finance Centre* (Stroudsburg, Penn.: Dowden, Hutchinson & Ross, 1972) p. 22.
53. Paul Einzig, *In the Centre of Things* (London: Hutchinson, 1960) p. 49.
54. John B. Wolf, 'The Diplomatic History of the Baghdad Railway', *University of Missouri Studies* (1936) vol. xi, pp. 13–15.
55. PRO FO 371/9146 70910. Memorandum for Lord Curzon, 22 October 1923.
56. PRO FO 371/9146 70910. Agreement between the Oriental Railways and the Anglo-Turkish Trust Company Ltd, 21 September 1923.
57. PRO FO 371/9146 70910. Memorandum for Lord Curzon, 22 October 1923.
58. Einzig, *Centre of Things* p. 48.
59. See Fritz Seidenzahl, *1870–1970: 100 Jahre Deutsche Bank* (Frankfurt-am-Main, 1970) pp. 268–9.
60. SA Agreement between J. Henry Schröder & Co. and the Deutsche Bank, 14 November 1924.
61. SA Agreement between J. Henry Schröder & Co. and the Deutsche Bank, 23 June 1926.
62. SA Henry Andrews, 'Memoir'.
63. Interview with Toby Caulfeild.
64. *The Times*, 18 September 1924.
65. SA Henry Andrews, 'Memoir'.
66. C. R. S. Harris, *Germany's Foreign Indebtedness* (Oxford University Press, 1935) pp. 116–18.
67. SA Robin Clutton, 'Potash Syndicate of Germany 25 year sinking fund gold loan' (unpublished typescript).
68. P. L. Cottrell, 'Aspects of Western Equity Investments in the Banking Systems of East Central Europe', in Alice Teichova and P. L. Cottrell (eds), *International Business and Central Europe, 1918 – 1939* (Leicester University Press, 1983) p. 341.
69. See Richard H. Meyer, *Bankers' Diplomacy: Monetary Stabilisation in the Twenties* (New York: Colombia University Press, 1970) pp. 1–15.
70. Interview with Henry Tiarks.
71. Ziegler, *Sixth Great Power* pp. 351–2.
72. Ziegler, *Sixth Great Power* p. 353.
73. PRO FO 371/7695. Memorandum by Sir H. Dering, Bucharest, for Foreign Office, London, 6 June 1922.
74. PRO FO 371/11418. Robert Greg, Bucharest, to Sir Austen Chamberlain, Foreign Office, London, 14 November 1926.
75. PRO FO 371/11418. Robert Greg, Bucharest, to Foreign Office, 19 November 1926.
76. PRO FO 371/11418. Orme Sargent, Foreign Office, to Robert Greg, 30 November 1926.
77. SA Henry Andrews, 'Memoir'.

78. Meyer, *Bankers' Diplomacy* p. 124.
79. See Leo Pasvolsky, *Bulgaria's Economic Position* (Washington DC: Brookings Institution, 1930).
80. SA Bond Book, 1921–32. This contains comments on the principal issues. No equivalent document exists for the earlier or later periods.
81. SA Henry Andrews, 'Memoir'.
82. Atkin, *British Overseas Investment* pp. 173–4.
83. J. W. F. Rowe, *Studies in the Artificial Control of Raw Materials. No. 3 – Brazilian Coffee* (London: London and Cambridge Economic Service, 1932) p. 36.
84. Ziegler, *Sixth Great Power* p. 351.
85. Interview with Henry Tiarks.
86. SA Norbert Bogdan, 'Schrobanco Recollections' (unpublished typescript, 1977).
87. *Quarterly Review*, November 1930.
88. *Quarterly Review*, May 1931.
89. *The Times*, 21 December 1932.
90. SA Letterhead of the Edward G. Budd Manufacturing Company.
91. SA Correspondence between J. Henry Schröder & Co., the Edward G. Budd Manufacturing Company and Morris Motors, 27 January 1926 – 18 February 1926.
92. See Pressed Steel, *Pressed Steel Company Limited* (Oxford: Pressed Steel, 1956).
93. SA Promotional pamphlet, 1930.
94. SA Letter from J. Henry Schröder & Co. to Baring Brothers Ltd about Pressed Steel, 6 May 1930.
95. See William Norris, *The Man Who Fell from the Sky* (London: Viking, 1987); *Illustrated London News*, 14 July 1928.
96. See Timothy B. Schroder, *The Art of the European Goldsmith: Silver from the Schroder Collection* (New York: The American Federation of Arts, 1983).

8   The New World Beckons: Schrobanco, 1923–35

1. Paul Einzig, *The Fight for Financial Supremacy* (London: Macmillan, 1931) p. 49.
2. M. F. Jolliffe, *The United States as a Financial Centre 1919–1933* (Cardiff: University of Wales Press Board, 1935) p. 7; Simon, 'New British Portfolio Foreign Investment', p. 39.
3. Jolliffe, *United States as a Financial Centre* p. 106
4. Estimated from figures in Jolliffe, *United States as a Financial Centre* p. 106, and Atkin, *British Overseas Investment* p. 61.
5. *Facts and Figures Relating to the American Money Market* (New York: American Acceptance Council, 1931) p. 8; Balogh, *Financial Organisation* p. 167.

6. Homer P. Balabanis, *The American Discount Market* (University of Chicago Press, 1935) p. 1.

7. Benjamin H. Bechart, *The New York Money Market*, vol. III (New York: Columbia University, 1932) p. 314.

8. 'Lombard Street and its Rivals', *The Economist*, 8 November 1930.

9. Jolliffe, *United States as a Financial Centre* p. 12.

10. See Lester V. Chandler, *Benjamin Strong, Central Banker* (Washington, DC: The Brookings Institution, 1958) pp. 86–93.

11. *Acceptance Bulletin*, 2 June 1919.

12. Interview with Henry Tiarks.

13. SA Memorandum of Intention from Helmut Schroder to Baring Brothers, 11 October 1951. In paragraph B, Helmut Schroder explained the origins of the establishment of Schrobanco.

14. FRBNYA C440. J. Henry Schroder Banking Corporation papers. Letter from E. R. Kenzal, Deputy Governor, to F. J. Zurlinden, Deputy Governor of the Federal Reserve Bank of Cleveland, Ohio, 4 February 1924, reporting Frank Tiarks' words.

15. E. N. White, *The Regulation and Reform of the American Banking System 1900–1929* (Princeton, NJ: Princeton University Press, 1983) p. 127.

16. FRBNYA Strong Papers 120.0. Paul M. Warburg to Benjamin Strong, 27 January 1925, with report enclosed.

17. Yale University. Manuscripts Collection. Manuscript Group 535. Letter from Paul Warburg to N. M. Rothschild & Sons reporting on Warburg's progress towards the establishment of the International Acceptance Bank (undated – probably summer 1920).

18. CMBA International Acceptance Bank. Minutes of first meeting of the board of directors, 5 March 1921, p. 10.

19. CMBA International Acceptance Bank. Box 3. List of Stockholders. 10 March 1921.

20. CMBA International Acceptance Bank. Minutes of first meeting of the board of directors, 5 March 1921, p. 11.

21. Sayers, *Bank of England* p. 269.

22. Unless otherwise indicated, all quotations from Frank Tiarks relating to his visits to New York in May and October 1923 are from the letters written to his wife, Emmy Tiarks. The letters were made available by his son, Henry Tiarks.

23. Benjamin Strong was recuperating from illness at the time of Frank Tiarks' arrival in New York.

24. Interview with Henry Tiarks.

25. Interview with Barbara Noble Robinson, daughter of Prentiss Gray.

26. SA John L Simpson, 'Activities in a Troubled World'. Copy of oral history memoir in University of California Bancroft Library, 1978. p. 74

27. Helbert Hoover, *An American Epic*, vol. II (Chicago: Henry Regnery Co., 1959) p. 32.

28. Quoted in Joseph S. Davis, *The World Between the Wars, 1919–39: an economist's view* (Baltimore, Md: Johns Hopkins University Press, 1975) p. 18.

29. Interview with Henry Tiarks; Einzig, *Financial Supremacy* p. 51.
30. Interview with Sherman Gray, son of Prentiss Gray.
31. SA John L. Simpson, 'Schrobanco Recollections'.
32. SA Schrobanco papers. Gerald F. Beal. 'Memorandum. Regarding Schroders, New York', 8 November 1943.
33. Yale University. Manuscripts Collection. Manuscripts Group 535. Paul Moritz Warburg Papers. Letter from Paul Warburg to N. M. Rothschild & Sons. No date.
34. CMBA International Acceptance Bank Organisation Papers. Box 3. Letter from Shattuck, Glenn & Ganter to George V. McLaughlin, 31 August 1923.
35. CMBA International Acceptance Bank Organisation Papers. Box 3. Letter from Shattuck, Glenn & Ganter, 31 August 1923.
36. SA Schrobanco papers. J. Henry Schroder Banking Corporation Organisation Certificate, 21 September 1923, p. 1.
37. At the time of McGarragh's appointment *The Banker* commented 'European interests have desired to see this office bestowed upon some American who stood well with the Reserve System and could exert a vigorous influence over it, and who at the same time, if possible, would be favourably regarded by the Administration at Washington. New York banks have desired to see the office in the hands of someone who would work harmoniously with them, and who would not fall into radical ways of doing things. They have found what is believed by all parties to be the proper selection fulfilling these requirements in the person of Mr Gates W. McGarrah'. H. Parker Willis, 'International American Banking', *The Banker* (1930) vol. xiv, pp. 47–8.
38. The outside subscribers who each took between 200 and 1,000 shares each (0.5 to 2.5 per cent of the equity) were Schröder Gebrüder, Deichmann & Co., Gebrüder Bethmann & Co., J. H. Stein; the Boden-Credit Anstalt, the Bankhaus Johann Liebig & Co., the Banque Privée de Glaris; and Staudt & Cia Buenos Aires.
39. Gray hired the clubhouse of the smart Larchmont Yacht Club near his home in Larchmont, New York State, for dinner after a summer swimming party. Although Prohibition was in force, a supply of bootleg liquor was acquired in large water cooler bottles. After chemical analysis, it was mixed with orange juice and served to the guests. Gray returned home after dinner leaving the party in full swing. The following morning he was awakened by the club secretary who informed him that his membership was suspended. On inspection of the clubhouse he found, as his son Sherman Gray put it, 'that the boys had had one hell of a good party'. A large donation to club funds mollified the secretary, but no more Schrobanco parties were held there.
40. SA William Tucker, 'Schrobanco Recollections'.
41. SA Schrobanco papers. Audit Department Memorandum, 8 May 1925.
42. SA Schrobanco papers. Memorandum from Mr Code, Audit Department, to Mr Gray, 23 January 1931.
43. SA John .L Simpson, 'Schrobanco Recollections'.

44. 'Honor Roll of Accepting Banks' published by the *Acceptance Bulletin*, 1924.
45. SA Carlos Lleras Restrepo, *Cronica de mi Propia Victa*, vol. I (date and place of publication unknown) pp. 371–2.
46. Interview with Polly Lada-Mocarski.
47. SA Schrobanco papers. President's Statement to Shareholders for the Year 1925.
48. FRBNYA C440. Letter from E. R. Kenzal, Deputy Governor, to F. J. Zurlinden, Deputy Governor, Federal Reserve Bank of Cleveland, 4 February 1924.
49. *New York Times*, 4 October 1923; 10 October 1923.
50. Jolliffe, *United States as a Financial Centre* p. 106.
51. Einzig, *Financial Supremacy* p. 53.
52. SA Schrobanco papers. Continental Securities Corporation file. Memorandum, December 1924.
53. Paul H. Nitze, *From Hiroshima to Glasnost: At the Centres of Decision, a memoir* (New York: Grove Weidenfell, 1989) p. xviii.
54. *New York Times*, 8 March 1933.
55. *New York Times*, 20 March 1933.
56. *New York Times*, 8 August 1934.
57. SA Simpson, 'Activities in a Troubled World', p. 79.
58. SA Schrobanco papers. Memorandum on Buenos Aires Note Issue, 1930.
59. SA Schrobanco papers. 'Memorandum'. Document prepared for Securities and Exchange Commission hearings on Standard Power and Light Corporation, May 1941.
60. SA Schrobanco papers. Letter from John Simpson, New York, to Prentiss Gray, London, 4 November 1929.
61. SA Schrobanco papers. Board Minutes. Haskins & Sells report on examination of accounts as of 31 December 1942, p. 8.
62. SA Schrobanco papers. Letter from Gerald Beal, London, to John Simpson, New York. 14 November 1929.
63. SA Letter from Henry Andrews, London, to John Simpson, New York, 30 November 1929.
64. SA Schrobanco papers. Cable from Prentiss Gray, New York, to Gerald Beal, Munich, 10 January 1930.
65. SA Schrobanco papers. Letter from John Simpson, New York, to Jerry Beal, London, 22 July 1931.
66. SA Simpson, 'Activities in a Troubled World', p. 106.
67. SA Schrobanco papers. Letter from John Simpson to Prentiss Gray, 8 June 1933.
68. SA E. Meili, 'Schrobanco Recollections'.
69. SA Schrobanco papers. Letter from Frederick Dolbeare, Berlin, to John Simpson, New York, 14 December 1928.
70. SA Schrobanco papers. Letter from Frederick Dolbeare, Berlin to John Simpson, New York, 9 January 1929.
71. SA Schrobanco papers. Letter from John Simpson to Gerald Beal, 21 October 1932.

72. SA Schrobanco papers. Letter from Norbert Bogdan, Paris, to John Simpson, New York, 25 September 1930.
73. SA Schrobanco papers. Letter from John Simpson to Gerald Beal, 4 November 1932.
74. SA Schrobanco papers. Letter from Gerald Beal to John Simpson, 10 July 1931.
75. SA Schrobanco papers. Letter from John Simpson to Gerald Beal, 4 November 1932.
76. SA Schrobanco papers. Letter from John Simpson to Gerald Beal, 19 October 1932.
77. SA Schrobanco papers. Letter from John Simpson to Gerald Donovan, August 1933.
78. SA Norbert Bogdan, 'Schrobanco Recollections'.
79. SA Peter Carpenter, 'Schrobanco Recollections'.
80. SA Norbert Bogdan, 'Schrobanco Recollections'.
81. SA Schrobanco papers. Letter from Frederick Dolbeare to John Simpson, 25 August 1933.
82. SA Schrobanco papers. Letter from John Simpson to Gerald Donovan, 13 June 1933.
83. SA Schrobanco papers. Letter from Frederick Dolbeare to John Simpson, 25 August 1933.
84. SA Schrobanco papers. Letter from Frederick Dolbeare to John Simpson, 25 September 1933.
85. SA Schrobanco papers. Letter from Prentiss Gray to John Simpson, 9 February 1934.
86. SA Schrobanco papers. Letter from John Simpson to Frederick Dolbeare, 14 September 1933.

9   'Standstill', Depression and War: 1931–45

1. See Richard Roberts, 'The City of London as a financial centre in the era of the depression, the Second World War and post-war official controls', in Anthony Gorst, Lewis Johnman and W. Scott Lucas (eds), *Contemporary British History, 1931–61* (London: Pinter Publishers, 1991) pp. 44–61.
2. League of Nations, *Monthly Bulletin of Statistics*, February 1934, p. 51.
3. Balogh, *Financial Organisation* p. 167.
4. United Nations, *International Capital Movements* p. 15.
5. Leonard Thompson Conway, *The International Position of the London Money Market 1931–1937* (unpublished dissertation: University of Pennsylvania, 1947) p. 55.
6. The chronology of events is derived from the Bank of England's diary of the crisis. BoEA OV 34/3. The German Crisis 1931. There are several detailed accounts of the Central European financial crisis in English. See Royal Institute of International Affairs, *Survey of International Affairs 1931* (London: RIIA, 1932); E. W. Bennett, *Germany and the Diplomacy of the Financial Crisis, 1931* (Cambridge, Mass.: Harvard University Press, 1962);

Harold James, *The German Slump: Politics and Economics 1924–1936* (Oxford: Clarendon Press, 1984); Sayers, *Bank of England* pp. 387–415.

7. *Quarterly Review*, 20 August 1931.
8. Harris, *Germany's Foreign Indebtedness* p. 23. The estimate was made by Robert Brand in 1935 and appears to exclude the clearing banks' short-term German debts.
9. *Quarterly Review*, November 1931.
10. *Quarterly Review*, November 1931.
11. BoEA OV 34/3. The German Crisis 1931.
12. BoEA C48/362. List of members of the Joint Committee, 22 July 1931.
13. BoEA C48/362. 13 July 1931.
14. BoEA C48/362. 18 July 1931.
15. Sayers, *Bank of England* p. 391.
16. 'The Conference and the Crisis', *The Economist*, 25 July 1931.
17. *Quarterly Review*, 20 August 1931.
18. Royal Institute of International Affairs, *Survey of International Affairs 1931* (London, RIIA, 1932) p. 8.
19. *Quarterly Review*, 20 August 1931.
20. BoEA C48/362. Memorandum of meeting with Joint Committee on 23 July 1931.
21. BoEA C48/362. 25 July 1931.
22. BoEA Diary of Montagu Norman, 2 July 1931. James Gannon had played an active part in the negotiations with Austria in May and June and had thereby become well known to Montagu Norman.
23. SA The details of Tiarks' activities in Berlin 26–30 July 1931 are derived from his cables via J. Henry Schröder & Co. and notes of his telephone messages.
24. 'The Credit Situation in Germany. Report of the Committee appointed on the Recommendation of the London Conference, 1931', *The Economist*, 22 August 1931.
25. SA Details of the conduct of these negotiations are derived from, 'Precis of Mr F. C. Tiarks' Telephone Reports from Basle to the Joint Bankers' Committee. Saturday 15th August–Wednesday 19th August 1931'.
26. 'The German Standstill Agreement', *The Economist*, 19 September 1931.
27. Harris, *Germany's Foreign Indebtedness* p. 27.
28. SA Telegram from Dr Luther to Frank Tiarks, 10 September 1931.
29. SA Standstill Press Cuttings, September 1931. Unidentified newspaper.
30. BoEA C48/363. Letter from Frank Tiarks to Montagu Norman, 17 October 1931.
31. James, *German Slump* p. 403.
32. BoEA C48/366. Telegram from the Reichsbank to the Bank of England, 16 May 1933.
33. BoEA C48/360. Telegram from the Bank of England to the Reichsbank, 18 May 1933; Paul Einzig, *Appeasement Before, During and After the War* (London: Macmillan, 1941) p. 72.
34. Hjalmar Schacht, *Confessions of the Old Wizard* (Boston: Houghton Mifflin, 1956) p. 283.

35. PRO T 160/465/F8 797/01. The Case Against Germany, 19 June 1933.
36. Harris, *Germany's Foreign Indebtedness* pp. 53.
37. Sayers, *Bank of England* pp. 509–10.
38. *Quarterly Review*, August 1934.
39. BoEA Colleagues File S–T. Letter from Frank Tiarks to Gustav von Mallinckrodt, 21 June 1934.
40. BoEA Colleagues File S–T. Letter from Montagu Norman to Frank Tiarks, 22 June 1934.
41. *Quarterly Review*, August 1934.
42. *Financial News*, 11 November 1934; The Treasury continued to make contingency plans for the introduction of a clearing despite the Anglo-German Transfer Agreement of July 1934. PRO T 160/670/13460. Anglo-German Clearing: explanation of scheme at present contemplated, 5 October 1934.
43. Harris, *Germany's Foreign Indebtedness* pp. 35–7, 51–3.
44. SA Henry Andrews, 'Memoir'.
45. Interview with Henry Tiarks; PRO T 160/818/12681. Letter from G. H. S. Pinsent, British Embassy Berlin, to S. D. Waley, Treasury, 18 January 1937.
46. BoEA Colleagues File S–T. Letter from Frank Tiarks to Montagu Norman, 2 March 1936.
47. PRO FO371/18878/70910. Anglo-German Fellowship: Minutes of the Meeting held at 2.45 pm on Monday 11th March 1935.
48. Einzig, *Appeasement* p. 82.
49. Interview with Henry Tiarks.
50. PRO T 160/818/12681. Letter from G. H. S. Pinsent, British Embassy Berlin, to S. D. Waley, Treasury, 18 January 1937.
51. PRO T 160/818/12681. Letter from S. D. Waley, Treasury, to Sir F. Phillips, Treasury, 14 January 1937. This was not the first instance of a difference of view between the clearing banks and the accepting houses. In 1933 Robert Brand of Lazards found it necessary to write a long letter to Frederick Hyde, Chief General Manager of the Midland Bank, requesting his agreement to the policy that he and Frank Tiarks were pursuing regarding rates of interest charged to Standstill debtors. Midland Bank Archive. 30/194, 27 February 1933.
52. PRO T 160/818/12681. Letter from G. H. S. Pinsent, British Embassy Berlin, to S. D. Waley, Treasury, 22 February 1937.
53. James, *German Slump* pp. 365–6.
54. PRO T 160/818/12681. Letter from S. D. Waley, Treasury, to Sir F. Leith Ross, Treasury, 4 November 1937.
55. MBA H. A. Astbury's Diary, 19 April 1939.
56. SA Standstill adherence documents.
57. BoEA C48/396. List of Creditors and their Acceptances, etc., 16 March 1937.
58. Diaper, 'History of Kleinwort Sons & Co.' p. 228.
59. Pointon, *Wallace Brothers* p. 69.
60. BoEA C48/396. Note re Standstill from A. C. Bull to Governor, 11 June 1936.

61. Sayers, *Bank of England* p. 511.
62. BoEA C48/396. Memorandum from A. C. Bull to Governor, 22 March 1937.
63. BoEA C48/45:2. Memorandum from A. C. Bull to Governor, 13 December 1938.
64. Sayers, *Bank of England* p. 511.
65. BoEA C48/45:3. Note on letter from Baron Bruno Schröder to Governor, 1 February 1939.
66. 'Decline of the Bill of Exchange', *The Economist*, 26 March 1938.
67. Stephanie Diaper, 'Merchant Banking in the Inter-War Period: the Case of Kleinwort, Sons & Co', *Business History* (1986) vol. xxviii, p. 63. For Japhets, see annual reports in *The Bankers' Magazine*.
68. Charles Gordon, *The Two Tycoons* (London: Hamish Hamiltion, 1985) p. 149.
69. SA 'Speech delivered by the Chairman at the Extraordinary General Meeting of Anglo-Foreign Securities Ltd . . . 26 February 1937'. The accounts of the development of Anglo-Foreign Securities and Compensation Brokers are based on this address.
70. PRO FO 371/19936/83513. Compensations Brokers (Limited). Record of Interdepartmental Meeting on November 17 1936. Annex B, letter from Mr Frank Tiarks of Messrs Schröders, to the Governor of the Bank of England, November 17 1936.
71. PRO FO 371/19936/83513. Compensation Brokers (Limited) Record of Interdepartmental Meeting on November 17, 1936.
72. SA Note from Montagu Norman to Frank Tiarks, 2 December 1936.
73. Robert B Stewart, 'Great Britain's Foreign Loan Policy', *Economica* (1938) vol. v, p. 60.
74. Atkin, 'Official Regulation' p. 331.
75. Robert B. Stewart, 'Great Britain's Foreign Loan Policy', *Economica* (1938) vol. v, p. 59.
76. Clay, *Norman* p. 329.
77. Burk, *Morgan Grenfell* p. 268–9.
78. SA Letter from Bank of England to J. Henry Schröder & Co., 12 December 1935.
79. See William Stevenson, *A Man Called Intrepid* (New York: Random House, 1976) During the war Ladenburg Thalmann assisted with the supply of currency to resistance fighters in occupied countries.
80. *Glasgow Herald*, 10 July 1935.
81. Committee on Finance and Industry, 1931. *Report*, Cmd 3897, para 404; W. A. Thomas, *The Finance of British Industry 1918–1976* (London: Methuen, 1978) pp. 116–21.
82. *The Economist*, 13 July 1935.
83. BoEA C48/45. Note by Mr M. Norman, 28 June 1935.
84. Interview with Edward Tucker, former managing director of Leadenhall Securities.
85. Interview with Sir John Mallabar.

86. SA Annual accounts of the Continental and Industrial Trust Ltd. Details of the investment portfolio are not available.
87. *Financial News*, 28 July 1941
88. Interview with Henry Tiarks.
89. Interview with Sir John Mallabar.
90. BoEA C48/45:7. Letter from Helmut Schroder to Governor, 8 July 1943.
91. SA Letter from Henry Tiarks to Helmut Schroder, 18 September 1951.
92. SA Partnership Agreement, 10 February 1951.
93. SA Letter from Helmut Schroder to Henry Tiarks, 12 June 1944.
94. SA Letter from Henry Tiarks to Helmut Schroder, 13 June 1944.
95. SA Letter from Helmut Schroder to Henry Tiarks, 15 June 1944.
96. SA Letter from Frank Tiarks to Henry Tiarks, 15 June 1944.
97. BoEA C48/45. Note re: call by Helmut Schroder on Governor and Deputy Governor, 8 September 1944.

10 Leadership from New York: Schrobanco, 1935–62

1. Interview with George Mallinckrodt.
2. SA Memorandum from Helmut Schroder to Baring Brothers, 11 October 1951.
3. Edward Tenenbaum, *National Socialism vs International Capitalism* (New Haven, Conn.: Yale University Press, 1942) p. 111.
4. *New York Times*, 4 October 1944; Charles Higham, *Trading With The Enemy* (London: Robert Hale, 1983) pp. 23–4.
5. USNA Department of State 862.20111 a/22. Letter from Edward L. Reed, US Embassy, Buenos Aires, to Secretary of State, Washington, 6 May 1942. Contains biographical details of Baron Otto Leithner.
6. SA Schrobanco papers. Letter from Norbert Bogdan, Berlin, to Schrobanco Senior Officers, New York, 28 June 1934; Memorandum 'Eastern European and South American Blocked Currencies', Valla Lada-Mocarski, Paris, 28 June 1934.
7. The average peso:sterling exchange rate for 1935 was 16.99. Information from Bank of England Reference Library; SA Schrobanco papers. Memorandum Mr Whall to Mr Shields, subject: Argentaria Share Distribution, 10 June 1937.
8. USNA Department of State 862.20211 A/30. Letter from Cecil M. P. Cross, American Consulate, Sao Paulo, to Secretary of State, Washington, 18 August 1942.
9. SA Schrobanco papers. Letter from Valla Lada-Mocarski to Kurt Boettscher, Banque des Pays de l'Europe Centrale, 6 August 1937.
10. USNA Department of State 740.00112A 1939/34790. Report of US Embassy in Buenos Aires Regarding Organisation and Activities of Argentaria SA de Finanza.
11. SA Norbert Bogdan, 'Schrobanco Recollections'.
12. SA Peter Carpenter, 'Schrobanco Recollections'.
13. SA Norbert Bogdan, 'Schrobanco Recollections'.

14. SA Schrobanco papers. Letter from Norbert Bogdan, New York, to J. Henry Schröder & Co., London, 11 February 1939.
15. SA Carlos Lleras Restrepo, *Cronica de mi Propia Victa*, vol. I (Date and place of publication unknown) pp. 370–2.
16. Notable amongst the commercial bank clients were the Banco de Bogota, the Banco de Colombia, the Banco Comercial Antiqueno, the Banco de los Andes and the Banco Central Hipotecario in Colombia; the Banco Popular, the Banco Internacional and the Banco de Credito del Peru in Peru; the Banco Union, the Banco Venezolano de Credito in Venezuela; the Banco de Chile, the Banco de Inversiones, and the Banco Sud Americano in Chile.
17. Interview with Alden B. Cushman.
18. Vincent Carosso, *Investment Banking in America* (Cambridge, Mass.: Harvard University Press, 1970) pp. 372–4; Harold Cleveland and Thomas Huertas, *Citibank 1812–1970* (Cambridge, Mass.: Harvard University Press, 1985) pp. 197–8.
19. *New York Times*, 9 July 1936.
20. Avery Rockefeller was the grandson of William Rockefeller, the younger brother of John D. Rockefeller. At the outset, Guinness, Mahon & Co. took a 10 per cent equity interest.
21. SA Schrobanco papers. 'Memorandum'. Document prepared for Securities and Exchange Commission hearings on Standard Power and Light Corporation, May 1941.
22. Interview with Alden B. Cushman.
23. USNA Department of State. 862.20211. Bogdan, Norbert A/1/4. Letter from William G. Burdett, US Embassy, Rio de Janeiro, to Secretary of State, Washington, 6 December 1940.
24. USNA Department of State. 164.12/4237. Copy of letter from G. F. Beal, president, J. Henry Schroder Banking Corporation to Dr Olavo Egydio de Souza Aranha, Monterio Aranha & Cia Ltda, Rio de Janeiro, 20 June 1941.
25. USNA Department of State. 862.20211. Bogdan, Norbert. Letter from Norbert Bogdan, New York, to R. B. Shipley, Chief Passport Division, Department of State, Washington DC, 20 August 1941.
26. Interview with Norbert Bogdan.
27. Interview with Henry Tiarks.
28. See Richard Sayers, *Financial Policy 1939–45* (London: Longmans, Green & Co., 1956) pp. 363–427.
29. BoEA C48/45.6. Memorandum from G. L. F. Bolton to S. Tink, 17 February 1941.
30. Interview with Henry Tiarks.
31. SA Norbert Bogdan, 'Schrobanco Recollections'.
32. *PM*, 9 January 1944.
33. SA Schrobanco papers. Report on Unfavourable Publicity. 1947.
34. See, Henry Ashby Turner, *Germany, Big Business and the Rise of Hitler* (Oxford University Press, 1985) pp. 314–17.
35. USNA RG 238. Records of the National Archives collection of World War II war crimes. Box 2 US Counsel for the Prosecution of Axis

Criminality 1945–1946. Miscellaneous Reference Materials. Transcripts of interrogations of Baron Kurt von Schröder.

36. *New York Times*, 14 December 1940.
37. Speech quoted in *The Christian Century*, 25 October 1944.
38. SA Schrobanco papers. Statement issued to press by Gerald F. Beal, 12 October 1944.
39. A. Leonidov, 'International role of the Anglo-American–German Schroder Bank (conclusion)', *New Times* (Moscow) 28 February 1947. See also edition of 21 February 1947 for first part of article; Leonard Mosley, *Dulles* (New York: The Dial Press, 1978) pp. 131–88 describes the activities of Allen Dulles in Switzerland during the war.
40. Interview with Peter Carpenter.
41. SA Schrobanco papers. Telegram to Gerald Beal and William Tucker from Colombian Ambassador, Washington, 29 April 1957.
42. Interview with Peter Carpenter.
43. Interview with George Mallinckrodt.
44. SA Officers' Meetings Minutes (hereafter OMM), 28 July 1947.
45. Interview with Henry Tiarks.
46. Interview with Donald Brown.
47. See Norman C. Miller, *The Great Salad Oil Swindle* (New York: Coward McCann, 1965).
48. Interview with Gerhard Laube.
49. Interview with R Canon Clements.
50. Beal's friendship with Albert L. Williams, as with Bertram Witham and Royal Firman Jr, who were appointed as non-executive directors in the 1960s, arose from their mutual interest in the Boy Scouts of America movement. See also, Charles W. V. Meares, *Looking Back* (New York: privately published, 1985).
51. Interview with Burges Coates.
52. SA Simpson, 'Activities in a Troubled World' p. 141.
53. SA Interview with James Madden, President of Schroder Rockefeller & Co. (no date, *c.* 1961).
54. See Cleveland and Huertas, *Citibank* pp. 243–57.
55. Cleveland and Huertas, *Citibank* pp. 243.
56. SA Schrobanco papers. 'Schroders – New York Management Structure and Organisation Plan', 1956, p. 1.
57. Ibid.
58. Ibid.
59. SA 'Policy of the Firm', draft memorandum by Helmut Schroder, 4 March 1959.
60. Interview with R. Canon Clements.
61. Return on all US National Banks calculated from Series X col.775, US Department of Commerce Bureau of the Census, *Historical Statistics of the United States: Colonial Times to 1970* (Washington DC: Department of Commerce, 1975) p. 1040.
62. Interview with Philip Robinson.

11 Recovery and Growth in London: 1945–59

1. E. Steffenburg, 'Merchant Banking in London', in *Current Financial Problems and the City of London* (London: Institute of Bankers, 1949) p. 66.

2. In 1928, J. Henry Schröder & Co. sent him to Hamburg to train with Schlubach, Thiemer & Co., the firm in which Helmut Schröder and Henry Tiarks had worked as volunteers in 1921.

3. Henry Tiarks was away from the office from 24 September 1948 to 28 March 1949, and Major Pam from 14 October to 17 December 1948.

4. Beal in New York received a letter, which he discussed with Tiarks and Pam, in which Helmut Schroder raised the possibility of inviting an outsider to become chief executive. The candidates he had in mind were Mark Turner of the issuing house Robert Benson, Gerard Koch de Gooreynd of stockbrokers Pamure Gordon, and Edwin Plowden, a civil servant formerly with the City firm C. Tennant & Sons, but no action was taken. Henry Tiarks' diary, 27 October 1948.

5. SA Letter from Helmut Schroder to Henry Tiarks, 24 March 1953.

6. SA OMM, 19 April 1955.

7. 'Potash Loan Offer', *The Economist*, 15 August 1953.

8. SA Agreement 1 August 1956 between Deutsches Kalisyndikat GmbH (Potash Syndicate of Germany), J. Henry Schroder & Co., 'the Receiving Bank', and Royal Exchange Assurance, 'the Trustee'.

9. SA OMM, 30 June 1947.

10. SA OMM, 28 July 1947.

11. Interview with Henry Tiarks.

12. SA OMM, 23 April 1948.

13. Interview with Dr Hermann J. Abs.

14. SA OMM, 21 April 1949.

15. SA OMM, 5 December 1949. An account was also opened simultaneously with Kleinworts.

16. SA OMM, 6 March 1950.

17. *The Economist*, 21 June 1952.

18. Interview with Henry Tiarks.

19. William Clarke, *The City's Invisible Earnings* (London: Institute of Economic Affairs, 1958) pp. 47, 96.

20. Evidence of Sir Edward Reid, Chairman of the Accepting Houses Committee, to the Committee on the Working of the Monetary System, 20 March 1958. Evidence, vol. II, part VI, cap. 5818 Cmnd 827 (London: HMSO, 1959).

21. 'Finance by Bills', *The Economist*, 29 August 1953.

22. Evidence of Sir Edward Reid, Chairman of the Accepting Houses Committee, to the Committee on the Working of the Monetary System, 20 March 1958. Evidence, vol. II, part VI, cap 5842–5844. Cmnd 827 (London: HMSO, 1959).

23. 'Latin American Market', *The Economist*, 18 August 1951.

24. SA OMM, 21 March 1946.

25. SA OMM, 14 October 1946.
26. SA OMM, 13 December 1951.
27. SA OMM, 17 August 1959.
28. SA OMM, 13 March 1950.
29. SA OMM, 4 December 1951.
30. SA OMM, 1 December 1959.
31. SA OMM, 22 February 1956.
32. SA OMM, 22 November 1957. The participants in the group were Rothschilds, Schroders, Lazards, Barings and the Bank of London & South America.
33. Interview with Jan Stuijt.
34. SA OMM, 28 October 1952.
35. SA OMM, 26 July 1957.
36. SA OMM, 10 October 1952.
37. Bank of England Reference Libary. The 'free market rate for financial remittances' during 1953 was 13.98 pesos to the dollar. The dollar–sterling sell rate on 31 March 1953 was $2.8106 to the pound sterling.
38. SA OMM, 16 June 1948. The interest in Cosalitre was sold to Robert Wigram & Sons.
39. SA OMM, 17 December 1947.
40. Henry Tiarks received the Chilean Order of Merit in June 1952 and was subsequently made a Grand Official; Helmut Schroder received the Chilean Order of Merit in July 1954. OMM, 13 June 1952, 19 July 1954.
41. SA OMM, 21 May 1946.
42. *The Times*, 2 April 1949.
43. SA OMM, 24 November 1949; 11 September 1953.
44. SA OMM, 21 December 1949.
45. SA OMM, 21 October 1952.
46. Interview with Lord Airlie (David Ogilvy).
47. SA OMM, 9 November 1954.
48. SA OMM, 8 August 1951.
49. Interview with Walter Gleich, Chairman of Norddeutsche Affinerie.
50. *The Times*, 10 June 1947.
51. SA OMM, 27 June 1947.
52. *The Bankers' Magazine* (1950) vol. 169, p. 248.
53. Interview with Toby Caulfeild.
54. SA OMM, 10 January 1957.
55. SA OMM, 20 April 1955.
56. SA OMM, 14 March 1956.
57. Interview with David Forsyth.
58. SA OMM, 28 June 1957.
59. SA OMM, 5 April 1955.
60. SA OMM, 12 June 1953.
61. SA OMM, 26 August 1954.
62. 'Extended credits for exports?', *The Economist*, 5 December 1953.
63. Report of the Committee on the Working of the Monetary System, Cmnd 827, cap. 868 (London: HMSO, 1959).

64. SA OMM, 1 July 1952; 4 July 1952.
65. SA OMM, 11 November 1953.
66. SA OMM, 20 November 1953.
67. SA OMM, 24 December 1953.
68. SA OMM, 3 December 1945.
69. SA OMM, 7 March 1946.
70. SA OMM, 17 September 1947.
71. SA OMM, 6 February 1948.
72. SA OMM, 20 September 1946.
73. 'Big Credit for French Trade', *The Times*, 21 January 1947.
74. SA OMM, 13 October 1947; 25 March 1948; 30 August 1949; 13 October 1949.
75. SA OMM, 7 December 1948.
76. SA OMM, 20 December 1948.
77. SA OMM, 9 October 1950.
78. SA OMM, 25 September 1951.
79. SA OMM, 10 June 1952.
80. SA OMM, 19 May 1952.
81. He later wrote a book on the subject, Rudi Weisweiller, *Introduction to Foreign Exchange* (Cambridge: Woodhead–Faulkner, 1983).
82. SA OMM, 15 November 1945.
83. Interview with Edward Tucker.
84. SA OMM, 19 April 1951; 11 September 1951.
85. Interview with Henry Tiarks; Henry Tiarks' diary, 27 June 1945.
86. Colin Fraser, *Harry Ferguson. Inventor and Pioneer* (London: John Murray, 1972) pp. 163–72.
87. SA Memo on issue written by Brian Girling, Head of the Issues Department.
88. SA OMM, 22 November 1950; interview with Henry Tiarks.
89. SA OMM, 25 November 1954.
90. Interview with Lord Perth.
91. Interview with Jonathan Backhouse.
92. Interview with Lord Richardson.
93. SA Schroder Reorganisation – General File. Proposed Reorganisation of Schroder banking businesses in London and New York, 25 June 1958.
94. SA Schroder Reorganisation – General File. Memorandum, 25 July 1959.
95. SA Report on Proposed Reorganisation Scheme by Cooper Brothers & Co., 27 March 1958.
96. SA Schroders Limited, prospectus, 25 September 1959.
97. *Daily Mail*, 24 September 1959.

12   Helbert, Wagg & Co.: 1848–1961

1. SA Alfred Wagg, 'The Wagg Family and its Connexions' (unpublished typescript, 1934) p. 2.

2. Marston Acres, *The Bank of England from Within, 1694–1900*, vol. I (London: Oxford University Press, 1931) p. 124.
3. 'Anglo-Jewish Coats of Arms', *Transactions of the Jewish Historical Society of England* (1894–95) vol. ii, p. 160.
4. Paul Emden, *The Jews of Britain* (London: Sampson Low, 1944) pp. 174–7.
5. John M. Shaftesley, 'Jews in English Regular Freemasonry', *Transactions of the Jewish Historical Society of England* (1973–75) vol. xxv, p. 189.
6. 'Selections from Sir I. L. Goldsmid's Correspondence', *Transactions of the Jewish Historical Society of England* (1899–1901) vol. iv, pp. 164–5.
7. SA Alfred Wagg, 'Autobiography' (unpublished typescript, *c.* 1958) p. 9.
8. Ibid.
9. Ibid.
10. GL Stock Exchange – General Purposes Committee Minutes, vol. 27, cap. 348. Arthur Wagg admitted to membership, 26 October 1863.
11. The text of the letter was published in the house magazine. *Wagtail* (Spring 1962) p. 8.
12. SA Wagg, 'Autobiography' p. 11.
13. *The Times*, 10 March 1933.
14. SA Wagg, 'Autobiography' p. 62.
15. Charles Duguid, *A History of the Stock Exchange* (London:Spottiswoode, 1900) p. 172.
16. *The Times*, 4 May 1889.
17. David Kynaston, *Cazenove & Co.: a history* (London: Batsford, 1991) p. 56.
18. Royal Commission on the London Stock Exchange. Minutes of Evidence, cap. 5935. BPP 1878 (xix).
19. Kynaston, *Cazenove* p. 74; Dorothy R. Adler, *British Investment in American Railways 1834 – 1898* (Charlottesville, Va: University Press of Virginia, 1970) p. 149.
20. Panmure Gordon & Co., *A Century of Stockbroking, 1876–1976* (London: Panmure Gordon, 1976) pp. 38–41.
21. SA Alfred Wagg, 'The History of the Firm' (unpublished typescript, no date).
22. GL Gibbs Manuscripts. MS 11,040, vol. 4, p. 175. Letter, Henry Gibbs to John Gibbs, 14 September 1900.
23. *Jewish Chronicle*, 13 December 1912.
24. Japhet, *Recollections* pp. 89,91.
25. Letter from Alfred Wagg, *Wagtail* (Spring 1955) p. 22.
26. *The Times*, 30 January 1903.
27. *The Statist*, 15 February 1908.
28. *The Statist*, 27 June 1908.
29. *Truth*, 27 March 1912.
30. SA Wagg, 'Autobiography' p. 14.; GL MS 14, 600/91 Stock Exchange Committee of General Purposes minute book, 9 December 1912, vol. 9.
31. *Evening Standard*, 8 December 1912.
32. SA Wagg, 'Autobiography' p. 14.
33. SA Wagg, 'Autobiography' p. 12.

34. L. E. Jones, *Georgian Afternoon* (London: Rupert Hart Davis, 1958) p. 72.
35. SA Wagg, 'Autobiography' p. 23
36. *The Times*, 22 September 1913.
37. SA Wagg, 'Autobiography' p. 25
38. SA Wagg, 'Autobiography' p. 26.
39. SA Wagg, 'Autobiography' p. 25.
40. SA Helbert, Wagg & Co. Ltd, board minutes, 10 July 1919.
41. *The Times*, 24 April 1919; SA Helbert, Wagg & Co. Ltd, board minutes, 20 June 1919.
42. Jones, *Georgian Afternoon* p. 73.
43. Lawrence Jones, 'The One and Only Alfred Ralph Wagg', *Wagtail* (1955) p. 2.
44. In 1928 he purchased 100 acres of Ashdown Forest, called the Isle of Thorns, which complete with club house, swimming pool and playing fields he gave to the Eton Manor Charitable Trust for the use of club members. Subsequently he presented the Trust with Broadstone Warren in Sussex as a camping site for Boys Scouts, which lent its name to the Broadstone Investment Trust.
45. W. Lionel Fraser, *All To The Good* (London: William Heinemann, 1963) p. 77.
46. Fraser, *All To The Good* pp. 79–80.
47. *The Times*, 5 March 1948.
48. Jones, *Georgian Afternoon* p. 120.
49. Fraser, *All To The Good* p. 84.
50. Jones, *Georgian Afternoon* p. 116.
51. *The Times*, 8 September 1969.
52. Fraser, *All To The Good* p. 87.
53. Palache's other continental bank directorships were the Rotterdamsche Bankvereniging NV, International Bodencredit, Banque de Crédit Roumain, British & Hungarian Bank Limited, and the Continental Gesellschaft für Bank und Industriewerke.
54. *The Times*, 27 March 1943.
55. Richard Fry (ed.), *A Banker's World: the revival of the City 1957–1970* (London, Hutchinson: 1970) p. 18.
56. Fraser, *All To The Good* p. 66.
57. Fraser, *All To The Good* p. 68.
58. Richard Davenport-Hines, 'Sir George Lewis French Bolton', *Dictionary of Business Biography*, vol. I (London: Butterworth, 1984) pp. 364–5.
59. *Financial Times*, 25 October 1920.
60. SA Letter from Arthur Gairdener, British Overseas Bank Ltd, to Alfred Wagg, Helbert, Wagg & Co. Ltd, 29 October 1920.
61. SA Letter from Foreign Office to Helbert, Wagg & Co. Ltd, 10 September 1921.
62. SA Letter from P. O. A. Anderson to The Minister for Iceland, S. Bjornsson, 26 July 1921.
63. SA Letter from Icelandic Envoy to the Court of Denmark to Helbert, Wagg & Co. Ltd, 27 August 1921.

64. SA 'Notes on Seine Negotiations', 11 January 1922. Memorandum marked 'Private and confidential', written by Max Bonn.
65. SA Wagg, 'Autobiography' p. 144.
66. Interview with Michael Verey.
67. *The Times*, 7 April 1922.
68. SA Letter from Dr Leopold Langer to Helbert, Wagg & Co., Ltd, 13 April 1922.
69. SA Letter from Albert Palache, Prague, to Helbert, Wagg & Co. Ltd, 15 June 1922.
70. Ziegler, *Sixth Great Power* p. 353.
71. *The Times*, 14 June 1922.
72. Jones, *Georgian Afternoon* pp. 102–5.
73. SA Romanian Ministry of Foreign Affairs, 'Expose of Reasons', 1 July 1922.
74. *Financial Times*, 6 November 1922
75. Fraser, *All To The Good* p. 93.
76. SA Letter from the Borneo Company Ltd to Helbert, Wagg & Co. Ltd, 18 April 1923.
77. *The Times*, 26 May 1925.
78. Edward Meigh, *The Story of the Glass Bottle* (Stoke-on-Trent: C. E. Ramsden, 1962) p. 76.
79. Noel Deerr, *The History of Sugar* (London: Chapman & Hall, 1950) p. 483.
80. The Ipswich Beet Sugar Factory; the Ely Beet Sugar Factory; the King's Lynn Beet Sugar Factory; English Sugar Beet.
81. SA Letter from W. B. H. Barrington to Öesterreichsche Credit-Anstalt, 25 January 1927.
82. *Financial Times*, 16 December 1925.
83. *The Times*, 23 April 1926.
84. SA Letter from Norddeutscher Lloyd, Bremen, to Helbert, Wagg & Co. Ltd, 19 April 1924.
85. SA Memorandum by Albert Palache, 27 July 1932.
86. *The Times*, 14 January 1933.
87. SA Letter from Cazenove, Akroyd & Greenwood & Co. to Helbert, Wagg & Co. Ltd, 7 February 1933.
88. *Financial Times*, 20 February 1933.
89. *The Times*, 22 February 1933.
90. SA Memorandum, 4 January, 1934.
91. SA HWBM, board minutes, 17 April 1947.
92. SA Letter from Cazenove, Akroyds & Greenwoood & Co. to Helbert, Wagg Co. Ltd, 14 December 1934.
93. Fraser, *All To The Good* pp. 110–1.
94. Fraser, *All To The Good* p. 103.
95. SA Memorandum by Albert Palache, 6 July 1933.
96. *Financial Times*, 26 January 1937.
97. Fraser, *All To The Good* p. 111.
98. Burk, *Morgan Grenfell* pp. 165–6.
99. SA Memorandum. The West India Sugar Company, 9 February 1937.

100. *The Times*, 15 March 1933.
101. SA Report on The Broadstone Investment Trust Ltd, Office of the Reichskommissar for the Treatment of Enemy Property, 14 March 1946.
102. *The Times*, 28 July 1932.
103. Jones, *Georgian Afternoon* p. 127.
104. SA Memorandum. Shaw, Strupp & Co. – Purpose of the Firm (no date).
105. SA HWBM, 12 August 1943.
106. SA HWBM, 4 January 1939.
107. SA HWBM, 5 October 1938.
108. SA HWBM, 26 June 1940.
109. Hugh Cudlipp, *At Your Peril* (London: Weidenfeld & Nicolson, 1962) p. 250.
110. Christine Shaw, 'William Lionel Fraser' *Dictionary of Business Biography*, vol. II (London: Butterworth, 1984) pp. 417–22.
111. *The Times*, 4 January 1965.
112. David Clutterbuck and Marion Devine, *Clore: the Man and his Millions* (London: Weidenfeld and Nicolson, 1987) p. 83.
113. SA HWBM, 22 February 1945.
114. SA HWBM, 18 April 1946.
115. SA HWBM, 24 May 1945.
116. SA HWBM, 12 October 1944.
117. *The Times*, 3 December 1945.
118. Fraser, *All To The Good* p. 181.
119. 'Capital issues in the United Kingdom', *Bank of England Quarterly Bulletin*, (1966) vol. 6, p. 154.
120. *The Times*, 9 March 1948; 12 March 1948. Another notable feature of this issue was that it was the first to be made in compliance with the recommendations of the Cohen Committee on Company law that eventually formed the basis of the 1948 Companies Act.
121. *The Times*, 6 December 1945.
122. *The Times*, 11 July 1947.
123. Fraser, *All To The Good* p. 230.
124. *The Times*, 6 February 1948.
125. Fraser, *All To The Good* p. 230.
126. *The Times*, 4 May 1949.
127. *The Times*, 11 August 1949.
128. *The Times*, 3 August 1949.
129. Fraser, *All To The Good* pp. 165–6.
130. *The Times*, 6 October 1955.
131. *The Times*, 27 November 1948.
132. *The Times*, 1 November 1954.
133. Fraser, *All To The Good* pp. 252–6.
134. *The Times*, 5 January 1952.
135. *The Times*, 1 January 1960.
136. Kathleen Burk, *The First Privatisation: the politicians, the City, and the denationalisation of steel* (London: Historians' Press, 1988) pp. 116–35.
137. *The Times*, 29 November 1957.

138. H. B. Rose and G. D. Newbould, 'The 1967 Take-Over Boom', *Moorgate and Wall Street* (Autumn 1967) p. 6.

139. See Richard Roberts, 'Regulatory Responses to the Rise of The Market for Corporate Control in Britain in the 1950s', *Business History* (1992) vol. 34 i, pp. 183–200.

140. George David Smith, *From Monopoly to Competition: the transformation of Alcoa, 1888–1986* (Cambridge University Press, 1988) pp. 322–6.

141. Jacques Attali, *A Man of Influence: Sir Siegmund Warburg, 1902–82* (London: Weidenfeld and Nicolson, 1986) p. 211.

142. David Kynaston, 'A City at war with itself', *Financial Times*, 7/8 January 1989.

143. Fraser, *All To The Good* p. 241.

144. Charles Gordon, *The Two Tycoons: a personal memoir of Jack Cotton and Charles Clore* (London: Hamish Hamilton, 1985) p. 105.

145. *The Times*, 24 April 1961.

146. *The Times*, 2 November 1959.

147. Cudlip, *At Your Peril* p. 199.

148. Cecil King, *Strictly Personal: some memoirs of Cecil H. King* (London: Weidenfeld & Nicolson, 1968) p. 125.

149. Fraser, *All To The Good* p. 246.

150. Interview with Michael Verey.

151. SA HWBM, 28 November 1946.

152. Interview with Michael Verey

153. *The Times*, 5 August 1954.

154. *The Times*, 15 May 1959.

155. *The Times*, 19 June 1959.

156. *The Times*, 1 February 1960.

13   Schroder Wagg: 1960–73

1. *Financial Times*, 21 May 1960.

2. *Evening Standard*, 24 May 1960.

3. SA Confidential memorandum from W. Lionel Fraser to Helbert, Wagg directors, 23 March 1960.

4. Interview with David Forsyth.

5. SA Confidential Report on Integration by Alan Russell, 8 August 1961.

6. SA Company Finance Department Memorandum on Integration, 26 March 1962.

7. SA Company Finance Department Memorandum on Organisation of Department, 18 May 1962.

8. *Wagtail*, Spring 1962.

9. Schroders Limited, Report and Accounts 1965, p. 4.

10. *Schroder Wagtail* (Winter 1964). A novel feature of the new building was the availability throughout of piped music. It was installed at the suggestion of John Bayley, who had observed the popularity of music-while-you-work amongst shop-floor workers while he was working in

manufacturing industry, for the benefit of staff engaged in routine tasks. It was discontinued after a few years.

11. Interview with John Kinross.
12. Gordon, *Two Tycoons* p. 143.
13. Interview with Lord Richardson.
14. Interview with David Forsyth.
15. Interview with Sir Charles Villiers.
16. SA 'The Organisation and Practice of Investment and Merchant Banking'. Paper delivered by Gordon Richardson to the London School of Economics and Political Science Seminar on Problems in Industrial Administration, 25 January 1966.
17. Both Bell and Cooper were authors of books and numerous articles on banking. See for instance, Geoffrey Bell, *The Euro-Dollar Market and the International Financial System* (London: Macmillan, 1973); John Cooper, *The Management and Regulation of Banks* (London: Macmillan, 1984).
18. SA Press Cuttings. Newspaper unidentified.
19. Burk, *Morgan Grenfell* p. 192.
20. SA 'The Organisation and Practice of Investment and Merchant Banking', paper delivered by Gordon Richardson to the London School of Economics and Political Science Seminar on Problems in Industrial Administration, 25 January 1966.
21. Ibid.
22. These are the operating profits of the London operating company Schroder Wagg *not* the holding company Schroders Limited.
23. *Daily Telegraph*, 30 December 1968; *Investors' Chronicle*, 25 December 1970.
24. Interview with Sir Charles Villiers.
25. Information from Schroder Wagg Management Accounts.
26. Interview with Lord Richardson.
27. Dennett, *Slaughter and May* p. 228.
28. Richard Spiegelberg, *The City: Power Without Accountability* (London: Quartet Books, 1973) p. 66.
29. Interview with John Hull.
30. D.C. Coleman, *Courtaulds; an economic and social history*, vol. III (Oxford University Press, 1980) p. 252.
31. *Daily Telegraph*, 30 December 1968.
32. *The Times*, 15 December 1970.
33. See Peter J.S. Dunnett, *The Decline of the British Motor Industry: the effects of government policy, 1945–1979* (London: Croom Helm, 1980) pp. 87–120.
34. See S.E. Boyle, 'A Blueprint for Competition: restructuring the motor vehicle industry', *Journal of Industrial Economics* (October 1975) pp. 21–41.
35. Interview with Sir Charles Villiers.
36. *The Times*, 13 May 1969.
37. Douglas Hague and Geoffrey Wilkinson, *The IRC – An Experiment in Industrial Intervention: a history of the Industrial Reorganisation Corporation* (London: George Allen & Unwin, 1983) pp. 91–118.

38. *Financial Times*, 31 January 1969.
39. *The Times*, 8 May 1969.
40. *Daily Telegraph*, 29 November 1968.
41. *Investors' Chronicle*, 17 January 1969.
42. *The Times*, 14 January 1969.
43. *Guardian*, 8 February 1969.
44. *Guardian*, 5 November 1969.
45. These were the takeovers of Meridian in 1964 and of Prew Smith in 1968.
46. *The Times*, 1 July 1969.
47. *Guardian*, 30 December 1969.
48. *Aberdeen Press and Journal*, 24 September 1970.
49. *The Times*, 20 December 1968.
50. See Joe Haines, *Maxwell* (London: Futura, 1988) pp. 297–334.
51. Nicholas Davenport, 'The end of the affair', *Spectator*, 18 October 1969.
52. *Times 500*; *The Banker* (1974) vol. 124, p. 1545.
53. Interview with Lord Airlie.
54. *The Times*, 23 December 1970.
55. *Manchester Daily Telegraph*, 30 December 1970.
56. Bank of England, *Statistical Abstract* (London: Bank of England, 1970) p. 54.
57. Schroders Limited, Report and Accounts for 1965. Chairman's statement to shareholders delivered on 23 February 1966.
58. For instance, in October 1972 a new subsidiary was formed named Wadkin Finance Ltd whose purpose was to lease equipment to the machine tool maker Wadkin Ltd. Schroder Finance subscribed the ordinary shares of Wadkin Finance while Wadkin Ltd took the preference shares.
59. Schroders Limited, Report and Accounts 1971. Chairman's statement to shareholders delivered on 27 March 1972.
60. John Grady, 'The Growth of the British Non-Clearing Banks, 1960–1975' (unpublished PhD thesis, Cambridge University, 1982) p. 115.
61. Interview with Lord Richardson.
62. Interview with Lord Airlie.
63. Leslie Hannah, *Inventing Retirement: the development of occupational pensions in Britain* (Cambridge University Press, 1986) p. 76.
64. Interview with Michael Verey.
65. *Schroder Wagtail*, Spring 1968.
66. H. Burton and D. C. Corner, *Investment and Unit Trusts in Britain and America* (London: Elek Books, 1968) p. 119.
67. *Investors' Chronicle*, 16 January 1970.
68. *Daily Telegraph*, 29 June 1968.
69. *Scotsman*, 11 January 1968.
70. *The Times*, 19 January 1970.
71. *Daily Telegraph*, 23 October 1968.
72. 'Unit trusts more attractive to the wealthier investor', *Financial Times*, 30 July 1973.
73. *Investors' Chronicle*, 25 October 1968.

74. Roy Levine, 'Unit trusts – poor relations?', *The Banker* (1973) vol. 123, p. 1499.
75. The first firm to take advantage of the relaxation of the regulations governing television financial advertising in April 1969 was Target, in the summer of 1969.
76. *The Times*, 12 September 1970; Schroder Wagg joined the Association of Unit Trust Managers in January 1970.
77. 'Evolution of the managed bond', *Investors' Chronicle*, 16 November 1973.
78. 'Managed bonds impress in bear market', *Financial Times*, 21 April 1973.
79. *The Times*, 22 February 1968.
80. Michael Stoddart, 'Pushing into the provinces', *The Banker* (1972) vol. 122, pp. 1661–3.
81. *Financial Times*, 30 January 1969.
82. *Scotsman*, 13 March 1968.
83. *Cork Examiner*, 7 March 1968.
84. C.J.J. Clay and B.S. Wheble, *Modern Merchant Banking* (Cambridge: Woodhead-Faulkner, 1983) pp. 127–30; John Grady and Martin Weale, *British Banking, 1960–85* (London: Macmillan, 1986) pp. 103–5.
85. Schroder Wagg board minutes, 28 September 1965.
86. Other merchant banks made similar moves: Charterhouse took a 25 per cent stake in Computer Systems and Programming Ltd; Rothschilds and ICFC acquired interests in Comperaid; and Hambros bought 40 per cent of Computer Resale Brokers. *Daily Telegraph*, 22 September 1969.
87. *Daily Telegraph*, 21 October 1969.
88. *Schroder Wagtail*, 1970.
89. *Gas World*, 27 June 1970.
90. The formation of the Industrial Department was preceded by the transfer of ownership of Leadenhall Securities, the dormant venture capital subsidiary formed by J. Henry Schroder & Co. in 1935, to Schroders Limited.
91. *Sunday Times*, 13 April 1969.
92. *Observer*, 13 July 1969.
93. Schroders Limited board minutes, 14 July 1971.
94. Interview with Geoffrey Williams.
95. *Financial Times*, 24 January 1973.
96. Interview with Sir Leslie Murphy.
97. *Toronto Financial Post*, 16 March 1974, contains a useful compilation of league tables.

14 International Expansion: 1960–73

1. Burk, *Morgan Grenfell* pp. 230–5; Attali, *A Man of Influence* pp. 230–1, 236–8.
2. Interview with George Mallinckrodt.
3. Schroders Limited, Report and Accounts 1961. Chairman's statement to shareholders, 22 February 1962.

4. Schroders Limited, Report and Accounts 1962. Chairman's Statement to shareholders, 26 February 1963.
5. Interview with Philip Robinson.
6. See, *The Development of a European Capital Market* (Brussels: European Economic Community, 1966).
7. *Schroder Wagtail* (Spring 1969).
8. See, for instance, the article by Schroder Wagg executive John Cooper, 'Common Market: what view should the City take?', *The Banker* (1970) vol. 120, pp. 1180–5.
9. SA SLBM, 26 April 1972.
10. *Schroder Wagtail* (Spring 1967).
11. By a remarkable coincidence it was Howell who, as a prefect at St Paul's School, Concord, New Hampshire, had been charged with the task of informing Sherman Gray, a junior boy, of the death of his father, Prentiss Gray, Schrobanco's first president, in 1935.
12. Interview with John I. Howell.
13. SA 'Schroder? What's that?', report on the *New York Times* advertising campaign of 1963.
14. Interview with Canon R. Clements.
15. Interview with John I. Howell.
16. Interview with Canon R. Clements.
17. SA 'Schrobanco Management Report' February 1968. The report was written by three middle-ranking Schrobanco officers: Francis Bessenyey, William Bethune and Michael Magdol, with outside assistance from Michael von Clemm.
18. Interview with Philip Robinson.
19. SA SLBM, 3 October 1973; John D. Wilson, *The Chase: the Chase Manhattan Bank NA, 1945–1985* (Cambridge, Mass.: Harvard Business School Press, 1986) pp. 193–4.
20. SA SLBM, 14 July 1971.
21. SA SLBM, 30 October 1972.
22. SA SLBM, 29 June 1973.
23. Interview with Gerhard Laube.
24. SA SLBM, 15 July 1969.
25. SA SLBM, 6 October 1972.
26. Interview with James D. Wolfensohn.
27. Interview with James D. Wolfensohn.
28. Interview with Lord Richardson.
29. Interview with David Forsyth.
30. David Montague, 'British merchant banking in Australia', *The Banker* (1969) vol. 119, pp. 1317–21.
31. SA SLBM, 14 July 1971.
32. SA SLBM, 2 April 1970.
33. *The Economist*, 23 January 1971.
34. SA SLBM, 18 January 1973.
35. Schroder Limited board minutes, 5 May 1966.

36. SA 'Schroder Group Management Structure', paper by John Bayley presented in June 1969 to the Schroder Board.
37. SA SLBM, 15 July 1969.
38. SA SLBM, 22 May 1971.
39. SA SLBM, 29 June 1973.
40. John Rule, 'Merchant banks' accounts – the need for disclosure', *The Banker* (1972) vol. 122, pp. 1645–51.
41. *The Economist*, 29 November 1969.
42. *The Times*, 9 February 1973.

Index

Note: In company names, the initials and forenames have been placed after the surname, e.g. Schröder, J. Henry, & Co.